NEW ENGLAND
Road Trip

JEN ROSE SMITH

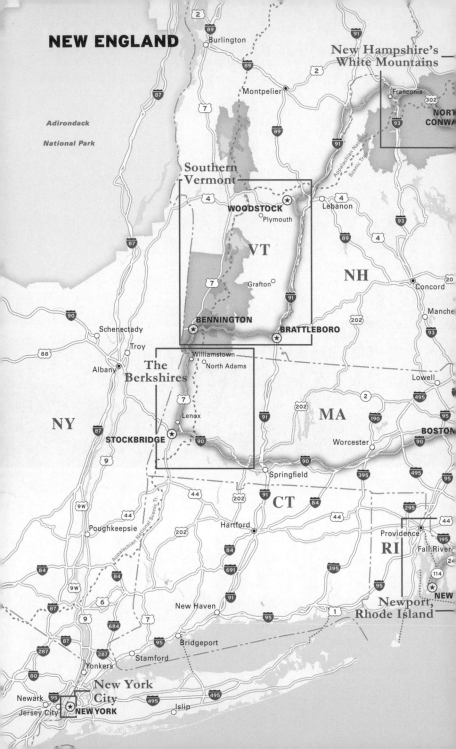

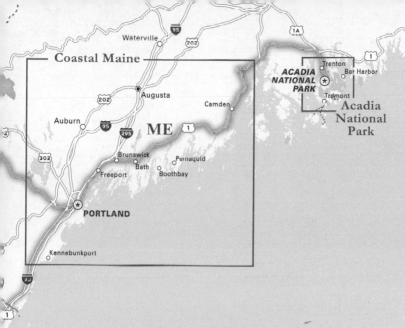

Coastal Maine

Waterville

Augusta

Camden

Auburn

ME

Acadia National Park

Trenton

Bar Harbor

Tremont

Acadia National Park

Brunswick
Bath
Pemaquid
Boothbay
Freeport

PORTLAND

Kennebunkport

ATLANTIC

OCEAN

Boston

Cape Cod
and the Islands

PROVINCETOWN

SANDWICH

Brewster
Yarmouth
Orleans

Hyannis
Chatham

Falmouth

Hole

Oak Bluffs

Nantucket

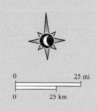

0   25 mi

0   25 km

CONTENTS

DISCOVER
New England

From pebble beaches to valley farms, clam shacks to Revolutionary War sites, a New England road trip is a drive through American history.

The coastline wraps around lonely lighthouses, Ivy League campuses, and the oldest mountains in the world, while country roads lead to time-lost villages. This is the land of the Wampanoag and Abenaki tribes, Pilgrims, whalers, and the founders of the United States.

But for all the well-worn trails and heritage, the Northeast is full of surprises. The White Mountains are wild and rugged, with howling weather and plants found nowhere else on earth. In big cities and rural communities, creative chefs are remaking Yankee cuisine with ingredients from the farm, sea, and forest. And there are endless ways to experience New England's landscapes, whether on a bicycle, schooner, or surfboard.

Pick and choose from the best the Northeast has to offer. Wander dirt trails or indulge in hipster chic. Dream up an easygoing getaway near the shore. Plan a whirlwind adventure to the edge of the map. This book is an invitation to hit the road and make a trip that's all your own.

PLANNING YOUR TRIP

Where to Go

Boston
Revolutionary history is layered with immigrant heritage and urban culture in this brassy, wisecracking city. Add in some of the **best art museums** in the country, the sound of bats cracking at **Fenway Park,** and **academic giants,** and Boston begins to feel like that "shining city upon a hill" Puritan settlers hoped to found—but with **cannoli.**

Coastal Maine
Maine's **3,478 miles of coastline** encompass **sandy beaches,** the hip and vibrant downtown of the **state's largest city,** and endless **rocky coves.** Life happens on the water here: Cozy harbors bristle with the masts of **sailboats** and **tall ships,** while many locals earn a living with fishing poles and lobster traps. Take to the sea to spot **humpback whales** and **puffin colonies,** paddle a **kayak** past wave-whipped points, and dive into the bracingly cold North Atlantic.

Acadia National Park
Wild scenery is set off by old-world elegance in this island park. **Carriage trails** wind through the bare, stone peaks, grand bridges arc across **forest streams,** and **historic hotels** overlook the shifting tides. Make a predawn drive up **Cadillac Mountain** to catch the **country's first sunrise,** go **tidepool-hopping** on the **Park Loop Road,** then head into the town of **Bar Harbor** for a *very* Vacationland blend of tourist shops, **ice cream,** and **lobster meals.**

New Hampshire's White Mountains
The gentle **Appalachians** erupt into jagged peaks in the White Mountains, and **Mount Washington** towers above them all. This range is remarkably accessible to visitors who can drive, ride, or walk to the top of **New Hampshire's highest peak** and hike along the blustery, alpine ridge linking the iconic **Presidential Range.** And while the Granite State's Old Man of the Mountain—those landmark granite cliff ledges—crumbled in 2003, there's plenty of rock left over to explore, along with **winding rivers, caves,** and **scenic drives.**

Southern Vermont
Take back roads and byways through Vermont at its most bucolic, and slow down to the pace of life in this tiny state. The trip from the starchy, small-town center of **Woodstock** to the **funky galleries** of **Brattleboro** passes **picture-book villages** and **winding rivers, rolling orchards,** and destination-worthy **craft breweries.**

The Berkshires
This countryside retreat offers refreshing contrasts: Old-fashioned charm abounds, but the Berkshires overflow with **cutting-edge art and culture,** including the glorious **Tanglewood Music Festival** in the summer months. In recent years, the Berkshires have become a **hot culinary destination,** and young chefs are drawing in crowds with New American fare sourced from the region's farm and barns.

Newport, Rhode Island
Newport is an unlikely setting for **Renaissance palazzos** and **Greek Revival chateaux,** but when 19th-century U.S. elite built summertime "cottages," they piled all their glamour and gaud into this charming colonial city. Those sprawling mansions are remarkably well preserved, and a trip through the lavish properties is a fascinating glimpse of **Gilded Age high society.**

Clockwise from top left: Boston's Harvard University; Newport's harbor; a serene scene in southern Vermont.

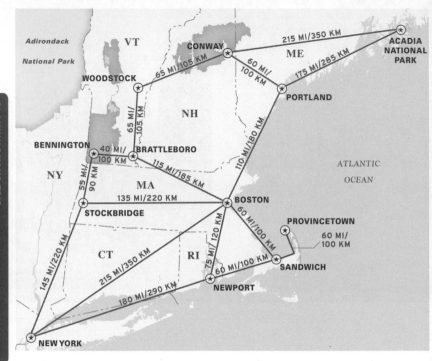

Cape Cod and the Islands

Just a few hours from downtown Boston, Cape Cod and the islands of **Nantucket** and **Martha's Vineyard** are a world unto themselves. Generations of artists, writers, and free spirits have escaped to their **dune shacks** and **beach retreats,** adding color to a centuries-old fishing community. Nantucket's **cobblestone streets** are infused with **whaling history,** and the harbors of Martha's Vineyard's bristle with **old-fashioned schooners.** Locals call Cape Cod's **Provincetown** "the end of the world," and it remains an artsy, liberal haven—and the East Coast's hottest **LGBT vacation and party spot.**

New York City

Cue the Sinatra (or Jay Z) for a whirlwind trip through the Big Apple. While New York isn't part of New England, it's a **convenient access point** to the region and offers a perfect contrast to the beaches, villages, and mountain charms of the Northeast with its **skyscrapers, museums,** and **monuments.** Leave plenty of time for **bagels** and **pizza.**

When to Go

With its long days, balmy weather, and warmer water, New England's **peak season** is during the school vacation **early July-late August.** While the cities can be sweleringly hot and hotels are often jam-packed, this is the ideal time to enjoy the **beaches** that stretch from Rhode Island to Acadia National Park.

Autumn is New England's showstopper, when quiet deciduous forests throw off their green for a lavish display of red, gold, and orange. **Fall color** depends on fickle weather conditions, but the season starts in **mid-September** in Vermont and

New England for Families

Get started on the ultimate kid-friendly road trip.

* **Boston Tea Party Ships and Museum, Boston:** Get a taste of Revolutionary history at a hands-on museum with costumed actors and interactive exhibits (page 50).

* **Dive-in Theater Boat Cruise, Acadia National Park:** See what's beneath the surface in this kid-focused, splashy nature outing from Bar Harbor with Diver Ed, who brings up touchable critters like sea stars, lobsters, and sea cucumbers (page 142).

* **Mount Washington Cog Railway, New Hampshire's White Mountains:** Aspiring engineers and mountaineers will love the slow-moving, scenic trip on this 150-year-old mountain railway (page 159).

* **Scott Farm Orchard, Southern Vermont:** Pick apples in a scenic orchard by Rudyard Kipling's Vermont home (page 201).

Boston Tea Party Ships and Museum

* **Cape Cod Baseball League, Cape Cod:** The free outdoor games held up and down the Cape are family-friendly ways to enjoy our national pastime without the crowds or hype—and you may just spot a future baseball great (page 302).

New Hampshire, and spends the next two months working its way south, with Rhode Island hitting its stride in the last two weeks of **October.**

For travelers hoping to catch a few waves in Rhode Island and see the turning of the leaves in the White Mountains, the **last week of September** can offer the best of both worlds; plus, the beaches are far more manageable when the kids are back in school. **Winter** and **spring,** while perfect for skiers and maple syrup aficionados, are notoriously terrible for driving, with roads stopped up by everything from snowdrifts to mud pits. By **April** and early **May,** even back roads have dried out and the first blossoms are opening up in the south—this is the ideal time to get rock-bottom rates on hotels around the region. And if you're willing to chance a stretch of rainy days, **June** is a glorious time for wildflowers, scented lilacs, and pastures full of newborn calves and woolly lambs.

Before You Go

The easiest place to **fly** into for launching a trip in New England is **Boston,** though **Portland, Maine,** is another major hub for the area. While it adds an extra half day of driving on either end of the trip, beginning or ending a New England road trip in **New York City** adds a nice counterpoint. If you are renting a car in any of these cities, plan to pick it up *after* spending time there, as **paid parking** and **crowded streets** makes it easier to explore by **public transport.**

BEFORE YOU GO

Clockwise from top left: lobster buoys on Mount Desert Island; fall colors on the coast of Maine; a New England moose.

When visiting during **high season** or **fall foliage season,** it's essential to book **accommodations** and **rental cars** well in advance, though impromptu **campers** can usually find somewhere to sleep without much notice. Unless you're planning to dine at a handful of elite **restaurants** in Boston and New York, it's unnecessary to make reservations more than a few days ahead of time.

Whenever you come, bring ample **layers of clothing,** as the weather is often changeable. If your itinerary includes visiting the high peaks of the White Mountains, keep in mind that temperatures can be chilly even in the middle of summer, and sailing in Maine, Massachusetts, and Rhode Island means blustery, ocean-cooled shore winds. On the other hand, you can't go far in New England before hitting an outdoor outfitters or gear store—anything left at home will be easy to find in a dozen shades of plaid.

Driving Tips

In New England, as in much of the United States, the finest roads are far from the interstate: winding, **two-lane highways** that define the "scenic route." When planning point-to-point drives, it's worth investing in a **detailed map of the area,** as the roads have a habit of merging, diverging, and changing names with little notice. Above all, don't assume you'll have **cell phone access,** as **rural swaths** of western Massachusetts, Vermont, New Hampshire, and inland Maine can have thin coverage.

Speed limits change from place to place. Unless otherwise marked, assume a maximum of 65 miles per hour on the interstate and 45 miles per hour on two-lane highways. Using a cell phone while driving can earn you a **hefty fine,** and seat belts are mandatory. Some Massachusetts, New Hampshire, New York, Rhode Island, and Maine highways have **tolls** (ranging from $1-10), so it's worth **traveling with cash.**

DRIVING TIPS

HIT THE ROAD

The 14-Day Grand Tour

A great loop through American history, high peaks, and picture-perfect country-side, this two-week trip is a "grand tour" in every sense. The full itinerary means quite a bit of time on the road, so those looking for a more leisurely vacation should snip out bits of this route in exchange for extra beach days, hikes, and free time to explore along the way. But if you've got an itchy pedal foot and the urge to put in miles, this gives you the lay of the land and the very best of New England.

Days 1-2
BOSTON
Get a crash course in Revolutionary history on the **Freedom Trail,** which stretches from the shiny dome of the **Massachusetts State House** to the **Bunker Hill Monument.** Don't tackle the whole thing at once—the trail isn't complete without a lunch break in the Italian American **North End** neighborhood. Try **Italian ice, cannoli,** or a classic **submarine sandwich** before crossing the Charles River toward the USS *Constitution.*

On your second day, hop a ride on a **swan boat** in the **Boston Public Garden.** Then explore **Back Bay**'s art and architecture; duck into the sanctuary of **Trinity Church,** soak up the scholarly atmosphere in the **Boston Public Library** reading room, then stand in the center of the world at the stained glass **Mapparium.** Spend the afternoon in one of Boston's fabulous museums, taking in ancient artifacts and contemporary art at the **Museum of Fine Arts**, or head to the **Boston Tea Party Ships and Museum** to reenact the city's favorite piece of colonial-era sabotage.

Days 3-5
COASTAL MAINE AND ACADIA
270 miles, 5.25 hours
Stop by **Caffe Vittoria** in the North End for an old-world cappuccino before picking up some wheels and heading to **Portland,** an easy, two-hour drive up the interstate. Before you reach the city, make a short detour to a trio of lighthouses in Cape Elizabeth. **Portland Head Light** is easily the most picturesque, but the pair of lighthouses known as **Two Lights** are a stone's throw from classic lobster rolls at **The Lobster Shack.**

Get a taste of Portland's maritime life on a **boat tour of Casco Bay**—hop a historic **schooner** or take a ride on the **mail boat** that connects the bay's islands to the mainland—then kick off the evening by visiting some of the city's award-winning **microbreweries.**

On your second day on the coast, make an essential breakfast stop at Portland's **Holy Donut,** then hit the road for a day of lighthouse-hopping and harbor-strolling. Drive up to **Bath** and work your way through the **Maine Maritime Museum,** or go a bit farther to **Rockland** and take in three generations of Wyeths at the **Farnsworth Art Museum** before visiting nearby **Owls Head Light.** Pick up a picnic lunch to eat near **Rockport**'s idyllic harbor, then visit the nautical boutiques in downtown **Camden.** Make the final push to **Acadia National Park** on Mount Desert Island, and turn in early if you're planning to catch **sunrise on Cadillac Mountain,** a pilgrimage place where you can see the first sunlight hit the coast.

After your morning's start, mountaintop sunrise or not, enjoy the rest of the day car-free in the national park; rent a bike, hop the free **Island Explorer shuttle,** and cruise the extensive network of **carriage trails** that link great stone bridges, viewpoints, and rolling mountains. For the real experience of a **Maine lobster dinner,** cross the island to **Thurston's Lobster Pound** to get one

Clockwise from top left: Trinity Church and the John Hancock Tower in Boston; hiking Cadillac Mountain in Acadia National Park; sunrise at Portland Head Light in Maine.

One Tasty Trip

You could spend a lifetime eating and drinking your way across New England.

lobster dinner

- **Boston's North End:** Discover the city's Italian heritage in its tastiest form: cannoli, wood-fired pizza, and hearty submarine sandwiches (page 58).

- **Portland Breweries:** From postage-stamp tasting rooms to behemoth breweries, this town is serious about good beer (page 89).

- **Maine Lobster:** Maine's most famous crustacean is also its favorite meal: Try a lobster roll at The Lobster Shack (page 93), or get the full dinner experience at Thurston's Lobster Pound (page 143).

- **Straight from the Farm:** A tiny restaurant with its own farm and winery, Woodstock's Osteria Pane e Salute (page 193) gives local Vermont produce a regional Italian twist. In Lenox in the Berkshires, Nudel (page 240) celebrates the twists and turns of the season with ultra-fresh, ingredient-focused fare.

- **Cape Cod Clam Shacks:** Seasonal clam-and-fry joints open their doors each spring with great piles of seafood. Two favorites: the Clam Shack of Falmouth (page 295) and Cap't Cass Rock Harbor Seafood (page 303).

with all the fixings at the edge of a scenic harbor.

Days 6-7
WHITE MOUNTAINS
215 miles, 4.75 hours

The route to the White Mountains crosses the dark, deep forests of inland Maine, ticking off a series of towns that recall the state's immigrant heritage: Pass Naples, Sweden, and Denmark on your way to the outdoor mecca of **North Conway.** Stretch your legs after the long drive on the easy walk to **Diana's Baths,** a series of small waterfalls perfect for an early evening dip (if there's enough water). Fortify yourself for a day in the mountains with dinner and a locally brewed beer in town.

Day two is all about mountain peaks and rugged scenery: Chug to the top of **Mount Washington** on the 150-year-old **cog railway,** or hike the mountain yourself—on a clear day at the summit you'll have views stretching from Maine to New York's Adirondack Mountains, and you can watch a steady stream of Appalachian Trail through-hikers pose for photos at the top. For all of the mountain scenery and fewer crowds, opt for a trek up **Franconia Ridge** instead, choosing from a series of 4,000-foot peaks with views of the valley below.

Days 8-9
SOUTHERN VERMONT
165 miles, 3 hours

Take the **Kancamagus Highway** for a swooping, scenic drive through the mountains on your way to **Woodstock,** where

Clockwise from top left: a trail in Cape Cod; walking the Freedom Trail in Boston; a footbridge in the Berkshires.

Coastal Charm

Sachuest Beach, Newport

New England's got beaches for days....

- **Popham Beach, Coastal Maine:**
  This stretch of shoreline offers the best of Maine, a sandy beach at the end of a scenic peninsula and a little rocky island to explore at low tide (page 102).

- **Bar Island, Acadia National Park:**
  The path from Bar Harbor to this forested islet only becomes a beach at low tide, which makes it the perfect place to find stranded sea creatures and tidepools (page 141).

- **Sachuest Beach, Newport:** Catch an easygoing summer swell at Sachuest Beach, a favorite surf spot just outside of downtown Newport (page 271).

- **Coast Guard Beach, Cape Cod:**
  Endless sand lined with wild roses, dramatic cliffs, and windswept lighthouses make this one of the best beaches in the East, and it's a favorite place for watching whales without leaving dry land (page 308).

- **Race Point Beach, Cape Cod:** The far tip of Cape Cod is nothing but beach, rolling dunes, and hidden shacks—for the ultimate "end of the world" experience, sleep at the remote Race Point Light (page 318).

you'll find a classic village green, art galleries, and farm-to-table restaurants in a lush river valley. Hop a wagon ride, learn to churn your own butter, and get friendly with some Jersey cows at the **Billings Farm & Museum,** then spend the afternoon visiting classic **covered bridges.**

The drive from Woodstock to **Brattleboro** is another stunner, especially if you take the scenic route: Visit the **President Calvin Coolidge State Historic Site** to see his family homestead on your way to Route 100, then wind through pretty villages like **Grafton.** Spend an evening exploring Brattleboro's **art galleries,** or catch a circus performance at the town's **New England Center for Circus Arts.**

Day 10
THE BERKSHIRES
80 miles, 2 hours
Watch the mountains taper into gentle hills as you make your way south, and choose a couple of the region's best destinations for a classic Berkshires day: Spend the morning with cutting-edge

modern art in **North Adams** at the **MASS MoCA** or follow in Thoreau's footsteps to the top of **Mount Greylock.** After lunch, continue south to **Lenox** to visit the elegant home of **Edith Wharton,** then spend a quiet evening in the **Brava** wine bar, mingling with musicians from nearby **Tanglewood.**

Day 11
NEWPORT
165 miles, 2.75 hours
Keep pointing for the coast and you'll wind up in this pretty port city, where the waterside **Cliff Walk** cuts past some of the grandest **Gilded Age estates** in New England. With just one day in town, pick a single mansion to explore before **hitting the beach** for **clam rolls,** sand, and sun. When the sun begins to slip, hop on scenic **Ocean Drive** to take in the coast with a stop at **Castle Hill Inn** for sundowners on **The Lawn.**

Days 12-13
CAPE COD
120 miles, 2.5 hours
Drive all the way to "the end of the world"—that's colorful, creative **Provincetown** to you—to spend your last days exploring **Cape Cod.** Make a beeline for the **Cape Cod National Seashore** when you arrive, where you'll find the finest beaches in New England, crumbling cliffs, and historic lighthouses, and spend a day wandering the sand.

The next day, get a taste of Provincetown's artistic heritage by strolling the **downtown galleries,** then join a tour of the rustic **artists' shacks** scattered through the rolling dunes. See if you can keep up with the locals at a raucous **tea dance,** then spend a night on the town in true **P-town** style with tickets to a **drag show.**

Day 14
BOSTON
115 miles, 2.25 hours
Start your last day of New England adventures with some pastries from the

Portuguese Bakery, then hit the **Cape Cod Rail Trail** for a morning of exploring on two wheels. If you have time, break up the return drive to Boston with stops in one or more of the villages that line the Inner Cape: Visit **Chatham**'s pretty **lighthouse,** play a round of pirate-themed minigolf in **Yarmouth,** or see a classic **saltbox home** in old-fashioned **Sandwich.**

Fabulous Foliage in a Week
Discover New England's brightest season on a seven-day leaf-peeping tour.

Day 1
NEW YORK CITY
Hit the Big Apple and enjoy classic NYC: Hop a ferry to the **Statue of Liberty,** get panoramic views of from the **One World Observatory,** then pick up bagels and lox for a picnic in **Central Park,** which is stunning under a canopy of colorful leaves.

Days 2-3
THE BERKSHIRES
140 miles, 2.75 hours
Follow the Hudson River Valley toward **Great Barrington,** Massachusetts, then leave the highway behind for the winding roads through the Berkshires. Stretch your legs on a hike up **Monument Mountain**, where you'll see bright leaves rolling through a series of quiet valleys. Visit the **Norman Rockwell Museum** for a glimpse of autumns past—many of his canvases feature bright New England falls. Settle into **Stockbridge** for a cozy evening of live music by the fire in **The Red Lion Inn's pub.**

Keep pointing north on back roads—or trade your car for a bike on the **Ashuwillticook Rail Trail**—leaving plenty of time to stop at **farm stands** along the way. Route 8 is particularly

Best Hikes

Hike White Mountain crags, walk a trail through rolling Cape Cod sand dunes, or catch America's first sunrise.

Boston

A pair of trails trace American history in Boston.

* **Freedom Trail:** Follow the red line on the sidewalk, and get a whiff of the Revolution (page 33).

* **Black Heritage Trail:** Learn about the separate struggle for freedom of African Americans on this path from memorial to museum (page 33).

Coastal Maine

* **Rockland Breakwater:** Walk along the breakwater and watch sailboats drift past on your way to a historic lighthouse (page 116).

* **Megunticook Trail:** Gain elevation and mountaintop views of Camden Harbor on this hike (page 124).

Acadia National Park

* **South Ridge Trail:** Tackle Cadillac Mountain and catch the country's first sunrise (page 139).

* **Beehive Trail:** Climb straight up a rock face, aided by iron rungs (page 141).

* **Bar Island Trail:** Take a low-tide stroll across the sandbar that links Bar Island to downtown Bar Harbor (page 141).

New Hampshire's White Mountains

* **Presidential Traverse:** Among the most ambitious hikes in New England is the trail that links every peak in the Presidential Range over almost 23 grueling miles, with views in every direction (page 164).

* **Diana's Baths:** A short stroll is the

perfect warm-up for a dip in the waterfall-fed wading pools for which this easygoing trail is named (page 165).

* **Franconia Ridge Loop:** Less crowded than the Presidential Range, and just as scenic, this challenging trail tackles three rocky peaks in a row (page 175).

Southern Vermont

* **Faulkner Trail:** Get an early start and catch sunrise from the summit of Mount Tom (page 192).

* **Quechee Gorge Trail:** Follow the mellow footpath into Vermont's deepest gorge (page 192).

The Berkshires

* **Bellows Pipe Trail:** Follow in the footsteps of Henry Thoreau on this 9.6-mile loop that links North Adams to the summit of Mount Greylock, or simply drive to the summit, where you enjoy the most dramatic section as an out-and-back (page 233).

* **Monument Mountain Trails:** Pass carriage roads and crumbling stone walls on Indian Monument Trail or Hickey Trail, which both earn you views of the rolling, southern Berkshires (page 248).

Newport, Rhode Island

* **Cliff Walk:** Walk all 3.5 miles of this path, or just snip off a section—you'll pass some of the grandest Gilded Age estates in New England and spot surfers off the rocky coast (page 264).

Cape Cod and the Islands

* **Snail Road Trail:** Trek across the sand in Provincetown on your way to a lonely beach, following a trail into the dunes (page 319).

Clockwise from top left: a craft distillery in Portland; the Sandwich boardwalk in Cape Cod; autumn apple picking in the Berkshires.

Art and Culture

Newport Folk Festival

Join colorful crowds on gallery walks, or brush up on high culture at music festivals and museums.

* **Museum of Fine Arts, Boston:** Stroll from the art of ancient Egypt to Impressionist masterpieces in this enormous, exquisite museum (page 47).

* **Massachusetts Museum of Contemporary Art, the Berkshires:** Follow the twists and turns of modern art through the sprawling MASS MoCA, which occupies a former factory in tiny North Adams (page 230).

* **Tanglewood Music Festival, the Berkshires:** Stretch out on the grass at the summer home of the Boston Symphony Orchestra in Lenox, where picnics are raised to fine art (page 238).

* **Music Festivals, Newport:** Watch marquee names from around the world as well as up-and-coming artists at the town's two historic musical blowouts, the Newport Folk Festival and Newport Jazz Festival (page 270).

* **Provincetown Galleries, Cape Cod:** Explore the creative culture of P-town, long a haven for artists and writers (page 315).

scenic from Pittsfield to **North Adams,** winding past the Cheshire Reservoir and slopes of Mount Greylock. In fine weather, drive all the way to the summit of **Mount Greylock,** which looks out over a landscape of brooding evergreens and colorful deciduous trees, but if you find yourself a cold, rainy afternoon, warm up in **MASS MoCA,** the sprawling modern art museum in the heart of workaday North Adams.

Days 4-5
SOUTHERN VERMONT
120 miles, 2.25 hours

Visit the site of Vermont's most famous Revolutionary-era battle in little **Bennington,** then follow Route 9—whose changing elevation offers a varied palette of colors—to **Brattleboro,** the hippie heart of southern Vermont's creative culture. Try to catch a **circus show** or **gallery walk** while you're there, join a tasting of unusual sour beers at **Hermit Thrush Brewery,** or spend the afternoon **picking heirloom apples** at **Scott Farm Orchard,** which offers a magnificent combination of fall fruit and foliage.

Take a roundabout way toward the town of **Woodstock,** tracing a route that includes **tasting aged cheddar** in Grafton's time-warp village center. Skip across to scenic Route 100, which ducks through deep valleys and over rushing mountain streams on its way to the **President Calvin Coolidge State Historic Site.** The historic site is tucked into a quiet hollow that's stunning in autumn and a good place to hear Yankee lore about Vermont's only presidential candidate. Then visit **Long Trail Brewing Company,** which often features special **autumn brews** like the Harvest Barn Ale.

Day 6
WHITE MOUNTAINS
120 miles, 2.75 hours
Take on the twists and turns of the Kancamagus Highway, where each roller-coaster dip brings fresh views of the rugged, high mountain landscape. There are plenty of trails and riverside picnic spots to relax at along the way, but save some daylight for an afternoon adventure: Peak baggers can zip to the top of **Mount Washington,** which feels like a slice of early winter with views of fall foliage in the surrounding valley floors. For a lower-elevation view of the trees, head to **Flume Gorge,** where a covered bridge glows bright red against a backdrop of vivid yellow and orange leaves.

Day 7
BOSTON
145 miles, 3 hours
Get an early morning start, and plan to drop your car off *before* exploring Boston on foot. With an afternoon in the city, plan to walk the **Freedom Trail,** winding from the bright trees of **Boston Common** through Revolutionary sites to the historic **North End** and concluding at the **Bunker Hill Monument.**

Boston

Big-city bluster, colorful neighborhoods, and a vivid Revolutionary past make Boston one of the most fascinating cities in the United States.

ME

COASTAL MAINE

VT

NH

NY

110 MI/180 KM
1.75 HOURS

ATLANTIC
OCEAN

135 MI/220 KM
2 HOURS

THE BERKSHIRES

MA

★ BOSTON

215 MI/350 KM
3.5 HOURS

60 MI/100 KM
1 HOUR

75 MI/120 KM
1.25 HOURS

CAPE COD

CT

RI

NEW YORK CITY

NEWPORT, RHODE ISLAND

Follow the Freedom Trail through Boston to find a city that's grown up alongside its history.

Skyscrapers and modern architecture tower over—yet don't overshadow—Victorian brownstones, colonial graveyards, crooked streets, and gracious squares.

Downtown is bustling and busy, but it wraps around a park that's older than the United States, where swan boats, pavilions, and quiet pathways provide an oasis of green grass and calm. And while Greater Boston sprawls across four New England states—in addition to Massachusetts, the metro area crosses into Rhode Island, New Hampshire, and Connecticut—its principal sights are concentrated on the tiny Shawmut Peninsula, making it easy to explore on foot or by public transport.

Crossing from one side to the other is a quick trip through the collective history and culture of the United States: See the Boston Red Sox's roaring fans in Fenway Park, visit the hushed reading room at the Boston Public Library, make way for ducklings in Boston Common, then walk the cobblestones where revolutionaries preached, fought, bled, and rebelled during the blazing hot summer months of 1776.

Boston's history is anything but simple, and those Revolutionary battles are entwined with a legacy of slavery, the massacres and abuse of Native Americans, and immigration-related racial strife. Today's city, though, is thrillingly diverse: Those ethnic enclaves are celebrated as Boston's collective heritage, the African American Heritage Trail highlights the legacies of Black Bostonians, and locals with roots from around the world blend with Boston's characteristic brass and bluster.

Planning Your Time

You could spend a week exploring all that Boston has to offer. The city's small size, however, makes it easy to see different parts on the same trip, no matter how much time you have. The only mandatory sightseeing destination is a walk along the Freedom Trail, which connects all of downtown's Revolutionary War sites. The city's cultural attractions, for the most part, are grouped on the outskirts of downtown in the Back Bay, South End, and Fenway districts. Art buffs can choose between several very different museums—the world-class Museum of Fine Arts, charming Isabella Stewart Gardner Museum, and cutting-edge Institute of Contemporary Art, while sports fans won't want to miss a guided tour of Fenway Park.

Even on a short trip, it's worth getting across the river to Cambridge, Boston's more bohemian "left bank." In addition to a more laid-back vibe, this sister city is home to Boston's most elite cultural institutions—Harvard University and the Massachusetts Institute of Technology.

Orientation

The bulk of Boston's downtown still takes up the Shawmut Peninsula, with Boston Common at the center. The downtown neighborhoods are organized around the Common, with Beacon Hill and the North End to the north, the Financial District and downtown to the east, and Back Bay and the South End to the west and south. East Boston, along with Logan International Airport, is across Boston Harbor to the northeast, while South Boston and the new Seaport District form a peninsula to the southeast. Across the river to the north are intellectual Cambridge and hip Somerville.

Highlights

★ **Freedom Trail:** Trace the thin red line from Boston Common to Bunker Hill (page 33).

★ **Boston Common and Boston Public Garden:** Catch a ride on a swan boat or watch some summertime Shakespeare in the oldest park in the United States (page 36).

★ **Boston Public Library:** With masterpiece paintings and exquisite architecture, this landmark library is far more than books but it's got millions and millions of those (page 45).

★ **Fenway Park:** From the Green Monster to the bleachers, this ball field is a pilgrimage place for baseball lovers (page 47).

★ **Museum of Fine Arts:** Discover Impressionist treasures and artifacts from around the world (page 47).

★ **North End Cuisine:** Pick up a cannolo, slurp an Italian ice, then watch the neighborhood drift by over a perfect cappuccino (page 58).

Boston

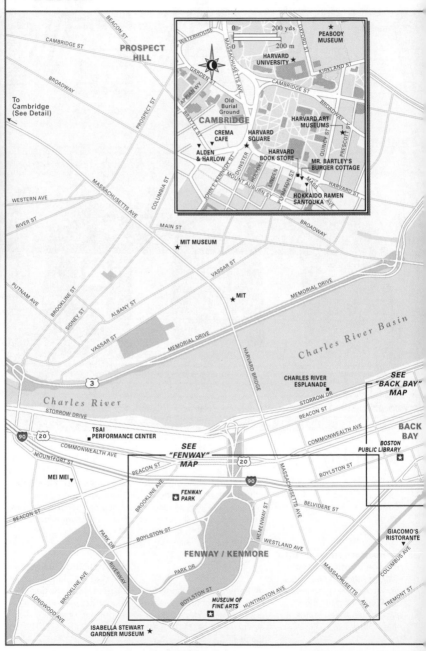

BOSTON

PROSPECT HILL

CAMBRIDGE ST

BEACON ST

BROADWAY

To Cambridge (See Detail)

PROSPECT ST

WATERHOUSE

GARDEN ST

APPIAN WY

BRATTLE ST

MASSACHUSETTS AVE

0   200 yds
0   200 m

★ PEABODY MUSEUM

HARVARD UNIVERSITY ★

CAMBRIDGE ST

KIRKLAND ST

BROADWAY

Old Burial Ground

CAMBRIDGE

CREMA CAFE ▼

HARVARD SQUARE

HARVARD ART MUSEUMS ★

PRESCOTT ST

QUINCY ST

ALDEN & HARLOW ▼

JOHN F. KENNEDY ST

DUNSTER ST

MOUNT AUBURN ST

HARVARD BOOK STORE

LINDEN ST

PLYMPTON ST

MR. BARTLEY'S BURGER COTTAGE ■

MASS. AVE

HARVARD ST

HOKKAIDO RAMEN SANTOUKA ■

WESTERN AVE

RIVER ST

MASSACHUSETTS AVE

COLUMBIA ST

MAIN ST

BROADWAY

★ MIT MUSEUM

VASSAR ST

PUTNAM AVE

BROOKLINE ST

SIDNEY ST

ALBANY ST

★ MIT

MEMORIAL DRIVE

VASSAR ST

MEMORIAL DRIVE

HARVARD BRIDGE

Charles River Basin

③

Charles River

STORROW DRIVE

CHARLES RIVER ESPLANADE

STORROW DR

SEE "BACK BAY" MAP

STORROW DRIVE

BEACON ST

90   20

TSAI PERFORMANCE CENTER ■

COMMONWEALTH AVE

COMMONWEALTH AVE

BACK BAY

BOSTON PUBLIC LIBRARY ✚

MOUNTFORT ST

SEE "FENWAY" MAP

BEACON ST

20

BOYLSTON ST

BELVIDERE ST

MEI MEI ▼

BEACON ST

BROOKLINE AVE

90

FENWAY PARK ✚

HEMENWAY ST

MASSACHUSETTS AVE

WESTLAND AVE

GIACOMO'S RISTORANTE ▼

COLUMBUS AVE

PARK DR

BOYLSTON ST

RIVERWAY

FENWAY / KENMORE

PARK DR

MASSACHUSETTS AVE

TREMONT ST

BROOKLINE AVE

LONGWOOD AVE

BOYLSTON ST

MUSEUM OF FINE ARTS ✚

HUNTINGTON AVE

ISABELLA STEWART GARDNER MUSEUM ★

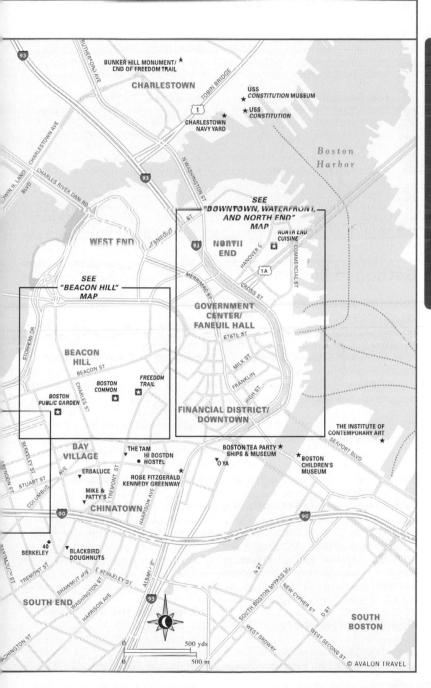

BUNKER HILL MONUMENT/ ★
END OF FREEDOM TRAIL

CHARLESTOWN

USS
★ *CONSTITUTION* MUSEUM

★ USS
CONSTITUTION

CHARLESTOWN
NAVY YARD

*Boston
Harbor*

WEST END

SEE
"DOWNTOWN, WATERFRONT,
AND NORTH END"
MAP

NORTH END
CUISINE

**NORTH
END**

SEE
"BEACON HILL"
MAP

**GOVERNMENT
CENTER/
FANEUIL HALL**

STATE ST

**BEACON
HILL**

BEACON ST

MILK ST

FREEDOM
TRAIL ★

FRANKLIN ST

BOSTON
PUBLIC GARDEN
★

BOSTON
COMMON
★

HIGH ST

**FINANCIAL DISTRICT/
DOWNTOWN**

THE INSTITUTE OF
CONTEMPORARY ART
★

**BAY
VILLAGE**

THE TAM
HI BOSTON ▼
● HOSTEL

BOSTON TEA PARTY ★
SHIPS & MUSEUM

SEAPORT BLVD

ERBALUCE ▼

O YA ▼

★ BOSTON
CHILDREN'S
MUSEUM

MIKE &
PATTY'S ▼

ROSE FITZGERALD ★
KENNEDY GREENWAY

CHINATOWN

40 ▼
BERKELEY

▼ BLACKBIRD
DOUGHNUTS

SOUTH END

**SOUTH
BOSTON**

0   500 yds

0   500 m

© AVALON TRAVEL

Best Accommodations

★ **John Jeffries House:** Simple, affordable rooms look out toward the Charles River from the heart of historic Beacon Hill (page 61).

★ **HI Boston Hostel:** Meet travelers from around the globe in this ultramodern hostel that's steps away from downtown sights (page 62).

★ **Liberty Fleet Tall Ships:** Wake up on the water after sleeping aboard a classic schooner on the Boston waterfront (page 62).

★ **Green Turtle Floating Bed and Breakfast:** Equal parts luxurious and offbeat, this trio of boats is moored at the Charlestown pier (page 63).

★ **College Club of Boston:** Sleep like a "Boston Brahmin" at a onetime private club with high ceilings, historic style, and a tony Back Bay location (page 64).

★ **The Verb:** Join a hip crowd of revelers at the pool, spin some vinyl on your personal turntable, and soak up the rock-and-roll vibe of Boston's edgiest boutique hotel (page 64).

Getting to Boston

Driving from New York City
215 miles, 3.5 hours

Leave New York City heading north on **FDR Drive.** Use the left lane to access Exit 17 to the **Robert F. Kennedy Bridge** ($8 toll, cash only), then stay left to merge onto **I-278 East.** After 4.5 miles, I-278 East merges with **I-95 North** ($1.75 toll, cash only). Follow I-95 North **46 miles** to Exit 27A in Bridgeport, Connecticut; exit right onto **Route 8 North,** which you'll follow 5.5 miles to Exit 9 and **Route 15 North.**

Take Exit 68 NE to merge onto **I-91 North** toward Hartford/Middletown, then stay right for Exit 29 and merge onto **Route 15 North** toward **I-84 East.** Use the left two lanes to continue onto I-84 East toward Boston. North of Sturbridge, I-84 East merges with **I-90** ($7.25 toll, cash only); stay right at the split for **I-90 East.** At Exit 24 use the middle lane to merge onto **I-93 North,** and take Exit 23 for all downtown Boston and North End destinations.

Driving from Newport
75 miles, 1.25 hours

Follow West Main Road north from downtown Newport, which turns into **Route 114 North.** Merge onto **Route 24 North** for about **37 miles.** Take Exit 21A for **I-93 North,** then take Exit 23 for all downtown Boston and North End destinations.

Driving from Cape Cod
60 miles, 1 hour

Starting at the **Sagamore Bridge** that links Sandwich and Sagamore across the Cape Cod Canal, follow **Route 3 North.** Use Exit 20B to merge onto to **I-93 North,** remaining on it until Exit 23 for all downtown Boston and North End destinations.

Driving from Coastal Maine
110 miles, 1.75 hours

From Portland, take **I-295 South** ($1 toll, cash only) to **I-95 South** ($3 toll at York Toll Plaza, $2 toll in Portsmouth, cash only), which you'll remain on for about **84 miles**; at Exit 46 merge onto **Route 1** South/Newbury St./Newbury Turnpike, which loops around to join **I-93 South** into downtown Boston. For downtown and North End destinations, take Exit 24.

Driving from the Berkshires
135 miles, 2 hours

From **Stockbridge,** follow Route 102 East to Lee for about 5 miles, where you'll use the right lane to merge onto I-90 East.

Best Restaurants

★ **Sam LaGrassa's:** It's worth the wait for classic deli sandwiches piled high with pastrami and all the fixings (page 58).

★ **Gene's Chinese Flatbread Cafe:** Broad, hand-pulled noodles are rolled in chili, garlic, and aromatic spices at this Chinatown landmark (page 58).

★ **O Ya:** Creative sushi gets museum-quality presentation in a hushed, elegant restaurant (page 58).

★ **Regina's Pizzeria:** Just-thin-enough crusts, fresh ingredients, and a bit of North End attitude have made this neighborhood pizza place a true classic (page 58).

★ **Neptune Oyster:** The lobster rolls alone would make this chic, North End restaurant a destination, and the raw bar is the best in the city (page 59).

★ **Modern Pastry:** The debate over the North End's best cannoli rages on, but the crispy, creamy version at this classic spot is a strong contender (page 59).

★ **Mei Mei:** Dig into a "Double Awesome" breakfast sandwich for the iconic experience at this eclectic, Chinese American café, or order from its creative, constantly changing menu (page 60).

★ **The Courtyard Restaurant:** Sip tea and nibble scones with a view of Boston Public Library's gracious courtyard (page 60).

★ **Blackbird Doughnuts:** Both sweet and savory doughnuts get rave reviews, but the doughnut ice cream sandwich is the real showstopper (page 60).

★ **Mike & Patty's:** This itsy-bitsy shop serves Boston's best breakfast sandwiches (page 61).

From **Lenox,** drive southeast on Walker Street/Route 183 North and stay right at Lee Road, following signs to Route 7 South. Merge onto **Route 7 South** to Lee.

From **Lee,** you'll take **I-90 East** ($11.10 toll, cash only), remaining on it for about **123 miles** before taking Exit 24 to merge onto **I-93 North.** Take Exit 23 for all downtown Boston and North End destinations (135 mi, 2 hrs).

If you're traveling from the northern part of the Berkshires, an alternate, more scenic route includes the **Mohawk Trail:** Leave **North Adams** on **Route 2 East** to Greenfield; when Route 2 bisects Interstate 91, continue straight onto **Route 2A,** which makes a sharp left turn before rejoining Route 2 a short distance later. From Greenfield through Erving, Route 2 and Route 2A are merged, but follow signs for the Mohawk Trail to continue on Route 2 when the roads diverge after Erving. After passing Concord,

merge onto **I-95 South** using the ramp toward Attleboro, then take Exit 25 to **I-90 East** ($3.55 toll, cash only). At Exit 24 use the middle lane to merge onto **I-93 North,** and take Exit 23 for all downtown Boston and North End destinations (145 mi, 2.75 hrs).

Getting There by Air, Train, or Bus
Air

Flights to Boston's **Logan International Airport** (www.massport.com/logan) are available from almost all major cities. From Logan, ground transportation can be arranged from the information desk at baggage claim. The most efficient way to get into the city is via taxi, though expect to pay a minimum of $25 for downtown locations, or shared van service to downtown and Back Bay for $20-25 per person.

Far cheaper (and almost as quick) is the MBTA Silver Line bus (www.mbta.

Two Days in Boston

Day 1

Start your day in America's oldest park, **Boston Common,** where you can sip a cup of coffee with a view of the gleaming, gilded **Massachusetts State House.** Get your bearings by following the **Freedom Trail** through the city's most important historic sites, with stops to pay your respects to Paul Revere and John Hancock at the **Granary Burying Ground,** visit the **Old State House** and site of the **Boston Massacre,** and stroll **Faneuil Hall.** By the time you reach the Italian American enclave of **North End,** you'll be ready for a sub sandwich with all the fixings from **Monica's Mercato** followed by a classic North End **dessert**— choose between a sugar-dusted cannoli from **Modern Pastry** or zesty Italian ice from **Polcari's Coffee** (or try them both).

Get back on the trail for an afternoon in **Charlestown,** where you can tour the USS *Constitution* and learn about real-life "Rosie the Riveters," then climb to the top of the **Bunker Hill Monument** to get a patriot's-eye view of the entire city. Head back into downtown Boston the easy way, on a ferry ride from the **Charlestown Navy Yard** to the waterfront, then finish the night in one of downtown's creative eateries.

Day 2

Now that you've covered the city's essential sights, slow down at one of Boston's great museums: see Impressionist masterpieces at the **Museum of Fine Arts,** learn about a history-making art heist at the **Isabella Stewart Gardner Museum,** or pitch some tea into the harbor at the **Boston Tea Party Ships and Museum.** If you're visiting Boston with kids, don't miss the fabulous **New England Aquarium,** where hands-on exhibits and walk-through tanks get you up close and personal with the East Coast's wildest underwater creatures.

For your last afternoon in the city, stock up on picnic supplies for an alfresco lunch in the **Boston Public Garden,** where you can watch the city drift by from a shady patch of grass, then take a lazy turn around the duck lagoon on a classic **swan boat.** When the sun goes down, join the boisterous local scene at one of Boston's many **dive bars,** where dim lights and televised sports pair well with pints of cheap beer or Irish whiskey. Start at **The Tam** and see where the night takes you, or go colonial-era at **Union Oyster House,** whose downstairs bar is the perfect place to slurp locally harvested oysters.

com); inbound rides on SL1 from Logan Airport to Boston's South Station are free, and leave from stops directly in front of each terminal. Buses leave several times an hour 5am-1am, and reach South Station in 15-25 minutes. If you're continuing to downtown stops or Cambridge, request a free transfer for the MBTA Red Line subway route.

Train

From most destinations, **Amtrak** (South Station, Summer St. and Atlantic Ave., 800/872-7245, www.amtrak.com) runs service to both the South Station and Back Bay Station. (Amtrak trains from all destinations in Maine run to the North Station.) The **Massachusetts Bay Transportation Authority** (617/222-5000, www.mbta.com) also runs commuter rail service from locations in Greater Boston for fares of up to $6.

Bus

Bus service arrives at the South Station. Most U.S. destinations are served by **Greyhound** (800/231-2222, www.greyhound.com). However, smaller bus companies also run from various locations around the region, such as the **BoltBus** (877/265-8287, www.boltbus.com), **Megabus** (www.megabus.com), and **Peter Pan Bus** (800/343-9999, www.peterpanbus.com).

Sights

Beacon Hill

Federal-style row houses and narrow brick sidewalks make this compact, exclusive district one of the most charming historic neighborhoods. The Black Heritage Trail goes right through the neighborhood, which also contains some of the earliest stops on the Freedom Trail. It's worth taking some time to simply wander, discovering picturesque Acorn Street, spotting the characteristic rippled purple glass in some of Beacon Hill's oldest homes, and making like a local in a café on Charles Street.

★ Freedom Trail

John Hancock, Sam Adams, Paul Revere—history has given the names of America's revolutionaries a nobility and purpose that might have surprised those early Bostonians. In fact, the months leading up to the War for Independence must have seemed more haphazard insurrection than organized battle for freedom to those who lived through them. Even in today's Boston, the passionate men and women who agitated for independence are vivid and accessible. It's easy to get drawn into the stories—both those that have become legendary and those that are less known.

A red line on the sidewalk connects 16 historic sites on a 2.5-mile walking trail ideal for getting your bearings in the city. Make your way from **Boston Common** to a series of churches, graveyards, and other early landmarks in downtown, then continue through the Italian American neighborhood of **North End** to visit **Paul Revere's House** and the church where he hung signal lights for Revolutionary commanders.

The trail then crosses the Charles River to the **Charlestown Navy Yard** and **Bunker Hill Monument,** where climbing 294 steep steps earns you panoramic views of the city from the top of a giant obelisk.

Visitors can walk the line themselves or take a 90-minute guided tour offered by the **Freedom Trail Foundation** (Boston Common Visitor Information Center, 148 Tremont St., 617/357-8300, www.the-freedomtrail.org, $12 adults, $10 students and seniors, $6 children) that covers the first 11 sites along the route; guides are costumed actors playing one of the lesser-known patriots. This is a good place to meet William Dawes, the "other" midnight rider; Abigail Adams, the intellectual letter writer and future first lady; or James Otis, who gave fiery, pro bono legal representation to colonists challenging British laws in court. The **National Park Service** (NPS, www.nps.gov/bost) also leads free tours and offers talks at sites along the Freedom Trail; check the website for schedules.

Perhaps the best way to take in the trail is to book the morning tour with the NPS or the Freedom Trail Foundation, then stop for lunch and an Italian ice in the North End. After lunch, continue across the Charles River to Bunker Hill and the Charlestown Navy Yard via the **ferry** (www.mbta.org, $3.50), which comes every 15-30 minutes, from **Long Wharf,** a waterfront transportation hub at the eastern end of Richmond Street.

Black Heritage Trail

Across from the Massachusetts State House is a life-size bas-relief bronze of Colonel Robert Gould Shaw by New England sculptor Augustus Saint-Gaudens. It depicts the commander of the Massachusetts 54th Regiment, the first all-black volunteer regiment to fight during the Civil War, marching out of Boston with his troops in March 1863. Two months later, Shaw and 271 of his men were killed during a suicide mission on Fort Wagner in South Carolina, galvanizing the country with the bravery of these soldiers. The sculpture is a powerful depiction of Shaw atop his horse, surrounded by soldiers carrying rifles, backpacks, and bedrolls. Above them

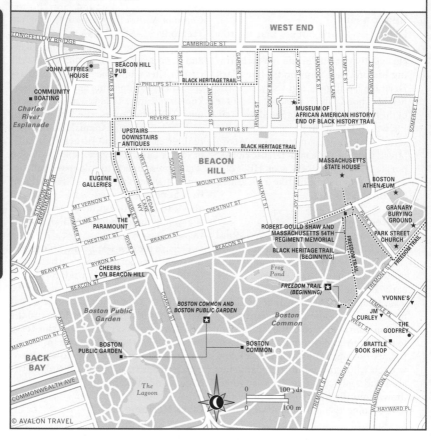

Beacon Hill

WEST END

CAMBRIDGE ST

LONGFELLOW BRIDGE

JOHN JEFFRIES HOUSE

BEACON HILL PUB

CHARLES ST

PHILLIPS ST

GROVE ST

GARDEN ST

SOUTH RUSSELL ST

JOY ST

HANCOCK ST

RIDGEWAY LANE

TEMPLE ST

BOWDOIN ST

SOMERSET ST

BLACK HERITAGE TRAIL

COMMUNITY BOATING

Charles River Esplanade

REVERE ST

ANDERSON ST

IRVING ST

MYRTLE ST

MUSEUM OF AFRICAN AMERICAN HISTORY/ END OF BLACK HISTORY TRAIL

UPSTAIRS DOWNSTAIRS ANTIQUES

PINCKNEY ST

BLACK HERITAGE TRAIL

HISTORY DR/EMBANKMENT DR

WEST CEDAR ST

LOUISBURG SQUARE

BEACON HILL

MOUNT VERNON ST

WALNUT ST

JOY ST

MASSACHUSETTS STATE HOUSE

BOSTON ATHENÆUM

EUGENE GALLERIES

CEDAR LANY

MT VERNON ST

CHARLES ST

LIME ST

THE PARAMOUNT

CHESTNUT ST

RIVER ST

CHESTNUT ST

BRANCH ST

BRIMMER ST

BEACON ST

PARK ST

GRANARY BURYING GROUND

PARK STREET CHURCH

FREEDOM TRAIL

ROBERT GOULD SHAW AND MASSACHUSETTS 54th REGIMENT MEMORIAL

BLACK HERITAGE TRAIL (BEGINNING)

BEAVER PL

BYRON ST

CHEERS ON BEACON HILL

BEACON ST

Frog Pond

FREEDOM TRAIL (BEGINNING)

FREEDOM TRAIL

YVONNE'S

TEMPLE PL

JM CURLEY

WEST ST

THE GODFREY

Boston Public Garden

ARLINGTON ST

CHARLES ST

BOSTON COMMON AND BOSTON PUBLIC GARDEN

Boston Common

BRATTLE BOOK SHOP

MARLBOROUGH ST

BACK BAY

BOSTON PUBLIC GARDEN

BOSTON COMMON

MASON ST

TREMONT ST

WASHINGTON ST

COMMONWEALTH AVE

The Lagoon

0   100 yds
0   100 m

HAYWARD PL

© AVALON TRAVEL

is an angel with an olive branch, symbolizing peace, and poppies, symbolizing death, and the inscription "Omnia Relinquit Servare Rempublicam," which means "He gives up everything to serve the republic."

The **Robert Gould Shaw and Massachusetts 54th Regiment Memorial** is the beginning of the **Black Heritage Trail** (www.afroammuseum.org/trail. htm), which traces the separate journey to freedom of African Americans, nearly 100 years after the events of the first Freedom Trail. Plaques at historic houses en route detail the lives of abolitionists and orators who lived on the back side of Beacon Hill, where Boston's more than 1,000 free African Americans lived and worked by the turn of the 19th century. Follow the trail to the end to visit the African Meeting House, once headquarters of the New England Anti-Slavery Society. Considered the "Black Faneuil Hall," the church now houses the **Museum of African American History,** which has exhibits and films dedicated to the story of Boston's abolitionists. The trail is also part of the **Boston African-American National Historic Site** (617/742-5415, www.nps.gov/boaf), and the

National Park Service runs free 90-minute tours along the route.

Museum of African American History

Small but fascinating, the **Museum of African American History** (46 Joy St., 617/725-0022, www.afroammuseum.org, Mon.-Sat. 10am-4pm, suggested donation $5 adults, $3 seniors and youth 13-17, under 13 free) has exhibits and films dedicated to the story of Boston's abolitionists. See the pulpit where Frederick Douglass recruited for the Massachusetts 54th Regiment, learn about the lives of activist pastors, and trace the roots of some of the United States' most prominent African American writers and thinkers to local Boston neighborhoods. It's worth seeing this museum as part of the free, National Park Service-run tours of the Black Heritage Trail (617/742-5415, www.nps.gov/boaf).

Massachusetts State House

On a sunny day, the shimmering gold dome of the state's capitol building can be seen from miles around. The brick building beneath it is the tidy federal-style structure of the **Massachusetts State House** (24 Beacon St., 617/727-3676, www.sec.state.ma.us/trs, tours Mon. Fri. 10am-3:30pm, free) designed by prominent Boston architect Charles Bullfinch and built in 1798. At the time, 15 white columns were pulled up Beacon Street in a procession of 15 white horses, one for each state. The wooden dome on top was sheathed in copper by Revolutionary renaissance man Paul Revere in 1802, then recovered with 23-karat gold leaf in 1948. Two marble wings were added at the turn of the 20th century.

An impressive selection of statutes graces the park side of the building. The equestrian statue in front of the main entrance depicts Joseph "Fighting Joe" Hooker, a Civil War general from Massachusetts who led the Army of the Potomac for all of six months. (There is no basis, however, to the myth that "hookers" are named after his troops, rumored to be frequent brothel patrons while on leave.) Other statues in front of the building are dedicated to 19th-century orator Daniel Webster and educator Horace Mann. In front of the wings are statues of two prominent women colonists: Anne Hutchinson, a freethinking Puritan who was banished to Rhode Island after nettling local ministers, and Mary Dyer, a prominent Quaker minister condemned for her religion and hanged on Boston Common in 1660.

There isn't much to see inside the building, outside of more statues of various Massachusetts politicians. Most interesting by far is the "Sacred Cod," a five-foot-long pinewood fish that hangs over the chamber of the state House of Representatives. Given to the state by a Boston merchant in 1784, it changes direction depending on which party is in control of the legislature.

Boston Athenaeum

The center of Boston's intellectual life during the early 19th century, this private library was a favorite of scholars like Ralph Waldo Emerson and Oliver Wendell Holmes who gathered to debate the political and philosophical issues of the day. Today, docents offer tours of the renovated **Boston Athenaeum** (10 Beacon St., 617/227-0270, www.boston-athenaeum.org, Mon.-Thurs. 9am-8pm, Fri. 9am-5:30pm, Sat. 9am-4pm, Sun. noon-4pm, free), including the study where Nathaniel Hawthorne reportedly saw the ghost of onetime library regular Reverend Harris (Hawthorne mused that the good reverend might have stopped by to read his own obituary). Among the library's more unusual holdings are the private library of George Washington and one of the world's largest collections of books about the Romany people. Art & Architecture tours of the library are offered Tuesday and Thursday at 3pm, Sunday at 1pm, and Monday at 5:30pm.

Park Street Church

The white-steepled church at the corner of Park and Tremont Streets looks particularly dramatic with a backdrop of downtown high-rises and has been a beloved landmark since its completion in 1809—the novelist Henry James once called it "the most interesting mass of brick and mortar in America." As legend has it, **Park Street Church** (1 Park St., 617/523-3383, www.parkstreet.org, mid-June-Aug. Tues.-Sat. 9:30am-3pm) was known as "brimstone corner" during the War of 1812 for the great stores of gunpowder in the basement, and the song *America (My Country 'Tis of Thee)* was sung on the steps of the church on July 4, 1831, the first public performance.

Granary Burying Ground

Three signers of the Declaration of Independence are interred in the tiny **Granary Burying Ground** (Tremont St. between School St. and Park St., daily 9am-5pm) surrounded by gleaming commercial buildings: Samuel Adams, John Hancock, and Robert Treat Paine. You'll also find Paul Revere, Ben Franklin's parents, and the victims of the Boston Massacre here, though this was far from being a cemetery for the elite—historians believe over 5,000 people were buried here, some in mass burial sites like the crowded Infants Tomb.

The grave markers of the patriots all date from the 20th century—the originals were either stolen or "lost." Many of the gravestones date from the 17th century, weather-beaten stone slabs inscribed with moving (and sometimes flippant) epitaphs and winged death skulls.

★ Boston Common and Boston Public Garden
Boston Common

Boston Common (139 Tremont St.) began its life as a sheep and cow pasture in 1634, just a few years after the city itself was founded. By Puritan law, it was legal for any resident of the city to graze their

autumn in Boston Public Garden

livestock on the common land (that law was repealed in 1833, so you now need to provide your own forage for your cows and sheep). These days, the Common feels like the city's collective backyard, with space for throwing Frisbees, spreading out picnics, and playing in the grass.

Several monuments within the park are attractions in and of themselves. The stunning fountain located just a few steps down from Park Street toward Boylston is named **Brewer Fountain,** a bronze replica of a fountain exhibited at the Paris World's Fair of 1855. The objects on its base depict sea gods and goddesses Neptune, Amphitrite, Acis, and Galatea. Opposite the gold-domed statehouse is the **Robert Gould Shaw and Massachusetts 54th Regiment Memorial,** a bas-relief by Augustus Saint-Gaudens that depicts the first all-black volunteer regiment in the Union army. Near the intersection of Park and Beacon Streets, the **Frog Pond** is an ice-skating rink in winter and a shallow fountain in summer, when it fills with kids cooling off. On the Tremont Street side, at the intersection with Boylston, the **Francis Parkman Bandstand** is used as the site for summer concerts, political rallies, and **Shakespeare in the Park** (www.commshakes.org).

Boston Public Garden

In contrast to Boston Common's open, parklike feel, the **Boston Public Garden** (4 Charles St.), right next door, is an intimate outdoor space, full of leafy trees and flower beds. Built on landfill in the 19th century, the garden was the country's first public botanical garden, envisioned by its creators as a respite from urban life. It's especially romantic at sunset, when the trees cast mysterious shadows over the walkways. The centerpiece is a lagoon, which is crossed by a fairy-tale bridge and surrounded by willow trees trailing their branch tips in the water—note the tiny island in the center of the lagoon which is used by ducks that pad up out of the water on an adorable, ducks-only ramp. Tracing lazy circles in the lagoon are Boston's famous **swan boats** (617/522-1966, www.swanboats.com, Apr.-mid-June daily 10am-4pm, mid-June-early Sept. daily 10am-5pm, early Sept.-mid-Sept. Mon.-Fri. noon-4pm, Sat.-Sun. 10am-4pm, $3.50 adults, $3 seniors, $2 children 2-15), a flotilla of six large paddleboats with the graceful white birds at the stern. The boats are a mandatory attraction if you are in Boston with children, as are the nearby bronze statues of Mrs. Mallard and her eight little ducklings: Jack, Kack, Lack, Mack, Nack, Ouack, Pack, and Quack. The statues pay homage to the children's book *Make Way for Ducklings,* which was partially set in the Boston Public Garden.

Downtown and the Waterfront

Downtown is where Boston's history and cutting edge coexist, an easily walkable district where colonial sites are densely packed amid skyscrapers. While not as

picture-perfect as Beacon Hill, it's the heart of the action. The waterfront is pedestrian-friendly, lined with parks, restaurants and attractions. Just east of Boston Common, the Downtown Crossing area has mega stores, boutiques, and landmark theaters.

King's Chapel

Boston's original Anglican church, **King's Chapel** (Tremont and School Streets, 617/523-1749, www.kings-chapel.org, Mon.-Sat. 10am-5pm, Sun. 1:30pm-5pm, $2 suggested donation), was founded in 1686, but the current stone church building dates to 1749 and holds a bell cast by Paul Revere that is still rung before services. The adjoining graveyard is the oldest in Boston; as such, it contains the graves of some of the original colonists of Massachusetts, including governor John "City on A Hill" Winthrop, and Anne Prine, said to be the real Hester Prynne on whom Nathaniel Hawthorne based his book *The Scarlet Letter*. Along with them are several lesser-known patriots like William Dawes, the "other rider" who raised the alarm on the eve of the battles of Concord and Lexington. There's a fascinating **"Bells and Bones" tour of the church's bell tower and 200-year-old crypt** (617/523-1749, tours at 11am, 1pm, 2pm, 3pm, and 4pm, $10 adults, $7 seniors, students, and military, $5 children under 13).

Old South Meeting House

The Boston Tea Party may have ended in the harbor, but it started at the brick church building with a grey-shingled tower known as the **Old South Meeting House** (310 Washington St., 617/482-6439, www.oldsouthmeetinghouse.org, Nov.-Mar. daily 10am-4pm, Apr.-Oct. daily 9:30am-5pm, $6 adults, $5 seniors and students, $1 children 5-17) dating from 1729. Led by Samuel Adams, over 5,000 patriots gathered here, overflowing into the streets, on the night of December 16, 1773. After fiery speeches, Adams spoke the code words: "This meeting can do no more to save our country." Those words were a prearranged signal to some members in the audience to don face paint and feathers and head down to Griffin's Wharf, where three ships stood loaded down with bins of loose tea. In all, $33,000 worth of tea was thrown into the harbor, setting the stage for the battles that followed. (As a postscript, when Queen Elizabeth II visited Boston for the Bicentennial in 1976, the mayor of the city presented her with a check for $33,000 to cover the cost of the tea—not counting inflation.)

The Old South still serves as a meeting place of sorts, offering (somewhat less rabble-rousing) lectures and classical music. The meeting house museum traces the events surrounding the tea party through an audio exhibit, with actors reading the words of Sam Adams and the other patriots along with sound effects to recreate the time period. A separate multimedia exhibit dubbed "Voices of Protests" focuses on Adams, statesman Ben Franklin, and abolitionist Phyllis Wheatley, who were all members of the Old South's congregation.

Old State House

Before construction of the new state house on Beacon Hill, both British and American governors ruled from the small brick **Old State House** (206 Washington St., 617/720-1713, www.bostonhistory.org, mid-May-early Sept. daily 9am-6pm, early Sept.-mid-May daily 9am-5pm, $10 adults, $8.50 seniors and students, free youth under 18) that's now surrounded by towering offices. On one side of the building are replicas of the standing lion and unicorn that signified the crown of England (the originals were torn down during the Revolution), while on the other is a gold-covered eagle signifying the new United States. On the 2nd floor of the building is the headquarters for the Bostonian Society, which runs a small museum full of artifacts including tea from the Boston Tea Party, weapons from the Battle of Bunker Hill, and clothing worn by John Hancock. Old State House tours are held daily at 10am, noon, 1pm, and 4pm, and meetings with colonial-costumed actors are at 11am, 12:30pm, 2pm, and 3:30pm.

Boston Massacre Site

On March 5, 1770, a group of angry Bostonians gathered in front of the Old State House to protest treatment by British regulars and royalists, and they soon began pelting the redcoats with a *very* Boston blend of dirty snowballs, cinders, and oyster shells.

British soldiers answered by firing their rifles into the crowd, and when the smoke cleared, five colonists lay dead, including Crispus Attucks, a former slave and whaler of African and Native American descent. The soldiers were later exonerated of the charges on the basis of self-defense; lawyer and future president John Adams defended them in court, giving a rousing oratory describing the protesters as "a motley rabble of saucy boys, Negroes and mulattos, Irish teagues and outlandish jack tars . . . the sun is not about to stand still or go out, nor the rivers to dry up, because there was a mob in Boston, on the 5th of March that attacked a party of soldiers. Such things are not new in the world."

There was spin and counter-spin, as the British government dubbed the event the "unhappy occurrence at Boston," while Paul Revere described it as the "bloody massacre." Patriot PR won out: Adams might have gotten the soldiers acquitted, but Revere's engraved images of soldiers firing into a defenseless crowd defined the encounter for Revolutionary Bostonians and posterity. A **Boston Massacre memorial marker** is on the Freedom Trail at the corner of State and Congress Streets.

Faneuil Hall

Peter Faneuil built this landmark building for two purposes: The ground floor would serve as a public food market, and the upstairs meeting hall would be a "marketplace of ideas." When **Faneuil Hall** (Congress St, 617/523-1300, www.nps.gov, daily 9am-5pm, free) was built in 1742, the most pressing issues were taxation on goods by the British government, and it became the main meeting space for protests and discussions by the Sons of Liberty—earning it the nickname the "Cradle of Liberty." After it was expanded in size by architect Charles Bullfinch, the hall was also the main venue for talks by William Lloyd Garrison, Frederick Douglass, and other antislavery activists. Public talks and citywide meetings are still held in the upstairs hall, lent more gravitas by the huge mural of Daniel Webster arguing against slavery that overlooks the stage. During the day, historic talks are given by National Park rangers every half hour. Downstairs, the stalls still exist, even though they have long since stopped selling food products; most are now the venue for souvenirs and other made in Boston goods.

Just behind Faneuil Hall is **Quincy Market** (367 South Market St., 617/523-1300, Mon.-Sat. 10am-9pm, Sun. noon-6pm), where farmers and butchers began selling their wares in 1826. Produce vendors have given way to food stalls, restaurants, and shops, making this a convenient place to grab a snack along the Freedom Trail.

Custom House Tower

Close to the waterfront is Boston's oldest "skyscraper," the 500-foot-tall **Custom House Tower** (3 McKinley Sq., 617/310-6300, www.marriott.com, lobby open daily 7am-11pm), which now houses a Marriott hotel. Built in 1915, the distinctive Beaux-Arts tower features a 22-foot-wide clock and pair of peregrine falcons who nest atop it during summer. You can try to catch a glimpse of them, along with knockout views of the harbor, on the **26th-floor observation deck** (Mon.-Thurs. and Sat.-Sun. 2pm and

6pm, $5-15). The deck on the 26th floor opens twice daily: Arrive at 1:45pm for the 2pm opening, which is $5, or come just before 6pm for the evening tour, which is $7.50 for admission, or $15 with an alcoholic beverage. Inside the tower is also a small museum with a few paintings and American historical artifacts on loan from the Peabody Essex Museum in Salem.

New England Aquarium

The centerpiece of the massive waterfront **New England Aquarium** (Central Wharf, 617/973-5200, www.neaq.org, July-Aug. Sun.-Thurs. 9am-6pm, Fri.-Sat. 9am-7pm, Sept.-June Mon.-Fri. 9am-5pm, Sat.-Sun. 9am-6pm, $27 adults, $25 seniors, $19 children 3-11, free children under 3, IMAX: $10 adults $8 seniors and children 3-11, whale watch: $50 adults $44 seniors, $33 children 3-11, $16 children 2 and under) is a 200,000-gallon tank full of sharks, sea turtles, and giant ocean fish that rises like a watery spinal column through the center of the building. A long walkway spirals around the tank, giving viewers a chance to see sealife on all levels of the ocean, from the toothy pikes that float on the surface to the 550-pound, 90-year-old sea turtle, Myrtle, often spotted snoozing on the floor. Other crowd-pleasers are the harbor seals in the courtyard and enormous open-air penguin pool, filled with three dozen rockhopper, little blue, and African penguins who fill the building with their raucous cries.

The aquarium is not just a museum, but also a research-and-rescue organization that finds stranded seals, dolphins, and other animals and nurses them back to health. You can see the aquarium's latest convalescents in a hospital ward on the 2nd floor. The aquarium also ventures out into the harbor itself for whale-watching trips, seeking out the humpbacks and right whales that make their way into Massachusetts Bay.

North End

Everyone from tour guides to locals will tell you the same thing about this historic neighborhood: "It's just like being in Italy!" The truth is, though, there's something essentially Bostonian about the Italian American North End—the home of the Celtics basketball team as well as numerous pastry shops, old-fashioned grocers, and classic red-sauce joints.

The area is the oldest part of the city, and its history overflows with Puritans and revolutionaries, including Paul Revere, whose house still stands. But by the mid-19th-century it was run-down and crime-ridden. Poor Irish immigrants settled here after fleeing famines at home and were joined by a wave of Jewish immigrants, and, finally the Italians, who reshaped the neighborhood in the image of Genoa, Palermo, Milan, and Naples.

Even as it's gentrified over the years, the North End has retained its cultural identity, with third- and fourth-generation Italians returning on Italian feast days, when churches and community clubs try to outdo each other with lavish parades full of floats, bunting, and sizzling Italian sausage. It's a fascinating place to eat, drink, and explore: With a cannoli in hand, taking in colonial architecture and dodging Boston traffic, you wouldn't mistake it for anywhere else in the world.

Paul Revere House

Every town in New England claims to have a Paul Revere bell in its belfry or a dusty bit of Revere silver in its historical museum. The patriot who made the famous midnight ride to warn the suburbs of the British march, however, was virtually unknown until before the Civil War, when Massachusetts poet Henry Wadsworth Longfellow made him the subject of a poem to stir up passion for the Union cause. Contrary to the poem's dramatic narrative, Revere never made it to Concord to warn the minutemen of the British approach; he was arrested by

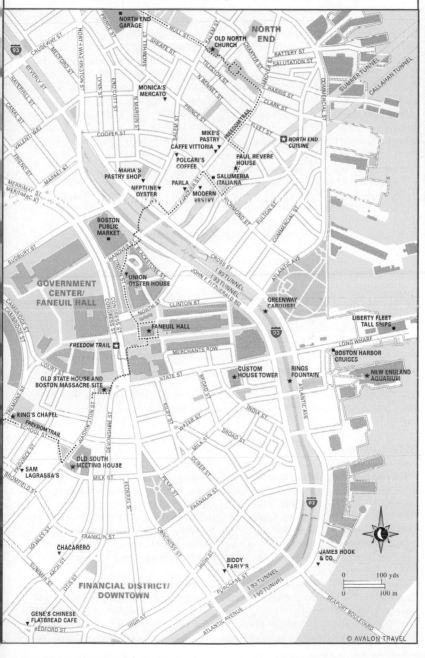

Downtown, Waterfront, and North End

NORTH END GARAGE

NORTH END

OLD NORTH CHURCH

MONICA'S MERCATO

MIKE'S PASTRY
CAFFE VITTORIA
POLCARI'S COFFEE

PAUL REVERE HOUSE

NORTH END CUISINE

MARIA'S PASTRY SHOP

PARLA

SALUMERIA ITALIANA

NEPTUNE OYSTER

MODERN PASTRY

BOSTON PUBLIC MARKET

UNION OYSTER HOUSE

GOVERNMENT CENTER/ FANEUIL HALL

GREENWAY CAROUSEL

LIBERTY FLEET TALL SHIPS

FANEUIL HALL

FREEDOM TRAIL

BOSTON HARBOR CRUISES

OLD STATE HOUSE AND BOSTON MASSACRE SITE

CUSTOM HOUSE TOWER

RINGS FOUNTAIN

NEW ENGLAND AQUARIUM

KING'S CHAPEL

FREEDOM TRAIL

OLD SOUTH MEETING HOUSE

SAM LAGRASSA'S

CHACARERO

BIDDY FARLY'S

JAMES HOOK & CO.

FINANCIAL DISTRICT/ DOWNTOWN

GENE'S CHINESE FLATBREAD CAFE

0   100 yds
0   100 m

© AVALON TRAVEL

the British after warning John Hancock and Sam Adams in Lexington. And he wasn't the only rider out that night. At least two other riders, William Dawes and Dr. Samuel Prescott, were also out warning the colonists.

Whatever the details of Revere's famous night, he was a riveting one-man band of the colonial world who earned his living as a silversmith, coppersmith, bell ringer, and dentist. He raised many of his 16 children in the house that still bears his name. The **Paul Revere House** (19 North Sq., 617/523-2338, www.paul-reverehouse.org, mid-Apr.-Oct. daily 9:30am-5:15pm, Nov.-mid-Apr. daily 9:30am-4:15pm, $3.50 adults, $3 seniors and students, $1 children 5-17, free children under 5) is a typical example of 17th-century architecture and the oldest house still standing in downtown Boston.

The house doesn't have many artifacts—the Museum of Fine Arts is the best place to go to see Revere silver—but it's an interesting window into the living quarters and implements of a typical family in colonial urban North America. Interpretive guides are on hand to lead guests up creaking narrow staircases into the snug quarters where Revere and his wife slept and entertained guests. On Saturday afternoons, artisans demonstrate colonial arts like silversmithing and gilding in the outdoor courtyards.

Old North Church
Paul Revere was a bell ringer in the landmark **Old North Church** (193 Salem St., 617/858-8231, www.oldnorth.com, Jan.-Feb. daily 10am-4pm, Mar.-May and Nov.-Dec. daily 9am-5pm, June-Oct. daily 9am-6pm, $3 donation) when he was a child, so he knew just where to hang his signal lights to warn the rebels that the British were moving by sea to Charlestown, then on to Concord and Lexington. The church sexton, Robert Newman, was the unsung hero in the story—he was arrested by the British the following morning and held in prison

until freed by General George Washington in an exchange. Inside the church, reproductions of colonial flags hang from the ceiling, and every half hour a guide tells Revere's story from the pulpit.

Between Old North and Hanover Street is the **Paul Revere Mall,** with a huge bronze statue of Revere on his horse, keeping watch over pigeons and wizened Italian ladies. Look for the plaques along the wall that honor other patriots who grew up in the North End or tell the stories of some of the original Puritan settlers of the neighborhood, including theologians Cotton and Increase Mather, governor John Winthrop, and Ann Pollard, the first woman settler to arrive in Boston.

Charlestown
The original settlement of the Puritans was named after the king they left behind. A swampy mess of a place without much access to fresh water, Charlestown was eventually abandoned when John Winthrop and company were invited over to the Shawmut Peninsula to found Boston. Charlestown, which is incorporated as a neighborhood of Boston, grew to be an important port in the 18th century. Then tragedy struck during the Revolutionary War, when the British fired cannonballs filled with incendiary oil across the channel and burned the city to the ground in retaliation for their losses at the Battle of Bunker Hill.

The city was rebuilt in the early 19th century about the same time as the brick mansions and brownstones were going up on Beacon Hill, and it shares that neighborhood's historic, cozy feel. Gas lamps, black shutters, and window boxes abound in the neighborhood that winds up toward the Bunker Hill Monument.

Bunker Hill Monument
High on the top of Breed's Hill stands the 221-foot granite obelisk of the **Bunker Hill Monument** (Monument Square, 617/242-5641, www.nps.gov/bost/historyculture/

bhm.htm, mid-Mar.-Nov. daily 9am-5pm, Dec.-mid-Mar. Mon.-Fri. 1pm-5pm, Sat.-Sun. 9am-5pm, free) to mark the misnamed first major battle of the Revolutionary War. In it, the patriots—while defeated—inflicted such high casualties upon the British army that thousands rushed to the colonial cause to begin a protracted siege of Boston. Climb the 294 steep, winding steps to the top of the monument for fine views of Boston Harbor and the city skyline.

Across the street, the impressive **Bunker Hill Museum** (43 Monument Sq., 9am-5pm daily, free) opened in 2007 with two floors of exhibits about the battle. In addition to artifacts such as a British cannonball, the museum features two dioramas with miniature figurines that perpetually fight the battle over again with the help of a sound and light display. The highlight, however, is the beautifully painted "cyclorama" on the 2nd floor, depicting the battle in breathtaking 360 degrees.

USS *Constitution*

The oldest commissioned ship in the American Navy, the **USS *Constitution***—also known as "Old Ironsides"—was named by President Washington and launched in 1798. In 17 years of active duty, it racked up a battle record as celebrated as any ship of its time, defeating the heavier British ships *Guerrière* and *Java* during the War of 1812, and leading a blockade of Tripoli during the War of the Barbary Coast.

She's now docked at Charlestown Navy Yard, where sailors give tours every half hour; it's thrilling to stand behind a long cannon on the gun deck or sit at the gambrel table in the captain's quarters. Some of the stones in the bilge are the originals placed there for ballast more than 200 years ago. The last time the *Constitution*

Top to bottom: Massachusetts State House; Paul Revere statue and the Old North Church; *USS Constitution*.

detached from a tugboat to sail freely under its own power was in 1997 during its 200th anniversary; the ship, however, is towed out into Boston Harbor and turned around with a 21-gun salute every year on July 4. (Members of the public can sign up on the ship's website for a lottery to board the ship for these cruises.)

Another warship living out her days in Charlestown is the **USS *Cassin Young,*** a Fletcher-class destroyer that was active in the Battle of Leyte Gulf and Battle of Okinawa, then stayed in service until 1960. The *Cassin Young* is one of just four Fletcher-class vessels still afloat, and it offers a glimpse of the cramped, tidy life aboard a naval vessel.

Get the background on the ships and the naval yard at the **Charlestown Naval Yard Visitors Center** (Charlestown Navy Yard, Building 5, 617/242-5601, www.nps.gov/bost/historyculture/cny.htm, mid-Mar.-Oct. daily 9am-5pm, Nov.-mid-Mar. Thurs.-Sun. 9am-5pm), which features a 10-minute video on the history of the yard, along with ropes, chains, uniforms, and other artifacts. Near the ship is a much larger **USS *Constitution* Museum** (Charlestown Navy Yard, 617/426-1812, www.ussconstitutionmuseum.org, Apr.-Oct. daily 9am-6pm, Nov.-Mar. daily 10am-5pm, suggested donation $5-10 adults, $3-5 children, $20-25 families) that displays swords, pistols, and cannonballs captured from the *Constitution*'s various engagements, along with a giant model of the ship under full sail. Several short films give more information about the ship and its history. Kids love the upper floor of the museum, which features a cannon they can swab, wad, and "fire" against an enemy ship and a rudimentary video game in which they can engage the HMS *Java* while learning the basic principles of battle under sail.

Fenway and Back Bay
Back Bay
In the most fashionable neighborhood in Boston, Back Bay's grand boulevards are lined with brownstones and large Victorian-style apartment buildings, linked by short side streets that are ordered alphabetically (Arlington, Berkeley, Clarendon . . .). Ironically, given how swanky the neighborhood has become, the area used to be one big disease-spreading swamp—it's no accident that the neighborhood's main drag, Boylston Street, is named after a doctor. In the days when Boston used to be a peninsula, Back Bay was literally a bay in the Charles River, where refuse would wash up with the tides, and men and boys—including a young Ben Franklin—would fish from shore. As the city expanded in the 1800s, the earth from Beacon Hill and other high ground was used for landfill to close up the bay, and a new neighborhood was born, quickly populated with larger and more impressive houses.

Arlington Street Church
Striking Tiffany windows depict Jesus's beatitudes—a series of blessings praising the meek, merciful, and peaceful — in the Unitarian Universalist **Arlington Street Church** (351 Boylston St., 617/536-7050, www.ascboston.com, open most mornings, free), where ministers like Theodore Parker and William Ellery Channing preached about abolition and social justice in the early 19th century.

Trinity Church
This Presbyterian landmark is the undisputed masterpiece of architect H. H. Richardson, whose bold style sparked a trend called "Richardson Romanesque" featuring massive blocks of stone, often worked in a contrasting "checkerboard" pattern with sweeping arches and towers. The inside of the **Trinity Church** (206 Clarendon St., 617/536-0944, www.trinitychurchboston.org, Tues.-Sat. 10am-5pm, Sun. 7:30am-8pm, $7, free children under 16) is calculated to impress, with a vaulted ceiling and a huge carved wooden pulpit in front of the altar. Classical music concerts are regularly offered here,

Back Bay

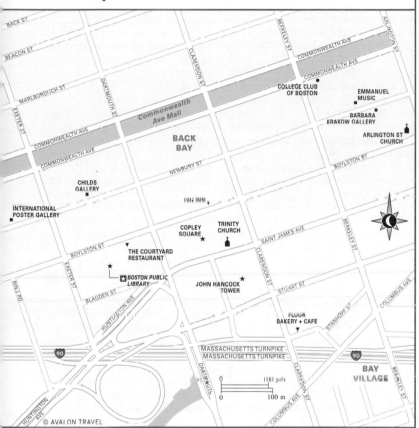

especially around the holidays, and volunteers lead tours twice a day (call for times).

★ Boston Public Library

The first municipal public library in the United States feels like a temple to learning and Western culture, from the bust of Athena watching over the entryway to stunning murals depicting vivid mythological scenes. The **Boston Public Library** (700 Boylston St., 617/536-5400, www.bpl.org, Mon.-Thurs. 9am-9pm., Fri.-Sat. 9am-5pm, Sun. 1pm-5pm, free) fills two city blocks on the south side of Copley Square, dividing its treasures into two buildings. The original, designed by Charles McKim and opened in 1895, is now the research library, with a more modern building next door holding the circulating collection.

While the library's collection is vast, its art and architecture make it destination-worthy as well; the exterior has classical proportions and is covered with names of great thinkers through the ages, and twin female statues of Art and Science keep guard outside. One of the best-kept secrets of the city is the library's central courtyard, an Italianate plaza that wraps around a central fountain (high tea at the courtyard restaurant is a special treat).

The hushed, studious heart of the McKim building is the Bates Reading Room, a 200-foot-long hall with a barrel-vaulted ceiling; high, arched windows; and long tables lined with dimly lit green lamps. One artistic highlight is the 80-foot-long Sargent Gallery, which features painter John Singer Sargent's fantastical mural sequence "Triumph of Religion," a sensual, often tempestuous journey through the gods, goddesses, and prophets of the ancient world. Other artistic works in the library include a mural sequence dedicated to the story of the search for the Holy Grail by American artist Edwin Austin Abbey, and a painting of George Washington at Dorchester Heights by Emanuel Gottlieb Leutze (who also did the famous painting of Washington crossing the Delaware). Free hour-long tours of the library's art and architecture are offered at various times daily; call for times.

John Hancock Tower

When it was first proposed in the 1970s, the 790-foot **John Hancock Tower** was met with fierce resistance by residents who feared it would wreck the historic ambience of Copley Square. In a stroke of genius, architect I. M. Pei covered the outside of the building with reflective glass, thereby enhancing rather than overshadowing the architectural beauty of Trinity Church, the Boston Public Library, and other nearby buildings. Not everything ended happily, however—due to a design flaw, many of the 10,344 panes of glass began falling out and shattering on the sidewalk below before the building was completed. Pei later corrected the technique for hanging the glass (which he also used on the pyramid for the Louvre), and the building is now one of the most striking in the city skyline.

Nearby, the much smaller "old" John Hancock building features a beacon on top that changes color depending on the weather forecast. Many older Bostonians can still recite the rhyme that cracks the code: "Steady blue, clear view / Flashing blue, clouds due / Steady red, rain ahead / Flashing red, snow instead." During summer and fall, flashing red means the Red Sox game is cancelled due to weather conditions.

Christian Science Center

With a towering dome and a grand organ, this "mother church" is the international center for the Church of Christ, Scientist (not, as docents are at pains to point out, the totally unrelated Church of Scientology). Founded in 1879 by Mary Baker Eddy, the religion is best known for its practice of "faith healing" that forbids its practitioners to take medicine for illnesses. Eddy, however, was once a larger-than-life figure in U.S. culture who was a leader of the early women's movement and a pioneering publisher. Visitors can learn more about Eddy's life at the eclectic **Mary Baker Eddy Library** (200 Massachusetts Ave., 617/450-7000, www.marybakereddylibrary.org, Tues.-Sun. 10am-4pm, $6 adults, $4 seniors, students, and youth 6-17, free children under 6). A series of multimedia exhibits encourages visitors to develop their own life philosophies while at the same time tracing the evolution of its matriarch's ideas with refreshingly little proselytizing. Another exhibit within the museum literally provides a window into the newsroom of the *Christian Science Monitor,* which has its headquarters in the complex.

Within the Christian Science Center, one hidden gem deserves special mention. The **Mapparium** (200 Massachusetts Ave., 617/450-7000, www.marybakereddylibrary.org, Tues.-Sun. 10am-4pm, $6 adults, $4 seniors, students, and youth 6-17, free children under 6) is a 30-foot-diameter globe with the countries of the world (circa 1935) displayed in vibrant stained glass around the walls. Standing on a clear bridge in the center offers a remarkable perspective on a globe whose borders have been dramatically rewritten by over 80 years of conflict. Twenty-minute tours of the Mapparium include a seven-minute light show with inspirational soundbites from Nelson Mandela, Eleanor Roosevelt, and other seminal thinkers.

Fenway

Upon first glance, the area of the city known as the Fenway doesn't seem to offer much. A gritty network of streets lined with pubs and discount stores, the neighborhood has traditionally been the stomping grounds for students of nearby Boston University. Scratch beneath the surface, however, and you'll find several of the city's premier cultural attractions, including the Museum of Fine Arts and the jewel-box Isabella Stewart Gardner Museum. The neighborhood gets its name from the Back Bay Fens, a winding, swampy greensward that serves as the drainage channel for the city. Today, The Fens is a rambling parkland, lined with ball fields and community gardens, including the hidden Kelleher Rose Garden, a dreamy garden full of vine-covered trellises and over 100 varieties of roses. The center of the neighborhood is Kenmore Square, a lively crossroads of student bars, discount stores, and burrito joints, just down the street from the historic home of the Boston Red Sox: Fenway Park.

★ Fenway Park

A new banner was flapping in the breeze here after the Red Sox's come-from-behind race to win the 2004 World Series. While the high of that victory infused **Fenway Park** (4 Yawkey Way, 617/226-6666, www.redsox.com, tours 9am-5pm, hrs differ on game days, $18 adults, $15 military, $12 children 3-12) with a new energy, Fenway has long been one of the most electric places to catch the national pastime. First opened in 1912, Fenway has a soul that none of the more modern parks can match. For the uninitiated,

the geography of the park—with its Green Monster, Pesky's Pole, and Ted Williams's seat—can seem a little arcane, but you can get your bearings with a tour led by one of the Fenway faithful. As good as those tours may be, however, nothing quite beats taking a seat in the bleachers, grabbing a Sam Adams, and waiting for the first crack of the bat.

★ Museum of Fine Arts

This grand, neoclassical museum's art collection is one of the best and most beloved in the country. The MFA, as it's known, is particularly noted for its French Impressionist works, but it also has outstanding Asian and Egyptian collections, as well as many celebrated early American paintings and artifacts. The **Museum of Fine Arts** (465 Huntington Ave., 617/267-9300, www.mfa.org, Sat.-Tues. 10am-5pm, Wed.-Fri. 10am-10pm, $25 adults, $23 seniors and students, $17 youth under 18, free for youth under 18 Mon.-Fri. after 3pm and on weekends, free for active-duty military from Memorial Day to Labor Day) began its life as the painting collection of the Boston Athenaeum, the private library on Beacon Hill. Under its current leadership, the museum has taken some gambles to bring more modern viewers into the galleries, staging artistic exhibitions of guitars and racecars alongside showstopping special exhibits featuring masterpieces by Monet, Van Gogh, and Gauguin.

At present, most visitors to the MFA make a beeline for the 2nd floor, which is home to several jaw-dropping rooms dedicated to works by French Impressionists Monet, Manet, Renoir, Van Gogh, and others. Less trafficked but equally rewarding are the American galleries, where you'll find what's arguably the most famous American painting ever: Gilbert Stuart's original unfinished painting of George Washington. The collection includes several paintings by John Singer Sargent, including the arresting *Daughters of Edward Darley Bolt,* as well

Fenway

PARK DRIVE

FENWAY

PARK DRIVE

KILMARNOCK ST

BOYLSTON ST

VAN NESS ST

BROOKLINE AVE

OVERLAND ST

BEACON ST

90

20

PETERBOROUGH ST

QUEENSBERRY ST

JERSEY ST

★ REGINA ▼
PIZZERIA

YAWKEY WAY

LANSDOWNE ST

MASSACHUSETTS TURNPIKE

COMMONWEALTH AVE

NEWBURY ST

★ THE VERB

★

✚ FENWAY
PARK

★

PARK DRIVE

PARK DRIVE

FENWAY

✚ MUSEUM
OF FINE ARTS

★

FORSYTH WAY

FENWAY

IPSWICH ST

BOYLSTON ST

Back Bay Fens

AGASSIZ ROAD

FENWAY /
KENMORE

★ FENWAY
VICTORY GARDENS

HEMENWAY ST

FENWAY

FENWAY

IPSWICH ST

NEWBURY ST

20

90

20

HUNTINGTON AVE

GAINSBOROUGH ST

SYMPHONY ROAD

WESTLAND AVE

BURBANK ST

HEMENWAY ST

BOYLSTON ST

MASSACHUSETTS AVE

0
0

100 yds
100 m

JORDAN
HALL ■

SAINT STEPHEN ST

■ BOSTON
SYMPHONY
HALL

HAVILAND ST

EDGERLY ROAD

MASSACHUSETTS AVE

SAINT GERMAIN ST

CLEARWAY ST

BELVIDERE ST

● OASIS GUEST
HOUSE

■ BERKLEE
PERFORMANCE
CENTER

▼ BUKOWSKI
TAVERN

NEWBURY ST

HEREFORD ST

GLOUCESTER ST

■ TRIDENT
BOOKSELLERS
& CAFE

NEWBURY
ST

90

★ CHRISTIAN SCIENCE CENTER
AND MAPPARIUM

HUNTINGTON AVE

SAINT BOTOLPH ST

MASSACHUSETTS AVE

WALLY'S ▼
■

WELLINGTON ST

CLAREMONT PK

GREENWICH PARK

WEST NEWTON ST

CUMBERLAND ST

COLUMBUS AVE

BACK
BAY

MASSACHUSETTS TURNPIKE

BOYLSTON ST

SOUTH
END

© AVALON TRAVEL

as those by Boston's own adopted artist, John Singleton Copley, including his portrait of Paul Revere. Several examples of the patriot silversmith's work are on display in adjoining galleries of colonial artifacts and furniture. Tours of various collections within the museum are offered free with admission throughout the day.

Isabella Stewart Gardner Museum

The small **Isabella Stewart Gardner Museum** (280 The Fenway, 617/566-1401, www.gardnermuseum.org, Fri.-Mon. and Wed. 11am-5pm, Thurs. 11am-9pm, $15 adults, $12 seniors, $5 students, free youth under 18) is filled with priceless European and American paintings. The most cherished work of art, however, may be the building itself, which is constructed around a plant-filled Italianate courtyard that may be the most pleasing indoor space in the city. The namesake socialite who built the museum was known as something of a brilliant eccentric who loved art and the Red Sox, and scandalized polite society by posing for a sensuous portrait by John Singer Sargent. (On display in the museum, the portrait was exhibited only once in Gardner's lifetime due to the wishes of her husband.) Other works of art in the collection include Titian's *Europa*, which may be the single most important work of art in Boston; Sargent's dynamic *El Jaleo*; Boticelli's *Virgin and Child with an Angel*; and an early Rembrandt self-portrait.

The building, where Gardner lived, has four floors of artwork organized as a living house museum, with some of the original typed labels still in place. Gardner's will stipulated that nothing in the museum be moved, or else the entire collection would be sold and the proceeds donated to Harvard's art faculty. The museum made headlines around the world for what's

Top to bottom: home game at Fenway Park; Museum of Fine Arts; Isabella Stewart Gardner Museum.

often called the largest art heist in history: As St. Patrick's Day revelers filled the streets during the early hours of March 18, 1990, two thieves disguised as police officers stole 13 works of art, including two Rembrandts and a stunning Vermeer. The empty frames for the stolen paintings still hang on the wall, and a five-million-dollar reward has never been collected. Keep your ticket stub from the MFA (or wear a piece of Red Sox gear) for a $2 discount on admission. Charmingly, anyone named Isabella gets free entry for life.

South End

Running along the southern edge of Fenway, Back Bay, and downtown, Boston's South End neighborhood doesn't have major sights, but with brick Victorian houses and a thriving arts community, it's an appealing place to wander. Pleasant parks are filled with young families. The hotel and restaurant options that spill out along the northern edge are convenient to downtown and Back Bay.

Seaport

Across Fort Point Channel from downtown, the South Boston waterfront district is a neighborhood in transition. For years, it has been home to New England's largest community of artists, who have taken advantage of the solid warehouses that once housed the stores for Boston's wool trade to build artist studios and performance spaces; the area itself is a visual artist's dream, with open spaces broken by iron girders and views of the harbor. It's now a darling of developers using the last bits of open space to create new hotels and condos.

Boston Tea Party Ships and Museum

The original three British ships that were the unwilling hosts to the Boston Tea Party were moored at Griffin's Wharf, which was later buried in landfill during the expansion of the city. The best

estimate of the location is near the present-day corner of Atlantic Avenue and Congress Street, near South Station. Not far from that spot, the **Boston Tea Party Ships and Museum** (306 Congress St., 617/338-1773, www.bostonteaparty-ship.com, daily 10am-5pm, $26 adults, $23 seniors, $16 children, purchase online for 10% discount) features replicas of the three original ships—the *Beaver,* *Dartmouth,* and *Eleanor*—but the real highlight is the vivid, and participatory, reenactment by actors in period dress. Among the items on display is the so-called "Robinson Tea Chest," which was recovered by a participant the day after the event, and one of only two original tea chests known to survive. Early American patriots drank coffee to signal their rejection of British traditions and sovereignty, but you can still find a nice cup of tea at the on-site **Abigail's Tearoom & Terrace** (daily 11:30am-3pm).

Institute of Contemporary Art

The **Institute of Contemporary Art** (ICA, 25 Harbor Shore Dr., 617/478-3100, www.icaboston.org, Tues.-Wed. and Sat.-Sun. 10am-5pm, Thurs.-Fri. 10am-9pm, $15 adults, $13 seniors, $10 students, free children under 17, free to all Thurs. after 5pm) was once viewed as being on par with New York's Museum of Modern Art (MoMA) on the vanguard of experimental modern art. While MoMA decided to collect the artists it exhibited and now boasts the likes of Jackson Pollock and Jasper Johns, the ICA felt that it could better remain on the cutting-edge by continually exhibiting new work. Making up for lost time, the ICA opened a new home on the waterfront in 2006, a space-age landmark that triples the size of the museum's old home in Back Bay, and more importantly adds a permanent collection for the first time. In its old location, the museum garnered a reputation for staging explosive exhibitions such as the first U.S. display of the photos of Robert Mapplethorpe in the 1980s;

in recent years, however, its exhibits of contemporary multimedia installations and photography have had a more uneven reception. The new building, designed by edgy architectural firm Diller Scofidio + Renfro, has reinvigorated the museum, providing dramatic views of the waterfront from flexible gallery spaces, and adding a 325-seat performing arts theater overlooking the harbor.

Boston Children's Museum
Kids can get their hands into giant bubbles, colorful art projects, and science exhibits at the fun **Boston Children's Museum** (308 Congress St., 617/426-6500, www.bostonchildrensmuseum.org, Sun.-Thurs. 10am-5pm, Fri. 10am-9pm, $16, free children under 1), which is best suited for children under the age of 11. Budding construction workers can build skyscrapers and jackhammer them down in the Construction Zone; little monkeys can tackle a brightly colored maze of tunnels, towers, and walkways called the Climb; and the nautically inclined can float their boats in a 28-foot-long model of the Fort Point Channel (visible outside the museum's walls) called Boats Afloat.

Cambridge
Two of the country's most iconic universities—Harvard and the Massachusetts Institute of Technology (MIT)—are just across the Charles River from downtown Boston in historic, quirky Cambridge. These are just the beginning of the over 100 colleges and universities in the greater Boston area, and a regular influx of students is part of what keeps Boston eternally young and energetic. Head across the river to get a taste of the intellectual scene; Cambridge is about three miles from downtown Boston and easily reached on the MBTA Red Line (Harvard station).

Harvard University
Download an audio tour and map to take a self-guided trip around the Harvard campus, or start the trip like a prospective student on a **Harvard Campus Tour** (1350 Massachusetts Ave., Cambridge, 617/495-1573, www.harvard.edu, free tours Mon.-Sat. 9am-5pm) that takes in the best of the university's green quads, landmark libraries, and that famous Harvard Yard.

Three separate facilities make up the **Harvard Art Museums** (617/495-9400, www.harvardartmuseums.org, daily 10am-5pm, $15 adults, $13 seniors, $10 students, free youth under 18), and Harvard's **Peabody Museum** (11 Divinity Ave., Cambridge, 617/496-1027, www.peabody.harvard.edu, daily 9am-5pm, $12 adults, $10 seniors and students, $8 children 3-18, under 3 free) is one of the oldest anthropological museums in the world.

Many of Boston and Cambridge's schools open their doors to the public for lectures by speakers from around the world. The **Harvard University Gazette** (www.news.harvard.edu/gazette) publishes a full schedule of talks. At Harvard you can even **attend a class** (www.college.harvard.edu/visitors-guide-larger-lectures) on anything from East Asian cinema to post-Hamlet literature and statistics. Contemporary readings and talks by authors are frequently held at the **Harvard Book Store** (1256 Massachusetts Ave., Cambridge, 800/542-7323, www.harvard.com).

Campus life spills into the streets at **Harvard Square** (Massachusetts Ave. and Brattle St.), a bustling plaza lined with shops and restaurants. Chain outlets have dimmed some of the spot's independent charm, but there are still enough buskers, artists, and studious undergraduates to make it an inviting destination.

Massachusetts Institute of Technology
Head to **MIT** (77 Massachusetts Ave., Cambridge, www.web.mit.edu, 617/253-1000, free tours call for times) for a tour of the striking campus, whose blend of old-fashioned architecture and

modernist, cutting-edge buildings offers a wonderful study in contrasts. No surprise: MIT's whiz engineers also designed a **mobile app campus tour** that you can download from iTunes and Google Play.

The **MIT Museum** (265 Massachusetts Ave., Cambridge, 617/253-5927, www.web.mit.edu/museum, daily 10am-5pm, $10 adults, $5 seniors, students, and children) traces the history of science, engineering, and research. The school also publishes a full schedule of talks (http://events.mit.edu).

Entertainment and Events

As a city that has always prided itself on culture, Boston rarely lacks for interesting arts and entertainment offerings. To find what's happening, check www.boston.com and www.thebostoncalendar.com, which has lots of free events. For tickets to theater performances, a great resource is **BosTix** (617/262-8632, www.calendar.artsboston.org), which offers half-price tickets the day of the show. Booths are located in **Faneuil Hall** (1 Faneuil Hall Sq., 617/262-8632, Tues.-Sun. 10am-4pm) and **Copley Square** (650 Boylston St., Thurs.-Sun. 10am-4pm) and only accept cash. Hours can vary, so call or check the website before stopping by.

Nightlife
Bars
Beacon Hill
Last call for the sitcom *Cheers* was in 1993, but the Beacon Hill bar where the exterior shots were filmed is still a serious destination. Life imitates art at **Cheers on Beacon Hill** (84 Beacon St., 617/22709605, www.cheersboston.com, daily 11am-1am), formerly the Bull & Finch Pub, where the upstairs has been reinvented as the fictitious television bar, complete with brass nameplates for the "regulars." There is a second location at Faneuil Hall, but it's worth heading to the original, which has a bit more charm to go with the cheese.

An oasis of blue-collar culture (or at least off-duty lawyers) with a tony address, **Beacon Hill Pub** (149 Charles St., 617/625-7100, Mon.-Sat. 11am-2am, Sun. noon-2am, cash only) is a great spot to pull up a stool and catch a game.

The menu at **No. 9 Park** (9 Park St., 617/742-9991, www.no9park.com, Tues.-Sat. 5:30pm-10pm, Sun.-Mon. 5:30pm-9pm) includes hard-to-find bottles and old-world varietals that earned the wine program a James Beard Award. Though it's primarily a restaurant, the quiet bar is an elegant place to enjoy a glass and a snack from the à la carte menu.

Downtown and the Waterfront
The most iconic bars in Boston fall firmly into "dive bar" territory—the kind of sticky, beer-soaked neighborhood joints where St. Patrick's Day memories are forged (or erased). One classic of the genre is **The Tam** (222 Tremont St., 617/482-9182, Sun.-Thurs. 8am-1am, Fri.-Sat. 8am-2am, cash only), a morning-to-night destination for cheap beer, loud music, and a gruff crowd of locals. Another downtown favorite is **Biddy Early's** (141 Pearl St., 617/654-9944, Mon.-Sat. 10am-2am, Sun. noon-2am), where Irish-themed decor and PBR Sriracha chicken wings pair beautifully with dartboards and arcade games.

All dark wood and scuffed signboards, the **Green Dragon Tavern** (11 Marshall St., 617/367-0055, daily 11am-2am) evokes the 1654 bar by the same name that Daniel Webster called the "Headquarters of the Revolution." The original was knocked down in 1854, but the new version is atmospheric and cozy, with an old-world feel and live music most nights.

There's an excellent selection of beers from around New England at **jm Curley** (21 Temple Pl., 617/228-5333, Mon.-Sat. 11:30am-1:30am, Sun. 11:30am-midnight), along with very credible cocktails and fresh bar food. Bacon popcorn is a favorite here.

Some of the finest cocktails in town are at the ultra-stylish, nostalgic **Yvonne's** (2 Winter Place, 617/267-0047, www.yvonnesboston.com, daily 4pm-2am), a Downtown Crossing supper club with two great places to drink (and take selfies): Settle in at the grand mahogany bar or grab a spot in the "library," which is lined with designer-selected vintage titles.

Quirky Victorian-era ephemera—black and white images of shirtless boxers, framed corsets—give **Stoddards Fine Food & Ale** (48 Temple Pl., 617/426-0048, www.stoddardsfoodandale.com, Thurs.-Sat. 11:30am-2am, Sun. 11:30am-midnight, Tues.-Wed. 11:30am-1am) a time-warp feel. Classic cocktails are listed by year, stretching back to the 1850s-era Sazerac, but the solid beer list is strictly 21st century.

Many of Boston's finest Irish bars are buried in hard-to-reach neighborhoods, but despite its downtown location, **Mr. Dooley's** (77 Broad St., 617/338-5656, www.somerspubs.com, Mon.-Fri. 11:30am-2am, Sat.-Sun. 9am-2am) is the real deal. Pints of Guinness and Jameson shots go well with live Irish music most weekend nights. Come ready to sing along to all the classics.

North End

Somewhere between chic Italian bistro and fantasy Prohibition-era speakeasy, **Parla** (230 Hanover St., 617/367-2824, www.parlaboston.com, daily 4pm-11pm) infuses its cocktail list with seasonal ingredients and offbeat flavors, but the gorgeous space alone is worth the visit.

The North End take on the Boston dive bar is **Corner Cafe** (87 Prince St., 617/523-8997, Mon.-Sat. 9am-2am, Sun. noon-2am), where locals scratch lottery tickets, drink cheap draft beer, and slurp up pudding shots (which are better than they sound). The real secret, however, is that Corner Cafe invites patrons to order food from outside, so you can grab a beer and call for a Regina's pizza.

Fenway and Back Bay

In the spirit of the raunchy, beer-loving poet, the **Bukowski Tavern** (50 Dalton St., 617/437-9999, Mon.-Sat. 11:30am-2am, Sun. noon-2am) has a gleefully unreconstructed feeling, but with a good draft list that transcends the usual dive bar pours.

Generic, somewhat corporate decor almost seems like a smoke screen for the incredible draft list at **The Lower Depths** (476 Commonwealth Ave., 617/266-6662, www.thelowerdepths.com, daily 11:30am-1am), which often includes cask beers and unusual brews from around the East.

I think outside the margarita at the gothic-themed **Lolita Cocina & Tequila Bar** (271 Dartmouth St., 617/369-5609, daily 5pm-2am), where tufted black leather and red lights meet a menu of sophisticated cocktails. Mixed drinks are both fresh and fierce, but there's also an appealing menu of house-made non-alcoholic drinks. The dessert menu is legendary.

Live Music

The South End's **Wally's** (427 Massachusetts Ave., 617/424-1408, www.wallyscafe.com) hosts jazz the way it was meant to be played, in a closet-sized room that heats up both on and off stage. Meanwhile, the nearby "Harvard of jazz," the Berklee School of Music, sponsors performances of both modern legends and up-and-coming prodigies at its **Berklee Performance Center** (136 Massachusetts Ave., 617/747-2261, www.berkleebpc.com), which also occasionally has folk and pop acts.

In addition to **Boston Symphony Hall** (301 Massachusetts Ave., 617/266-1492, www.bso.org), Boston has many excellent smaller halls that regularly offer classical concerts. These include: New England Conservatory's acoustically refined **Jordan Hall** (30 Gainsborough

St., 617/585-1260, www.newengland-conservatory.edu/concerts) and Boston University's **Tsai Performance Center** (685 Commonwealth Ave., 617/353-8725, www.bu.edu/tsai).

A little-known choral gem, **Emmanuel Music** (15 Newbury St., 617/536-3356, www.emmanuelmusic.org) performs entire Bach masses on Sundays at Emmanuel Church. **Trinity Boston** (206 Clarendon St., 617/536-0944, www.trinitychurchboston.org) performs half-hour recitals on Fridays at noon, as well as occasional choral concerts in one of the most beautiful settings in Boston—Copley Square's Trinity Church.

Festivals and Events

Everyone gets a little Irish for **St. Patrick's Day** in Boston, which is celebrated with a parade through South Boston streets decked in shamrock green. In April, runners come from around the world to compete in the **Boston Marathon,** the oldest (and some say toughest) marathon in the United States. Spectators start lining the route to cheer along Beacon and Boylston Streets, all the way to Copley Square, where the finish line is painted in the street. Americans from around the country tune in to the Boston Pops performance on the **Fourth of July,** when the esplanade becomes a gallery for a fabulous fireworks show.

Numerous (often free) events take place throughout the summer months, from **open-air Shakespeare on Boston Common** (www.commshakes.org) to **outdoor concerts.** A good resource for finding current listings is www.bostonusa.com.

Shopping

Faneuil Hall Marketplace

Touristy? Yes. Pricey? Also. But the **Faneuil Hall Marketplace** (4 South Market St., 617/227-3962, www.faneuilhallmarketplace.com, Mon.-Sat. 10am-9pm, Sun.

noon-6pm) is an outdoor mall where you can pick up all of your Boston-themed souvenirs. **Best of Boston** (1 Faneuil Hall Marketplace, 617/227-3962, Mon.-Sat. 10am-9pm, Sun. noon-6pm) has a colorful selection of lobster shot glasses, Red Sox gear, saltwater taffy, and "Boston Tea Party"-brand tea for drinking or throwing in the harbor.

Charles Street

Charles Street in Beacon Hill has some 40 antiques stores crammed to into one-third of a mile; one of the best is **Upstairs Downstairs Antiques** (93 Charles St., 617/367-1950, Sun.-Fri. 11am-6pm, Sat. 10am-6pm) a warren of rooms stuffed with tableware, glassware, and other knickknacks from a dozen decades. Armchair historians and explorers alike thrill at the selection of antique maps and charts at **Eugene Galleries** (76 Charles St., 617/227-3062, Mon.-Sat. 11am-6pm, Sun. 11am-5pm), which cover Boston, New England, and the rest of the world.

Newbury Street

The place to shop for high-end, stylish clothes is Back Bay's stylish **Newbury Street,** which carries outposts of international designers from Armani to Zegna, alongside local boutiques.

Newbury Street also hosts the most prestigious art galleries in the city. The biggest name on the street is the **Barbara Krakow Gallery** (10 Newbury St., 617/262-4490, www.barbarakrakow-gallery.com, Tues.-Sat. 10am-5:30pm), which draws nationally known contemporary artists. More traditional paintings and prints are on display at the venerable **Childs Gallery** (169 Newbury St., 617/266-1108, www.childsgallery.com, Tues.-Fri. 9am-6pm, Sat. and Mon. 10am-5pm), which focuses on pre-WWII American and European work. The **International Poster Gallery** (205 Newbury St., 617/375-0076, www.internationalposter.com, Mon.-Sat. 10am-6pm, Sun. noon-6pm) is a treasure trove of original French liquor prints and Russian propaganda posters.

The kind of shop where you can settle in with a coffee and a good read, **Trident Booksellers & Cafe** (338 Newbury St., 617/267-8688, www.tridentbookscafe. com, daily 8am-midnight) has a wonderful selection of titles and hosts frequent author events and reading.

Downtown Crossing

Most of the shopping in this bustling district is of the big-name, big-store variety, with names like H & M and Primark lining Washington Street, Summer Street, and Winter Street. One long-standing exception to downtown's plate glass window displays is **Brattle Book Shop** (9 West St., 617/542-0210, www.brattlebookshop.com, Mon.-Sat. 9am-5:30pm) where three stories cannot contain a collection of books that spills beyond the bookstore and into the adjoining alley, whose brick walls are painted with the images of iconic authors.

Harvard Square

There are still some locally owned gems among the chain stores that have crept into this triangular plaza. The thoughtfully curated **Black Ink** (5 Brattle St., Cambridge, 617/497-1221, www.blackinkboston.squarespace.com, Mon.-Sat. 10am-8pm, Sun. 11am-7pm) is ideal for gifts, pretty stationery, and what the shop accurately calls "unexpected necessities." With time-warp charm and all sorts of quirk, **Leavitt & Peirce** (1316 Massachusetts Ave., Cambridge, 617/547-0576, www.leavitt-peirce.com, Mon.-Sat. 9am-6pm, Sun. noon-5:30pm) has been Harvard's tobacconist since 1884, but also stocks a trove of games and gentlemanly gifts like cuff links and shaving brushes. Another fun place to browse is **Goorin Bros. Hat Shop** (43 Brattle St., Cambridge, 617/868-4287, www.goorin.com, Mon.-Sat. 10am-8pm, Sun. 11am-7pm), which has everything from ball caps to fedoras to and Kentucky Derby wear.

Sports and Recreation

Hiking and Biking

Watch pink- and white-sailed dinghies tack and jibe along the shore from the **Charles River Esplanade** (www.esplanadeassociation.org), which has three miles of waterfront trails that stretch from the Museum of Science to the Boston University Bridge. The trails are especially charming in the springtime, when blossom-laden cherry trees arch over the path.

Landscape architect Frederick Law Olmsted designed a series of parks known as the **"Emerald Necklace"** (www. emeraldnecklace.org) that stretches from the Back Bay Fens to Forest Hills and the Arnold Arboretum, with walking and biking trails throughout. One highlight of the Back Bay Fens park is the **Fenway Victory Gardens**—while it's indistinguishable from the many community gardens that have been appearing in cities across the United States, this 7.5-acre plot was planted during World War II to supplement strained food supplies. It's the oldest continually operating such garden in the country, and the 500 garden plots are now waitlist-only growing spaces for Boston residents.

When the "Big Dig" construction project put I-93 underground, it created 15 acres of surface-level space that's been transformed into the **Rose Kennedy Greenway** (www.rosekennedygreenway. org), a slender line of parks that runs 1.5 miles from the Chinatown Gate to North End Park. One highlight of the parks is the **Greenway Carousel** (Atlantic Ave. and Cross St., 888/839-7616, $3), whose colorful animals are all Massachusetts natives—don't miss the chance to ride a codfish, peregrine falcon, whale, or lobster. You'll also find some wonderful art along the way; exhibits change seasonally, but past installments have featured Chinese artist Ai Weiwei and abstract pieces with a focus on local history and nature. Many of the seven water fountains along the greenway are strategically designed for cooling off in the Boston summer. Favorites with the wading toddler crowd include the **Rings Fountain** (Central St. and Cross St.), **North & South Canal Fountains** (Cross St. and Hanover St.) and interactive **Harbor Fog Fountain** (High St. and Cross St.), whose movement sensors trigger great billows of cooling mist.

Boating

Boston Harbor remains a transportation hub for the region, and **Boston Harbor Cruises** (www.bostonharborcruises.com) runs convenient boat service to **Salem** (1 hr, round-trip ticket $45 adults, $41 seniors, $35 children 3-11) and **Provincetown** (1.5 hrs, round-trip ticket $58 adults, $53 seniors, $39 children 3-11) that are a good alternative to driving. To simply get views of the city from the water, though, take a turn on its **Historic Sightseeing Cruise** (1.5 hrs,

tickets $27 adults, $25 seniors, $23 children 3-11), which loops along the shoreline of the inner and outer harbor to the historic Boston Light and the Harbor Islands.

Take in the harbor under sail with the **Liberty Fleet** (617/742-0333, www.libertyfleet.com, cruises $35-40 adults, $19-24 children under 12), which offers day sails, sunset sails, and a "Rum and Revelry" sail with costumed actors and drinks. The schooner *Liberty Clipper* is the flagship, a 125-foot gaff-rigged replica of the Baltimore Clipper-style ships prized by fast-moving privateers during the American Revolution and War of 1812. Her little sister is the 67-foot *Liberty Star*, whose classic lines are modeled on 19th-century coastal schooners—crews on board both ships are friendly and experienced, and the sails can be as hands-on (or off) as desired.

All those postcard-ready sailboats on the Charles River belong to **Community Boating** (21 Mugar Way, 617/523-1038,

Rose Kennedy Greenway in the North End

www.community-boating.org, Apr.-Oct. Mon.-Fri. 3pm-sunset, Sat.-Sun. 9am-sunset), an institution on the Charles River Esplanade since the 1940s. Experienced sailors can rent a sailboat for $84, and kayaks are available at $43—a single and a double kayak cost the same, so paddling with a friend is half the price.

Spectator Sports

With baseball, hockey, and basketball, Boston has an almost year-round sports season, with fervor to match. Most iconic are the **Red Sox** (877/733-7699, www.redsox.com) baseball team, and after suffering through the 86-year-long "Curse of the Bambino," it can finally bring home pennants again (the Red Sox sold the legendary player Babe Ruth to the New York Yankees after winning the 1918 championship, and didn't catch a break until the 2004 World Series). The hockey-playing **Bruins** (617/624-2327, www.bostonbruins.com) are another passion-inspiring team and the oldest NHL team in the United States. And while the 1980s heyday of Larry Bird, Kevin McHale, and Robert Parrish has not returned, the **Celtics** (866/423-5849, www.nba.com/celtics) still pack the TD Garden to the gills.

Food

Beacon Hill

The open kitchen at **The Paramount** (44 Charles St., 617/720-1152, www.paramountboston.com, Mon.-Fri. 7am-10pm, Sat.-Sun. 8am-10pm, $6-27) slings fresh, flavorful diner fare at breakfast and lunch: Try caramel banana French toast, huevos rancheros, hefty salads, and sandwiches. Dinner gets a bit more grown-up with pasta dishes and entrées like miso-glazed shrimp and Sriracha coconut chicken. Lines can get long at this neighborhood favorite, so it's a good option to call ahead for sandwiches and have a picnic in Boston Public Garden, which is just a couple of blocks away. If you do dine in, you'll order and pay for your food at the counter, then sit down when your meal arrives.

Tucked down a brick-lined side street, **75 Chestnut** (75 Chestnut St., 617/227-2175, www.75chestnut.com, dinner Sun.-Thurs. 5pm-midnight, Fri.-Sat. 5pm-1am, brunch Sat. 10:30am-3pm Sept.-June only, Sun. 10:30am-2:20pm, $23-32) is a cozy neighborhood bistro that's refined enough for a romantic evening out. The dinner menu includes classic seafood dishes and pasta, salads, steaks, and a few burgers. Brunch is especially popular here, with a short, but appealing menu and a Bloody Mary bar.

Bright and stylish, **Tatte Bakery & Café** (70 Charles St., 617/723-5555, www.tattebakery.com, Mon.-Fri. 7am-8pm, Sat. 8am-8pm, Sun. 8am-7pm, $3-9) is a good spot to nibble something sweet and watch locals drift in and out of the cozy space. Pastries are the star of the show, but there's also an appealing lineup of sandwiches and lunch items.

Downtown and the Waterfront

Daniel Webster downed brandy and oysters here, and John F. Kennedy loved to sip lobster bisque in booth 18; **Union Oyster House** (41 Union St., 617/227-2750, www.unionoysterhouse.com, Sun.-Thurs. 11am-9:30pm, Fri.-Sat. 11am-10pm, bar open until midnight, $9-34) is the oldest operating restaurant in the United States, and if it's acquired a few overpriced dishes, a cheesy gift shop, and a pile of Olde New Englande tat over the years, it's easy to forgive over a bowl of super-creamy clam chowder. Find all the classics here, from Boston baked beans to baked scrod, but if you just want to soak up the historic atmosphere, grab a drink and a half-dozen oysters at the downstairs raw bar or the darkly colonial-looking Union Bar.

One might never suspect this laid-back, counter service lunch place of having the "World's No. 1 Sandwiches," but ★ **Sam LaGrassa's** (44 Province St., 617/357-6861, www.samlagrassas.com, Mon.-Fri. 11am-3:30pm, $9-13) has a passionate following that lines up for enormous deli sandwiches and chowder. Roast beef and Reubens are served in classic style here, piled high with deli meat, but it's the pastrami that made this place famous. Most sandwiches can easily serve two people.

Find Chilean sandwiches piled with freshly grilled meat, veggies, and muenster cheese at **Chacarero** (101 Arch St., 617/542-0392, www.chacarero.com, Mon.-Fri. 11am-6pm, $7-10), a pocket-sized sandwich shop beloved by locals. The secret ingredient: green beans.

A little, family-run "shack" on the waterfront, **James Hook & Co.** (440 Atlantic Ave., 617/423-5501, www.jameshooklobster.com, $18-20) sells live lobsters and seafood, but it's worth stopping by for the truly satisfying (though quite pricey) lobster rolls—just mayonnaise, hot dog bun, fresh meat, and no fuss. A few tables for sitting are located outside, or you can bring your roll down to the waterfront harborwalk.

It *is* possible to order the namesake sandwiches at ★ **Gene's Chinese Flatbread Cafe** (86 Bedford St., 617/482-1888, www.genescafe.com, Mon.-Fri. 11am-6:30pm, Sat. 11:30am-7pm, $5-11), but the real draw is the hand-pulled noodles that come doused in garlicky oil, mild chili powder, fresh herbs, and green onions. The noodles are a chewy delight, and Gene's is one of the only places in New England where you can find the traditional food.

The sushi and Japanese small plates at ★ **O Ya** (9 East St., 617/654-9900, www.oya.restaurant, Tues.-Thurs. 5pm-9:30pm, Fri.-Sat. 5pm-10pm, $50-70) are both creative and exquisite, and meals here are consistently ranked among the best in the city. For an all-out feast, try the 17-course tasting menu that includes one of the chef's signature dishes: Kumamoto oyster *nigiri* is a warm, fried oyster atop a tiny bed of rice and seaweed, topped with a froth of ethereal squid ink. In keeping with the culinary artistry, the decor is modern, simple, and elegant.

North End trattorias have the low lights and Chianti candles on lock, but **Erbaluce** (69 Church St., 617/426-6969, www.erbaluce-boston.com, Tues.-Thurs. and Sun. 5pm-10pm, Fri.-Sat. 5pm-11pm, $30-50) offers a more contemporary, sophisticated experience. Minimalist decor pairs well with the chef's use of simple, full-flavored northern Italian recipes and super-fresh ingredients.

Boston Public Market (100 Hanover St., 617/973-4909, www.bostonpublic-market.org, Mon.-Sat. 8am-8pm, Sun. 10am-8pm) is a covered, year-round market space with dozens of local vendors selling prepared foods, products, and groceries.

★ North End

There's always a line out the door of ★ **Regina's Pizzeria** (11½ Thatcher St., 617/227-0765, www.reginapizzeria.com, Sun.-Thurs. 11am-11:30pm, Fri.-Sat. 11am-12:30am, $8-16), but joining the line is part of the fun at this landmark destination. The kitchen turns out blistered, lightly blackened pies topped with traditional Neapolitan ingredients, but it's the crust that really shines: The *pizzaoli* in the open kitchen throw disks of dough that are chewy, thin, and just slightly uneven, truly some of the best in town. Walls are decked with streamers and signs from neighborhood saints' days, tables are closely packed, and service is brusque—with a bit of a North End swagger (either native or adopted). When waits are long, large groups might do well to go elsewhere, but someone regularly goes down the line plucking out pairs and singles for seats at the bar.

Stop by **Monica's Mercato** (130 Salem St., 617/742-4101, www.monicasboston.com, daily 9am-11pm, $6-12) at lunchtime, and you'll order your sub alongside a line of North End cops, construction workers, and longtime locals—it's a good omen that doesn't disappoint. Sandwiches are layered with freshly sliced prosciutto, salami, and Italian cheeses, bathed in extra virgin olive oil and balsamic vinegar and wrapped to go. There's no seating in this shoebox-size deli, but it's a five-minute walk to the North End Park, where you'll find shaded tables, park benches, and a series of fountains that keep things cool on the steamiest Boston afternoons.

It would be easy to miss little **Polcari's Coffee** (105 Salem St., 617/227-0786, www.polcaris.com, Mon.-Fri. 10am-6:30pm, Sat. 9am-6pm, Italian ice $2-3), a shop that's weighed out the neighborhood's espresso beans and spices since 1932. In the warm months, though, Polcari's scoops cups full of fine grained, lemony Italian ice that's unbelievably refreshing on a hot day.

Whether you're sipping a morning cappuccino or an *amaro* nightcap, the marble-topped tables at **Caffè Vittoria** (290 Hanover St., 617/227-7606, www.caffe-vittoria.com, Sun.-Thurs. 7am-midnight, Fri.-Sat. 7am-12:30am, $3-9) are perfect for watching North End life drift by. Every surface of this old-world café is covered in antique espresso machines, vintage Italian posters, and other memorabilia. Cappuccinos come under a melting layer of powdered chocolate, and the late-night menu of cordials—these include herbal *amari* and sweet sips like *crema di limoncello*—are perfect with traditional Italian desserts.

An island of contemporary style in the thoroughly old-school North End, ★ **Neptune Oyster** (63 Salem St., 617/742-3474, www.neptuneoyster.com, Sun.-Thurs. 11:30am-10pm, Fri.-Sat. 11:30am-11pm, $22-39) gets a lot of hype and deserves every bit of it. The big, buttery lobster rolls are the best in Boston, but the creative seafood menu skims through the world's great coastal cuisines: Try sea urchin ditalini, Veracruz-style mackerel, or shrimp and grits. Raw bar offerings include East and West Coast oysters along with a rotating lineup of what's fresh. The line starts well before the doors open for lunch, and the tiny space can be cramped and loud.

Another neighborhood favorite with a constant line, **Giacomo's Ristorante** (355 Hanover St., 617/523-9026, Mon.-Thurs. 4:30pm-10pm, Fri.-Sat. 4:30pm-10:30pm, Sun. 4:30pm-9:30pm, $16-26) serves huge portions of Italian American favorites like baked ziti, eggplant parmesan, and veal marsala in a simple brick dining room. Cash only.

Don't leave the North End without a string-wrapped box filled with traditional Italian sweets. The classic cannoli rivalry is between a pair of legendary shops geographically close enough to a head-to-head comparison. The versions at **Mike's Pastry** (300 Hanover St., 617/742-3050, www.mikespastry.com, Sun.-Thurs. 8am-10pm, Fri.-Sat. 8am-11:30pm, $2-8) are hefty and sweet, overflowing with ricotta filling. ★ **Modern Pastry** (257 Hanover St., 617/523-3783, www.modernpastry.com, daily 6:30am-11:30pm, $2-8) has a slight edge, serving smaller, more delicate cannolo that are filled on the spot.

Far less flashy and famous, **Maria's Pastry** (46 Cross St., 617/523-1196, www.mariaspastry.com, Mon.-Sat. 7am-7pm, Sun. 7am-5pm, $2-8) has a passionate cadre of supporters who swear by the *sfogliatelle* that overflow with luscious vanilla cream.

In the North End, little Italian markets are the ideal place to stock up for a picnic of cured meats and imported cheeses; one favorite is **Salumeria Italiana** (151 Richmond St., 617/523-8743, www.salumeriaitaliana.com, Mon.-Sat. 8am-7pm, Sun. 10am-4pm), which also has fabulous deli sandwiches.

Fenway and Back Bay

In a convenient spot by Copley Square, **Dig Inn** (557 Boylston St., www.diginn.com, Mon.-Fri. 7am-10pm, Sat.-Sun. 9am-10pm, $8-14) has a fresh menu of mix-and-match dishes that emphasize sustainable values and ingredients sourced directly from producers. Choose from a list of proteins including include wild-caught fish, tofu, and farm-raised meats, and add whole grains and sides, or snack on lighter options like avocado toast or a roasted kale salad. This restaurant is part of a small chain based in New York City.

Another fabulous place for something sweet is **Flour + Bakery Cafe** (131 Clarendon St., 617/437-7700, www.flourbakery.com, Mon.-Fri. 7am-8pm, Sat. 8am-6pm, Sun. 9am-5pm, $3-9), one of four locations in the Boston area run by master pastry chef Joanne Chang. You'll find sandwiches and salads enough for a fine, upstanding lunch, but it's the lusciously sugary tarts, rolls, buns, and pies that bring in the crowds—a particular favorite is Chang's sticky bun, a mammoth treat that's surprisingly light beneath a coating of caramel and pecans.

Somewhat out of the way on the western side of Fenway, ★ **Mei Mei** (506 Park Dr., 857/250-4959, www.meimeiboston.com, Sun. and Tues.-Wed. 11am-9pm,

Mon. 11am-2:30pm, Thurs.-Sat. 11am-10pm, $7-19) is worth the trek and an easy, five-minute walk from the Fenway T station. It's a fun, welcoming place run by the Li siblings—one brother and two sisters—who bring a lighthearted approach to a menu that leans Chinese American but doesn't shy away from eclectic dishes like pierogi or mac and cheese (which gets a whiff of Chinese heat from spicy *gochujang* cheese sauce). Mei Mei's most famous creation, though, is its oozy, savory breakfast sandwich, the Double Awesome: pesto, cheese, eggs, and meat are layered between two flaky scallion pancakes.

The Boston Public Library's Italianate courtyard is a glorious place to linger in the summer—the fountain and deep shady arcades keep it cool on even the hottest days—but many visitors never discover the restaurant overlooking the elegant spot. Stop by ★ **The Courtyard Restaurant** (700 Boylston St., 617/859-2282, www.thecateredaffair.com, Mon.-Sat. 11:30am-3:30pm, afternoon tea $35) for the elegant high tea, and nibble on tiered platters of savory sandwiches, sweet petit fours, and scones with cream . . . and a freshly brewed pot of tea.

Small markets abound in the city, but the most convenient is the **Copley Square Boston Farmers Market** (early May-late Nov. Tues. and Fri. 11am-6pm), where farmers, bakers, and chefs set up right across the street from the Boston Public Library.

South End

The treats at ★ **Blackbird Doughnuts** (492 Tremont St., www.blackbirddoughnuts.com, Mon.-Fri. 7am-6pm, Sat.-Sun. 8am-8pm, $3-5) are displayed individually on cake pedestals, speared with tiny flags that make them look like tiny, recently discovered islands. Pillowy raised doughnuts come in flavors like salted toffee, passion fruit, and the oozing PB&J Bismarck, but the namesake sweet is a cake doughnut. The Blackbird signature flavor is a combination of old-fashioned vanilla bean with vanilla bean glazed. Pick up treats to go, as this tiny shop has no seating.

A strong competitor for Boston's best breakfasts, ★ **Mike & Patty's** (12 Church St., 617/423-3447, www.mikeandpattys. com, Mon.-Tues. 8am-2pm, Wed.-Fri. 7:30am-2pm, Sat.-Sun. 7:30am-2:30pm, $5-11) is a hole-in-the-wall corner café with just a handful of stools—which is why the sidewalk is filled with patrons on sunny days, enjoying egg sandwiches fresh from the griddle. Order it "classic" with American cheese and egg on an English muffin, or go "fancy" to get the works. Orders for pickup can be placed on the website.

An "indie diner" with a colorful, irreverent attitude, **Myers + Chang** (1145 Washington St., 617/542-5200, www.myersandchang.com, Sun.-Thurs. 11:30am-10pm, Fri.-Sat. 11am-11pm, $15-20) has a generous menu that ranges from dim sum brunch (on weekends) to noodle soup, Asian-influenced mains, homestyle Indonesian food, and anything else that appeals to the talented kitchen. This is an especially good choice on Monday and Tuesday's "cheap dates nights," with $45 prix fixe menus for two.

Cambridge

Harvard Square is jam-packed with places to recover from hard-core learning (and sightseeing). For something that transcends the budget student joints, **Alden & Harlow** (40 Brattle St., Cambridge, 617/864-2100, www.aldenharlow.com, Mon.-Wed. 5pm-1am, Thurs.-Fri. 5pm-2am, Sat. 10:30am-2pm and 5pm-2am, Sun. 10:30am-2:30pm and 5pm-1am, $25-35) serves exquisite, ingredient-focused small plates like fried quail, bass crudo, and chicken liver pâté.

Nostalgic alumni are sure to stop by **Mr. Bartley's Burger Cottage** (1246 Massachusetts Ave., Cambridge, 617/354-6559, www.mrbartley.com, Mon.-Sat. 11am-9pm, $11-17) for burgers with jokey names and wonderfully crispy onion rings.

Sunny **Crema Café** (27 Brattle St., Cambridge, 617/876-2700, www.cremacambridge, Mon.-Fri. 7am-9pm, Sat.-Sun. 8am-9pm, $3-6) has big communal tables that give the independent coffee shop a friendly, social feel; you'll also find breakfast sandwiches and sweet treats.

Fill up on great bowls of ramen and snacks like *takoyaki* (octopus-filled battered balls) and *gyoza* (dumplings) at **Hokkaido Ramen Santouka** (1 Bow St., Cambridge, 617/945-1460, www.santouka-usa.com, Mon.-Thurs. and Sun. 11am-9pm, Fri.-Sat. 11am-10:30pm, $12-20), a chic, modern outpost of a Japanese chain that's popular with just about everybody.

Accommodations

Because Boston is so compact, all the following listings are good choices for accessing the city's main sights and attractions. They won't come cheap—Boston is among the most expensive cities in the United States for hotels and Airbnb. There are some wonderful options, however, and it's worth booking well in advance to secure a spot.

Beacon Hill
$150-250

A quaint bed-and-breakfast on the back of Beacon Hill, the ★ **John Jeffries House** (14 Mugar Way, 617/367-1866, www.johnjeffrieshouse.com, $137 s, $169-205 d) has spartan but comfortable rooms that were originally quarters for nurses at the nearby Massachusetts Eye and Ear Infirmary. There are small kitchenettes in each room and a continental breakfast is served in the common space, and guests get a discounted rate at the Charles Street garage ($27 for 24 hrs). Try for a room with a view of the Charles River.

$250-350

The **Beacon Hill Hotel and Bistro** (25 Charles St., 617/723-7575, www.beaconhillhotel.com, $249-449) is right in the heart of the action in this fashionable, historic neighborhood. The rooms at are smallish, but charming and sweetly decorated. A full breakfast is served in the downstairs bistro, or can be brought to your room. The real star of this boutique hotel is the rooftop terrace, which offers perfect people-watching down toward Charles Street. It's an ideal spot to bring a bottle of wine at the end of the day.

Downtown and the Waterfront
$50-150

On the edge of downtown, with a great location between the theater district and Chinatown, ★ **HI Boston Hostel** (19 Stuart St., 617/536-9455, www.boston-hostel.org, dorms $55-80, private rooms $230) sets the standard for large, urban hostels, and it's easily the best budget option in the city. Dormitory rooms range from eight-bed economy options to four-bed premium rooms, both gender-specific and co-ed, and the thoughtful design makes them comfortable spaces to sleep for all kinds of travelers. Beds have assigned lockers, small reading lights, and charging stations, and the shared hallway bathrooms are always immaculate; private rooms have en suite bathrooms and a spare, modern style. Self-serve breakfasts of toast, cereal, and fruit are offered in the large common dining room, where there are hot drinks all day and a big kitchen for guest use. Employees organize guided walks or group activities from brewery tours to bar hops and movie nights, which makes this a great place to meet other visitors. There's no parking on-site, but hostel staff directs guests to the **Boston Common Parking Garage** (0 Charles St., overnight $18), which is a 0.4-mile walk from the hostel.

One of the most unusual places to sleep on the waterfront is aboard one of the ★ **Liberty Fleet tall ships** (67 Long Wharf, 617/742-0333, www.libertyfleet.com, two-person shared bunk-room $65 pp, private s $98, private d $130), which moor at a centrally located

dock by the New England Aquarium. Accommodations are somewhat rustic with shared bathroom and shower and no wireless Internet—the experience is somewhere between floating hostel and tour of duty, but it's completely charming to wake up to the sounds of the Boston waterfront and lapping waves. Guests spending their first night aboard must meet a crew member for a short evening orientation but on subsequent nights may come and go freely after the last sail of the day and first morning outing (typically between 8pm and 10am), and receive a 30 percent discount on a sailing trip. The closest parking is at the **Harbor Garage** (70 East India Row, 24 hrs $36).

$250-350

Old-world elegance is faded but still enchanting at the **Omni Parker House** (60 School St., 617/227-8600, www.omnihotels.com, $260-390), one of downtown Boston's most storied hotels. The waitstaff have included Malcom X and Ho Chi Minh, both of whom presumably ferried countless baskets of the Parker House Rolls that were invented here. The hotel regularly lands on the list of Boston's most haunted places (paranormal activity is said to be particularly high on the 3rd floor). If you book Table 40 in the Parker Restaurant, you'll dine where J.F.K. proposed to the future Jackie Kennedy. In keeping with the historic building, rooms are rather small, and while they're pleasantly furnished, they're neither as historic nor as luxurious as the public spaces. Valet parking is available for $46 per person.

Over $350

One of Boston's new crop of boutique hotels, **The Godfrey** (505 Washington St., 617/804-2000, www.godfreyhotelboston.com, $315-400) is chic and modern, and right in the thick of the Downtown Crossing shopping area. You'll find all the luxe amenities—valet parking, spa services, fitness center—along with rooted-in-Boston flourishes such as local art and designs. Splash out for a corner room for wraparound views of the city below.

North End
$250-350
Just across the bridge in Charlestown, ★ **Green Turtle Floating Bed and Breakfast** (1 13th St., Pier 8, 617/340-2608, www.greenturtlebb.com, $280-375) offers a novel solution to Boston's perennial lack of space. Accommodations are in a two-bedroom houseboat or one of two motor yachts, pulling off an unusual blend of luxury and quirk. Rooms are very comfortable and well appointed, a full breakfast is delivered each morning by the friendly hosts, and the boats' kitchenettes are stocked with snacks and drinks. The bed-and-breakfast is a 1-mile walk from North End sights and close to the public ferry dock on Pier 4. A taxi from Logan costs approximately $32, and a water taxi is $12 per person (inquire at the airport).

Over $350
Striking a pleasant balance between boutique style and corporate suave, **The Boxer Boston** (107 Merrimack St., 617/624-0202, www.theboxerboston.com, $300-450) is an appealing choice within easy walking distance of North End sights. In addition to more traditional king rooms, doubles, and suites, the Boxer has bunk rooms with a double bed on the bottom, and a twin-sized bed on top—a good option for couples traveling with one child. The compact, comfortable, and modern rooms have flat-screen televisions and coffeemakers. Valet parking with in-and-out service is available for $44 a night, though there are more affordable North End parking garages a short distance away.

While not a traditional hotel or inn, the North End's famous "spite house," aka **Skinny House** (44 Hull St., www.vrbo.com/247506, $325, 5-night minimum stay) is available to rent. Just over nine feet wide at its largest point, the house dates back to a colonial-era family spat, when one brother was left just a slice of land to built on. Beds for five are shared across two bedrooms, alongside a full kitchen and laundry facilities. It's across the street from Copps Hill Burial Ground. Shorter stays are possible during the winter months.

Fenway and Back Bay
$50-150
The bare-bones **Boston Fenway Inn** (12 Hemenway St., 857/250-2785, www.bostonfenwayinn.com, dorms $40-50, private rooms $120-169) is a decent option for budget travelers if the more appealing HI Boston is fully booked. All rooms have shared baths, and a basic continental breakfast is provided. Some travelers have found that rooms aren't cleaned as frequently as they'd like.

$150-250
With a quiet location, **Oasis Guest House** (22 Edgerly Rd., 617/267-2262, www.oasisguesthouse.com, shared bath $179-189, private bath $259-280, three-person suite $280 with breakfast and two-night minimum on weekends) is walking distance to Fenway Park and public transportation. The somewhat faded decor leans old-fashioned, but it's a perfectly tidy, friendly place to land, whether you're in the Oasis property itself or Adams Bed and Breakfast, a neighboring outpost with similar facilities and the same management. A small continental breakfast is served, limited parking is available on-site on a first-come, first served basis for $25, and there's a public garage nearby with $35, 24-hour parking.

Though technically in Kenmore Square, **Abigayle's Bed and Breakfast** (72 Bay State Rd., 617/720-0522, www.bnbboston.com, $125 s, $175 d) is easy walking distance to destinations in Fenway and Back Bay. Friendly hosts and a simple continental breakfast make this a comfortable place to stay. All rooms have private baths (though the single room has a detached private bath in the hallway). The four-story house does not have an elevator. One parking space is available for $14 a night.

$250-350

Part of the charm of a Boston neighborhood is imagining the elegant homes behind the brownstones, but there aren't many ways to get past the doorstep. With elegant furnishings and a wonderfully historic feel, the ★ **College Club of Boston** (44 Commonwealth Ave., 617/536-9510, www.thecollegeclubofboston.com, s with shared bath $199, d with private bath $270-310) is like an invitation into one of those houses. The 11 guest rooms are named for colleges and universities, and each is furnished with unique style and charm; you'll find high ceilings and windows throughout the house, pretty secretary desks, and thoughtful touches. Shared bathrooms are pristine, and a generous continental breakfast is served in a downstairs dining room.

A trio of Back Bay town houses are linked up to make the **Newbury Guest House** (261 Newbury St., 617/670-6000, www.newburyguesthouse.com, $299-400). This bed-and-breakfast is walking distance from an appealing array of shops and cafés. Breakfast includes hot options like eggs and bacon along with croissants, fruit and yogurt, and hot drinks. Rooms are clean, light, and airy, and some have in-room fireplaces—welcome on blustery fall evenings. A few parking spaces are available on-site for $20/night; call when booking to reserve.

The Gryphon House (9 Bay State Rd., 877/375-9003, www.innboston.com, $275-350) is a turn-of-the-20th-century Victorian brownstone that has been painstakingly preserved, with historic wallpaper and atmospheric paintings. The eight suites are spacious and well-appointed, with gas fireplaces, flat-screen televisions with DVD players, wet bars, and refrigerators. The "extended continental" breakfast is an ample spread of yogurt, fruit, toast, hot and cold cereal, juice, and hot drinks, and parking is available on-site for $15 a night.

Over $350

Achingly cool and Instagram-ready, ★ **The Verb** (1271 Boylston St., 617/566-4500, www.theverbhotel.com, $300-700) combines a colorful rock-and-roll aesthetic with high-end service and style. The poolside scene is fun and occasionally boisterous; the bar serves strong, creative cocktails; and you can browse the lobby's vinyl library for something to spin on your in-room Crosley record player. Before a stem-to-stern overhaul, this was a Howard Johnson hotel, and The Verb raises a glass to that history at Hojoko, its on-site Japanese tavern. Valet parking is $45 per night, and you're a baseball-throw's distance away from Fenway Park.

South End
$150-250

There's still a roller-skating rink beneath the armchairs and coffee tables at **40 Berkeley** (40 Berkeley St., 617/375-2524, www.40berkeley.com, $145-165), an enormous YWCA-turned hotel. Rooms are somewhat institutional and shared baths are basic, but management is installing wall-mounted air-conditioning units by spring 2017. While all rooms are private, the overall effect is hostel-like, with a room for movie nights, games, and convivial common spaces. This is a good choice for families, as triples and quads are available with no additional charge for extra guests.

$250-350

The bright units at **Chandler Studios** (54 Berkeley St., 617/482-3450, www.chandlerstudioboston.com, $239-409) are enlivened by grainy scenes from historic Boston, giving the modern decor a bit more personality. Studios have fully equipped kitchenettes, and the one-bedroom suite has a one-bedroom sitting room with a pullout couch. Hot drinks are available 24 hours a day in the lobby. Guests get a reduced rate at a nearby parking garage ($28 for 24 hrs), and the location is within easy walking distance from public transport and Back Bay sights.

Logan Airport
The hotels around Boston's Logan Airport are corporate bland, but for early morning flights or avoiding city traffic, these can be a convenient option.

$150-250
Eight miles north of the airport, **Red Roof Plus Boston Logan** (920 Broadway, Saugus, 937/969-6166, www.redroof.com, $140-200) is a clean, easy-to-reach, budget option, convenient for anyone who is flying into Boston and leaving the next morning. Taxi service from the airport is $25 and takes 15-30 minutes, while the MBTA station is an $18 taxi ride away. Free parking is available. While the neighborhood is not much of a destination, there are stores and restaurants within walking distance of the hotel.

$250-350
The **Hilton Boston Logan Airport** (1 Hotel Dr., Logan International Airport, 617/568-6700, www.hilton.com, $240-300) is connected to the A and E terminals by a sky bridge and has 24-hour shuttle service to the airport, the MBTA Blue Line, and to water taxis, which makes it straightforward to get into downtown Boston. Hot breakfast is available, though not included with rates, and the hotel also has a fitness room and indoor pool. Parking is available for $37.

Information and Services

Information
A good place to get oriented is the **Boston Common Visitor Information Center** (148 Tremont St., 888/733-2678, www.bostonusa.com, daily 9am-5pm), located in the park halfway between the Park Street and Boylston Street T stops. There you can pick up maps and guides, along with discount museum coupons and brochures for major attractions. It's also the starting place for the Freedom Trail and several trolley tours around the city. The National Park Service runs its own **Faneuil Hall Visitor Center** (1 Faneuil Hall, 617/242-5642, www.nps.gov/bost, daily 9am-5pm), which includes a good collection of books on Boston and Massachusetts. If you are planning ahead, you can contact the **Greater Boston Convention & Visitors Bureau** (800/733-2678, www.bostonusa.com) for additional publications with the latest tourist information. The NPS also has a Boston-specific **app** with tours, maps, and info.

Attraction Passes
While many of Boston's most appealing experiences are free (or just the cost of a cannoli), seeing the city's museums and attractions can add up quickly. A couple of cards and passes bundle attractions under a single price, often with a dizzying array of variations: The **All-Inclusive Go Boston Card** (www.smartdestinations.com, $55-170 adults, $37-115 children) has passes in increments ranging from a single day to a week and includes admission to many of the city's best sites, with no limits on the number you can visit each day. The three-, five- and seven-day options include one "premium attraction"— the aquarium's whale-watching boat tour, tickets to a Red Sox game, or the surf and turf-style Boston Duck Tour. Verdict: If you're a fast-moving sightseer and plan to see these sites anyway, this is a great deal. For those who like to take more time at museums and historic sites, though, it's hard to get enough value for the cost.

If just a couple of specific places are on your list, it's definitely worth purchasing tickets to them via the same company's **Build Your Own Go Boston Card,** where

◈ Side Trip to Walden Pond

The writer **Henry David Thoreau** built a cabin by this small, wooded pond in **Concord** "to live deliberately, to front only the essential facts of life . . . to live deep and suck out all the marrow of life, to live so sturdily and Spartan-like as to put to rout all that was not life." *Walden,* his 1852 book chronicling a year in the woods, has become a classic of American literature, beloved by generations of naturalists and armchair homesteaders. Thoreau's minute observations of passing seasons and the natural world are particularly beautiful, and his social criticisms cut as deeply today as they did in the mid-19th century.

It might come as a surprise, then, to see the bustling boat ramp, swimming beach, and grassy slopes filled with picnicking families of today's **Walden Pond State Reservation** (915 Walden St., Concord, 978/369-3254, www.mass.gov, Mon.-Fri. 5am-8pm, Sat.-Sun. 7am-8pm, $10/vehicle). While it may no longer be the place to contemplate Thoreau's "tonic of wildness," you can follow a path through the woods to the former site of his cabin, now marked with granite posts, visit a reconstruction of the cabin, and learn the natural and literary history of Walden Pond at a new visitors center.

And if Thoreau would have grumbled about the fuss and crowds at Walden Pond (the writer was certainly fond of grumbling), scholars of his life often point out that even in his day the small woods were no howling wilderness. He frequently walked home to Concord to drop his laundry at his mother's house or raid her cookie jar, and he was rumored to have slipped away with pies left unguarded on windowsills. Thoreau enjoyed visitors at his one-room cabin and made frequent calls at the home of fellow writer Ralph Waldo Emerson. For Thoreau was not Concord's only great thinker: The small community was also home to Nathaniel Hawthorne and Amos Bronson Alcott, a political reformer and father of Louisa May Alcott, and the writers were part of a vibrant Transcendentalist community committed to self-reliance, social justice, and spiritual experiences.

After exploring Walden Pond, lovers of American literature can pick up the trail of Concord letters on the **Emerson-Thoreau Amble** (www.concordma.gov), a 1.7-mile walking path that winds from Walden Pond to **Heywood Meadow** (Heywood St. at Lexington Rd.). The path goes by Thoreau's cabin site and bean field, a pond where Thoreau took the Alcott and Emerson children on berry-picking outings, and a partial view of Ralph Waldo Emerson's house.

Getting There from Boston: Follow I-93 North to Route 16 West and Route 2 West. In Concord, turn south onto Route 126. Walden Pond State Reservation is on the right (19 miles, 0.5 hr).

you select your destinations and save 15-20 percent by purchasing in advance. Another option is the **Boston City Pass** (www.citypass.com, $55 adults, $42 children), which includes the New England Aquarium, Museum of Science, Skywalk Observatory, and either the Museum of Fine Arts or a harbor cruise over a nine-day period. Who it works for: anyone already planning to visit two of the higher-dollar attractions on a more relaxed schedule.

Services
Emergencies

For medical emergencies, call 911. Boston has many hospitals with 24-hour emergency rooms, including **Massachusetts General Hospital** (55 Fruit St., off Cambridge St., 617/726-2000, www.massgeneral.org) and **Beth Israel Deaconess Medical Center** (330 Brookline Ave. at Longwood Ave., 617/667-7000, www.bidmc.org).

Getting Around

Car

Ask local drivers about Boston's behind-the-wheel style, and they'll describe their competitive, fast-moving traffic as part of the city's Hobbesian soul and panache. Ask anyone else in New England, and they'll explain how Bostonians earned their regional nickname: Massholes.

If you can get around without it, it's far easier and cheaper to leave your car in a garage while in Boston. Check with your accommodations first, as many often have a deal with a nearby location.

Parking

It's possible to find street parking in Boston, but regulations can be byzantine, with varied time limits and many resident-only zones. If you do find on-street parking, meters are active Monday-Saturday, 8am-8pm, and most take both coins and credit cards, as well as payment through the **Park Boston app.**

In downtown, **Boston Common Garage** (0 Charles St., 617/954-2098, weekdays $28 for 3-10 hrs, $32 for 10-24; weekends $14 for 1-3 hrs, $18 overnight) is large, convenient, and affordable. The **North End Garage** (600 Commercial St., 617/723-1488, $24 for 2-10 hrs, $34 for 10-24 hrs) is close to TD Garden and North End sights. Prices fluctuate and some small lots offer good discounts: Parking app **SpotHero** (www.spothero. com) is an excellent way to search for nearby spots using custom time parameters, often at discounted prices—though some garages require you to print your pass. Most garages do not include "in and out" privileges.

One other option is to leave your car outside of the city entirely. Some MBTA stations have enclosed garages that are much cheaper than city parking: **Alewife Station** (11 Cambridgepark West, Cambridge, www.lazparking.com, overnight parking $8) is convenient and big, with 2,733 spaces in an enclosed garage. Alewife is at the end of the Red Line, and frequent trains make the 20-minute trip to downtown Boston.

Public Transit

For peace of mind (and to save on parking costs), use public transport. The "T," which is short for MBTA, or **Massachusetts Bay Transportation Authority** (617/222-5000, www.mbta. com) is cheap, safe, and easy to use. Subway fares are $2.75 with a ticket—or $2.25 with a reloadable Charlie Card you can pick up at major stations. More out-of-the-way locations require taking one of the MBTA buses, which are often slow but give good coverage across the city. Fares are currently $2, or $1.70 with a Charlie Card. Often overlooked as a means of transportation are the ferries that ply Boston Harbor. A trip from Charlestown Navy Yard to Long Wharf (perfect after completing the Freedom Trail) costs $3.50.

Taxi

Keep in mind that the MBTA doesn't run 12:30am-5:30am. The only option at that time is to take a taxi, which isn't cheap. Fares start at $2.60 for the first one-seventh mile, and add $2.60 for each additional mile, with $28 for each hour of waiting time. Also note that trips to Logan are saddled with an additional $2.75 for tolls, while trips from Logan cost an extra $6.

Call a cab from the hybrid fleet of **Boston Cab Dispatch** (617/536-5010, www.bostoncab.us), which also has wheelchair-equipped cars, or try **Boston Logan Taxi Service** (617/499-7770, www. bostonairportexpresscar.com), whose website allows pre-booking for airport pickups. **Uber** and **Lyft** services are also available in Boston.

Coastal Maine

Wild and vast, Maine's sprawling coast is full of castaway lighthouses, pebble beaches, and picture-perfect seaside villages.

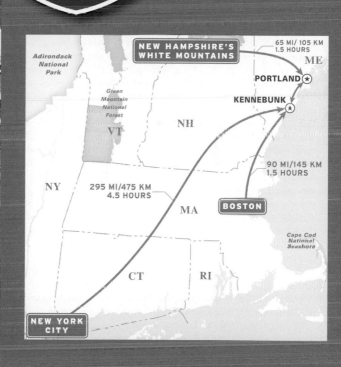

NEW HAMPSHIRE'S WHITE MOUNTAINS

65 MI/ 105 KM
1.5 HOURS

ME

PORTLAND ★

KENNEBUNK

Adirondack National Park

Green Mountain National Forest

VT

NH

90 MI/145 KM
1.5 HOURS

NY

295 MI/475 KM
4.5 HOURS

MA

BOSTON

Cape Cod National Seashore

CT

RI

NEW YORK CITY

Trace a route along Maine's 3,500-mile waterfront, and you'll find fishing towns, far-flung beaches, and one of New England's most vibrant small cities.

Within day-tripping distance from Boston, the south coast is a classic vacation getaway for city crowds who come to sail and socialize in grand seaside inns. This is the pinnacle of Maine beach chic, with perfect sand, gentle surf breaks, and elegant waterside dining. A few lighthouses up the coast, Portland is the cultural capital of the state, with a fabulous setting and quality of life that draw creative talent from around the country. Framed by a pair of scenic parks, downtown overflows with boat-to-table restaurants, microbreweries, and art.

After Portland, the shoreline goes wild, fracturing into deep coves and bays; proud shipwright towns stand back from the sea on tidal rivers that sent merchant vessels and warships to every corner of the globe. Roads to the shore dead-end in seasonal lobster shacks where you can dine "in the rough" as fishers unload the day's catch.

From Rockland's working waterfront to pretty Camden, the towns lining Penobscot Bay are home to lobster-boat captains, sailors, and summer people, and their harbors shelter grand old schooners and elegant luxury yachts. This is the beginning of Down East, the far stretch of the Maine coast that extends to the most easterly point in the United States. From Penobscot Bay, the coast gets increasingly remote, the towns divided by long passages of deep forest and rugged shoreline leading onward to the scenic jewel of Acadia National Park.

Planning Your Time

Even more than other destinations in New England, the true high season in Maine is during the summer school vacation, when families descend on beaches in hordes. Visiting in late June or late August offers the best weather without the crowds, though many locals say September is the finest month, with still-warm days and cooler nights. At any time of year, however, the weather can be unpredictable, and Maine can seemingly pass through multiple seasons in a single day, with sunshine giving way to fog and rain before turning again.

Experiencing the highlights of coastal Maine takes at least a week, especially when summer crowds turn Route 1 into a series of bottlenecks. Allot this much time, and you can take in the region in a series of clusters (with less time, perhaps focus on one, and avoid Route 1 when possible for expediency).

Spend a couple of days exploring south coast lighthouses, beaches, and restaurants from the Kennebunks—Kennebunkport and Kennebunk—or Portland, with time to visit the outdoors or go outlet shopping in Freeport. Make your second destination one of the towns of Maine's Mid-Coast, such as Brunswick, Bath, Wiscasset, and Damariscotta. Plenty of museums and historic downtowns are along Route 1, but don't miss the chance to get off the main road, following quiet highways to island communities and seaside lobster shacks.

After making its way through inland forests, Route 1 finds the coast in Penobscot Bay, where a trio of wonderful towns is perched on picturesque harbors: Rockland, Rockport, and Camden are ideal places to trade your car for a kayak or berth on a historic schooner and explore islands dotting the coast.

Highlights

★ **Whale-Watching:** Spot the humpback whales that spout and breach above offshore banks (page 78).

★ **Lighthouse Bagging:** Every rocky peninsula and outcropping's got its very own lighthouse, from hidden gems to crowd favorites (page 84).

★ **Portland's Breweries:** Taste your way through microbreweries in a beer-obsessed city by the sea (page 89).

★ **Lobster Feast:** Dig into great piles of steamed lobster and clams at a rustic island dinner (page 111).

★ **Paddling Penobscot Bay:** The best way to see Maine's rocky coves and historic harbors is by boat, so you can get a seal's-eye view of the coast (page 123).

Coastal Maine

© AVALON TRAVEL

Orientation

Perched just before the coastline crumbles into a squiggly line of bays and peninsulas, Portland is the cosmopolitan hub and gateway to Maine's endless shoreline. Beyond the city, other destinations on the Maine coast lie along Route 1, a two-lane highway lined with banks of wildflowers and thick forest. Traffic slows to a crawl in each of the towns along the way, where coastal roads sheer off into fishing villages and deep inlets.

Getting to Coastal Maine

Driving from Boston
90 miles, 1.5 hours

To get to Maine's south coast from Boston, head out on **I-93 North,** then take Exit 37A to merge onto **I-95 North** ($2 toll in New Hampshire, cash only). For **Kennebunk,** take **Exit 25** ($3 toll, cash only), and follow **Route 35** into downtown (90 mi, 1.5 hrs). For **Portland,** stay

Best Accommodations

★ **Seaside Inn, Kennebunk:** Catch sunrise—and sunset—on the beach from this perfectly placed, old-fashioned hotel (page 83).

★ **Pomegranate Inn, Portland:** Hand-painted walls and modernist touches set this elegant neighborhood inn apart (page 95).

★ **Inn by the Sea, Cape Elizabeth:** Luxurious rooms, rescue puppies, and ecofriendly policies? A location on the south coast's best beach doesn't hurt either (page 95).

★ **Hermit Island Campground, Phippsburg:** Fabulous campgrounds can be found up and down the coast, but this one's got an island to itself (page 105).

★ **1774 Inn, Phippsburg:** This historic, Georgian mansion on the Kennebec River is full of traditional charm (page 105).

★ **Beach Cove Waterfront Inn, Boothbay Harbor:** Start the day with a morning paddle at this family-friendly (and budget-friendly) lakeside institution (page 112).

★ **The Inn at Cuckolds Lighthouse, Southport:** Take a private island escape with boat service, afternoon cocktails, and a bed in a classic lighthouse (page 112).

★ **Old Granite Inn, Rockland:** Homey and historic, this laid-back inn is perfect for watching sails and seabirds drift by (page 121).

★ **Oakland Seashore Cabins, Rockport:** Somewhere between quaint and rustic, these sweet and affordable cabins have access to a private beach and a million-dollar view (page 126).

★ **16 Bay View, Camden:** Wake up to the sounds of schooner lines and lapping waves at a boutique hotel with a rooftop terrace (page 127).

on I-95 until **Exit 44** ($3 toll, cash only), merging onto **I-295**. Stay right and take Exit 7 for downtown locations (110 mi, 1.75 hrs).

Driving from New Hampshire's White Mountains
65 miles, 1.5 hours
Driving to coastal Maine from the White Mountains means a trip through rural farmlands and mountains on two-lane roads. To drive to **Portland** from **Conway, New Hampshire,** take **Route 113 East** until it merges briefly with **Route 25 East,** then make a slight right in Gorham to continue onto **Route 112 North.** When Route 112 intersects **Route 114 South,** turn right on Route 114, following it beneath the interstate. Turn left onto Mussey Road, which becomes West Broadway, following signs to **I-295 North.** Merge onto I-295 North for 3.3 miles and take Exit 7 to downtown Portland.

To reach the Kennebunks from Conway, leave town on **Route 113 East** across the border into Maine, turning right in Fryeburg to continue onto **Route 113 South** for 18 miles. Turn right onto **Route 117 South/Route 5 South** into Cornish, where you'll turn left to stay on **Route 117.** After 2.5 miles, turn right to stay on Route 117 for another 16 miles, then turn right onto **Route 35 South** for 18 miles into downtown **Kennebunk.** It's approximately 65 miles and 1.5 hours of driving time to reach either Portland or Kennebunk from Conway.

Driving from New York City
295 miles, 4.5 hours
The drive from New York City to coastal Maine takes around 4.5-5 hours, though

Best Restaurants

★ **The Clam Shack, Kennebunk:** The lobster rolls and fried clams at this seasonal fry-joint make annual best-of lists throughout the region (page 80).

★ **The Wayfarer, Kennebunkport:** New England meets Southern comfort at this small-town eatery minutes from the water (page 82).

★ **Eventide Oyster Co., Portland:** Come to explore Maine's bays and oyster beds and stay for the brown butter lobster roll (page 92).

★ **Duckfat, Portland:** Much of the casual fare at this cozy bistro emerges from a boiling vat of flavorful duck fat, and the milk shakes have a cult following (page 93).

★ **Fore Street, Portland:** Local seafood and produce go haute at the Portland institution that put Maine on the foodie map (page 94).

★ **Five Islands Lobster Co., Georgetown:** In a crowded field, this rustic seaside shack tops many local lists for lobster "in the rough" (page 104).

★ **Pemaquid Fisherman's Co-op, Pemaquid:** Bring your own side dishes to go with lobsters and clams at a harbor-side picnic table (page 114).

★ **Primo, Rockland:** Make your reservations well in advance to dine at this beautiful farm restaurant with an Italian soul (page 120).

★ **Rhumb Line, Camden:** Dine on super-fresh seafood on the edge of a working boatyard (page 124).

★ **Nina June, Rockport:** Views of a picturesque harbor go perfectly with seasonal trattoria fare from a Maine-born, Manhattan-trained chef (page 126).

can be significantly longer with **traffic.** Leave New York City heading north on **FDR Drive.** Use the left lane to access Exit 17 to the **Robert F. Kennedy Bridge** ($8 toll, cash only), then stay left to merge onto **I-278 East.** After 4.5 miles, I-278 East merges with **I-95 North** ($1.75 toll, cash only). Follow I-95 North **46 miles** to Exit 27A in Bridgeport, Connecticut; exit right onto **Route 8 North,** which you'll follow 5.5 miles toward Exit 9 to **Route 15 North.**

Take Exit 68 NE to merge onto **I-91 North** toward Hartford/Middletown, then stay right for Exit 29 onto **Route 15 North** toward **I-84 East.** Use the left two lanes to continue onto I-84 East. North of Sturbridge, I-84 East merges into **I-90** ($7.25 toll, cash only); stay right at the split for **I-90 East.** In Auburn, use the right two lanes to take Exit 10 to merge onto **I-290 East.** Use the left lane to take Exit 26B to **I-495 North,** then merge onto **I-95 North** at Exit 60. For **Kennebunk,**

take **Exit 25** ($3 toll, cash only), and follow Route 35 into downtown (295 mi, 4.5 hrs). For **Portland,** stay on I-95 until **Exit 44** ($3 toll, cash only), merging onto **I-295.** Stay right and take Exit 7 for downtown locations (315 mi, 5 hrs).

Getting There by Air, Train, or Bus
Air
Maine's largest airport is **Portland International Jetport** (1001 Westbrook St., 207/774-7301, www.portlandjet-port.org), with service from American Airlines, Delta, JetBlue, Southwest, and United. There you'll find national car rental agencies Alamo, Avis, Budget, Enterprise, Hertz, and National, and the **Greater Portland Transit District METRO** (207/774-0351, www.gpmetro-bus.net), which has a bus from the airport to downtown Portland (Route #5, 6-15 buses daily).

Two Days in Coastal Maine

Day 1

Flip a coin: small-town escape or city experience? Choose the more urban option, and kick off your time in **Portland** with a trip to the **Portland Museum of Art,** taking in the Maine coast through the keen eyes of Edward Hopper and Rockwell Kent. Grab a quick cup of **chowder** in the **Old Port** before starting a tour of the city's excellent **microbreweries.** Shoppers might be craving a side trip to **Freeport's outlet stores** by now, and aspiring yachties can end the afternoon with a **cruise on Casco Bay;** either way, you'll have worked up an appetite for dinner at one of the city's many **boat-to-table restaurants.**

If your quarter came up small town, make a beeline for **Penobscot Bay.** Get the lay of the land by following a trail (or auto road) to the top of **Mount Battie** or **Mount Megunticook,** then descend to the coast for a seafood lunch on **Camden Harbor.** History buffs should make a detour to the **Penobscot Marine Museum,** but there's no better way to enjoy the coast than from a boat: Grab a **paddle** or head out on an afternoon **sailing trip.**

Day 2

On day two, Portland adventurers can pick up pastries or doughnuts at one of the city's fabulous bakeries on their way to the **lighthouses** lining the rocky shoreline, then settle on pretty Crescent Beach at **Cape Elizabeth** for an afternoon of sun and sea. When the sun goes down, head back to the historic town center for dinner: Choose between gorgeous oyster joint **Eventide Oyster Co.** and upscale **Fore Street,** two of the best destinations for well-prepared seafood in coastal Maine. Rubbing shoulders with the colorful downtown crowd is part of the experience.

Small-town escapists can make their way to **Rockland** for a morning walk down the **Rockland Breakwater,** which crosses the harbor to a pretty, brick lighthouse, then find a restaurant in the vibrant downtown. Explore paintings by three generations of Wyeths in the wonderful **Farnsworth Art Museum,** and take in a classic Maine sunset at **Owls Head Lighthouse.**

Train

The Amtrak **Downeaster** (800/872-7245, www.amtrakdowneaster.com) runs from Boston to Portland five times a day, with two trains making an extended trip to Freeport and Brunswick. The Portland stop is at the **Portland Transportation Center** (100 Thompson's Point Rd.) two miles outside of downtown. Trolleys link **Wells Regional Transportation Center** with the Kennebunks, and the **Freeport station** is within walking distance of downtown shops.

Bus

Concord Coach Lines (100 Thompson's Point Rd., Portland, 800/639-3317, www.concordcoachlines.com) operates buses from Boston and New York City; long-distance routes connect to Portland, then continue to many towns along Route 1, including Brunswick (16 Station Ave.), Bath (Mail It 4 U, 10 State Rd.), Rockland (Maine State Ferry Terminal, 517A Main St.), and Camden/Rockport (Maritime Farms, 20 Commercial St./Rte. 1, Rockport).

Greyhound (950 Congress St., Portland, 207/772-6588 or 800/231-2222, www.greyhound.com) has services to Portland and Brunswick from Boston.

The Kennebunks

The two towns that make up Maine's toniest seaside destination—Kennebunk and Kennebunkport—are filled with luxurious inns featuring platoons of beach chairs on the waterfront. A great, sweeping curve of beach in Kennebunk is one of the best on the southern coast, with plentiful sand and sunrise views of the bay. And Kennebunk River, a spidering tidal waterway that divides the pretty villages, also offers places to swim and sit away from the blustering waves of the sea.

While the Kennebunks' reputation is for blue bloods and well-heeled preppies (an image bolstered by the presence of the Bush clan in an eye-catching compound on Ocean Avenue), it's not that much more expensive than destinations up the coast. Ways to get on the water here include helming a sailboat, searching for whales on the offshore banks, and paddling into knee-high rollers on a surfboard. Streets are lined with old-fashioned colonial and federal homes, the whitewashed facades and bright shutters of which are classic New England. Even travelers blazing a path for Down East islands could while away an afternoon in Kennebunkport's Dock Square, with its nautical boutiques, galleries, and riverside cafés, or spend some time in Cape Porpoise, a village within Kennebunkport just a few miles up the coast from the city center.

Sights

You won't find the usual local historic paraphernalia at the **Brick Store Museum** (117 Main St., Kennebunk, 207/985-4802, www.brickstoremuseum.org, Tues.-Fri. 10am-4:30pm and Sat. 10am-1pm, $7.50 adults, $6 seniors, $3 children 6-16, families $20). Instead, the staff gets creative with frequently rotated themed displays such as *The Kennebunks During the Civil War* and *Kennebunks A-Z*. The museum also runs a walking tour of the historic district every Friday at 11am throughout the summer and a tour of historic homes around nearby Mother's Beach at 2pm on Thursdays; maps of the sites are also available if you'd prefer to explore the areas on your own (guided tours $5, maps $5).

Step back into the golden days of narrow-gauge rail at the **Seashore**

Trolley Museum (195 Log Cabin Rd., Kennebunkport, 207/967-2800, www.trolleymuseum.org, summer daily 10am-5pm, weekends only May and Oct., closed Nov.-Apr. except during Christmas Prelude, $10 adults, $8 seniors $7.50 children 6-16, $5 children 3-5, free children under 3). With a collection of more than 200 trolleys (some of which you can ride through nearby woods from the museum), plus a gift shop dedicated entirely to streetcars, the museum is well suited to enthusiastic kids and train aficionados alike.

The 1825 **Wedding Cake House** (104 Summer St., Kennebunkport) has become an essential sight for many visitors, who stop along the road to peer through the fence (the house is no longer open to the public). On a street with trim and tidy colonial gems, the overwrought Carpenter Gothic exterior *is* eye-catching, though the building sinks deeper into disrepair with each passing winter.

Entertainment and Events
Nightlife

While there's plenty of nightlife in the Kennebunks to go around, the main event is sunset, when boat drinks and microbrews flow at packed waterside bars. For a local vibe, flotsam-inspired decor, and Geary's beer on draft, the **Pilot House** (4 Western Ave., Kennebunk, 207/967-9961, Mon.-Sat. 11am-1am, Sun. 11am-midnight) is right by a marina and often has live music on weekend afternoons. The cavernous **Federal Jack's** (8 Western Ave., Kennebunk, 207/967-4322, www.federaljacks.com, daily 11:30am-1am) is less atmospheric but has plenty of seating on deep balconies overlooking the water. A little farther into Kennebunk, **Old Vines Wine Bar** (173 Port Rd., Kennebunk, 207/967-2310, www.oldvineswinebar.com, Mon.-Thurs. 5pm-11pm, Fri.-Sat. 5pm-midnight, Sun. 5pm-10pm) makes up for an inland location with a rooftop patio, gorgeously crafted cocktails, and the best wine list

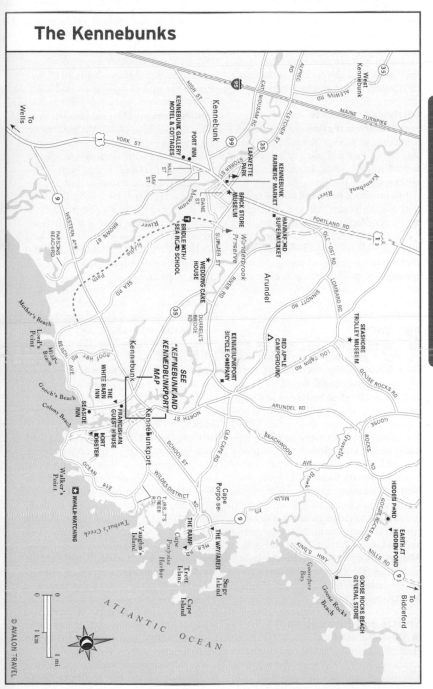

The Kennebunks

in town. On the other end of the spectrum, the **Arundel Wharf** (43 Ocean Ave., Kennebunkport, 207/967-3444, daily 11:30am-9pm) is more rum-and-coke than riesling, but you'll be served on a floating dock in the Arundel River.

Festivals and Events
Free **Concerts in the Park** (Lafayette Park, Kennebunk, Wed. 6:30pm-7:30pm) feature classic rock and jazz bands, mid-June to mid-August; bring a picnic blanket to spread out on the grass. In early June, the **Kennebunk Food and Wine Festival** (www.kennebunkportfestival.com) gathers local celebrity chefs and winemakers for a series of tastings and themed dinners. Later that month, **Launch! Maritime Festival** (www.gokennebunks.com) celebrates the Kennebunks' nautical heritage with seafood cook-offs, boat parties, and the annual Blessing of the Fleet.

Shopping
Packed with adorable gift shops and maritime galleries, Kennebunkport's **Dock Square** easily offers a day's worth of window-shopping. Equal parts hip and classic, **Daytrip Society** (4 Dock Sq., Kennebunkport, 207/967-4440, www.daytripsociety.com, daily 10am-7pm) is full of sweet treasures, nautical doodads, and stylish little books. Among the galleries scattered around downtown, **Landmark Gallery** (31 Ocean Ave., Kennebunkport, 207/967-0020, www.landmarkgallery.net, daily 10am-5:30pm) has one of the finest collections of maritime art, mostly paintings by regional artists. Find whimsical crafts and gifts at **Abacus** (2 Ocean Ave., Kennebunkport, 207/967-0111, www.abacusgallery.com, daily 10am-6pm), a sprawling store ideal for aimless browsing.

Sports and Recreation
★ Whale-Watching
Humpback, finback, and minke whales congregate and feed at offshore banks, where they luxuriate in a whale's dream buffet of tiny sea creatures. Try to catch a glimpse aboard *Nick's Chance* (4 Western Ave., Kennebunk, 207/967-5507, www.firstchancewhalewatch.com, 4.5-hr trip $48 adults, $28 children 3-12), an 87-foot vessel that makes daily trips mid-June-September and weekend trips in the shoulder season. The boat goes up to 20 miles offshore, so even if the weather on the beach is balmy, bring plenty of warm clothing (and your favorite seasickness remedy). No refunds are given for trips when no whales are spotted, but passengers get a free pass for a second outing. The same company also runs 1.5-hour cruises on a **lobster boat** that's a fun, inexpensive way to explore the coast and see what's on the other end of all those colorful lobster buoys ($20 adults, $15 children 3-12).

Beaches
The 1.5-mile stretch of coastline known as **Kennebunk Beach,** located where the Kennebunk River reaches the ocean and about 1.2 miles away from Dock Square, is actually a series of three beaches, scalloped curves neatly separated by small, rocky outcroppings. Farthest east and easily the most popular of the three, **Gooch's Beach** is long and easy to access (if you've already secured a parking place downtown, it's easy to reach Gooch's Beach by bicycle or on foot: Leave Dock Square heading west on Western Ave., then turn left onto Beach Ave.) but dwindles to a thin strip of sand at high tide. Next in line is **Middle Beach,** a quieter portion where the sand gives way to smooth stones that keep away sunbathers and sandcastle builders. **Mother's Beach** is small and sandy, with a good playground that makes it a hit with young families. A $20 parking fee for Kennebunk Beach is charged from mid-June to mid-September. The local Intown Trolley also makes stops at the three beaches.

On busy summer weekends, it's often worth making the trip to **Goose Rocks**

Beach in Cape Porpoise. Wide and scenic, the beach is rimmed with dune grass and perfect for strolling or taking a dip into the bracingly cold water. Parking at the beach is limited, and passes are required 8am-6pm, late May-early September; buy a sticker at **Goose Rocks Beach General Store** (3 Dyke Rd., Kennebunkport, 207/967-2289, May-June Mon.-Thurs. 7:30am-2pm and Fri.-Sat. 7:30am-7pm, July-Sept. daily 7:30am-7pm, $15). A pass doesn't guarantee you'll find a spot, and the store advises showing up before 8:30am for the best chance at parking.

Biking

Back roads and trails around the Kennebunks invite endless exploration on two wheels. Though the way is narrow, winding, and sometimes clogged with sightseers, the eight-mile one-way ride down Ocean Avenue from Kennebunkport to **Cape Porpoise** via Wildes District Road is among the most scenic in town; the jewel-box seaside village has a few good seafood restaurants and an ice cream shop for mid-ride recovery. A gentler option is the flat, dirt **Bridle Path** that runs two miles along the Mousam River; the main access point and parking is at **Sea Road School** (29 Sea Rd., Kennebunk).

The 65-mile **Eastern Trail** (www.easterntrail.org) stretches along the coast from Kittery to South Portland, including 22 miles of smooth, off-road trail between Kennebunk and Bug Light in South Portland (parking available at Kennebunk Town Hall). Rent a hybrid, road, or mountain bike at **Kennebunkport Bicycle Company** (34 Arundel Rd., Kennebunkport, 207/385-4382, www.kennebikeport.com, Mon.-Sat. 10am-5pm, Sun. 8am-3pm, bikes from $19 half day, $26 full day), which also offers guided tours of local trails.

Boating

All eyes are on 55-foot schooner *Eleanor* when she cruises down the coast with gaff-rigged sails flying, and a trip with Captain Woody feels like stepping back into the grand old days of New England sailing. *Eleanor* (43 Ocean Ave., Kennebunkport, 207/967-8809, www.schoonereleanor.com, $45 day cruise, $55 sunset sail) makes two-hour outings daily May-September, and passengers are welcome to bring snacks and drinks aboard.

Hiking

Kennebunk Beach makes a great place to start the day with a sunrise walk. Just outside of downtown Kennebunk, **Wonder Brook Reserve** (www.kennebunk-landtrust.org, parking on Plummer Lane) has 2.5 miles of footpaths through shady upland forest and banks of rustling ferns.

Old, sandy roads-turned-walking-trails run through pine barrens and grassland at **Kennebunk Plains** (Rte. 99, www.nature.org), which the Nature Conservancy bought in order to protect the endangered Morefield's leather flower, threatened northern blazing star plants, and endangered grasshopper sparrows. The reserve also has a treasure trove of **wild blueberries,** and late summer brings a luxurious crop of the tiny, intensely flavored fruit (it's essential to stay on the trail when picking, however, as some of the plains' most vulnerable birds make their nests on the ground Apr.-Sept.).

Paddling

Paddle the Kennebunk River or follow the shoreline to **Goat Island Light** on a guided kayak outing with **Coastal Maine Kayak & Bike** (8 Western Ave., Kennebunk, 207/967-6065, www.coastalmainekayak.com, three-hr tours $85; kayak rentals from $45 half day and $80 full day), which also has a fleet of stand-up paddleboards. The Arundel River winds through scenic forest as it leaves the coast and is the most popular place for independent kayak trips, but outings must be timed to the tides (some paddlers have found themselves stuck in the mud).

Surfing

Unless there's a hurricane sending giants swells to shore (and sending expert surfers to the beach) the Kennebunks' waves are relatively gentle and beginner-friendly. Learn your way around the break at Gooch's Beach with one of the instructors from **Aquaholics Surf Shop** (166 Port Rd., Kennebunk, 207/967-8650, www.aquaholicsurf.com, 1.5-hr private lesson $110 1 person, $170 for 2, $230 for 3, rental boards from $25 half day and $35 full day), which also rents soft and hard-top boards.

Food
Kennebunk

The main competition for best lobster roll in town is ★ **The Clam Shack** (2 Western Ave., 207/967-3321, www.theclamshack. net, May-Oct. daily 11am-8pm, $12-25), which has gotten top scores from a who's who of food magazines and television shows. The riverside spot charges a premium for its version, but stuffs the toasted hamburger buns with a pound of lobster in large, meaty chunks bathed in your choice of mayonnaise or butter.

It's a travel truism that nothing says "tourist trap" like a giant board screaming: "Locals eat here!" The thing about the **Pilot House** (4 Western Ave., Mon.-Sat. 11am-1am, Sun. 11am-midnight, $8-22), though, is that locals really do spend their time on the riverside patio or bellied up to the inside bar outfitted with outboard motors and fishing gear. Geary's beer on tap, a convivial atmosphere, and a decent menu of fried grub (which many regulars like to cap off with a Jell-O shot, or three) make this a fine place to nurse a pint at the end of the day, listening to conversations about tourist foibles and fishing.

Grab a few basic foods, along with deli sandwiches and some prepared items

Top to bottom: Maine seafood shack; Kennebunk Beach; Dock Square in Kennebunkport.

Kennebunk and Kennebunkport

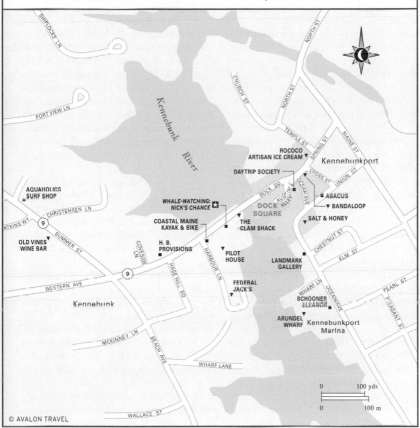

at **H. B. Provisions** (15 Western Ave., 207/967-5762, www.hbprovisions.com, daily 6am-9pm). For a more extensive selection, a **Hannaford Supermarket** (65 Portland Rd., 207/985-9135, Mon.-Sat. 7am-10pm, Sun. 7am-9pm) is on Route 1. Meet local bakers, farmers, and artisans at the **Kennebunk Farmers' Market** (3 Wells Ct., www.kennebunkfarmersmarket.org, May-Nov. Sat. 8am-1pm), rain or shine.

Kennebunkport

There's nowhere to sit at **Port Lobster** (122 Ocean Ave., 207/967-2081, www.

portlobster.com, daily 9am-6pm, $9-16), but you can bring your takeout lunch across the street to the edge of the Arundel River and find park benches and views of the local fishing fleet. This seafood shop buys lobster and fish straight from the boat, and its lobster roll is simple and to-the-point: toasted white hot dog bun and tender meat just kissed with mayonnaise. The short menu also includes crab rolls, seafood salads, and chowder that come highly recommended.

Funky and offhandedly cool, **Bandaloop** (2 Dock Sq., 207/967-4994, www.bandaloop.biz, Oct.-May

Wed.-Sun. 5pm-11pm, June-Sept. daily 5pm-11pm, $19-31) is an airy, energetic place to catch dinner made from organic, all-natural, and local foods served by a young, hip waitstaff. The menu changes frequently but includes creative dishes like tandoori-grilled salmon and pan-seared halibut with pepitas and pineapple chutney. Bandaloop also has beautifully prepared vegan options and is easily the best choice in town for non-meat options.

The lighthearted **Salt & Honey** (24 Ocean Ave., 207/204-0195, www.thesalt-andhoney.com, Mon.-Tues. 8:30am-2pm, Wed.-Sun. 8:30am-2pm and 5pm-9pm, breakfast $9-22, lunch $7-18, dinner $15-26) has fresh food and ambience offering a refreshing change from the seafood shack scene. Fish tacos and crab cakes are immensely popular, and you can start the day like a high-roller with a lobster omelet dripping with caramelized onions and havarti cheese.

A long-standing fine dining destination, **The White Barn Inn** (37 Beach Ave., 207/967-2321, www.whitebarninn. com, Mon.-Thurs. 6pm-9:30pm, Fri.-Sun. 5:30pm-close, four-course prix fixe $109, nine-course tasting menu $155, wine pairing $48-85) has won seemingly every award and honor a restaurant can earn in the United States. It has impeccable service, and the 19th-century barn setting makes a luxurious backdrop for the food, which balances classic and creative flavors.

With offbeat offerings ranging from Lemon Pink Peppercorn to Malbec & Berries, **Rococo Artisan Ice Cream** (6 Spring St., 207/251-6866, www.rococoi-cecream.com, daily 11am-7pm, $4-6) is the sweetest game in town. Lucky for wafflers, the shop serves ice cream in "flights" including four small scoops of different flavors.

Cape Porpoise

Though it's only three miles down the road from the center of Kennebunkport, the village of Cape Porpoise is a place apart, with salt marshes and just a few places to eat in between the vacation homes lining the waterfront.

★ **The Wayfarer** (2 Pier Rd., Kennebunkport, 207/967-8961, www. wayfarercapeporpoise.com, daily 7am-2pm and 5pm-9pm, breakfast $7-14, dinner $15-25) brings a southern twist to New England cuisine in a charmingly hip spot full of light and nautical flourishes. Brunch items like eggs Benedict and blueberry pancakes drenched in maple syrup are favorites here, and the milk-marinated fried lobster is completely outrageous.

On a coast where flotsam-chic is a competitive sport—everything from clam shacks to inns are draped in fishing net, buoys, and other marine paraphernalia—**The Ramp** (77 Pier Rd., Kennebunkport, 207/967-8500, www.pier77restaurant. com, daily 11:30am-9pm, $14-25) might take the prize. Crushed shells cover the ground and rowboats stand guard over the parking lot. The menu of pub classics and seafood is solid, but it's the Portuguese-style mussels that win raves.

Out a bit farther, **Earth at Hidden Pond** (354 Goose Rocks Rd., Kennebunkport, 207/967-6550, www.earthathiddenpond. com, daily 5:30pm-9:30pm, $40-65) is a top contender for a night of splashing out with its exquisite food and modern-design-meets-rustic-chic decor. Its menu of contemporary cuisine is rooted in local products and flavors, and while any spot in the restaurant makes a lovely place to spend the evening, two private screened-in shacks (first-come, first-served) are the most stunning places to enjoy a meal.

Accommodations and Camping
Camping

The hospitable ★ **Red Apple Campground** (111 Sinnott Rd., Kennebunkport, 207/967-4927, www.re-dapplecampground.com, $48 tent, $57 RV, $62 full-service) has neat and tidy campsites set on a grassy clearing in the forest, as well as comfortable **cabins** ranging from four-person units with air-conditioning, cable TV, and a refrigerator to six-person options with a small kitchen, barbecue area, and outdoor fire pit ($175-220 cabins, 3-day minimum, 1-week minimum in high season). A heated pool, camp store, and rec room give this spot a convivial feel, and if you order in the morning, the friendly owners will bring a fresh-cooked lobster dinner to your site at far-below Kennebunkport prices.

With slightly fewer amenities, **Yankeeland Campground** (1 Robinson Way, Kennebunk, 207/985-7576, www.yankeelandcampground.com, $32/34 for two adults in partial/full-hookup sites, $3 extra adult, $3 extra child) is still an appealing option, especially at the lower price.

$100-150

There's nothing fancy about **Kennebunk Gallery Motel & Cottages** (65 York St., Kennebunk, 207/985-4543, www.kennebunkcottages.com, May-Oct., $80-164), but the friendly staff and location just outside town make it an excellent find. Larger cottages have small, simple kitchens, and a volleyball court and pool keep things cheery.

$150-250

Set on the serene grounds of a Lithuanian Franciscan monastery, the nonprofit **Franciscan Guest House** (26 Beach Ave., Kennebunk, 207/967-4865, www.franciscanguesthouse.com, $117-175) is a converted boardinghouse that hosts retreats and a regular crowd of Lithuanian summer people. The dated, very simple rooms are not for everybody—same goes for faux wood paneling and flaxen-haired figurines—but it's a half-mile walk to town or to Kennebunk Beach, and the guesthouse is a good deal for the location, with prices that fall to $69 in the shoulder season. A simple, continental breakfast is included, and a hot breakfast buffet is available for an additional donation, with

homemade Lithuanian bread, pancakes, and sometimes Ukininku Suris, a rustic farmer cheese; dinner may be served during high season. All rooms have a fridge, cable television, and in-room bathrooms, and there's an unheated pool that's a treat for lounging.

Perfectly tidy and well-maintained, the **Port Inn** (55 York St., Kennebunk, 855/849-1513, www.portinnkennebunk.com, $105-200) has flourishes of contemporary style and color that keep it from feeling generic. A generous, hot buffet breakfast is served in a bustling dining room and, given the location, this spot feels a bit more luxurious than the price would suggest.

Over $250

Common spaces at the ★ **Seaside Inn** (80 Beach Ave., Kennebunk, 207/967-4461, www.kennebunkbeachmaine.com, $259-369) are somewhere between dated and homey, but rooms are comfortable and bright, and oceanfront rooms have big sliding doors that let in the sound of rolling waves and scent of the sea. For access to the beach, this spot is unmatched, with a private, sandy path that leads straight to the water. The breakfast buffet is classic, old-fashioned Maine: whole grain oatmeal, French toast with blueberries and syrup, and bowls of fresh fruit in a convivial dining room.

The closest thing in adult life to an indulgent, sleep-away summer camp may be **Hidden Pond** (354 Goose Rocks Rd., Kennebunkport, 888/967-9050, www.hiddenpondmaine.com, bungalows from $299, cottages from $499), a dreamy resort tucked into a quiet patch of woods. Guests ride cruiser bikes down the dirt roads between bungalows and gather each night to toast s'mores at a lakeside bonfire. The two-bedroom cottages have small kitchens and are clustered near the all-ages pool, while the bungalows are strolling distance from the adults-only pool and a spa. Each of the buildings has distinctive style and decor, but chic, vintage flair and a keen eye for style make the whole place picture-perfect.

Information

All the usual pamphlets, along with maps and good advice, are available at the **Chamber of Commerce** (16 Water St., Kennebunk, 207/967-0857, www.gokennebunks.com, Mon.-Fri. 9am-4pm).

Getting Around

Intown Trolley (207/967-3638, www.intowntrolley.com, June-Oct., $16 adults, $6 children 3-17, free children under 3, $45 family of two adults and up to four children) follows a fixed route through town that takes in Kennebunk and Kennebunkport's main sights and beaches, with narration. Fares are good for one whole day, making this a useful option if you plan on doing a lot of sightseeing. **Shuttle-Bus** (207/282-5408, www.shuttlebus-zoom.com) operates buses around the southern coast. Fares and schedules vary.

Portland

Perched at the aft end of Casco Bay, Portland's the last bit of solidly built earth before the coastline splinters into the bays, inlets, and islands of Mid-Coast Maine. Look closer, though, and the city itself seems all shoreline: heads, breakwaters, and lighthouses wrap in on themselves, pinching Portland's peninsular center between Back Cove and the Fore River. Downtown bristles with schooner masts and wharves that give way to a rugged, working waterfront.

That blend of picturesque charm and real-world maritime culture infuses the city, and wherever you go in the Old Port and peninsula, the sea is not far away. Cobblestone streets are lined with galleries, museum, and boutiques celebrating Maine's seafaring traditions, and many of the city's chic bars and restaurants have a boat-to-table philosophy boasting

chefs on a first-name basis with fishers, long-liners, and sea captains. The effect is utterly entrancing: When the weather is fine and Casco Bay sparkling, and the air smells of salt and fresh seafood, many visitors find themselves at Old Port brewpubs or on the deck of a sailing ship thinking up ways to move to Portland.

Sights

To orient yourself in Portland, find its two major thoroughfares: Commercial Street runs between the Old Port and working waterfront, which anchor the heart of Portland's peninsula. The Arts District centers around Congress Street, with a collection of fine art galleries, studios, and the excellent Portland Museum of Art. Meanwhile, to the west, up-and-coming areas Munjoy Hill and West Bayside are primarily residential, with a handful of art galleries and cafés. Cape Elizabeth is part of the greater Portland area, about a 20-minute drive south of the city down Route 77.

Lighthouses

With a craggy shoreline that's often wrapped in thick fog, it's no wonder the Portland area needs half a dozen lighthouses to keep boats off the rocks. Even with their blinking beacons, the city's seen centuries of dramatic and often tragic wrecks: the *Annie C. Maguire* ran aground right at the base of Portland Head Light on Christmas Eve, 1886, and **Cape Elizabeth**'s two lights didn't save the RMS *Bohemian*, which struck an underwater ledge just off the coast. Set on pretty capes and outcroppings, lighthouses are part of the Maine landscape at its most picturesque, but even on sunny days, their powerful lenses and stout architecture serve as a reminder that sailing Maine's waters has always been a dangerous undertaking.

★ Lighthouse Bagging

The most iconic among Portland's lighthouses is the **Portland Head Light** (1000

Greater Portland

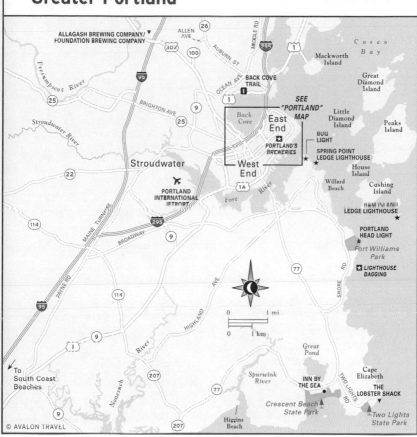

Shore Rd., Cape Elizabeth, www.portlandheadlight.com, museum and gift shop daily 10am-4pm, park sunrise-sunset); its slender proportions and red-roofed keeper's house are perfectly offset by jagged outcroppings and crashing waves. It was the first lighthouse completed by the U.S. government and has been guiding ships on Casco Bay since 1791; the rocky head is rich with history, including shipwrecks and daring, stormy rescues, and some believe it's haunted by the benevolent ghost of a former lighthouse keeper. One frequent visitor was hometown poet Henry Wadsworth Longfellow, who liked to drink with the lighthouse keeper and later wrote:

Steadfast, serene, immovable, the same
Year after year, through all the silent night
Burns on forevermore that quenchless
flame,
Shines on that inextinguishable light!

Another favorite spot for lighthouse bagging is **Two Lights** (Two Lights Rd., Cape Elizabeth), a pretty pair of private lighthouses with a small beach and rocks perfect for hopping around and scouting for sea creatures. Confusingly, neither of the two lights is visible from Two Lights State Park, so just keep on down the road

Portland

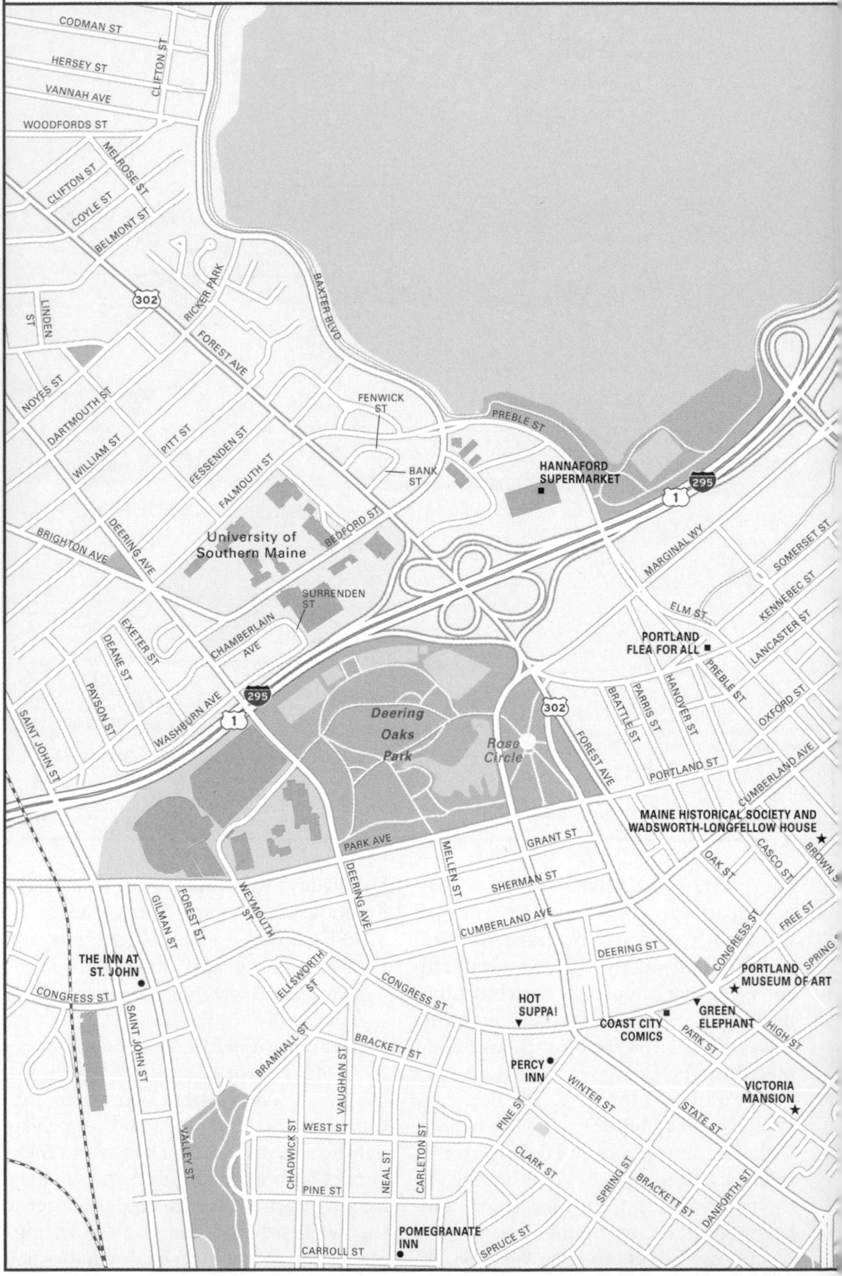

CODMAN ST
HERSEY ST
VANNAH AVE
WOODFORDS ST
CLIFTON ST
CLIFTON ST
MELROSE ST
COYLE ST
BELMONT ST
302
RICKER PARK
FOREST AVE
LINDEN ST
BAXTER BLVD
NOYES ST
DARTMOUTH ST
PITT ST
FESSENDEN ST
FENWICK ST
PREBLE ST
WILLIAM ST
FALMOUTH ST
BANK ST
HANNAFORD SUPERMARKET
1
295
BRIGHTON AVE
DEERING AVE
BEDFORD ST
University of
Southern Maine
MARGINAL WY
SOMERSET ST
EXETER ST
SURRENDEN ST
CHAMBERLAIN AVE
ELM ST
KENNEBEC ST
PORTLAND FLEA FOR ALL
DEANE ST
LANCASTER ST
PAYSON ST
WASHBURN AVE
295
1
Deering Oaks Park
Rose Circle
302
BRATTLE ST
PARRIS ST
HANOVER ST
PREBLE ST
OXFORD ST
PORTLAND ST
FOREST AVE
CUMBERLAND AVE
SAINT JOHN ST
PARK AVE
MELLEN ST
GRANT ST
SHERMAN ST
MAINE HISTORICAL SOCIETY AND
WADSWORTH-LONGFELLOW HOUSE
OAK ST
CASCO ST
BROWN S
DEERING AVE
CUMBERLAND AVE
CONGRESS ST
FREE ST
FOREST ST
WEYMOUTH ST
DEERING ST
CONGRESS ST SPRING
THE INN AT ST. JOHN
GILMAN ST
ELLSWORTH ST
CONGRESS ST
PORTLAND MUSEUM OF ART
CONGRESS ST
SAINT JOHN ST
BRACKETT ST
HOT SUPPA!
COAST CITY COMICS
GREEN ELEPHANT
PARK ST
HIGH ST
BRAMHALL ST
VAUGHAN ST
PERCY INN
PINE ST
WINTER ST
STATE ST
VICTORIA MANSION
WEST ST
CHADWICK ST
NEAL ST
CARLETON ST
CLARK ST
SPRING ST
BRACKETT ST
DANFORTH ST
VALLEY ST
PINE ST
CARROLL ST
POMEGRANATE INN
SPRUCE ST

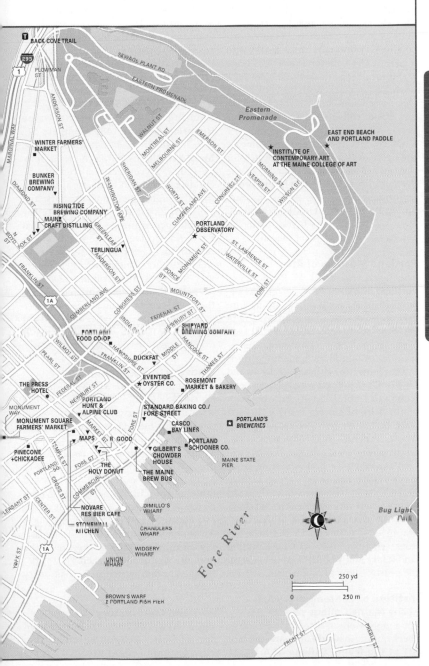

BACK COVE TRAIL

PLOWMAN ST

SEWAGE PLANT RD

EASTERN PROMENADE

Eastern Promenade

WALNUT ST

MONTREAL ST

MELBOURNE ST

EMERSON ST

EAST END BEACH
AND PORTLAND PADDLE

INSTITUTE OF
CONTEMPORARY ART
AT THE MAINE COLLEGE OF ART

MORNING ST

YESPER ST

WILSON ST

WINTER FARMERS'
MARKET

SHERIDAN ST

WASHINGTON AVE

NORTH ST

CUMBERLAND AVE

CONGRESS ST

BUNKER
BREWING
COMPANY

DIAMOND ST

RISING TIDE
BREWING COMPANY

MAINE
CRAFT DISTILLING

GREENLEAF ST

PORTLAND
OBSERVATORY

ST. LAWRENCE ST

N BOYD ST

FOX ST

TERLINGUA

ANDERSON ST

MONUMENT ST

PONCE ST

WATERVILLE ST

FORE ST

FRANKLIN ST

CUMBERLAND AVE

CONGRESS ST

INDIA ST

MOUNTFORT ST

FEDERAL ST

NEWBURY ST

PORTLAND
FOOD CO-OP

SHIPYARD
BREWING COMPANY

WILMOT ST

HAMPSHIRE ST

FRANKLIN ST

MIDDLE ST

HANCOCK ST

THAMES ST

PEARL ST

DUCKFAT

THE PRESS
HOTEL

FEDERAL ST

NEWBURY ST

EVENTIDE
OYSTER CO.

ROSEMONT
MARKET & BAKERY

MONUMENT
WAY

PORTLAND
HUNT &
ALPINE CLUB

MONUMENT SQUARE
FARMERS' MARKET

MARKET ST

FORE ST

STANDARD BAKING CO./
FORE STREET

CASCO
BAY LINES

PORTLAND'S
BREWERIES

MAPS + R GOOD

PINECONE
+CHICKADEE

TEMPLE ST

PORTLAND
SQ

FORE ST

GILBERT'S
CHOWDER
HOUSE

PORTLAND
SCHOONER CO.

THE
HOLY DONUT

MAINE STATE
PIER

THE MAINE
BREW BUS

CROSS ST

COMMERCIAL ST

NOVARE
RES BIER CAFE

DIMILLO'S
WHARF

Fore River

Bug Light
Park

PLEASANT ST

CENTER ST

STONEWALL
KITCHEN

CHANDLERS
WHARF

WIDGERY
WHARF

YORK ST

UNION
WHARF

0   250 yd

0   250 m

BROWN'S WARF
& PORTLAND FISH PIER

FRONT ST

PREBLE ST

MARGINAL WAY

until it ends in a small parking lot. Since neither lighthouse is open to the public, the views (and photo opportunities) aren't quite as good as elsewhere, but this shortcoming is easily made up for nearby with a visit to **The Lobster Shack** (225 Cape Lights Rd., Cape Elizabeth, 207/799-1677, www.lobstershacktwolights.com, Mar.-Oct. daily 11am-8pm, $12-18), which offers lobster rolls considered some of the best in Maine.

Of course, these are only some of the lights dotting Casco Bay; watch for the squat **Bug Light** at the edge of the Portland Breakwater, **Ram Island Ledge Lighthouse** on its own tiny island, and **Spring Point Ledge Lighthouse,** which looks like a stubby, cast-iron spark plug and has excellent views of the bay.

Portland Museum of Art

The highly regarded I. M. Pei-designed **Portland Museum of Art** (7 Congress Sq., 207/775-6148, www.portlandmuseum. org, mid-Oct.-late May Mon.-Wed. and Sat.-Sun. 11am-6pm; late May-mid-Oct. Wed. and Sat.-Sun. 11am-6pm, Thurs.-Fri. 11am-8pm; $15 adults, $13 seniors, $10 students, free children under 14 and free to all Fri. 5-9pm) is a world-class collection of Impressionist and American work. A highlight for many visitors is work by Maine artist Winslow Homer, whose dramatic images of rescues at sea, windy shorelines, and small boats are seen as among the best American landscapes. Other noteworthy artists include Mary Cassatt, Claude Monet, Edward Hopper, and Auguste Renoir, but don't miss the dramatic engravings, lithographs, and paintings by Maine artist Rockwell Kent, many of whose mythic landscapes and woodcuts were made on the nearby island of Monhegan.

Institute of Contemporary Art at the Maine College of Art

For a more modern slice of the art scene, check out the **Institute of Contemporary Art at the Maine College of Art** (522 Congress St. or 87 Free St., 207/879-5742 or 207/669-5029, www.meca.edu, Wed.-Sun. and Fri. 11am-5pm, Thurs. 11am-7pm, first Fri. of the month 11am-8pm, free). The school's galleries draw cutting-edge installations from local and global artists, both established and aspiring.

Maine Historical Society

Rotating exhibitions at the **Maine Historical Society** (489 Congress St., 207/774-1822, www.mainehistory.org, Mon.-Sat. 10am-5pm, Sun. noon-5pm, $8 adults, $7 seniors and students, $2 children under 17) illustrate the state's past through collections, exhibits, and lectures. Particularly riveting are the exhibits pertaining to the shelling that Portland received at the hands of the British during the Revolutionary War, when the port, then known as Falmouth, was burned to the ground in October 1775. The British captain offered mercy if the townspeople would swear allegiance to King George. No oath came, and the city was destroyed—only to be rebuilt over the next two decades.

Wadsworth-Longfellow House

Next door, the **Wadsworth-Longfellow House** (487 Congress St., 207/774-1822, www.mainehistory.org, May tours daily noon-4pm, June-Oct. tours Mon.-Sat. 10:30am-4pm and Sun. noon-4pm, $15 adults, $12 seniors and students, $3 children 6-17, $30 family of 2 adults and up to 3 children) was built in 1786 and achieved fame as the childhood home of poet Henry Wadsworth Longfellow. It's been restored to the time of the early 1800s, when Longfellow lived there. Tours lasting 45 minutes take in the life of the poet, as well as other members of the Longfellow family, such as Revolutionary War general Peleg Wadsworth.

Portland Observatory

Tired of waiting for boats to round Spring Point Ledge and come into view, Captain Lemuel Moody built the

★ Portland's Breweries

In recent years, Portland has established itself as one of the best U.S. cities for beer, with microbreweries and tasting rooms cropping up on the margins of downtown and clustered around an industrial complex north of the peninsula.

* **Rising Tide Brewing Company** (103 Fox St., 207/370-2337, www.risingtidebrewing.com, Mon.-Sat. noon-7pm, Sun. noon-5pm, free tours daily at 3pm, additional tours Fri.-Sat. 1pm and 5pm, Sun. 1pm, flights of four beers $8) has a diverse list of beers on tap, including the flagship Daymark American Pale Ale, a gorgeously balanced brew made with locally grown rye. The tasting room is cavernous and a bit gritty, and in summer months the outdoor beer garden is flanked by food trucks. Even devoted beer geeks should head next door to **Maine Craft Distilling** (101 Fox St., 207/798-2528, www.mainecraftdistilling.com, Sun.-Thurs. noon-5pm, Fri.-Sat. noon-7pm, free tastings), which uses many local ingredients in its offerings, which include whiskey, rum, gin, and the unusual Black Cap Barley Spirit, made entirely with Maine-grown barley and filtered through Maine maple charcoal.

* **Shipyard Brewing Company** (86 Newbury St., 207/761-0807, www.shipyard.com, Mon.-Wed. 11am-5pm, Thurs.-Sat. 11am-6pm, Sun. noon-4pm, tours $7 with tastings mid-May-Oct. Tues. 5pm, reserve online well in advance, flight of four beers $4) started in Kennebunkport, but the heart of Maine's largest brewery is just on the edge of downtown Portland. The tasting room has more of a finished brewpub feel, with barrels of aging beers stacked high against the walls, and a huge selection of brews (and a few craft sodas) on draft.

* **Bunker Brewing Company** (17 Westfield St., Unit D, 207/613-9471, www.bunkerbrewingco.com, Wed.-Thurs. 3pm-8pm, Fri.-Sat. noon-10pm, Sun. noon-6pm, flights of three beers $3) offers mainstay Machine Czech Pilz as well as constantly turns out funky one-offs and collaborations like the Long Island Potato Stout.

* **Foundation Brewing Company** (1 Industrial Way, 207/370-8187, www.foundationbrew.com, Thurs. 3pm-7pm, Fri.-Sat. noon-7pm, self-guided tours, 4-oz. pour $2, 10-oz pour $4) is teeny-tiny and friendly, with a rotating cast of beers on draft that's been winning raves. Don't miss Zuurzing, a refreshing and bright sour farmhouse ale.

* **Austin Street Brewery** (1 Industrial Way, 207/200-1994, www.austinstreetbrewery.com, Thurs. 3pm-7pm, Fri.-Sat. noon-7pm, 5-oz. pours $2) is another diminutive spot with brews that run the gamut from the citrusy, piney Patina Pale to the dark-as-espresso Milk Stout with its sweet, richly toasted flavor.

* **Allagash Brewing Company** (50 Industrial Way, 207/878-5385, www.allagash.com, daily 11am-6pm, check website for tour hours and registration, free tastings) turns out beers beloved across New England, especially the refreshing Allagash White and a rich-tasting tripel that packs a malty wallop. Aside from tastings, beer is not sold for consumption on-site.

An excellent way to soak up (so to speak) the Maine brewing scene is on a tour, so you can sip flights to your heart's content without worrying about cabs, buses, or wobbly bikes. **The Maine Brew Bus** (111 Commercial St., 207/200-9111, www.themainebrewbus.com, tours from $55) runs fun, highly regarded tours to the best taprooms in town, with food and drinks included.

Portland Observatory (138 Congress St., 207/774-5561, www.portlandlandmarks. org, May-Oct. tours daily 10am-4:30pm; sunset tours late July-early Sept. Thurs. 5pm-8pm, $10 adults, $8 seniors and students, $5 children 6-16, $30 families) in 1807 so he could see harbor arrivals—and pass along the news to other shipowners for a tidy $5 annual fee. Climb the cheery red tower for Cap'n Moody's coveted lines of sight across Casco Bay and beyond, a vantage point especially sublime at sunset, when the waterfront and islands seem to glow on the sparkling water.

Victoria Mansion

Fans of Italianate architecture (or anyone who likes a pretty building) can swing by the **Victoria Mansion** (109 Danforth St., 207/772-4841, www.victoriamansion. org, tours May-Oct. Mon.-Sat. 10am-4pm, Sun. 1pm-5pm; late Nov.-early Jan.1Tues.-Sun. 1pm-5pm , $15 adults, $13.50 seniors, $5 students 6-17, free children under 6, $35 family). Built by a hotel magnate between 1858 and 1860, the mansion is considered the greatest surviving example of pre-Civil War architecture in the country. Ahead of its time, it employed central heating, running water, and gas lighting in an era when such efficiencies were virtually unknown luxuries. These days the house is particularly impressive at Christmastime, when it's decorated from baseboards to ceilings with ornaments and wreaths.

Entertainment and Events
Nightlife

Even if it weren't for all its breweries, Portland would have an amazing bar scene. Some of the most popular places to grab a drink are also restaurants, like **Eventide Oyster Co., Duckfat,** and **Terlingua,** but there are a few that go right to the point.

Nordic chic and Scandinavian-themed small bites prevail at the stylish **Portland Hunt & Alpine Club** (75 Market St., 207/747-4754, www.huntandalpineclub.

com, daily 3pm-1am), and a happy hour lineup of four $6 cocktails is available daily until 6pm. Unless you're really looking, you'll walk right by **Novare Res Bier Cafe** (4 Canal Plaza, 207/761-2437, www. novararesbiercafe.com, Mon.-Thurs. 4pm-1am, Fri. 3pm-1am, Sat.-Sun. noon-1am), which is tucked down an alley between Union and Exchange Streets. Between the shady beer garden and cave-like interior, it works in any weather, and has an enormous list of beers from around the world. Drinkers who like their music on vinyl and decor eclectic will *love* **Maps** (64 Market St., 207/272-9263, Wed.-Sun. 4pm-midnight), which feels like a basement apartment owned by a fashionable friend, but with drinks, cake, and grilled cheese sandwiches.

Festivals and Events

With such a deluge of art venues, it's no surprise Portland offers a slew of performances, concerts, openings, and other events over the course of every year. One of the most regular—and festive—is the **First Friday Art Walk** (www.firstfridayartwalk.com, 5pm-8pm on the first Fri. of every month). In early June, the waterfront pulls out all the stops for the **Old Port Festival** (www.portlandmaine.com), an outdoor event packed with musicians, public art, and a Ferris wheel at the water's edge. Another favorite is the **Maine Brewers Festival** (www.mainebrewersfestival) in early November, which assembles the best of local beer in one place.

Shopping

Pretty shops line the cobblestone streets of Portland's Old Port. For the most efficient browsing, make your way along Exchange and Congress Streets. One local favorite is the sweetly hipster **Pinecone + Chickadee** (6 Free St., 207/772-9280, www.pineconeandchickadee.com, daily 10am-6pm), which stocks unique clothing, vintage finds, and doohickeys that make perfect gifts. Comic book lovers from around the East come to **Coast**

City Comics (634 Congress St., 207/899-1505, www.coastcitycomics.com, daily 11am-8pm) for its collection not only of comics but pinball and arcade games and vintage toys so fun the store could charge admission. Vintage and antiques hounds shouldn't miss the **Portland Flea For All** (585 Congress St., 207/370-7570, www.portlandfleaforall.com, Fri. noon-6pm., Sat.-Sun. 10am-5pm but hours can change without notice so call to confirm) for treasures covering three sprawling floors. Loved for classic jams and jellies, **Stonewall Kitchen** (182 Middle St., 207/879-2409, www.stonewallkitchen.com, daily 10am-6pm) is one of Maine's most recognizable brands, and the company store in Portland is a wonderland of free samples and things to buy.

Sports and Recreation
Beaches
With great sunset views and a skinny strip of sand, **East End Beach** is pleasant for walking and kayaking, and more to the point, it's Portland's only public beach. It's set on the southern end of the **Eastern Promenade,** where monuments, cliffs, and smooth trails make for a haven from the city.

For the real Maine beach experience, it's worth heading out of town. Eight miles south of Portland, **Crescent Beach** (66 Two Lights Rd., Cape Elizabeth, 207/767-3625, www.maine.gov, $8 adults, $2 seniors, $1 children 5-11) is all dune grass and soft sand, a gorgeous place to watch the fishing fleet cross the horizon.

Boating
Take a turn hoisting the gaff-rigged sails—or let someone else do the work—on a two hour cruise aboard the *Bagheera* or *Wendameen,* the 72- and 88-foot schooners operated by **Portland Schooner Co.** (Maine State Pier, 56 Commercial St., Portland, 207/766-2500, www.portlandschooner.com, $42 adults, $31 children 3-13, under 3 free).

An affordable way to get some water views is with a ticket for one of the ferries connecting Portland with the islands speckling Casco Bay. **Casco Bay Lines** (56 Commercial St., 207/774-7871, www.cascobaylines.com, passenger ferries $7-12, mailboat run $16 adults, $14 seniors, $8 children) runs trips to seven islands, from a quick hop to Peaks Island to the longer trip to Chebeague. The ferry service still delivers the mail to offshore communities, and you can tag along on the **mailboat run,** which lasts 2.5-3.5 hours; while the boat doesn't linger long enough for you to explore the islands, you'll get great views, and the crew narrates the whole experience on a loudspeaker (bring your own food and drinks).

Hiking and Biking
Walking and biking paths wind through Portland's streets, and much of the scenic waterfront is pedestrian-accessible. One of the finest places to walk or bike is **Back Cove Trail,** a 3.6-mile paved trail that circles a small estuary just north of downtown. Hop on (and leave your car) at Payson Park, the northern access point, or Preble Street. If you're headed from north to south, the Back Cove Trail connects to the **Eastern Promenade,** a slender, waterfront park that caps Portland's East End neighborhood; 2.1 miles end-to-end, the park has walking trails, a popular swimming beach, and showstopping sunrise views. **Portland Trails** (207/775-2411, www.trails.org) maintains a website with maps and directions to many of the city's best offerings.

Paddling
Rent a kayak (or stand-up paddleboard) from **Portland Paddle** (East End Beach, Eastern Promenade, 207/370-9730, www.portlandpaddle.net, kayaks $30 2 hrs, $40 half day, $55 full day, SUP $20 1 hr or $35 3 hrs) to explore Casco Bay on your own. Paddlers with basic skills can poke along the coast and beaches, while more experienced kayakers can visit uninhabited islands, the historic Fort Gorges, and

offshore communities. The company also offers guided tours: Family paddles, moonlight outings, and sunset trips are just a hair more expensive than renting the equipment alone (tours from $40 adults, $35 children 10-17).

Food

From old-school seafood joints to achingly hip bistros, Portland punches far above its weight in the restaurant department, and deciding where to apportion your limited meals in the city can be agonizing. Oysters and cocktails? Super-fresh salads packed with ingredients from local farms? How about a creamy bowl of chowder within earshot of the waterfront's clanging masts and foghorns?

Seafood

A refreshing throwback to Portland's pre-hipster, rough-hewn days, **Gilbert's Chowder House** (92 Commercial St., 207/871-5636, www.gilbertschowderhouse.com, daily 11am-9pm, $7-21) slings fresh corn and clam chowders in a thoroughly unpretentious space. The crisp, flaky haddock sandwiches are another treat, as is the open terrace behind the restaurant; when the restaurant is packed, order a cup of soup to go and find a spot on the nearby wharves for a very Maine picnic.

The interior of the ★ **Eventide Oyster Co.** (86 Middle St., 207/774-8538, www.eventideoysterco.com, daily 11am-midnight, $16-25) is almost too gorgeous: bright teal walls setting off a mammoth chunk of granite filled with crushed ice and sea creatures. The oysters—which mostly come from Maine, with a few out-of-state additions—are the obvious choice and centerpiece, and come with anything from "Kim Chee Ice" to classic mignonettes and cocktail sauce. Other

Top to bottom: lobster roll at The Lobster Shack; downtown Portland; sailing on historic schooner *Wendameen*.

options include small plates like duck confit salad and tuna crudo, but Eventide is famed for its lobster roll, a luscious combination of sweet lobster meat, brown butter, and chives in a soft Chinese-style steamed bun.

If you'd prefer a mini road trip with your seafood, **The Lobster Shack** (225 Cape Lights Rd., Cape Elizabeth, 207/799-1677, www.lobstershacktwolights.com, Mar.-Oct. daily 11am-8pm, $12-18) is a worthy goal. Nine miles south of Portland, this teeny restaurant is located by a pair of lighthouses and has some of Maine's most beloved lobster rolls. The interior is decked out in marine bric-a-brac, and the outdoor picnic tables overlook crashing waves and the lighthouses—but be vigilant about seagulls to avoid losing bits of your meal. While the lobster roll is the main attraction here, The Lobster Shack also serves the standard lineup of market-price seafood, and a homemade strawberry rhubarb pie that gets rave reviews.

Bakeries

From dark chocolate with sea salt to maple bacon, the flavors of the soft, crisp-crusted treats at **The Holy Donut** (7 Exchange St., 207/775-7776, www.theholydonut.com, Mon.-Thurs. 7:30am-4pm, Fri.-Sun. 8am-5pm, $2-5) are some of the best around—for doughnut lovers, this shop is a pilgrimage place. Arrive early to get the best selection, and avoid coming at the end of the day, as the doors close when the last doughnut sells.

A rustic, French aesthetic means great piles of croissants and fruit galettes at **Standard Baking Co.** (75 Commercial St., 207/773-2112, www.standardbakingco.com, Mon.-Fri. 7am-6pm, Sat.-Sun. 7am-5pm, $3-9), a beloved local institution walking distance from the Old Port. Breads and pastries are made with organic wheat flour from regional growers, and all the delightfully crusty loaves are naturally leavened.

Casual Fare

Just a few doors down, you'll find fresh fare to offset any doughnut guilt; **B. Good** (15 Exchange St., 207/747-5355, www.bgood.com, Mon.-Thurs. 11am-9pm, Fri.-Sat. 11am-10pm, Sun. 11am-8pm, $7-12) is a chain with a couple dozen locations across the East, but the concept of healthy food with local roots means the ingredients are sourced from Maine farmers and producers. Come for bowls of kale and quinoa, bright salads, simple burgers, and healthy smoothies, and find a seat upstairs when the place is hopping—a quiet bar and window-side tables overlook the action on Exchange Street.

Cheerful and welcoming, **Hot Suppa!** (703 Congress St., 207/871-5005, www.hotsuppa.com, Tues.-Sat. 7am-2pm and 4pm-9pm, Sun.-Mon. 7am-2pm, breakfast $5-11, lunch $7-12, dinner $15-24) serves an eclectic selection of comfort food with Southern flair, like pork belly with red beans and rice, catfish and grits, chicken and waffles, and some of the best corned beef hash in New England. Waits can get long, so aim to come early or late.

Named for a map-dot Texas town that hosts a yearly chili cookout, **Terlingua** (52 Washington Ave., 207/808-8502, www.terlingua.me, $14-20) is a warm, vivid antidote to all that seafood. The barbecue fare at this laid-back restaurant is executed with a reverence for smoke and meat and Tex-Mex flair, from butternut squash empanadas to red and green chilis. Menu items like Frito pie (in the bag) lean cheeky, and regulars wash it all down with the killer house margaritas and solid beer choices.

Just down the road is another local favorite: ★ **Duckfat** (43 Middle St., 207/774-8080, www.duckfat.com, daily 11am-10pm, $8-14) serves a casual lineup of paninis, salads, and golden french fries redolent of—you guessed it—duck fat. Decor is exposed brick and magnetic poetry tiles, and the poutine topped with cheese curds, gravy, and a fried egg would fortify you for a week of lighthouse bagging. If at all possible, save room for one of the shop's luxurious milk shakes, and come prepared to wait most nights.

Fine Dining

Vegetarians weary of meat-heavy Yankee fare shouldn't miss **Green Elephant** (608 Congress St., 207/347-3111, www.greenelephantmaine.com, $12-15), a top-notch Asian bistro with stenciled green walls and chandeliers. The spicy ginger noodles are a favorite with regulars, as are the tofu tikka masala and crispy wontons filled with soy cheese and spinach.

Often credited with putting Portland on the international foodie map, ★ **Fore Street** (288 Fore St., 207/775-2717, www.forestreet.biz, Sun.-Thurs. 5:30pm-10pm, Fri.-Sat. 5:30pm-10:30pm, bar opens 5pm daily, $28-40) could rest on its locally sourced, hand-crafted laurels for a decade. That makes it all the more refreshing that the kitchen continues to turn out such high-quality fare. An open kitchen keeps the industrial chic space from seeming too hushed as diners tuck in to seafood roasted in a wood-fired oven or house-made charcuterie paired with a serious wine list.

Markets

Conveniently located in the Old Port, **Rosemont Market & Bakery** (5 Commercial St., 207/699-4560, www.rosemontmarket.com, Mon.-Sat. 9am-7pm, Sun. 9am-6pm) is "human sized" and stocked with regional vegetables, cheese, meat, and house-made baked goods as well as pizza and sandwiches. The **Portland Food Co-op** (290 Congress St., 207/805-1599, www.portlandfood.coop, daily 8am-8pm) has aisles stuffed with local and organic products plus healthy, premade food. More basic options are available at **Hannaford Supermarket** (295 Forest Ave., 207/761-5965, daily 7am-11pm), at the edge of Back Cove.

Portland has three farmers markets overflowing with everything from local veggies to goat yogurt and kimchi. A carnival atmosphere commands at the downtown **Monument Square market** (456 Congress St., Apr.-Dec. Wed. 7am-1pm), while the market at **Deering Oaks Park** (late Apr.-Nov. Sat. 7am-1pm) is a bit more relaxed. The **Winter Farmers' Market** (84 Cove St., Dec.-Apr. Sat. 9am-1pm) also has live music and food trucks.

Accommodations

Though Portland has some wonderful top-end offerings, a lack of reasonably priced accommodations in the city makes sites like Airbnb and VBRO good options for travelers on a budget.

$100-150

Ask a local about **The Inn at St. John** (939 Congress St., 207/773-6481, www.innatstjohn.com, $105-250), and he or she will likely recall its seedy years when the West End was decidedly downmarket. It's been overhauled one room at a time, however, retaining flourishes of Gilded Age glamour and gaining much-needed updates like wireless Internet, coffeemakers, and a bit of contemporary style. Continental breakfast is served in a downstairs dining room, and the rooms vary widely, from more luxurious king rooms boasting en suite baths and views of the street to somewhat garret-like singles with shared baths. The narrow, steep stairs are not for everyone.

$150-250

Set on a quiet side street in the West End, the **Percy Inn** (15 Pine St., 207/871-7638, www.percyinn.com, $129-219) is in a renovated 1830s federal-style brick house that feels like pure, old-fashioned Portland. The house has some quirks and could use a bit of updating, but the overall effect is lovely; rooms are named for famous writers, and the firelit library and spacious common room are welcoming.

Over $250

Somewhere between bohemian whimsy

and design-chic, ★ **Pomegranate Inn** (49 Neal St., 207/772-1006, www.pomegranateinn.com, $279-359) is settled on a pretty corner in a historic neighborhood and full of visual treasures. Every room has unique hand-painted walls, and antiques are displayed alongside modern art. A 3rd-floor lounge is stocked with games, and a quiet back patio makes an ideal spot for enjoying the daily cookies, tea, and coffee. "The Pom" is now operated by Lark Hotels, and serves the group's characteristic small-plate breakfast that will charm your socks off (and leave some hungry travelers looking for a bit more).

Flying typewriters and wordy art are reminders that **The Press Hotel** (119 Exchange St., 207/808-8800, www.thepresshotel.com, $225-450) was once the home of the *Portland Press Herald,* and the journo-chic theme runs throughout the property. Excellent service gives the large property a boutique feel, and the Inkwell coffee and wine bar feels like just the place to type up some hotel poetry of your own—local touches are everywhere and, all in all, Press offers some of the coolest new digs in New England.

Twenty minutes south of town (and a world away), ★ **Inn by the Sea** (40 Bowery Beach Rd., 207/779-3134, www.innbythesea.com, $450-700) has a perfect location set back from Crescent Beach, the finest stretch of sand in the greater Portland area. The luxurious resort has family-friendly bungalows and cottages as well as beautiful rooms in the main inn and perks like outdoor pools, a fireplace stocked with s'mores, and a spa. What sets the inn apart from other top-notch properties, though, is a remarkable focus on conservation; the on-site wetlands and meadows were overhauled to create habitat for the endangered New England cottontail rabbit, the inn runs environmental science education programs, and the chef works with local fishers to source from underutilized fish populations. It's also easy to leave the inn with an unusual

memento of your stay—the staff fosters friendly dogs from the local humane society that can be adopted by guests; hundreds find new homes each year.

Information

The remarkably helpful and informative **Visitors Bureau** (207/772-5800, www.visitportland.com) has a website full of information and links, and runs information centers on the waterfront at 14 Ocean Gateway Pier (207/772-5800, Mon.-Fri. 9am-5pm, Sat.-Sun. 9am-4pm, winter hours vary) and in the Jetport Terminal next to baggage claim (207/775-5809, Mon., Thurs., Fri. 8am-midnight, Sat.-Sun. 10am-midnight, winter hours vary).

Getting Around

Portland's local bus company is **Metro** (114 Valley St., 207/774-0351, www.gpmetrobus.net, $1.50 adults, $0.75 seniors, free children under 6, $5 all-day pass), which runs out of its downtown station to points including the airport. Compared to most capital cities, Portland has a decent amount of metered street parking, which doesn't guarantee you'll find any right away (particularly in the summer), but the odds are good. That said, the city has pay lots and garages set up every few blocks. Local taxis to call are **ABC Taxi** (207/772-8685) and **Town Taxi** (207/773-1711).

Freeport

Just 20 minutes up the coast from Portland, Freeport is a shipbuilding and fishing village turned New England-themed outlet shopping destination, a transformation that's left some interesting quirks, with boutiques, outlets, and even a McDonald's restaurant tucked into historic homes. Visitors tend to love it or hate it, but whether you're planning an all-day shopping itinerary or just want a home base for exploring Portland, it's a good place to stay, with more affordable accommodations than the city.

Entertainment and Events

For a town that's made shopping its raison d'être, it only makes sense that **Black Friday**—the massive sales following Thanksgiving—would be a kind of official carnival, with midnight trains of shoppers arriving from Boston to live music and a celebratory atmosphere.

Shopping

The undisputed headliner of Freeport's retail scene is the **L.L. Bean Flagship Store** (95 Main St., 877/755-2326, www.llbean.com), which is open 24 hours a day, 365 days a year. If the appeal of buying waterproof boots at 3am isn't enough to tempt you, the indoor trout pond or archery and clay shooting lessons might.

Many of the other big-name outlets are clustered in the **Freeport Village Station** (1 Freeport Village Station, www.onefreeportvillagestation.com, Sun.-Thurs. 10am-7pm, Fri.-Sat. 10am-8pm) or along **Main Street,** including the Gap, Patagonia, Bass, and the North Face. Most stores open at 9am or 10am and remain open until 6pm or 7pm.

Food

Downtown Freeport is packed with national chain restaurants—like that olde New Englande McDonald's—but there are plenty of local spots to recover from your shopping.

One favorite is the hunting lodge-like **Broad Arrow Tavern** (162 Main St., 207/865-9377, www.harraseeketinn.com, daily 11:30am-10:30pm, $15-30), where Maine classics line up alongside brick-oven pizza, hearty salads, and soups.

Get a taste of Freeport's maritime past at **Harraseeket Lunch and Lobster** (36 Main St., South Freeport, 207/865-3535, www.harraseeketlunchandlobster.com, Apr.-Oct. or end of season, daily 11am-7:45pm, $9-25), which leans a bit pricey for an outdoor lobster shack but has an unbeatable location at the edge of the marina.

For a quick, healthy lunch of sandwiches and salad, L.L. Bean's **1912 Café** (95 Main St., inside the store, daily 9am-7pm, $6-12) is a convenient option in the heart of the action, or head outside of town for a great bistro meal at **Conundrum** (117 Rte. 1, 207/865-0303, www.conundrumwinebistro.com, Tues.-Sat. 4:30pm-10pm, $14-30), a cozy wine joint in the shadow of the "Big Indian," a beloved local landmark.

Accommodations and Camping

A shady cluster of quiet roads on 626 waterfront acres makes **Recompence Shore Campground** (134 Burnett Rd., 207/865-9307, www.freeportcamping.com, $28-52) a haven from the bustling downtown, with fun lobster bakes most Saturday nights and **waterfront cottages** from $130.

Clean and family-run, **Casco Bay Inn** (107 Rte. 1, 207/865-4925, www.cascobayinn.com, $101-145) may not be fancy, but it's a short drive to downtown Freeport and a good value, with coffeemakers and fridges in the rooms as well as a basic continental breakfast. Wonderfully friendly hosts and a hearty fresh breakfast make the **Nicholson Inn** (25 Main St., 207/618-9204, www.nicholsoninn.com, $130 s, $160 d) a relaxing option with a good location, period furnishings, and private baths, though young children may not be allowed. Once the home of Arctic explorer and Bowdoin grad Donald MacMillan, the **White Cedar Inn Bed and Breakfast** (178 Main St., 207/865-9099, www.whitecedarinn.com, $199-379) combines Victorian charm with modern touches like comfy beds, a guest pantry, common spaces, and a great breakfast, walking distance from downtown.

Bath and Brunswick

The scattershot coast that spreads south from Route 1 is anchored by a pair of solid brick towns, and they're a study in contrasts. Brunswick is home to Bowdoin College, which rambles outward from a picturesque campus filled with elite undergraduates and grand buildings named for famous alums. Nine miles west, Bath is all union halls, shipyards, and hulking ironworks, an industrial town that once launched the world's grandest schooners.

Look closer, however, and the distinction blurs. Until it closed in 2011, the local naval air station meant that downtown pubs and cafés were likely to have as many service members as students, keeping Brunswick from feeling too precious. And while Bath's riverfront still rings with the sound of shipbuilding and workers, the pretty center is full of cafés, shops, and bookstores run by the liberal-leaning, creative community.

On a state-sized map of Maine, both towns seem to be a breath away from the sea, but it would be easy to pass through Bath and Brunswick with nothing but river views. To experience the best parts of this scenic stretch of coast, drive south, looping into the long peninsulas; the tangled coastlines are classic Maine, with fishing villages, lobster shacks, and sheltered bays that appear around every bend in the road, making for idyllic driving at a leisurely pace.

Brunswick
Sights
Bowdoin College
The pretty campus of **Bowdoin College** (255 Maine St., 207/725-3000, www.bowdoin.edu) is all soaring oaks and grassy quads, and would be a worthwhile place to stroll even without the college's two fascinating museums. The tiny **Peary-MacMillan Arctic Museum** (9500 College Station, 207/725-3416, www.bowdoin.edu/arctic-museum,

Tues.-Sat. 10am-5pm, Sun. 2pm-5pm, free) traces the Arctic adventures of two Bowdoin graduates and explorers, Donald MacMillan and Robert Peary. In addition to stuffed arctic animals and one of the original dog sledges from the Peary expedition, a display honors Matthew Henson, an African American explorer who was the first known person to set foot at the pole and whose contributions to exploration went unrecognized until late in his life, when he was accepted to the New York Explorers Club at age 70. The other highlight on campus is the **Bowdoin College Museum of Art** (9400 College Station, 207/725-3275, www.bowdoin.edu/art-museum, Tues.-Wed. and Fri.-Sat. 10am-5pm, Thurs. 10am-8:30pm, Sun. 1pm-5pm, free), where an eclectic—and sometimes exquisite—permanent collection is on display alongside exhibits encompassing everything from Renaissance painting to edgy critiques of contemporary culture.

Food
Brunswick
While great views and a picturesque setting count for a great deal with most casual foodies, among devoted lobster roll hounds there's a special thrill that comes with discovering a diamond in the rough. **Libby's Market** (42 Jordan Ave., 207/729-7277, Tues.-Sat. 3am-7:30pm, Sun.-Mon. 3am-5pm, $6-20) is a classic example: The unprepossessing convenience store has a short-order counter and a couple of picnic tables outside, but aside from a great pile of lobster traps and early, fisher-friendly hours, passersby would never guess it's a lobster roll mecca. The classic rolls come in small, medium, or large, and the meat is more finely chopped than usual, with a heavier dose of mayo. A real locals' favorite.

The best Mexican food in the Mid-Coast is served from a shiny truck just a few blocks from the Bowdoin campus. **Taco the Town** (205 Maine St., 207/632-4740, Tues.-Sat. 11am-3pm, $4-9) has

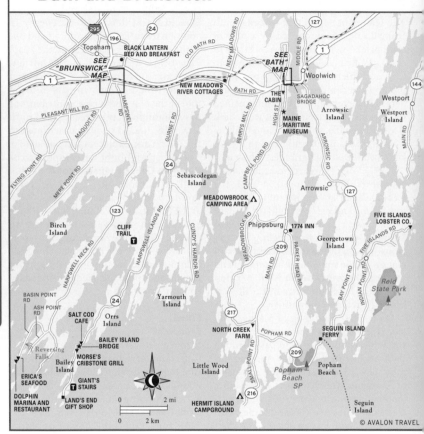

Bath and Brunswick

burritos, quesadillas, and classic tacos served with four kinds of house-made salsa. Cool off with a sweet, cinnamon-spiced *horchata* or "cochata," a delightfully innovative coffee-*horchata* blend.

Tucked into the back of a little gourmet and kitchen store, ★ **Local Market** (148 Maine St., 207/729-1328, www.localmarket04011.com, Mon.-Sat. 9:30am-6pm, Sun. 9:30am-5pm, $6-12) has a pair of big communal tables and a deli counter with sandwiches, salads, and soups prepared with plenty of fresh, local, and organic ingredients. The Cobb salad gets raves, as do hearty sandwiches made

with bread from Portland's Standard Baking Co.

The North Indian food at **Shere Punjab** (46 Maine St., 207/373-0422, www.sherepunjabme.com, lunch Mon.-Wed. 11am-3pm; dinner Sun.-Thurs. 5pm-9pm, Fri.-Sat. 5pm-10pm, $8-16) is full of rich flavors and spices—though the chef deftly tempers the heat for all palates. The vast menu includes a good selection of vegetarian options and ranges from familiar classics like butter chicken to dishes less frequently seen on American menus such as aromatic, steamed lamb *dilruba* (a preparation including garlic,

Brunswick

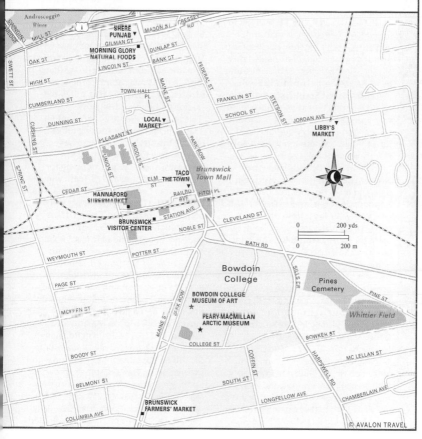

onion, ginger, and Indian spices), or syrupy, fried *gulabjamun* (a popular, milk-based Indian dessert). Decor is casual and cozy, and brightened up with Punjabi paintings and handicrafts.

Little **Morning Glory Natural Foods** (60 Main St., 207/729-0546, www.moglonf.com, Mon.-Sat. 9am-7pm, Sun. 10am-5pm) is stocked with local and organic options, as well as a good selection of picnic-ready items; also nearby is a **Hannaford Supermarket** (35 Elm St., 207/725-6683, Mon.-Sat. 6am-11pm, Sun. 6am-9pm). Find cheese, lobsters, and locally baked bread at the **Brunswick**

Farmers' Market (Maine St., May Nov. Tues. and Fri. 8am-2pm).

South of Brunswick

A pair of seafood stops anchors each side of the cribstone bridge to Bailey Island. The **Salt Cod Cafe** (1894 Harpswell Island Rd., Orr's Island, 207/833-6210, late May-early Oct. daily 8am-5pm, hours vary at the beginning and end of season) has blueberry pie and quick bites that can be eaten by the shore. Across the bridge is **Morse's Cribstone Grill** (1495 Harpswell Island Rd., Bailey Island, 207/833-7775, Mon.-Thurs. 11:30am-8pm, Fri.-Sat.

Scenic Drive: To Land's End and Back

Finding the best bits of the Maine coast means getting off Route 1 and following the curving, narrow roads that stretch into the sea, skipping from peninsulas to islands and back again. For aimless driving and views of tattered coast, nothing beats **Route 24** and **Route 123,** which flank **Harpswell Sound,** south of Brunswick. Following these two country highways, you can make an H-shaped journey using the connecting Mountain Road for a 48-mile, 1.5-hour trip to both Bailey Island and Harpswell.

Route 24 is particularly lovely, passing deep bays rimmed with evergreen trees and rocky beaches as it passes from **Sebascodegan Island** to **Orr's Island** and, finally, **Bailey Island,** the prettiest and smallest of the three. Just before you reach the **Bailey Island Bridge,** the charming **Salt Cod Cafe** (1894 Harpswell Island Rd., Orr's Island, 207/833-6210, late May-early Oct. daily 8am-5pm, hours vary at the beginning and end of season) sells some of the finest slices of blueberry pie along the coast, and the other side of the bridge is flanked by **Morse's Cribstone Grill** (1495 Harpswell Island Rd., Bailey Island, 207/833-7775, Mon.-Thurs. 11:30am-8pm, Fri.-Sat. 11:30am-9pm, Sun. noon-8pm, $8-30), a beloved spot with great piles of seafood and views of the water. Even if you're not hungry, it's worth pausing to take a gander at the 1,150-foot bridge itself, which is a Historic Civil Engineering Landmark. In order to withstand the waves and powerful tides, it was built with 10,000 tons of locally quarried granite; the large slabs, known as cribstones, are laid without mortar or cement in a crosshatched pattern that allows the water to flow freely through, and it's thought to be the only granite cribstone bridge in the world. Keep going straight to reach the **Land's End Gift Shop** (2391 Harpswell Island Rd., Bailey Island, 207/833-2313, Apr.-Oct. daily 9am-5pm, limited hours in off-season) at the tip of the island, or turn left on Washington Street (1.5 miles south of the bridge) to reach the **Giant's Stairs,** a 0.25-mile seaside trail across jutting rocks.

Head back up Route 24 to Mountain Road, which connects the two lobes of land; this stretch of road crosses **Strawberry Creek** and the **Ewin Narrows,** and it's worth stopping for the excellent 2.3-mile **Cliff Trail,** which has views of Long Reach to the west. The trailhead and parking lot are located behind the **Harpswell Town Office** (263 Mountain Rd., 207/833-5771). Continue on Mountain Road to Neck Road, or Route 123, and follow it south into map-dot **West Harpswell,** where the land splits into a Poseidon's trident of Basin Point, Pott's Point, and Ash Point, three smaller promontories that jut into the ocean. At the tip of the westernmost point is **Dolphin Marina and Restaurant** (515 Basin Point Rd., Harpswell, 207/833-6000, daily 11:30am-8pm, $12-28), an upscale spot for seafood with showstopping views. A stone's throw up the peninsula is **Erica's Seafood** (6 Malcolm Dr., Harpswell, 207/833-7354, www.ericasseafood.com, May-Oct. daily 11am-7pm, $7-16), a casual spot with fried food and views of the working marina. There's not much on the next point east, but the narrow channel between the two creates an unusual **reversing falls** or **tidal waterfall** at the narrows, visible from the parking lot of the commercial **Interstate Lobster Pound** (Ash Point Rd., Harpswell).

11:30am-9pm, Sun. noon-8pm, $8-30), whose deck has perfect views back toward the water. Morse's serves the usual seafood fare, plus "twin" lobster dinners for ambitious eaters.

With views to Bailey Island and beyond, **Dolphin Marina and Restaurant** (515 Basin Point Rd., Harpswell, 207/833-6000, daily 11:30am-8pm, $12-28) is also south of Brunswick in Harpswell, and would be a sublime place to dine on a plate of rocks, so the nice quality of the international seafood menu is an added bonus. Nothing is too flashy or creative, but solid, and many entrées come with a mystifying (but welcome) blueberry muffin on the side.

If you'd prefer your eats from a take-out window, the nearby **Erica's Seafood** (6 Malcolm Dr., Harpswell, 207/833-7354, www.ericasseafood.com, May-Oct. daily 11am-7pm, $7-16) is a popular shack with haddock sandwiches, lobster rolls, and crisp, slender fries. The outdoor picnic tables are right by a working wharf, so you can watch the day's catch arrive on local fishing boats.

Accommodations

The **Travelers Inn** (130 Pleasant St., 207/729-3364, www.travelersinmc.com, $99-133) is an old-fashioned motel with well-kept rooms. This is an especially good option for families, as some rooms have two beds, with cribs or roll-away cots available. The helpful staff is knowledgeable about the area, and a basic continental breakfast of bagels, fruit, coffee, and juice is served in the lobby.

Just across the Androscoggin River from downtown Brunswick, the **Black Lantern Bed and Breakfast** (57 Elm St., Topsham, 207/725-4165, www.blacklanternbandb.com, $125-140) is walking distance from a scenic bit of riverbank and a gracious, welcoming place to stay. Comfortable beds, en suite baths, hearty breakfasts, and old-fashioned charm are highlights, as are Judy and Tom, the super-friendly innkeeps.

With a location in the heart of downtown, the **Brunswick Hotel & Tavern** (4 Noble St., 207/837-6565, www.thebrunswickhotelandtavern.com, $175-350) is often filled with families visiting the nearby college, and it's a comfortable place to enjoy the town. A gracious porch has rocking chairs and plenty of shade, well-appointed rooms are on the luxurious side of comfortable, and the train station is easy walking distance away. Don't look for a mint on your pillow, but the homemade whoopie pies on the nightstand earn fervent praise.

Information

The **Brunswick Visitor Center** (16 Station Ave., 207/721-0999, daily 10am-6:30pm) is adjacent to the Amtrak station.

Bath

Bath offers numerous diversions for visitors, as well as grants access to other coastal pleasures. South of town, the land splits into two squiggly peninsulas, named for their largest towns, each about 15 minutes from Bath: Phippsburg, down Route 209, and Georgetown, down Route 127.

Sights

Maine Maritime Museum

Wide, deep, and sheltered from the raging sea, the Kennebec River is the perfect place for building and launching ships; indeed, the first ocean-going ship built by English shipwrights in the Americas—the *Virginia of Sagadahoc*—was constructed here, a 30-ton pinnace measuring less than 50 feet from stem to stern. That ship was just the beginning, and in the mid-18th century, shipbuilding was a roaring industry, with a couple dozen shipyards launching merchant, naval, and pleasure vessels connecting this clattering town in rural Maine with every corner of the globe.

One of those shipyards, Percy & Small, has been transformed into the wonderful **Maine Maritime Museum** (243 Washington St., 207/443-1316, www.mainemaritimemuseum.org, daily 9:30am-5pm, $15.50 adults, $14 seniors, $10 youth 6-12, free children under 6), a sprawling 20-acre site with exhibits on the state's seafaring traditions.

The yard is dominated by a soaring, metal skeleton that evokes the Percy & Small-built *Wyoming*, the largest schooner ever made. (Most of the sculpture's proportions are true-to-size, but the masts stop short of *Wyoming*'s 177 feet, as the full-sized version would require warning lights for passing aircraft.) Other highlights include reproductions

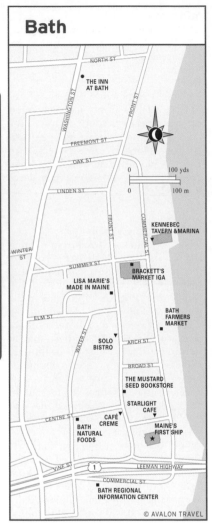

Bath

© AVALON TRAVEL

reconstructing the *Virginia of Sagadahoc* based on the (very) sketchy descriptions that have survived from colonial times. In keeping with the lighthearted, ad hoc attitude of the group, some building materials are recycled, and bits of the ship's framework retain printing from former lives. But the wooden-pegged skeleton is smart as can be, and it's a treat to stop by during construction. Meet the building crew of **Maine's First Ship** (1 Front St., 207/433-4242, www.mfship.org, Wed. and Sat. 9am-3pm) on open build days, or visit anytime to peek through the fence as the pinnace takes shape.

Entertainment and Events

Most of the year, **Bath Iron Works** (700 Washington St., 207/443-3311, www.gdbiw.com) is off-limits to the public. That changes during one of its infrequent but spectacular ship launchings. Then the whole town comes out for the celebration, and flags, food, and local dignitaries fill the waterfront to break champagne on the hull.

Shopping

Downtown Bath is perfect for browsing and gallery carousing. Find books and music (and some sweetly old-fashioned tea service) at **The Mustard Seed Bookstore** (74 Front St., 207/389-4084, www.themustardseedbookstore.com, Mon.-Sat. 10am-5pm), or browse the souvenirs at **Lisa Marie's Made in Maine** (170 Front St., 207/443-2225, www.lisamariesmadeinmaine.com, Mon.-Sat. 10am-6pm, Sun. 10am-4pm), which stocks work from a vast range of local artisans, crafters, and artists.

Sports and Recreation

Beaches

South of Bath, the Phippsburg and Georgetown peninsulas each end in a charming beach. The larger of the two, **Popham Beach** (10 Perkins Farm Ln., Phippsburg, 207/389-1335, $8 adults, $2 seniors, $1 children 5-11, under 5 free),

of a shipyard's various workstations, in-depth explorations of lobstering on the Maine coast, and exhibits illustrating the many sides of New England's maritime traditions. Tickets are good for a second visit within a seven-day period, and the museum also operates scenic cruises.

Maine's First Ship

In a tiny shipyard in downtown Bath, a quixotic, creative group of volunteers are is more Miami than Mid-Coast, the kind of broad, sandy swath most Mainers can only dream of. Tiny **Fox Island** is just off the beach, and it's possible to walk to it at low tide (beware of getting stranded, which would mean a long wait for the water to drop once again). Popham's charms mean it can be jam-packed on busy days, so arrive early, or head to **Reid State Park** (375 Seguinland Rd., Georgetown, 207/371-2303, 9am-sunset, $8 adults, $2 seniors, $1 children 5-11, under 5 free), where you'll find two sandy beaches framed by rocky outcroppings, a headland with great views to Seguin Island lighthouse, and breaking waves for some of the best surfing in Maine.

Boating

Get an up close look at the hulking naval ships in Bath's floating dry docks on one of Maine Maritime Museum's hour-long **Shipyards & Lighthouses Cruises** (243 Washington St., 207/443-1316, www.mainemaritimemuseum.org, mid-June-early Sept. daily noon and 2pm, $32 adults, $18.50 youth 6-12, $5 children under 6, ticket prices include museum admission), which also passes by the Doubling Point Lighthouse and Kennebec Range Lights. Check the website for longer tours that go farther afield, which are available more sporadically.

Another wonderful way to explore the coastline is by hopping a boat to **Seguin Island** (207/443-4808, www.seguinisland.org), where Maine's tallest lighthouse sends beams over 20 miles to sea from a first-order Fresnel lens that's been used since 1857. Make the 30-minute trip on the passenger only **Seguin Island Ferry** (Popham Beach, 207/841-7977, www.fishntripsmaine.com, Sun.-Tues. and Thurs.-Fri., round trip $30 adults, $25 children 12 and under, $40 overnights), and spend the day exploring beaches, trails, and the lighthouse itself.

Food
Bath

Exposed brick and contemporary art make ★ **Solo Bistro** (128 Front St., 207/443-3373, www.solobistro.com, Mon.-Sat. 5pm-9pm, $18-33) feel fresh and modern on Bath's historic Front Street, and the farm-to-table restaurant serves bistro food of a consistently high quality. Small plates of greens, grilled seafood, and local cheeses lead into a dinner menu featuring hangar steaks and seared boat scallops. At $25 ($18 on Wed.), the three-course prix fixe dinner is an excellent value for money.

While the menu of pub classics and seafood is pretty ordinary (and reportedly inconsistent), that's not really the point at **Kennebec Tavern & Marina** (119 Commercial St., 207/442-9636, www.kennebectavern.com, Sun.-Thurs. 11am-10pm, Fri.-Sat. 11am-11pm, $9-30), which boasts a fabulous outdoor seating area that juts out into the current of the Kennebec River offering great views of passing boats. On cool days, there's not much to tempt diners into the bland dining room, but summer afternoons are the perfect time to relax in the shade with a cold beer and a pile of fried scallops.

Tucked below ground on a sloping side street, **Starlight Cafe** (15 Lambard St., 207/443-3005, Tues.-Fri. 7am-2pm, Sat. 8am-2pm, $6-13) has a quirky dining room filled with hand-painted chairs and vintage Trivial Pursuit cards so diners can pass the time while waiting for hearty breakfasts and comforting lunch plates. Enormous raspberry pancakes, the turkey-stuffed Thanksgiving Sandwich, and haddock chowder are all favorites, and the friendly staff is pure local charm.

As the name suggests, stepping into **The Cabin** (552 Washington St., 207/443-6224, www.cabinpizza.com, Sun.-Thurs. 10am-10pm, Fri.-Sat. 10am-11pm, $8-14) feels like ducking below the deck of an old ship. Nautical bric-a-brac and dark wood complete the effect, and while the pizza might not live up to its claims of

"Best in Maine," it's pretty darn good all the same. Chewy crusts, generous toppings, and addictive, bready garlic knots keep this a favorite with locals and visitors. No credit cards.

With views of the action in the heart of historic Bath, **Café Crème** (56 Front St., 207/443-6454, Mon.-Sat. 7:30am-5:30pm, Sun. 8:30am-5:30pm, $2-8) is the place to watch the town drift by with a cup of chai or cappuccino. This little coffee shop has wireless Internet, plenty of tables, and sweet and savory treats made by a local baker.

Pick up organic produce and bulk items at **Bath Natural Foods** (36 Centre St., www.bathnaturalmarket.com, Mon.-Fri. 9am-6pm, Sat. 9am-5pm, Sun. noon-4pm), or visit **Brackett's Market IGA** (185 Front St., 207/443-2012, daily 7am-8pm), a small, locally owned grocery store by the waterfront. Local farmers and producers operate the thriving, year-round **Bath Farmers Market** (Waterfront Park, Commercial St., May-Oct. Sat. 8:30am-noon; Bath Freight Shed, 27 Commercial St., Nov.-Apr. Sat. 9am-noon, www.bathfarmersmarket.com). Ten minutes south of downtown Bath, the **Winnegance General Store** (36 High St., 207/443-3300, Sun.-Wed. 6am-4pm, Thurs.-Sat. 6am-8pm, $4-11) is a popular stop-over for day-trippers on their way to Popham Beach. Scones and muffins are baked fresh in the back of the old-fashioned shop, and a few small tables are available for enjoying breakfasts of pancakes or eggs and bacon or homemade soup and sandwiches.

South of Bath
South of Bath in Georgetown, ★ **Five Islands Lobster Co.** (1447 Five Islands Rd., Georgetown, 207/371-2990, check website or call for hours before visiting,

Top to bottom: mapping out lobster at the Maine Maritime Museum; one of the state's scenic beaches; reconstructing Maine's First Ship in Bath.

$8-18) regularly makes "best of" lists for lobster rolls, steamers, and fried oysters, and it's right on the way to Reid State Park. This is a classic waterside joint with picnic tables and views of a picture-perfect bay dotted with tiny forested islands.

Cheerfully quirky and fresh as can be, **North Creek Farm** (24 Sebasco Rd., Phippsburg, 207/389-1341, www.north-creekfarm.org, daily 9am-6:30pm, $3-12) is a little bit flower nursery, a little bit country store, and a little bit café. Order a Reuben sandwich with kimchi and it comes decked in blossoms, or get slices of hearty quiche to go. Don't miss out on the homemade baked goods and fruit pies. A Sunday morning brunch menu includes sweet and savory treats and farm eggs every way. With just a couple of small tables in the café, ordering food to-go is a good option.

Accommodations and Camping

Many bed-and-breakfasts in the area are members of **Mid-Coast Maine Inns** (www.midcoastmaineinns.com), which posts a helpful spreadsheet of available rooms in the area that is usually up to date. While staying in Bath is most convenient, a few wonderful campgrounds and a historic inn are tucked down the peninsula by the water, away from the bustle of Route 1.

Camping

Splash out for an oceanfront spot at ★ **Hermit Island Campground** (6 Hermit Island Rd., Phippsburg, 207/443-2101, www.hermitisland.com, $39-63) and you'll get prime views of sandy beaches and coastline. This is a 25-minute drive from Bath, and snagging one means planning ahead (the reservation rules are byzantine), but even the "value" sites are within easy strolling distance of the shore. No credit cards.

A little bit closer to Route 1, **Meadowbrook Camping Area** (33 Meadowbrook Rd., Phippsburg, 207/443-4967, www.meadowbrookme.com, tent sites $31-33, hookups $35-43)

has smallish sites that are a tad too closely set in woods and an open meadow, with many campers who come for the whole season, but you can sign up for daily lobster dinners and have a feast at your site or the communal outdoor seating area.

Camping is permitted on **Seguin Island,** accessible by ferry from Phippsburg's Popham Beach, mid-May-early October (207/443-4808, www.seguinisland.org, minimum $50 donation). There's no running water, but composting toilet facilities are provided. Reservations are required.

Under $100
Simple, sweet, and neat as a pin, **New Meadows River Cottages** (4 Armstrong Way, West Bath, 207/442-9299, www.newmeadowsrivercottages.com, $89-99) are nothing fancy, but the stand-alone rooms have a double bed or double and single as well as air-conditioning, coffeemakers, fridges, and little sitting areas; higher rates are for cottages with little kitchenettes.

$150-200
Gardens surrounding **The Inn at Bath** (969 Washington St., Bath, 207/808-7904, www.innatbath.com, $170-190) are overflowing with blooming rhododendrons and wild mountain laurel, and the interior of the Greek Revival-style building is full of art and unfussy antiques. The quiet neighborhood is about a 15-minute walk from downtown Bath, and breakfasts are an appealing spread of fresh fruit, granola, and one hot option. All rooms have private baths and air-conditioning, but they differ widely in style and decor, and one room opens onto the kitchen.

$200-250
Historic and beautiful, the ★ **1774 Inn** (44 Parker Head Rd., Phippsburg, 207/389-1774, www.1774inn.com, $180-260) is among the most romantic places

to stay along the coast, with chairs tucked around its sprawling grounds that abut the Kennebec River. Though the inn is just 7.5 miles south of Bath, the experience is serene and secluded. Many of the rooms, which vary widely in style, are exquisite, and guests rave about the thoughtful breakfasts. For an ultra-private experience, book the more rustic Woodshed Room, a self-contained suite near the river with a private veranda and stunning views.

Information
The **Bath Regional Information Center** (15 Commercial St., 207/442-7291, www.visitbath.com, mid-Apr.-Dec. daily 9am-7pm, Jan-mid-Apr. Mon.-Fri. 9am-7pm) has great resources and advice for the entire Mid-Coast area, and its website is frequently updated with tours and events in town.

Getting Around
Parking in Bath is free for up to two hours on the street or in municipal lots on Commercial, School, and Water Streets. The **town website** (www.cityofbath.com) has maps for both "Parking" and "Secret Parking." A convenient way to see Bath car-free is the **Bath Trolley** (207/443-8363, www.cityofbath.com, $1), which runs every 30 minutes on a fixed loop that connects the Winnegance General Store with the Maine Maritime Museum and downtown.

Boothbay and Pemaquid

Ask a native Mainer for directions on the Mid-Coast, and you're likely to hear the classic refrain: "You can't get there from here!" The Boothbay and Pemaquid Peninsulas, accessible from Route 1 via Wiscasset and Damariscotta, respectively, are separated by a river that opens onto jagged bays, which means the lobster shacks, gardens, and lighthouses that rim the sea are much farther apart then they appear on a map.

Boothbay is by far the more popular of the two, a scenic stretch of bays that culminates in the town of Boothbay Harbor, the pinnacle of Maine's fudge and T-shirt shop kitsch. It's beyond hectic during school vacation months, but with dozens of ways to get out on the water, it's easy to see why the spot is so beloved. By contrast, Pemaquid is decidedly laid-back, and most visitors head straight down the forested peninsula for Pemaquid Point Light, a classic lighthouse and the stuff of Yankee pinups with its white-washed tower, picket fence, and snapping American flag.

These two peninsulas are also the primary access points for boat tours to Eastern Egg Rock, a seven-acre island whose granite shoreline offers a unique habitat for puffins, guillemots, and dozens of other nesting and migratory birds. It's the first of its kind, a restored colony, the success of which inspired dozens of imitators worldwide, as scientists work to protect the dwindling seabird population.

Boothbay Region
Sights
Wiscasset's self-branding as the "prettiest village in Maine" might not convince passing visitors, who often remember the map-dot town more for its notorious bottleneck traffic. Get away from the backup, though, and the old-fashioned community is perfectly charming, with much of its downtown listed on the National Register of Historic Places. The town's **self-guided walking tour** offers a ramble through old captain's homes and federal-style mansions, with informative plaques along the way. Start the tour at the large plaque adjacent to **Sarah's Cafe** (45 Water St., Wiscasset), and pick up a brochure that traces the picturesque route. Most of the stops are great for just wandering by, but it's worth popping inside **Castle Tucker** (2 Lee St., Wiscasset, 207/882-7169, Jun.-mid-Oct. Wed.-Sun.

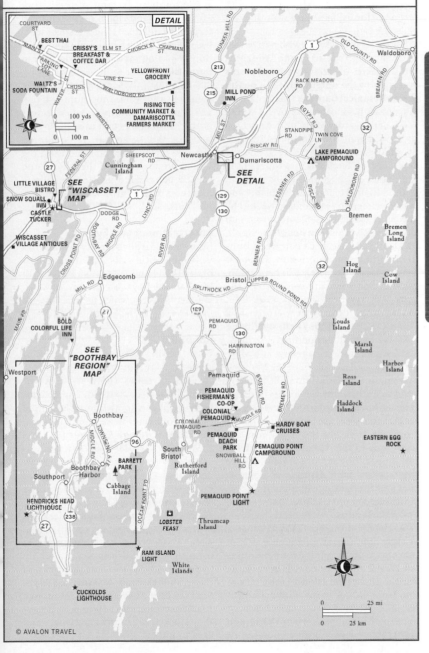

Boothbay and Pemaquid

© AVALON TRAVEL

11am-4pm, tours every 30 minutes, $8 adults, $7 seniors, $4 students), an 1807 captain's home overlooking the river with Victorian furnishings and a stunning spiral staircase.

Pathways overflowing with native species, shady groves of rhododendrons, and 125 acres of carefully tended plants roll right to the water's edge at **Coastal Maine Botanical Gardens** (132 Botanical Gardens Dr., Boothbay, 207/633-8000, www.mainegardens.org, mid-Apr.-Oct. daily 9am-5pm, $16 adults, $14 seniors, $8 children 3-18, under 3 free), one the finest in New England. Free tours of the highlights are scheduled daily at 11am, with additional tours of native plants and rare specimens offered once a week. The garden also organizes one-hour tours up the Back River on *The Beagle,* a small, blessedly quiet electric boat; when bundled with garden admission, the boat tour costs approximately $20 per person, making it an affordable way to enjoy the coast.

Halfway down the Boothbay Peninsula, the **Boothbay Railway Village** (586 Wiscasset Rd., Boothbay, 207/633-4727, www.railwayvillage.org, late May-mid-Oct. daily 10am-5pm, $12 adults, $10 seniors, $6 children 3-18, under 3 free) is a highlight for many families with children. The narrow-gauge steam train that circles the village might be the star attraction, but trains are just the beginning of this 10-acre village. Old-fashioned filling stations and homes are interspersed with displays of antique cars and firefighting equipment, blacksmithing demonstrations, baby goats, and model trains.

At the tip of the Boothbay Peninsula are five **lighthouses,** of which four can be spotted by driving around Routes 96, 27, and 238. At the very tip of Route 96, the little **Ram Island Light** is visible from Ocean Point. Make a counterclockwise loop of the more westerly Southport Island to see **Hendricks Head Light** off Beach Road in West Southport;

the offshore **Cuckolds Lighthouse,** visible from the tip of Town Landing Road at the southern extreme of the island; and **Burnt Island Light,** best seen from Capitol Island Road. Get a taste of what life was like on an island lighthouse station by joining a fascinating boat tour to **Burnt Island** (Pier 8, Boothbay Harbor, 207/633-2284, www.balmydayscruises.com, Jul.-Aug. Mon. and Thurs. 1:45pm, $25 adults, $15 children), where actors portray the family of an early 20th-century lighthouse keeper. It's common to spot seals and porpoises during the 15-minute boat ride to the island, and the 2.5-hour island portion includes a nature walk and time to explore the scenic trails.

Entertainment and Events

Boothbay Harbor's pretty waterfront is bright with sails and flying colors as the town kicks off summer with **Windjammer Days** (late June, www.windjammerdays.org), which includes the annual Blessing of the Fleet.

Shopping

Unsurprisingly, Wiscasset is a major center for antiquing, with more than two dozen shops filled with everything distressed, restored, and charmingly shabby. A sprawling collection of pieces from many dealers can be found at **Wiscasset Village Antiques** (536 Rte. 1, Wiscasset, 207/882-4029, www.wiscassetvillageantiques.com, daily 9am-7pm); find a more curated collection of European textiles and furnishings at **The Marston House** (101 Main St., Wiscasset, 207/882-6010, www.marstonhouse.com, Thurs.-Sun. noon-5pm, or by appt.), which specializes in homespun pieces from the 18th-19th centuries. Pick up treasures with a more contemporary aesthetic at **Rock Paper Scissors** (68 Main St., Wiscasset, 207/882-9930, Mon.-Sat. 10am-5pm, Sun. noon-5pm), a pretty gift shop stocked with quirky stationery and dreamy gifts.

Boothbay Region

West Side Rd
Miles Island
BACK RIVER RD
HARDWICK RD
★ BOOTHBAY RAILWAY VILLAGE
27
LEDGES RD
Oak Hill
ADAMS POND RD
BOOTHBAY RD
BUTLER RD
PENSION RIDGE CR
Trevett
KNICKERBOCKER RD
COUNTRY CLUB
BEATH RD
TREVETT COUNTRY STORE
BOOTHBAY CRAFT BREWERY
WATERSHED TAVERN
Porter Preserve
WINTER'S ISLAND RD
BARTER ISLAND RD
Boothbay
BOOTHBAY FARMERS' MARKET
BACK NARROWS RD
★ COASTAL MAINE BOTANICAL GARDEN RD
COASTAL MAINE BOTANICAL GARDENS
SAWYER'S ISLAND RD
TAVENNER RD
Ram Islands
Indiantown Preserve
SAMOSET RD
MIDDLE RD
27
TOWNSEND AVE
96
LAKESIDE DR
BOOTHBAY HARBOR REGION CHAMBER OF COMMERCE
OCEAN POINT RD
EASTERN AVE
KENNYFIELD DR
Bayville
Spectacle Islands
LAKEVIEW RD
REED RD
DORY PUB
PARK ST
BEACH COVE WATERFRONT INN
Boothbay Harbor
OAK ST
Mount Pisgah
ATLANTIC AVE
OAK POINT RD
MADDOCKS RD
WESTERN AVE
MC KOWN ST
PORTS OF ITALY
CAP'N FISH'S
LOBSTER COVE RD
BARRETT PARK
CAM RONS POINT RD
West Boothbay Harbor
WESTERN AVE
CABBAGE ISLAND CLAMBAKES
Sprucewold
Cabbage Island
Southport
MC KOWN POINT RD
HENDRICKS HILL RD
PLUMMER RD
CAPE NEWAGEN RD
238
Mouse Island
GRANVIEW AVE
MADDOCKS RD
DOGFISH HEAD RD
EBEN COOK RD
21
CRUCS RD
Pine Cliff
CAPITAL ISLAND RD
SALT POND RD
BEACH RD
West Southport
CAPE NEWAGEN RD
ALL SAINTS RD
DUNNT ISLAND LIGHT ★
★ HENDRICKS HEAD LIGHTHOUSE
PRATT'S ISLAND RD
HENDRICKS HILL RD
Hendricks Harbor
GRAY
GRAY'S HOMESTEAD CAMPGROUND

0   0.5 mi
0   0.5 km

© AVALON TRAVEL

Sports and Recreation
Beaches

The Boothbay Peninsula doesn't have much sand to break up its rocky headlands, but **Barrett Park** (Lobster Cove Rd., Boothbay Harbor) is a nice place to enjoy the water views. Two rock beaches make for good tidepooling at low tide and have shady picnic tables, swings, and bathroom facilities.

Boating

A seven-acre sprawl of granite boulders and low-lying vegetation, **Eastern Egg Rock** doesn't look like a very cozy nesting ground, but the wildlife sanctuary was the first restored seabird colony in the world. Nesting seabird populations have been hard-hit by hunters, egg collectors, fishing practices, and pollution, and until the restoration process began, puffins hadn't shacked up here since 1885. **Puffins** are now on the island mid-June-August.

From Boothbay Harbor, book a trip with **Cap'n Fish's** (42 Commercial St., Boothbay Harbor, 207/633-3244, www.mainepuffin.com, 2.5-hr puffin tour $35 adults, $20 children 12 and under, $15 dog, 4-hr puffin and whale tour $75 adults, $45 youth 6-14, $30 children 5 and under, $15 dogs), whose puffin cruises, accompanied by an Audubon naturalist, pass three lighthouses and scattered islands on the way out to Eastern Egg Rock. The company's combination puffin and whale cruises commonly spot finback and minke whales, as well as the humpback whales that arrive on the coast in July.

Food

Another top contender on annual "best lobster roll" lists, **Red's Eats** (41 Water St., Wiscasset, 207/882-6128, daily 11:30am-10pm, $7-25, cash only) is a James Beard Award-winning shack that fills its buns with a pound of drawn (not chopped) meat, served with a little cup of clarified butter on the side. Picnic tables and

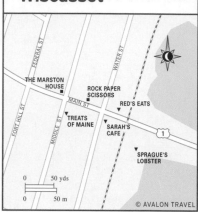

umbrellas with views of the water are available on-site, but note two drawbacks to eating at Red's: The line can stretch upward of an hour at busy times, and it's right beside the idling cars stuck in Wiscasset traffic. Just across the street is **Sprague's Lobster** (22 Main St., Wiscasset, 207/882-1236, daily 11am-8pm, $7-20); it hasn't racked up the same list of awards as Red's, but sells a similar style of lobster rolls at a lower price (albeit with somewhat less meat).

Half country bakery, half gourmet store, **Treats of Maine** (80 Main St., Wiscasset, 207/882-6192, www.treatsofmaine.com, Mon.-Sat. 7:30am-6pm, Sun. 10am-4pm, $3-7) serves pastries ranging from down-home to gourmet, with hefty chocolate babkas, fruit scones, muffins, and layered French confections. The long counter is a welcome place to enjoy a sweet and cup of coffee, but this place excels at takeout feasts of quiche, wine, cheese, and dessert.

A nondescript exterior hides the tasteful dining room at **Little Village Bistro** (65 Gardiner Rd., Wiscasset, 207/687-8232, http://littlevillagebistro.com, Tues.-Sat. 4:30pm-9pm, $11-20), which turns out to be a sweet haven with well-prepared, classic cuisine. Regulars love the crab cake appetizers and wild mushroom pizza, and the menu of simple pastas, braised Italian-style meats, and fresh seafood is full of flavor and thoughtful touches. Reservations are recommended.

With a mid-peninsula location just past the Boothbay botanical gardens, **Trevett Country Store** (381 W. Barter's Island Rd., Trevett, 207/633-1140, daily 7am-7:30pm, $5-20) might seem like a back road convenience store, but it's a local favorite for sandwiches, simple breakfasts, and fresh seafood. In warm months, the outdoor sundeck is a charming place to eat with water views and a cool breeze.

All cedar shake and dark wood, the **Watershed Tavern** (301 Adams Pond Rd., Boothbay, 207/633-3411, www.boothbaycraftbrewery.com, Wed.-Thurs. 3pm-8:30pm, Fri.-Sat. 11:30am-8:30pm, $12-29) has the kind of cave-like interior best enjoyed when the weather turns blustery. The food includes a fairly standard pub lineup of burgers, salads, and pizzas, but with some meat from local farms and appealing house-made additions. This is the brewpub side of **Boothbay Craft Brewery** (www.boothbaycraftbrewery.com, 207/633-3411, tours $5), which runs 30-minute tours daily at 3pm, followed by a beer tasting. Naturally, those beers are on tap at the tavern: Brews range from super-drinkable session ales to imperial stouts and red IPAs.

A destination for sophisticated, traditional food, ★ **Ports of Italy** (47 Commercial St., Boothbay, 207/633-1011, www.portsofitaly.com, May-Dec. daily 4:30pm-close, $18-34) stands head and shoulders above the crowded Boothbay Harbor restaurant scene. Thoughtful service and consistently high-quality food, an excellent wine list, and pleasant seating on an outdoor patio make this a good choice for a romantic evening or celebration. Reservations are essential.

Casual cousin to the attached Thistle Inn, the **Dory Pub** (55 Oak St., Boothbay Harbor, 877/633-3541, www.thethistle-inn.com, Tues.-Sat. 5pm-close, $10-16)

serves a simpler, solid menu in a fun space. Cozy up to the bar—made from an actual dory boat—for burgers, crab cakes, or piles of Maine mussels steamed in white wine. Great cocktails and an extensive beer and wine list make this a nice first stop of the evening for drinks and snacks.

Vendors from around the region set up stalls at **Boothbay Farmers' Market** (1 Common Dr., Boothbay, www.boothbayfarmersmarket.com, mid-May-early Oct., Thurs. 9am-noon).

★ Lobster Feast

Like a Polynesian *imu* or Maya *p'ib*, the classic method of cooking up a New England lobster is using a pit oven lined with rocks and heated with a blazing fire. The pit is then filled with seaweed, lobster, clams, and corn on the cob, covered with more seaweed (along with some sand or tarps), and left to cook for hours, infusing everything inside with a briny tang. Aside from swapping out the sand pit for some giant, wood fired steamers, **Cabbage Island Clambakes** (Pier 6, Boothbay Harbor, 207/633-7200, www.cabbageislandclambakes.com, mid-June-mid-Oct., four-hr boat tour and clambake $63) does them in classic, Maine style. The family-run operation takes a slow cruise to **Cabbage Island**, where you'll sit down to two steamed lobsters, white clams, fish chowder, new potatoes and corn, followed by blueberry cake and coffee. The experience is simply one of the finest ways to get a taste of this traditional feast in Maine.

Accommodations and Camping
Camping

Drift off to the sound of crashing waves at **Gray's Homestead Campground** (21 Homestead Rd., Southport, 207/633-4612, www.graysoceancamping.com, tent sites $38, RV sites $41, full hookups $51), an old-fashioned and friendly spot four miles south of Boothbay Harbor. Fire rings and a swimming beach give the campground a holiday atmosphere, and it also has laundry facilities, hot showers, and a dump station.

$100-150

By a quiet lake between the botanical gardens and downtown Boothbay Harbor, the motel-like ★ **Beach Cove Waterfront Inn** (48 Lakeview Rd., Boothbay Harbor, 207/618-8003, www.beachcovehotel.com, $99-215) is a great budget option. All rooms have views of the water and come stocked with a fridge, microwave, and coffeemaker, and a small continental breakfast is served in the lobby. Decor is simple and a bit dated, and some visitors find the walls overly thin, but staying at the inn gets you free access to a fleet of canoes and rowboats to enjoy on the lake.

$150-250

Walking distance from Wiscasset's historic downtown, the **Snow Squall Inn** (5 Bradford Rd., Wiscasset, 207/882-6892, www.snowsquallinn.com, $117-180) is all comfort and relaxation. Rooms are bright and uncluttered, with soft linens and simple furnishings, and the well-traveled, gracious owners prepare a fabulous breakfast each morning, with hot and cold options. The property includes a barn that's been converted into an airy yoga studio, and classes are offered throughout the day (www.wickedgoodyoga.com, $14).

Gorgeous lawns roll from a rambling farmhouse to the water's edge at the **Bold Colorful Life Inn** (802 Back River Rd., Boothbay, 207/633-6566, www.boldcolorlifeinn.com, $159-209), a laid-back estate that's halfway down the Boothbay Peninsula. Enjoy the quiet spot in a hammock, or wander the trails and gardens. Common spaces include a great room with a piano and bookshelves, and the unsurprisingly bright and colorful rooms each have private baths. The inn is run by a welcoming psychotherapist and life coach.

Over $250

Isolated and luxurious, ★ **The Inn at Cuckolds Lighthouse** (40 Town Landing Rd., Southport, 855/212-5252, www.innatcuckoldslighthouse.com, $500-600) is on a small island south of Boothbay and among the most romantic places to stay in Maine. The 1892 lighthouse has just two suites—book the whole darn island if you want a *really* private experience—and high-end amenities. Boat transportation to the island, afternoon tea and cocktails, and views of crashing waves make this a place apart, and all transportation and treats are included in the price of a night's stay.

Information

The **Boothbay Harbor Region Chamber of Commerce** (192 Townsend Ave., Boothbay Harbor, 207/633-2353, www.boothbayharbor.com, mid-May-early Oct. Mon.-Fri. 8am-5pm, Sat.-Sun. 10am-4pm; early Oct.-mid-May Mon.-Fri. 8am–5pm) runs a visitors center at its office.

Getting Around

The only place in this region where parking is an issue is in Boothbay Harbor, where it's worth leaving your car in one of the town's metered lots; the largest is adjacent to the town office (11 Harbor St., Boothbay Harbor, $1/hr to $7 full day). That town also has the only noteworthy in-town transit, the **Rocktide Trolley,** a free sightseeing trolley that makes a limited loop through downtown starting from the **Rocktide Inn** (35 Atlantic Ave., Boothbay Harbor, 207/633-4455, www.rocktideinn.com).

Pemaquid Region
Sights
Pemaquid Point Light

Crashing waves and jagged rocks are the perfect setting for **Pemaquid Point Light** (3115 Bristol Rd., New Harbor, 207/677-2492, www.visitmaine.com, early May-late Oct. daily 9am-5pm, $2). Classic calendar material, it was commissioned by John Quincy Adams and is considered by many the loveliest of New England's lights—by popular vote, its image landed on the Maine state quarter. Climb a wrought-iron spiral staircase to the top of the tower for a seagull's-eye view of the craggy headland, and get an up close look at the fourth-order Fresnel lens, one of just six in the state. After exploring the tower and clambering around the rocks, it's worth stopping in to the adjoining keeper's house, where the **Fisherman's Museum** (207/677-2494, mid-May-mid-Oct. daily 10:30am-5pm, free) displays mementos of the lobstering life. Also on-site is the **Pemaquid Art Gallery** (207/677-2752, early June-late Oct. daily 10am-5pm), which displays juried work from local artists.

Colonial Pemaquid

Three forts were raised and destroyed at the gaping mouth of the Pemaquid River as fur traders, pirates, the English, Native Americans, the French, and early settlers scrapped for control of the strategic stronghold. **Colonial Pemaquid** (2 Colonial Pemaquid Dr., New Harbor, 207/677-2423, www.friendsofcolonialpemaquid.org, late May-late Aug., daily 9am-5pm, $4 adults, $1 seniors, children under 12 free) offers a look at those tumultuous times, with historic reenactments, demonstrations, and nicely preserved structures. **Fort William Henry** is the centerpiece of the site (and a reconstruction of the second fort built here), where a trio of flags flies above a stone tower; the fort's permanent exhibit explores the intersection of fur trading and politics in the early years of European settlement. The sprawling grounds offer plenty to explore, including a visitors center museum, an 18th-century cemetery, and an herb garden stocked with plants that 17th-century settlers used for food and medicine, and the seaside site is a pleasant place to bring a picnic.

Sports and Recreation
Beaches

Just south of Colonial Pemaquid is the appealing **Pemaquid Beach Park** (Snowball Hill Rd., Bristol, 207/677-2754, daily 8am-5pm, $4, children under 12 free), a quarter-mile of pristine white sands with a concession stand, boogie board rentals, and nice views along the coast.

Boating

Hardy Boat Cruises (132 Rte. 32, New Harbor, 207/677-2026, www.hardyboat.com, 1.5-hr puffin tour $30 adults, $12 children under 12, under 2 free) is just five miles from Eastern Egg Rock and run its trips in the early evening, with an Audubon naturalist aboard, to catch the puffins rafting together in the water and lounging on the rocks. Hardy operates a somewhat smaller boat, meaning fewer crowds and a slightly rougher ride when waves are choppy.

Food

The old-timey treats at **Waltz's Soda Fountain** (167 Main St., Damariscotta, 207/563-7632, Mon.-Sat. 8am-5pm, Sun. 8am-3pm, $2-9) are right at home in Damariscotta's brick-and-window glass downtown. Twirl on the red leather stools, sip an egg cream or ice cream soda, or go all-out with a sundae under gobs of hot fudge sauce. A simple menu of sandwiches and snacks is also available, albeit overshadowed by the creamier options.

An outlier among Mid-Coast lobster shacks and bistros, **Best Thai** (74 Main St., Damariscotta, 207/5633-1440, www.bestthaimaine.com, Tues.-Fri. 11am-3pm and 4pm-9pm, Sat. noon-3pm and 4pm-9pm, Sun. 4pm-9pm, lunch $8-11, dinner $12-17) really does serve the best Thai food in the region (until you hit its sister restaurant in Bath). Panang curry and noodle dishes are consistently good, and the *tom kha* (chicken soup) gets rave reviews.

Find sweet treats and the best breakfasts in town at **Crissy's Breakfast &**

Coffee Bar (212 Main St., Damariscotta, 207/563-6400, www.cbandcb.com, daily 8am-2pm, $3-11). Gluten-free rice bowls are piled with meat, eggs, and veggies, while breakfast sandwiches are generous and served alongside crispy home fries. The lunch menu is also served all day, a savory mix of sandwiches, burritos, and salads.

Pemaquid's take on lobster "in the rough," the ★ **Pemaquid Fisherman's Co-op** (32 Co-op Rd., Pemaquid, 207/677-2642, daily 11am-8pm, $7-25) has the seafood, and you can bring the fixings. Bring beer or wine—some regulars even bring their own side salads—to go with whole lobsters swabbed in melted butter, steamers, and crabs. Outside seating offers great views of the Pemaquid River.

Find all the basics at **Yellowfront Grocery** (5 Coastal Market Dr., Damariscotta, 207/563-3507, Mon.-Sat. 7am-9pm, Sun. 8am-8pm), or visit **Rising Tide Community Market** (323 Main St., Damariscotta, 207/563-5556, www.risingtide.coop, daily 8am-8pm), a cooperatively owned natural food store that also has a deli and café.

The **Damariscotta Farmers Market** (www.damariscottafarmersmarket.org) has two locations for its Monday and Friday markets. On Mondays from early June-late September, find the vendors at the **Rising Tide Community Market** (323 Main St., Mon. 3pm-6pm), and on Fridays from mid-May-late October, farmers set up at **Round Top Farm** (3 Round Top Rd., Fri. 9am-noon).

Accommodations and Camping

Quiet and filled with shade trees, **Pemaquid Point Campground** (9 Pemaquid Point Campground Rd., New Harbor, 207/677-2267, www.pemaquidpointcampground.com, tent sites $27, RV sites $37, no credit cards) has hot showers, a playground, horseshoe pits, and easy access to the beach, Colonial Pemaquid, and the lighthouse, so you can beat the crowds coming from Boothbay. If you're just passing through and don't want to make the 20-minute trek down the peninsula, book a site at **Lake Pemaquid Campground** (100 Twin Cove Rd., Damariscotta, 207/563-5202, www.lakepemaquid.com, $36-48) whose 200 sites surround a pleasant, freshwater lake.

Leave the crowds (and any hope of cell service) behind at ★ **Mill Pond Inn** (50 Main St., Nobleboro, 207/352-4044, www.millpondinn.com, $150-160), which has five guest rooms on the shore of Damariscotta Lake. Fresh flowers in each room and a wonderfully peaceful setting make this feel like a retreat from the world. The full country-style breakfast often includes blueberry pancakes or French toast, bacon, and eggs, and the friendly innkeepers have a great collection of books, games, and music to enjoy during your stay. The house was built in 1780, and retains a wonderfully historic feel.

Information

Information on the area is available through the **Damariscotta Region Chamber of Commerce** (15 Courtyard St., Damariscotta, 207/563-8340, www.damariscottaregion.com, Mon.-Fri. 8:30am-4:30pm).

Penobscot Bay

Down East begins where the Penobscot River opens onto a scenic bay filled with low-lying rocky islands. This is classic sailing territory, though submerged shoals and the maze-like geography make navigation difficult. Lobster boat captains work hundreds of traplines passed down through generations. Much of the bay's edge is thoroughly rural, with forest broken only by the occasional village, but at the southern end is a trio of beautiful communities—Rockland, Rockport, and Camden—each with a scenic harbor and plenty to explore.

Penobscot Bay

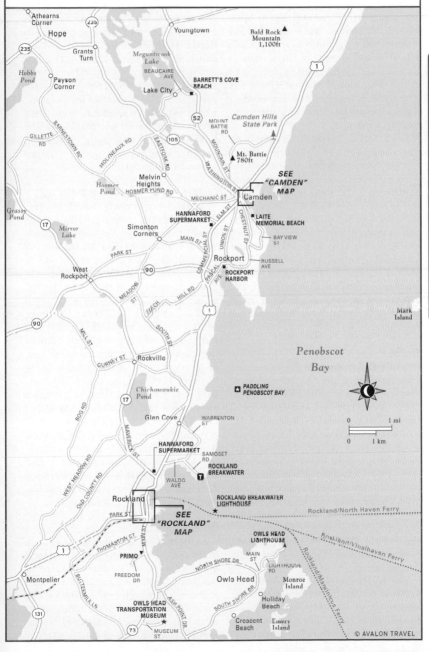

© AVALON TRAVEL

Rockland

A thriving commercial fishing fleet has long been the heart of this working harbor, and at first glance the sturdy brick Main Street has a staid, old-fashioned look. It's got a deep history with the sea: The Abenaki name for the harbor is Catawamtek, "great landing place," and in the 19th century, the waterfront was alive with shipbuilding and lime production as fishing boats arrived laden with cod and lobster.

Rockland's charms have long been overshadowed by picture-perfect Camden and Rockport, but in recent years the storefronts have filled up with destination restaurants and cozy bistros, and it has begun to feel unexpectedly chic. It's a good home base for exploring Penobscot Bay, and remains fairly low-key. Even if you're making tracks for Acadia or other parts of Down East Maine, it's worth stopping to see the fabulous collection of Andrew Wyeth paintings at the Farnsworth Art Museum and walk the breakwater to the harbor lighthouse.

Sights
Farnsworth Art Museum

The main draw may be the unparalleled collection of works by the artists of the Wyeth family, but the wonderful **Farnsworth Art Museum** (16 Museum St., 207/596-6457, www.farsworthmuseum. org, Nov.-Dec. and Apr.-May Tues.-Sun. 10am-5pm, Jan.-Mar. Wed.-Sun. 10am-5pm, July-Oct. daily 10am-5pm, $20 adults, $18 seniors, $15 students 17 and older, 16 and under free) encompasses far more. Explore beautifully curated works depicting Maine's landscape and people, including pieces by Robert Bellows, Eastman Johnson, Winslow Homer, and George Inness.

The **Wyeth Center at the Farnsworth Art Museum** highlights the very different works of Andrew Wyeth's father, N. C., and his son Jamie. Andrew Wyeth's best-known work, *Christina's World,* isn't here

(it's at MoMA in New York City), but the next best thing is—the house that inspired the arresting and melancholy character study. Docents can give you directions to the museum-operated **Olson House** (Hathorn Pt. Rd., Cushing, $5), a half-hour drive away; it was once home to Christina Olson, disabled by illness, and her eccentric brother Alvaro. On-site guides tell the story of the painting, which was based on an actual event when Wyeth came across Christina crawling home from her parents' graves. From June-September, admission to museum is free on Wednesdays 5pm-8pm.

Owls Head Transportation Museum

The little town of Owls Head, a 10-minute drive south from Rockland, seems an unlikely place for the sprawling **Owls Head Transportation Museum** (117 Museum St., Owls Head, 207/594-4418, www.shead.org, daily 10am-5pm, $14 adults, $10 seniors, free youth under 18), whose remarkable collection of pre-1940s vehicles celebrates everything that whirs, sputters, rolls, and glides. Aircraft, automobiles, and motorcycles are all fully functional, and the bicycle exhibit covers everything from an 1868 velocipede "boneshaker" to a turn-of-the-20th-century dual propulsion tricycle. Ask upon arrival about riding in a Ford Model T; if a staff member is available, he or she will take you for a turn around the grounds. Aircraft—including 19th-century gliders, a Wright flyer, biplanes, and a "Red Baron"-style triplane—get off the ground during outdoor events that take place frequently during the summer months.

Other Sights

Almost 700,000 tons of granite were sunk off Jameson Point to create the **Rockland Breakwater** (207/785-4609, www.rocklandharborlights.org), a 4,346-foot pile of rocks with a pretty brick lighthouse at the end. The scale of the building project, which was completed in 1900, is staggering, and the bulk of the structure is

Rockland

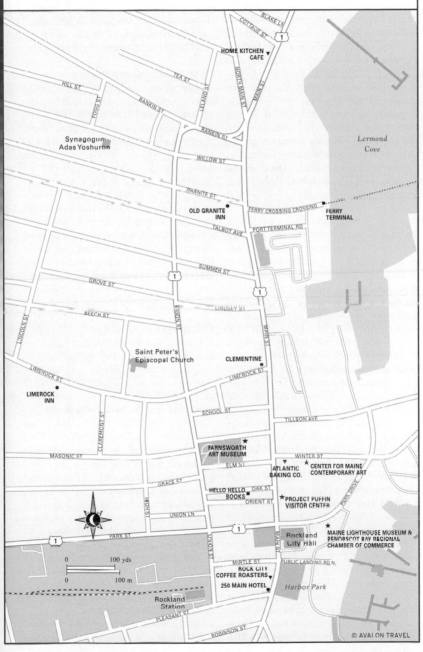

BLAKE LN

COTTAGE ST

HOME KITCHEN
CAFE

TEA ST

HILL ST

FOGG ST

RANKIN ST

LELAND ST

NORTH MAIN ST

MAIN ST

RANKIN RD

Synagogue
Adas Yoshuron

Lermond
Cove

WILLOW ST

GRANITE ST

OLD GRANITE
INN

FERRY CROSSING CROSSING

FERRY
TERMINAL

TALBOT AVE

PORT TERMINAL RD

SUMMER ST

GROVE ST

LINDSEY ST

BEECH ST

UNION ST

MAIN ST

LINCOLN ST

Saint Peter's
Episcopal Church

CLEMENTINE

LIMEROCK ST

LIMEROCK ST

LIMEROCK
INN

CLAREMONT ST

SCHOOL ST

TILLSON AVE

MASONIC ST

FARNSWORTH ★
ART MUSEUM

WINTER ST

ELM ST

ATLANTIC ★ CENTER FOR MAINE
BAKING CO. CONTEMPORARY ART

GRACE ST

HIGH ST

OAK ST

HELLO HELLO
BOOKS

ORIENT ST

★ PROJECT PUFFIN
VISITOR CENTER

PARK DRIVE

UNION LN

PARK ST

MAINE LIGHTHOUSE MUSEUM & ★
PENOBSCOT BAY REGIONAL
CHAMBER OF COMMERCE

Rockland
City Hall

UNION ST

MAIN ST

0   100 yds

0   100 m

MYRTLE ST

PUBLIC LANDING RD N.

ROCK CITY
COFFEE ROASTERS ▾

250 MAIN HOTEL

Harbor Park

Rockland
Station

PLEASANT ST

ROBINSON ST

© AVALON TRAVEL

underwater—a cross section of the breakwater would be trapezoidal, with the base measuring 175 feet across. Walking the breakwater is an experience in itself, as sailboats, seabirds, and seals add to the scenery, and the **Rockland Breakwater Lighthouse** is fun to visit when open (if the flag is flying, the lighthouse is open—sharp-eyed visitors can spot the flag from Jameson Point, or check out the oddly hypnotizing live webcam feed on the breakwater website). Don't set out down the breakwater during storms, though, as heavy waves can wash over the rocks.

Short and pert, the **Owls Head Lighthouse** (Lighthouse Rd., Owl's Head, free) commands beautiful views of the rocky coastline, and is accessible via a short, gentle walk through coastal forest. Over the years, the lighthouse has collected a remarkable list of legends and ghost stories. The light is said to be haunted by two ghosts (one helpful spirit left one-way tracks in the snow when he visited to polish the brass and clean the lens), and the lighthouse has been the site of some remarkable rescues. In a December 1850 storm, a small schooner smashed up on the rocks near Owls Head, and two survivors huddled on the rocks while a third sought help. By the time a search party arrived, the two are said to have been fully encased in a block of frozen sea spray; the rescuers chipped off the ice, and dunked the victims in cold water to revive them. According to legend, the two survivors later married and had four children.

While it might not thrill the casual visitor, lighthouse aficionados shouldn't miss the **Maine Lighthouse Museum** (1 Park Dr., 207/594-3301, www.mainelighthousemuseum.com, Mon.-Fri. 10am-5pm, Sat.-Sun. 10am-4pm, $5 adults, $4 seniors, free children under 12), which bills itself as the country's most significant collection of lenses and artifacts. The attached chamber of commerce has brochures and maps for lighthouse hopping up the coast. If puffins are more your thing, stop by the **Project Puffin**

Visitor Center (311 Main St., 207/596-5566, www.projectpuffin.audubon.org, May Wed.-Sun. 10am-5pm, June-Oct. daily 10am-5pm, free), which has a small but interesting exhibit on the birds and their habitat on Eastern Egg Rock.

Entertainment and Events

Lobster lovers arrive from all over for the five days of cook-offs and contents at the **Maine Lobster Festival** (800/596-0376, www.mainelobsterfestival.com, early Aug.) which has been held in Rockland since 1947. The event doesn't really get going until King Neptune crowns the Maine Sea Goddess on Wednesday night, and then it's a frenzy of pancake breakfasts, music, and 20,000 pounds of lobster that goes straight from the boats into the world's largest lobster pot. It ends on Sunday with the "International Great Crate Race," where fleet-footed contestants run across lobster crates suspended in the harbor, overseen—and sometimes fished out—by umpires in rowboats.

Shopping

If you're looking for a place to browse or buy, **Main Street** around the Farnsworth Art Museum has a profusion of little boutiques and shops interspersed with small galleries. Find summer reads and literature at the adorable **hello hello books** (316 Main St., 207/593-7780, www.hellohellobooks.com, Mon.-Thurs. 9am-7pm, Fri.-Sat. 9am-8pm, Sun. 9am-6pm), an indie shop with a good selection of new and used titles. Quilters and DIY fashionistas will love **Clementine** (428 Main St., 207/596-3905, www.clementineme.com, Mon.-Sat. 9am-5pm, Sun. 9am-4pm), a boutique fabric shop that overflows with color, and you can find pretty, handmade beauty products at **Trillium Soaps** (216 Main St., 207/593-9019, www.trilliumsoaps.com, Wed.-Sat. 10am-5pm).

Sports and Recreation

Unlike more cumbersome square-rigged ships, Maine's "windjammer" schooners

The Lobstering Life

Leah and Lesley Ranquist, living the lobstering life

Leah and Leslie Ranquist got their first taste of lobstering as children when their grandfather took them out in his skiff to bait traps and band lobsters. After completing a strenuous apprentice program, the two sisters, who both prefer the traditional term "lobsterman," began carrying on the family tradition from their home on Swan's Island, where each captains a lobster boat. Following a long day of hauling some of her 600 traps, Leah shared a bit about the lobstering life:

What's a typical day like for you?

It's pretty repetitive—at 5 or 5:30 I'll head out and haul through 180-250 traps, depending on the day, then I head back in. My sternman is there to bait the pockets and band the lobsters, and I fish singles, pairs, and triples. A triple is three traps on one buoy, so when that first trap comes up, I'll have him grab the first trap, and I'll grab the second trap.

What do you like about lobstering?

I like a lot about lobstering! I mostly like

that I'm my own boss, and I can make my own schedule. It's pretty relaxed, and I like being out on the water. The beautiful days are really worth the not-so-good ones. I'll be fishing five or six days a week for six months a year, then I haul my traps out in November, and I pick away at them and fix them through the winter. I do have to work in the winter, but that's my version of taking a break.

What are some challenging things facing the Maine lobster industry in coming years?

We're trying to prepare for uncertainly. Lobsters have been doing very good the last few years, and not knowing if it's going to keep up, or if they'll disappear like other fisheries have, we have to plan for disaster just to keep in mind that it might not be there forever.

What's your favorite way to eat a lobster?

Steam it in a pot, then eat it hot with hot butter! I also enjoy a lobster roll here and there.

can sail close-hauled to the wind, making them remarkably nimble and fast for their size. Five of the nine ships that make up the **Maine Windjammer Association** (207/374-2993, www.sailmainecoast. com) are National Historic Landmarks, and they're overhauled each spring with fresh paint, polished brass, and gleaming wood. Without a steady stream of tourists, it's hard to imagine these ships staying afloat; even a small wooden sailboat is a labor of love, and a grand, historic schooner even more so.

Cruises range from 3-6 days in length, poking around rocky islands, sailing into coves in search of seals, and providing evening deck views under brilliant stars. Accommodations are cramped, but increasingly the schooners are creating a more luxurious experience, with wine tastings and thoughtfully prepared food. Guests can lend a hand in hoisting sails and anchors, or just lay back and watch the show.

The *J. & E. Riggin* (207/594-1875, www. mainewindjammer.com, 3-day trips from $596) leaves from Rockland and is known for the best schooner food on the coast, and the 1922 *Ladona* (207/594-4723, www.schoonerladona.com, 3-day trips from $968) has cornered the upper end of the market after a recent overhaul, with wonderfully pristine deck chairs, luxurious beds, and elegant tiled showers.

Food

The beans and brews at **Rock City Coffee Roasters** (252 Main St., 207/594-5688, www.rockcitycoffee. com, Sun.-Thurs. 6:30am-7pm, Fri.-Sat. 6:30am-9pm, $2-6) are fresh as can be, and you can watch the roasters at work in the back of the little café. Fresh, locally baked pastries are available, and Rock City hosts frequent live shows.

A huge menu of hearty breakfasts and lunch plates is the draw at **Home Kitchen Café** (650 Main St., 207/596-2449, www. homekitchencafe.com, Wed.-Sat. and Mon. 7am-3pm, Sun. 8am-3pm, $7-13),

a bright, friendly spot with a sunny rooftop patio. The recurring lobster tacos special is legendary, but the café's homemade sticky buns and corned beef hash also have passionate fans.

The busy bakers at **Atlantic Baking Co.** (351 Main St., 207/596-0505, www. atlanticbakingco.com, Mon.-Sat. 7am-6pm, Sun. 8am-4pm, $3-11) turn out an impressive display of sweets, breads, and savory pastries. This centrally located spot is a favorite for quick, simple lunches of soups, salads, or sandwiches on housemade bread and also good for picnic supplies if you're headed out to Owls Head Lighthouse or the Rockland Breakwater.

Superb, farm-to-table cuisine is beautifully presented at ★ **Primo** (2 South Main St., 207/596-0770, www.primorestaurant.com, Wed.-Sun. 5pm-10pm, $32-40), an Italian restaurant on a four-acre farm. James Beard Award-winning chef Melissa Kelly creates a menu that changes with the season, and plates are a heady blend of classic flavors and Maine ingredients, like seared scallops with morel mushrooms and fiddleheads, or a branzino fillet with local whelks, shrimp, and clams. Reservations are recommended: Book the downstairs dining room for a romantic, more formal feel, or dine in the upstairs lounge, full of colorful nooks, bar seating, and a convivial atmosphere. Cocktails are as garden-fresh as the food.

On the north end of town is a **Hannaford Supermarket** (75 Maverick St., 207/594-2173, Mon.-Sat. 6am-11pm, Sun. 7am-9pm), and the tiny **Good Tern Natural Foods Co-op and Café** (750 Main St., 207/594-8822, www.goodtern.com, Mon.-Sat. 8am-7pm, Sun. 9am-5pm) has a good selection of organic, GMO-free foods, a deli, and a small café with a sitting area.

Accommodations

Rockland has few accommodations compared to Rockport and Camden, making Airbnb a good option here.

$150-200

Modern touches and eclectic, original art keep the ★ **Old Granite Inn** (546 Main St., 207/594-9036, www.oldgraniteinn. com, $150-215) from feeling fusty, but the common spaces of the granite colonial house retain a historic feel. Rooms range from a compact queen with detached private bath to four-person suites that are an excellent value for families; some have electric fireplaces and whirlpool tubs, while two rooms on the 2nd floor boast views of the Rockland Harbor Lighthouse. The hearty breakfasts served in the communal dining room get raves from guests.

$200-250

The elegant Queen Anne architecture of **LimeRock Inn** (96 Limerock St., 800/546-3762, www.limerockinn.com, $169-249) is brightened up with an eye-popping coat of teal paint and garden full of blooming plants. Welcoming owners and a location that's walking distance from downtown restaurants and the Farnsworth Art Museum make this a good choice for exploring Rockland, but the gracious wraparound porch, living room, and comfortable rooms are tempting reasons to stay in as well. All rooms have a private bath and fun, varied decor that ranges from a somewhat princess-y pink suite to staid, Yankee plaid.

Over $250

Luxurious and ultramodern, **250 Main Hotel** (250 Main St., 207/594-5994, www.250mainhotel.com, $279-400) offers stunning views of the harbor from many rooms, some of which feature floor-to-ceiling glass. Clever, nautical touches and original art are everywhere in the hotel's 26 rooms and common spaces. Don't miss the wonderful rooftop patio.

Information

The **Penobscot Bay Regional Chamber of Commerce** (1 Park Dr., 207/596-0376, www.therealmaine.com) runs a large and well-stocked information center in a new building by the harbor.

Rockport and Camden

Forested, sloping hills running straight to the water are the perfect frame for Camden's sheltered harbor and picturesque downtown; the elegant little community is one of New England's most beautiful. Schooners and sleek yachts stand to attention at mooring buoys and floating docks, and on quiet mornings you can hear spanking lines and outboard motors from all over town. There's no finer place on the coast to see Maine's windjammer fleet, breathtaking wooden vessels crowned with acres of flying sails and trim lines.

All that beauty has made Camden a tourist destination since the mid-19th century, and downtown can be a madhouse in the heat of summer. When the ice cream shop has a line out the door and there's nowhere to park within a mile of the water, it's worth taking in your harbor views from the relative quiet of Camden Hills State Park, where Mount Megunticook and Mount Battie look out on Penobscot Bay.

Just down the coast, tiny Rockport feels like Camden in dollhouse scale: Turn away at the wrong moment, and you'd totally miss the perfect little harbor and downtown. There are just a few restaurants on the little Main Street, and no sights to speak of, but the waterfront park is ideal for watching lobster boats and sailors.

Sights

Starting in the 18th century, Mainers produced lime by burning locally quarried limestone in wood- and coal-fired kilns. At the time, lime was an essential part of almost any construction project, and, at the industry's peak in 1892, millions of casks of lime left the Maine coast. Keep an eye out and you'll see traces of the lime business everywhere, including a ruined

Camden

© AVALON TRAVEL

lime kiln by the river in the Rockport Harbor. Featuring Maine's best artists, the **Center for Maine Contemporary Art** (162 Russell Ave., Rockport, 207/236-2875, www.artsmaine.org, late May-Oct. Tues.-Sat. 10am-5pm, Sun. 1pm-5pm; closed Tues.-Wed. in winter, $5 adults, free children) is worth a look for its dozens of summer art shows held in a converted firehouse.

While it's not quite as extensive as the maritime museum in Bath, the collection of nautical treasures, art, and artifacts at the **Penobscot Marine Museum** (2 Church St., Searsport, 207/548-0334, www.penobscotmarinemuseum.org, late May-mid-Oct. Mon.-Sat. 10am-5pm, Sun. noon-5pm, $12 adults, $10 seniors and students, $8 children 8-15, $30 family, free children under 8) is fascinating. You'll find a trove of model ships and scrimshaw here, along with practical tools and navigation equipment. The museum is about 30 minutes up the coast from Camden in Searsport, so makes a stop on the way to Acadia National Park.

Entertainment and Events

Like the other tourist towns on the coast, Camden's summer is a whirl of themed weekends and small festivals. The real centerpiece of the season, though, is the **Camden Windjammer Festival** (early Sept., 207/236-4404, www.camden-windjammerfestival.org) when the harbor fills with two dozen magnificent schooners. Boat parades, fireworks, and a lobster-trap race make this a fun time to visit, but book accommodations far in advance.

Shopping

Downtown Camden is stuffed with little shops and boutiques selling everything from tourist kitsch to luxury goods. On the latter end are the handwoven wool blankets from **Swans Island Company** (2 Bay View St., Camden, 207/706-7926, www.swansislandcompany.com, Mon.-Sat. 9am-5pm). One of Maine's best independent bookstores, the **Owl & Turtle Bookshop** (32 Washington St., Camden, 207/236-4769, www.owlandturtle.com, daily 8am-4pm) has a "marine room" full of nautical books and charts, and a children's room with a view of the river below. Sweets lovers shouldn't miss **Uncle Willy's Candy Shoppe** (57 Bay View St., Camden, 207/230-2470, www.unclewillyscandyshoppe.com, Wed.-Sat. 10am-6pm, Sun. noon-6pm), two whole floors of old-fashioned penny candy, fudge, and brittle.

Sports and Recreation
★ Paddling Penobscot Bay

As beautiful as Rockport and Camden are, getting out on a boat is the only way to really take in Penobscot Bay. Tiny forested isles and town-sized islands are dreamlike on sunny days, when the sparkling water lights up the coast. But the bay is a sprawl of rocky shoals and hazards, and a thick layer of fog can turn even familiar harbors into a dangerous maze. Would-be adventurers shouldn't be deterred local captains and kayak guides are well versed in keeping people safe.

The lacy, rock edges of the Penobscot Bay are perfectly suited to kayaks, which can nose in and out of coves too small for bigger boats. **Maine Sports Outfitters** (24 Main St., Camden, 207/236-8797, www.mainesport.com, kayak trips $40-125 adults, $35-75 kids 10-15) runs trips ranging from two hours to a full day. A two-hour Camden Harbor Tour is a good way to see the schooners and yachts from the water as you work your way to a small island at the mouth of the harbor, but the half-day Harbor-to-Harbor paddle goes farther afield, starting in Rockport Harbor and going to Camden Harbor, with a picnic lunch on Curtis Island.

Experienced kayakers can rent from the same company (full-day sea kayak rental $45/single, $55/tandem), which is full of good advice on day trips and overnight paddles from Camden Harbor.

Beaches

The Camden area isn't known for great beaches, but there are some fine places to cool off on a hot day: At the eastern end of Megunticook Lake, **Barrett's Cove Beach** (Beauclaire Ave. off Route 52) has a bit of sand and picnic tables. By midsummer, the water here is far warmer than the bay, making it a good choice for families. A one-mile walk from downtown Camden, **Laite Memorial Beach** (south side of Camden Harbor, off Bay View St.) is a pleasant, grassy park with a sandy beach that narrows to a sliver at high tide.

Boating

Sailing out of Camden, the 1871 **Lewis R. French** (270/230-8320, www.schooner-french.com, three-night trips from $590) is the oldest windjammer in the United States, and still has no inboard engine; with all sails set, she flies a remarkable 3,000 square feet of canvas. Another Camden favorite is the **Angelique** (800/282-9989, www.sailangelique.com, three-night trips from $595), a modern vessel that's particularly dramatic under deep red, gaff-rigged sails.

Hiking

Aside from Mount Desert Island, **Camden Hills State Park** (280 Rte. 1, Camden, 207/236-3109, www.maine. gov, 9am-sunset, $6 adults, $2 seniors and children) is the only place in Maine where the mountains hew so closely to the coast, and the views of Penobscot Bay are unmatched. You'll earn your views on the steep 2.6-mile round-trip **Megunticook Trail** as you climb almost 1,000 feet in elevation on your way to the summit. Another good choice for views of the bay is the 3-mile loop trail up the 1,200-foot **Bald Rock Mountain,** where two rustic Adirondack shelters are set just below the bare crest. Unless you're a very brisk walker, set aside two hours for either hike, and be sure to pick up a free hiking map at the entrance to the park.

Of course, you also don't have to walk anywhere for views in this park. An auto road to the summit of **Mount Battie** climbs from just inside the state park entrance. The 19-year-old Edna St. Vincent Millay, a Rockland native who would go on to win the 1923 Pulitzer Prize for poetry, was inspired by Mount Battie when she wrote her poem "Renascence":

> "All I could see from where I stood
> Was three long mountains and a wood;
> I turned and looked the other way,
> And saw three islands in a bay."

Not much has changed.

Food
Camden

Even when you are looking for ★ **Rhumb Line** (59 Sea St., 207/230-8495, www.rhumblinecamden.com, Wed.-Mon. 11:30am-9pm, $7-25), it's easy to miss, tucked between the waterfront and a cavernous working boatyard. The small seafood restaurant is across the harbor from the core of downtown, and it's a pleasure to enjoy the alternative vantage point from the outdoor bar and patio seating. Opened in 2016, the restaurant generated buzz with creative cocktails and fresh boat-to-table seafood.

schooner *Angelique*, Penobscot Bay

The menu includes the usual fried fare, along with offbeat sashimi and ceviche, and the rustic-chic interior is right at home on the water's edge.

Find great coffee and something to read at **Owl & Turtle Bookshop** (33 Bay View St., 207/230-7335, www.owlandturtle.com, daily 8am-4pm, $2-5), which also has a small selection of fresh pastries. Friendly staff and a good crowd of locals make this a nice place to linger with a crossword puzzle.

No one goes to **Cuzzy's** (21 Bay View St., 207/236-3272, www.cuzzysrestaurant.com, daily 11am-1am, $5-20) for a gourmet meal, but that's somewhat beside the point. There's a huge menu of affordable pub food, very decent chowder, and all kinds of fried seafood to eat at the bar, where fishers and schooner crews come to relax in a cave-like interior or on the sunny back patio. Happy hour specials on cheap beer and pizza are available daily 3pm-6pm.

With a solid menu of seafood

standards and patio seating that juts over the harbor, **Waterfront** (40 Bay View St., 207/236-3747, www.waterfrontcamden.com, daily 11am-9:30pm, $9-30) is a perennial favorite. No individual dish seems to blow anyone away, but watching the boats roll in and out of the harbor over a glass of local beer and plate of oysters is a true Camden experience. On busy nights, waits can get very long, and since the interior seating is a bit lackluster, it's often worth going elsewhere.

Reasonably priced sandwiches, soups, and salads at **Camden Deli** (37 Main St., 207/236-8343, www.camdendeli.com, daily 7am-10pm, $7-10) are a simple option right downtown. Limited seating is available inside (window seats have great views of the harbor), but this is a nice place to pick up sandwiches to take around the corner to the small park where paths and benches face the water.

In a cheerfully decorated, historic brick building, **Fresh** (1 Bay View Landing, 207/236-7005, www.freshcamden.com, Mon.-Tues. and Thurs. 5pm-8pm, Fri. Sun. 11:30am-2:30pm and 5pm-8pm, $21-28) is just that, with an eye-opening menu of international food that skews Asian. The huge, homemade lobster ravioli with wonton wrappers is a favorite here, as is the "deconstructed" lamb moussaka as well as tiger shrimp with black rice and ginger barbecue sauce. Despite the upscale food (and prices), this restaurant has a casual atmosphere, with outdoor seating and the occasional live act.

Find high-quality baked goods, meat, cheese, and drinks at **French & Brawn Marketplace** (1 Elm St., 207/236 3361, www.frenchandbrawn.com, Mon.-Sat. 6am-8pm, Sun. 8am-8pm), which is the only market in downtown Camden. More basic goods are available from **Hannaford Supermarket** (145 Elm St., 207/236-8577, Mon.-Sat. 7am-10pm, Sun. 7am-9pm), on the main road south of town. Small but vibrant, the **Camden Farmers Market** (Knox Mill between Washington and Knowlton, May-Nov. Sat. market 9am-1pm; mid-June-Nov. Wed. market 3:30pm-6pm) has local breads, cheeses, vegetables, and fruit.

Rockport

Tiny Rockport doesn't have much of a dining scene, but ★ **Nina June** (24 Central St., 207/236-8880, www.nina-junerestaurant.com, Wed.-Fri. 5:30pm-9pm, Sat. 9am-2:30pm and 5pm-9:30pm, Sun. noon-3pm and 5:30pm-9:30pm, brunch $6-18, lunch/dinner $20-30) is a noteworthy exception. A deck overlooking the Rockport Harbor makes a sublime setting for a Mediterranean menu that changes with the season. On a recent September evening, the menu included bucatini with lamb neck ragu and grilled swordfish beside a pile of shaved cucumber and cherry tomatoes. Saturday lunch means a hearty menu of Italian specialties, while Sunday brunch ranges from traditional breakfasts like strata or pancakes to white-almond gazpacho and other savory entrées.

Accommodations and Camping
Camping
Set in the rolling forest along the coast, ★ **Camden Hills State Park** (280 Rte. 1, 207/236-3109, www.maine.gov, $38-49) has amazing views of Penobscot Bay, trails to explore, and level campsites that range from simple tent pads to extra large options with water, electric, and space for a 35-foot camper. The campground is divided into reservable sites that must be booked 48 hours in advance (though it's worth planning ahead for peak season), and a smaller number of sites set aside on a first-come, first-served basis.

Under $100
The trim little cottages at ★ **Oakland Seashore Cabins** (112 Dearborn Ln., Rockport, 207/594-8104, www.oakland-seashorecabins.com, $70-140) are rustic and a bit of a tight squeeze, but they're set right on the edge of a private pebble beach

between Rockland and Rockport, making them a fabulous value and wonderfully peaceful place to stay. This property also includes motel rooms at a similar price, and while they're a decent option, the cabins are the clear winner. The cottages with kitchenettes are stocked with very basic cooking equipment, and the largest sleep up to five people. No televisions, telephones, or coffeepots here (and the wireless access is hit or miss).

$100-150
A quiet, 15-minute walk from Rockport's gem of a harbor, **Schooner Bay Motor Inn** (337 Commercial St., Rockport, 888/308-8855, www.sbaymotorinn.com, $119-179) has trim furnishings and a thoughtful, local character that sets it apart from the other motels along Route 1. Light sleepers should request a room at the forested back of the property, where there's a small, shady creek. A breakfast of fresh pastries, fruit, and homemade quiche is served May-December.

If you're looking for a lower-budget place to stay in downtown Camden, the **Towne Inn** (68 Elm St., Camden, 207/236-3377, www.camdenmotel.com, $124-139) is hard to beat. The super-clean, motel-style rooms are nothing fancy, but the friendly owners are gradually overhauling them; updated rooms are the same price as the older ones, but with smart, fresh colors and little artistic flourishes. All rooms have coffeemakers, cable televisions, air-conditioning, wireless Internet, and small fridges, and an appealing breakfast is served during summer months; in the off-season, the owners deliver a little breakfast packet to each room that includes their killer homemade granola.

$150-250
Find Maine country style with a few nautical touches at the **Blue Harbor House Inn** (67 Elm St., Camden, 207/236-3196, www.blueharborhouse.com, $155-199), a homey spot that's a short walk from

downtown. Rooms are stocked with coffeemakers and comfortable beds, and afternoon tea and the innkeeper's two-course breakfast are served in a welcoming common room. All rooms have en suite bathrooms, and more expensive options have steam showers or claw-foot soaking tubs.

An expansive lawn rolls all the way to a private beach, a wonderful perk that makes the **High Tide Inn** (505 Rte. 1, Camden, 207/236-3724, www.hightide-inn.com, $175-195, deck house $170-260) feel like a retreat just a few minutes' drive from downtown Camden. A handful of options are available on this property: a somewhat lackluster Oceanview Motel (where you can just spy a bit of blue); the sweet, compact rooms in the old-fashioned inn; a collection of oceanfront rooms a stone's throw from the water; and six little cottages, nostalgic and rustic. A homemade continental breakfast is served on a glass-enclosed porch with views to the water.

Over $250
Find all the top-end perks at ★ **16 Bay View** (16 Bay View St., Camden, 207/706-7990, www.16bayview.com, $300-500),

a 21 room boutique hotel with perfect views of the harbor from ocean-side rooms and the rooftop bar. Great piles of silky pillows, gas fireplaces, spa bathrooms, and balconies are luxurious, and the hotel, which opened in early 2016, is beautifully decorated. A continental breakfast is served in the Prohibition-themed Vintage Room.

Information
The **Camden-Rockport-Lincolnville Chamber of Commerce** (Public Landing, 800/223-5459 or 207/236-4404, www.visitcamden.com, Mon.-Sat. 9am-4pm) runs a helpful information center on the Camden waterfront.

Getting Around
No real in-town public transit is available in any of the Penobscot Bay locales, but they're small enough to explore on foot. In Camden, free parking is available at two public lots (Washington Street, turn north when Route 1 passes the Camden Village Green). In Rockland, there's free, two-hour parking on Main Street, and a larger lot at **Oceanside High School** (400 Broadway, Rockland, July and Aug. only).

Acadia National Park

A rugged, scenic coastline wraps around granite peaks, glacier-carved valleys, and a classic Maine vacation town.

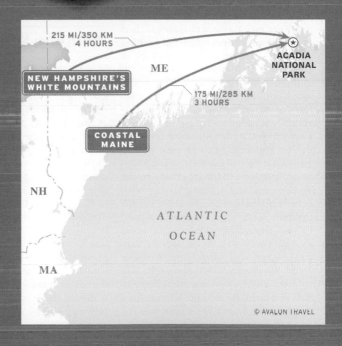

215 MI/350 KM
4 HOURS

ME

NEW HAMPSHIRE'S
WHITE MOUNTAINS

ACADIA
NATIONAL
PARK

175 MI/285 KM
3 HOURS

COASTAL
MAINE

NH

ATLANTIC
OCEAN

MA

© AVALON TRAVEL

Maine's scenic drama comes to a head in Acadia National Park, a 47,000-acre preserve that spills across Mount Desert Island to the surrounding islets and shoreline.

Twenty-four mountain peaks describe the island's dramatic history in sparkling granite: 450 million years ago, mini continent Avalonia rammed into the hulking North American plate, forming a platform that would be buried under sand, silt, volcanic lava, and ash, then raked by a series of massive glaciers. Geologic clues are everywhere here, from odd-looking rocks left perched on mountaintops to ice-carved U-shaped valleys and deep gouges in bare granite. A deep, fjord-like bay nearly splits the island in two. For oceanview hiking, rocky trail exploration, and tidepooling, New England's only national park is incomparable.

The Wabanaki people have inhabited this stretch of coast for thousands of years, hunting and fishing in year-round settlements and trading widely with other regional groups. In 1604, French explorer Samuel de Champlain stopped by long enough to record a name—*Isles des Monts Déserts,* or islands of bare peaks—and was followed by waves of Jesuit missionaries, French and British soldiers, and European settlers eager to fish and farm. By the mid-18th century, though, the dramatic scenery was the main draw, as a generation of "rusticators," city people seeking simpler country pleasures, came by steamship for entire summers of hiking, sailing, and painting by the sea. Those early lodges were replaced by grander hotels and Gilded Age homes, and Bar Harbor became a favorite retreat of the East Coast elite. By the turn of the 20th century, some of those landowners began to set aside large tracts of land for public use, then finally turned the land over to the federal government for the 1919 creation of the first national park east of the Mississippi River.

It remains an extraordinary place, with rugged mountains, beaches, and headlands so tightly packed they can be explored in a single day. Acadia is glorious in the summer sunshine, but it's equally entrancing when thick fog creeps across the water, isolating the island into a world of its own. One vibrant town and a handful of scattered communities are interwoven with the park land, so your experience in Acadia can be as luxurious, or remote, as you choose.

Planning Your Time

Mount Desert Island is 108 square miles, and accounting for winding roads and slow-moving traffic, it can take quite a while to drive from one side to the other. When visiting, then, it's worth choosing one of the two sides as a home base: Opt for Bar Harbor for great access to kid-friendly activities, shops, and restaurants, or sleep on the western "quiet side" to escape the crowds. From spring to fall, the free Island Explorer shuttle makes frequent loops of the island following eight different routes; if you'd like to explore car-free (highly recommended), choose accommodations on a shuttle route. As in other destinations on coastal Maine, the true high season is during the school vacation months of July and August. Many prices drop substantially in June and September, whose mild weather and sunshine also make them some of the prettiest months on the island. The leaves begin to change color towards the end of September, reaching a brilliant peak in mid-October. While the Park Loop Road is open year-round, many restaurants and hotels close their doors between November and May.

Highlights

★ **Driving the Park Loop Road:** Find ocean views and sheer cliffs around every corner of this 27-mile drive, which loops through the heart of Acadia National Park (page 137).

★ **Sunrise at Cadillac Mountain:** Catch first light from the tallest peak on the Eastern Seaboard (page 139).

★ **Carriage Roads:** Walk or bike this extraordinary network of car-free roads—or hop a horse-drawn carriage to a rocky summit (page 139).

★ **Tidepooling:** The sandbars and rocky inlets around Mount Desert Island trap diverse sea creatures every time the tide goes out (page 141).

★ **Bar Harbor's Ice Cream Shops:** Line up for cones and cups in this classic Vacationland town, where a pair of beloved ice cream shops serve everything from Moose Tracks to lobster ice cream (page 148).

Acadia National Park

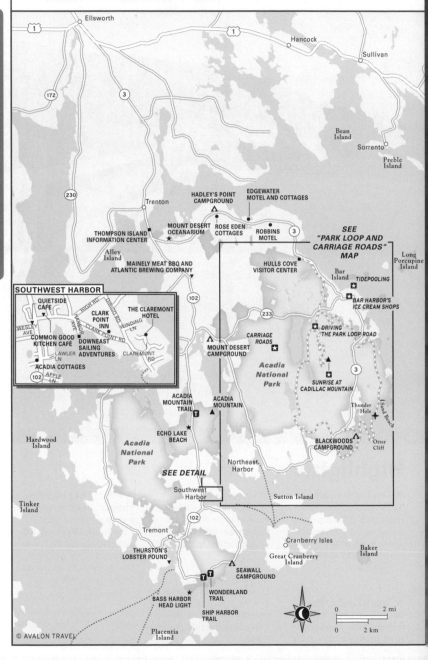

Ellsworth

Hancock

Sullivan

Bean Island

Sorrento

Preble Island

Trenton

HADLEY'S POINT CAMPGROUND

EDGEWATER MOTEL AND COTTAGES

MOUNT DESERT OCEANARIUM

ROSE EDEN COTTAGES

ROBBINS MOTEL

THOMPSON ISLAND INFORMATION CENTER

Alley Island

MAINELY MEAT BBQ AND ATLANTIC BREWING COMPANY

HULLS COVE VISITOR CENTER

SEE "PARK LOOP AND CARRIAGE ROADS" MAP

Bar Island

Long Porcupine Island

TIDEPOOLING

BAR HARBOR'S ICE CREAM SHOPS

SOUTHWEST HARBOR

QUIETSIDE CAFE

CLARK POINT INN

THE CLAREMONT HOTEL

WESLEY AVE

COMMON GOOD KITCHEN CAFE

DOWNEAST SAILING ADVENTURES

CLAREMONT RD

LAWLER LN

ACADIA COTTAGES

APPLE LN

CARRIAGE ROADS

DRIVING THE PARK LOOP ROAD

MOUNT DESERT CAMPGROUND

Acadia National Park

SUNRISE AT CADILLAC MOUNTAIN

Thunder Hole

Sand Beach

ACADIA MOUNTAIN TRAIL

ACADIA MOUNTAIN

ECHO LAKE BEACH

Hardwood Island

Acadia National Park

BLACKWOODS CAMPGROUND

Otter Cliff

SEE DETAIL

Northeast Harbor

Tinker Island

Southwest Harbor

Sutton Island

Tremont

Cranberry Isles

Baker Island

THURSTON'S LOBSTER POUND

Great Cranberry Island

SEAWALL CAMPGROUND

BASS HARBOR HEAD LIGHT

WONDERLAND TRAIL

SHIP HARBOR TRAIL

Placentia Island

© AVALON TRAVEL

0   2 mi

0   2 km

Best Accommodations

★ **Mount Desert Campground, Central Island:** Start your day with a chilly dip in Somes Sound at a campground that's perfectly placed at the center of the island (page 144).

★ **Acadia Cottages, Southwest Harbor:** Sweet cottages scattered through the woods make this a true "quiet side" destination (page 144).

★ **The Claremont Hotel, Southwest Harbor:** One of two surviving hotels from the elegant years of Gilded Age

getaways, this old-fashioned gem is a gentle time machine by the sea (page 144).

★ **Acacia House Inn, Bar Harbor:** Fabulous breakfasts, welcoming hosts, and comfortable rooms are a find in downtown Bar Harbor (page 149).

★ **Edgewater Motel and Cottages, Bar Harbor:** Strike a balance between town and country with a sweet cottage on a private beach (page 149).

Orientation

For many people, Acadia National Park and Mount Desert Island are synonymous, but the national park is a patchwork that covers much of the island and a bit of mainland coast. The bulk of the park territory is on the eastern side of Mount Desert Island, where the Park Loop Road circles some of the most dramatic scenery and best-known hiking trails. On the other side of Somes Sound is the "quiet side," good for less-frequented hikes. The remaining parkland is on the harder-to-reach Isle au Haut, and the Schoodic Peninsula, which is linked by passenger ferry to Bar Harbor.

Getting to Acadia National Park

Driving from Coastal Maine
175 miles, 3 hours

Coastal Maine's **Route 1,** which you can take almost the entire way up to Acadia National Park, passes through **pretty villages** and **forests,** occasionally breaking out into **shoreline views.** Sections of this road, especially from **Rockland** to **Lincolnville** and at the **Penobscot Narrows Bridge,** are very scenic, and there are plenty of places to stop along

the way for window-shopping and walks along the ocean. For this drive, take Route 1 all the way to Ellsworth, turning right onto High Street in town to stay on Route 1, then continue straight for **Route 3,** which crosses the **Trenton Bridge** onto Mount Desert Island and into **Bar Harbor** (190 mi, 4.25 hrs).

While Route 1 is undeniably lovely, it's also **notoriously congested** and may be worth avoiding on crowded weekends. Without accounting for traffic, using the inland interstate highway saves about an hour. When traffic is at its worst, it would be easy to spend an additional two hours sitting in Route 1 **traffic jams** in **Wiscasset** and **Camden.** If you're headed straight to Acadia from destinations between the Kennebunks and Bath, you can avoid frequent congestion by following the quicker, less-trafficked I-95 (and I-295). This route passes mostly through thick forest, missing the towns and harbors along Route 1, but it's worth considering on busy weekends and during high season when traffic slows to a crawl.

To follow this inland route from **Portland** (175 mi, 3 hrs) or **Kennebunkport** (205 mi, 3.5 hrs), travel north on **I-295** until it merges with **I-95 North** in **Gardiner** ($5 toll, cash only). Stay on I-95 for **79 miles,** then take Exit

Best Restaurants

★ **Jordan Pond House, Acadia National Park:** Steaming popovers and strawberry jam with a view are a long-standing tradition at Acadia National Park's only restaurant (page 142).

★ **Common Good Kitchen Café, Southwest Harbor:** While it lacks the dramatic setting of Jordan Pond House, the popovers shine at this nonprofit café on a quiet side street (page 143).

★ **Thurston's Lobster Pound, Bernard:** Get all the fixings and a million-dollar view at this longtime favorite near a sheltered harbor (page 143).

★ **2 Cats, Bar Harbor:** Find a spot on the shady porch to enjoy the best breakfast on the island (page 147).

★ **Terrace Grille at the Bar Harbor Inn, Bar Harbor:** Tuck into a lobster dinner on a sunny patio, then nibble blueberry pie as the sun sets (page 147).

182A in Bangor to merge onto **I-395 East.** After 4.7 miles, merge onto **Route 1A East** at Exit 6A. Follow **Route 1A** as it changes into **Route 3** in Ellsworth, then crosses the **Trenton Bridge** onto Mount Desert Island and into **Bar Harbor.**

Driving from New Hampshire's White Mountains
215 miles, 4 hours

Several routes link **Conway, New Hampshire,** with Mount Desert Island, on roads that wind through Maine's **deep, inland forest.** The most straightforward way to reach the coast is to take **Route 113 East** from Conway, turning right in Fryeburg, Maine, for **Route 113 South.** In Brownfield, you'll turn left on **Route 160 North,** which merges into **Route 117 North** in Denmark. Follow signs and turn right to stay on Route 117, then make another right onto **Route 302 East.** You'll next turn left onto **Route 11 North** (watch closely for signs, as the route zigzags for the 10 miles you'll be on it) before turning right onto **North Raymond Road,** then left onto Cleve Tripp Road after 1.7 miles, then right onto Range Hill Road after 1.3 miles. Next, turn left onto **Carpenter Road/Route 122,** then right at Poland Spring Road to stay on Route 122. Make a left onto Washington Street, then merge onto **I-95 North** (toll $1.75, cash only).

Stay on I-95 for about **106 miles,** then take Exit 182A in Bangor to merge onto **I-395 East.** After 4.7 miles, merge onto **Route 1A East** at Exit 6A. Follow **Route 1A** as it changes into **Route 3** in Ellsworth, then crosses the **Trenton Bridge** onto Mount Desert Island and into **Bar Harbor.**

Getting There by Air, Train, or Bus
Air
It's relatively easy to reach Bar Harbor without wheels of your own. **Cape Air** (a JetBlue affiliate) and **Pen Air** offer direct flights from Boston to **Bar Harbor-Hancock County Airport** (www.bhbairport.com); during its months of operation between June and mid-October, the **Island Explorer** (www.exploreacadia.com) shuttle has free service from the airport to Bar Harbor. Hertz and Enterprise both offer car rentals at the airport.

Train
Amtrak's **Downeaster line** (800/872-7245, www.amtrakdowneaster.com) runs from Boston along the coast as far as Brunswick, where it's possible to rent

One Day in Acadia National Park

Morning
Ambitious visitors can rise in the dark for a predawn pilgrimage to **Cadillac Mountain,** where sunrise reveals thick forests, remote islands, and granite peaks. Wait out the crowds for a quiet walk around the short **Summit Loop** before descending into Bar Harbor for a well-deserved stack of Maine blueberry pancakes and coffee at the quirky **2 Cats.**

Afternoon
Take a stroll around town to pick up a picnic lunch for a day in the park, then get your bearings with a scenic drive around

Park Loop Road, stopping for views and time on the beach. Leave your vehicle behind in the afternoon and explore the **carriage roads,** 47 miles of car-free bliss: Walk, bike, or ride a horse-drawn carriage to sweeping views of the mountainous interior, hulking granite bridges, and hidden streams.

Evening
Head to the quiet side of the island for an early dinner at **Thurston's Lobster Pound,** then take in sunset on the water at the nearby **Bass Harbor Head Light.**

a car or connect with a twice daily bus service to Bangor on **Concord Coach Lines** (800/639-3317, www.concordcoachlines.com).

Bus
Greyhound (800/231-2222, www.greyhound.com) offers bus service to Bangor from Brunswick and Portland, as does **Concord Coach Lines** (800/639-3317, www.concordcoachlines.com). From Bangor, **Downeast Transportation** (207/667-5796, www.downeasttrans.org) operates an afternoon bus to Bar Harbor on Mondays and Fridays from the Concord Coach station. You can also take the **Bar Harbor-Bangor Shuttle** van service (207/479-5911, www.barharborshuttle.com, $45, advance reservation required).

Visiting the Park

Entrances
Because of the patchwork way Acadia National Park was stitched together, driving around Mount Desert Island means passing in and out of park territory, often without notice. The only real gateways to the park are the kiosks at the on-ramps to Park Loop Road, where you'll be asked to

present your pass; otherwise, leave it displayed in your car (park rangers suggest that cyclists and motorcyclists carry their pass with them on hikes).

Park Passes and Fees
From May to October, the entrance fee for a private vehicle seating 15 people or fewer is $25. Motorcycles with one or two passengers pay $20, cyclists and pedestrians pay $12 each, and individuals 15 years old and younger are admitted free of charge. Most passes are valid for seven days; annual passes to Acadia National Park are $50, while an Interagency Annual Pass is $80 and covers all National Park Service and Forest Service entrance fees. Active military, people with disabilities, and U.S. fourth-grade students are eligible for a free Interagency Annual Pass; a lifetime interagency pass is available to seniors for $10. Passes are sold at all park visitors centers, campgrounds, and information booths, but for trips during peak season, it's worth purchasing online to avoid lines (www.yourpassnow.com).

Visitors Centers
As Route 3 crosses the Mount Desert Narrows, the small **Thompson Island Information Center** (mid-May-mid-Oct.

daily 8:30am-5:30pm) is on the left, and it's a useful stop for passes and maps if you're making a beeline to a trail or campground on the west side of the island. Otherwise, keep going to **Hulls Cove Visitor Center** (Rte. 3, 207/288-3338, Apr.-mid-June daily 8:30am-4:30pm, mid-June-Aug. daily 8:30am-6pm, Sept.-Oct. daily 8:30am-4:30pm), which has several exhibits orienting visitors to Acadia's natural and cultural history, including a 15-minute film about the park. It's also possible to sign up for guided naturalist and history programs here; multiple ranger-led programs are held each day throughout the summer in Acadia National Park, from walks and demonstrations to outdoor art lessons. Many of these are free; for more information, visit the events webpage (www.nps.gov/acad/planyourvisit).

Reservations

Reservations are essential for the two campgrounds—Blackwoods and Seawall—inside the national park, which can be made through the **National Recreation Reservation Service** (877/444-8777, www.recreation.gov). A small number of sites in each campground is set aside for day-of arrivals with no reservations; call each location first thing in the morning to inquire about openings, though sites don't become available every day. When visiting the island during school vacations, it's important to reserve in advance almost everywhere, but there are many rooms on the island, and it's generally possible to find something during shoulder seasons.

Information and Services

While there are no markets, banks, or other services within Acadia National Park itself, they can be found in nearby **Bar Harbor,** or in **Southwest Harbor** on the western side of the island. Southwest Harbor has two **banks,** a small **market,** and a **public library** (338 Main St., Southwest Harbor, 207/244-7065, www.

swhplibary.org, Mon.-Tues. and Thurs.-Fri. 9am-5pm, Wed. 9am-8pm, Sat. 9am-1pm) with free **Internet access.**

Getting Around

While a car is convenient for reaching less-frequented trailheads, and for early morning trips up Cadillac Mountain, limited parking and congestion during busy months make it worth parking your vehicle and exploring on public transport. Late June-early October, the free, convenient **Island Explorer** (207/667-5796, www.exploreacadia.com) makes it easy to get around Acadia without a car. The fleet of propane-powered buses follows eight fixed routes all over the island and on the Schoodic Peninsula, and covers most of Park Loop Road and all the villages, hotels, campgrounds, and trailheads. While there are automatic stops at many of the most notable destinations, drivers will stop to let you out whenever it's safe. Likewise, many hotels can recommend spots to flag down passing buses, even if there's not an official stop nearby.

To see the only part of Acadia National Park that's on the mainland, take the **Bar Harbor Ferry** (Bar Harbor Inn Pier, 7 Newport Dr., 207/288-2984, www.bar-harborferry.com, late June-Sept., round-trip tickets $24 adults, $14 children under 12, $75 family) to the tiny town of **Winter Harbor** on the **Schoodic Peninsula.**

Even more so than other destinations in New England, this is an excellent place to have a bicycle, as the slow-moving traffic on Park Loop Road and extensive network of car-free carriage roads are ideal for riders of all skill levels. If you'd like to combine shuttling with bicycling, note the Island Explorer buses have racks that accommodate up to six bikes, but popular routes (particularly afternoon return trips from Jordan Pond) can fill up quickly. For a better chance of catching a ride with your bike, look up the schedule for the **Island Explorer Bicycle Express** bus, which has a trailer that fits 12 bikes.

To take in the main sites in 2.5-3 hours, **Acadia National Park Tours** (207/288-0300, www.acadiatours.com, $30 adults, $17.50 children 12 and under) runs a bus contracted with the NPS to give sightseeing tours of Park Loop Road. The 2.5-hour narrated trip includes three 15-minute stops to stretch your legs and snap photos, and tickets can be purchased from **Testa's Restaurant** (53 Main St., Bar Harbor, 207/288-3327, daily 8am-9pm).

Sights and Recreation

Park Loop Road

Passing headlands, trailheads, beaches, and stunning views of Penobscot Bay, the 27-mile Park Loop Road winds through some of Acadia's finest scenery. Traffic moves one way—clockwise—from the main entrance near Hulls Cove Visitor Center to Jordan Pond, then two-way traffic completes the loop and heads all the way up to the summit of Cadillac Mountain. Alternate entrances, where passes are also checked, are at Sieur des Monts, south of Bar Harbor; Sand Beach; Stanley Brook, by Seal Harbor; and off Route 233, just north of Cadillac Mountain Road. For much of the one-way section, parking is allowed in the right-hand lane, which makes it easy to spot a view and pull over for a closer look. It also means the road is often full of unexpected parked cars, pedestrians, and cyclists (along with the occasional moose), so it's important to take the Park Loop Road at a careful pace. There are also several low bridges which may be a problem for some RVs—the lowest of these is the 10-foot by four-inch span across the Stanley Brook Entrance.

★ Driving the Park Loop Road

Driving the whole road at once is a nice way to get an overview of the park, but allow plenty of time to stop for picture-taking, tidepooling, walking, and otherwise exploring. From the main entrance

at Hulls Cove, the road rises steeply to **Sieur de Monts,** where the small **Wild Gardens of Acadia** recreates typical habitats found on Mount Desert Island from heath to coniferous forest, with over 400 species of indigenous plants.

One of the finest places to swim on the whole island is **Sand Beach,** where a parking lot and short walking trail lead to a pleasant stretch of beach and **Great Head.** Along the rocky coast that follows, be sure to stop at **Thunder Hole,** a deep inlet with a submerged cavern that can roar and send water 40 feet into the air when waves hit just right; for the best show, try to visit two hours before high tide.

The horizon opens back up at **Otter Cliff,** a 110-foot granite wall that's one of the tallest coastal headlands this side of Rio de Janeiro. After the turn back inland, the **Jordan Pond House** is a traditional stopping-off point for afternoon tea and hot popovers with a view of a glacial tarn and distant mountains. Finally, a side road rises through a series of switchbacks to the park's grand attraction, the road to the top of **Cadillac Mountain.**

Cadillac Mountain

At 1,528 feet, this rounded granite mountain is the highest point on the United States' Atlantic Seaboard. The summit is gouged with deep, north-south scratches left by retreating glaciers, and leathery, subalpine plants sprout from the rocky crevices. Even on a summer day, it's easy to imagine the icy winds that howl across the mountain in the winter, stunting spruce and pitch pine trees into gnarled miniatures. In the booming tourist years of the late 19th century, a narrow-gauge cog railway was built to the top of the mountain, much like the railway up Mount Washington, but those tracks are long gone. These days, visitors hike or drive to the summit, where there's a gentle, scenic trail and views across Penobscot Bay.

Park Loop and Carriage Roads

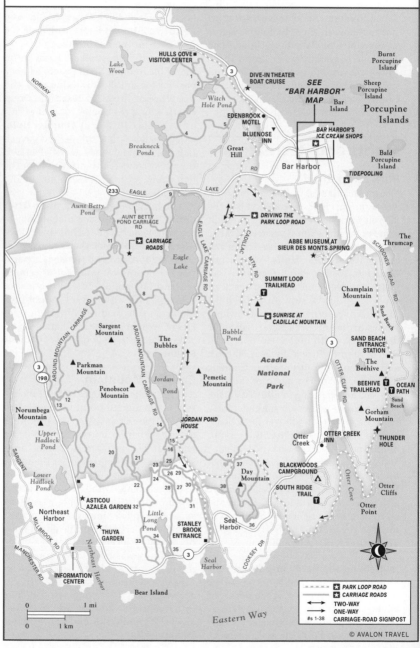

Lake Wood

NORWAY DR

HULLS COVE VISITOR CENTER

3

DIVE-IN THEATER BOAT CRUISE

SEE "BAR HARBOR" MAP

Burnt Porcupine Island

Sheep Porcupine Island

Porcupine Islands

Bar Island

Witch Hole Pond

1
2
3

EDENBROOK MOTEL

5

BLUENOSE INN

BAR HARBOR'S ICE CREAM SHOPS

Bar Harbor

Bald Porcupine Island

TIDEPOOLING

Breakneck Ponds

4

Great Hill

RD

233 EAGLE   LAKE

6
9

Aunt Betty Pond

AUNT BETTY POND CARRIAGE RD

11   CARRIAGE ROADS

Eagle Lake

The Thrumcap

SCHOONER HEAD RD

DRIVING THE PARK LOOP ROAD

ABBE MUSEUM AT SIEUR DES MONTS SPRING

CADILLAC MTN RD

SUMMIT LOOP TRAILHEAD

Champlain Mountain

EAGLE LAKE CARRIAGE RD

8

7

SUNRISE AT CADILLAC MOUNTAIN

Sand Beach

AROUND-MOUNTAIN CARRIAGE RD

10

Sargent Mountain

The Bubbles

Bubble Pond

Acadia National Park

SAND BEACH ENTRANCE STATION

3

The Beehive

Parkman Mountain

Jordan Pond

Pemetic Mountain

OTTER CLIFF RD

BEEHIVE TRAILHEAD   OCEAN PATH

3
198

Penobscot Mountain

AROUND-MOUNTAIN CARRIAGE RD

14

JORDAN POND HOUSE

Sand Beach

Gorham Mountain

Norumbega Mountain

12
13

15
16

Otter Creek

OTTER CREEK INN

THUNDER HOLE

Upper Hadlock Pond

20

21

23 25
26 29
28 27 30

17

37

Day Mountain

38

BLACKWOODS CAMPGROUND

Otter Cove

19

22

24

SOUTH RIDGE TRAIL

Otter Cliffs

Lower Hadlock Pond

ASTICOU AZALEA GARDEN 32

Little Long Pond

31

Seal Harbor

Otter Point

SARGENT DR

Northeast Harbor

THUYA GARDEN

33

34

STANLEY BROOK ENTRANCE

35

3

36

COOKSEY DR

MILLBROOK RD

MANCHESTER RD

INFORMATION CENTER

Northeast Harbor

Bear Island

Seal Harbor

Eastern Way

0   1 mi
0   1 km

PARK LOOP ROAD
CARRIAGE ROADS
TWO-WAY
ONE-WAY
#s 1-38 CARRIAGE-ROAD SIGNPOST

© AVALON TRAVEL

★ Sunrise at Cadillac Mountain

Watching the sun come up from the peak of Cadillac Mountain is an iconic part of the Acadia National Park experience. In the fall and winter months it's the first place in the United States to see the sunrise.

The 3.5-mile **Cadillac Mountain Road,** off the Park Loop Road, winds up the mountain, which is how most visitors arrive in the early morning hours, though there are also several walking trails to the summit. The most scenic of these is the **South Ridge Trail,** a 7-mile round-trip hike that starts near Blackwoods Campground and climbs 1,050 feet at a steady, moderate pace. If you're hoping to catch the sunrise after hiking the trail, plan to bring lights and warm clothing, and allow 2-4 hours each way, depending on your hiking speed.

Although it is often crowded, it's possible—especially outside of high season—to find yourself alone on the summit as dawn breaks over Penobscot Bay, lighting up islands and deep forests. A more likely scenario involves clusters of chatting families and several sleepy hikers who started up the peak in the middle of the night. Inevitably, though, the crowd begins to thin as soon as the sky lights up, and one of the nicest times to enjoy the short 0.3-mile **Summit Loop** is when everyone else heads to Bar Harbor for breakfast.

★ Carriage Roads

Concerned that Mount Desert Island would be destroyed with the introduction of automobiles, John D. Rockefeller Jr. started building a vast network of roads in 1913, determined they would remain closed to motorized traffic. Today, the 47 miles of crushed-stone roads are perfect for walking and biking as well as a favorite destination of cross-country skiers in the winter. The roads curve gently through a forest of birch, beech, and maple trees, over beautifully crafted granite bridges, and through tunnels and arches, perfect for exploration by bicycle. Numbered wooden signposts at each intersection make it easy to find your way around. A park map, available at the visitors center, is essential for exploring the carriage roads, which continually intersect with the Park Loop Road and other roads on the island. Two of the most popular **parking areas** for accessing the carriage roads are at Sieur de Monts and the Jordan Pond House.

To really immerse yourself in Rockefeller's vision of Acadia, though, take an actual carriage ride: **Carriages of Acadia** (Wildwood Stables, Park Loop Rd., 207/276-3622, tours from $20 adults, $12 children 6-12, and $7 children 4-5) offers a range of jaunts in horse-drawn carriages, including tours of stone bridges, trips to Jordan Pond for popovers, and a climb to the top of Day Mountain.

Thuya Garden and Asticou Azalea Garden

This pair of tranquil gardens is a must-see for plant lovers and a convenient side trip from the Park Loop Road.

Thuya Garden (Rte. 3, Northeast Harbor, www.gardenpreserve.org, May-Oct. daily 7am-7pm, trails and garden accessible during the off-season weather permitting, $5 requested donation) is in the semiformal English style, with butterfly gardens, pavilions, and a pretty reflecting pool. To approach the gardens from Park Loop Road, head southwest and continue on Stanley Brook Road, turning right onto Route 3. A sign on the harbor side of Route 3 marks a small parking area opposite the Asticou Terrace Trail, whose great, granite switchbacks climb 0.25 mile to the Thuya Garden gates, passing a trailside shelter and lookout.

For Asticou Azalea Garden parking, head north on Route 3 and turn right on Route 198. Beginning in late May, the **Asticou Azalea Garden** (Rte. 3 and Rte. 198, Northeast Harbor, www.

gardenpreserve.org, May-Oct. daily during daylight hours, free) is a riot of bright blooming rhododendrons and azaleas that give way to irises and water lilies in July and August. Its design celebrates attributes of Japanese gardens—circular paths, garden rooms, and carefully tended views—and it was built in 1956 using plants from the Bar Harbor garden of Beatrix Farrand, a groundbreaking gardener who was a founding member of the American Society of Landscape Architects.

To visit the gardens on the Island Explorer shuttle, ask the driver on Route #5 or Route #6 to drop you at either location, and flag a passing bus to continue onward. It is possible to connect the two gardens on foot by taking the sidewalk on Route 3 from the Asticou Azalea Garden to the Asticou Terrace Trail.

Bass Harbor Head Light

Set on the edge of a rocky sea cliff, the scenic **Bass Harbor Head Light** (Bass Harbor Head Rd., off 102A) is at the southern extreme of Mount Desert Island. The lighthouse itself is a private residence, but it's a scenic spot to catch the morning light. For the classic photograph of the lighthouse above the rocks, take the staircase at the eastern end of the parking lot and shoot back toward the cliffs.

Hiking

There is a lifetime of hiking available in Acadia National Park, and the park rangers are experts at helping you find just the right one. The following are a few favorites on Mount Desert Island; for all of these hikes, it's essential to bring an **Acadia National Park map** (available for free at all information centers). While most of the trails are easy to follow, the many trails that intersect within the park

Top to bottom: Bass Harbor Head Light; carved door at the gatehouse to Thuya Garden; an elegant stone bridge on the carriage roads.

would be impossible to navigate without a map.

Sure-footed walkers can head up one of the island's "iron rung" trails, where the paths are supplemented by metal bars set directly in the granite. The strenuous **Beehive Trail** is one of these, with exposed, stony sections along the south face of the 520-foot peak that make the hike seem longer than its 1.6 miles round-trip. To reach the trailhead, leave your car in the Sand Beach parking lot (which is also a stop on the Island Explorer shuttle bus), and cross the Park Loop Road.

One of the easiest trails to hop on for a leisurely walk is **Ocean Path,** which follows the Park Loop Road for about two miles between the Sand Beach parking lot and Otter Cliff, with lots of ocean views and rocks for scrambling.

The "quiet side" of Mount Desert Island has plenty of hikes as well, and these are often less busy than the eastern trails. On the southern edge of the island, the 1.3-mile round-trip **Ship Harbor Trail** is a good place to walk through scenic coastal forest offering views along a deep inlet, and the 1.5-mile round-trip **Wonderland Trail** is just up the road, with great tidepools on a rocky beach, and a jumble of granite boulders. For the trailheads, drive south from Southwest Harbor, and turn left onto Route 102A to follow the coast. The clearly marked Wonderland Trailhead is 4.1 miles past the turnoff onto Route 102A, and the Ship Harbor Trailhead is a short distance further. Both have parking lots.

For fabulous views to Somes Sound and the ocean, the 1.8-mile round-trip walk up **Acadia Mountain** is a favorite; with 500 feet of elevation gain, it's an easier peak to hike than Cadillac Mountain. The clearly marked parking lot for the Acadia Mountain trail is on Route 102, 3.1 miles north of Southwest Harbor.

Biking

By far the best place to ride a bike in Acadia is on the network of **carriage trails**—the crushed stone surface is well suited to mountain bike tires and medium-width road bike tires, and it's a joy to explore the island away from car traffic. A *Carriage Road User's Map* is available from the Park Service, and bicycles can be rented in Bar Harbor from **Acadia Bike** (48 Cottage St., 800/526-8615, www.acadiabike.com, $23 full day, $18 half day).

One favorite activity on the **Schoodic Peninsula** is cycling the scenic roads, which tend to be less trafficked than those on Mount Desert Island. Options are endless, but a pair of loops covering 12 or 24 miles is a good starting point (www.exploremaine.org/bike/downeast).

★ Tidepooling

Fluctuating water levels strand sea creatures in rocky pools all along the Mount Desert Island coast, but finding them involves careful planning. Pick up a copy of the *Acadia Weekly* or stop by any of the ranger stations for information on the tides, which range between 10 and 15 feet around the island. The best time to spot wildlife is 1.5 hours before and after extreme low tide.

When searching for tidepools, bring a pair of shoes with good traction that you don't mind getting wet and sandy, and pay close attention to water levels, as some rocky outcroppings can be stranded by rising water.

One favorite way to explore is by walking to **Bar Island** from downtown Bar Harbor (follow Bridge St.); for 1.5 hours before and after low tide, a 0.8-mile gravel bar that leads from the end of Bridge Street is exposed. There are walking trails on the tiny island, and the outgoing tide usual leaves some sea stars and crabs in sandy tidepools along the bar.

On the southwest side of the island, **Ship Harbor** and **Wonderland Trails** are also good choices, with plenty of nooks and crannies to trap interesting things in the intertidal zone. **Ranger-led tidepool programs** (www.nps.gov/acad/

planyourvisit/calendar.htm) are held at Ship Harbor and Sand Beach in July and August. Drive south from Southwest Harbor and turn left onto Route 102A to find the well-marked Wonderland Trailhead 4.1 miles past the turnoff onto Route 102A, and the Ship Harbor Trailhead a short distance farther. Both have parking lots.

Paddling

Get a harbor seal's view of the island's rugged coast by touring in a sea kayak. A handful of well-regarded operators lead trips open to paddlers of all skill levels. Visit the remoter western side of the island with **National Park Sea Kayak Tours** (39 Cottage St., Bar Harbor, 800/347-0940, www.acadiakayak.com, $48-52), which plans its trips through Western Bay and Blue Hill Bay so you head downwind. Tours last 2.5-3 hours. **Acadia Park Kayak Tours** (Bar Harbor, 207/266-1689, www.acadiaparkkayak.com, $45-60) launches right in downtown Bar Harbor and schedules exciting nighttime stargazing tours. Tours run 3.5-4 hours.

Swimming

There are two beaches in Acadia with summer lifeguards. The water at **Sand Beach,** just off the Park Loop Road, stays in the high 50s throughout the summer, but that's warm enough for plenty of visitors; come here for saltwater, views, and a beach vacation atmosphere. Find (somewhat) warmer water at **Echo Lake Beach,** on the west side of Route 102 between Somesville and Southwest Harbor. The lake floor drops gradually from the shoreline, making this a good choice for families with children.

Boating

If Maine's lobstermen had a celebrity spokesperson, it would have to be Captain John Nicolai of *Lulu* **Lobster Boat Ride** (55 West St., Bar Harbor, 207/963-2341, www.lululobsterboat.com, two-hr tour $35 adults, $32 seniors and U.S. military,

$20 children 6-12), who keeps up a great running patter about the lobstering life (and the life of a lobster). Come April-early June to spot adorable baby seals lolling around near Egg Rock Lighthouse.

By far one of the best things to do on the island with nature-loving kids is head out on a **Dive-In Theater Boat Cruise** (105 Eden St., Bar Harbor, 207/288-3483, www.divered.com, $42 adults, $37 seniors, $32 children 6-11, $16 children under 6) with "Diver Ed." Ed (and his sidekick "mini Ed") suit up in scuba gear equipped with underwater microphones and cameras. The crowd on decks can follow along, then Ed reappears with underwater creatures that kids can touch before sending them back to the ocean floor. The boat departs from the College of the Atlantic, where you can park for free in the North Lot.

A classic style of sailboat along the East Coast is the Friendship sloop, a graceful, gaff-rigged boat that originated in Friendship, Maine, in the late 19th century. Friendship sloop *Surprise,* operated by **Downeast Sailing Adventures** (Cranberry Island Dock, Southwest Harbor, 207/288-2216, www.downeast-sail.com, two-hr sail $35-50 pp, private sail $200 up to six people), has been sailing the Maine coast since 1964 and offers an intimate, beautiful way to experience it.

Food

The Jordan Pond House is the only restaurant in the park proper, but there are places to eat scattered around the island, and some make great destinations unto themselves.

Enjoying popovers and tea on the lawn at ★ **Jordan Pond House** (2928 Park Loop Rd., Seal Harbor, 207/276-3316, www.acadiajordanpondhouse.com, daily 11am-9pm, $7-25) is a classic Acadia experience: The warm, oversized pastries are perfect with melting butter and house-made strawberry jam, and the restaurant has stunning views of the glacial tarn with the granite "bubbles" in the background. The restaurant itself was rebuilt in 1979 and the interior is fairly charmless, but the afternoon tea experience is delightful and should not be missed.

But Jordan Pond House doesn't completely own the popover world on Mount Desert Island. While it has no views to speak of, everyone agrees ★ **Common Good Kitchen Café** (19 Clark Point Rd., Southwest Harbor, 207/266-2733, www. commongoodsoupkitchen.org, May-Oct. daily 7:30am-11am, by donation) would win hands down in a popover-to-popover showdown. A simple menu of oatmeal, coffee, and popovers is served by volunteers on a sunny patio, with all proceeds going to a meal delivery service for disadvantaged islanders during the winter months.

With a location between Route 102 and Route 3, **Mainely Meat BBQ** (15 Knox Rd., Bar Harbor, 207/288-9200, www.atlanticbrewing.com, May-Oct. daily 11:30amclose, $11-19) is the convenient and casual on-site restaurant of **Atlantic Brewing Company** (May.-Oct. daily 10am-6pm, free tastings). Large portions of barbecue basics come with coleslaw, potato salad, and baked beans; ribs are a favorite for many visitors. Tours of the brewery are at 2pm, 3pm, and 4pm daily during peak season, and are capped at 25 people.

A menu of sandwiches, seafood, and pizza served in a family-run diner setting makes the **Quietside Café** (360 Main St., Southwest Harbor, 207/244-9444, Mon.-Sat. 11am-10pm, Sun. 11am-8pm, hours vary in off-season, $6-12) a mainstay for laid-back lunches, dinners, and ice cream. The butter lobster stew is a favorite, and the blueberry pie à la mode also gets rave reviews.

If this lobster-loving author had to choose just one of the many lobster places to eat in Maine, it would be ★ **Thurston's Lobster Pound** (9 Thurston Rd., Bernard,

207/244-7600, www.thurstonforlobster. com, daily 11am-9pm, $7-30), just outside the park off Route 102 in Bernard. Consider arriving early or late to avoid the line, which can stretch far out the door, but it's worth making an evening trip to the quiet side for a traditional lobster dinner or an overstuffed lobster roll (perhaps followed by sunset at the Bass Harbor Head Light). The restaurant has two sides: Line up on the right to order a whole lobster dinner or sit in the main dining area, or head to the left to sit in the bar, where the rest of the menu is available. You can also sit in the bar with a lobster dinner—it just needs to be ordered in that long line. It's not an unpleasant wait, though, as it's fascinating to watch the servers run in and out with great bags of clams and lobsters to drop in the industrial-size boiler outside. A casual atmosphere, local beers on tap, and views of the pretty harbor make this a true gem.

Accommodations and Camping

A couple of campgrounds are within Acadia National Park's boundaries, but there are no hotels or inns within the park itself; lodging listings below cover places to stay on the "quiet side" that are still convenient to park activities and sights.

Camping

Only two of the campgrounds on Mount Desert Island are inside the park proper, set on the southernmost part of Mount Desert Island on opposite sides of Somes Sound. It's worth reserving either of these far in advance for busy times, but each sets aside a small number of non-reservable sites. Call first thing in the morning to check availability. **Blackwoods Campground** is right on Park Loop Road (Rte. 3, 207/288-3274, www.nps. gov/acad, May-Oct. $30; Apr./Nov. $15;

free, primitive sites available Dec.-Mar.), adjacent to an Island Explorer shuttle stop and convenient to Bar Harbor and Cadillac Mountain. The 306 forested sites often fill up; the campground can feel busy and noisy during peak season. No hookups or showers, but free firewood is provided, and a spot just outside the entrance offers hot, coin-operated showers. Or set up your tent on the "quiet side" at **Seawall Campground** (Rte. 102A, 207/244-3600, www.nps.gov/acad, late May-early Sept., $22-30), 18 miles from Bar Harbor, and a prime location for beautiful sunsets on the shore as well as access to less-trafficked hikes and Bass Harbor Head Light. Like Blackwoods, Seawall has no hookups or showers, but it offers coin-operated showers and a general store five minutes away. Many cell phones get no reception on this side of the island.

The privately owned ★ **Mount Desert Campground** (516 Sound Dr., off Rte. 2, 207/244-3710, www.mountdesertcampground.com, late May-early Oct., $33-59) splits the difference, with a superb location at the head of Somes Sound that's the perfect jumping-off point for exploring all of the island. Tent sites roll right up to the water (pricing varies depending on the season and proximity of the site to the water), hookups are available, and the campground rents all kinds of boards and boats for getting in the sound, as well as a launching ramp for private boats. Bathhouses have free hot showers, and the small, convivial "gathering place" offers wireless Internet, snacks, coffee, and ice cream.

There's a summer camp atmosphere at **Hadley's Point Campground** (33 Hadley Point Rd., off Rte. 3, 207/288-4808, www.hadleyspoint.com, mid-May-mid-Oct., tents $26-29, hookups $35-46, cabins $55-80), making it a good choice for families, though tent sites are set close together and don't provide much privacy. A heated swimming pool, coin-operated showers, laundry facilities, a playground, and

wireless Internet are available. The campground is on the Island Explorer shuttle bus route for easy access to Bar Harbor, and there's a public beach within easy walking distance. The rustic, tidy cabins have private bathrooms, three beds, and a fire pit (bring your own linens).

$100-150

Completely surrounded by national park land, the **Otter Creek Inn** (47 Otter Creek Dr., 207/288-5151, www.ottercreekme.com, May-Oct., $124-180) is a perfect place (almost) for non-campers to stay in Acadia. The rooms and cabins are simple but sufficient, and a continental breakfast is served in the attached market. Some guests have noted the rooms' thin walls, though the price, which drops below $100 outside of peak season, is hard to beat.

$150-250

The self-contained units at ★ **Acadia Cottages** (410 Main St., Southwest Harbor, 207/244-5388, www.acadia-cottages.com, $145-170) are simple and old-fashioned, but well-appointed kitchens, outdoor fire pits, and comfortable mattresses are a cut above other cabins on the island. Wooded grounds make these feel relatively private, and the cottages are walking distance from Southwest Harbor.

Views of Southwest Harbor and a friendly, hospitable atmosphere are the draws at **Clark Point Inn** (109 Clark Point Rd., Southwest Harbor, 207/244-9828, www.clarkpointinn.com, $169-239), which has five guest rooms cheerfully decorated in country style. Three-course breakfasts, afternoon cookies and snacks, and welcoming common spaces make this a favorite with adults-only guests.

Over $250

Perched on the end of Somes Sound, ★ **The Claremont Hotel** (22 Claremont Rd., Southwest Harbor, 207/244-5036, www.theclaremonthotel.com, inn $220-342, cottages $318-444) is an 1884 grande dame that rambles across a six-acre, waterfront property. The 24 rooms in the main house have been recently renovated, but are full of historic charm, their old-fashioned quirks left intact (which is not necessarily to everyone's taste). This feels like a glimpse of old Maine, and for afternoons on the porch, games of croquet on the perfectly trimmed lawn, and sunset drinks at a dockside bar, it remains a wonderful destination.

Bar Harbor

Times have changed since the first 19th-century "rusticators" came to Bar Harbor for society parties with wilderness views. The stunning landscape of forested islands is still there, but the town itself can feel overstuffed and kitschy, an ice cream-fueled frenzy of T-shirt shops and minigolf. Still, Bar Harbor is the "town" for Mount Desert Island, with restaurants, museums, services, and loads of places to stay. This is the jumping off point for many boat cruises and activities and a perfect foil to the quiet trails and mountaintops inside Acadia National Park.

Sights

Step into the world of Mount Desert Island's earliest locals at the **Abbe Museum,** which has two campuses focusing on modern-day and bygone Wabanaki lives. Visit the **Abbe Museum downtown location** (26 Mount Desert St., 207/388-2519, www.abbemusuem.org, May-Oct. daily 10am-5pm, call for off-season hours, $8 adults, $4 children 11-17, free 10 and under and Native Americans) for a stronger focus on today's Wabanaki, along with stories from the past and a few artifacts. Located inside Acadia National Park, the **Abbe Museum at Sieur des Monts Spring** (Sieur des Monts, Park Loop Road and Route 3, late May-mid-Oct. daily 10am-5pm, $3 adults, $1 children 11-17, free 10 and under and Native

Americans) is much smaller, but has fascinating artifacts and depictions of archaeological digs in the area. A ticket to Abbe Downtown also includes admission to the Sieur des Monts Spring venue, and the cost of the Abbe Museum at Sieur de Monts Spring ticket is deducted from the admission price if you visit the downtown location as well.

Small but interesting, the **Bar Harbor Historical Society Museum** (33 Ledgelawn Ave., 207/288-3807, www.bar-harborhistorical.org, June-Oct. Mon.-Sat. 1pm-4pm, by appt. in winter, free) has a remarkable collection of images from the town's Gilded Age heyday—think lots of full-length tennis skirts and boating parties. The 1916 building in which it's housed is as intriguing as the contents. It was built by Colonel and Louise Drexel Morell (who appear in stained glass windows on the 2nd floor). Louise was sister to Saint Katherine Drexel, who gave up her share of the family's considerable fortune to become a missionary in the American Southwest. She was a strong advocate for Native American and African American rights and was canonized in 2000.

Watch the ships come in and out of the harbor from Bar Harbor's gentle **Shore Path,** a paved walking trail that stretches 0.75 mile from the town pier to Wayman Lane. It's especially nice as a morning walk, when the harbor begins to flood with early sunshine.

Follow the life of a lobster from itsy-bitsy hatchling to full-grown, claw-snapping adult at **Mount Desert Oceanarium** (1351 Rte. 3, 207/288-5005, www.the-oceanarium.com, mid-May-late Oct. Mon.-Sat. 9am-5pm, $15 adults, $10 children), a bayside nature center with a lobster hatchery, live seals, and marsh trails. The museum tour, a series of three 30-minute presentations, is a bit long and stationary for active kids, but Audrey and David Mills have been talking lobsters for years and are a great source of info about Maine's marine ecology.

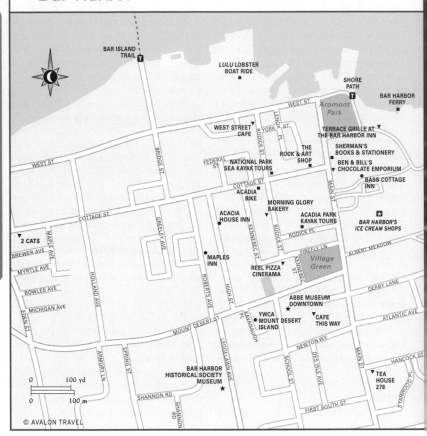

Bar Harbor

BAR ISLAND
TRAIL

LULU LOBSTER
BOAT RIDE

SHORE
PATH

BAR HARBOR
FERRY

WEST ST

Aromont
Park

WEST STREET
CAFE

YORK ST

LENOX PL

TERRACE GRILLE AT
THE BAR HARBOR INN

RODICK ST

THE
ROCK & ART
SHOP

SHERMAN'S
BOOKS & STATIONERY

FEDERAL
ST

NATIONAL PARK
SEA KAYAK TOURS

BEN & BILL'S
CHOCOLATE EMPORIUM

WEST ST

BRIDGE ST

COTTAGE ST

BASS COTTAGE
INN

ACADIA
BIKE

MORNING GLORY
BAKERY

MAIN ST

COTTAGE ST

GREELEY AVE

ACACIA
HOUSE INN

ACADIA PARK
KAYAK TOURS

RODICK PL

BAR HARBOR'S
ICE CREAM SHOPS

2 CATS

MAPLE AVE

BREWER AVE

KENNEBEC ST

RODICK ST

FIREFLY LN

ALBERT MEADOW

MYRTLE AVE

MAPLES
INN

REEL PIZZA
CINERAMA

KENNEBEC

Village
Green

HOLLAND AVE

BOWLES AVE

ROBERTS AVE

HIGH ST

DERBY LANE

MICHIGAN AVE

ABBE MUSEUM
DOWNTOWN

EDEN ST

MOUNT DESERT ST

KAVANAUGH
PL

YWCA
MOUNT DESERT
ISLAND

CAFE
THIS WAY

ATLANTIC AVE

ARMORY LN

SPRING ST

LEDGELAWN AVE

NEWTON WY

SCHOOL ST

DES ISLE AVE

MAIN ST

HANCOCK ST

STANWOOD PL

BAR HARBOR
HISTORICAL SOCIETY
MUSEUM

TEA
HOUSE
278

0   100 yd
0   100 m

SHANNON RD

SHANNON
RD

FIRST SOUTH ST

© AVALON TRAVEL

Entertainment and Events

After a day of hiking peaks and ocean swimming, **Reel Pizza Cinerama** (33 Kennebec Pl., 207/288-3811, www.reel-pizza.net, pizzas $14-23) beckons; the single-screen theater is stocked with comfy, mismatched couches and counter seats for settling in with pizza and beer. From the end of June through mid-August, the **Bar Harbor Town Band** (www.townband. org) plays hour-long concerts on the Village Green; shows are on Mondays and Thursdays at 8pm. Another summer tradition is heading to the **Great Room** lounge at the **Bluenose Inn** (90 Eden St.,

800/445-4077, www.barharborhotel. com), where pianist Bill Trowell plays laid-back favorites every night at 7pm from late May to October.

Shopping

Many of the shops in Bar Harbor sell variations on a theme—lobster and moose stuffed animals, T-shirts, Christmas ornaments. Find these along Main Street. Before you go on a wildlife expedition, stop by **Sherman's Books & Stationery** (56 Main St., 207/288-3161, www.sher-mans.com, daily 9am-10:30pm), which carries an exceptional selection of bird-watching and wildlife guides and trail maps in addition to a full stock of books and cards. Another fun stop is **The Rock & Art Shop** (13 Cottage St., 207/288-4800, www.therockandartshop.com, daily 9am-8pm, hours vary seasonally), which does have both rocks and art, but also stuffed fish, skulls, and other fascinating, odd treasures.

Food

In a bright, rambling home on the edge of downtown, ★ **2 Cats** (130 Cottage St., 207/288-2808, daily 7am-1pm, $4-9) is a funky gem and the best place for breakfast on the island. Simple breakfast classics like eggs Benedict and blueberry pancakes are done nicely, and the café's fresh, flaky biscuits come with a dreamy side of homemade strawberry butter. Come early to snag a spot on the deep, wraparound porch.

For fresh pastries, espresso, and sandwiches on bagels and house-made bread, **Morning Glory Bakery** (39 Rodick St., 207/288-3041, Mon.-Fri. 7am-5pm, Sat.-Sun. 8am-5pm, $3-12) is a longtime favorite. You'll find a few tables inside (and wireless Internet) at this casual, counterservice spot, but don't miss the back patio on sunny days, where comfy Adirondack chairs and a little garden await.

A menu of classic seafood options, salads, and pasta is surprisingly reasonable at this waterside spot, given that the ★ **Terrace Grille at the Bar Harbor Inn** (7 Newport Dr., 207/288-3351, www.barharborinn.com, daily 11:30am-dark, $12-30) has the best outdoor seating in town. Tables on the lawn and patio overlook the harbor and Bar Island, making this a great place to catch a sunset over a bowl of chowder or lobster stew. At $39, the lobster bake—a boiled lobster with chowder, clams, mussels, sides, and blueberry

Top to bottom: downtown Bar Harbor; Mount Desert Ice Cream; outdoor dining at the Terrace Grille at the Bar Harbor Inn.

pie—is an excellent deal for downtown Bar Harbor.

A quiet atmosphere, simple decor, and a pretty garden make **Tea House 278** (278 Main St., 207/288-2781, www. teahouse278.com, mid-May-early Oct. Wed.-Sat. 11am-7pm, Sun. 11am-5pm, $3-13) a respite from bustling Bar Harbor, and servers are trained in the traditional preparation of Chinese teas. A small menu of snack food includes tea eggs, sweets, nuts, and egg rolls.

Simple, sunny and laid-back, **West Street Cafe** (76 West St., 207/288-5242, www.weststreetcafe.com, daily 11am-8:30pm, $14-30) has a big menu of beef and chicken dinners, pastas, and seafood. The lunch menu of "Earlybird Specials" is served until 6pm, and an excellent value for an early dinner, especially the $20 lobster plate and $25 lobster dinner with chowder and blueberry pie.

It would be easy to miss **Cafe This Way** (14 Mt. Desert St., 207/288-4483, www. cafethisway.com, Tues.-Sat. 7am-11:30am and 5:30pm-9pm, Sun. 8am-1pm and 5:30pm-9pm, breakfast $6-12, dinner $19-28), a restaurant with art nouveau flair that's tucked down an alley between School and Main Streets. Breakfast omelets, burritos, and blueberry pancakes get raves, and a menu of grilled seafood and salads is full of fresh flavors. While most Bar Harbor kids' menus are identical lists of fried food and cheesy pasta, Cafe This Way stands out with small plates of grilled meat and seafood served with mashed potatoes and corn on the cob.

Farmers and artisans from around Penobscot Bay attend the **Eden Farmers Market** (YMCA, 21 Park St., mid-May-Oct. Sun. 9am-noon), which is a great place to find farm-fresh Maine blueberries in season.

★ Ice Cream Shops

There are two ice cream greats in downtown Bar Harbor: The granddaddy is **Ben & Bill's Chocolate Emporium** (66 Main St., 207/288-3281, www.benandbills.com,

daily 8am-11:30pm, $3-7), a candy store with a zillion flavors (including Maine lobster), big servings, and a landmark lobster sculpture out front that's a classic Bar Harbor selfie spot. The scoop-wielding young Turks of the waffle cone scene are at **Mount Desert Ice Cream** (7 Firefly Ln., 207/801-4001, www.mdiic. com, daily 11am-10pm, $3-7), where flavors range from Maine Sea Salt Caramel to Blueberry Sour Cream and Chocolate Wasabi. Not all the flavors are quite so offbeat—President Obama ordered a scoop of plain ol' coconut while visiting with his family in 2010.

Accommodations
Under $100

Seriously no frills, **Robbins Motel** (Rte. 3, 207/288-4659, www.acadia.net/robbins, May-mid-Oct., $55-65) features the rates of yesteryear and rooms to match. Amenities include cable TV, a pool, and wireless Internet, but the overall experience is pretty bare bones.

Right in the heart of Bar Harbor, the **YWCA Mount Desert Island** (3 Mount Desert St., 207/288-5008, www.ywcamdi. org, $44, discounts for longer stays) has dorm-like housing for women only with a large communal kitchen and shared baths. It's generally important to book well in advance to stay here, but worth asking about last-minute availability.

$100-150

The smallest cottages at **Rose Eden Cottages** (864 Rte. 3, 207/288-3038, www.roseeden.com, $75-128) are like nautical dollhouses, with just enough room for a double bed, coffeemaker, and compact bathroom. Each of the 11 cottages is different, some with kitchenettes, second bedrooms, and sitting areas; the largest has a full kitchen. A location on the main road 7.5 miles outside of Bar Harbor means that the sounds of traffic are an issue for some guests, but the owners provide white noise machines, and some units are set farther back on the grassy property, which has a gas grill and laundry facilities for guests. The friendly owners also prepare good-value lobster dinners to go.

One of the best values among the generic digs that line Route 3 is **Edenbrook Motel** (96 Rte. 3, 800/323-7819, www.edebrookmotelbh.com, $85-130), which is adjacent to the College of the Atlantic and 1.5 miles outside of Bar Harbor. The simple, superclean rooms have air-conditioning, a television, and a coffeemaker, and the Island Explorer shuttle stops right in front, making it a breeze to head into town or the park.

$150-250

With a location right in downtown Bar Harbor, the ★ **Acacia House Inn** (6 High St., 800/551-5399, www.acaciahouseinn.com, $155-195) is a wonderful value, with sweet, simple decor and great breakfasts cooked with lots of local and organic ingredients, including eggs from the friendly innkeepers' own chickens. All rooms have private bathrooms, organic cotton sheets, and cable TV. The quiet side street the inn sits on lends a surprisingly laid-back atmosphere given the downtown location.

Smart, whitewashed cottages and tidy motel-style rooms look out on Frenchman's Bay at ★ **Edgewater Motel and Cottages** (137 Old Bar Harbor Rd., 207/288-3941, www.edgewaterharbor.com, cottages $119-186, motel $154-186), where a broad lawn dotted with Adirondack chairs give a resort feel to this five-acre property that's 6.5 miles from Bar Harbor. The cottage kitchens are stocked with cooking equipment and coffeemakers, and you can spot harbor seals and porpoises from the outdoor decks.

Another downtown gem is the **Maples Inn** (16 Roberts Ave., 207/618-6823, www.maplesinn.com, $119-219), a charming Victorian bed-and-breakfast with seven well-appointed rooms (one has a detached, private bath, while others have private in-room baths). One of the owners is a professional chef who prepares personalized menus and afternoon cookies for guests, and the rocking chairs on the shady front porch are an idyllic place to relax after a day of exploring.

Over $250

Stylish and luxurious, the **Bass Cottage Inn** (14 The Field, 207/288-1234, www.basscottage.com, $260-400) strikes a balance between the personal experience of a bed-and-breakfast and thoughtful service of a top-end hotel. The inn is tucked down a private lane a few minutes' walk from the waterfront, so it feels like a retreat in downtown Bar Harbor. The 1885 building has been carefully restored with a clean, airy design and comfortable common spaces. Breakfast is prepared to order and evening wine and snacks create a convivial atmosphere.

Information and Services

The **city's informative website** (www.barharborinfo.com) has useful walking maps of the town, and there's a **visitors center** (19 Firefly Ln., 207/288-3338, June-Oct. daily 8am-5pm) on the Bar Harbor Green. There are several **banks** and **ATMs** located along Main Street and Cottage Street in downtown, and free wireless Internet is available at **Jesup Public Library** (34 Mt. Desert St., 207/288-4245, www.jesuplibrary.org, Wed.-Thurs. 10am-8pm, Fri.-Sat. and Tues. 10am-5pm).

Getting Around

As in the national park, the **Island Explorer** (207/667-5796, www.exploreacadia.com) is the best way to get around Bar Harbor. The **Eden Street route** connects major hotels along Route 3 with the Bar Harbor Green. For the most part, though, the town is easy to walk on foot. Metered parking is available throughout downtown, but the only RV parking is on Main Street south of Park Street on the way out of town.

New Hampshire's White Mountains

Alpine peaks tower over wooded valleys, mountain rivers, and a lifetime of hiking trails in New Hampshire's White Mountains.

FRANCONIA

White Mountain National Forest

CONWAY

ME

65 MI/105 KM
1.25 HOURS

60 MI/100 KM
1.5 HOURS

VT

COASTAL MAINE

SOUTHERN VERMONT

NH

185 MI/300 KM
3.25 HOURS

135 MI/220 KM
2.5 HOURS

THE BERKSHIRES

ATLANTIC OCEAN

330 MI/535 KM
6.5 HOURS

MA

NEW YORK CITY

BOSTON

In this unique mountain environment you'll find staggering extremes of weather, fiercely pitched trails, and flowers that grow nowhere else in the world.

After winding through the trees for many hundreds of miles, the 2,160-mile Appalachian Trail hits sunshine, rocks, and sweeping views in the White Mountains, one of the most dramatic parts of a footpath that stretches from Georgia to Maine. More like the Alps or the Dolomites than other North American mountain ranges, the White Mountains are filled with backcountry huts maintained by the Appalachian Mountain Club (AMC), off-grid stations which in the summer become small communities that welcome hikers from around the world.

What really sets these mountains apart, though, is how easy it is for visitors of any ability (or motivation) to get to a peak. In the 19th century, Americans fell hard for the wilderness of New Hampshire, which became a favorite destination for escaping hot, crowded cities. They took to the hills in woolen knickers and hiking gowns, capturing images of the sublime landscape and weather on portable easels and with early cameras. Those first tourists left paths that can still be followed today: They forged scenic roads that wind to mountain peaks, built a railway that runs straight to the top of Mount Washington, and slept in grand hotels offering all the views with none of the sweat. To discover the best of the White Mountains, simply choose a trail, pick a road, or take a seat on the cog railway to get a taste of New England rock laid bare.

Planning Your Time

The White Mountains are popular for summer hiking, foliage trips, and skiing, so most restaurants and accommodations are open year-round, and rooms tend to be more affordable than elsewhere in New England. It's also generally possible to find a place to stay on short notice.

Orientation

Two great ranges hold down opposite sides of the White Mountains, and a series of valley highways wind from peak to peak. On the northeastern side is Mount Washington and the Presidential Range, neatly bordered by Route 302 and Route 16. These mountains are most easily accessed from Gorham or the Conways—Conway and North Conway—where many of the region's services, hotels, and attractions are based. Using the vocabulary of mountain terrain, the most important landmarks are peaks and "notches," a New England term for mountain passes. Route 302 has Crawford Notch, where there's an information center and lodge, while Route 16 passes Pinkham Notch, a similar destination not far from the Mount Washington Auto Road.

On the west side, along I-93, is the Franconia Range. Here the peaks are smaller (though by no means unimpressive), and the highway is studded with family-style attractions and trailheads. Running along the southern edge of both ranges, the Kancamagus Highway—or "the Kanc"—cuts through the most dramatic terrain in the White Mountains, following the Swift River past rolling hills and notches. The towns of Franconia and Littleton are the principal gateways to the Franconia Range, with trailheads, campgrounds, and accommodations. South of Franconia, the road passes through Franconia Notch State Park, a valley with high mountains that rise on both sides.

Highlights

★ **Mount Washington Cog Railway:** Chug to the top of the highest peak in the East in colorful carriages pushed by coal and biodiesel engines (page 159).

★ **Mount Washington Summit:** Explore wind-whipped ridges, learn about Mount Washington's extreme weather, and take in views across three states (page 161).

★ **Hiking the Presidentials:** Take a stroll along a mountain ridge, or tackle the 23-mile, 10-peak "Death March" (page 164).

★ **Kancamagus Highway:** This winding road offers a cross section of the White Mountains' rugged terrain and is one of the best places in New England to see the colorful display of autumn foliage (page 170).

★ **Flume Gorge:** Walk to dramatic waterfalls and covered bridges on an easy-going, family-friendly trail (page 173).

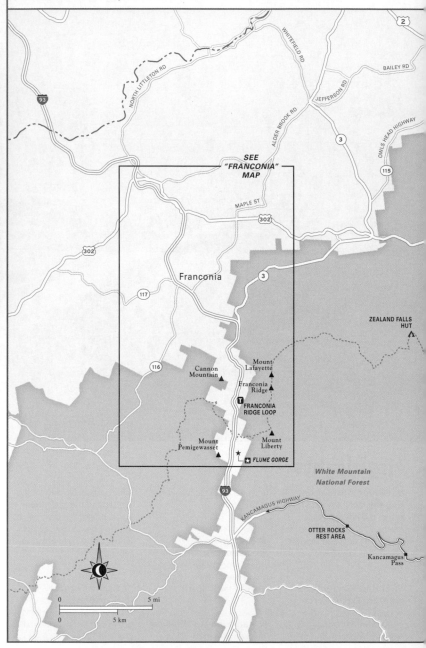

New Hampshire's White Mountains

NORTH LITTLETON RD

WHITEFIELD RD

BAILEY RD

93

JEFFERSON RD

ALDER BROOK RD

3

OWLS HEAD HIGHWAY

115

SEE
"FRANCONIA"
MAP

MAPLE ST

302

302

Franconia

3

117

ZEALAND FALLS
HUT

116

Cannon
Mountain

Mount
Lafayette

Franconia
Ridge

FRANCONIA
RIDGE LOOP

Mount
Pemigewasset

Mount
Liberty

FLUME GORGE

White Mountain
National Forest

93

KANCAMAGUS HIGHWAY

OTTER ROCKS
REST AREA

Kancamagus
Pass

0   5 mi

0   5 km

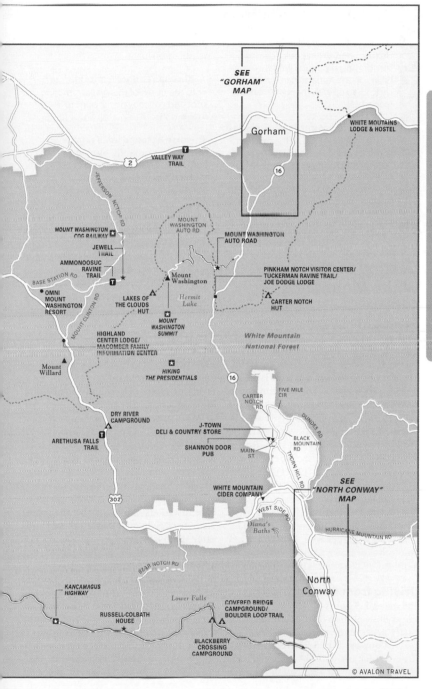

Best Accommodations

★ **White Mountains Lodge and Hostel, Shelburne:** Bunk down in a friendly hostel popular with through-hikers on the Appalachian Trail, then try to keep up with them at breakfast (page 169).

★ **Red Elephant Inn Bed & Breakfast, North Conway:** Find all the modern comforts in this cozy inn stocked with gourmet treats (page 169).

★ **Omni Mount Washington Resort, Bretton Woods:** Step into New Hampshire's grand and elegant past at this historic hotel at the foot of Mount Washington (page 170).

★ **Kinsman Lodge, Franconia:** Settle onto the porch of this rustic, rambling spot and you may never want to leave (page 177).

★ **Horse & Hound Inn, Franconia:** Strolling the grounds, playing games in the library, and enjoying brandy nightcaps will leave you feeling like a country squire at this lovely inn (page 177).

Getting to the White Mountains

Driving from Coastal Maine
60 miles, 1.5 hours

Conway is the entry point to the White Mountains when driving from **Portland, Maine.** Leave downtown Portland on **I-295 South,** then take Exit 5B onto **Route 22 West,** Congress Street, which becomes County Road. Turn right onto **Route 114 North,** which you'll follow to a traffic circle; take the second exit onto **Route 112 South.** At the next traffic circle, stay straight to continue on 112. At the following traffic circle, you'll take the second exit onto **Route 25 West.** Next, turn right onto **Route 113 North.** In Fryeburg, turn left on Main Street to stay on Route 113, which here merges with **302** and takes you into downtown Conway after about 8 miles.

Driving from Boston
135 miles, 2.5 hours

From Boston, the White Mountains are easily accessible via the interstate. To reach **Conway,** take **I-93 North** out of the city, then use Exit 37A to merge onto **I-95 North.** Stay on I-95 North for **48.5 miles,** ($3.40 toll, cash only), then merge left at Exit 4 onto **Route 16 North,** which brings you to Conway (135 mi, 2.5 hrs). For **Franconia** (150 mi, 2.5 hrs), take **I-93 North** from the city to **Exit 38** ($1 toll, cash only).

Driving from Southern Vermont
65 miles, 1.25 hours

From the southern Vermont hub of **White River Junction,** about 14 miles northeast of **Woodstock** via **Route 4,** leave town on **I-91 North.** For **Franconia,** follow **I-91 North** for about **38 miles.** Take Exit 17 to **Route 302 East,** in Wells River turning right onto Main Street North and left onto Railroad Street to stay on Route 302, then turning left at the next juncture in Woodsville to stay on the route. Next, turn right onto **Route 117 East** and, after about 8 miles, right onto **Route 116** to reach downtown Franconia (65 mi, 1.25 hrs).

For **Conway,** take **I-91 North** to Exit 15. In Fairlee, turn right onto Lake Morey Road, then left onto Main Street for half a mile before turning right onto **Route 25A East.** Turn right for a brief bout on **Route 10/Route 25A** before turning left to continue on **Route 25A.** In Wentworth, turn left onto **Route 118 North,** merging

Best Restaurants

★ **May Kelly's Cottage, North Conway:** Hearty plates of Irish food and pub fare go perfectly with live music sessions and a deck with mountain views (page 166).

★ **Stairway Café, North Conway:** A little bit country and a little bit rock and roll, this cozy breakfast spot is the place to rub shoulders with everyone from spandex-wearing cyclists to leather-clad bikers (page 166).

★ **Libby's Bistro, Gorham:** An elegant gem in the mountains, this bistro serves creative cuisine in a romantic setting (page 167).

★ **Omni Mount Washington Resort, Bretton Woods:** Pinkies out for the elegant drink of your choice at New Hampshire grande dame Omni Mount Washington Resort: high tea at the Princess Room or cocktails, wine, and beer at the Rosebrook Bar (page 168).

★ **Horse & Hound Inn, Franconia:** All warm wood and New England cuisine, this classic inn's restaurant combines old-fashioned charm and hospitality with garden-fresh ingredients (page 175).

★ **Polly's Pancake Parlor, Sugar Hill:** Legendary pancakes made from flour ground on-site collide with rivers of maple syrup from the on-site sugarhouse (page 175).

★ **Schilling Beer Co., Littleton:** Fresh, offbeat beers served in a rambling old farmhouse go perfectly with Neapolitan-style flatbreads from a wood-fired oven (page 176).

with **Route 112** just outside of Lincoln. Continue on Route 112 for about **39 miles,** then turn left onto **Route 113,** Main Street, for downtown Conway (95 mi, 2.25 hrs).

Driving from the Berkshires
185 miles, 3.25 hours

To reach **Franconia** from **North Adams,** leave the city on **Route 2 East,** the scenic **Mohawk Trail,** for **34 miles.** At the traffic circle, use the third exit to merge onto **I-91 North,** following the interstate for **122 miles.** Take Exit 17 to **Route 302 East,** in Wells River turning right onto Main Street North and left onto Railroad Street to stay on Route 302, then turning left at the next juncture in Woodsville to stay on the route. Next, turn right onto **Route 117 East** and, after about 8 miles, right onto **Route 116** to reach downtown Franconia (185 mi, 3.25 hrs).

To reach **Conway** from **North Adams,** follow **Route 8 North** out of town, and turn right when it intersects with **Route 9.** After about 25 miles, turn left to enter

I-91 North for 2.7 miles, then take Exit 3 for **Route 9 East,** making a sharp left after about 15 miles, in Keene, to remain on the route. In Hopkinton, merge onto **I-89 South** for 8 miles, then exit onto **I-93 North,** which you'll follow for **33 miles.** Take Exit 23 to **Route 104 East/Route 132 North,** then turn left onto **Route 3 North** for 1 mile, and make a right onto **Route 25 East,** which you'll continue on for about **19 miles.** Turn left onto **Route 113,** turning left again on Tamworth Road then right on Chocorua Road, which becomes Page Hill Road, to remain on Route 113. Turn left onto **Route 16 North,** which continues into downtown Conway (190 mi, 4 hrs).

Driving from New York City
330 miles, 6.5 hours

From New York City to **Franconia,** leave the city heading north on **FDR Drive.** Use the left lane to access Exit 17 to the **Robert F. Kennedy Bridge** ($8 toll, cash only), then stay left to merge onto **I-278 East.** After 4.5 miles, I-278 East merges

Two Days in the White Mountains

Day 1

With two days in the Whites, head straight for the highest point—**Mount Washington.** The summit of this commanding peak combines history and a rugged alpine landscape and is easily accessible by car or the cog-driven train to the top. If you're feeling ambitious, though, make a day of it by walking up the **Jewell Trail** that pitches straight up the rocky mountain slopes. Either way, by the time the sun gets low you'll be ready for a snack at the **Omni Mount Washington Resort,** where you can take an elegant afternoon tea in the **Princess Room** or settle into the gracious veranda for a cocktail with perfect views of the peak.

Day 2

On day two, rise early for a beautifully backlit drive along the **Kancamagus Highway,** leaving plenty of time to stop at the river swimming holes that pock the cool Swift River. Turn north for the **Franconia Notch,** where you can shed a tear for the Old Man of the Mountain, slip into **Flume Gorge,** and take an afternoon tram ride to the top of **Cannon Mountain** before heading to the **Horse & Hound Inn** for a garden-fresh meal in the dining room.

with **I-95 North** ($1.75 toll, cash only). Follow I-95 North **46 miles** to Exit 27A in Bridgeport, Connecticut. Keep right for **Route 8 North,** which you'll follow 5.5 miles to Exit 9, merging onto **Route 15 North.** Take Exit 68 NE to merge onto **I-91 North,** and stay on I-91 North for about **200 miles.** Take Exit 17 to **Route 302 East,** in Wells River turning right onto Main Street North and left onto Railroad Street to stay on Route 302, then turning left at the next juncture in Woodsville to stay on the route. Next, turn right onto **Route 117 East** and, after about 8 miles, right onto **Route 116** to reach downtown Franconia (330 mi, 6.5 hrs).

For **Conway** from New York City, you'll stay on **I-91 North** for about **105 miles** before taking Exit 3 for **Route 9 East.** Make a sharp left after about 15 miles, in Keene, to remain on Route 9. In Hopkinton, merge onto **I-89 South** for 8 miles, then exit onto **I-93 North,** which you'll follow for **33 miles.** Take Exit 23 to **Route 104 East/Route 132 North,** then turn left onto **Route 3 North** for 1 mile, and make a right onto **Route 25 East,** which you'll continue on for about **19 miles.** Turn left onto **Route 113,** turning left again on Tamworth Road then right on Chocorua Road, which becomes Page Hill Road, to remain on Route 113. Turn left onto **Route 16 North,** which continues into downtown Conway (350 mi, 6 hrs).

Getting There by Air, Train, or Bus
Air

The White Mountains' closest commercial airport is **Portsmouth International Airport at Pease** (PSM, www.flyportsmouthairport.com), which is primarily served by Allegiant Air, but for convenience and price, flying into **Boston Logan International Airport** (www.massport.com) is a much better option, with direct flights from around the world and across the United States.

Train

There's no train service to New Hampshire; the closest station is White River Junction in Vermont, which is served by **Amtrak** (800/872-7245, www.amtrak.com) on its Vermonter route.

Bus

Concord Coach Lines (800/639-3317, www.concordcoachlines.com) runs a daily bus from Boston through the White

Mountains, stopping at Conway (First Stop Market & Deli, 13 W. Main St.), North Conway (Eastern Slope Inn, 2760 Main St./Rte. 16), and Gorham (Irving Oil, 350 Main St.). A more westerly route heads to Franconia (Mac's Market, 347 Main St.). **Greyhound** (800/231-2222, www.greyhound.com) also runs buses to Conway (First Stop Market & Deli, 13 W. Main St.).

Mount Washington and the Presidential Range

A series of bare peaks pushing high above the tree line, the Presidential Range is the heart of White Mountain National Forest (WMNF), a rugged spine that culminates in Mount Washington, the highest summit in the northeastern United States. While the area isn't vast—the entire Presidential Range can be hiked in one punishing, 23-mile day—it has the feel of true wilderness. Trails tackle slopes head-on or hop from one rock to another without a scrap of flat, even ground. Visitors used to hiking the higher-elevation Rockies, Sierras, and Cascades are often surprised by how challenging the White Mountains can be; though they're less than half the size of the Western peaks, the Presidential summits are serious climbs.

Even in summer, the temperature difference between the peak of Mount Washington and neighboring valleys averages around 30 degrees. The tree line, the altitude where trees go from stunted to nonexistent, is around 4,400 feet in the White Mountains, in contrast to 11,000-12,000 feet in Colorado's Rocky Mountains; that difference shows how harsh the conditions are in New Hampshire's relatively low lying alpine areas. The weather observatory on that peak has recorded some of the world's most extreme weather, including the highest wind speeds on record, and the Presidentials get hammered by winter storms that coat them in thick layers of rime ice, snow, and frost.

If that were the end of the story, these peaks would be strictly for ropy-legged adventurers, but the White Mountains have a fascinating legacy of travel that opens their wildest places to all comers. By the mid-19th century, the area was a favorite destination for U.S. artists and tourists eager to explore the wilderness. Dozens of trains came to the Whites from Boston each day, stopping at a series of elegant hotels, nearly self-contained cities with their own train stations and hundreds of staff. An auto road and cog railway brought visitors to the summit of Mount Washington in open train cars, horse-drawn carriages, cars, and motorized stages.

Anyone with time and strong legs can find lonely trails and solitude in the White Mountains, and it can be a sublime experience. But for all the carnival atmosphere atop Mount Washington, it's pure, giddy fun to enjoy the Presidential Range in 19th-century style, chugging up slope in "The Cog," bagging a few stony summits, then taking high tea in the Princess Room at Bretton Woods.

Sights
★ Mount Washington Cog Railway
When Chicago meatpacking baron Sylvester Marsh first presented his idea for a railway to the top of Mount Washington, the state legislature told him he might as well "build a railway to the moon." In the spirit of the times, he was undeterred and began work on the world's first mountain-climbing train using materials hauled through thick forest by oxen teams. When the railway first opened in 1869, it was the first in the world to employ toothed gears, or cogs, that meshed with a pinion on the track to prevent the train from slipping backward. In those early years, the railway was powered with staggering quantities of wood, which gave way to coal in 1908.

These days the historic coal-fired trains alternate with more ecofriendly biodiesel engines, and though the railway is slower (and more expensive) than the auto road, it's wonderfully fun to chug your way up Mount Washington as the steam whistle echoes off the surrounding peaks. The trains of the **Mount Washington Cog Railway** (Base Rd., off Rte. 302, Bretton Woods, 603/278-5404, www.thecog.com, 3-hr round-trip on steam/biodiesel, $75/$69 adults, $69/65 seniors, $39 children 4-12, free children under 4, one-way $48, discount with military ID) run late April-November; daily service June-October tapers to weekends during April-May and November. After reaching the top of Mount Washington, it's worth asking the engineer for a peek inside the engine to see the coal bin, brakes, levers, and gauges. Trips allow for one hour on the summit, so if you'd like to spend the day hiking, you'll have to book a standby return ticket—though you're guaranteed to get down by the end of the day, it's not possible to reserve a spot on any given train.

Mount Washington Auto Road

You'll see the bumper stickers as soon as you start driving around New England: "This Car Climbed Mount Washington." It doesn't seem like much to brag about until you're white-knuckling the steering wheel around the zigzag highway to the summit, earning breathtaking views with every turn of the **Mount Washington Auto Road** (Rte. 16, Pinkham Notch, 603/466-3988, www.mountwashingtonautoroad. com, early May-late Oct. variable hours, $29 car and driver, $9 each adult, $7 each child, children under 5 free, $17 motorcycle and driver, no bicycles). The 7.6-mile trip, off Route 16, goes by at a snail's pace, taking about 30 minutes on the way up, 40 on the way down, and it's not for everyone—both drivers and passengers who are unnerved by heights may be better off in one of the guided van tours (from $36 adults, $31 seniors, $16 children 5-12, under 5 free). The driver shares stories and anecdotes on the way up the mountain, and groups have one hour on the

Mount Washington summit from Lakes of the Clouds

summit before heading back downslope. For hikers who'd like to make a one-way trip up or down Mount Washington, there's an irritatingly expensive one-way shuttle ($31 adults, $26 seniors, $13 children 5-12); hitchhiking is prohibited. At the bottom of the road, the **Red Barn Museum** (1 Mount Washington Auto Rd., 603/466-3988, ,late May-early Oct., Mon.-Sun. 10am-4pm, free) displays objects relating to the auto road's past, including antique cars and a carriage that used to climb the mountain.

★ Mount Washington Summit

With views stretching from the Adirondacks to Maine, the Mount Washington summit is unlike any mountain peak in the United States: It's the high point of the 2,160-mile Appalachian Trail, a day trippers' destination complete with gaily painted steam engines and the site of an extraordinary weather station that records storms that can howl in on any day of the year. When going

to the summit, it's worth bringing more clothing than seems necessary, as temperatures can be bone-chilling when the valley is balmy. For all the train tracks, crowds, and postcard racks, this is a mountain that commands respect, and seasoned hikers and climbers die here every year, usually from hypothermia.

Learn about the scientists who live and work at the top at the **Mount Washington Observatory Weather Discovery Center** (summit building, daily 10am-5pm, $2 adults, $1 children 7-17, free children under 7), which has interactive displays explaining the mountain's wild weather and telling the story of the day in 1934 when a record-breaking 231 miles-per-hour wind was recorded at the summit. There's also a good visual guide to the alpine plants that grow on the summit, including the dwarf cinquefoil, a tiny flower that grows only in the alpine zones of the Presidential Range and Franconia Ridge. Those willing to join the observatory's membership program can register for a tour of the **Weather Station** (www.mtwashington.org, 603/356-2137, ext. 211, membership $50 individual, $75 couple or family) itself; unfortunately, the station is closed to the public, though the observatory recently began partnering with the Cog Railway so that several railway trips a week include a tour of the weather station (call for details).

The oldest surviving building on the summit is the **Tip Top House,** a rustic stone lodge built in 1853 as a hotel, which then became the office for *Among the Clouds,* a mountain newspaper that chronicled social events, train schedules, weather, and gossip 1888-1915. Tiny bunks, communal tables, and a few dusty reproductions of the newspaper are on display.

Other Sights

In many ways, the White Mountains were easier to reach a century ago than today—frequent trains made the trip from Boston a breeze, with whistle stops

Gorham

at lodges and hotels. The small, volunteer-run **Gorham Historical Society & Railroad Museum** (25 Railroad St., Gorham, 603/466-5338, www.gorham-newhampshire.com, May-Oct. Tues.-Sat. 10am-3pm, free) preserves artifacts from that era in Gorham's 1907 railway station. Call before visiting, as hours can vary with volunteer availability.

Entertainment and Events

What nightlife there is in this corner of the mountains is firmly based in the Conways, the cultural hub of the Whites. It's not really "night" life, but you can try local beers well into the early evening at **Tuckerman Brewing Company** (66 Hobbs St., Conway, 603/447-5400, www.tuckermanbrewing.com, daily noon-6pm, tours 2pm and 4pm daily), where you taste your way through a lineup of stouts, ales, and IPAs. A good way to meet some locals is at the Sunday night Irish session at **May Kelly's Cottage** (3002 Rte. 302, Conway, 603/356-7005, www.maykellys.com, Tues.-Thurs. 4pm-9pm, Fri.-Sat. noon-10pm, Sun. noon-8pm), which has a pleasant porch for afternoon beers and a convivial feel. Another favorite watering hole is **Muddy Moose Restaurant & Pub** (2344 Rte. 302, North Conway, 603/356-7696, www.muddymoose.com, Sun.-Thurs. 11:30am-9pm, Fri.-Sat. 11:30am-10pm), whose antler chandelier and raw wood interior evoke an oversize summer cottage. Up the road in little Jackson, the **Shannon Door Pub** (Rte. 16, Jackson, 603/383-4211, www.shannondoor.com, Mon.-Wed. 4pm-10pm, Thurs. and Sun. 4pm-11pm, Fri.-Sat. 4pm-midnight) has live music nightly Thursday-Saturday, and a fun, country Irish atmosphere.

Shopping

While there are plenty of shops for poking around in the Conways, the most useful stores in the White Mountains are gear shops stocked with everything you need to walk, ride, or climb your way into the hills. The Conways have a plethora: **International Mountain Equipment** (2733 Rte. 302, North Conway, 603/356-7064, www.ime-usa.com, Sun.-Thurs. 9am-6pm, Fri. 9am-9pm, Sat. 8am-8pm) is a well-stocked gear shop run by the International Mountain Climbing School, which also rents hiking and camping equipment. **Stan & Dan Sports** (2936 Rte. 302, North Conway, 603/356-6997, www.stananddansports.com, Mon.-Sat. 9am-6pm, Sun. 9am-5pm) is a go-to for bike and ski gear. In Gorham, stop by **Gorham Hardware & Sport Center** (96 Main St., Gorham, 603/466-2312, www.nhhockeyshop.com, Mon.-Fri. 8am-5pm, Sat. 8am-4pm, Sun. 8am-1pm, hours may vary seasonally) for hiking, climbing, skiing, and camping setups.

Sports and Recreation
Hiking
There are endless ways to enjoy these mountains, but before setting out it's worth stopping by one of the ranger stations or visitors centers for maps and updated advice; some trails are closed seasonally to protect wildlife, and it's especially important to learn mountain weather forecasts before setting out above the tree line. In Conway, the White Mountain National Forest **Saco Ranger Station** (33 Rte. 112, Conway, 603/447-5448, late May-mid Oct. daily 8am-5pm, closes at 4:30 Oct.-May) has maps, advice, and updated weather reports, as does Gorham's White Mountain National Forest **Androscoggin Ranger Station** (300 Glen Rd., Gorham, 603/446-2713, May Oct. daily 8am-4:30pm). On Route 16, the Appalachian Mountain Club's **Pinkham Notch Visitor Center** (361 Rte. 16, 603/466-8116, www.outdoors.org, daily 6:30am-10pm) has plenty of the same, along with a small trading post for supplies, and the

Top to bottom: Omni Mount Washington Resort at Bretton Woods; hiking Mount Washington; the Presidential Range.

AMC **Macomber Family Information Center** (3575 Rte. 302, Crawford Notch, 603/466-2727, 9am-4pm, closes earlier in off-season) is a popular trailhead and hiker information spot. The AMC also has a trail information and weather hotline (603/466-2721).

For hikers who want to do longer, one-way hikes, it's worth looking into the **AMC Hiker Shuttle** (www.outdoors.org, early June-Oct., $23) which has a fixed route that accesses many popular trailheads in the area, especially those that lead to the AMC's mountain huts.

★ Hiking the Presidentials

Bar none, the most iconic hike in the White Mountains is the **Tuckerman Ravine Trail,** a 4.2-mile route to the summit of Mount Washington, which leaves from the **Pinkham Notch Visitor Center** (361 Rte. 16). Doing this hike as a round-trip is a full-day outing of at least six hours, and it's especially important to bring extra clothes, water, and a headlamp for this strenuous trail. After some initial switchbacks through thick forest, the trail rises fairly gradually, following the route of the Cutler River and reaching the **Hermit Lake Shelter** after 2.4 miles, which has lean-tos, tent platforms, and potable water from a hand-operated pump. This scenic spot is the jumping-off point for many of the backcountry skiers who tackle the famous headwall of Tuckerman Ravine each spring. After the lake, the trail begins to climb in earnest, then aims straight up the western edge of Tuckerman Ravine, earning elevation and views with every step. Upon cresting the valley headwall, the trail reaches a junction that's clearly signed for the Mount Washington summit (0.6 mi) and Lakes of the Clouds (0.8 mi), the most spectacular of the White Mountains' AMC huts, and a pleasant spot to stop for hot drinks (and sometimes freshly baked treats from the hut staff). For a return trip to Pinkham Notch that's easier on the knees, it's possible to descend via

the more moderate **Boott Spur** or **Lion Head Trail.**

It's also possible to ascend Mount Washington by a pair of trails on the **Crawford Notch** side, accessible from Route 302; parking for these routes is at the Cog Railway station, and you should allow a full day for a round-trip hike up either trail. The most direct route is the 4.4-mile **Ammonoosuc Ravine Trail,** which climbs steeply to Lakes of the Clouds, then continues up a rocky path to the summit; in addition to passing scenic ponds and the AMC hut, this trail has gorgeous views as it works its way up the southwest face of the mountain. Somewhat longer and more gradual, the 5.1-mile **Jewell Trail** ascends the western slope of Mount Clay, then skirts the summit to join a ridge trail to the top of Mount Washington. This is another stunner on clear days; it's delightful to hike parallel to the Cog Railway for views of the brightly colored trains with an endless backdrop.

Strictly for extremely fit, experienced hikers, the **Presidential Traverse,** is a remarkable, 23-mile hike that goes up and over every peak in the range—tellingly, this hike is often referred to as the **Death March,** and many hikers begin and end in the dark (although the classic Death March is a long day hike, it's possible to break it up with a night in the **Lakes of the Clouds** hut). Most hikers go north to south, taking the **Valley Way Trail** from the Appalachia parking lot (Rte. 2, 5 miles west of the intersection with Rte. 16) up Mount Madison before ticking off a who's-who of American presidents, ending with Mount Jackson, then descending into Crawford Notch. The one-way hike requires a car on either end, or you can use the **AMC Hiker Shuttle** (603/466-2727, www.outdoors.org, $23). More information can be obtained at the **Pinkham Notch Visitor Center** (361 Rte. 16, 603/466-8116, www.outdoors.org, daily 6:30am-10pm).

Another option is the full-day, 10-mile

The Appalachian Mountain Club's White Mountain Huts

The Appalachian Mountain Club has maintained a system of nine backcountry huts in the White Mountains since 1888, making the wilderness accessible for hikers without the gear and experience to rough it on their own. Spending a night at one of the AMC huts is a great deal like alpine summer camp, with bunk beds, communal meals, and a convivial atmosphere among the tired hikers. While rates can seem high (especially given the rustic experience), you're paying for meals hiked in by hardy college students in a wild, scenic place, and staying in the backcountry is an unforgettable experience.

The most famous—and perhaps most spectacular—among the AMC huts is **Lakes of the Clouds,** set by a cluster of alpine ponds just a ridgeline away from the top of Mount Washington. The trail to pretty **Zealand Falls Hut** is far less challenging, a relatively gradual 2.8-mile hike that ends at a perfect river swimming spot. Less popular (and crowded) than those two all-stars, **Carter Notch Hut** is the easternmost hut in the AMC system, a 1914 stone structure set between Wildcat Dome and Carter Mountain.

One of the Appalachian Mountain Club's most easily accessible huts from the Franconia Range side is **Lonesome Lake Hut,** which is a 1.6-mile hike from the trailhead in Lafayette Campground with fabulous views of the mountains, naturalist programs, and rustic co-ed bunkrooms. Another favorite in the Franconia area is **Greenleaf Hut,** which is at the end of a moderate, 2.7-mile walk and offers equally spectacular perspective on the rugged terrain.

Rates include dinner the night of arrival and breakfast the morning after, and **reservations** (www.outdoors.org, 603/466-2727, $105-131) can be made online or by phone. Visitors must bring their own sleeping bags, though additional wool blankets are provided, and guests share simple, often solar-powered bathrooms with cold running water. The most popular huts, and especially Lakes of the Clouds, are often booked months in advance, but there's almost always last-minute space if you're flexible about where you stay.

round-trip hike to Mount Jefferson, which is equal parts challenging and rewarding, following a rocky ridge that looks out across the White Mountains. The **Castle Trail** takes off from Route 2, 9.2 miles west of the junction between Route 2 and Route 16 in Gorham; a brown sign on the south side of the road marks the entrance, and a parking area is at the end of the road.

Other Hikes

Not all the hikes in the White Mountains are quite so strenuous. One favorite option for families is the 3.2-mile round-trip hike up **Mount Willard,** which earns fabulous views of Crawford Notch with more gradual slopes (for that reason, this hike tends to be crowded on busy days in the Whites, so don't expect solitude). Park at the railroad depot information center adjacent to the **AMC Highland Center** on Route 302.

Another good choice for hiking with kids is the gentle, 0.6-mile walk to **Diana's Baths** between North Conway and Bartlett, which has an enchanting series of waterfalls ideal for cooling off in wading pools (the baths vary greatly with water level, though, and by late summer the waterfalls can be mere trickles). To reach the parking area from North Conway, take Route 302 north out of town, then turn left on River Road (which becomes West Side Rd. after a mile) for 2.5 miles. A large parking lot is on the left with a self service, cash only parking fee station ($3).

Find the highest single-drop waterfall in New Hampshire at the end of the **Arethusa Falls** trail, a 2.6-mile round-trip hike along Bemis Brook. Park on the west side of Route 302 about a mile south of Dry River Campground in Crawford Notch State Park. The hike is fairly steep but well suited for families with older kids, and it's possible to extend it into a 4.7-mile loop by returning via **Frankenstein Cliff Trail,** which has lovely views of the valley. The falls' musical name is said to be taken from a poem by Percy Bysshe Shelley about a Greek nymph who was transformed into a flowing spring, and the lines evoke the spot beautifully:

Arethusa arose
From her couch of snows
In the Acroceraunian mountains,
From cloud and from crag,
With many a jag,
Shepherding her bright fountains.
She leapt down the rocks,
With her rainbow locks
Streaming among the streams;
Her steps paved with green
The downward ravine
Which slopes to the western gleams

Food
The Conways

A year-round favorite is ★ **May Kelly's Cottage** (3002 Rte. 302, 603/356-7005, www.maykellys.com, Tues.-Thurs. 4pm-9pm, Fri.-Sat. noon-10pm, Sun. noon-8pm, $9-22), which serves hearty Irish classics and American pub fare in a relaxed, old-world setting. With fabulous mountain views and shaded tables, the outdoor patio is perfect for an early evening meal, while the interior is decked with a pleasant jumble of Americana and Irish bric-a-brac. Shepherd's pie, soups, and hearty salads all come with homemade, grainy bread, and regulars love the fried potato cakes with spinach and horseradish sauce. On Sunday evenings, a fun group of Irish musicians holds a relaxed live session, playing around a table over beers.

Fresh, simple breakfasts and hearty lunches at ★ **Stairway Café** (2649 Rte. 302, North Conway, 603/356-5200, www.stairwaycafe.com, daily 7am-3pm, $7-18) are the main draw, but the atmosphere is pretty great too—the decor strikes a curious balance between country kitchen and rock and roll (imagine a bacon and egg skull on a floral print menu). Both the breakfast and lunch menus are served all day and include plenty of basic egg plates, burgers, and sandwiches, along with offbeat additions like wild game sausage and Maine lobster Benedict.

The unassuming **Leavitt's Country Bakery** (564 Rte. 302, Conway, 603/447-2218, daily 4am-5pm, $2-7) turns out great piles of doughnuts, fritters, and Bismarck pastries—regular visitors fill boxes full of sweets before leaving the Whites. With no seating and little fuss, Leavitt's is perfect for picking up pre-hike treats and coffee, and it also prepares a mean breakfast sandwich to go.

Part of a small chain of earthy pizza joints with a focus on natural, organic ingredients, **Flatbread Company** (2760 Rte. 302, North Conway, 603/356-4470, www.flatbreadcompany.com, daily 11:30am-9pm, $9-13) pulls thin-crust pies from a wood-fired oven, topped with homemade pepperoni and sausage, piles of fresh vegetables, and tomato sauce that bubbles away in a cauldron by the fire. The very casual spot is rustic and a little loud, a good choice for larger groups and families with children.

With a bit more polish and creative food, **Chef's Bistro** (2724 Rte. 302, North Conway, 603/356-4747, www.chefsbistronh.com, Sun.-Fri. 11am-9pm, Sat. 11am-10pm, $9-28) serves eclectic dinners ranging from a vegetarian Thai curry to Asian beef salad and bistro-style steaks with great piles of hand-cut fries. Lunch is simpler, with unfussy and appealing sandwiches, burgers, and salads.

North Conway

This is an especially good place for those with dietary restrictions, and the restaurant has a basic kids' menu.

Conway is the main base for services in the area, with a **Shaw's** grocery store (1150 Eastman Rd., Conway, 603/356-5471, daily 7am-9pm) and **The Local Grocer** (3358 Rte. 302, North Conway, 603/356-6068, www.nhlocalgrocer.com, daily 8am-8pm), a smaller store that stocks natural and organic options.

Gorham

Amid the generic chains lining Route 2 through Gorham, **White Mountain Café & Bookstore** (212 Rte. 2, 603/466-2511, www.whitemountaincafe.com, daily 7am-4pm, $4-11) stands out with personality and charm. Head to the counter for sandwiches, burritos, pastries, and salads, then settle in at a small café table or the sunny front lot. The café also has solid espresso and wireless Internet, making it a good spot to sit a spell and catch up on emails.

For pizza lovers of a certain age, it's hard not to love **Mary's Pizza** (9 Cascade Flats Rd., 603/752-6150, www.maryspizzanh.com, Tues. 4pm-9pm, Wed.-Sat. 11am-9pm, $6-18), an old-school Italian American joint that recalls the years before "flatbread" began to appear covered with gourmet toppings. Pizzas and pastas are simple and come piled with lots of cheese, meat, and vegetables, with decor to match; red and white checkered vinyl tablecloths, red Coke glasses, and a jukebox stocked with country and rock-and-roll CDs are right at home here.

If you've taken some time to explore Gorham, then ★ **Libby's Bistro & SAaLT Pub** (111 Rte. 16, 603/466-5330, www.libbysbistro.org, bistro Fri.-Sat. 5pm-8pm, $10-24, pub Wed.-Sun. 5pm-9pm, $9-15) will come as something of a surprise. The more upscale bistro and the clubby, convivial pub both have outstanding food, as well as a full bar menu. Even the burgers have creative flair, like the Korean burger topped with kimchi coleslaw and chili mayo or a Peruvian fish sandwich daubed with spiced tartar sauce, but the kitchen really gets going with the global mains: ricotta gnocchi with veal meatballs, Mumbai cakes, and Middle Eastern-spiced fried chicken strike a balance between thoughtful and satisfying.

For groceries in Gorham, you'll find a **Save-A-Lot** (491 Main St., 603/752-1248, daily 8am-8pm) discount grocery and **Walmart Supercenter** (561 Main St., 603/752-4621, daily 7am-10pm).

Off Routes 16 and 302

Between the Conways and Gorham are a cluster of shops and restaurants in Jackson, on Route 16, that make a good stopping point. Among the most convenient is **J-Town Deli & Country Store** (174 Main St., Jackson, 603/383-8064, www.jtowndeli.com, Sun.-Thurs. 7am-6pm, Fri.-Sat. 7am-7pm, $5-8), where you can pick up breakfast and lunch to eat at on-site picnic tables or take with you—breakfast sandwiches, subs, and wraps include gluten-free and vegetarian-friendly options, and the store also prepares dinners to go, which are good value if your accommodation has a kitchen.

If you visit the **White Mountain Cider Company** (207 Rte. 302, Bartlett, 603/383-9061, www.ciderconh.com, deli Thurs.-Fri. and Sun.-Mon. 7am-3pm, Sat. 7am-5pm; restaurant Sun.-Thurs. 5pm-9pm, Fri.-Sat. 5pm-10pm, $12-30) mid-September-early winter, you'll find it pressing apple cider with an old-fashioned mill and serving the unbeatable pairing of fresh juice and apple cider doughnuts. The deli side of the operation offers doughnuts, cider, sandwiches, and coffee, and by night the restaurant serves gourmet bistro fare in a charmingly rustic setting. Menu items change frequently, but the pan-roasted duck breast is a favorite, as are the creative burgers. A full menu of beer, wine, and cocktails makes this a good spot for a night out, as well.

Thirty-four miles up Route 302 from Conway, the ★ **Omni Mount Washington Resort** (Rte. 302, Bretton Woods, 603/278-1000, www.mountwashington-resort.com) would be out of the way if it weren't such a worthwhile destination of its own. The giant hotel has a small city's worth of restaurants, but two stand out as destination-worthy. For alpine elegance, you can't beat high tea in the **Princess Room** (Fri.-Sat. 3pm, $20 adults, $12 children 10 and under): Grown-ups sip their brews along with ceviche, savory tartlets, scones, and sweets, while kids get mini marshmallows in their hot chocolate, and a menu of tiny sandwiches, savory muffins, macarons, and strawberry tarts. The elegant room is named for Princess Caroline, the eccentric, glamorous wife of the hotel's original owner. As charming as those princess-worthy tea parties can be, though, the finest seats in the hotel are on the broad back veranda, where comfortable wicker chairs are pointed straight at the southern slope of Mount Washington. Sunsets are spectacular here, and sharp-eyed visitors can spot the glint and smoke of the Cog Railway as it chugs up the slope. Guests on the veranda can order from the **Rosebrook Bar** (noon-10pm, $9-15), and sip wine, beer, and cocktails along with savory nibbles that would seem overpriced in a different venue.

Accommodations and Camping
Camping

In the White Mountain National Forest, backcountry camping is allowed below the tree line, as long as tents are over 200 feet from trails and water. WMNF also operates a number of excellent campgrounds: Six miles south of Gorham, **Dolly Copp Campground** (Rte. 16, 877/444-6777, mid-May-mid Oct., reservations accepted with some sites first-come, first-served, $22) is one the largest in the forest, with vault toilets, campfire rings, and ranger-run programs. No showers are on-site, but coin-operated showers are available five miles south at the AMC's **Pinkham Notch Visitor**

Center (361 Rte. 16, 603/466-2721, www.outdoors.org, daily 6:30am-10pm, $1 for 3 minutes, quarters only).

For good access to the Cog Railway and hikes on the Crawford Notch side of Mount Washington, Crawford Notch State Park's **Dry River Campground** (2057 Rte. 302, Bartlett, 877/647-2757, www.nhstateparks.org, May-Oct., $23) is a good option, with 36 primitive sites, good bathroom facilities, and showers.

Under $100

Compare blisters with fellow travelers at the **White Mountains Hostel** (36 Washington St., Conway, 866/902-2521, www.wmhostel.com, dorms $31, private rooms $59), a super-friendly spot with a communal kitchen, comfortable common areas, and very clean (if rather plain) quarters. The six-bed dorms include female-only, male-only, and co-ed options, and the private rooms are an excellent choice for families—each has a full bed, and some have an additional twin or bunk bed (prices are for two adults, and there's a supplemental charge of $20 per adult or $10 per child).

Four miles east of Gorham, ★ **White Mountains Lodge and Hostel** (592 Rte. 2, Shelburne, 603/466-5049, www.whitemountainlodgeandhostel.com, $35 with breakfast) is another excellent option for budget travelers, and as it's popular with through-hikers on the Appalachian Trail, it's a good place to hear tales from the woods. The co-ed rooms have 2-6 beds, and the huge, home-cooked breakfasts are perfect fuel for a day on the trail. The rambling, 19th-century building is both gracious and homey, with a patio, pond, and fire pit.

$100-150

In addition to remote, backcountry huts, the AMC runs a pair of front country lodges that are fun and convenient to hikes—it's something of a hostel experience, but an especially good fit for families. The older of the two is **Joe Dodge Lodge** (Rte. 16, Pinkham Notch, 603/466-2727, www.outdoors.org, room with dinner and breakfast from $92 pp), where both private rooms and bunk rooms share bathrooms, and there's often a blazing fire in the living room and library. Meals are served family-style at big tables, and knowledgeable staff lead guided hikes and give talks on the natural world. On the other side of Mount Washington is the newer **Highland Center Lodge** (Rte. 302, Crawford Notch, 603/466-2727, www.outdoors.org, room with dinner and breakfast from $109 pp), which has all the communal joys of Joe Dodge (fireplaces, friendly cafeteria), but with a few private bathrooms for those who prefer not to share sinks. If you're staying at the Highland Center, you get free access to the gear room, which has all the warm layers and hiking boots you need for tackling some peaks.

$150-250

With a central location in North Conway, the ★ **Red Elephant Inn Bed & Breakfast** (28 Locust Ln., North Conway, 603/356-3548, www.redelephantinn.com, $129-209) combines the best of a classic bed-and-breakfast—giant breakfast spread, a friendly atmosphere, and cozy common spaces—with the amenities and style of a more luxurious inn. Complementary afternoon wine and snacks are just the thing after a day spent on the trails, and the big library is stocked with local maps and books to read by the unheated outdoor pool. A hot drink and snack bar is available throughout the day for guests to help themselves, and rooms balance a warm wood-and-plaid White Mountains aesthetic with bits of art deco flair that keep things fresh and contemporary.

Fireplaces in every room and elegant, four-poster beds make the **Riverside Inn Bed & Breakfast** (372 Rte. 16, Intervale, 866/949-0044, www.riverside-inn-bed-breakfast.com, $119-225) one of the more romantic places to stay in the White

Mountains. A river runs through the serene backyard, which is stocked with well-placed lawn chairs and a hammock, and the cooked-to-order breakfasts use lots of local ingredients, organic veggies, and seasonal fruits. Fresh cookies are served at afternoon teas in the old-fashioned sitting room.

Over $250

Of the dozens of grand hotels that dotted the mountains at the turn of the 20th century, the 1902 ★ **Omni Mount Washington Resort** (Rte. 302, Bretton Woods, 800/843-6664 or 603/278-1000, www.mountwashingtonresort.com, $179-469) is the most perfectly preserved, and discovering the gorgeous historic touches throughout the building could easily occupy a rainy afternoon. A gracious veranda runs the length of the rambling hotel, with comfortable chairs that look straight out on Mount Washington. Even if you're not staying here, stopping by for a drink on the deck—or an utterly charming high tea in the Princess Room—is a wonderful experience, and a gracious counterbalance to the White Mountains' rugged scenery.

If you come for the night, be sure to head outside to watch the stars from the outdoor fireplace or pool, and enjoy the period feel of the rooms—while the usual contemporary amenities have been added, the rooms are still thoroughly old-fashioned. For much of the year, the most desirable are those facing the mountain, which get stunning sunrise views, but for trips during foliage season, book the front of the hotel, which looks across the valley at a slope crowded with flaming maple trees. Bretton Woods, as it's still called by many, is a city unto itself, complete with post office in the basement, golf courses, a zip line, riding stables, and a handful of restaurants on-site. While much of Bretton Woods is beautifully done, meal service is inconsistent and the main dining room seems overpriced for quality. Many visitors prefer to duck into the downstairs pub, which is less grand but more reliable.

Information

For everything in the White Mountain National Forest, the **Saco Ranger Station** (33 Rte. 112, Conway, 603/447-5448, late May-mid-Oct. daily 8am-5pm, closes at 4:30 Oct.-May) is the place to start. Get brochures, maps, and advice at the **North Conway Village information center** (2617 Rte. 302, North Conway, 603/356-5947, daily 10am-6pm).

Getting Around

While it's only really useful for longer, point-to-point hikes, the **AMC Hiker Shuttle** (www.outdoors.org, early June-Oct., $23) stops at trailheads throughout the mountains.

★ Kancamagus Highway

Between Conway and Lincoln, 35 miles of tightly inscribed switchbacks, swooping valleys, and perfect mountain views make the Kancamagus Highway among the most iconic drives in New England. Route 112, affectionately known as "the Kanc," rolls through the heart of White Mountain National Forest, following the twists and curves of the Swift River and climbing to almost 3,000 feet—at 2,855 feet, the Kancamagus Pass has fabulous views, especially when autumn turns the surrounding forest into a riot of color.

Sights and Recreation

There are plenty of places to stop along the way on the Kancamagus Highway—look for clusters of cars along the side of the road, which often signals a favorite local swimming spot—including a series of scenic overlooks, hiking trails, and historic sites.

Driving from Conway to Lincoln, mile zero is at the White Mountain National Forest ranger station, making it easy to find landmarks along the way. Six miles after leaving Conway, the **Boulder Loop Trail** is a moderate, three-mile hike that takes 2-3 hours and has good views of rocky ledges and forest. A series of interpretive signs illustrates the geologic history, flora, and fauna of the White Mountains. At 7.0 miles, **Lower Falls** is a popular spot for swimming in the Swift River and has bathrooms and a picnic area near a small, scenic falls. You can peer into daily life in 19th-century New Hampshire at 12.7 miles in the volunteer-run **Russell-Colbath House,** which is open when staff are available. It's small but free, and docents are happy to share the mysterious story of Thomas Colbath's years-long disappearance and possible reappearance.

Keep winding up to the **Kancamagus Pass,** which at 2,855 feet is the highest point on the road, then you'll find the **Otter Rock Rest Area** at 26 miles, with restrooms and a short trail to another lovely swimming area in the Swift River.

Camping

Six miles west of Conway on the Kancamagus Highway are a pair of appealing campgrounds, the 49-site **Covered Bridge** (Rte. 112, 877/444-6777, mid-May-mid-Oct., reservations accepted, $22), as well as the smaller, walk-up only **Blackberry Crossing** (Rte. 112, 877/444-6777, mid-May-mid-Oct., $22).

The Franconia Range

An alpine backbone runs along this compact range from Mount Lafayette to Mount Flume, a 2.5-mile sprint of rock with fabulous views. While the Presidential Range outdoes the highest of these by a cool 1,000 feet, the Franconia Range is just as rugged; there's no way to drive to the top of these mountains, so if you sweat to the top of Mount Lafayette,

you won't need to share the view with crowds in flip-flops.

Set dramatically between the Franconia Range and the Cannon Cliffs, Franconia Notch State Park runs along the Pemigewasset River, with easily accessible hiking trails to waterfalls, lakes, and a deep, natural gorge. This used to be the home of New Hampshire's most recognizable landmark, the "Old Man of the Mountain," a series of granite ledges whose profile resembled a craggy old Yankee until they came tumbling down in 2003 despite elaborate efforts to hold the stony face together.

The towns of Littleton and Franconia are the main bases for visiting Franconia Notch, and the road into the park is an especially dramatic one, twisting between high peaks. Franconia Notch itself is a bustling vacation spot, with an enormous campground, a lake with a swimming beach, a mountain tram, and trailhead after trailhead heading up into the hills.

Sights
Frost Place

From 1915-1920, Robert Frost lived in a small house with views of the mountains, and his spirit lives on at the secluded farmstead, now a museum and poetry center. Each year, the museum invites a poet to live in the house for six weeks, writing and working in Frost's former home of **Frost Place** (Ridge Rd., Franconia, 603/823-5510, www.frostplace.org, late May-June Thurs.-Sun. 1pm-5pm; July-mid-Sept. Wed.-Mon. 1pm-5pm; mid-Sept.-mid-Oct. Wed.-Mon. 10am-5pm, $5 adults, $4 seniors, $3 students 12 and above, under 12 free), which retains a peaceful, contemplative feel. The museum has signed first editions of Frost's poetry, as well as other memorabilia from his life, and there's a half-mile nature trail winding through the property with poems from the Franconia years. The trail, grounds, and

Franconia

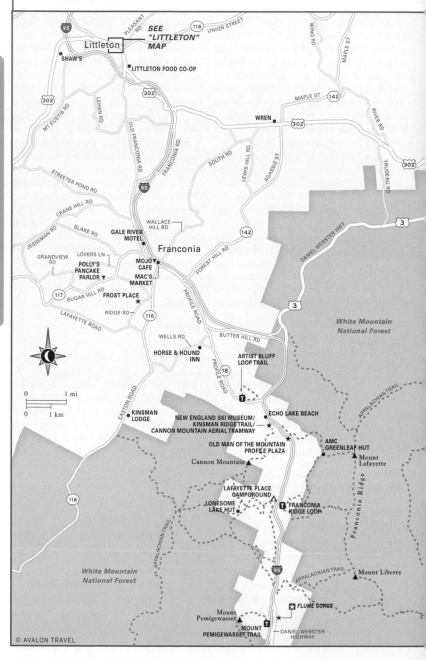

© AVALON TRAVEL

peaceful front porch of the house are always open to the public.

★ Flume Gorge

Narrow, wooden walkways lead through this natural chasm, accessible from a **visitors center** (852 Rte. 3, Lincoln, 603/745-8391, www.nhstateparks.org, early May-late Oct. daily 8:30am-5pm, open until 5:30 mid-June-early Sept., $16 adults, $13 children 6-12, under 6 free). Its high, Conway granite walls shelter covered bridges, mossy walls, and waterfalls, including the spectacular 45-foot-high Avalanche Falls. The gorge was formed before the last Ice Age, when a fin of basalt was forced into the vertically fractured granite; the basalt weathered away more quickly than the surrounding granite, leaving a winding slot in its place. A two-mile trail leads through the gorge, with a few places to duck off the path and explore, such as the Wolf's Den, a narrow, one-way route that involves squeezing yourself through cracks in the rock, and crawling on hands and knees. As the story goes, Flume Gorge was discovered by 93-year-old Jess Guernsey when she was looking for a new spot to drop a fishing line, and it still holds the thrill of discovery: It's cool between the rock walls, and birch trees worm out of stony cracks. Don't miss the visitors center's display case full of old-timey Flume Gorge postcards that 19th-century vacationers sent to their friends back home.

Cannon Mountain

Get your bearings from the top of this bare granite dome—on a clear day, views stretch to four states and Canada, and you can enjoy the scene from an observation deck. You'll also find a café at the top of Cannon Mountain, and walking trails that cross the 4,080-foot summit. Zip up to the top in fewer than 10 minutes on the **Aerial Tramway** (260 Tramway Dr., Franconia, 603/823-8800, www.cannonmt.com, late May-mid-June 9am-5pm, mid-June-mid-Oct.

8:30am-5:30pm, round-trip ride $17 adults, $14 children 6-12; one-way $13 adults, $10 children 6-12, free children under 6), or you can hike to the top on the **Kinsman Ridge Trail,** a 2.2-mile one-way hike that leaves from the tramway parking lot and has great perspectives on Franconia Notch.

Other Sights

Relive the glory days of New Hampshire's rocky mascot at the **Old Man of the Mountain Profile Plaza** (Tramway Drive, Exit 34B from I-93), where you can line up just right and get a glimpse of what the cliffs looked like before they collapsed in 2003. You can watch ski technology progress from furry boots and wool knickers to high-tech jumpsuits at the diminutive **New England Ski Museum** (Tramway Drive, Franconia, 603/823-7177, www.newenglandskimuseum.org, late May-end of ski season, daily 10am-5pm, free) whose koan-like motto is "preserving the future of skiing's past." The museum has medals and trophies from New Hampshire-native skier Bode Miller and a short movie about his career.

Entertainment and Events

Up the road in picturesque Littleton, the **Schilling Beer Co.** (18 Mill St., Littleton, 603/444-4800, www.schillingbeer.com, Sun.-Thurs. noon-11pm, Fri.-Sat. noon-midnight) brews small-barrel batches of European-style beers that range from more familiar Hefeweizens to offbeat pours; on a recent summer afternoon, the family-owned brewery was pouring a sour brown wild ale, Leipzig-style gose, and Czech black lagers in a historic, riverside barn.

The mountain meadows north of the notch are filled with violet blossoms every year in time for the **Lupine Festival** (603/823-8000, www.franconianotch.org, mid-June), a street festival and art show with events throughout the region. By governor's decree, each year in early July, Frost Place holds **Frost**

THE FRANCONIA RANGE

Day (603/823-5510, www.frostplace.org), with readings of poetry by the poet-in-residence and musical performances at the farmstead. Littleton author Eleanor H. Porter created the super-chipper Pollyanna in a pair of children's novels, and the town has adopted the character as a kind of local mascot. The official **Pollyanna Glad Day** (www.golittleton. org, early June) celebrates her optimistic legacy with readings, awards, and festivities.

Shopping

Shopping in this area usually means picking up an extra layer for a hike, so stores lean more toward gear than souvenirs. In Littleton, stop by the little, employee-owned **Badass Outdoors** (17 Main St., Littleton, 603/444-9445, Tues.-Thurs. 11am-5pm, Fri.-Sat. 10am-6pm, Sun. 11am-5pm). Bethlehem, a cute little town five miles down Route 302 from Littleton, has a supercool shop stocked with work by local artists and artisans, a worthwhile exception to the mostly gear rule; visit **WREN** (2011 Main St., Bethlehem, 603/869-9736, www.wren-works.org, daily 10am-5pm) to pick up truly local gifts, which are otherwise hard to find in the area.

Sports and Recreation
Beaches

Set just at the base of Cannon Mountain, **Echo Lake Beach** (Exit 34C, Franconia Notch State Park, 603/823-8800, $4 adults, $2 children 6-11, under 6 free) is sandy and scenic, with a lifeguard on duty during the day; it's possible to rent canoes, kayaks, and pedal boats here for $20/hour.

Hiking

For hikes in the area, stop by the hiker cabin at **Lafayette Place Campground**

Top to bottom: driving the Kancamagus Highway in autumn; Franconia Notch; Artist Bluff Loop Trail.

Littleton

(Franconia Notch State Park, 603/823-5884, www.nhstateparks.org, daily 8am-3pm) for updated trail conditions, maps, and alpine weather reports—even when valley weather is blissful, the exposed alpine trail can get howling wind and whiteout fog. For the ultimate Franconia hike, plan for at least 6 hours on the 8.2-mile **Franconia Ridge Loop,** a rugged New Hampshire classic that goes up and over three peaks: Little Haystack Mountain, Mount Lincoln, and Mount Lafayette. The trail starts on the east side of I-93, opposite Lafayette Place Campground, and starts straight up the fall line, climbing 3,480 feet in around four miles, passing a series of scenic waterfalls on the way up Little Haystack. The ridgeline trail between Mount Lincoln and Mount Lafayette is a highlight, a knife-edge ridge that's all exposed rock and perfect views.

Earn your views with (somewhat) less work on the **Mount Pemigewasset Trail,** a moderate, 3.3-mile out-and-back that takes roughly 2-3 hours to complete from the Flume Gorge Visitor Center parking lot. Much of the way is wooded and shady, and the trail crosses a series of pretty brooks, but the summit is bare rock, and though the mountain tops out at 2,557 feet, it feels like a real adventure.

For more information on this hike, ask at the on-site visitors center.

Easy enough for younger children, the 1.5-mile **Artist Bluff Loop Trail** looks out toward Cannon Mountain and Franconia Notch from the valley floor. To access the trailhead from Littleton or Franconia, take Exit 34C from I-93, then take Route 18 west for 0.5 mile, and park in the large lot on the right. This trail is particularly nice in early spring, when wildflowers bloom along the edge of Echo Lake.

Food
Franconia

For takeout sandwiches, strong coffee, ice cream, and pizza, the colorful **Mojo Cafe** (334 Main St., Franconia, 603/823-5697, Tues.-Thurs. 7am-3pm, Fri.-Sat. 7am-7pm, Sun. 8am-noon, $3-12) is a convenient stop, and it's something of a local icon, with rock-and-roll memorabilia and random knickknacks covering every surface. Limited counter seating is available inside, and there are a few tables on the sunny front porch.

The elegant dining room at the ★ **Horse & Hound Inn** (205 Wells Rd., Franconia, 800/450-5501, www.horseandhoundnh.com, reservations recommended, $20-33) has a refined menu that changes with the season, using plenty of fresh, local ingredients, some of which come from the on-site garden. A recent menu included lobster corn custard, fresh handkerchief pasta with wild mushrooms, and a roasted half rack of lamb with mint pesto. On warm days, the outdoor terrace is serene and sunny, and the more casual tavern has a full bar and wonderfully cozy, historic feel.

Two miles west of Franconia, ★ **Polly's Pancake Parlor** (672 Rte. 117, Sugar Hill, 603/823-5575, www.pollyspancakeparlor.com, daily 7am-3pm, $7-13) serves legendary stacks of three-inch cakes with house-made maple syrup ("the fake stuff" is available on request, but it's sure to come with a tart helping of side eye). Buckwheat, cornmeal, and whole wheat flours are stone-ground on-site, and while some nostalgic visitors note that the newly renovated building doesn't have the down-home charm of the original, it has loads of seating, which reduces the impressive lines on weekend mornings.

Find basic groceries in Franconia at **Mac's Market** (347 Main St., Franconia, 603/823-7795, daily 7am-8pm), which is small, but has beer, wine, and deli products.

Littleton

In addition to its brews, the ★ **Schilling Beer Co.** (18 Mill St., Littleton, 603/444-4800, www.schillingbeer.com, Sun.-Thurs. noon-11pm, Fri.-Sat. noon-midnight, $9-18) serves Neapolitan-style pizza from a wood-fired oven, and when the riverside patio is open, it's easily the most pleasant, relaxing place to eat in town.

For hearty American breakfasts and lunch at old-fashioned prices, **The Coffee Pot** (30 Main St., Littleton, 603/444-5722, www.thecoffeepotrestaurant.com, Mon.-Fri. 6:30am-4pm, Sat. 6:30am-2pm, Sun. 6:30am-noon, $4-10) is beloved, with tightly packed tables, a diner counter, and paper place mats advertising local lawn mower repair services. The blueberry pancakes are chock-full of fruit and served with maple syrup, hearty sandwiches are made using house-baked bread, and a fresh fruit pie is always on the menu.

Exposed brick walls, white tablecloths, and refined service make **Tim-Bir Alley** (7 Main St., Littleton, 603/444-6142, Wed.-Sun. 5pm-9pm, $19-30) easily the most romantic place to eat in Littleton, and the small, handwritten menu changes frequently to reflect the season. Tournedos of beef, ocean fish with fresh herbs, and wild mushroom soup were included on a recent springtime menu, and it's a genuine challenge not to fill up on the breadbasket full of fresh-baked biscuits and butter.

The back porch of **Miller's Cafe and Bakery** (16 Mill St., Littleton, 603/444-2146, www.millerscafeandbakery.com,

Tues.-Sun. 8am-3:30pm, $5-9) overlooks the Ammonoosuc River just as it makes its way under a bright red-covered bridge, so the views alone make this a charming place for breakfast or lunch. Sandwiches, quiche, salads, and a bakery case full of toothsome, old-fashioned sweets are hearty and simple.

Find big-city style and beans from Intelligentsia Coffee at **MZO Tea + Coffee** (81A Main St., Littleton, 603/575-5433, www.mzoteaco.com, daily 8am-5pm, $3-8), along with a long menu of loose leaf teas and locally baked pastries. Comfy chairs and wireless Internet make this a good place to catch up on the world outside the White Mountains. The owner, who hails from Bangkok, also started **Chang Thai Café** (77 Main St., Littleton, 603/444-8810, www.changthaicafe.com, Mon.-Fri. 11:30am-3pm and 4pm-9pm, Sat.-Sun. noon-9pm, lunch $9-13, dinner $9-19), a casual, laid-back place with a menu that includes the American Thai classics—pad thai, drunken noodles—as well as some unexpected additions, like Massaman avocado curry with black tiger shrimp. Lunch specials are a great deal, and the café serves bento boxes with teriyaki and sushi.

Stock up on groceries at **Shaw's** (625 Meadow St., Littleton, 603/444-1017, daily 7am-9pm) or the **Littleton Food Co-op** (43 Bethlehem Rd., Littleton, 603/444-2800, www.littletonfoodcoop.com, daily 8am-8pm), which has a very good selection of local and organic products, a bulk department, and prepared foods.

Accommodations and Camping
Camping

The sites at **Lafayette Place Campground** (1 Franconia Notch State Park, Franconia, 603/823-9513, www.nhstateparks.org, $25) are right in the heart of the action, with quick access to the trails and destinations within Franconia Notch State Park and hiker information on-site. The location also means the campground has quite a bit of road noise, contained by the high valley walls, but the 97 sites have showers, a camp store, and fire rings, and are ideal for an early start up the Franconia Ridge.

Under $100

Claiming the title of "oldest motel in New Hampshire," the **Littleton Motel** (166 Main St., Littleton, 603/444-5780, www.littletonmotel, May-Oct. $68-108, two-bedroom suites $98-158) does have time-warp pine walls and floral bedspreads, but the friendly management has added welcome updates like in-room coffeemakers and fridges, wireless and cable television. There's a grill and fire pit on the grounds, and it's walking distance from downtown shops and restaurants—all in all, this clean, well-run place is an excellent value.

Find country hospitality at the ★ **Kinsman Lodge** (2165 Easton Rd., Franconia, 603/823-5686, www.kinsmanlodge.com, $55 s, $95 d), which Chet and Sue Thompson run with a minimum of fuss in a rambling historic building. Guest rooms share superclean bathrooms in the hallway, and the accommodations are simple but comfortable. After a hot day of hiking it's hard to beat a rocking chair on the broad, shady porch, or a seat in the library, which is stocked with books and games. A big breakfast is served in the sunny dining room.

$100-150

Simple motel rooms and cottages have views of Mount Lafayette and Franconia Notch at **Gale River Motel** (1 Main St., Franconia, 603/823-5655, www.galerivermotel.com, rooms $90-105, cottages $140-220), where fairly basic accommodations are set on a six-acre property with a shuffleboard, pool, and barbecue area. Rooms have coffeemakers, fridges, wireless Internet, and televisions; the lobby always has fresh baked cookies, cocoa, and tea; and the friendly owner is happy to lend out a DVD player and board games. This motel attracts many guests with pets and kids.

$150-250

As in the wonderful restaurant on-site, lodgings at the ★ **Horse & Hound Inn** (205 Wells Rd., Franconia, 800/450-5501, www.horseandhoundnh.com, $130-195) are full of well-polished rustic charm. Hardwood floors, locally handmade maple furniture, organic soaps, and beautiful linens are right in keeping with the inn's nostalgic, lodge-like feel. There's a bottle of brandy for nightcaps, a library stocked with books and games, and a fireplace that roars away on cold nights; a breakfast of fresh baked pastries, egg dishes, granola, and fruit is served.

Information and Services

The **Franconia Notch Chamber of Commerce** (603/823-8000, www.franconianotch.org), on I-93 just north of the notch, runs an unstaffed **information center** stocked with brochures, open 24 hours a day. The booth is right next door to the **Abbie Greenleaf Library** (439 Main St., Franconia, 603/823-8424, Mon.-Tues 2pm-6pm, Wed. 10am-noon and 2pm-6pm, Thurs.-Fri. 2pm-5pm, Sat. 10am-1pm). In downtown Littleton, stop by the **information center** (124 Main St., Littleton, 603/444-0616, late May-June Fri.-Sat. 9am-4pm., Sun. 11:30am-3pm; July-Oct. Mon.-Sat. 9am-4pm, Sun. 11:30am-3pm) run by the **Littleton Area Chamber of Commerce** for a self-guided walking tour of town and information on area businesses. During the months the center is closed, information is available at the **chamber office** (2 Union St., Littleton, 603/444-0616, www.littletonareachamber.com, Mon.-Fri. 9am-5pm). Another good source of outdoors info is the hiker cabin at **Lafayette Place Campground** (Franconia Notch State Park, 603/823-5884, www.nhstateparks.org, daily 8am-3pm).

Getting Around

It's generally easy to find street parking in both Littleton and Franconia; neither town has public transit.

Southern Vermont

*S*outhern Vermont's back roads and byways lead to picturesque villages, winding rivers, and orchards hung with heirloom fruit.

NEW HAMPSHIRE'S WHITE MOUNTAINS

Adirondack National Park

WOODSTOCK

80 MI/130 KM
1.5 HOURS

ME

NY   VT

NH

BENNINGTON

BRATTLEBORO

115 MI/185 KM
2.25 HOURS

40 MI/65 KM
1 HOUR

THE BERKSHIRES

MA

BOSTON

CT   RI

Just a few hours away from New England's biggest cities, southern Vermont remains fundamentally rural. Spaces between towns are filled with rolling farms and forests.

The Green Mountains extend nearly from one edge to the other, rearing up between the Battenkill valley in the west and the Connecticut River Valley that shapes Vermont's eastern border.

The region's towns offer vivid contrasts. In the foothills of the central Green Mountains, Woodstock is one of the state's most picturesque spots: a cluster of old-fashioned mansions, covered bridges, and galleries that evoke Vermont's history as a rural escape for the East Coast elite. Then as now, farmers shared fences with small-scale sugarmakers and family-run dairies, a fascinating blend that gives the area an uncommon vigor—artisanal cheese and Jersey cows from this part of the state snag top prizes at Vermont country fairs.

Follow the Connecticut River downstream to reach artsy, creative Brattleboro, whose compact downtown is a testament to quirk that feels wholly authentic, with delightful art galleries and farm-to-table restaurants. In the 1930s, pioneering academics Helen and Scott Nearing settled near Brattleboro to farm, write, and live free, and the "back to the land" movement has lingering roots in the hills around town. Get a glimpse of that spirit as Brattleboro celebrates its own slow pace of life at the annual Strolling of the Heifers, Vermont's tongue-in-cheek, ambling retort to Pamplona's Running of the Bulls.

The road across the Green Mountains rises to stunning views from Hogback Mountain before dropping toward quiet Bennington, a working-class town steeped in Revolutionary history. It's the western end of the Molly Stark Trail, a warpath turned scenic byway that's named for a general's wife. John Stark crossed the mountains in 1777 to defeat the British troops at the Battle of Bennington, a rebel victory that resulted in increased support for independence and a monumental obelisk that pokes high above the forested landscape. Beyond the battlefield, modern-day Bennington is the unassuming home of a wonderful art museum, a dense cluster of covered bridges, and the birch-ringed churchyard where the poet Robert Frost is buried.

It's an intriguing trio of towns, but many visitors to southern Vermont find that their most lingering impressions are of a countryside veined with brooks and back roads through villages that seem unchanged by modern life. The Molly Stark Trail is a breathtaking passage across the mountains when fall kindles the trees, and in any season at all, Route 100 is a beautiful way to traverse the state. For adventurous travelers looking to leave the beaten path behind, drive until the pavement gives way and discover a wandering web of smooth dirt roads that beg to be explored.

Planning Your Time

You could breeze through the slender southern end of Vermont in a couple of days, but travelers who slow down to the pace of this area will discover back roads to explore, a fascinating rural culture, and endless spots to linger.

Orientation

Logical bases are Woodstock—a jewel-box village at the edge of the Green Mountains—and funky Brattleboro, Vermont's beguiling, pint-sized cultural mecca. They offer intriguing contrasts, and since they're just over an hour apart, it's easy to explore one or the other as a

Highlights

★ **Billings Farm & Museum:** Experience Vermont's agricultural heritage with wagon rides, award-winning cheddar, and a picture-perfect herd of Jersey cows (page 187).

★ **President Calvin Coolidge State Historic Site:** Explore "Silent Cal's" rural roots at the president's boyhood home, then snack your way through the nearby cheesemaking factory (page 197).

★ **Grafton Village Cheese Company:** Taste some of Vermont's finest cheddar in a picture-perfect, time-warp village (page 198).

★ **Apple Picking at Scott Farm Orchard:** Fill up on heirloom fruit and literary history at this stunning property, where Rudyard Kipling's Vermont home presides over rolling lanes of apple trees (page 201).

★ **Brattleboro's Gallery Walk:** Mingle with world-class artists, hippie farmers, and circus students at this monthly event, when Brattleboro throws open its doors to celebrate local art (page 203).

★ **Bennington Museum:** An excellent collection of work by folk artist Grandma Moses is just the beginning at this fascinating museum, whose exhibits trace the history of Bennington's Gilded Age industrialists and modernist movement (page 211).

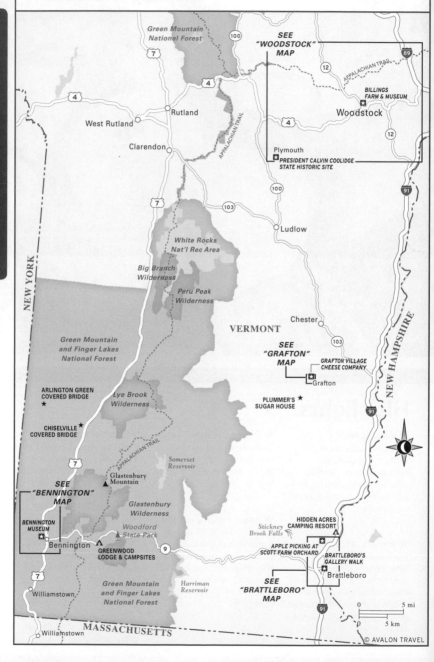

Southern Vermont

Green Mountain
National Forest

SEE
"WOODSTOCK"
MAP

APPALACHIAN TRAIL

BILLINGS
FARM & MUSEUM

Woodstock

Rutland

West Rutland

Clarendon

Plymouth

PRESIDENT CALVIN COOLIDGE
STATE HISTORIC SITE

Ludlow

White Rocks
Nat'l Rec Area

Big Branch
Wilderness

Peru Peak
Wilderness

Chester

VERMONT

SEE
"GRAFTON"
MAP

GRAFTON VILLAGE
CHEESE COMPANY

Grafton

Green Mountain
and Finger Lakes
National Forest

NEW HAMPSHIRE

ARLINGTON GREEN
COVERED BRIDGE
★

Lye Brook
Wilderness

PLUMMER'S ★
SUGAR HOUSE

CHISELVILLE ★
COVERED BRIDGE

APPALACHIAN TRAIL

Somerset
Reservoir

SEE
"BENNINGTON"
MAP

Glastenbury
▲ Mountain

Glastenbury
Wilderness

HIDDEN ACRES
CAMPING RESORT

BENNINGTON
MUSEUM

Woodford
▲ State Park

Bennington

GREENWOOD
LODGE & CAMPSITES

9

Stickney
Brook Falls

APPLE PICKING AT
SCOTT FARM ORCHARD

BRATTLEBORO'S
GALLERY WALK

Brattleboro

SEE
"BRATTLEBORO"
MAP

Williamstown

Green Mountain
and Finger Lakes
National Forest

Harriman
Reservoir

MASSACHUSETTS

Williamstown

NEW YORK

0   5 mi
0   5 km

© AVALON TRAVEL

Best Accommodations

★ **Jackson House Inn, Woodstock:** Start your day with a hearty, homemade breakfast made with locally sourced ingredients at this charming and historic B&B (page 195).

★ **Woodstock Inn & Resort, Woodstock:** Channel Vermont's county gentry at this elegant property on the village green, and unwind with afternoon teas, luxurious rooms, and an intriguing roster of posh activities (page 195).

★ **Latchis Hotel, Brattleboro:** Enjoy popcorn-scented dreams in an art deco building with a grand old movie theater on the bottom floor (page 210).

★ **Naulakha, Dummerston:** Work on your novel—or just enjoy the view—with a few days' stay at Rudyard

Kipling's meticulously restored former home (page 210).

★ **Harwood Hill Motel, Bennington:** A roadside motel meets local art and million-dollar views (page 216).

★ **Greenwood Lodge & Campsites, Woodford:** The fresh mountain air and hiking trails that surround southern Vermont's only hostel make this Green Mountain whistle-stop an appealing place to linger (page 216).

★ **Eddington House Inn, Bennington:** After a day exploring Revolutionary battle sites and Robert Frost's Vermont digs, history buffs can relax in comfortable suites furnished with plush linens and beautifully chosen antiques (page 217).

day trip, with a dozen ways to go from one to the other on scenic back roads. History-rich Bennington is right on the way for travelers continuing to the Berkshires from southern Vermont, but it's also an easy day trip from Brattleboro across a classic mountain road lined with tempting lakes and sweeping views.

Getting to Southern Vermont

Driving from New Hampshire's White Mountains
80 miles, 1.5 hours

To get to **Woodstock** from **Franconia** (80 mi, 1.5 hrs), head out of town on **Route 18 North,** and take **Route 117 West** to **Route 302.** Turn left to merge onto **I-91 South,** and remain on it for about **40 miles.** Exit to **I-89 North,** taking Exit 1 to **Route 4 West** into the center of town. For **Brattleboro,** remain on **I-91 South** for

101 miles, then take Exit 2 for **Route 9 East** into town (130 mi, 2.25 hrs).

For **Woodstock** from **Conway** (115 mi, 2.5 hrs), take the **Kancamagus Highway** (Rte. 112) west and remain on it for about **48 miles** before turning left onto **Route 116 West,** staying on it for 10 miles. Turn left onto **Route 10 South,** then right onto Newbury Road and left onto **Route 5 South.** You'll next turn right on South Main Street, left onto Mill Street, left again onto Old Creamery Road, and then right onto **Route 25 North.** Merge onto **I-91 South** and stay on it for about **28 miles.** Exit to **I-89 North,** taking Exit 1 to **Route 4 West** into the center of town. For **Brattleboro,** remain on **I-91 South** for **88 miles,** then take Exit 2 for **Route 9 East** into town (160 mi, 3 hrs).

Driving from Boston
115 miles, 2.25 hours

To get to **Brattleboro** from Boston (115 mi, 2.25 hrs), head out of town on **I-93 North,** then take Exit 31 for **Route 16**

Best Restaurants

★ **Osteria Pane e Salute, Woodstock:** Regional Italian flavors take center stage at this tiny Woodstock restaurant, which sources many of its ingredients at its Barnard farm and vineyards (page 193).

★ **Worthy Kitchen, Woodstock:** Woodstock locals unwind with hearty burgers and creative pub fare in a convivial space, but the real star is a head-spinning selection of Vermont craft beers (page 193).

★ **Phelps Barn Pub, Grafton:** Country-style dining means heaping plates of pub food in this historic barn (page 200).

★ **T. J. Buckley's Uptown Dining, Brattleboro:** The unassuming exterior of this restored 1925 railway car makes the elegant interior and fine seasonal fare an even sweeter surprise (page 208).

★ **duo, Brattleboro:** Farm to table gets a modern twist at this stylish downtown restaurant (page 208).

★ **Three Stones Restaurant, Brattleboro:** *Salbutes, panuchos,* and *cochinita adobado* are on the menu at an authentic Yucatec joint that's an unexpected highlight of Brattleboro's culinary scene (page 208).

★ **Superfresh! Organic Café, Brattleboro:** A painter's box of bright, vegan food keeps Brattleboro bohemians well fed (page 209).

★ **Sonny's Blue Benn Diner, Bennington:** This real-deal diner has a jukebox and an enormous menu of hearty classics (page 215).

★ **Bakkerij Krijnen, Bennington:** Don't leave Bennington without stocking up on kuchen and *stroopwafels* from these friendly Dutch bakers (page 216).

West, using the second exit at the traffic circle for Alewife Brook Parkway before merging onto **Route 2 West.** Continue on Route 2 to **Greenfield,** then follow signs to merge onto **I-91 North.** Take Exit 1, and follow Canal Street into town.

To get to **Woodstock** from Boston, head out of town on **I-93 North** and stay on it for about **62 miles** ($1 toll, cash only). Exit onto **I-89 North** for **65 miles**, then take Exit 1 for **Route 4 West** (150 mi, 2.75 hrs).

Driving from the Berkshires
40 miles, 1 hour
Coming from the Berkshires, **Bennington** is a short and scenic drive north on **Route 7** from **Lenox** (40 mi, 1 hr), on a sweetly curving road across the Housatonic floodplain. Just north of Pittsfield, the road passes Pontoosuc Lake; turn left on **Hancock Road** for a pleasant sandy swimming beach.

To get to **Brattleboro** from **Stockbridge** (95 mi, 1.5 hrs), take **Route 102 East** to **I-90 East,** staying on it for **34.5 miles** ($2.75 toll, cash or EZ-Pass). Take Exit 4 for **I-91 North,** remaining on it for about **52 miles** until **Exit 1,** and then follow Canal Street into town. Add 30 minutes and some appealing countryside views by taking the **scenic route** (80 mi, 2 hrs): Take **Route 7 North,** and continue on to **Route 8** to Searsburg, then turn onto **Route 9** for a rolling descent into the Connecticut River Valley.

For **Woodstock,** continue on **I-91 North** for **105 miles** to **Exit 9,** turning left onto **Route 5 North** and continuing onto **Route 12 North.** Turn left onto **Route 4 West** into town (160 mi, 2.75 hrs).

It's worth leaving the highway for the stretch between Brattleboro and Woodstock; see *Getting to Woodstock* on page 196 and *Getting to Brattleboro* on

Two Days in Southern Vermont

With a couple of days to explore the area, stick to the eastern side of the Green Mountains and discover art, farms, and historic villages, with plenty of time to take the long way home.

Day 1

Enjoy a leisurely, maple syrup-drenched breakfast at one of Woodstock's gracious B&Bs, then head to **Billings Farm & Museum** to meet a beauty queen herd of Jersey cows, ride a hay wagon, and learn to churn your own butter. History buffs can continue next door to the well-preserved mansion at **Marsh-Billings-Rockefeller National Historical Park,** but if you're primed for more agricultural excitement, opt for a quick trip to **Sugarbush Farm** to learn about the sugarmaking process while sampling farm-made cheese and syrup.

Pick up some picnic supplies at the **Woodstock Farmers' Market** store as you head back through town to **President Calvin Coolidge State Historic Site,** where outdoor tables have an idyllic view of "Silent Cal's" childhood home. Trace his path from the rural family homestead to the White House, then graze award-winning cheddar at nearby **Plymouth Artisan Cheese.**

Turn back up Route 100A toward Bridgewater Corners, where you'll toast Vermont's thriving beer scene at **Long Trail Brewing Company,** then spend the rest of the afternoon strolling Woodstock's **art galleries** and **shops,** or cooling off in an Ottauquechee River swimming hole. If you're feeling romantic, cozy up over regional Italian fare at itsy-bitsy **Osteria Pane e Salute;** if not, join a friendly crowd of locals for craft beer and burgers at **Worthy Kitchen,** Woodstock's unofficial living room.

Day 2

Wake up early for a sunrise hike up **Mount Tom,** then hit the road to explore some of Vermont's most scenic byways. If you've already visited Plymouth Notch, the best way to Grafton is south on Route 106 to Route 10 and Route 35 South. Stroll through the perfectly preserved village center, and eat enough of the excellent aged cheddar at **Grafton Village Cheese Company** to keep you going to **Brattleboro,** where **Superfresh! Organic Café** is the perfect place to meet the locals over vegan grain bowls, "mylk," and hearty salads.

Use the café Wi-Fi to download a map of Brattleboro's latest **art gallery** exhibits, then visit the remarkable collections of fine arts, crafts, and photography in the walkable downtown. If it's apple picking season (mid-August through October), trace the Connecticut River Valley north to Dummerston, where **Scott Farm Orchard** is a sublime place to fill your suitcase with a funky variety of apples, quince, and medlar.

Take I-91 all the way to Route 4 west so you can visit the tiny town of **Quechee.** Hike into Vermont's deepest gorge at **Quechee State Park,** then head to **Simon Pearce** to watch a team of expert glassblowers shape the elegant wineglasses for sale upstairs in the gallery showroom. Stay in Quechee for dinner—Simon Pearce has a beautiful on-site restaurant—or head back to Woodstock for a meal at **Richardson's Tavern,** an informal pub inside the elegant Woodstock Inn.

page 210 for routes that trace some of the state's prettiest roads.

Getting There by Air, Train, or Bus
Air

It's easy to fly *near* to southern Vermont, but unless you packed your pilot's license, the region's postage-stamp airports won't be much use. The largest selection of flights connects to Boston's **Logan International Airport** (BOS, www.massport.com/logan-airport), which is served by every major airline (3 hrs, 147 mi to Brattleboro, 2.5 hrs, 142 mi to Woodstock). Get a little bit closer by booking to **Bradley International Airport** (BDL, www.bradleyairport.com), which has nonstop flights to locations within the United States and Canada (1.25 hrs, 78 mi to Brattleboro; 2.25 hrs, 142 mi to Woodstock), or **Albany International Airport** (ALB, www.albanyairport.com, 1.75 hrs, 80 mi to Brattleboro; 2.5 hrs, 128 mi to Woodstock).

Train

Amtrak (800/872-7245, www.amtrak. com) offers service to Vermont from Washington DC that also passes through New York City and New Haven on its way to Brattleboro, White River Junction, and the Burlington area. The aptly named **Vermonter** isn't the quickest (or cheapest) way to get into the Green Mountain State, but the trains have space for bicycles and excellent views (book bicycle spots in advance).

Bus

Greyhound (www.greyhound.com) has daily bus service between Brattleboro, Woodstock, and Bennington, and to all over New England.

Woodstock

With a bit of starch and a lot of history, this picture-book village is among the prettiest in New England. Rolling hills and farms are the perfect backdrop for Woodstock's covered bridges, elegant homes, and tiny town center. That "country gentleman" feel is no accident—this part of Vermont was a rural escape for some of the 19th-century's most affluent U.S. families, and names like Rockefeller, Billings, and Marsh continue to define today's landscape of historic inns, parks, and farms.

In part due to its carefully maintained past, Woodstock attracts transplants from urban areas around the East. This blend of new and old lends an unusual vitality to the small town, where upscale

Jersey cows at Billings Farm & Museum

restaurants, art galleries, and boutiques cheerfully coexist with farm stores and a quirky "town crier," a community black-board listing contra dances and church suppers. Nestled at the foot of the Green Mountains, Woodstock's surrounded by farms and breweries to visit, and endless back roads invite lazy drives with no destination. It's an alluring base for explorers who like to finish a day of adventure with white tablecloth dining and a well-curated wine list.

Sights

★ Billings Farm & Museum

One of Woodstock's most successful native sons was Frederick Billings, who made his money as a San Francisco lawyer in the heat of the gold rush. In the 1870s he returned to Woodstock and bought the old Charles Marsh Farm, which he transformed into a model dairy farm complete with imported Jersey cows. Today visitors to the grounds of the **Billings Farm & Museum** (53 Elm St.,

802/457-2355, www.billingsfarm.org, May-Oct. daily 10am-5pm, Nov.-Feb. Sat.-Sun. 10am-4pm , $14 adults, $13 seniors, $8 children 5-15, $4 children 3-4, children under 3 free) can tour the property in wagons drawn by Percheron draft horses, meet the well-groomed herd of milking cows, and churn fresh cream into butter. The farm produces two varieties of cheddar from a herd of all Jersey cows: full-flavored and creamy sweet cheddar and butter cheddar that is slightly salty with a rich, melting texture.

Next door, **Marsh-Billings-Rockefeller National Historical Park** (54 Elm St., 802/457-3368, www.nps.gov/mabi, Memorial Day-Oct. daily 10am-5pm, $8 adults, $4 seniors, children 15 and under free) is home to the mansion built by natural philosopher Charles Marsh during 1805-1807 and bought by Billings in 1861. The mansion, open for tours by advance reservation, has a Tiffany stained glass window and an extensive collection of American landscape paintings. In 1934, Billings's granddaughter married Laurance Rockefeller, and they donated the land to the National Park Service in 1992. The main visitors center is the former Carriage Barn, which houses a permanent exhibit about conservation history, a reading library, and bookstore. Combination tickets ($19 adults, $15 seniors) include two-day admission to both Billings Farm and Marsh-Billings-Rockefeller National Historical Park.

Sugarbush Farm

Cows and other farm animals can be found at **Sugarbush Farm** (591 Sugarbush Farm Rd., 802/457-1757, www.sugarbush-farm.com, Mon.-Fri. 8am-5pm, Sat.-Sun. and holidays 9am-5pm), which produces excellent cheddar cheese and keeps their maple sugar shack open all year (though syrup is made between February and April). Set atop a scenic hill, the farm also produces maple syrup, mustards, and jams—all of which are free to sample. To get here, take a right across the covered

Woodstock

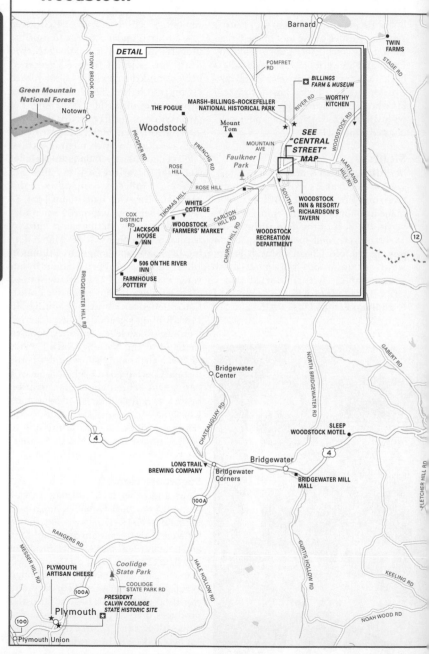

Barnard

TWIN FARMS

STAGE RD

STONY BROOK RD

POMFRET RD

BILLINGS FARM & MUSEUM

Green Mountain National Forest

Notown

THE POGUE

MARSH–BILLINGS–ROCKEFELLER NATIONAL HISTORICAL PARK

RIVER RD

WORTHY KITCHEN

WOODSTOCK RD

Woodstock

Mount Tom

SEE "CENTRAL STREET" MAP

PROSPER RD

FRENCHS RD

MOUNTAIN AVE

Faulkner Park

HARTLAND HILL RD

ROSE HILL

ROSE HILL

SOUTH ST

WHITE COTTAGE

12

COX DISTRICT RD

THOMAS HILL

CARLTON HILL RD

WOODSTOCK INN & RESORT/ RICHARDSON'S TAVERN

JACKSON HOUSE INN

WOODSTOCK FARMERS' MARKET

CHURCH HILL RD

WOODSTOCK RECREATION DEPARTMENT

506 ON THE RIVER INN

FARMHOUSE POTTERY

BRIDGEWATER HILL RD

Bridgewater Center

NORTH BRIDGEWATER RD

GABERT RD

CHATEAUGUAY RD

SLEEP WOODSTOCK MOTEL

4

LONG TRAIL BREWING COMPANY

Bridgewater

4

Bridgewater Corners

BRIDGEWATER MILL MALL

FLETCHER HILL RD

100A

RANGERS RD

CURTIS HOLLOW RD

KEELING RD

MESSER HILL RD

PLYMOUTH ARTISAN CHEESE

Coolidge State Park

100A

COOLIDGE STATE PARK RD

HALE HOLLOW RD

PRESIDENT CALVIN COOLIDGE STATE HISTORIC SITE

100

Plymouth

NOAH WOOD RD

Plymouth Union

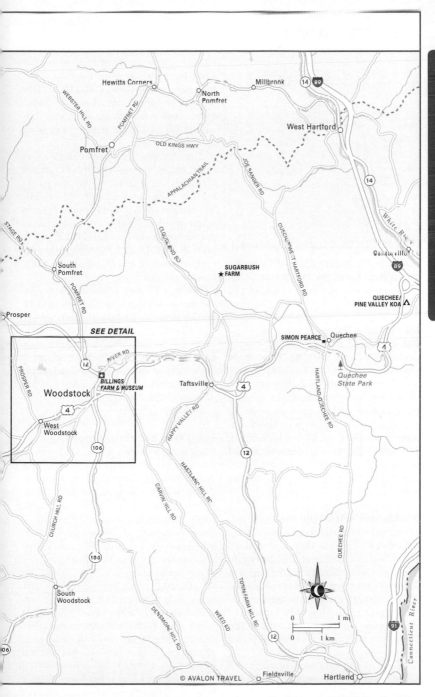

Hewitts Corners

North Pomfret

Millbrook

14 89

West Hartford

WEBSTER HILL RD

POMFRET RD

OLD KINGS HWY

Pomfret

APPALACHIAN TRAIL

JOE RANGER RD

14

White River

STAGE RD

CLOUDLAND RD

GULF-WEST HARTFORD RD

South Pomfret

SUGARBUSH
★ FARM

Quechee Hills

89

POMFRET RD

Prosper

QUECHEE/
PINE VALLEY KOA

SEE DETAIL

RIVER RD

SIMON PEARCE   Quechee

12

4

BILLINGS
FARM & MUSEUM

Taftsville

4

Quechee
State Park

PROSPER RD

Woodstock

HARTLAND-QUECHEE RD

West
Woodstock

4

HAPPY VALLEY RD

106

12

CHURCH HILL RD

HARTLAND HILL RD

QUECHEE RD

CARVIN HILL RD

106

South
Woodstock

DENSMORE HILL RD

WEED RD

TOWN FARM HILL RD

0   1 mi

0   1 km

12

91

Connecticut River

© AVALON TRAVEL   Fieldsville   Hartland

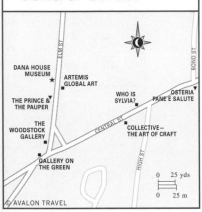

Central Street

© AVALON TRAVEL

bridge at the small village of Taftsville and follow the signs to the farm. Call ahead for road conditions in winter and early spring.

Dana House Museum

For a glimpse into Woodstock's non-agricultural past, visit the **Dana House Museum** (26 Elm St., 802/457-1822, www.woodstockhistorical.org, June-late Oct. Wed.-Sat. 1pm-5pm, Sun. 11am-3pm , free), a federal-style home once owned by a prosperous local dry goods merchant. Now a museum run by the Woodstock Historical Society, it contains period rooms full of fine china, antique furniture, kitchen instruments, and children's toys.

Woodstock's Art Galleries

It's easy to visit the town's vibrant art galleries on foot, as they're in a compact cluster at the center of town, on Elm and Center Streets. Start on Elm at **Artemis Global Art** (23 Elm St., 802/457-7199, www.artemisglobalart.com, daily 11am-5pm), an airy, light-filled space that displays the work of Dutch painter **Ton Schulten** and a handful of other abstract artists.

Walk in the direction of the town green to reach **The Woodstock Gallery** (6

Elm St., 802/457-2012, www.woodstock-galleryvt.com, Mon.-Sat. 10am-5pm, Sun. noon-4:30pm), where the imagery is closer to home. Fine and folk artists offer their takes on the New England landscape and other themes, and the gallery stocks a good selection of work by **Sabra Field,** a beloved Vermont artist who captured the spirit of the state with striking woodblock prints.

Turn left on Center Street for a short stroll to **Collective—the art of craft** (46 Central St., 802/457-1298, www.collective-theartofcraft.com, Mon.-Sat. 10am-5pm, Sun. 11am-4pm), where a small group of local artists and artisans display their work in an old stone mill. Handwoven fabrics, blown glass, pottery, woodwork and metal work are of a remarkably high quality.

Make a U-turn (or, as they say in these parts, bang a uey) and head back up the street to **Gallery on the Green** (1 The Green, 802/457-4956, www.gallery-onthegreen.com, Mon.-Sat. 10am-6pm, Sun. 10am-4pm), which has an extensive collection of sweetly pastoral paintings by Chip Evans, as well as other fine examples of the New England "red barns and Holsteins" genre.

Long Trail Brewing Company

Back before there was a craft brewery in almost every village, there was **Long Trail Brewing Company** (5520 Rte. 4, Bridgewater Corners, 802/672-5011, www.longtrail.com, daily 10am-7pm, free) 15 minutes west of Woodstock. Long Trail started filling kegs in 1989, and their flagship amber ale is now ubiquitous in Vermont. If that's the only Long Trail brew you've tried, you'll be astounded by the selection at the brewery, which keeps around 13 beers on tap. Standouts include the barrel-aged triple bag, but the bartenders are through-and-through beer geeks who can guide your selection. The brewery also has a menu of pub food served 11am-7pm, featuring wings, burgers, and other beer-friendly meals. A raised walkway overlooks the bottling and brewing facility, giving you a fascinating bird's-eye view of the action.

Entertainment and Events

Each year toward the end of sugaring season (late Mar.-early Apr.), many of Vermont's sugarhouses open their doors for the **Maple Open House Weekend** (www.vermontmaple.org/events), which is an excellent chance to rub shoulders with sugarmakers and sample the state's sweetest treats, like sugar on snow . . . with a pickle.

Billings Farm & Museum sponsors many special events throughout the summer, including **Cow Appreciation Day** every July, which includes a judging of the Jerseys, ice cream and butter making, and (always gripping) dairy trivia, as well as a **Harvest** celebration in October with husking competitions and cider pressing. In late July, Woodstock gets wordy during **Bookstock** (www.bookstockvt. org), a festival that attracts an intriguing lineup of writers. While the town maintains an events page, the best resource is kept up by the helpful owner of **Sleep Woodstock Motel** (www.sleepwoodstock. com/upcoming-events).

Shopping
Downtown Woodstock

Handmade pottery with a gorgeously modern aesthetic is the main draw at **Farmhouse Pottery** (1837 Rte. 4, 802/774-8373, www.farmhousepottery.com, Mon.-Sat. 10am-5pm, Sun. 11am-5pm), where you can watch the artisans at work. The store also stocks maple rolling pins, candles, and a seemingly endless array of beautiful things.

Not your average vintage store, **Who Is Sylvia?** (26 Central St., 802/457-1110, Mon.-Tues. 11am-5pm, Thurs.-Sun. 10am-6pm, closed Tues. Jan.-Apr.) stocks flapper dresses, pillbox hats, brocade jackets, and other hard-to-find items dating back more than a century.

Bridgewater Mill Mall

Six miles west of Woodstock on Route 4, **Bridgewater Mill Mall** is filled with studio space for artisans and craftspeople. A highlight is **Shackleton Thomas** (102 Mill Rd., Bridgewater, 802/672-5175, www.shackletonthomas.com, Mon.-Sat. 10am-5pm, Sun. 11am-4pm), where Charles Shackleton—a distant relation of Antarctic explorer Ernest Shackleton—crafts simple but elegant Shaker and modern-style furniture. It's fascinating to watch the woodcarvers, who train for years, and the display room is also stocked with eclectic gifts with unusual charm.

Simon Pearce

Even if you're not in the market for their high-end glassware, **Simon Pearce** (1760 Main St., the Mill at Quechee, 802/295-2711, www.simonpearce.com, daily 10am-9pm) is a fascinating stop that's seven miles east of Woodstock in the village of Quechee. Located in an old mill building run entirely by hydroelectric power, the studio is open to the public, who can watch glassblowers blow bubbles into glowing orange balls of 2,400-degree silica. It's an extraordinary sight, especially the way multiple craftspeople coordinate individual components of a delicate wineglass, with precise timing and handiwork. If they slip up, of course, that's one more glass for the shelf of perfect-seeming "seconds" which are available for purchase at somewhat lower prices.

Sports and Recreation
Hiking

In addition to the exhibits at **Marsh-Billings-Rockefeller National Historical Park** (54 Elm St., 802/457-3368, www. nps.gov/mabi, Memorial Day-Oct. 10am-5pm, $8 adults, $4 seniors, children 15 and under free), the preserve has 20 miles of walking trails, which are accessible from the park entrance on Route 12 and a parking lot on Prosper Road. The roads

circle around the slopes of Mount Tom, which is forested with old-growth hemlock, beech, and sugar maples. Popular hikes include the 0.7-mile loop around the mountain pond called **The Pogue** and the gentle, 1-mile climb up to the **South Summit** of Mount Tom, which lords over Woodstock and the river below. No mountain bicycles are allowed on the trails; in the winter, they are groomed for cross-country skiing.

It's also possible to walk 2.75 miles round-trip to the summit of **Mount Tom** starting at the centrally located **Middle Covered Bridge** on Mountain Avenue. Cross the bridge and follow Mountain Avenue as it curves around to the left along a rock wall. An opening in the rock wall leads to the **Faulkner Trail** at Faulkner Park, where it begins to switchback up the gentle south flank of the peak. The last 300 feet of the trail get a bit steeper, giving wide views of the Green Mountains. Allow an hour for the hike.

East of Woodstock's town green 7.7 miles, **Quechee State Park** (5800 Woodstock Rd., Hartford, 802/295-2990, www.vtstateparks.com/htm/quechee.htm, May 20-Oct. 16, $4) has a pleasant 2.2-mile round-trip trail into Vermont's deepest gorge, starting at the informative visitors center. The **Quechee Gorge Trail** hike takes about an hour.

Swimming

There's an actual swimming pool inside the **Woodstock Recreation Department** (54 River St., 802/457-1502, www.woodstockrec.com, Mon.-Fri. 6am-8pm, Sat. 8am-2pm, Sun. 9am-1pm), but the real treat is a dip in the Ottauquechee River. There's a short path that leaves from right behind the Rec Department, descending to a gentle swimming area that's suitable for families.

Top to bottom: glassblowing at Simon Pearce; Woodstock house; antique cheese press.

Food

Dining on mostly fried, salty fare at a "snack bar" is a quintessential summer experience in Vermont and **White Cottage** (863 Woodstock Rd., 802/457-3455, May-Oct. daily 11am-10pm, $3-22, cash only) is a fine place to get your fix. Golden mounds of fried clams come with tartar sauce and lemon, maple creemees are piled high on sugar cones, and hamburgers are simple and to-the-point. Snack bar food doesn't vary much from place to place, but White Cottage's outdoor tables, riverside location, and friendly staff make it a favorite—and you can wade in the river while you wait for your order.

Pick up supplies at the confusingly named **Woodstock Farmers' Market** (979 W. Woodstock Rd., 802/457-3658, www.woodstockfarmersmarket.com, Tues.-Sat. 7:30am-7pm, Sun. 8am-6pm), which turns out to be a specialty food shop that stocks plenty of locally made treats, cheese, beer, wine, and everything else you might need for a showstopping picnic on the road.

Great piles of pancakes and home fries make **Mountain Creamery** (33 Central St., 802/457-1715, www.mountaincreameryvt.com, daily 7am-3pm, $6-14) a breakfast favorite in downtown Woodstock, and many of the ingredients come from the owners' Killington farm. When local fruit is ripe, don't miss the "Mile High Apple Pie."

★ **Osteria Pane e Salute** (61 Central, 802/457-4882, www.osteriapaneesalute.com, Dec.-Mar. and May-Oct. Thurs.-Sun. 6pm-close, $13-25) is a gem, and aficionados come here from all over New England. Owners Deirdre and Caleb blend their love of regionally driven Italian food with hyper local and sustainable ingredients. The menu changes constantly, but the prix fixe menu ($48) is always a good option. A recent evening featured duck leg in red wine and spices, a selection of elegant pizzas, and a rustic apple *crostata*. The wine list is dreamy, as you might expect from a restaurant with its own vineyard, but the country-chic space itself is very small; reservations are available 30 days in advance, and they book up quickly.

Sedate and sophisticated, **The Prince & The Pauper** (24 Elm St., 802/457-1818, www.princeandpauper.com, daily 5pm-9pm, $18-25) serves fine dining classics—don't miss the restaurant's signature *carré d'agneau royale*, a tender dish of lamb, spinach, and mushrooms wrapped in puff pastry—in a candlelit country setting. Think high-backed wooden booths, exposed beams, and local art for sale on the wall. It's an ideal date setting, though families and groups are also welcome.

If you've had enough of Woodstock's white tablecloth scene, you may be ready for a meal at the relaxed and convivial ★ **Worthy Kitchen** (442 E. Woodstock Rd., 802/457-7281, www.worthyvermont.com, Mon.-Fri. 4pm-10pm, Sat. 11am-10pm, Sun. 10am-9pm, $8-15), a "farm diner" that has a hearty selection of pub food with flair, from fried chicken to poutine. Burritos, nachos, and burgers are other favorites, and there's an excellent beer selection.

Scope out the elegant digs at the Woodstock Inn & Resort on your way into **Richardson's Tavern** (14 The Green, 888/338-2745, www.woodstockinn.com, Sun.-Thurs. 5pm-9pm, Fri.-Sat. 5pm-10pm, bar 5pm-close, $15-27), which offers an appealing blend of pub fare and hearty, grown-up options. Tuck into seafood stew with sourdough crostini, a lamb flatbread or shepherd's pie in a cozy, dimly lit booth; on chilly fall evenings, arrive early to snag a prime table by the open fireplace.

Accommodations and Camping

Woodstock has some of the most appealing accommodations in the state. Prices tend to be higher than elsewhere and rise dramatically during peak foliage season, while off-season prices may be significantly lower than those listed.

Making the Grade . . .

maple syrup's many colors

Vermont is the largest producer of maple syrup in the country, but these days even die-hard Yankees can't keep the syrup grades straight. Starting in 2014, the old grading system—which sorted syrups into Grade A Light Amber (or Fancy), Grade A Medium Amber, Grade A Dark Amber, Grade B, and the hair-raising, commercial Grade C—was replaced by a new one:

* **Grade A Golden Color, Delicate Taste:** Once called "Fancy," this is the lightest syrup grade, with a delicate flavor that often has notes of vanilla. This syrup is best enjoyed with relatively mild foods that won't overwhelm its subtleties; try it with Greek yogurt or poured over vanilla ice cream (Ben & Jerry's, of course).

* **Grade A Amber Color, Rich Flavor:** This grade combines Medium Amber and Dark Amber, and tends to have the most classic "maple" flavor, though some tasters will notice butterscotch or buttery notes. This is classic pancake syrup, and can be swapped for cane sugar or honey in sweet and savory recipes.

* **Grade A Dark Color, Robust Flavor:** Formerly called Grade B, this syrup

has the fullest flavor of the "sipping syrups." This is a favorite among many syrup aficionados, and is ideal for baking, as the more delicately flavored grades may be harder to detect in the finished product.

* **Grade A Very Dark Color, Strong Flavor:** Mostly used for commercial purposes, the syrup-formerly-known-as-Grade C has a powerful taste and can be substituted in recipes that call for molasses.

Maple syrup is produced in March and April by boiling sap collected from sugar maples, and changing temperatures result in a fluctuating spectrum of colors and flavors. While the overall trend is to start the season with pale syrup and end with the darker stuff, a cold snap in April can easily produce a batch of straw-colored syrup with that "delicate taste." The new names may be unwieldy, but the previous system seemed to imply that "Fancy" was superior to "Grade B," which is simply a question of personal preference. The best way to explore Vermont's sweetest product is to find a sugarmaker at a shop or farmers' market; just sample the sweet stuff until you find your favorite.

Camping

Quechee State Park (5800 Woodstock Rd., Hartford, 802/295-2990, www.vt-stateparks.com/htm/quechee.htm, May 20-Oct. 16, $4) has some excellent spots for river **swimming** near a bustling, friendly **campground,** with lean-tos and 45 RV and tent sites along a forested loop (tents $18-22, lean-tos $25-29). There is a dump station, but no hookups; fully powered sites in this area are limited, and the closest option is 2.6 miles farther east, at the **Quechee/Pine Valley KOA** (3700 East Woodstock Rd., White River Junction, May 1-Oct. 15, tents $28-36, RVs $45-70).

$100-150

There's nothing fancy about **Sleep Woodstock Motel** (4324 West Woodstock Rd., 802/332-6336, www.sleepwoodstock.com, $88-158, 2-bedroom suite $250-400), but it's friendly, the rooms are clean and comfortable, and you can use the extra cash for cheddar cheese. This is Woodstock's only budget offering, and the roadside motel evokes another era of travel: It was built in 1959, and as the owners renovate, they're adding flourishes with retro style. The motel is a short drive west of the center.

$150-250

Elegant, well-appointed rooms at the ★ **Jackson House Inn** (43 Senior Ln., 802/457-2065, www.jacksonhouse.com, $189-249) manage to avoid fussiness. Quarters in the main house are somewhat more in keeping with the old-fashioned style of the place, but new additions come with perks like massage tubs. Each one is different, so peek into a few before making your choice. The crackling fire is an appealing place to thaw, but in summer months the broad porch entices. The congenial owners, Rick and Kathy, are devoted to local food, and Rick prepares sumptuous breakfasts with ingredients from area farms.

The **506 on the River Inn** (1653 Rte. 4, 802/457-5000, www.ontheriverwoodstock.com, $169-289) was renovated in 2014 and has an appealingly chic take on Woodstock's genteel country style. Throw pillows are emblazoned with folksy Vermont expressions, antiques are used with restraint, and welcome extras include a game room, library, and toddler play room. Breakfast is well prepared and lavish, served in a dining room and bar that open to the public at night. The inn's bistro menu covers classed-up pub food and child-friendly diner standbys like mac and cheese.

Over $250

You can't miss the elegant ★ **Woodstock Inn & Resort** (14 The Green, 802/457-1100 or 800/448-7900, www.woodstockinn.com, $235-820), which dominates the green in the heart of the village. The rooms and facilities are some of the prettiest in Vermont, full of thoughtful touches and design. This location has been a tourist destination since a tavern with accommodations was established in 1793, but Laurance Rockefeller built the current structure in the 1970s. There are seemingly endless facilities: spa, fitness center, cruiser bikes for exploring the town, organic gardens, and a celebrated 18-hole golf course. You can come take courses on farming and falconry, or just watch the weather from the glassed-in conservatory.

The exquisite and extravagant **Twin Farms** (452 Royalton Turnpike, Barnard, 800/894-6327, www.twinfarms.com, $1,450-2,800) is the former home of journalist Dorothy Thompson and Nobel laureate Sinclair Lewis, who was known for his stirring critiques of capitalism and materialism. Even he might be tempted by this alluring and romantic resort, where the rooms are kitted out with four-poster beds, fireplaces, whirlpool tubs, rare woods, and museum art, with views over a breathtaking property. Twin Farms is all-inclusive and offers an impressive suite of activities, along with remarkable food and drink.

Information and Services

The **Woodstock Area Chamber of Commerce** (888/469-6378, www.woodstockvt.com) runs a **welcome center** (3 Mechanic St., 802/432-1100, daily 9am-5pm) and an information booth (on the green). The well-stocked, independent **Woodstock Pharmacy** (19 Central St., 802/457-1306, Mon.-Sat. 8am-6pm, Sun. 8am-1pm) is conveniently located in the center of town, as are the ATM machines at **People's United Bank** (2 The Green, 802/457-2660, Mon.-Thurs. 8:30am-5pm, Fri. 8:30am-5:30pm) and **Citizens Bank** (431 Woodstock Rd., 802/457-3666, Mon.-Fri. 9am-5pm). In an emergency, contact the **Woodstock Police** (454 Rte. 4, 802/457-1420).

Getting Around
Getting to Woodstock

To get to Woodstock from **Brattleboro** (70 mi, 1.25 hrs) head up I-91 North to Exit 9 to Route 12 North, then turn left onto Route 4 East. **Scenic versions** of this route are almost endless; one option follows Route 30 North to Route 35 North into **Grafton,** then traces Route 103 North to Route 100 to **Plymouth** and continues onto Route 100A North and Route 4 East (75 mi, 2 hrs). Alternately, leave town heading west on the winding Route 9 to **Wilmington,** and take Route 100 North all the way through the mountains to Plymouth, before continuing onto Route 100A North and Route 4 East (100 mi, 2.5 hrs).

Getting Around Woodstock

Most of Woodstock's main attractions are clustered in the small town center, but a number of inns are on Route 4 (also known as W. Woodstock Rd.) that winds west from the Town Green along the Ottauquechee River.

Parking in the village is metered Monday-Saturday 10am-4pm, but it's

President Calvin Coolidge State Historic Site

often possible to find free parking on the west side of town. Woodstock also has an unusual parking validation policy—if you get a ticket in a metered spot, you can bring it to any merchant or restaurant, who can validate it (cancel it) for free.

Plymouth Notch

Tucked into a lush, intimate valley, Plymouth Notch doesn't seem to have changed much since President Calvin Coolidge took office in 1923. The family homestead has been scrupulously maintained, and the nearby state park has miles of hiking trails. Despite being near to one of the state's most important historic sites, Coolidge State Park tends to be overlooked by summer crowds, making it an excellent place to find a trail to yourself. There are only limited services—and no restaurants, so plan on eating in nearby Woodstock.

★ President Calvin Coolidge State Historic Site

One of the best presidential historic sites in the country, the **President Calvin Coolidge State Historic Site** (3780 Rte. 100A, 802/672-3773, www.vtstateparks. com/htm/coolidge.htm, late May-mid-Oct. daily 9:30am-5pm, office exhibits only Mon.-Fri., $9 adults, $2 children 6-14, children under 6 free, $25 family pass) is situated on the grounds of the 30th president's boyhood home, a sprawling collection of houses, barns, and factories in a mountain-ringed valley. The exhibits inside give a rare intimate look into the upbringing of the president known as "Silent Cal" for his lack of emotion, but who restored the dignity of the office during a time of widespread scandal. The family parlor preserves the spot where Coolidge was sworn into office—by his father, a notary public. Even in 1924, when Calvin Coolidge ran for reelection, the homestead swearing-in must have seemed like a scene from a simple, earlier time—one radio campaign ad described it in heavily nostalgic terms, pitching Cal as a rustic counterpoint to Washington DC's modernity and urban sophistication.

Nearby **Plymouth Artisan Cheese** (106 Messer Hill Rd., 802/672-3650, www.plymouthartisancheese.com, daily 10am-5pm) was founded in 1890 by John Coolidge, Calvin Coolidge's father. Their granular curd cheeses were once relatively common in the United States, but are now rare. Learn about the cheesemaking process at the on-site museum, then sample everything from squeaky-fresh cheese curds to granular aged cheeses that have been hand dipped in wax.

Sports and Recreation

Travelers who packed their gold panning kits can prospect for nuggets in **Coolidge State Park** (855 Coolidge State Park Rd., 802/672-3612, www.vtstateparks.com/htm/coolidge.htm, Memorial

Day weekend-Columbus Day), which is at the epicenter of the (very) short-lived Vermont gold rush. No one got rich then and you probably won't either, but locals still find bits of precious metal in the area streams. The park's hiking trails are a safer bet—the 3.6-mile round-trip up **Shrewsbury Peak Trail** takes about two hours and is an appealing way into the forest; the trail gains elevation slowly as it climbs through the trees, and there are views to the south and east from the mostly wooded summit at 3,681 feet. If you're tempted into spending the night in the park, the **campground** has 26 tent sites and 32 lean-to shelters that are among the most appealing in the Vermont state park system (tent sites $18-22, lean-tos $25-29).

Getting Around

To get to Plymouth Notch from **Woodstock,** take Route 4 west to Route 100A South. Turn right on Route 100 to reach the **President Calvin Coolidge State Historic Site.**

Grafton

Once a country crossroads, the village of Grafton hosted presidents and poets as they traveled through 19th-century Vermont. Theodore Roosevelt, Ralph Waldo Emerson, Woodrow Wilson, and Oliver Wendell Holmes all stayed here, but by the 1960s the town's population had dwindled and the village was lapsing into dereliction.

It's a familiar story in rural communities across the state, but Grafton's decline was reversed by Dean Mathey, a New Jersey investment banker with family ties to the region. In 1963 he established the Windham Foundation to "promote the vitality of Grafton and Vermont's rural communities," and it essentially bought and restored the entire place to a high shine, including the elegant Grafton Inn, which has been in business since 1801.

The result is a company town with undeniable charm, an extraordinary cheesemaking company, and a 2,000-acre recreation area: the Grafton Ponds Outdoor Center, with cross-country skiing, hiking, mountain biking, and paddling. It's the perfect excuse to avoid the interstate while traveling between Woodstock and Brattleboro.

Sights
★ Grafton Village Cheese Company

The **Grafton Village Cheese Company** (56 Townshend Rd., 802/843-1062, www.graftonvillagecheese.com, daily 10am-5pm) singlehandedly revived the Grafton cheesemaking tradition. The original, farmer-founded cooperative burned down in 1912, but the Windham Foundation rebuilt in the 1960s, with a vision of making cheese in the rural tradition, with raw milk from family farms. Graze samples of all of their cheeses—don't miss the four-year cheddar—and peer down at workers that are making the stuff. You may wish to dive in the vat when you see the cheesemakers "cheddaring," or turning, blocks of soft curd.

Plummer's Sugar House

There's not much overlap between road-tripping season and sugarmaking season, when the early spring thaw turns Vermont's back roads into churning mud. Any time of the year, though, you can get a glimpse of Vermont's sweetest crop at **Plummer's Sugar House** (2866 Townshend Rd., 802/843-2207, www.plummerssugarhouse.com, daily 8am-5pm), where the owners will walk you through the process with a purchase from the maple store.

Nature Museum

Grafton is home to a small **Nature Museum** (186 Townshend Rd., 802/843-2111, www.nature-museum.org, Thurs. and Sat.-Sun. 10am-4pm, free), which is filled with dioramas and stuffed

Grafton

examples of the local fauna. While some of the exhibits are a bit mangy, the museum is worth a look for its impressive catamount. According to scientists, Vermont's only mountain lion has been extinct for 50 years, despite the dozens of locals that claim to see them each year—those sightings are likely western mountain lions, whose population has been expanding eastward.

Shopping

Once you've stopped by the cheese shop, you can line your walls with art at Grafton's galleries. The diversity and high quality of work available at **Gallery Northstar** (151 Townshend Rd., 802/843-2465, www.gnsgrafton.com, daily 10am-5pm) make it one of the best in southern Vermont. Art is displayed in six rooms of an 1877 village house.

Many of the sculptures at the **Jud Hartmann Gallery** (6 Main St., 802/843-2018, www.juddhartmanngallery.com, mid-Sept-early Nov. daily 10am-5pm; mid-Nov.-Memorial Day by appointment) are vivid renderings of Native Americans from northeastern tribes. They're full of life and exquisite details; particularly dynamic are those that

Say Cheese!

It's only fitting that a place speckled with dairy cows should have cheesemakers to match, and Vermont's got more of them (per capita) than any other state. Cheddar has marquee appeal, but local artisans are producing everything from richly veined blues to creamy chèvres and racking up international awards that have put Green Mountain cheese on the world stage. The Vermont Cheese Council maintains a **Cheese Trail map** (www.vtcheese.com) of the cheesemakers that welcome visitors, and the truly dedicated can hopscotch across the state filling their luggage with tangy wedges.

The **Grafton Village Cheese Company** (56 Townshend Rd., Grafton, 802/843-1062, www.graftonvillagecheese.com, daily 10am-5pm) is a delightful place to start. You can graze samples at the retail store, and the factory is just a short walk down the road, with a viewing window to watch the action most weekdays 7am-2pm. While you're there, don't miss the **Shepsog,** a blended sheep's and cows' milk cheese that's cave aged for five months. The firm, earthy cheese has brought home a shelf full of trophies and awards for its standout flavor.

There's nothing but beautiful back roads from there to **Plymouth Artisan Cheese** (106 Messer Hill Rd., Plymouth Notch, 802/672-3650, www.plymouthartisancheese.com, daily 10am-5pm), which has been operating continuously since John Coolidge (father to President Calvin Coolidge) founded it in 1890. Their distinctive granular curd cheeses are made with raw cows' milk, which you can learn about and sample in the on-site museum and store. Try the **Plymouth Original** or the sharp **Plymouth Hunter.** They don't make cheese every day, so call ahead to find out when they're producing.

Cows might be Vermont's marquee attraction, but even die-hard cheddar lovers should consider the options at **Vermont Shepard** (281 Patch Farm Rd., Putney, 802/387-4473, www.vermontshepard.com, farm store daily 9am-5pm). The family-owned business makes aged and fresh sheep cheeses that have racked up national accolades. Their flavors are inspired by Spanish-style cheeses from the Pyrenees, and the aged versions have a richly flavored, nutty quality. A highlight is the aged **Invierno,** a natural rind cheese that's heavenly with a pint of cider or beer. The shop is self-service, but visitors are welcome to bring a picnic to enjoy the picturesque spot.

depict Iroquois lacrosse players. The hours can vary, so call ahead to confirm that the gallery is open.

Sports and Recreation

A sprawling expanse of fields and forest, **Grafton Ponds Outdoor Center** (783 Townshend Rd., 802/843-2400, www.graftonponds.com, May-Oct. daily 9am-4pm, $5 half day, $7 full day, bike rental $20 half day, $40 full day) has nine miles of hiking and mountain biking trails, and a mountain bike terrain biker. On warm days, the pond is tempting and cool, with a floating dock for basking.

Food

The Windham-owned **Grafton Inn** (92 Main St., 800/843-1802, www.graftoninnvermont.com) dominates the dining scene in Grafton, but fortunately for hungry visitors, they serve commendable food in both of their establishments. The more casual of the two is the ★ **Phelps Barn Pub** (92 Main St., Tues.-Sun. 4pm-10pm, $11-30) serving comfort food that is remarkably refined for something dubbed "pub grub." Burgers and mac and cheese line up alongside options like sole *meunière* (a French preparation involving butter, parsley, and lemon) with barley and roasted fennel, and beef tenderloin in a red wine sauce. The pub is in the inn's onetime carriage barn and retains an appealingly rustic ambience.

The inn's fine dining option is the **Old Tavern Restaurant** (92 Main St., daily 8am-10am daily, plus Fri.-Sat. 6pm-9pm, Sun.-Mon. 5:30pm-8pm, $22-30), whose menu overlaps with the Phelps Barn Pub, but offers a wider range of plated entrées in a beautiful dining room in keeping with the inn's historical feel.

Grab some delicious made-to-order sandwiches at **Grafton Grocery Market** (162 Main St., 802/843-1196, Mon.-Sat. 8am-6pm, Sun. 8:30am-5pm, $5-9). The atmospheric deli also sells excellent cheeses, wines, and sweets—along with any other fixings you might need for a country picnic.

Accommodations

If you like Grafton enough to stick around, the **Grafton Inn** (92 Main St., 802/843-2231, www.graftoninnvermont. com, $165-420) is just as sweetly historic as the village, with period antiques and tasteful country style. Rooms have been updated with luxurious beds and modern bathrooms. Rates include a hearty breakfast with freshly baked pastries and plenty of maple syrup.

Getting Around

If you're looking for a scenic route between **Woodstock** and **Brattleboro**, Plymouth and Grafton are perfect destinations (75 mi, 2 hrs). From the north, head west on Route 4 to VT 100A South, which passes through **Plymouth** before turning into Route 100. Take Route 103 South to Route 35 South and Route 35 South into **Grafton**.

Brattleboro

Brattleboro's brick-lined center is rimmed by gentle mountains that lend the town a dreamy, insular feel. The Connecticut River drifts right through the heart of downtown, where locals linger in cozy cafés, farm-to-table restaurants, and a remarkable collection of galleries with work by local artists. A heady blend of art and ideas infuse life in this famously progressive community, partly driven by students that come to study everything from international development to circus skills. Maybe there's just something in that fresh Green Mountain air, because even the prolific author Rudyard Kipling came here to be inspired and penned some of his best-loved work from a desk at Naulakha, his home just outside of town.

For the visitor, Brattleboro is the perfect place to experience Vermont's free-spirited, intellectual side by rubbing elbows with unreconstructed hippies, professors, and aspiring clowns at one of the town's frequent community events. Strap on dancing shoes, join the lineup and do-si-do in a traditional contra dance, browse organic apples at the vibrant farmers' market, or time your visit to attend the monthly gallery walk, when dozens of local venues unveil exhibits that they'll display throughout the month.

And if you'd like to explore the serious work of the good life in Brattleboro, plan to attend the annual Slow Living Summit, when academics, artists, and activists hash out a game plan for a better world. If that sounds too serious, you can just fall in line behind the cows that lead the Strolling of the Heifers parade, a slo-mo, Green Mountain take on a bull run.

Sights

★ Apple Picking at Scott Farm Orchard

Just north of Brattleboro is the magnificent **Scott Farm Orchard** (707 Kipling Rd., Dummerston, 802/254-6868, www. scottfarmvermont.com, July-Nov. daily 8am-5pm), a rolling expanse of apple trees, forest, and fields dotted with fascinating historic structures. It's a memorable experience to pick your own fruit from the trees that march up and down

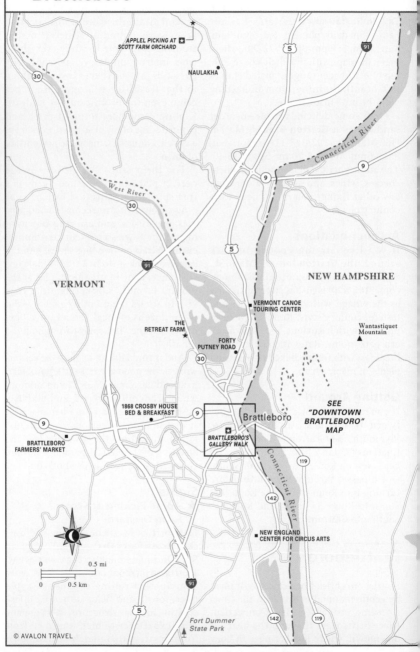

Brattleboro

Sweet Inheritance: Heirloom Apples

The wax-shined, blemish-free apples that gleam in grocery store coolers are a far cry from the fruits that early New Englanders baked into pies and pressed into cider. Nineteenth-century farmers grew hundreds of varieties of apples chosen for their unique flavor profiles and uses, but over time those diverse varieties have been passed over for fruit that's easy to grow and can withstand months of shipment and cold storage. In recent years, a new crop of growers is putting heirloom varieties back on the shelf, growing old cultivars kept alive by generations of farmers.

These heirloom apples can seem homely in contrast with widely distributed Red Delicious and Granny Smith varieties, but many Vermonters have learned to love the nubbly, colorful, russeted fruits for their extravagantly varied flavor and appearance. And a bowl of heirloom apples is a sweet testament to the painstaking work of dedicated farmers. Because apples are grown from cuttings, rather than seed, every single apple represents an unbroken chain of cultivation—one generation of fruit trees lost to disease or frost means the end of that particular variety.

And for heirloom apple lovers, it doesn't get better than **Scott Farm Orchard,** a shrine to eclectic fruit that's worthy of a pilgrimage. Orchardist Zeke Goodband grows over 100 varieties

with intriguing names like Lamb Abbey Pearmain and Zabergau Reinette along with other offbeat tree fruits like quince and medlar. The farm is open for pick-your-own and during harvest season, Scott Farm distributes to stores around Vermont.

Don't miss these favorite heirloom varieties:

+ **Ananas Reinette:** Fine fleshed and crisp, this small, yellow apple is named for the faint pineapple flavor that some tasters can detect—it's a zesty, bright-tasting fruit that's wonderful eaten out of hand.

+ **Blue Pearmain:** With sweet-tart, dry flesh and a beautifully deep color, this apple was a favorite of the writer Henry David Thoreau, who loved to gather them from a tree near his home, saying: "I fill my pockets on each side, and . . . I eat one first from this side, and then from that, to keep my balance."

+ **Esopus Spitzenberg:** Thomas Jefferson grew this aromatic, faintly spicy apple in his orchard at Monticello.

+ **Hubbardston Nonesuch:** Red-gold skin dappled with freckles and russet make this dessert apple as pretty as it is sweet, but it's notoriously hard to grow, making it a rare find.

the hills in parallel lines, and the on-site Farm Market sells jugs of unpasteurized cider made from the farm's dozens of heirloom varieties (unlike most ciders, which are made from easier-to-grow Macintosh apples). Pick-your-own season usually extends from Labor Day through mid-September, but call ahead for apple updates.

The rambling property is also home to **Naulakha,** where author Rudyard Kipling lived from 1893 through 1896. He built the vaguely ship-shaped building on a promontory with stunning views of the

Connecticut River and named it for an Indian adventure story he wrote with his brother-in-law, then penned the *Jungle Book* and *Captains Courageous* at his heavy desk in the "bow." The only way to visit the home is as an overnight guest with a three-night minimum stay.

★ Gallery Walk
Snow, sleet, or shine, crowds throng the center of town on the first Friday of every month for the **Gallery Walk** (802/257-2616, www.gallerywalk.org, 5:30pm-8:30pm, free), Brattleboro's signature

social event. Everyone in town comes out for it, and no other experience will give you a better feel for Brattleboro's unique spirit. The streets take on a festival atmosphere as neighbors catch up on news and pore over their friends' latest creations while juggling snacks and wine. A free map and guide (available online) will help you plot a course through the 50-some venues, which are mostly concentrated on Elliot and Main Streets.

Don't miss the exquisite **Gallery in the Woods** (145 Main St., 802/257-4777, www.galleryinthewoods.com, Mon.-Sat. 11am-5:30pm, Sun. noon-5pm), whose focus on the "Visionary, Surreal, Fantastic and Sacred" results in surprisingly grounded and relatable exhibits that range from folk traditions to fine art. Another gem is the **Vermont Center for Photography** (49 Flat St., 802/251-6051, www.vcphoto.org, Fri.-Sun. noon-5pm), which hosts work by some of the region's most skilled and creative photographers. There's a broad range of mediums on display at **Vermont Artisan Designs** (106 Main St., 802/257-7044, www.vtart.com, Mon.-Thurs. and Sat. 10am-6pm, Fri. 10am-8pm, Sun. 10am-5pm), and it's an ideal place to browse for unique handmade gifts.

Brattleboro Museum & Art Center

Recent exhibits at the eclectic **Brattleboro Museum & Art Center** (10 Vernon St., 802/257-0124, www.brattleboromuseum. org, Wed.-Mon. 11am-5pm, $8 adults, $6 seniors, $4 students, under 18 free; first Fri. of the month 11am-8:30pm free after 5:30pm) included photographs of a local drag troupe and work from an experimental weaving studio in Egypt. The museum's unusual location in a renovated railway station is a draw, as are the one-off events, like yo-yo tutorials, poetry readings, and lectures. On the first Friday of the month, the galleries and gift shop stay open until 8:30pm, with free admission after 5:30pm.

Hermit Thrush Brewery

The diminutive brew house at **Hermit Thrush Brewery** (29 High St., 802/257-2337, www.hermitthrushbrewery.com, Mon.-Thurs. 3pm-8pm, Fri.-Sat. noon-7pm, Sun. noon-5pm, tours at 2pm, 4pm, and 6pm Fri.-Sat., samples $2) makes Belgian-inspired ales in a tiny, rustic space downtown. Try samples of their seasonal options, but don't miss the flagship Brattlebeer, a tart, refreshing sour ale brewed with 20 percent cider and aged in wine barrels. Tart, dry, and slightly fruity, it was "inspired by the town of Brattleboro." During winter months, the brewery closes one hour earlier.

The Retreat Farm

On the outskirts of town, **The Retreat Farm** (350 Linden St., 802/257-2240, www.theretreatfarm.com, late May-Oct. Wed.-Sat. 10am-4pm, Sun. noon-4pm, $6 adults, $5 children 12 and under) has a family-friendly "petting farm" with dozens of animals that range from familiar to exotic. The 475-acre property is still a working farm owned by the Windham Foundation, a private foundation dedicated to preserving Vermont's rural traditions. In the spirit of being a "gateway farm," the Retreat offers plenty of ways to interact with the resident critters, so you can scratch a pig's belly, go eye-to-eye with a one-ton ox, and snag a selfie with an impossibly adorable dwarf goat.

All year round, the **Retreat Trails** are accessible from the main visitors center or from several other entry points. The network includes about nine miles of trails. One popular walk travels 1.15 miles from the farm to scenic **Ice Pond** via **Morningside Trail.** A recent addition is the **Woodlands Interpretive Trail,** a 1-mile loop that is accessed at the Solar Hill trailhead off of Western Avenue; the trail has folksy, 30-minute audio guide that can be downloaded from the farm website, with idiosyncratic stories from locals.

Downtown Brattleboro

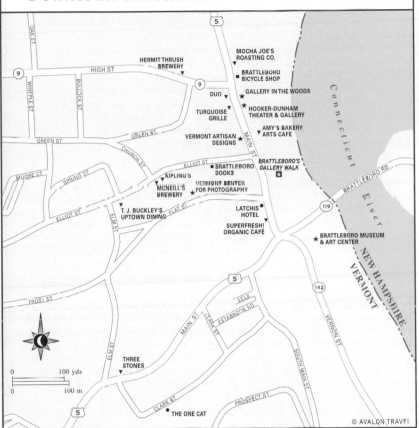

Entertainment and Events
Nightlife
There's always a friendly crowd at **McNeill's Brewery** (90 Elliot St., 802/254-2553, Mon.-Thurs. 4pm-2am, Fri.-Sun. 1pm-2am) which serves its own beers alongside taps from a slew of local breweries. It's an English taproom crossed with a college bar, with plenty of salty pub fare to help soak it all up.

There are bars named for Rudyard Kipling in places from Michigan to Mumbai, but **Kipling's** (78 Elliot St., 802/257-4848, Mon.-Tues. 11:30am-8pm, Wed.-Fri. 11:30am-2am, Sat. 3pm-2am)

has a distinctively Brattleboro feel. Maybe it's the unexpected mashup of Irish bar, fish-and-chip joint, local hangout, and literary mecca (try the James Joyce burger).This is the sort of bar where regulars bang out tunes on the piano.

The Arts
The landmark art deco building that houses the **Latchis Theatre** (50 Main St., 802/254-6300, www.latchis.com, $9 adults, $7 children and seniors, $7 matinees) is as much a part of the show as anything on the screen. Its 750-seat main theater has an iridescent mural of

the zodiac on the ceiling and frolicking Greeks along the walls. Three movie theaters show a mix of first-run and independent films. The 1938 building is also a hotel.

On the other end of the spectrum, patrons of the **Hooker-Dunham Theater & Gallery** (139 Main St., 802/254-9276, www.hookerdunham.org, events $5-20, gallery admission free) enjoy its funky subterranean feel. This venue showcases art-house films, folk and chamber music, and avant-garde theater.

Jugglers, acrobats and trapeze artists take center stage at the **New England Center for Circus Arts** (209 Austine Dr., www.necenterforcircusarts.org, $10-20), a serious training camp for performers both silly and spectacular. Shows are held at the end of school sessions, or when a visiting circus troupe is in town, with one or two performances a month through the summer.

Festivals and Events

Follow step-by-step instructions from the caller, and you'll be twirling and swinging along with a crowd at **The Brattleboro Dance** (118 Elliot St., www.brattcontra. org, 7pm-10pm, $8 students, $10-12 adults), a bi-monthly traditional contra dance with live music and a welcoming set of regulars. Beginners can show up at 6:45pm for a bit of practice. Dancers should bring a pair of clean, soft-soled shoes to change into.

Each June the cows take over for the **Strolling of the Heifers** (www.strollingoftheheifers.org, early June), a parade that celebrates the area's agrarian history and draws attention to the challenges faced by local farmers. In an opening parade, the pride of the pastures saunter down the street, followed by cow floats and kids in cow costumes. During the day, a Dairy Fest features free ice cream, cheese tastings, and a "celebrity" milking contest. Events recently added to the celebration include a Green Expo showcasing environmentally sustainable products

and lifestyles and a fiercely competitive Grilled Cheese Cook-off, pitting professional and amateur chefs against each other for the coveted Golden Spatula. For a true taste of country living—and some enthusiastic swing and twirls—don't miss the evening community contra dance.

Taking place concurrently is the **Slow Living Summit** (www.slowlivingsummit.org), where issues like sustainability, mindfulness, and the good life get serious attention, and keynote speakers come from around the world.

Shopping

Downtown Brattleboro has an eclectic mix of shops that invites leisurely browsing, like **Boomerang** (12 Elliot St., 802/257-6911, www.boomerangvermont. com, Mon.-Thurs. and Sat. 10am-6pm, Fri. 10am-7pm, 11am-5pm Sun.) which stocks new, used, and vintage clothing for men and women and many picks with flair.

Books tower from floor to ceiling at **Brattleboro Books** (36 Elliot St., 802/257-7777, www.brattleborobooks.com, Mon.-Sat. 10am-6pm, Sun. 11am-5pm), an independent store with the best selection in town, including many used and out of print copies.

You can find one-of-a-kind gifts at **Vermont Artisan Designs** (106 Main St., 802/257-7044, www.vtart.com, Mon.-Thurs. and Sat. 10am-6pm, Fri. 10am-8pm, Sun. 10am-5pm), which features pottery, furniture, and other crafts made by artisans from across the state.

Sports and Recreation
Biking

With easygoing traffic and loads of scenic country roads, Brattleboro is the perfect place to ditch four wheels for two. If you've got your own bike, the Windham Regional Commission creates a useful pdf bicycle suitability map (www.windhamregional.org/bikemap), and 21-speed hybrid bikes are available to rent at **Brattleboro Bicycle Shop** (165 Main St.,

Salamander Crossing

It might look like a practical joke, but if you see a "Salamander Crossing" sign, don't laugh—just ease off the gas pedal and watch for slow-moving amphibians. Every spring, salamanders—including the strikingly spotted red eft—trek to vernal pools to lay their eggs after a sleepy winter below the frost line. When warming weather gets them moving, they start to walk to their pool of choice over the course of several rainy nights in April. But if the migration route crosses a road, entire populations risk being wiped out by passing cars.

To protect the amphibious creatures, volunteers around the state post signs to alert cars of their presence, and on the "Big Nights" when they start to migrate, an ad hoc platoon of crossing guards slow traffic and run a salamander shuttle service. The poky salamanders get scooped up one at a time and carried to the opposite side of the road, where they can continue to mosey through forests and fields to lay their eggs. If you're in southern Vermont in salamander season, you can sign up to receive updates on all things salamander from the **Bonnyvale Environmental Education Center** (www.beec.org) and even volunteer to help the adorable amphibians get to where they're going.

802/254-8644, www.bratbike.com, $25/ day). The friendly staff is happy to suggest rides in the area, which are either flat out-and-backs in the Connecticut River Valley, or hilly climbs into the Green Mountains. As is the case throughout Vermont, some of the finest riding is on unpaved dirt roads, which outnumber the nearby asphalt options three to one, and these are an ideal way to escape into quiet country hollows.

Boating

Canoes, kayaks, and tubes can be rented from the **Vermont Canoe Touring Center** (451 Putney Rd., 802/257-5008, www.vermontcanoetouringcenter.com; kayak: $20 for 2 hrs, $30 for 4 hrs., $40 for a full day; canoe: $25 for 2 hrs, $35 for 4 hrs., $45 for a full day; tube: $20/day; appointments required) at the intersection of the Connecticut and West Rivers. The stretch of the Connecticut above Vernon Dam is wide and pleasant, with some small islands along the way for paddlers to get out and explore; the West River is smaller but similarly peaceful, though it can also offer some great class II and III whitewater in the early spring when the snow melts, or on one of a few release dates from the upstream dam each year.

Hiking

Three short, gentle nature trails leave from the Fort Dummer State Park Campground; the 1-mile long **Sunrise Trail** and the 0.5-mile **Sunset Trail** loop through the forest, and the 0.5-mile **Broad Brook Trail** leads from the southern edge of the campground loop to a river swimming hole that's a pleasantly shady haven on a hot summer day.

Brattleboro's rolling skyline is dominated by **Wantastiquet Mountain,** but the trail to the top of the 1,368-foot peak starts in New Hampshire, just across the Connecticut River. To reach the trailhead take Rte. 119 across the river from downtown Brattleboro, and turn left onto Mountain Road just after the second bridge. The trailhead is 0.9 miles from downtown Brattleboro at a small parking area on the right side of the road. The 1.5 miles of switchbacks earn you sweeping views of the Connecticut valley from the summit, where an exposed granite slab makes an excellent picnic spot.

Swimming

The Connecticut River looks temptingly cool as it burbles past town, but there are cleaner, more peaceful options a short drive outside of city limits.

Though the river is generally too shallow for swimming, just flopping into a pool at **Stickney Brook Falls** is a delightful way to spend a hot afternoon. The series of gentle falls is on the left hand side of Stickney Brook Road; from downtown Brattleboro, drive north on Route 30, and continue 3.7 miles past the I-91 underpass. Turn left on Stickney Brook Road, and watch for cars parked along the road.

Stickney Brook is a tributary of the **West River,** which runs parallel to the Route 30 north of Brattleboro. There are excellent swimming holes all along the waterway, notably just under the West Dummerston covered bridge (7.3 miles north of Brattleboro, with a sometimes strong current).

Half an hour west of Brattleboro, the sinuous **Harrington Reservoir** is pocked with pleasant spots to slip into the water. To reach the reservoir, drive west on Route 9 to the intersection with Route 100 in Wilmington. Access points and swimming beaches are located on the right side of Route 100, several with picnic areas and grills. The reservoir's most famous swim spot is **The Ledges,** a pristine, clothing-optional crook in the shoreline that's back in the buff after losing its nudist privileges in a hotly contested town vote. Thanks to support from groups like A.A.N.R.—that's the American Association for Nude Recreation—the vote was eventually overturned.

Food
Fine Dining
The contrast between the thoughtful menus and the offbeat setting—a 1925 Worcester diner car—only heighten the experience at ★ **T. J. Buckley's Uptown Dining** (132 Elliot St., 802/257-4922, Thurs.-Sun. 5:30pm-9:30pm, $40), a long-standing Brattleboro favorite. There are just eight tables, so chef-owner Michael Fuller gives personal attention to each dish and offers a handful of options nightly. All of them feature bold flavor combinations, such as venison with

eggplant caponata, truffle oil, and fresh currants, or the quail with duck leg confit and root vegetables.

Exposed brick and an open kitchen making dining at ★ **duo** (136 Main St., 802/251-4141, www.duorestaurants.com, Mon.-Thurs. 5pm-9pm, Fri. 5pm-10pm, Sat. 9am-2pm and 5pm-10pm, Sun. 9am-2pm and 5pm-9pm, $18-24) a convivial and cozy experience. Their fresh, farm-to-table menus bring diverse influences to bear on seasonal ingredients. Recent starters included fried pickled radishes and potted hot pastrami served with remoulade, sauerkraut, and rye. The pork chop is perfectly prepared and arrives alongside cornbread, bacon, and rhubarb chow chow.

International
With a brightly lit industrial chic space right in the center of town, **Turquoise Grille** (128 Main St., 802/254-2327, www.turquoisegrille.com, Mon.-Sat. 11am-3pm and 5pm-9pm, Sun. 9:30am-3pm, $7-18) beckons on gray afternoons. The menu has global versions of meat on bread, with Turkish flair: kofte and kebabs alongside pulled pork, bratwurst, and burgers.

The unexpectedness of ★ **Three Stones Restaurant** (105 Canal St., 802/246-1035, www.3stonesrestaurant. com, Wed.-Sun. 5pm-9pm, $12-16) is enchanting. A ramshackle exterior gives way to a warm and vivid interior with a decidedly casual feel. This family-run joint prepares classic foods of the Yucatán Peninsula in southern Mexico, like *panuchos,* a stuffed, refried tortilla; *salbutes,* fried maize cakes piled high with meal and vegetables; and *cochinita adobado,* slow-cooked pork that melts in your mouth. Don't miss the *onzicil,* a sauce made from toasted pepitas and tomatoes.

Cafés and Bakeries
The town's unofficial meeting hall is **Amy's Bakery Arts Cafe** (113 Main St.,

802/251-1071, Mon.-Sat. 8am-6pm, Sun. 8am-5pm, $7-10), where locals catch up over freshly baked bread, pastries, and coffee at tables overlooking the Connecticut River.

Tucked into a cozy basement nook, **Mocha Joe's Roasting Co.** (82 Main St., 802/257-7794, www.mochajoes.com, Mon.-Thurs. 7am-8pm, Fri. 7am-9pm, Sat. 7:30am-9pm, Sun. 7:30am-8pm) roasts coffee sourced from around the world, with direct trade programs in Cameroon and Nicaragua. The café serves pastries and snacks but the brews are the real focus, and the friendly space may tempt you to while away the morning.

Vegetable lovers who've tired of Vermont's typically meat-heavy menus should head to ★ **Superfresh! Organic Café** (30 Main St., 802/579-1751, www. superfreshcafe.com, Mon.-Wed. 10am-4pm, Thurs. 10am-9pm, Fri.-Sat. 10am-10pm, Sun. 10am-9pm, $7-14), which fills plates with vibrant salads, filling sandwiches and wraps, and ample gluten-free options. You'll find plenty of smoothies, vegan "mylks," and elixirs for what ails you. The laid-back, artsy style is right at home in downtown Brattleboro, attracting a colorful crowd of locals.

Markets

The **Brattleboro Farmers' Market** (www.brattleborofarmersmarket.com, May-Oct. Sat. 9am-2pm; June-Oct. Tues. 10am-2pm) is the best in southern Vermont, with piles of local produce, cheese, and meat from local farms, crafters, and producers. Snap up artisanal kimchi, gelato, and pasta, among many other things. The Saturday market is on Route 9 near the covered bridge; the Tuesday market is at Whetstone pathway, on lower Main Street.

Accommodations and Camping
Camping

A 1908 dam on the Connecticut River flooded Fort Dummer—Vermont's first

permanent European settlement—but the area around it has been preserved as **Fort Dummer State Park** (517 Old Guilford Rd., 802/254-2610, www.vt-stateparks.com/htm/fortdummer.htm, mid-May-Labor Day, campsites and lean-tos $18-27). The 217-acre forest is just south of downtown, with a pleasant mix of oak, beech, and birch trees that shelter wild turkey and ruffed grouse. The campground's 50 wooded tent sites are comfortable, if not particularly private, or you can spend the night in one of 10 more secluded lean-tos. Hot showers and a dumping station are available, but no hookups.

While somewhat less centrally located than Fort Dummer, **Hidden Acres Camping Resort** (792 Rte. 5, Dummerston, 802/254-2098, www.hiddenacresvt.net, Apr. 15-Oct. 15, tents $28, sites with hookups $40) is a family-friendly place to plug in your RV, with a snack bar, swimming pool, and miniature golf. Sites don't offer much privacy, but pets are welcome.

$100-150

Diminutive and homey, **The One Cat** (34 Clark St., 802/579-1905, www.theonecat-vermont.com, $132-165) is as funky as Brattleboro itself. The two guest rooms—New England and Brighton—are named for the Anglo-American couple's homes, with according decorative flourishes. The tiny library is full of intriguing books and calls out for intimate wintertime reading. A full English breakfast is served, and a 20 percent discount is available for guests that arrive without cars.

$150-250

Despite the confusing name—which has led some guests to look for the wrong street address—**Forty Putney Road** (192 Putney Rd., 800/941-2413, www.fortyputneyroad.com, $189-299) is at 192 Putney Road, and the meticulous bed-and-breakfast couldn't be cuter. The pristine white house is surrounded by specimen trees and meticulous gardens outside and filled with serenely decorated rooms evocative of the Provencal and English countryside. A full gourmet breakfast is included.

The lobby at the ★ **Latchis Hotel** (50 Main St., 802/254-6300, www.latchis. com, $115-190) retains art deco flourishes from its heyday in the 1930s, and for some, it doesn't get any better than a room at a downtown movie theater. Period details like terrazzo floors and chrome fixtures maintain historical cool, ongoing renovations are sprucing up the down-at-the-heel rooms, and suites with small sitting rooms are available.

Sweet old-fashioned rooms have romantic appeal at the **1868 Crosby House Bed & Breakfast** (175 Western Ave., 802/257-7145, www.crosbyhouse.com, $160-199). Three individual rooms each have queen-size beds and fireplaces; the largest has a double-whirlpool bath. Fans of dress-up will love the special afternoon tea at which the innkeepers lay out a selection of gloves and hats for guests, along with feathers and other accessories for decorating. The nearby Retreat Trails are perfect for morning walks.

Over $250

Slow down for a few days on the property that surrounds **Scott Farm Orchard** (707 Kipling Rd., Dummerston, 802/254-6868, www.scottfarmvermont.com), and you'll be rewarded with a sublimely peaceful retreat into scattered apple orchards and shady forests. The **Landmark Trust USA** (www.landmarktrustusa. org) maintains five historic buildings that are destinations worth planning a trip around, especially the exquisite ★ **Naulakha** (sleeps 8, 3-night minimum stay, $390-450), Rudyard Kipling's scrupulously maintained home. The property favors historical preservation over modern-day comforts, but the grounds offer sweeping views of Wantastiquet Range, where Kipling loved to watch

Mount Monadnack break the clouds "like a giant thumb-nail pointing heavenwards." The other on-site rentals include the Kiplings' charming **Carriage House** (sleeps 4, 3-night minimum stay, $275), a renovated sugarhouse, and two historical farmhouses. All properties must be booked in advance, and have minimum stay requirements.

Information and Services

The **Brattleboro Area Chamber of Commerce** (180 Main St., 802/254-4565, www.brattleborochamber.org, Mon.-Fri.-9am-5pm) runs a visitors center downtown.

The area's premier hospital is **Brattleboro Memorial Hospital** (17 Belmont Ave., 802/257-0341, www. bmhvt.org). For pharmacy needs, there's **Rite Aid Pharmacy** (499 Canal St., 802/257-4204, Mon.-Sat. 8am-9pm, Sun. 9am-5pm, pharmacy Mon.-Fri. 9am-9pm, Sat. 9am-6pm, Sun. 9am-5pm), which also offers faxing services, and **Walgreens** (476 Canal St., 802/254-5633, daily 8am-10pm, pharmacy Mon.-Fri. 8am-10pm, Sat.-Sun. 9am-6pm). For nonmedical emergencies, contact the **Brattleboro Police** (230 Main St., 802/257-7946).

Banks are found all over the downtown area, particularly on Main Street. ATMs are plentiful around retail stores, in and around hotels, and in convenience stores. Most cafés have **wireless Internet.** Computers are available for public use at **Brooks Memorial Library** (224 Main St., 802/254-5290, Mon.-Wed. 10am-9pm, Thurs.-Fri. 10am-6pm, Sat. 10am-5pm).

Getting Around
Getting to Brattleboro

To get to Brattleboro from **Bennington** (40 mi, 1 hr), drive east on Route 9, the **scenic Molly Stark Byway** which links both towns' downtown areas. The most direct route from **Woodstock** (65 mi, 1.25 hrs) is to follow Route 4 East to Route

12 South, then cruise south along I-91. With a bit of extra time, however, it's worth taking the **scenic route** through the mountains. Take Route 4 West to the 100A through bucolic Plymouth, then turn onto Route 100 South. There are two excellent options for reaching Brattleboro: stay on Route 100 South through Weston and catch up to Route 9 in **Wilmington** (100 mi, 2.5 hrs), or take Route 103 to Route 35 and Route 30, which passes through the cheesemaking village of **Grafton** (75 mi, 2 hrs).

Getting Around Brattleboro

Metered parking is available all over downtown Brattleboro, and the town's small downtown is compact and easy to navigate. Three city bus lines connect at the Flat Street Transportation Center in downtown; rides within town are $1, buses operate Monday-Saturday, and a service map is available at www.crtransit.org.

Bennington

Bennington has a long and rich history, but the town is best known for a battle that took place 12 miles to the west, just over the New York border. The Battle of Bennington was a defining moment for the American Revolutionary cause, a fascinating clash between the pro-British forces—a mixed group of German dragoons, Native Americans, Canadians, and loyalists—and a rebel force led by General John Stark and reinforced by Ethan Allen's Green Mountain Boys.

Tensions have simmered down since 1777, and modern day Bennington is a tranquil former mill town with a liberal arts college and a number of attractions worth a visit, including an excellent art and history museum, Robert Frost's gravesite and nearby home, and a towering monument that commemorates the famous battle.

Sights
Bennington Battle Monument

It's hard to miss the **Bennington Battle Monument** (15 Monument Cir., 802/447-0550, www.historicsites.vermont.gov/directory/bennington, mid-Apr.-Oct. daily 9am-5pm , $5 adults, $1 children), a 306-foot-tall limestone obelisk that's the tallest structure in the state. Inside is a diorama of the second engagement of the Battle of Bennington, along with an elevator that takes visitors two-thirds of the way up for a knockout view of the Green Mountains, Berkshires, and Taconic Range (in Vermont, Massachusetts, and New York, respectively). Statues of the battle's heroes, General John Stark and Colonel Seth Warner, strike dashing poses on the monument grounds, and a kitschy gift shop occupies the site of the storehouse the British had hoped to capture in the skirmish.

★ Bennington Museum

The art-filled **Bennington Museum** (75 Main St., 802/447-1571, www.benningtonmuseum.org, June-Oct. daily 10am-5pm, Nov.-Dec. and Feb.-May Thurs.-Tues. 10am-5pm , $10 adults, $9 students and seniors, under 18 free) is a detour-worthy destination. The museum has the largest public collection of work by folk artist Grandma Moses, along with her sweetly decorated painting desk and chair. Anna Mary Robertson Moses lived in Bennington for eight years, from 1927 to 1935, and developed a simple (some might say simplistic) style that celebrated America's rural roots—harvests, mills, sleigh rides, and ice skating during a time when the United States was undergoing rapid industrialization.

The museum's scope extends beyond folk art: Exhibits opened in 2013-14 include a permanent selection of artwork by the "Bennington Modernists," a vibrant group of avant-garde artists that worked in Bennington from the early 1950s to the mid-1970s, many with a connection to artist Paul Feeley, the head of

Bennington

© AVALON TRAVEL

the Bennington College Art Department. The *Gilded Vermont* exhibit offers insight into the town's history by skillfully juxtaposing elaborate relics of Bennington's mill-owning upper crust with images of the workers that labored in their factories.

Bennington Potters

The first pottery in Bennington was made by a Revolutionary War veteran in 1793. Since then, the town has become famous for its chunky, speckled earthenware, a tradition that is carried on at **Bennington Potters** (324 County St., 802/447-7531 or 800/205-8033, www.benningtonpotters.com, Mon.-Sat. 9:30am-6pm, Sun. 10am-5pm), which is equal parts outlet store and museum. You can browse several rooms of mugs, bowls, and plates made in the company's distinctive "speckleware" patterns and then watch artisans at work spinning clay in the potters' yard.

Main Street

Old First Congregational Church

Robert Frost once wrote, "one could do worse than be a swinger of birches," and his beloved trees keep watch above his gravesite, where he was buried alongside his wife, Elinor, behind the **Old First Congregational Church** (1 Monument Cir., 802/447-1223, www.oldfirstchurch-benn.org, late May-July Sat. 10am-noon and 1pm-4pm, Sun. 1pm-4pm; July-mid-Oct. Mon.-Sat. 10am-noon and 1pm-4pm, Sun. 1pm-4pm , donations welcome). In addition to Frost's grave, the cemetery also contains those of American, British, and Hessian soldiers killed at the Battle of Bennington.

Park-McCullough House

One of the most impressive Victorians in New England is the **Park-McCullough House** (1 Park St., 802/442-5441, www.parkmccullough.org, May-Dec. Fri. 10am-4pm, $15 adults, $12 seniors, $8 students and youth 8-17, under 8 free), a Second Empire mansion filled with lavish antiques and period furniture. The grounds and gardens are open year-round and can be accessed free of charge, as can the neighboring **Mile-Around Woods,** a forested idyll looped with a carriage path that is precisely one mile around.

Covered Bridges

The country roads around Bennington are the perfect place to explore Vermont's distinctive covered bridges, wooden structures built to withstand harsh winter weather that became icons of the New England landscape. Start at the elegantly trussed **Silk Road Covered Bridge** across the Walloomsac River, a single-lane "town lattice truss" that dates to 1840; follow Route 7 north from downtown Bennington to Route 67A, and turn left onto Silk Road (3.9 mi from the intersection of Route 7 and Route 9). Continue northeast on Route 67A to a left turn on Murphy Road, where the **Paper Mill Village Bridge** stretches over the river (0.2 mi).The original bridge construction was in 1889, but the existing structure was rebuilt in 2000.

Drive across the Paper Mill Village Bridge, and continue south on Murphy Road, which loops around to **Burt Henry Covered Bridge,** another 1840 structure with town lattice trussing (1.3 mi). Keep an eye out for **Henry House,** to the left of the road just south of the bridge; built in 1769, it is one of the oldest surviving houses in Vermont.

The area's other two covered bridges are 15 miles north, in the village of Arlington. Cross the Burt Henry Bridge and turn right on River Road, then follow Route 67A to Route 67 and 7A North. Just before the Stewart's shop in Arlington, turn right on East Arlington Road, which turns into Sunderland Road before reaching the **Chiselville Covered Bridge** across Roaring Branch Brook (15.3 mi). Set over a steep embankment, this 1870 bridge features a threatening one-dollar fine for crossing above a walking pace.

Retrace your path back to Route 7A, and go north for 0.2 mile before turning left on Route 313. Take a left onto the aptly named Covered Bridge Road after 4.2 miles, and you'll find the **Arlington Green Covered Bridge** (6.3 mi). With a bucolic view of West Arlington's town green and forested hills, this bridge is

among Vermont's most photogenic, especially when fall colors highlight it's iconic rust red color. The bridge is a stone's throw from the home where artist Norman Rockwell lived and painted for 15 years, now the Inn on Covered Bridge Green.

Robert Frost Stone House Museum

After visiting his gravesite at the Old First Church, follow the footsteps of New England's favorite poet to the sweetly simple home, where he lived for several years. Today, it's the **Robert Frost Stone House Museum** (121 Rte. 7A, Shaftsbury, 802/447-6200, www.frostfriends.org, May-Nov. Tues.-Sun. 10am-5pm, $6 adults, $5 seniors, $3 students under 18, children under 10 free). Several rotating exhibits at this small museum explore Frost's life and work, and a permanent display is dedicated to the poem "Stopping by Woods on a Snowy Evening," which he wrote at the dining room table here "on a hot June morning in 1922." Some of Frost's own apple trees remain on the slightly ramshackle grounds, along with crumbling stone walls and groves of birch.

Entertainment and Events

On August 16 of every year, Vermont celebrates its very own holiday, **Bennington Battle Day** (802/447-3311 or 800/229-0252, www.bennington.com), during which the town holds an annual parade along with battle reenactments on the monument grounds.

A few weeks later, bring your breath mints to the **Southern Vermont Garlic and Herb Festival** (802/447-3311, www.lovegarlic.com), an annual Labor Day weekend celebration that offers up plenty of piquant samples of garlic spreads, garlic jellies, garlic salsas, and even garlic ice cream (don't miss the tent with garlic

Top to bottom: statue of Revolutionary brigadier General John Stark; Bennington Battle Monument; Robert Frost Stone House Museum.

margaritas) at a fairground off Route 9 west of town. In between eating and not kissing, fairgoers can take in musical performances, face painting, and a hay maze.

Set in a nondescript brick building in workaday downtown Bennington, it's hard not to love that **Oldcastle Theatre Company** (331 Main St., 802/447-0564, www.oldcastletheatre.org) has been putting on professional caliber performances since 1972. Catch shows that range from Shakespeare to show tunes and slapstick.

Shopping

The shelves at **Bennington Bookshop** (467 Main St., 802/442-5059, www.benningtonbookshop.com, Mon.-Thurs. and Sat. 9am-5:30pm, Fri. 9am-6pm, Sun. noon-4pm) are built for browsing, with an ample selection of children's books, beach reads, and serious literature, along with plenty of local subject matter.

Browse a fun collection of jewelry, art, and crafts at **Fiddlehead at Four Corners** (338 Main St., 802/447-1000, daily 10am-5pm), a friendly store set into an old bank with a slate-lined vault where visitors can scrawl messages in chalk. The friendly, knowledgeable owner makes this shop a local favorite, and he's an excellent source of local lore and attractions.

Sports and Recreation

The Appalachian Trail becomes the **Long Trail** when it passes into Vermont. The closest access point to Bennington is where the trail crosses Route 9—drive 5.2 miles east of the intersection of Route 9 and Route 7, and park in the small roadside lot. To follow a bit of the famous trail, you could head north or south, though the Long Trail mostly winds through thick forest on either side of the road.

Northbound, the Long Trail climbs to **Glastonbury Mountain,** where hikers earn panoramic views of the Green Mountain National Forest from a rickety fire tower. The hike is 7.3 miles one-way, and should only be attempted as a full-day walk.

Southbound, the Long Trail climbs more steeply, pitching up **Harmon Hill;** the round-trip hike from Route 9 is 3.7 miles round-trip; plan for 2.5-3 hours. The trail switchbacks and steps its way up 1,200 feet of elevation gain to an open meadow that peers down on the town of Bennington, where the Bennington Battle Monument pokes high above the trees.

For maps and hiking information, contact the **Manchester Ranger District** (2538 Depot St., Manchester Center, 802/362-2307, www.fs.usda.gov/greenmountain).

Food
Casual Fare

If you don't know what to order at ★ **Sonny's Blue Benn Diner** (314 North St./Rte. 7, 802/442-5140, Mon.-Tues. 6am-5pm, Wed.-Fri. 6am-8pm, Sat. 6am-4pm, Sun. 7am-4pm, $3-12), just look up. Every inch of wall space in this prefab 1940s diner car is covered with specials. Especially to-die-for are the waffles and French toast, topped with every imaginable combination of syrups, fruits, and nuts.

Just up the road in North Bennington about six miles from downtown Bennington, **Kevin's Sport Pub & Restaurant** (27 Main St., North Bennington, 802/442-0122, www.kevinssportpubandrestaurant.com, daily 11am-2am, $8-19) is a neighborhood bar and restaurant that's fiercely beloved by locals. They come for burgers, fried chicken, and steak or just to lean an elbow on the bar and watch the whole town come and go. There's usually live music on Friday and Saturday nights, and the game is always on.

International

The authentic Italian at **Allegro Restaurant** (520 Main St., 802/442-0990, www.allegroristorante.com, daily 5pm-10pm, $14-23) has a huge local following, as evidenced by the oft-packed dining room. Settle in for the homemade specialty ravioli of the day or main courses such as diver scallops with lemon risotto.

The convivial **Madison Brewing Company** (428 Main St., 802/442-7397, www.madisonbrewingco.com, Sun.-Thurs, 11:30am-9:30pm, Fri.-Sat. 11:30am-10:30pm, $8-15) serves handcrafted beers along with pub grub from around the world: cottage pie, mezze platters, Irish lounge fries, and pork schnitzel are among the democratic offerings. The malty, smooth Old 76 Strong Ale is a standout among their brews, many of which change with the season.

Bakeries
Most days, **Crazy Russian Girls Neighborhood Bakery** (443 Main St., 802/442-4688, Mon.-Fri. 7am-4pm, Sat. 8am-4pm, $3-10) serves classic American baked goods with a few soup and sandwich options available before 3pm. The pastries are sweet and satisfying, but don't miss the Peasant Lunch that happens each Friday, when homemade pierogi and and the hearty Ukrainian soup known as *kapusta* fill the cozy space with the scent of Eastern Europe.

Hard to pronounce and easy to love, ★ **Bakkerij Krijnen** (1001 Main St., 802/442-1001, Wed.-Sun. 9am-5pm, $3-10) combines classic pastries and breads from around Europe with Dutch favorites, like dense squares of almond-filled spice cake and apple kuchen. The bakery also has creative soups and sandwiches, including vegan options, and a remarkably friendly staff.

Accommodations and Camping
Camping
Eleven miles east of the town of Bennington on Route 9, the solitude and integrity of **Woodford State Park** (142 State Park Rd., 802/447-7169, www.vtstateparks.com/htm/woodford.htm, Memorial Day-Columbus Day) are magnified by its location at the heart of the 400,000-acre Green Mountain National Forest.

The park maintains a wooded, 103-site **campground** (tent sites $18-22, lean-tos $27-29), which has an RV dump station, but no hookups. Rowboats, canoes, and kayaks are available to rent at the park ($10/hr, $40/full day), and there's a family-friendly swimming beach and picnic area.

You can plug in your rig a few miles west at **Greenwood Lodge & Campsites** (311 Greenwood Dr., Woodford, 802/442-2546, www.campvermont.com/greenwood, mid-May-late Oct., tent sites $27/29, 20- to 30-amp sites $34/36, 50-am sites $36/38 for one/two people, no credit cards) where the 40 wooded campsites have full hookups with 20, 30, and 50 amps. There's also a hostel on-site.

Under $100
The new owners at the ★ **Harwood Hill Motel** (864 Harwood Hill Rd., 802/442-6278, www.harwoodhillmotel.com, $80-115, two-bedroom suite $175) have spruced up their rooms with paintings by local artists and added appealing splashes of color to the simple roadside motel, which has a sweeping view over the town. All rooms have coffeemakers and refrigerators, and rollaway beds are provided for no extra charge. The two-bedroom farmhouse suite was renovated in 2015 and includes a full kitchen and living room. If you're staying for two nights and plan to take in the sights, the Arts Package is an amazing deal: $285 covers both evenings as well as admission and discounts at a laundry list of local attractions.

Just down the hill from the Bennington Battle Monument, the **Knotty Pine Motel** (130 Northside Dr., 802/442-5487, www.knottypinemotel.com, $96-99) offers good value and spotless rooms, including queens, doubles, and efficiencies with kitchenettes.

Eight miles outside of town, ★ **Greenwood Lodge & Campsites** (311 Greenwood Dr., Woodford, 802/442-2546, www.campvermont.com/greenwood, mid-May-late Oct., dorms $32 HI members or $35 nonmembers, private rooms $72-79) is an unbeatable deal set in a serene mountain property. Female and male dorms are four and five beds, respectively, and share a bathroom down the hall. Rustic, mountain cottage decor makes this a cozy place to relax after a day exploring the area's many hiking trails and lakes, and the hostel has a shared kitchen and common area. There is a $3 discount for travelers with their own linens and towels, and dinner supplies are available at the nearby general store.

$150-250

The sweetly restored ★ **Eddington House Inn** (21 Main St., North Bennington, 800/941-1857, www.eddingtonhouse inn.com, $159-199) is full of thoughtful touches; handmade truffles, afternoon snacks, and delicious breakfasts make it a welcoming place, as do the friendly owners. The rooms are decorated with beautiful taste, antiques are atmospheric but uncluttered, and each one includes a sitting area that's perfect for curling up with a book. The Eddington House is in North Bennington, a village that's about six miles north of downtown Bennington.

Four chimneys really do project from the roof of **The Four Chimneys Inn** (21 West Rd./Rte. 9, 802/447-3500, www. fourchimneys.com, $159-299), a sprawling Revolutionary-era parsonage that has been converted to an upscale bed-and-breakfast. As might be expected, many of the rooms have fireplaces, including one with a real wood-burning hearth. The white-cloth dining room has French doors looking out on the grounds and serves a menu of refined New England cuisine, with specialties such as grilled apple cider salmon and mushroom and leek risotto.

Information and Services

The **Bennington Area Chamber of Commerce** (100 Veterans Memorial Dr., 802/447-3311, www.bennington.com) runs a visitors center in town. Emergency medical services are handled by **Southwestern Vermont Medical Center** (100 Hospital Dr., East Bennington, 802/442-6361, www. svhealthcare.org). For medications, **Extended Care Pharmacy** (207 North St., 802/442-4600) is located in the center of town, along with the chain **Rite Aid Pharmacy** (194 North St., 802/442-2240, Mon.-Fri. 9am-9pm, Sat. 9am-6pm, Sun. 9am-5pm). On the north side of town is **CVS Pharmacy** (8 Kocher Dr., 802/442-8369). For nonmedical emergencies, contact **Bennington Police Department** (118 South St., 802/442-1030).

Several banks with ATM machines are located at the corner of Route 7 and Route 9, including **Chittenden Bank** (401 Main St.), **Sovereign Bank** (107 N. Side Rd.), and **Merchants Bank** (406 Main St., 802/442-8321, 8:30am-5pm Mon.-Thurs., 8:30am-6pm Fri.). Free Internet use is offered at the **Bennington Free Library** (101 Silver St., 802/442-9051, www.benningtonfreelibrary.org, Mon. 10am-7pm, Tues.-Wed. 10am-5pm, Thurs. 1pm-7pm, Fri. 1pm-5pm; Sat. 10am-1pm).

Getting Around

To get to Bennington from **Brattleboro** (40 mi, 1 hr), drive east on **Route 9,** the **scenic Molly Stark Byway,** which links both towns' downtown areas. Precisely halfway between the two, the diminutive town of **Wilmington** is the perfect place to pause for a swim or take in views to the south from the Hogback Mountain overlook.

The Berkshires

The Berkshires are New England country life at its most elegant, with summers full of world-class music and art in charming villages.

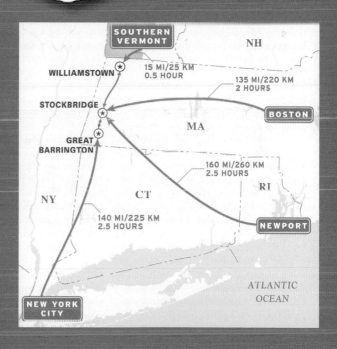

SOUTHERN VERMONT

NH

WILLIAMSTOWN

15 MI/25 KM
0.5 HOUR

135 MI/220 KM
2 HOURS

STOCKBRIDGE

BOSTON

MA

GREAT
BARRINGTON

160 MI/260 KM
2.5 HOURS

RI

NY

CT

NEWPORT

140 MI/225 KM
2.5 HOURS

ATLANTIC
OCEAN

NEW YORK
CITY

All rolling hills and twisting rivers, the Berkshires' gentle landscape shelters quaint villages, grand mansions, and one of New England's most vibrant arts communities.

It's an unexpected mix, but one that's thrived since the days of Edith Wharton and Nathaniel Hawthorne, and the region's artists, farmers, and well-heeled Yankees seem to get along just fine. Berkshire County stretches all along the western edge of Massachusetts, defined by the silhouette of the Taconic Range, where the occasional rocky peak breaks the forest canopy for views of the Catskills and Green Mountains.

In the north, pretty Williamstown and industrial North Adams are just a few miles apart, a town-and-gown matched set with museums that draw art lovers from around New England. Follow the Hoosic River down county to discover the extravagant mansions where 19th-century socialites escaped the heat and noise of the city, establishing a creative connection to Boston and New York that thrives to this day. In the summer season here, the hills of are filled to the brim with music and dance, when the Boston Symphony Orchestra plays for a sea of picnickers on the lawn at the Tanglewood music venue, and the Jacob's Pillow Dance Festival brings world-class performers onto a forest stage.

With all those high-brow cultural attractions, it would be easy to while away a trip focusing on art alone, so for culture-savvy visitors, the real surprise is that the headlining acts are set in one of New England's truly bucolic settings. In between the museums and shows, find a back road to follow at a country pace, leaving plenty of time to take in the views.

Planning Your Time

Compact and simple to navigate, the Berkshires are easy to see from a single home base: Choose one of the towns in the northern part for access to fabulous art museums and the trails of Mount Greylock, or stay in the more southerly section for a taste of Gilded Age glamour and village life.

As with other summer destinations in New England, July and August are peak season in the Berkshires, but the whirlwind schedule of concerts and performances at Tanglewood—which lasts eight weeks from the end of June to the beginning of September—makes everything a little more intense, from hotel prices to traffic. Attending a Tanglewood concert is an unforgettable experience, worth planning far ahead to get tickets and a place to stay. But if you're not coming for a show, consider visiting outside of that frenetic time, when lines dwindle and prices return to earth. Lilacs and tulips burst into bloom in late May, and autumn is an enchanting time to visit, with bright foliage and roaring fires in many bed-and-breakfasts. In the true off-season of late fall and winter, many destinations are closed or have reduced hours (sometimes unpredictably), and it's essential to call ahead before visiting.

Orientation

Berkshire County stretches from the northern to southern edges of Massachusetts on the state's west side, but the key destinations are a series of villages mostly accessible along Route 7. In the north, Williamstown and North Adams are side by side; about an hour south, Lenox and Stockbridge are on opposite sides of I-90, with Great Barrington an additional 20-minute drive down Route 7.

Highlights

★ **Massachusetts Museum of Contemporary Art (MASS MoCA):** Explore a sprawling complex of former mill buildings filled with modern art, installations, and performances (page 230).

★ **Mount Greylock:** Tackle a steep trail to the top of the highest point in Massachusetts (or take a leisurely drive to the same place), and earn views that

stretch to Vermont and New York (page 233).

★ **The Mount:** Tour the gorgeously understated country home that Edith Wharton designed herself, where she gathered a who's who of intellectuals and artists (page 236).

★ **Tanglewood Music Festival:** Spread your blanket and pour the wine for

the summer's most glamorous picnic at the warm weather home of the Boston Symphony Orchestra (page 238).

★ **Norman Rockwell Museum:** Learn about the art and life of an artist enchanted by small-town living and the New England landscape (page 242).

The Berkshires

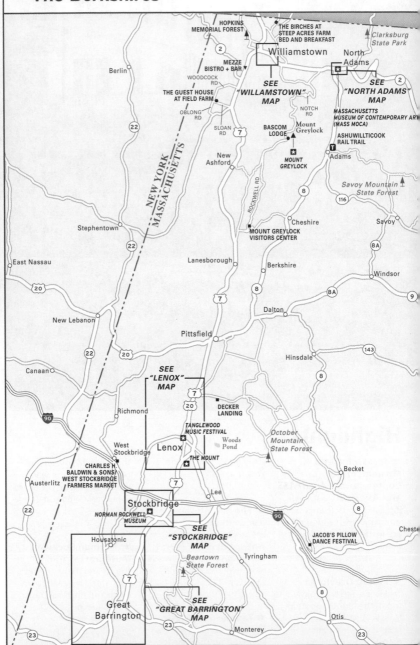

HOPKINS MEMORIAL FOREST

THE BIRCHES AT STEEP ACRES FARM BED AND BREAKFAST

Clarksburg State Park

2

Williamstown

North Adams

Berlin

MEZZE BISTRO + BAR

WOODCOCK RD

SEE "WILLIAMSTOWN" MAP

2

SEE "NORTH ADAMS" MAP

THE GUEST HOUSE AT FIELD FARM

OBLONG RD

NOTCH RD

MASSACHUSETTS MUSEUM OF CONTEMPORARY ART (MASS MOCA)

ASHUWILLTICOOK RAIL TRAIL

22

SLOAN RD

7

BASCOM LODGE

Mount Greylock

Adams

New Ashford

ROCKWELL RD

MOUNT GREYLOCK

Savoy Mountain State Forest

8

116

Savoy

Stephentown

22

MOUNT GREYLOCK VISITORS CENTER

Cheshire

8A

East Nassau

Lanesborough

Berkshire

Windsor

20

New Lebanon

7

8

8A

9

Dalton

143

Canaan

20

22

Pittsfield

Hinsdale

8

90

SEE "LENOX" MAP

Richmond

7

20

DECKER LANDING

October Mountain State Forest

West Stockbridge

TANGLEWOOD MUSIC FESTIVAL

Woods Pond

Becket

CHARLES H. BALDWIN & SONS/ WEST STOCKBRIDGE FARMERS MARKET

Lenox

THE MOUNT

Austerlitz

22

7

Lee

90

8

Stockbridge

NORMAN ROCKWELL MUSEUM

JACOB'S PILLOW DANCE FESTIVAL

Cheste

SEE "STOCKBRIDGE" MAP

Housatonic

Beartown State Forest

Tyringham

23

Great Barrington

SEE "GREAT BARRINGTON" MAP

8

Otis

23

23

Monterey

NEW YORK

MASSACHUSETTS

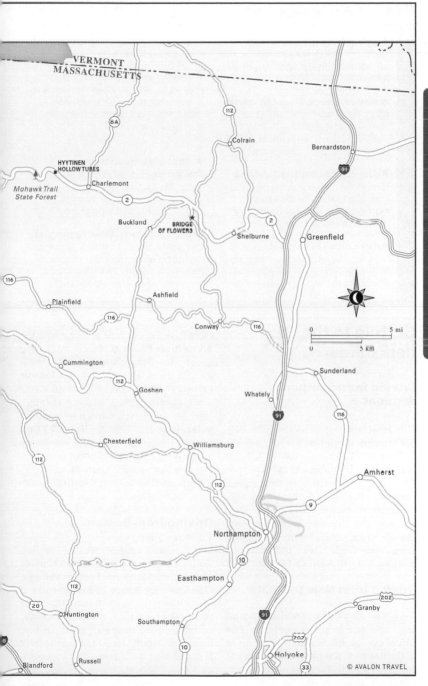

VERMONT
MASSACHUSETTS

112

8A

Colrain

Bernardston

91

HYYTINEN
HOLLOW TUBES

Charlemont

Mohawk Trail
State Forest

2

Buckland

BRIDGE
OF FLOWERS

Shelburne

2

Greenfield

116

Plainfield

Ashfield

116

Conway

116

Cummington

112

Goshen

Whately

Sunderland

91

116

Chesterfield

Williamsburg

112

112

Amherst

9

Northampton

10

112

20

Huntington

Easthampton

202

Granby

Southampton

91

10

202

Blandford

Russell

Holyoke

33

0   5 mi
0   5 km

© AVALON TRAVEL

Best Accommodations

★ **Clover Hill Farm, Williamstown:** Make friends with horses, ducks, and a surly goat at this wonderfully friendly family farm (page 229).

★ **Bascom Lodge, Mount Greylock:** Watch the sun set over the Catskills from a rustic stone lodge built by the Civilian Conservation Corps in the1930s (page 235).

★ **The Porches Inn, North Adams:** Thoughtful design and bits of Americana make this the Berkshires' most exciting hotel, just steps away from MASS MoCA (page 235).

★ **The Cornell Inn, Lenox:** Carefully chosen antiques, self-serve lemonade and snacks, and a manicured garden contribute to the getaway feel of this inn, which has a convenient location by the highway (page 241).

★ **Brook Farm Inn, Lenox:** A classic country inn with modern comforts and historic charm, Brook Farm overflows with poetry books perfect for reading over the afternoon tea service (page 242).

★ **1862 Seasons on Main, Stockbridge:** Enjoy all the frills (and none of the fuss) of a romantic bed-and-breakfast, with gorgeous rooms and thoughtful perks (page 245).

★ **Briarcliff Motel, Great Barrington:** This run-of-the-mill roadside motel at the foot of Monument Mountain took on new life with modern decor and homemade breakfasts (page 251).

Getting to the Berkshires

Driving from Southern Vermont
15 miles, 0.5 hour
Williamstown is just across the border from **Bennington** (15 mi, 0.5 hr), a short drive south on **Route 7.** From **Brattleboro,** drive about **23 miles** west on **Route 9** to Searsburg, then turn left on **Route 8.** After about 5 miles, turn right to remain on Route 8. After 8.5 miles and crossing the state line, turn right onto Middle Road, which becomes Franklin Street, then Eagle Street, and leads into downtown **North Adams** (45 mi, 1.25 hrs).

Driving from New York City
140 miles, 2.5 hours
From New York City to **Great Barrington,** leave the city heading north on **FDR Drive.** Use the left lane to access Exit 17 to the **Robert F. Kennedy Bridge** ($8 toll, cash only), then stay left to merge onto

I-278 East. Take Exit 52 to merge onto the **Bronx River Parkway** for 8.4 miles, continuing onto **Sprain Brook Parkway** north for 12.5 miles. Proceed onto the **Taconic Parkway North**—among New York state's most **scenic** drives, passing through Hudson Valley farms and forest—for **85 miles,** then exit right for **Route 23 East** toward Claverack/Hillsdale. Continue on Route 23 though South Egremont, where it merges with **Route 41,** following it until turning left onto Main Street in Great Barrington.

Driving from Boston
135 miles, 2 hours
Leave Boston on **I-90 West,** following the highway for approximately **125 miles** ($11.70 toll, cash only). For **Stockbridge,** take Exit 2 for **Route 20 East,** then keep right to merge onto **Route 102 West** into downtown Stockbridge. For **Lenox,** take Exit 2 for **Route 20 West.** In Lee, turn right onto Main Street, following it slightly left to Center Street to remain on Route 20. After about 3 miles, turn

Best Restaurants

★ **Mezze Bistro + Bar, Williamstown:** Local ingredients and a creative international menu make this elegant restaurant a regional favorite (page 229).

★ **Bright Ideas Brewing, North Adams:** A community-minded brewery that's equal parts art and industry, Bright Ideas offers a lineup of craft beers for every taste (page 235).

★ **Public Eat + Drink, North Adams:** Industrial cool meets farm to table, just down the street from MASS MoCA (page 235).

★ **Nudel, Lenox:** Score a table in the diminutive dining room and settle in for an evening of cutting-edge cuisine that places local farmers and artisans front and center (page 240).

★ **Haven Cafe and Bakery, Lenox:** Watch the whole town come and go at this relaxed, centrally located hangout (page 240).

★ **Once Upon a Table, Stockbridge:** Tucked into a sweet, sunny alley, this friendly bistro is a longtime favorite for locals and visitors alike (page 244).

★ **rubi's coffee & sandwiches, Great Barrington:** Simple grilled cheese and deli sandwiches are elevated by top-quality cheeses and charcuterie from the attached cheesemonger (page 249).

★ **The Bistro Box, Great Barrington:** The casual fare at this roadside stand is a Berkshires take on the New England snack bar done right (page 249).

★ **The Meat Market, Great Barrington:** Stellar burgers and cauldron-fried chicken make this a carnivore's dream (page 249).

left onto Walker Street, which leads into Lenox. It's about the same amount of driving time and distance from Boston to either Stockbridge or Lenox.

Driving from Newport
160 miles, 2.5 hours

From Newport, take Farewell Street north from downtown and follow it as it becomes **Route 238 North,** then merge onto **Route 138 West,** which leads across the **Newport Bridge** ($4 toll, cash only). Exit onto **Route 1 North** toward Provincetown, then use the left two lanes to turn onto **Route 4 North.** After 10 miles, merge onto **I-95 North** for 2.8 miles, staying left to continue on **I-295 North** for 18.6 miles. Take Exit 9B and keep left for **Route 146 North,** which you'll follow for about 25 miles, crossing into Massachusetts.

Exit toward Route 20/I-90, then use the left two lanes to enter **I-90 West** ($2.95 toll, cash only), on which you'll remain for approximately **83 miles.** For **Stockbridge,** take Exit 2 for **Route 20 East,** then keep right to merge onto **Route 102 West** into downtown Stockbridge. For **Lenox,** take Exit 2 for **Route 20 West.** In Lee, turn right onto Main Street, following it slightly left to Center Street to remain on Route 20. After about 3 miles, turn left onto Walker Street, which leads into Lenox. It's about the same amount of driving time and distance from Newport to either Stockbridge or Lenox.

Getting There by Air, Train, or Bus
Air

The closest airport to the region is **Albany International Airport** (737 Albany Shaker Rd., Albany NY, 518/242-2200, www.albanyairport.com). Taxi service from the airport is available from a variety of car services including **Capitaland Taxi Services** (518/242-4222, www.

Two Days in the Berkshires

Day 1
Work your way from north to south—or reverse the trip—and experience the best of the Berkshires' art, nature, and culture. First, though, choose your style: Modern art lovers should head straight for North Adams's **MASS MoCA** for a morning of wild installations and contemporary masterpieces, while those more interested in the classics can go up the Hoosic River to **The Clark Art Institute** in Williamstown. In the afternoon, drive to the summit of **Mount Greylock** for sweeping views of the mountains and lunch at a communal dining table in **Bascom Lodge,** then strike out along the **Appalachian Trail** to tick off a few of its 2,181 miles; keep an eye on the time, and head back to the peak in time for its showstopping sunsets. Dine in town,

then perk up with a cup of after-dinner coffee—the grounds at The Clark Art Institute are open all night for **stargazing** by the reflecting pools.

Day 2
Continue south for a taste of classed-up country life, starting with **The Mount,** Edith Wharton's gorgeous estate and grounds. If you're ready for more art, don't miss the collection at the **Norman Rockwell Museum,** or join a **canoe trip** down the Hoosic River, whose gentle curves and oxbows offer unmatched perspectives on the mountains, waterside forests, and fields. Finish the day with a slow-moving meal of farm-to-table food at **Nudel,** or catch some tunes in the lair-like basement bar of the historic **Red Lion Inn.**

capitalandtaxi.com), which charges $116 to Williamstown and $126 to Lenox.

Train
Amtrak (800/872-7245, www.amtrak.com) offers service to from Boston to Pittsfield, a somewhat gritty town on Route 7, 17 miles north of Lenox (4 hrs, from $18), and from New York City to Hudson, New York (2 hrs, from $37), 32 miles east of Stockbridge. New York's **Metropolitan Transit Authority** runs trains from the city to Wassaic (2.5 hrs, $21), 50 miles south of Lenox.

Bus
Peter Pan Bonanza (800/343-9999, www.peterpanbus.com) connect Boston's South Station with Lenox (3.25 hrs, $29) before continuing to Williamstown (4 hrs, $40) and North Adams (5.25 hrs, $46). Peter Pan also runs buses from New York City's Port Authority Bus Terminal to Great Barrington and Stockbridge (3.5 hrs, $36), Lenox (4 hrs, $37), North Adams (6.75 hrs, $23), and Williamstown (5 hrs, $40).

Williamstown

A sign at the crossroads of Williamstown's center designates the town "the village beautiful," and few would dispute the claim. Completely ringed by mountains, it's dominated by Williams College, and the green lawns, old-fashioned architecture, and student-filled cafés conjure pure New England college nostalgia. The school is one of the oldest in the country, founded in 1791 through the will of Colonel Ephraim Williams, who was killed during the French and Indian Wars, but left his money for the establishment of a "free school" in the town of West Hoosac—provided it changed its name to Williamstown. Just 30 years after its founding, the president and half the student body left to found Amherst College in the southeast, thus ensuring a rivalry that continues through sports to the present day. Today, the town is well known for its art museums and theater festival, which brings theatergoers from New York and Boston every summer.

Williamstown

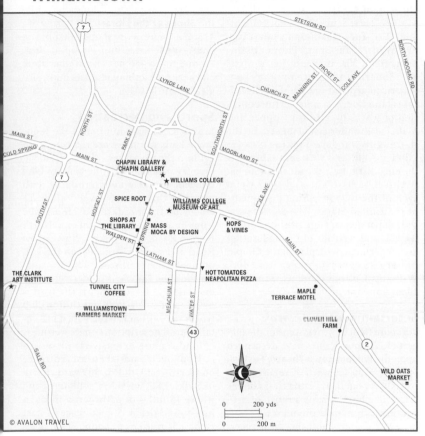

STETSON RD

NORTH HOOSAC RD

FRONT ST

COLE AVE

MANNING ST

CHURCH ST

LYNDE LANE

SOUTHWORTH ST

MOORLAND ST

MAIN ST

COLD SPRING

NORTH ST

PARK ST

MAIN ST

7

SPICE ROOT

HOXSEY ST

SPRING ST

SOUTH ST

CHAPIN LIBRARY &
CHAPIN GALLERY

★ WILLIAMS COLLEGE

WILLIAMS COLLEGE
★ MUSEUM OF ART

SHOPS AT
THE LIBRARY

MASS
MOCA BY DESIGN

WALDEN ST

LATHAM ST

HOPS
& VINES

COLE AVE

MAIN ST

THE CLARK
ART INSTITUTE
★

TUNNEL CITY
COFFEE

WILLIAMSTOWN
FARMERS MARKET

MEACHUM ST

WATER ST

HOT TOMATOES
NEAPOLITAN PIZZA

MAPLE
TERRACE MOTEL

CLOVER HILL
FARM

2

43

GALE RD

WILD OATS
MARKET

| 0 | 200 yds |
| 0 | 200 m |

© AVALON TRAVEL

WILLIAMSTOWN

Sights
The Clark Art Institute

The extensive collection of high-quality art at **The Clark Art Institute** (225 South St., 413/458-2303, www.clarkart. edu, Tues.-Sun. 10am-5pm, $20 adults, free students and children under 18) is remarkable, as is the institute's park-like setting. The Clark is simply one of the best small museums in the country, with a collection full of gems by Renoir, Monet, Degas, Copley, Remington, and other well-known artists that seem hand-picked for their individual beauty or interest. Beyond the gallery walls are 140 acres of walking trails, meadows, and forest, free to access at any time; one of the most romantic ways to enjoy the campus is to make a late-night trip to the Clark's reflecting ponds, where comfortable Adirondack chairs invite all comers for an evening of stargazing.

Williams College

Historic buildings and a picture-perfect backdrop make the **Williams College campus** (880 Main St., 413/597-3131, www.williams.edu) an excellent place to explore on your own, with a few highlights not to be missed. Rounding out the town's reputation as a showstopping arts destination is the **Williams College Museum of Art** (15 Lawrence Hall Dr., 413/597-2429, Sept.-May Thurs. 10am-8pm, Fri.-Tues. 10am-5pm; June-Aug. Fri.-Wed. 10am-5pm, Thurs. 10am-8pm, free). The museum has a focus on modern and contemporary art, American art, and the art of world cultures, and houses a noteworthy collection of works by Edward Hopper and Maurice Prendergast. Housed in the thoroughly modern-looking Sawyer Library, Williams's **Chapin Library** is the only institution outside the National Archives to have an original copy of each of the four founding documents of the United States: The Declaration of Independence, Constitution, Bill of Rights, and Articles of Confederation are on permanent display in the **Chapin Gallery** (Sawyer Library, Rm. 406, Williams College Campus, Mon.-Fri. 10am-5pm, free).

Entertainment and Events

For more than 60 years, some of the biggest Hollywood names have descended upon the **Williamstown Theatre Festival** (413/458-3200, www.wtfestival.org, June-Aug.) to try out their acting chops on the stage. The festival runs a range of productions, from gala premieres to intimate play readings, allowing theatergoers a chance to see a different side of well-known and up-and-coming stars.

Shopping

The main drag of **Spring Street** is full of college-themed shops geared to alumni and stocked with gear in Williams College's single color: purple. Unfortunately, the school's traditional rivals at Amherst College opted for purple and white, so the "Ephs" (that's short for Ephraim Williams, the college founder) tend to spruce up their gear with some yellow to underscore the difference. For gifts in other hues, **MASS MoCA by Design** (50 Spring St., 413/652-2143,

Mon.-Sat. 10am-6pm, Sun. noon-5pm) carries a carefully curated selection of art books, decor, and doodads, while the **Shops at the Library** (70 Spring St., 413/458-3436, www.shopsatthelibrary.com, Wed.-Sat. 10am-5:30pm, Sun. 11am-5pm) combines an antiques store and a pair of clothing retailers into a single, eclectic location.

Sports and Recreation

Mount Greylock dominates the landscape here, but there are many ways to get into the woods from Williamstown. One favorite outing is the trail up **Pine Cobble,** a quartzite outcropping with views of the Hoosic River Valley. To reach the trailhead, take Cole Avenue from Route 7 and turn right onto North Hoosic Road. Turn left on Pine Cobble Road and park 0.2 mile up on the left, opposite the trailhead. The 1.6-mile trail to Pine Cobble is moderately steep and takes at least an hour; the trail is maintained by the **Williams Outing Club** (www.woc.williams.edu), which has detailed trail descriptions on its website.

Find a more extensive trail system in **Hopkins Memorial Forest** (entrance on Northwest Hill Rd., 109 yards north of Bulkley St., www.hmf.williams.edu), where 15 miles of paths wind through forests and fields. A good place to start is the 1.5-mile **Lower Loop,** which takes roughly one hour, and the hike can be extended by connecting to the 2.6-mile **Upper Loop,** which takes an additional two hours; together, the two loop trails form a figure-eight shape.

Food

The floor-to-ceiling windows at **Tunnel City Coffee** (100 Spring St., 413/458-5010, daily 6am-6pm, $2-7) are flung wide open on warms days, and students kick back in comfortable couches and armchairs. Aside from the people-watching, locally roasted coffee is the draw, along with pastries and snacks.

Chewy crusts and freshly prepared

saucics make **Hot Tomatoes Neopolitan Pizza** (100 Water St., 413/458-2722, www. hottomatoespizza.com, Mon.-Fri. 11am-2pm and 4pm-9pm, Sat.-Sun. noon-9pm, $10-14) a perennial favorite. This is primarily a takeout place, but outdoor picnic tables offer fine river views, and the adjoining park is a nice place for a picnic and a stroll.

The village's culinary jewel is ★ **Mezze Bistro + Bar** (777 Rte. 7, 413/458-0123, www.mezzerestaurant.com, Sun.-Thurs. 5pm-9pm, Fri.-Sat. 5pm-10pm, $15-30), a sophisticated restaurant in a beautifully renovated 19th-century home just south of town. Local ingredients are transformed on an international menu with an Italian emphasis; small plates, mains, and pasta dishes star alongside an extensive (and very reasonable) wine list.

In the persistently quaint Berkshires, the colorful decor and bold Indian flavors at **Spice Root** (23 Spring St., 413/458-5200, www.spiceroot.com, Tues.-Sat. 11:30am-2:30pm and 5pm-10pm, Sun. noon-3pm and 5pm-10pm, $12-19) are a tonic. The ample vegetarian and vegan choices are popular here, and the weekday lunch buffet is a fabulous deal.

The classed-up bar food at **Hops & Vines** (16 Water St., 413/884-1372, www. hopsandvinesma.com, Tues.-Sat. 4pm-9pm, $19-25) is served in a relaxed, modern dining room and on a garden-like patio. The menu is brief—favorites include a lamb burger, smoked bacon macaroni, and brussels sprouts—but the wine and beer lists are long and thoughtful.

Grab provisions at **Wild Oats Market** (320 Main St., 413/458-8060, www.wildoats.coop, Mon.-Sat. 7am-8pm, Sun. 9am-8pm), where some produce, prepared foods, and other groceries are sourced locally. Shop for bread, crafts, honey, produce, local arts, and crafts at the **Williamstown Farmers Market** (125 Spring St., late May-Oct. Sat. 9am-1pm), which also has prepared foods.

Accommodations and Camping
Camping
Shady and quiet, the campground at **Clarksburg State Park** (1199 Middle Rd., Clarksburg, 413/664-8345, www.mass. gov, late May-early Sept., $20) has 44 sites, five miles northeast of Williamstown's center. The park also has extensive hiking trails and a tempting pond (where swimming is not allowed).

Under $100
Simple rooms are clean and well appointed at **Maple Terrace Motel** (555 Main St., 413/458-9677, www.mapleterrace.com, $89-109), whose convenient Main Street location is walking distance to the Williams College campus. The continental breakfast of good coffee and fresh bread is an unexpected treat, but the real treasure is behind the motel, where a swimming pool and lawn abut a rolling horse pasture that feels like a bit of country in the middle of town.

$100-150
Just a mile outside of town, **The Birches at Steep Acres Farm Bed and Breakfast** (520 White Oaks Rd., 413/207-9211, www. birchesbb.com, $125-195) is full of charm and hospitality. The 30-acre property has a pond with rowboats for rent, trails, and apple trees, and the fabulous homemade breakfasts are served in a bright, cheerful dining room.

$150-250
While scores of "farms" to stay at abound in the Berkshires, you'll find the real thing at ★ **Clover Hill Farm** (249 Adams Rd., 413/458-3637, www.cloverhillfarm. net, $135-215), home to horses, chickens, ducks, and an adorably grouchy goat named Susie (after she took on a few too many cars, her horns were wrapped in soft cloth—bottles labeled "Goat H2O" are stashed all over the farm to rebuff her mostly harmless butts). The wonderful owners have two single rooms, a five-person suite, and a guesthouse

that are casual, comfortable, and dog-friendly. This is a great choice for families, and riding lessons can be arranged in advance.

A tiered, cubist exterior, painted in hues of teal and mauve, is your first sign that **The Guest House at Field Farm** (554 Sloan Rd., 413/458-3135, www.thetrustees.org/field-farm, $195-350) is not your ordinary bed-and-breakfast. A Bauhaus-inspired modernist masterpiece, the home is full of modern art and design-conscious period furniture. A heated outdoor pool, private decks, and terry-cloth robes create a sense of peaceful refuge, combined with the natural setting—300 protected acres surround the house.

Information

The **Williamstown Chamber of Commerce** (413/458-9077, www.williamstownchamber.com) runs a small information booth which, as of late 2016, is slated to be moved from the corner of Routes 2 and 7 to 100 Spring Street. No hours have yet been set, but the booth is going to be seasonal and volunteer-staffed.

Getting Around

Buses throughout the region are run by the **Berkshire Regional Transit Authority** (413/449-2782 or 800/292-2782, www.berkshirerta.com). Williamstown itself is easily walkable, and metered parking is available on Spring Street.

North Adams

With hulking factory buildings and and a gritty, rustbelt mood, North Adams isn't a place you'd expect to find the largest collection of modern art in the United States, and the Massachusetts Museum of Contemporary Art can seem like a colonial outpost of some hip, faraway community. But if you take the time to explore the town, you'll find art entwined with the old brick structures, vibrant

murals brightening up highway bridges, and studios tucked above Main Street shops. MASS MoCA brought energy, visitors, and an infusion of much-needed cash after the town's leading employer, Sprague Electric, shut its doors in the 1980s, ending North Adams's long history as a mill and manufacturing town. Faded Victorian homes and an elegant public library are legacies of those prosperous years, when whirring woolen mills, shoe factories, sawmills, and ironworks were powered by the twin branches of the Hoosic River.

Sights
★ Massachusetts Museum of Contemporary Art (MASS MoCA)

Built on the sprawling campus of Sprague Electric, the size of the **Massachusetts Museum of Contemporary Art** (1040 MASS MoCA Way, 413/662-2111, www.massmoca.org, late June-Sept. Wed.-Mon. 11am-5pm, Sept.-late June Sun.-Wed. 10am-6pm, Thurs.-Sat. 10am-7pm, $18 adults, $16 seniors, $12 students, $8 children 6-16, free for children under 6) is stunning. Composed of 27 redbrick former factory buildings and connected by an interlocking network of bridges, walkways, and courtyards, it has vast gallery spaces that allow for artwork of an unusually epic scale—from enormous installations to expansive performance art. The scale of the museum also affords more inclusiveness than many institutions, and MASS MoCA has a lack of pretension and takes an infectious delight in the creative process: small, unexpected touches abound, like the sidewalk cracks that employees fill in with gleaming gold paint.

Other Sights

The Barbara and Eric Rudd Art Foundation transformed a historic church into the **Berkshire Artists Museum** (159 E. Main St., 413/664-9550, www.bamuseum.org, mid-June-early Sept. Wed.-Sun. noon-5pm, Sept.-Oct.

North Adams

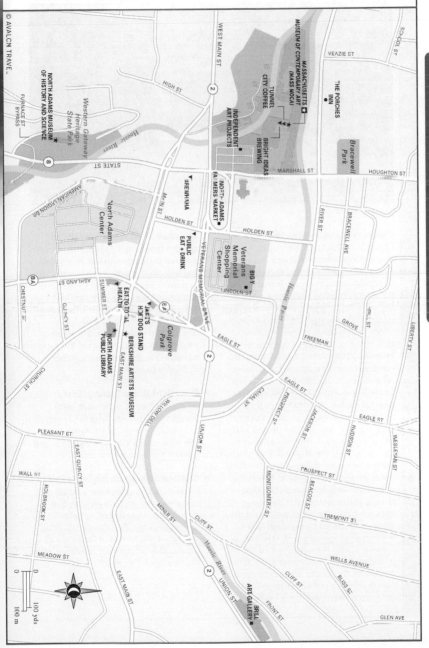

© AVALON TRAVEL

Scenic Byway: Driving the Mohawk Trail

driving the Mohawk Trail

The soul of travel may be in the journey rather than the destination, but it's not always easy to keep that in mind when flying past the off-ramps and strip malls lining the Massachusetts Turnpike. For drivers coming from the east, the Mohawk Trail is a scenic alternative that evokes the golden age of road-tripping, winding through 63 miles of rolling hills, villages, and gorgeous scenery on its way from Athol, a small town in north-central Massachusetts, to North Adams. The route alternates between Route 2 and Route 2A, following a traditional Native American path through the mountains, and was one of the first auto-tourism roads in the United States when it opened in 1914. In contrast to the Berkshires, the Mohawk Trail still has a retro feel, with motor lodges, trading posts, and scenic overlooks lining the roller-coaster ride through the mountains. If you're driving the trail as an out-and-back, the finest portion is the eight-mile stretch from North Adams to the trail's highest point, Whitcomb Summit, which is marked with a bronze statue of an elk. It's a lovely stretch for some Sunday driving, or easy to incorporate if you're coming from Boston. Here are some of the trail's highlights:

- **Mohawk Trail State Forest:** Old-growth forest, mountains, and streams are shot through with five miles of hiking trails that connect to a much larger system in Savoy Mountain State Forest. A favorite hike is the Mahican-Mohawk Trail, which offers access to meadows buzzing with life and a path to the top of Todd Mountain; there are also hiking trails and family-friendly places to swim (Rte. 2, Charlemont, 413/339-5504, day pass $8).

- **Deerfield River Tubing:** Rent an inner tube in Charlemont from **Hyytinen Hollow Tubes** (7 Tea St. Ext., 413/339-4786, www.hyytinenhollow.com, tubes $10, car shuttle $5), and cool off in a leisurely current.

- **Shelburne Falls:** Pretty and old-fashioned, this village has a creative, castaway feel, and the picturesque downtown is lined with art galleries and workshops. The main attraction, though, is the Bridge of Flowers, a disused trolley bridge that overflows with blooms April-October.

Sat.-Sun. noon-5pm, free), a home for local contemporary work. Eric Rudd's own work is on display in a moving, spiritually focused space at the same site, in the **Chapel for Humanity** annex.

Housed in the grand former home of local factory owner Sanford Blackinton, the **North Adams Public Library** (74 Church St., 413/662-3133, www.naplibrary.com, Mon.-Wed. and Fri. 9am-5pm, Thurs. noon-8pm, Sun. 10am-1pm) is a beautiful old building worth a look. Free wireless Internet and cozy reading chairs make this a comfortable place to wait out a rainy day.

For a trip back in time, the **North Adams Museum of History and Science** (W. Gateway State Park, 413/664-4700, www.northadamshistory.org, Thurs.-Sat. 10am-4pm, Sun. 1pm-4pm., free) evokes small-town Americana, and the homemade quality of its exhibits is just part of the old-fashioned charm. Three floors of old photos, clothing, Native American artifacts, and kitschy dioramas tell the story of the town from its founding.

Entertainment and Events

In addition to its art exhibits, **MASS MoCA** serves as the cultural center of the community, staging silent movies accompanied by a string quartet, cutting-edge dance performances, and musical performances by the likes of Yo La Tengo and Laurie Anderson.

Bring a picnic for the weekly shows at **Windsor Lake** (www.explorenorthadams.com, mid-June-Aug. Wed. 6:30pm, free), where local bands play under a small shelter at the water's edge.

Shopping

North Adams isn't much of a shopping destination, but even if you're skipping the whole MASS MoCA experience, the **museum store** could supply a year's worth of creative Christmas presents. Take home a piece of the North Adams art scene from **Independent Art Projects** (1315 MASS MoCA Way, 413/346-4004,

www.independentartprojects.com, Sept.-June Wed.-Sun. 11am-5pm, July-Aug. daily 11am-5pm), a gallery with beautifully curated works in a museum-like space. Another good spot for contemporary work is the **Brill Art Gallery** (243 Union St., 413/664-4353, www.brillgallery109.com, daily 10am-5pm), which often has standout photography shows.

Sports and Recreation
Biking

The 11.2-mile **Ashuwillticook Rail Trail** runs from just behind the **Adams Visitor Center** (3 Hoosac St., Adams, 413/743-8358), about a 15-minute drive south of North Adams, to the small town of Lanesborough, with views of mountains, rivers, and lakes. It's a pleasant, easy trail, and you can rent a bike just off it at **Village Bike Rental** (31 Park St., Adams, 413/743-2453, www.villagebikerental.com, late May-Oct. Mon. 10am-6pm, Tues.-Sun. 9am-6pm, hybrid bikes $22 for 2 hrs, $32 for 4 hrs, $45 for 24 hrs).

Hiking
★ Mount Greylock

The 3,491-foot summit of **Mount Greylock** (Rockwell Rd., Lanesborough, 413/499-4262, www.mass.gov, access free, summit parking $6), the highest peak in Massachusetts, is both accessible and wild, and it and the surrounding peaks are favorites for overnight hikes or leisurely afternoon drives. Several trails lead up into the mountains from both North Adams and Williamstown: Trace some of Henry David Thoreau's 1844 hike to the peak on a challenging 9.6-mile loop, which takes about 6-8 hours, from Notch Road in North Adams—follow **Bellows Pipe Trail** to the **Appalachian Trail** (A.T.)., and return via the A.T. and **Bernard Farm Trail.**

Or try the slightly easier, 6.2-mile round-trip summit hike that takes 4-5 hours from the Mount Greylock Campground. This route starts off signed as the **Campground Trail,** then follows

Hopper Trail for 1.4 miles, and links up with the Appalachian Trail for the final 1.1 miles.

As there are many trails in the area, it's essential to have a detailed map, available at the **Mount Greylock Visitor Center** (30 Rockwell Rd., 413/499-4262, late May-early Sept. daily 9am-5pm, Sept.-May daily 9am-4:30pm).

If all that sounds a bit strained, you can take a scenic, winding road straight to the top of Mount Greylock, where there's a snack bar and visitors center with information on short hikes and nature activities.

Food

Locals have been sidling up to the counter at **Jack's Hot Dog Stand** (12 Eagle St., 413/664-9006, www.jackshotdogstand. com, Mon.-Sat. 10am-7pm, $1-4) since 1917 for a simple menu of hot dogs, burgers, and fries. If the microwave figures more visibly into kitchen prep than is conducive to misty-eyed nostalgia, Jack's is right at home in gritty North Adams, and the friendly service and vintage pricing are unbeatable.

Just down the street (and in a different world entirely) is the vegan, "allergy-free" **Eat to Total Health** (14 Ashland St., 413/346-4357, www.eattototalhealth. com, Mon.-Thurs. 11am-7pm, Fri. 11am-6pm, Sat. 11am-2pm, $5-11), which sells fresh smoothies, prepared foods, and assorted healthy groceries in a small shop with a friendly staff.

Like its sister café in Williamstown, North Adams's **Tunnel City Coffee** (87 Marshall St., 413/398-5304, Mon.-Fri. 7:30am-5pm, Sat.-Sun. 9am-5pm, $2-7) serves pastries, snacks, and locally roasted coffee. This one, however, is inside the MASS MoCA complex (though the café can be accessed without buying a museum ticket), which means your

---

Top to bottom: summit marker at Mount Greylock; Appalachian Trail marker; Bascom Lodge.

cappuccino comes with a side of world-class people-watching, as the museum employees and visitors come and go.

Also in the MASS MoCA complex, ★ **Bright Ideas Brewing** (111 MASS MoCA Way, 413/346-4460, www.bright-ideasbrewing.com, check website for hours, $3-7) is full of references to North Adams's industrial past, with gorgeous brick walls and a 40-foot bar made by local workers. Its diverse lineup of beers manages to bridge the divide between the town's art lovers and townies.

Modern, industrial decor and a gastropub menu make ★ **Public Eat + Drink** (34 Holden St., 413/664-4444, www.publiceatanddrink.com, $10-20) the most stylish place to eat in town, and regulars love the fish-and-chips, burgers, and great drink menu, which includes beers from around New England.

Popular with the locals, the casual **Brewhaha** (20 Marshall St., 413/664-2020, daily 7am-5pm, $3-10) serves coffee, sandwiches, salads, and excellent soups in a small café. Music, friendly staff, and bright posters on the wall make this a welcoming spot.

Pick up the essentials at **Big Y** (45 Veterans Memorial Dr., 413/663-6549, daily 7am-9pm), a basic grocery store in the center of town. Or if you're in town on a Saturday in season, head to the **North Adams Farmers Market** (intersection of Rte. 8 and St. Anthony Drive, 413/664-6180, early June-late Oct. Sat. 9am-1pm), a producers-only market, which also has live music 10am-noon.

Dine on top of Mount Greylock at **Bascom Lodge** (30 Rockwell Rd., Lanesborough, 413/743-1591, www.bascomlodge.net, June Tues.-Sun and July-Oct. daily, breakfast 8am-10:30am, lunch 11am-4:30pm, sunset drinks Wed.-Sun. 5pm-7pm, dinner seating 7pm, breakfast/lunch $4-10, prix fixe dinner $35-45), an Arts and Crafts-style mountain hut with an unbeatable location. The simple breakfast and lunch menus include basic sandwiches, egg dishes, hot dogs, and hamburgers, and the fixed price dinner includes a salad and dessert. While the food gets mixed reviews, dining at heavy communal tables in a mountaintop dining room is the real experience, and the "sunset beverage hour" commands some of the finest views in the Berkshires.

Accommodations and Camping

There aren't many places to stay in North Adams, so unless you're splashing out at The Porches Inn, it's worth booking a room in Williamstown. Alternately, there are quite a few places listed on Airbnb and other private rental sites, for significantly less than the local hotels, and if you're prepared to drive to the summit of Mount Greylock, you'll find a historic Arts and Crafts-style lodge with unforgettable views.

If you've come prepared with backpacking gear, the remote tent sites at **Mount Greylock Campground** (park 413/499-4262 or reservations 877/422-6762, www.mass.gov, mid May-Oct. $8, free off-season) are blissfully backcountry, and a series of five **lean-to shelters** within the park are open year-round (register at 413/499-4262, free).

One remarkable way to experience the Mount Greylock State Reservation is by spending the night at ★ **Bascom Lodge** (30 Rockwell Rd., Lanesborough, 413/743-1591, www.bascomlodge.net, May-Nov., bunks $40, private rooms $125), on the mountain's summit, which also serves meals in the on-site dining room. The Arts and Crafts-style lodge has shared bathrooms, and staying in it provides a hostel-like experience, a chance to rub shoulders with ropy Appalachian Trail through hikers, and the best views in the county. The lodge is a 25-minute drive from downtown North Adams.

With a focus on design and impeccable comfort, ★ **The Porches Inn** (231 River St., 413/664-0400, www.porches.com, $299-485) stands out for channeling the spirit of North Adams—both old and new. Workers' row houses from the 1890s have been transformed into luxury guest rooms with ultrasoft sheets and light-hearted touches. Each room is different, with vintage decor and thoughtfully chosen color schemes (and just about everything that's not bolted to the floor is for sale). Rates include a fresh, appealing continental breakfast, and coffee and baked goods are available in-room by request.

Information
The **Adams Visitors Bureau** (3 Hoosac St., Adams, 413/743-8353, www.berkshires.org) runs a mammoth visitors center providing information on the entire Berkshires region, open seasonally.

Getting Around
Bus services for the region are provided by **Berkshire Regional Transit Authority** (413/449-2782 or 800/292-2782, www.berkshirerta.com).

Lenox

In the midst of the glamourous Gilded Age excess of the late19th century, Boston's barons of industry erected palatial homes in the Berkshires, which became their carefully sculpted haven from city life. For that very small, exclusive society, it was one of a few summertime escapes along with places like Newport, Rhode Island, and Bar Harbor, Maine—where the wealthy made extended visits surrounded by small armies of servants. More than any other town in the area, Lenox retains that sheen of upscale country living, and when the Boston Symphony Orchestra takes up its annual summertime residence at Tanglewood, the town is packed to the gills. Lenox also has the greatest concentration of places to stay in the area, along with a thriving arts scene, dance festival, and celebrated yoga retreat.

Sights
★ The Mount
Edith Wharton's incisive, prolific writing is among the best in American literature, but she once contended that she was "a better landscape gardener than novelist." Judge for yourself at **The Mount** (2 Plunkett St., 413/551-5100, www.edithwharton.org, mid-May-Oct. daily 10am-5pm, $18 adults, $17 seniors, $13 students, $10 military, youth under 18 free), the gorgeously restored estate she designed from the ground up. With the exception of the library, most of the author's personal belongings and furniture are long gone, but Wharton's taste for symmetry, balance, and allusion are everywhere. And while visiting the house takes just an hour or so, the expansive grounds are an inviting place to linger—in the cool sunken garden, by a blossom-fringed fountain, or on the trails that wrap through the woods and past neat lines of tilia trees. On weekends in July and August, there are informal jazz sessions on the outdoor terrace, and professional actors perform readings of Wharton's writing on Wednesdays in the summer ($5, check website for events calendar). The grounds are open from sunrise to sunset all year and free to access outside visiting hours, which make this a perfect place for a quiet, early morning or evening walk.

Other Sights
Part of the movie *The Cider House Rules* was filmed at the **Ventfort Hall Mansion and Gilded Age Museum** (104 Walker St., 413/637-3206, www.gildedage.org, Mon.-Sat. 10am-4pm, Sun. 10am-3pm, tours hourly, $18 adults, $17 seniors and students, $7 youth 5-17, under 5 free), a celebration of all things Victorian. The restored mansion was once owned by J. P. Morgan's sister, and tours bring alive the 1890s, when the Berkshires were the playground of the superrich.

Explore the gorgeous Bauhaus-style home that artists George L.K. Morris

Lenox

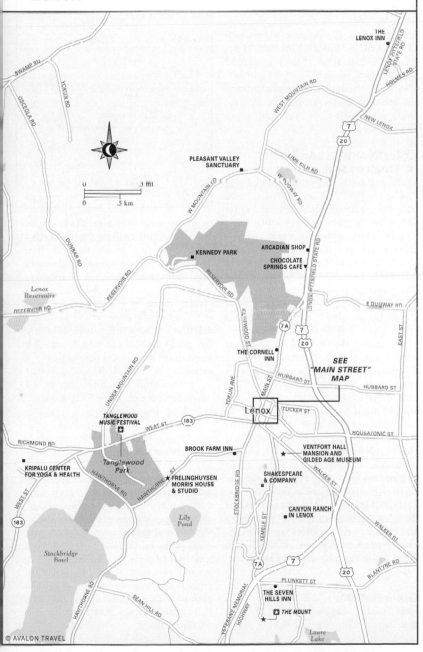

THE LENOX INN

SWAMP RD

YOKUN RD

OSCEOLA RD

WEST MOUNTAIN RD

NEW LENOX

7
20

PLEASANT VALLEY SANCTUARY

LIME KILN RD

W DUGWAY RD

DUNBAR RD

W MOUNTAIN RD

KENNEDY PARK

ARCADIAN SHOP

CHOCOLATE SPRINGS CAFÉ

LENOX PITTSFIELD STATE RD

Lenox Reservoirs

RESERVOIR RD

RESERVOIR RD

RESERVOIR RD

E DUGWAY RD

7A

7
20

EAST ST

THE CORNELL INN

SEE "MAIN STREET" MAP

UNDER MOUNTAIN RD

YOKUN AVE

MAIN ST

HUBBARD CT

HUBBARD ST

TANGLEWOOD MUSIC FESTIVAL

WEST ST

183

Lenox

TUCKER ST

RICHMOND RD

Tanglewood Park

BROOK FARM INN

VENTFORT HALL MANSION AND GILDED AGE MUSEUM

HOUSATONIC ST

WALKER ST

KRIPALU CENTER FOR YOGA & HEALTH

HAWTHORNE RD

HAWTHORNE ST

FRELINGHUYSEN MORRIS HOUSE & STUDIO

SHAKESPEARE & COMPANY

WEST ST

183

STOCKBRIDGE RD

Lily Pond

CANYON RANCH IN LENOX

WALKER ST

Stockbridge Bowl

KEMBLE ST

7A

7

20

BLANTYRE RD

HAWTHORNE RD

BEAN HILL RD

VETERANS MEMORIAL HIGHWAY

PLUNKETT ST

THE SEVEN HILLS INN

THE MOUNT

Laurel Lake

© AVALON TRAVEL

0   .3 mi

0   .5 km

and Suzy Frelinghuysen built to live and work in at **Freylinghuysen Morris House & Studio** (92 Hawthorne St., 413/637-0166, www.frelinghuysen.org, late June-Oct. Thurs.-Sun. 10am-3pm, closed Sun. in Sept., $15 adults, $14 seniors, $7.50 students, children under 12 free). In addition to the couple's own abstract art, the house has a noteworthy collection of works that include Picasso, Braque, and Gris as well as beautiful period furniture.

Entertainment and Events
★ Tanglewood Music Festival
During summer, the Boston Symphony Orchestra (BSO)—along with a suite of other performers—brings world-class music to **Tanglewood** (297 West St., 413/637-1600, www.bso.org), a sprawling venue named for a collection of stories by Nathaniel Hawthorne, who spent a summer writing on the property. The Tanglewood season runs late June-early September, and popular shows often sell out within a week of their first availability in January, as do rooms in town.

Music, however sublime, is only part of the experience. Elegant picnics at Tanglewood have been a tradition since the BSO performed here in the late 1930s, and afternoons on the lawn have a nostalgia-tinged, languid charm. Show up several hours early to stretch the picnic into an all-afternoon affair, or explore the Tanglewood campus on a 1.5-hour, volunteer-led tour; tours depart from the on-site visitors center during the music season (for more information, call 617/638-9394). Part of the thrill of Tanglewood is heading out on the town in Lenox to rub shoulders with the musicians (the local wine bar, Brava, is said to be especially popular with the musical set).

Other Festivals
Stars of the dance world invigorate the tiny, nearby town of Becket every

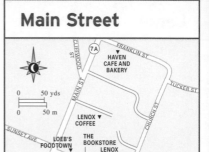

summer with the internationally renowned **Jacob's Pillow Dance Festival** (358 George Carter Rd., Becket, 413/243-9919, www.jacobspillow.org, mid-June-Aug., free-$55), founded by modern-dance pioneer Ted Shawn. Every style from hip-hop to ballet gets its time in the spotlight during the two-month celebration, which includes dozens of free performances and gallery talks. The main draw, however, is the showcases of artists from around the world, featuring both established companies such as Mark Morris and Alvin Ailey alongside emerging choreographers.

Some of the best summer Shakespeare in the country is performed by **Shakespeare & Company** (70 Kemble St., 413/637-3353, www.shakespeare.org, free-$60) in an air-conditioned scaffold-and-canvas theater. In addition to plays by the Bard, the company also stages premieres by area playwrights and special events, for instance one-acts by Edith Wharton or interpretations of Edgar Allan Poe stories by actor F. Murray Abraham. The company is in the process of an ambitious plan to build a replica of the 1587 Rose Playhouse, surrounded by a mock-Elizabethan village.

Shopping

The main street of Lenox is packed with little boutiques that invite browsing, mostly clustered along **Church Street** and **Housatonic Street.** Only at **The Bookstore** (11 Housatonic St., 413/637-3390, www.bookstoreinlenox.com, Mon.-Thurs. 9am-6pm, Fri.-Sat. 9am-9pm, Sun. 10am-3pm, open late on busy summer evenings), though, can you browse the shelves with a glass of wine in your hand from the house wine bar.

Sports and Recreation
Biking

Right in the center of town, **Kennedy Park** (275 Main St., www.townoflenox.org) has over 10 miles of old carriage roads, multiuse trails, and singletracks popular for mountain biking. The trails, which connect to more extensive singletracks outside the park's boundaries, aren't particularly well marked, but it's hard to get lost for too long without crossing a road. For rental bikes, maps, and friendly advice about where to ride, the **Arcadian Shop** (91 Pittsfield Rd., 413/637-3010, www.arcadian.com, $45 mountain bike or $35 hybrid bike full-day rentals) is a great resource.

Boating

The gentle Housatonic River is scenic and approachable for boaters of all skill levels, and one of the prettiest stretches is the meandering section between **Decker Landing,** between Lenox and Pittsfield, and **Wood's Pond** in Lenox, a 4.6-mile trip that takes 2-3 hours and has great views of the mountains. **Arcadian Shop** (91 Pittsfield Rd., 413/637-3010, www.arcadian.com, $35 single or $60 tandem kayak) rents boats, and will drop your boat at Decker Landing and pick it up at Wood's Pond for $20. Another good option is to join a group from **Berkshire Canoe Tours** (413/442-2789, www.berkshirecanoetours.org, $50 adults, $30 children), which makes a 2-hour trip from Decker Landing multiple times

daily during summer months in canoes and kayaks.

Hiking

Just a few miles north of town, Massachusetts Audubon's **Pleasant Valley Sanctuary** (472 West Mountain Rd., 413/637-0320, www.massaudubon.org, Nov.-Apr. Tues.-Sun. 10am-4pm, May-Oct. Mon.-Fri. 9am-4pm and Sat.-Sun. 10am-4pm, $5 adults, $3 seniors and youth 2-12, sunrise-sunset) has over 1,000 acres of wetlands, forests, and meadows with seven miles of trails for exploring the eastern slope of Lenox Mountain. The strenuous, three-mile **Ledges-Overbrook Loop** goes to the 2,126-foot summit for views of Mount Greylock, the Taconic Range, and the Catskills, while the gentler 1.5-mile **Yokun-Beaver Lodge Trails Loop** is popular for birding.

Spas and Yoga

East meets western Massachusetts at the **Kripalu Center for Yoga & Health** (297 West St., 413/448-3152, www.kripalu.org, day-pass $125), one of the foremost yoga training centers in the country. The sprawling campus has fabulous views and lots of places to lounge on the grass between workshops on yoga, meditation, and mindfulness, and offers healthy meals in the dining room as well as dormitories and private rooms for those who want to stay over.

At the other end of the spectrum, the ultra-luxe **Canyon Ranch in Lenox** (165 Kemble St., 413/637-4100, www.canyonranchdestinations.com, day-pass $370) opens its elegant spa to the public for daytime access including classes, use of spa pools and gyms, lunch in the Canyon Ranch restaurant, and treatments like massages and facials.

Food

In a strip mall just north of town, **Chocolate Springs Café** (55 Pittsfield Rd., 413/637-9820, www.chocolatesprings.com, Sun.-Fri. 9am-9pm, Sat. 9am-10pm,

$3-9) is a cozy little space devoted to all things chocolaty, from rich gelato to truffles with whisper-thin shells. A comfortable seating area makes this a nice place to read, and the café often hosts local musicians at night.

Picture-perfect French pastries are the highlights of **Patisserie Lenox** (30 Church St., 413/551-9050, www.patisserielenox.com, Mon.-Sat. 8:30am-7:30pm, Sun. 8:30am-6:30pm, may close early in off-season, $3-12), whose brioche, macarons (French meringue-based confections), and éclairs will leave you dreaming of Paris. The shop also has prepared salads and light lunch items, though the intimate tables for two fill up quickly.

The farm-to-table superstar of the Berkshires is ★ **Nudel** (37 Church St., 413/551-7183, www.nudelrestaurant.com, Tues.-Sat. 5pm-9:30pm, Sun. 5pm-9pm, $19-28), whose diminutive, modern dining room displays artistic portraits of ingredients. Chef Bjorn Somlo's thoughtful, creative menu changes frequently and reads like an ode to the twists and turns of New England seasons.

Appealing small plates and a show-stopping wine list make **Brava** (27 Housatonic St., 413/637-9171, www.bravalenox.com, daily 5pm-1am, $14-22) a treat for a slow dinner, and the tiny spot keeps the lights on far later than anyone in town; many Tanglewood musicians make this their hangout while summering in the Berkshires, so it's a good place to rub shoulders with the performers at the casual bar.

For an easy, fresh breakfast or lunch, ★ **Haven Cafe and Bakery** (8 Franklin St., 413/637-8948, www.havencafebakery.com, Mon.-Fri. 7:30am-3pm, Sat.-Sun. 8am-3pm, $4-12) is the hands-down locals' favorite. It has laid-back counter service, plenty of seating, and a menu of burgers, salads, and sandwiches, as well

Top to bottom: picnicking at Tanglewood; Jacob's Pillow Dance Festival; downtown Lenox.

as a pleasant outdoor patio for warm afternoons.

Tucked back from the main drag in a shingled house, **Lenox Coffee** (52 Main St., 413/637-1606, Mon.-Sat. 7am-6pm, Sun. 8am-6pm, $2-5) has a good selection of pastries and the best espresso in town, made from locally roasted coffee, in addition to seats on a shady porch, wireless Internet, and fun local art on the walls.

Friendly and locally owned, **Loeb's Foodtown** (42 Main St., 413/637-0270, www.loebsfoodtown.com, Mon.-Thurs. and Sat. 7am-6pm, Fri. 7am-7pm, Sun. 7am-4pm) has all the usual groceries along with deli foods and snacks; just down the block, **Lenox Natural Foods** (11 Housatonic St., 413/637-2721, www.lenoxnaturalfoods.com, Mon.-Sat. 10am-6:30pm, Sun. 10am-5pm) is diminutive but all organic. Local farmers and other artisans ply their wares each week at the **Lenox Farmer's Market** (Roche Reading Park, Main St., May-Oct. Fri. 1pm-5pm), a good place for an outdoor lunch.

Accommodations and Camping

The region's travel department estimates the Berkshires offer 4,500 hotel rooms, and that 30,000 people descend on the area during busy summer weekends. Lenox is the heart of the action, and prices spike during Tanglewood season. Many locals list their guest bedrooms on Airbnb, which can be a convenient alternative to commercial options.

Camping

October Mountain State Forest (317 Woodland Rd., Lee, 413/243-1778, www.mass.gov, May-Oct., yurts $45-55, tent sites $20) is just seven miles west of town, with hiking trails, a scenic gorge, and a secluded campground with 47 sites, rustic yurts, and bathrooms with hot showers. Book yurts well in advance, and bring your own sleeping bags or bedding.

$100-150

Clean rooms and affordable prices make **The Lenox Inn** (525 Pittsfield Rd., 412/499-0324, www.thelenoxinn.com, $65-155) a decent option, and the roadside motel has an outdoor pool, welcoming after a day of exploring.

The three carefully restored historic buildings at ★ **The Cornell Inn** (203 Main St., 413/637-4800, www.cornellbb.com, $135-179) have an ideal location walking distance from downtown Lenox and Kennedy Park's trails. In warm months, the fresh breakfasts are served on an outdoor deck, and the friendly, accommodating owners infuse the inn with hospitable spirit.

$150-200

Elegant and historic, the manor house at **The Seven Hills Inn** (40 Plunkett St., 413/207-9330, www.sevenhillsinn.com, $130-255) is full of antiques and old-world charm, and surrounded by perfectly manicured grounds. When booking a room in the manor house, review the online gallery, as decor varies from charmingly restrained to somewhat lurid boudoir plush. In addition to rooms in the manor house are motel and carriage house options. The least expensive rooms are in the on-site **Terrace Country Motel,** and though they're somewhat dated and dingy, the high-rent setting makes this spot a good choice if you're not planning to linger in your room. A third option is the **Carriage House,** where prices fall in between the inn and motel, and furnishings are light, pretty, and modern (and a suite with a kitchenette is also available).

It's possible to spend the night at the **Kripalu Center for Yoga & Health** (297 West St., 413/448-3152, www.kripalu.org), which has somewhat charmless dormitories and more appealing private rooms. All-inclusive retreats start at $376 for two nights; if you're booking within a week of your visit, however, one night stays may be available from $189.

Over $250

The comfortable, welcoming rooms at ★ **Brook Farm Inn** (15 Hawthorne St., 413/637-3013, www.brookfarm.com, $198-415) are full of country charm, ruffles, and floral wallpaper. The house has a few barrier-free rooms that are fully accessible, and the appealing breakfasts incorporate food from local farms and artisans. The inn has a long literary tradition dating back to the art-loving original owners, and one highlight for many guests is the wonderful collection of poetry books; the inn hosts occasional poetry readings.

Information

The **Lenox Chamber of Commerce** (12 Housatonic St., 413/637-3646, www.lenox.org, mid-May-mid-Oct. daily 9am-5pm, mid-Oct.-mid-May Mon.-Thurs. 10am-5pm) runs a visitors center in town.

Getting Around

Berkshire Regional Transit Authority (413/449-2782 or 800/292-2782, www.berkshirerta.com) provides bus services throughout the region.

Stockbridge

On quiet summer mornings before the tour buses arrive, the quaint town of Stockbridge looks unchanged since Norman Rockwell captured its postage-stamp downtown in *Main Street, Stockbridge,* and you could easily use the painting to find your way around the historic center. Rockwell painted here for the last 25 years of his life in a 19th-century carriage-barn-turned-studio behind Stockbridge center, and the museum dedicated to his work is one of the region's most popular attractions. The town has gone to great lengths to preserve its Rockwellian character, with white picket fences and a general store packed with nostalgic bits and bobs. You could walk the strip in a few

minutes flat, and there isn't much in the way of nightlife or events in town, but it's a nice place to linger; from the shady porch at the Red Lion to the alleyway cafés, time in Stockbridge is all about watching life drift by.

Sights
★ Norman Rockwell Museum

With his sweet depictions of soda fountains, small towns, and kids goofing around, Norman Rockwell can elicit strong reactions, from nostalgic sighs to eye rolls. With the world's largest collection of the artist's original work, the **Norman Rockwell Museum** (9 Rte. 183, 413/298-4100, www.nrm.org, Nov.-Apr. Mon.-Fri. 10am-4pm, Sat.-Sun. 10am-5pm; May-Oct. daily 10am-5pm, $18 adults, $17 seniors, $10 students, $6 children 6-18, under 6 free) may surprise viewers who know the artist from his *Life* magazine covers alone. Among the paintings on exhibit is the series Rockwell did on civil rights, including a haunting depiction of the three civil rights workers killed in Mississippi; the artist emerges as someone who cared deeply about social justice, even as he looked toward the past.

Behind the museum is the artist's barn studio (open May-mid-Nov.), preserved almost identically to when Rockwell painted here, with lovely views of rolling forest and lawns. The grounds are speckled with sculptures by his son, Peter Rockwell, whose work shows a refreshing taste for the weird.

Other Sights

Even if you've never heard of sculptor Daniel Chester French, you've likely seen images of his work, from the Lincoln Memorial in Washington DC to *Minute Man* in Concord, Massachusetts. His country home and "heaven" was **Chesterwood** (4 Williamsville Rd., 413/298-3579, www.chesterwood.org, May-Oct. daily 10am-5pm, $18 adults, $17 seniors, $9 youth 13-17, under 13 free). Tours take visitors through his

Stockbridge

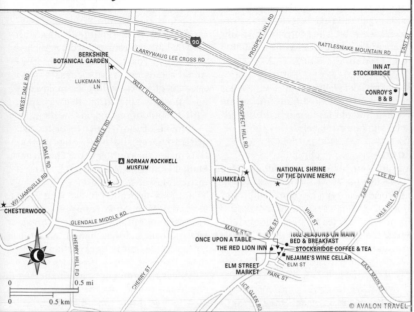

elegantly appointed house, intimate studio, and 122 acres of grounds designed by the artist.

Another of the Berkshire's Gilded Age "cottages," **Naumkeag** (5 Prospect Hill Rd., 413/298-8146, www.thetrustees.org, Apr.-May. Sat.-Sun. 10am-5pm; June-Oct. daily 10am 5pm, $15, children under 13 free) stands out for being preserved in its entirety, with gorgeous original furnishings that make visiting the house a transporting experience. For many visitors, though, the grounds are the real draw, with deep pools, rustling groves of birch trees, and great mounds of blooming flowers that are perfectly manicured and maintained.

The flowers at the **Berkshire Botanical Garden** (5 West Stockbridge Rd., 413/298-3926, www.berkshirebotanical.org, May-Oct. daily 9am-5pm, $15 adults, $14 seniors, $12 students, under 12 free) are carefully chosen so that each week brings fresh blooms, and the 15-acre

grounds are a pleasure for plant lovers. Tables and benches invite afternoon picnics, and many of the trails are wheelchair accessible.

While the **National Shrine of the Divine Mercy** (Eden Hill, 413/298-3931, www.thedivinemercy.org, free) might not be well known outside the Catholic Church, it's an important pilgrimage place for American Roman Catholics. Thousands flock to the shrine's Easter Services, and during the 2015-2016 Extraordinary Jubilee of Mercy, the church offered plenary indulgences that used to be available only at the four papal basilicas in Rome. Non-pilgrims can enjoy the beautiful main church and large, peaceful grounds.

Shopping

Stock up on penny candy, gadgets, and old-fashioned knickknacks at **Charles H. Baldwin & Sons** (1 Center St., West Stockbridge, 413/232-7785, www.

baldwinextracts.com, Mon.-Sat. 9am-5pm, Sun. 11am-3pm), a family-owned country store that also dispenses homemade syrups and extracts that Berkshire bakers swear by. The center of the frilly, flounced **Country Curtains** (The Red Lion Inn, 30 Main St., 800/937-1237, www.countrycurtains.com, Thurs. 9:30am-8pm, Fri.-Wed. 9:30am-6pm) universe is in the back of The Red Lion Inn, where you can find old-fashioned bedding, pillows, and everything else.

Food

Just off Main Street, **Stockbridge Coffee & Tea** (6 Elm St., 413/931-7044, www.stockbridgecoffeeandtea.com, daily 7am-5pm, $2-8) serves espresso drinks and Harney & Sons tea in a cozy bookshop, where the small collection of volumes is unusually well chosen and organized. Locally made pastries and quiche of the day are available.

Bright yellow walls and vintage French posters give ★ **Once Upon a Table** (36 Main St., 413/298-3870, www.onceuponatablebistro.com, Sun.-Thurs. 11am-3pm and 4:30pm-8pm, Fri.-Sat. 11am-3pm and 4:30pm-8:30pm, $14-29) the cheerful feel of a country bistro, with food that ranges from decidedly French—escargot or roasted duck—to international salads and sandwiches. A good selection of wines by the glass makes this an especially appealing alleyway spot, with its outdoor seating on fine days.

A menu of short-order favorites like grilled cheese and hearty egg breakfasts makes the counter at the **Elm Street Market** (4 Elm St., 413/298-3634, www.elmstreetmarket.com, mid-June-Oct. Sun.-Thurs. 6am-6pm and Fri.-Sat. 6am-7pm, Nov.-May Mon.-Sun., 6am-6pm, $4-13) a convenient option for a simple breakfast or lunch, and the stools at the counter have a pleasantly Rockwellian feel to them. It also sells basic groceries.

It's easy to imagine any of the five American presidents that have stayed at **The Red Lion Inn** (30 Main St.,

The Red Lion Inn

413/298-5545, www.redlion.com, daily 7:30am-9:30pm, $23-34) tucking into the dining room menu of meat and potatoes, which combines with dark wood, old china, and white tablecloths to thoroughly old-fashioned effect. If that's not your scene, you can head down the hall to the casual and atmospheric **Widow Bingham's Tavern** (daily 5pm-8:45pm, $11-17) for burgers, sandwiches, and salads under a ceiling bristling with beer steins. A similar menu is available downstairs at the pleasantly cave-like **Lion's Den** (food served daily 5pm-8pm, $9-20), a pub popular with locals and visitors alike, and it hosts live music nightly (Sun.-Thurs. 8pm-11pm, Fri.-Sat. 9pm-midnight, free).

Nejaime's Wine Cellar (3 Elm St., 413/298-3454, www.nejaimeswine.net, Mon.-Sat. 9am-9pm, Sun. 11am-6pm) has a great selection of wine, spirits, and beer, including some local varieties. A few miles outside of downtown Stockbridge, the **West Stockbridge Farmers Market**

(Harris St., West Stockbridge, late May-early Oct. Thurs. 3pm-7pm) brings in vendors, crafters, and farmers from around the Berkshires.

Accommodations
$150-250
Somewhat homier than other rooms in Stockbridge, **Conroy's B & B** (11 East St., 413/298-4990, $118-225) is full of laid-back country charm. The helpful owner cooks breakfast each morning and is an excellent resource for things to do, and there are gardens full of blooming perennials and an outdoor pool in the summer.

The wraparound veranda at **The Red Lion Inn** (30 Main St., 413/298-5545, www.redlioninn.com, $115-390) is a relaxing place to sink into a rocking chair and watch the passersby, and the warren-like inn is a fascinating place to explore. Rooms in the main building are furnished with appealing antiques, and the bowed floors and crackled portraits give the hotel a deliciously "olde New England feel." Stockbridge is something of a company town, and the Red Lion owns much of the block it occupies, with annexes, guesthouses, and a wonderful turn-of-the-20th-century firehouse that was the subject of a Rockwell painting.

Over $250
The friendly innkeepers at ★ **1862 Seasons on Main Bed & Breakfast** (47 Main St., 413/298-5419, www.seasonsonmain.com, $245-395) strike a welcoming balance of luxury and leisure at a convenient location in town; each of the seasonally themed rooms is beautifully decorated but completely livable, and the historic house is full of places to enjoy the inn's morning coffee, afternoon wine, and ice cream nightcaps. Breakfasts are cooked to order and served at the enormous dining room table, and the inn has a private theater furnished with comfy armchairs.

On the road from Stockbridge to Lenox, the **Inn at Stockbridge** (30 Rte.

7, 855/713-0473, www.stockbridgeinn. com, $250-472) is another plush find, with inviting common spaces and treasures from the owners' travels around the world. Home-cooked breakfasts, a heated pool, all-day snacks, and an exercise room are appealing perks, but the inn's location by the highway means more noise than elsewhere.

Information

The **Stockbridge Chamber of Commerce** (413/298-5200, www.stockbridgechamber.org) has a small, unstaffed visitors booth on Main Street with information.

Getting Around

Regional buses are run by the **Berkshire Regional Transit Authority** (413/449-2782 or 800/292-2782, www.berkshirerta.com).

Great Barrington

Trees and picket fences give way to faded mill buildings along the Housatonic River when you cross the border into Great Barrington, an appealing blend of tourist town and rural hub that offers a real glimpse of life in the Berkshires. With restored brick buildings and a mix of old-fashioned hardware stores, boutiques, and restaurants, downtown Great Barrington is a refreshing change of scene from the curated centers of Lenox and Stockbridge, and a good base for exploring if you need a break from all the quaintness. Just up the road, the village of Housatonic is an unexpected gem, a tiny satellite of Great Barrington where disused railway depots and crumbling factory buildings keep watch over a tiny downtown with a celebrated bakery and a hip café. Not much remains beside a few signs and markers, but Great Barrington was the childhood home of the great African American writer and academic W.E.B. DuBois, who attended an integrated public school in the late

19th century and left for college with the support of the local church.

Sights

The tiny spire and whitewashed facade of the old Trinity Lutheran Church seem an unlikely place to celebrate a raucous, rebellious folk singer—but peace sign windows offer a hint of what's inside **The Guthrie Center** (2 Van Deusenville Rd., 413/528-1955, www.guthriecenter. org, Tues.-Sat. 10am-4pm, free). Arlo Guthrie's album covers and posters decorate every surface of the church's small welcome center, which hosts interfaith services on Sundays 11am-noon (services are "BYOG," or "bring your own god"). Free lunch is served to all comers each Wednesday at noon, and local musicians gather for an informal hootenanny on Thursday nights (doors 7pm, show 8pm, $5, performers free). Back when Arlo Guthrie was a student at a progressive boarding school in Stockbridge, the church was home to Alice and Ray Brock, and was immortalized in the rambling, shaggy-dog, antiwar song "Alice's Restaurant."

Fill your bags with blueberries and crisp fall apples at **Windy Hill Farm** (686 Stockbridge Rd., 413/398-3217, www. windyhillfarminc.com, Apr.-Dec. daily 9am-5pm), where pretty rows of Paula Red and Gingergold apples give way to stunning views of nearby Monument Mountain and rolling berry fields. Blueberry season opens around the beginning of July, and apples are ripe from September until late autumn.

Entertainment and Events

Pronounced muh-HAY-wee, **The Mahaiwe Performing Arts Center** (14 Castle St., 413/528-0100, www.mahaiwe. org) is located in a restored 100-year-old theater and presents a first-rate, if eclectic, lineup of music, spoken-word, and theater performances. The 2016 season included Bach, zydeco performances, and a show by local hero Arlo Guthrie.

Great Barrington

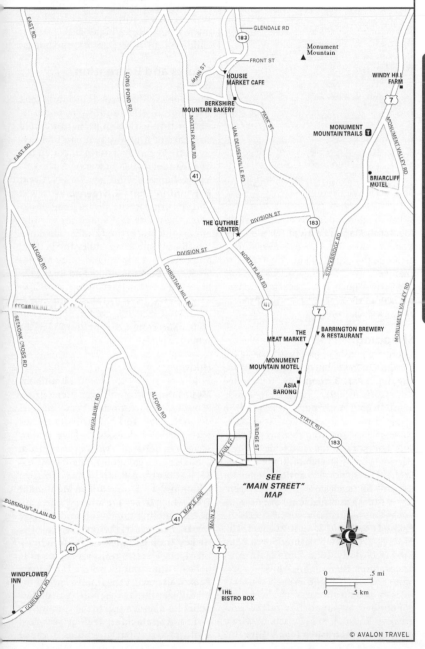

GLENDALE RD
183
Monument Mountain ▲
FRONT ST
MAIN ST
EAST RD
LONG POND RD
HOUSIE MARKET CAFE
WINDY HILL FARM
7
BERKSHIRE MOUNTAIN BAKERY
PARK ST
MONUMENT MOUNTAIN TRAILS T
MONUMENT VALLEY RD
NORTH PLAIN RD
VAN DEUSENVILLE RD
41
BRIARCLIFF MOTEL
EAST RD
THE GUTHRIE CENTER ★
DIVISION ST
183
ALFORD RD
DIVISION ST
CHRISTIAN HILL RD
NORTH PLAIN RD
STOCKBRIDGE RD
SEEKONK RD
41
7
MONUMENT VALLEY RD
SEEKONK CROSS RD
THE MEAT MARKET ▼
BARRINGTON BREWERY & RESTAURANT
HURLBURT RD
ALFORD RD
MONUMENT MOUNTAIN MOTEL
ASIA BARONG
STATE RD
BRIDGE ST
183
MAIN ST
SEE "MAIN STREET" MAP
EGREMONT PLAIN RD
41
MAPLE AVE
MAIN ST
41
MAIN S
7
0   .5 mi
0   .5 km
WINDFLOWER INN
S. EGREMONT RD
THE BISTRO BOX
© AVALON TRAVEL

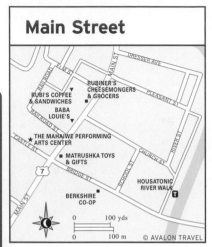

Main Street

What Tanglewood is to symphony music, the **Aston Magna Festival** (Daniel Arts Center, Alford Rd., 413/528-3595, www. astonmagna.org, $35 per concert) is to chamber music. During weekends in July and early August, both vocal and instrumental masters of the form perform at Simon's Rock College.

Shopping

There are plenty of places to browse for antiques in town, but one of the most intriguing is **Asia Barong** (199 Stockbridge Rd., 413/528-5091, Thurs.-Sun. 11am-5pm), an enormous multilevel collection of art from all over Asia that encompasses everything from treasures to trinkets. For more antiques, outside of Great Barrington, the stretch of Route 7 down to Sheffield is known as **antiques alley** for its many fine such stores (maps of the antiques stores are available at most destinations). One particularly worthy stop is the **Painted Porch** (102 S. Main St., Sheffield, 413/229-2700, www.paintedporch.com, Jun.-Dec. daily 10am-5pm; Jan.-May Thurs.-Mon. 10am-5pm), whose owners scour the English and French countrysides for rare furniture.

Founded by supporters of the progressive Rudolph Steiner school, Great Barrington's **Matrushka Toys & Gifts** (309 Main St., 413/528-6911, www.berkshiretoys.com, Mon.-Sat. 10am-5pm, Sun. 11am-4pm) is strictly electronics-free, instead filled with hand-crafted toys made from natural materials, as well as children's costumes, clothes, and books.

Sports and Recreation
Biking

The plentiful back roads around Great Barrington offer endless opportunities for riding, though it's hard to avoid stretches of highway that can be heavily trafficked and narrow (and often full of meandering sightseers). An excellent resource for finding a route is **Great Barrington Trails & Greenways** (www.gbtrails.org), whose online map designates the roads best suited for cycling; among the best is the 15-mile ride down the Housatonic River Valley to Sheffield and back. Get a bike (and some helpful advice) at **Berkshire Bike and Board** (29 State Rd., Great Barrington, 413/528-5555, www.berkshirebikeandboard.com, Mon.-Sat. 10am-6pm, Sun. 11am-5pm, bikes from $20 4-hr and $35 24-hr rental).

Hiking

Find a clear day to ascend **Monument Mountain,** and you'll get views from Mount Greylock on the Vermont border to the New York Catskill Mountains, with plenty of Housatonic River Valley scenery in between. Two trails leave from a small parking lot on Route 7 (parking $5, just north of Briarcliff Motel): Turn left onto the 1.5-mile **Indian Monument Trail,** which traces a relatively gentle path past crumbling stone walls and carriage roads, or head right on the 0.8-mile **Hickey Trail,** and pick a line straight up the slope. The two trails join at 0.6 mile beneath the summit, where the **Squaw Peak Trail** reaches the finest views of the hike. Regardless of the route, plan on two hours for a return trip to the summit.

The **Appalachian Trail** passes just south of Great Barrington as it winds from Georgia to Maine, and you can get a taste of the 2,160-mile trail in **Beartown State Forest** (69 Bluehill Rd., Monterey, 413/528-0904, $10), which has miles of hiking and multiuse trails. Walking on the Appalachian is generally an out-and-back that can be as long, or short, as you like, but the forest's most popular trail is the gorgeous **Benedict Pond Loop Trail,** an easy hike which wraps 1.5 miles around a tree-fringed lake.

Right in the center of Great Barrington, the **Housatonic River Walk** (www.gbriverwalk.org) runs a half-mile along the riverbed. The shady trail has plenty of comfortable benches and places to enjoy the view and is divided into two sections. The **upstream** portion can be accessed behind 195 Main Street, or the church parking lot at 15 Dresser Avenue, and the **downstream** segment continues to Bridge Street.

Food

Simple grilled sandwiches are transformed by beautiful cheeses and cured meats at ★ **rubi's coffee & sandwiches** (256 Main St., 413/528-0488, www.rubiners.com, Mon.-Fri. 7am-6pm, Sat. 8am-6pm, Sun. 8am-5pm, $5-13), the café cousin of Great Barrington's cheesemonger, Rubiner's. The tuna melt oozes with rich comté and crisp baby dill pickles, and a country-style pâté gets a vinegar bite from rustic Dijon mustard. The small café serves espresso and natural wines by the glass, and the small outdoor courtyard is an appealing place to enjoy a meal.

Great Barrington's answer to the New England snack bar is ★ **The Bistro Box** (937 S. Main St., 413/717-5958, www.thebistrobox.rocks, May-Nov. Mon.-Sat. 11am-7pm, Sun. 11am-4pm, $4-10), run by a pair of married chefs with serious kitchen chops. Hand-cut truffle fries are luxurious alongside grass-fed burgers topped with tomato jam and garlic aioli, and the chefs incorporate fresh and for aged foods into specials like wild ramp

pesto and blueberry lemonade. Lawn seating and picnic tables are available.

The thin and crusty sourdough pizza at **Baba Louie's** (286 Main St., 413/528-8100, www.babalouiessourdoughpizzacompany.com, Mon.-Sat. 11am-9:30pm, $8-13) is a strong contender for the best in the Berkshires, and the cozy, hole-in-the-wall restaurant is impressively laid-back for the quality of its pies. Gluten-free crusts get raves, and the fig, Gorgonzola, and prosciutto pizza is an outrageously flavorful blend of sweet and savory.

Picky carnivores should make a detour to ★ **The Meat Market** (389 Stockbridge Rd., 413/528-2022, www.themeatmarketgb.com, Wed.-Sat. 11am-6pm, Sun. 11am-4pm, $8-13), a butcher shop that sources whole grass-fed animals from local farms, serving up meals such as as liverwurst and onions on rye, roast pork with broccoli rabe, and a completely fabulous, slightly messy half-pound burger. Limited seating is available in the back of the simple market or on the patio, and it's worth calling to find out about regular fried chicken dinners that involve a giant, cast-iron cauldron, hand-cut fries, and open flames.

The sprawling menu of sandwiches, salads, burgers, and other classic American mains might not make any headlines in Great Barrington's food scene, but **Barrington Brewery & Restaurant** (420 Stockbridge Rd., 413/528-8282, www.barringtonbrewery.net, $5-20) is relaxed and appealing and offers a serious list of great beers. Head straight through the dining room for the bar, where regulars' potter mugs hang overhead and coasters from breweries around the world are tacked onto every possible surface. The tap lists changes with the season, but the Black Bear Stout and Barrington Brown are local favorites.

Young, hip, and totally unexpected, **Housie Market Cafe** (226 Pleasant St., Housatonic, 413/274-0261, Mon.-Fri. 7am-6pm, Sat. 8:30am-5pm, Sun. 8:30am-4pm, $3-9) is right at home in

Housatonic's cheerfully ramshackle downtown. Breakfasts bowls, sandwiches, and hearty lunches range from comforting to offbeat: Local workers come in for the "contractors special" of eggs, cheddar, and bacon between two slabs of bread, but some regulars swear by the peanut butter and kimchi sandwich.

Pack the picnic hamper of your dreams at **Rubiner's Cheesemongers & Grocers** (246 Main St., 413/528-0488, www.rubiners.com, Mon.-Sat. 10am-6pm, Sun. 10am-5pm), which stocks cheese from farms in the Berkshires, Vermont, and beyond, along with a charcuterie case stocked with rich pâtés, dried sausages, and duck confit. Then find award-winning wholesome loaves in Housatonic's **Berkshire Mountain Bakery** (367 Rte. 136, Housatonic, 413/274-1313, www.berkshiremountainbakery.com, Mon.-Sat. 8am-7pm, Sun. 8:30am-6pm), where baker Richard Bourdon has been making artisanal bread since long before it was cool. Many grains are sprouted and

ground on-site, and breads are naturally fermented. Cooperatively owned and stocked with piles of local food, **Berkshire Co-op** (42 Bridge St., 413/528-9697, www.berkshire.coop, daily 8am-8pm) also has a good deli with smoothies, sandwiches, and salads.

Accommodations and Camping

Beartown State Forest (69 Bluehill Rd., Monterey, 413/528-0904, $16) has just 12 sites (and no showers), but the 10,000-acre preserve is a wonderfully quiet place to spend the night about 30 minutes outside of Great Barrington, especially if you can snag site #11, which occupies an idyllic, private spot on the edge of a lake.

The sweet country style at **Windflower Inn** (684 S. Egremont Rd., 413/528-2720, www.windflowerinn.com, $175-235) perfectly befits the Berkshires' old-fashioned charm. Fires blaze in a stone fireplace in one room, an outdoor swimming pool is ringed by perennial blooms, and

hiking Monument Mountain

homemade breakfasts and comfortable beds are divine.

Bright white bedspreads and a few recent touches set **Monument Mountain Motel** (247 Stockbridge Rd., 413/551-4615, www.monumentmountainmotel.com, $190-215) apart from the other motels that line Route 7 on the outskirts of Great Barrington. Rooms are a bit dated, but neat as a pin, and the in-ground pool, play area, and basketball court make it a nice choice for families.

The standard, roadside exterior of the ★ **Briarcliff Motel** (506 Stockbridge Rd., 413/207-9420, www.thebriarcliffmotel.com, $175-240) offers few clues to the freshly renovated rooms, which are decorated with modern flair and a great sense of style. Each is unique, with artwork on the walls and small sitting areas, as well as several barrier-free, accessible bathrooms, a rarity in the Berkshires. Great coffee and homemade

granola are served along with pastries, organic yogurt, and hard-boiled eggs for the continental breakfast, and DVD players, a fire pit, and a pleasant wooded location outside of town make this a nice place to relax.

Information

The **Southern Berkshires Chamber of Commerce** runs a **visitors center** (326 Main St., 413/528-1510, www.southernberkshirechamber.com, Sat.-Mon. 11am-5pm) with information on the town as well as the rest of the region. The hours at this small office can vary somewhat unpredictably, especially during off-season months, so call before visiting.

Getting Around

The **Berkshire Regional Transit Authority** (413/449-2782 or 800/292-2782, www.berkshirerta.com) runs buses throughout the region.

Newport, Rhode Island

Explore a historical city dotted with clam shacks, outrageous mansions, and dozens of ways to get in and on the water.

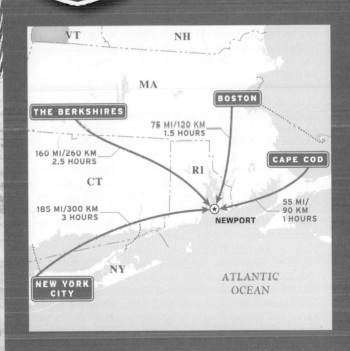

VT

NH

MA

THE BERKSHIRES

BOSTON

75 MI/120 KM
1.5 HOURS

160 MI/260 KM
2.5 HOURS

CAPE COD

RI

CT

185 MI/300 KM
3 HOURS

55 MI/
90 KM
1 HOURS

NEWPORT

NY

NEW YORK CITY

ATLANTIC OCEAN

Rhode Island's 400-mile coastline curves around sandy beaches, seaside cliffs, and picturesque lighthouses on its way to the historic city of Newport.

From its early days in the 17th century, Newport was a haven for freethinkers, heretics, and dissidents drummed out of Puritan settlements, who thrived and intermingled while the town gradually grew into a bustling port city. Wharves hummed with activity as pirates, fishers, and whalers brought their cargoes in and out of the sheltered harbor, and tiny Newport led New England's grimmest market, a booming trade in enslaved Africans.

When the U.S. economy turned to railroads and industry, Newport became a summertime escape for Eastern elite, whose opulent "cottages" were the toast of New York's polite society. Their surviving homes are maintained to a high gloss and filled with antiques and designs that offer a fascinating glimpse of what Mark Twain sardonically dubbed the "Gilded Age," a time of runaway fortunes, dollar princesses, and raw inequality.

But beyond the flash ballrooms and boudoirs, summer in Newport is pure New England, and it would be easy to spend a week sailing Narragansett Bay, surfing beach breaks, and taking in ball games at Cardines Field. The city has a thriving arts scene from a year-round film festival to a pair of destination-worthy museums. While Newport has long boasted some of the coast's most authentic clam shacks and chowder joints, a new wave of creative chefs has placed Rhode Island in the vanguard of New England cuisine. Despite the summer crowds and attractions, though, crossing the Newport Bridge onto Aquidneck Island is like being let in on a delicious secret—the smallest state in the United States is still overshadowed by her heavyweight neighbors, and almost 400 years after its founding, Newport feels like a discovery.

Planning Your Time

With two days in Newport, it's possible to see a few of the town's historic mansions, then save time for sandy beaches, and waterside trails. To explore all the most important of the Newport Historic Society mansions, however, plan to spend two full days visiting the properties. While Providence is a worthwhile place to spend a day, it's also easy to tack on a visit while on your way to destinations in New York and Massachusetts.

Orientation

Newport occupies the southern tip of Aquidneck Island, a vantage point that dominates the two major channels into Narragansett Bay, which is New England's largest estuary. Within city limits, the majority of sights are clustered around the Thames Street waterfront and the historic district along Bellevue Avenue, with a smattering of parks and inns along Ocean Drive, which traces the bottom edge of the peninsula.

Getting to Newport

Driving from Boston
75 miles, 1.5 hours

Newport is an easy drive from Boston. From downtown, follow **I-93 South** for 12 miles to **Route 24 South.** Stay on Route 24 for about **38 miles** before exiting onto **I-195 West** toward Fall River and then, after another 0.9 mile, taking Exit 8A to remain on Route 24, which merges with **Route 114 South** when you reach Aquidneck Island heading into town.

Highlights

★ **Newport's Mansions:** Channel the 19th-century elite while visiting their sprawling summer homes that combine Gilded Age glamour, exquisite art, and monumentally bad taste (page 258).

★ **Cliff Walk:** Stroll between the mansions and the sea on this seven-mile walking path (page 264).

★ **Ocean Drive:** Trace the southern tip of Aquidneck Island on a scenic 10-mile drive past a historic fort, elegant inns, and Rhode Island's finest kite-flying (page 265).

★ **National Museum of American Illustration:** Works by N.C. Wyeth, Norman Rockwell, and Maxfield Parrish are just the beginning of a remarkable collection in a Gilded Age setting (page 265).

★ **Touro Synagogue:** Discover Newport's Jewish heritage in an elegant historic synagogue (page 266).

★ **Newport's Music Festivals:** Watch musicians from around the world at the legendary festivals where performers like Miles Davis and Bob Dylan have made musical history (page 270).

Newport, Rhode Island

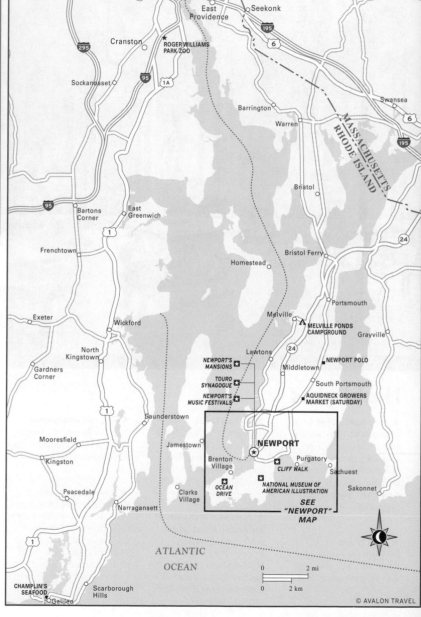

Best Accommodations

★ **Crow's Nest at the Seaman's Church Institute:** Browse a sailor's library and dream of the ocean in this historic, nonprofit hotel that also offers services to the "men and women of the sea" (page 278).

★ **Forty 1° North:** Boats pull right up to the waterside lounge at this modern hotel filled with iridescent touches and design books (page 278).

★ **Castle Hill Inn:** Watch the sails drift by from Grace Kelly's beach, where drinks on the lawn feel like a glamorous garden party (page 278).

★ **Gilded:** Bright colors, designer flair, and plenty of gold offer an irreverent take on Newport's Gilded Age with all the comforts of a boutique hotel (page 278).

Driving from New York City
185 miles, 3 hours

Coming from New York City, Newport is a half-day drive up the coast. Head north on **FDR Drive,** using the left lane to access Exit 17 to the **Robert F. Kennedy Bridge** ($8 toll, cash only), then stay left to merge onto **I-278 East.** After 4.5 miles, I-278 East merges into **I-95 North** ($1.75 toll, cash only). Follow I-95 North for **137.5 miles.** Take Exit 4 for **Route 3** and, after about 4 miles, turn right onto **Route 102 North,** then merge onto **Route 4 South,** continuing on as it becomes **Route 1 South.** Shortly after, turn onto **Route 138 East** to cross the **Newport Bridge** ($4 toll, cash only), then turn right onto **Route 238 South** into downtown Newport.

Driving from Cape Cod
55 miles, 1 hour

To reach Newport from Cape Cod, make your way to the **Bourne Bridge,** which connects Cape Cod and the mainland across the southerly side of the Cape Cod Canal. From there, continue onto **Route 25 West** for 9.1 miles, then use Exit 1 to merge onto **I-195 West** toward New Bedford/Providence. After **26 miles,** use Exit 8A for **Route 24 South** toward Tiverton, which merges onto **Route 114 South** and continues into downtown Newport.

Driving from the Berkshires
160 miles, 2.5 hours

To reach Newport from **Stockbridge,** follow **Route 102 East** 5.3 miles before merging onto **I-90 East** for **83 miles** ($4.75 toll, cash or EZ-Pass). Use exit 10A to turn onto **Route 146 South.** Follow Route 146 South for 25 miles, crossing the state line into Rhode Island, then exit onto **I-295 South** toward Warwick. After 18.6 miles, merge onto **I-95 South** for 3 miles, then stay left to continue onto **Route 4 South.** Route 4 merges with **Route 1 South.** Shortly after, turn onto **Route 138 East** to cross the **Newport Bridge** ($4 toll, cash only), then turn right onto **Route 238 South** into downtown Newport.

Getting There by Air, Train, or Bus
Air

United, JetBlue, Delta, American and Southwest Airlines offer service to **T.F. Green Airport** (2000 Post Rd., Warwick, 888/268-7222, www.pvdairport.com) though fares tend to be higher than flying into Boston.

Train

Amtrak (800/872-7245, www.amtrak.com) connects Providence with **New York City** (frequent trains, 3-3.5 hrs, $65-150) and **Boston** (frequent trains, 1 hr, $11-40).

Best Restaurants

★ **Tallulah on Thames:** Slow down for five courses of local food with creative flair in a modern dining room (page 273).

★ **The Black Pearl:** Grab a seat at the bar and a bowl of award-winning chowder at this sailor joint just a stone's throw from the water's edge (page 274).

★ **Mission:** Belly up to Newport's best burger at this place, where the local, organic food comes with a minimum of fuss—and some excellent beers (page 274).

★ **Meg's Aussie Milk Bar:** Recover from mansion hopping or beach-exhaustion with a Tim Tam Slam and a smoothie (page 276).

★ **Flo's Clam Shack:** Join the summer pilgrimage across Easton Bay to indulge in piles of crisply fried seafood, served amid 80 years of buoys, awards, and maritime kitsch (page 276).

The Providence train station is a short walk from Kennedy Plaza, where frequent buses depart for Newport.

Bus
Megabus (866/488-4452, www.megabus.com) has service between Newport and **New York City** (twice weekly, 5 hrs, $40), and **Peter Pan Bus Lines** (800/343-9999, www.peterpanbus.com) has buses to **New York City** (thrice daily, 6.5 hrs, $46), **Boston** (twice daily, 1.75 hrs, $30), **Cape Cod** (twice daily, Provincetown: 3.5 hrs, $28) and **the Berkshires** (twice daily, Stockbridge: 3.5 hrs, $28).

Rhode Island Transportation Authority (RIPTA, 401/781-9400, www.ripta.com) #60 connects Providence and Newport (frequent buses, 1 hr, $2) leaving from the centrally located Kennedy Plaza in Providence and arriving at the Gateway Center adjacent to the Newport Visitors' Center.

Sights

★ Newport's Mansions
When Newport was *the* place to spend the summer season, the wealthiest families in the United States piled their money into ostentatious "cottages"—sprawling mansions whose gilt, gaud, and grandeur are truly something to behold. The most famous of these date to the Gilded Age, a period in the late 19th century that saw extraordinary income inequality, when industrialists—sometimes called robber barons—made stunning fortunes from railroads, finance, and monopolies on natural resources. From an aesthetic perspective alone, Newport's mansions are fascinating, and it's easy to while away a few afternoons exploring dozens of rooms packed with art from around the world and manicured grounds designed by some of the United States' most famous architects.

But beyond the golden frames and marble flourishes, the mansions tell a story about a singular moment in U.S. history, when American wealth was ascendant, but European culture reigned supreme. The houses are packed with art brought back from European travels, and many are designed to resemble the French and Italian palaces that Americans encountered during their time abroad. That blend of American money and European heritage defined much of elite social life at the time, as newspaper headlines announced the marriages of wealthy "dollar princesses" to impoverished European aristocrats.

The **Preservation Society of Newport County** (401/847-1000, www.

Two Days in Newport

Choose a few historic sites, then save some time for the beach.

Day 1

Start your day early with a morning stroll on **Cliff Walk,** and watch the sun light up the mansions along this scenic coastal path. Once you've worked up an appetite for breakfast, head to friendly **Meg's Aussie Milk Bar** for a meat pie or a smoothie, then pick a pair of **Newport mansions** to explore. Start with **The Breakers,** Newport's ne plus ultra of historic ostentation, then continue to **Marble House, The Elms,** or the intriguing Gothic Revival **Kingscote.**

Watch for surfers as you cross the bay toward **Flo's Clam Shack** for great piles of clam cakes, lobster rolls, and stuffed quahogs before heading to the beach to while away the day in the sand. Join the action by signing up for surf lessons at **Sachuest Beach,** or opt for **Easton's Beach** and alternate rides on a **vintage carousel** with time in the water.

Join the crowds on Thames Street to browse souvenir shops and watch the yachties try to dock their powerboats, then climb to the 3rd floor at **Fluke Wine, Bar & Kitchen** for sunset cocktails and an oyster dinner.

Day 2

Enjoy a friendly, old-fashioned breakfast at **Corner Café,** then stroll back to downtown past **Touro Synagogue** and **Trinity Church.** Hop a trolley back to the Bellevue Historic District, then visit another mansion or the extraordinary **National Museum of American Illustration,** where N.C. Wyeth and Norman Rockwell's work is displayed in a finely restored Gilded Age home.

Pick up supplies for an elegant picnic at **Picnic Gourmet** or the **Newport Wine Cellar & Gourmet,** and find the perfect stretch of grass at **Fort Adams State Park,** at the start of the 10-mile Ocean Drive. When the sun begins to sink low over the harbor, continue along the scenic route. Pause for drinks on the **The Lawn at Castle Hill Inn** or fly kites at **Brenton Point State Park,** two of the best spots in town for a spectacular sunset.

Kick off your last night on Broadway, starting with a pint at **The White Horse Tavern,** a strong contender for the oldest bar in the United States. Continue to **Mission,** a casual burger joint that serves locally sourced, organic food, then loop back to Thames Street to catch a live show in one of the bustling waterside pubs.

newportmansions.org) maintains eight remarkable mansions that can be visited with guided tours or self-guided audio tours (not all locations offer both options). Each is fascinating, but after three in a row, the wainscoting starts to swim before your eyes and you can't tell neo-Gothic from Louis XIV. Fortunately, the society's two- and five-house tickets ($25.99 or $32.99 adults, $7.99 or $11 youth 6-17, free children under 6) are not limited to a single day, so tours of aristocratic boudoirs can be interspersed with time at the beach. Tickets to The Breakers are sold separately, but to visit any other single house, purchase a one-house ticket

at any mansion ($15.99 adults, $6.99 youth 6-17, free children under 6).

With time for just one mansion, however, **The Breakers** (44 Ochre Point Ave., Sept.-late June daily 9am-5pm, late-June-Aug. daily 9am-6pm, $20 adults, $6.99 children 6-17, free children under 6) is Newport's showstopper. Commodore Cornelius Vanderbilt II built the Italianate behemoth to resemble an open-air palazzo, and downy clouds arc above the central Great Hall. The house was created by Richard Morris Hunt, founder of the first American architectural school, and he wove the story of the Vanderbilt fortune into his design,

Newport

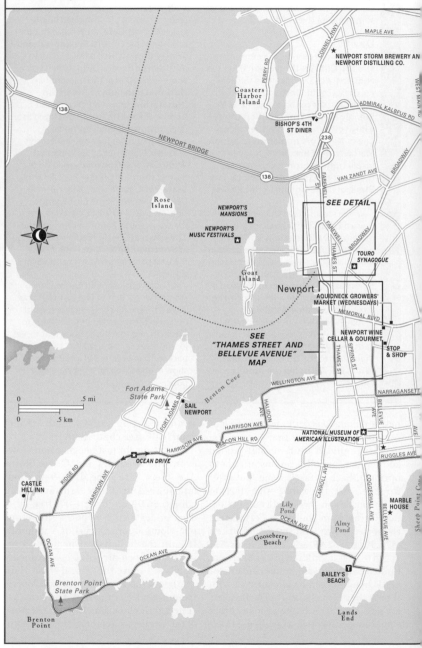

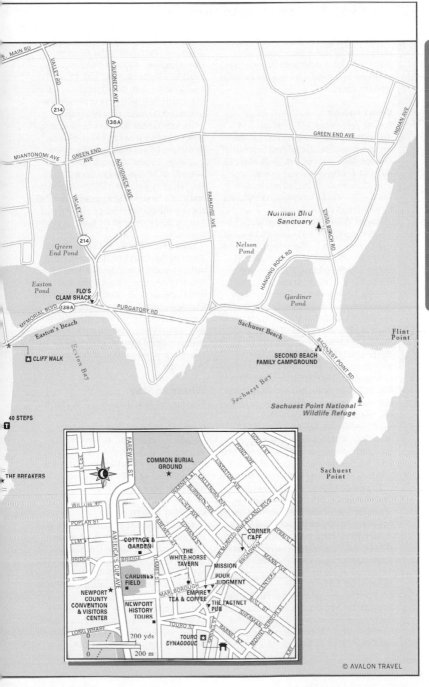

© AVALON TRAVEL

◆ Side Trip to Providence

In recent years, Providence has become unexpectedly hip. A vibrant culinary scene, beautiful architecture, and easy-to-access historical sites make it a worth-while day trip.

What to See

Browse art by ancient Egyptians and mid-century modern designers at the extraordinary **Rhode Island School of Design Museum of Art** (20 N. Main St., 401/454-6500, www.risdmuseum.org, Tues.-Sun. 10am-5pm, $12 adults, $10 seniors, $5 college students, $3 children 5-18, children under 5 free).

  Roger Williams Park Zoo (1000 Elmwood Ave., 401/785-3510, www.rwpzoo.org, Oct.-Mar. daily 10am-4pm, Apr.-Sept. daily 10am-5pm, $14.95 adults, $12.95 seniors, $9.95 children 2-12) was one of the first in the United States and remains among the best in New England. Highlights include a miniature Nubian goat, red pandas, wildebeest, cotton top tamarin, and a Linne's two-toed sloth.

  It's easy to explore downtown Providence's historic sites on foot, starting with the grassy quads and brick buildings of **Brown University** (1 Prospect St., 401/863-1000, www.brown.edu/about/visit), where you can take a self-guided tour. Head down College Street toward the **Providence Athenaeum** (251 Benefit St., 401/421-6970, www.providenceathenaeum.org, Mon.-Thurs. 9am-7pm, Fri.-Sat. 9am-5pm, Sun. 1pm-5pm), a historic library that was a favorite haunt of Edgar Allan Poe and H. P. Lovecraft. Continue one block farther on College Street until you cross the inscribed green line of the **Independence Trail** (www.independencetrail.businesscatalyst.com, 401/441-6401), a 2.5-mile route that takes you through downtown Providence.

Where to Eat

Dine on farm-to-table fare at **Nick's on Broadway** (500 Broadway, 401/421-0286, www.nicksonbroadway.com, Wed.-Sat 8am-3pm and 5:30pm-10pm, Sun. 8am-3pm, brunch $7-13, dinner $18-26).

The airy dining room at the eclectic vegetarian restaurant **The Grange** (166 Broadway, 401/831-0600, www.providencegrange.com, Sun.-Thurs. 8am-midnight, Fri.-Sat. 8am-1am, $10-17) feels like a rustic loft, with lots of pockmarked wood and railroad spike beer taps.

  Standard diner fare and a postage-stamp seating area can't keep **Haven Brothers Diner** (Fulton St. between Exchange St. and Memorial Blvd., 401/603-8124, Sun.-Thurs. 5pm-3am, Fri.-Sat. 5pm-4am, $4-10) from legendary status. It's been slinging meals since 1893, though the onetime horse-drawn food truck is now a shiny silver trailer with seating inside.

  Local chain **Olneyville New York System Restaurant** (18 Plainfield St., 401/621-9500, www.olneyvillenewyorksystem.com, Sun.-Thurs. 11am-2am, Fri.-Sat. 11am-3am, $3-8) won an "America's Classic Award" from the James Beard Foundation in 2014 for its distinctive take on the Rhode Island wiener, which comes topped with mustard, meat sauce, chopped onions, and a bit of celery salt.

Where to Stay

The hippest spot in town is **The Dean** (122 Fountain St., 401/455-3326, www.thedeanhotel.com, $99-179), where vintage furniture and artwork meet a modern aesthetic. A downtown classic is the Hilton-run **Providence Biltmore** (11 Dorrance St., 401/421-0700, www.providencebiltmore.com, $199-400).

Getting There

To reach Providence from Newport, take Farewell Street north from downtown, then merge onto Route 138 West, which leads across the Newport Bridge ($4 toll, cash only). Exit onto Route 1 North, then use the left two lanes to turn onto Route 4 North. After 10 miles, merge onto I-95 North, which leads to Providence. For downtown sights, merge right in Providence onto Route 6 West/Route 10 West, then keep right to take Exit 22A.

Thames Street and Bellevue Avenue

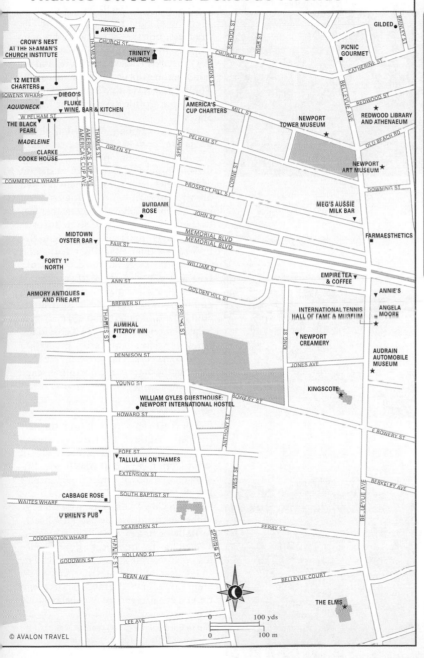

ARNOLD ART
CHURCH ST
GILDED
CROW'S NEST
AT THE SEAMAN'S
CHURCH INSTITUTE
PICNIC
GOURMET
TRINITY
CHURCH
CHURCH ST
CATHERINE ST
12 METER
CHARTERS
BELLEVUE AVE
REDWOOD ST
BOWENS WHARF
DIEGO'S
AQUIDNECK
W PELHAM ST
FLUKE
WINE, BAR & KITCHEN
MILL ST
AMERICA'S
CUP CHARTERS
NEWPORT
TOWER MUSEUM
REDWOOD LIBRARY
AND ATHENAEUM
THE BLACK
PEARL
OLD BEACH RD
MADELEINE
PELHAM ST
SPRING ST
CLARKE
COOKE HOUSE
GREEN ST
NEWPORT
ART MUSEUM
COMMERCIAL WHARF
AMERICA'S CUP AVE
CORNE ST
PROSPECT HILL ST
DOWNING ST
DUNDANK
ROSE
JOHN ST
MEG'S AUSSIE
MILK BAR
MIDTOWN
OYSTER BAR
MEMORIAL BLVD
MEMORIAL BLVD
FARMAESTHETICS
FAIR ST
FORTY 1°
NORTH
GIDLEY ST
WILLIAM ST
ANN ST
EMPIRE TEA
& COFFEE
ANNIE'S
ARMORY ANTIQUES
AND FINE ART
BREWER ST
GOLDEN HILL ST
INTERNATIONAL TENNIS
HALL OF FAME & MUSEUM
ANGELA
MOORE
THAMES ST
ADMIRAL
FITZROY INN
SPRING ST
KING ST
NEWPORT
CREAMERY
AUDRAIN
AUTOMOBILE
MUSEUM
DENNISON ST
JONES AVE
YOUNG ST
WILLIAM GYLES GUESTHOUSE:
NEWPORT INTERNATIONAL HOSTEL
BOWERY ST
KINGSCOTE
HOWARD ST
ANTHONY ST
E BOWERY ST
POPE ST
TALLULAH ON THAMES
EXTENSION ST
WEST ST
BERKELEY AVE
CABBAGE ROSE
SOUTH BAPTIST ST
WAITES WHARF
O'BRIEN'S PUB
BELLEVUE AVE
DEARBORN ST
PERRY ST
CODDINGTON WHARF
THAMES ST
SPRING ST
GOODWIN ST
HOLLAND ST
DEAN AVE
BELLEVUE COURT
THE ELMS
LEE AVE
0   100 yds
0   100 m

© AVALON TRAVEL

with marble railcars and dozens of stylized acorns and oak leaves.

Marble House (596 Bellevue Ave., daily 10am-5pm) can't rival the scale of The Breakers, but the sumptuous, French-inspired home is filled with extraordinary art, extravagant furniture, and an imposing amount of gold leaf and marble. The remarkable Gothic Room is a famous example of Gothic Revival in the United States.

A favorite among mansion aficionados is **The Elms** (367 Bellevue Ave., Sept.-late June daily 9am-5pm, late June-Aug. daily 9am-6pm), one of the most elegant of the Newport homes. French-inspired architecture and furnishings are set amidst Classic Revival gardens that feature grand old trees and some surprising statuary—don't miss the imaginative bronze of a tiger attacking an alligator. Darker and more subdued, **Kingscote** (253 Bellevue Ave., daily 10 am-5pm) is among the earliest mansions in Newport, and it's set apart by Gothic Revival architecture and older technologies. Built by plantation owner George Noble Jones, Kingscote dates to an earlier generation of Newport elite, when wealthy, antebellum Southerners came north to escape the heat.

★ Cliff Walk

Get the best views in town from the narrow path that threads between Newport's most elegant homes and the rocky edge of the Atlantic Ocean. **Cliff Walk** (www.cliffwalk.com) winds 3.5 miles from **Easton's Beach** (175 Memorial Blvd., signed entrance to Cliff Walk at the western edge of the beach), also known as First Beach, to **Bailey's Beach** at Bellevue Avenue, known locally as "Reject's Beach" since it's open to, you know, the public. The finest stretch of scenery starts at the 40 Steps, an engraved granite staircase at the end of Narragansett Avenue. Heading

Top to bottom: the dining room at The Breakers; Cliff Walk; Touro Synagogue.

north, the path is smooth and well-constructed for a half mile and passes behind The Breakers, Rosecliff, and Marble House. After Ruggles Avenue, the going gets a bit harder, and a sturdy pair of walking shoes is required.

Limited street parking is available at First Beach and on Narragansett Avenue, but it can be challenging to find a parking spot in the popular Bellevue Avenue area. The #67 **RIPTA bus** (www.ripta.com/67, $2, full-day pass $6) is convenient for making a one-way trip from 40 Steps to Ruggles Avenue or Bailey's Beach; buses run every 20-30 minutes and pass close by the entry and exit points.

★ Ocean Drive

The perfect Newport day might start with early morning light at Cliff Walk, but the scenic, 10-mile **Ocean Drive** (www.oceandrivenewport.com) has got sunset on lock. To begin, follow **Thames Street** south from downtown, turning right onto **Wellington Avenue**, continuing on as it becomes **Halidon Avenue,** then making a right onto **Harrison Avenue.** While Ocean Drive follows various roads, it's clearly **signposted** at every turn.

Keep watch for fainting goats, llamas, and sheep as you pass the **Swiss Village Foundation** (www.svffoundation.org) on Harrison Avenue; the foundation is an egg and sperm bank for endangered livestock breeds that's open to the public just one day each year.

Duck off the main road onto Fort Adams Drive for a side trip through historic **Fort Adams** (401/847-2400, www.riparks.com, free), then continue south along Harrison Avenue to Ridge Road. Turn right onto Castle Hill Avenue then right again onto Ocean Avenue to pause for a drink on **The Lawn at Castle Hill Inn** (590 Ocean Dr., 401/849-3800, www.castlehillinn.com), one of the most elegant stretches of grass in Newport. After your break at the inn, turn right on **Ocean Avenue** to stay on the Ocean Drive route to **Brenton Point State Park** (Ocean Ave., 401/849-4562, www.riparks.com, free), which wraps all the way around the point where Narragansett Bay meets the Atlantic Ocean. Brenton Point's consistent winds make it the best **kite-flying** spot around, so bring your own or pick one up at the park's small shop, then grab a **Del's Lemonade** from one of the trucks that prowl the parking lot. For an interesting glimpse of a once-grand Newport mansion, peek through the fence at **The Bells,** now crumbling into a creepy, atmospheric ruin on the park's grounds. To find the building, follow the grassy road behind the restrooms.

You'll eventually loop up by way of **Bellevue Avenue.** Ocean Drive can take a brisk 35 minutes or extend through a leisurely afternoon.

★ National Museum of American Illustration

In 1998, one of Newport's great mansions was transformed into the **National Museum of American Illustration** (492 Bellevue Ave., 401/851-8949, www.americanillustration.org, late May-early Sept. Thurs.-Sun. 11am-5pm, Sept.-late May Fri. 11am-5pm, guided tours year-round Fri. 3pm, $18 adults, $16 seniors, $12 students, $8 children 5-12, under 5 not admitted), the first museum in the country devoted to illustration art. The collection includes work by N.C. Wyeth, Maxfield Parrish, and Norman Rockwell, the most iconic names from the golden age of American illustration, which stretched from the post-Civil War era to the 1950s. It's a fascinating look at the intersection of popular culture, propaganda and fine art, and the knowledgeable docents offer insight into U.S. art history. Don't leave the museum without exploring the grounds of Vernon Court; a romantic rose garden, terraces, and a sunken garden are beautifully maintained in the neoclassical style.

Fort Adams State Park

As the British navy set up floating blockades during the War of 1812, the militia at Fort Adams manned an impressive array of 17 cannons that would give any invading fleet a rough welcome to the Newport Harbor. Join a guided tour at **Fort Adams State Park** (90 Fort Adams Dr., 401/841-0707, www.fortadams.org, May-Oct. daily, tours hourly 10am-4pm; Nov.-Jan. Sat.-Sun. tours at noon and 2pm; late May-late March daily, tours at noon and 2pm, $30 families, $12 adults, $6 youth 6-17, self-guided tours $15 families, $6 adults, $3 youth 6-17, children under six free) to explore officers' quarters, the ramparts, and fascinating tunnels to the outer defenses, or visit the fort at your own pace (though tunnels aren't accessible on self-guided tours).

The rest of the park is free to explore, and swimming beaches, picnic areas, and rolling grass make it a pleasant spot on warm afternoons. The 2.2-mile **Bay Walk** loops along the shoreline, up the western side of the park with views of the Narragansett Bay, and back down the eastern edge, where you can see the bristling masts and white sails of Newport Harbor.

Newport Art Museum

Browse modern and historic art in (yet another) historic mansion at the **Newport Art Museum** (76 Bellevue Ave., 401/848-8200, www.newportartmuseum.org, Tues.-Sat. 10am-4pm, Sun. noon-4pm, $10 adults, $8 seniors, $6 students and military, children under 6 free). The John N. A. Griswold house was built Richard Morris Hunt (of Breakers fame), and is one of earliest and best-known American Stick-Style buildings. It's an atmospheric place to see works by William Trost Richards, Gilbert Stuart, and other New England artists, and the rotating exhibitions are a highlight.

★ Touro Synagogue

Rhode Island is thought to be the first civil authority in the world to guarantee religious freedom to all citizens, and it became a haven for Quakers, Jews, and freethinkers that Puritans saw as a threat to their social fabric. Perhaps the most vivid place to hear about this part of Rhode Island's legacy is at the historic **Touro Synagogue** (85 Touro St., 401/847-4794, www.tourosynagogue.org, May-June Sun.-Fri. noon-1:30pm, July-Aug. daily 10am-3:30pm, Sept.-Oct. Sun.-Fri. 10am-1:30pm, Nov.-Apr. Sun. noon-2pm, $12 adults, $10 seniors, $8 students and military, under 14 free), the only surviving colonial-era synagogue in the United States.

Construction on the building began in 1759, and the layout resembles those of synagogues in the Caribbean islands and Amsterdam; Newport's Jewish community was descended from the Sephardic people expelled from Spain by the Inquisition, who continued to more tolerant homes in the Netherlands and the New World. The synagogue itself is a stunning building, with an airy balcony for the formerly gender-divided congregation, a 500-year-old Torah, and a framework of 12 Ionic columns—one for each tribe of Israel.

Each year, community members gather to celebrate Rhode Island's spirit of religious liberty by reading a historic letter from George Washington to the congregation, expressing his support for their freedom. "It is now no more that toleration is spoken of as if it were the indulgence of one class of people," he wrote, "the Government of the United States . . . gives to bigotry no sanction, to persecution no assistance."

Newport Storm Brewery and Newport Distilling Co.

Sample locally made beer and rum at **Newport Storm Brewery and Newport Distilling Co.** (293 J.T. Connell Hwy., 401/849-5232, www.thomastewrums.com, Sun.-Thurs. noon-5pm, Fri.-Sat. noon-6pm, beer tastings $9, rum tastings $10). Guided tours are available

Newport's Legacy of Slavery

Rhode Island's founders came to Aquidneck Island to find freedom from the strictures of Puritan society, but the first recorded slaves arrived less than 15 years later. The colony became a leader in the New England slave trade—between 1709 and 1807, local merchants sent 930 slave ships to Africa—and by the mid-18th century, it had the highest percentage of enslaved inhabitants in the North.

While many slaves were forced to work in Rhode Island homes and plantations, much of the area's involvement in human trafficking was a part of New England's "triangle trade." Newport rum distilleries imported molasses from Caribbean sugar plantations that depended on enslaved laborers, and shipped rum to Africa to trade for slaves who'd be brought back

to the Caribbean to swap for molasses. That tragic commerce permeates Rhode Island's history; Brown University, Touro Synagogue, and the Redwood Library and Athenaeum were built with money from slave-trading families, and Newport's Brick Market and Old Colony House was constructed in part by enslaved workers.

Many Newport slaves were buried in the **Common Burial Ground** (Warner St. and Farewell St., www.colonialcemetary.com), known by the local African American community as "God's Little Acre." **Newport History Tours** (127 Thames St., 1.25-hr tours $15 adults, $5 children 5-12) offers guided visits to the cemetery, as well as an **African American History Tour.**

each day at 3pm, but you can explore the brewing and distilling processes anytime with a self-guided option; the tour climbs to a balcony above the brewery floor, past a towering stack of oak barrels filled with enough rum for a lifetime of daiquiris. A couple centuries ago, Newport had 22 rum distilleries, but things got pretty dry for local spirit lovers after 1842—Newport Distilling Co. is the first legal Newport distillery since then. Its Thomas Tew rum is distilled from domestically produced blackstrap molasses and got its name from a local privateer-turned-pirate.

Trinity Church

Just down the street from the synagogue is another beautiful and historic house of worship. The airy, light-filled sanctuary of **Trinity Church** (141 Spring St., 401/846-0660, www.trinitynewport.org, late May-Oct. Mon.-Sat. 10am-4pm, Sun. 11:30-12:30pm, Nov.-May. Sun. 11:30am-12:30pm, $5, under 13 free) is occupied by fascinating architectural details and artwork that can be explored with a self-guided tour. George Washington, Queen

Elizabeth, and the Anglican bishop Desmond Tutu have all attended worship here, and the public is welcome to join services at 10am on Sundays.

Redwood Library and Athenaeum

Leather-bound books and historic portraits line the walls at the **Redwood Library and Athenaeum** (50 Bellevue Ave., 401/847-0292, www.redwoodlibrary.org, Mon.-Tues. 9:30am-5:30pm, Wed. 9:30am-8pm, Thurs.-Sat. 9:30am-5:30pm, Sun. 1pm-5pm., $10, students and youth under 18 free), the oldest surviving lending library in the United States. Though the admission fee seems high for this relatively diminutive spot, it's still an intriguing place to explore; come at 10:30am to join a guided tour (free with admission), or find the library's artistic and architectural highlights with a self-guided brochure. Don't miss the self-portrait of Gilbert Stuart, a native Rhode Islander and 18th-century portraitist who created the most famously unfinished canvas of George Washington.

Newport's Mysterious Tower

Newport Tower

The round stone structure in Touro Park looks harmless enough, but the 28-foot tower has been the source of endless speculation, study, and a bit of intrigue. Over the years, it's been variously attributed to ancient seafaring Norsemen, pre-Colombian Chinese sailors, 17th-century English settlers, Knights Templar, Portuguese explorers, and an Elizabethan astronomer and natural philosopher. Radiocarbon dating of the tower's mortar suggests that it was constructed between the mid- and late-17th century, but those tests haven't put the controversy to rest. An important clue is a reference by Benedict Arnold—Rhode Island's first governor and great grandfather of the famously traitorous American general—to a stone windmill on his property, which included present-day Touro Park. Elements of the tower's construction differ from other windmills of the time, however, prompting some to ask: "what did Benedict Arnold have to hide?"

Visitors ready for a deep dive into the subject are welcome at the **Newport Tower Museum** (152 Mill St., Newport, 401/447-6757, www.newporttower-museum.com, Mon.-Sat. 10am-5pm, free), where curator Jim Egan offers a passionate and detailed analysis of the possibilities. The short version is this: Egan believes that the tower is a horologium, a building that allows for detailed astronomical observations and functions as a timepiece and calendar. According to Egan, holes in the tower walls aren't built to support mill infrastructure, but are a camera obscura that projected outside images into the tower's interior. He proposes that Elizabethan scientist and occult philosopher **John Dee** designed the tower, which was then constructed as part of an abortive early effort to colonize the Americas, at a time that coincided with a broad interest in improving the calendar system. Egan's spent years researching and reading about the topic, and his explanation includes a dramatic demonstration of a camera obscura, a side trip into theoretical math, and a fascinating glimpse of John Dee's life and work.

International Tennis Hall of Fame and Audrain Automobile Museum

In the heart of Bellevue Avenue's shops and cafés is a pair of museums that may split the true aficionados from their less dedicated companions (who may be more interested in an "awful awful" shake across the road at **Newport Creamery**). Tennis fans won't want to miss the **International Tennis Hall of Fame Museum** (194 Bellevue Ave., 401/849-3990, www.tennisfame. com, Sept.-June daily 10am-5pm, July-Aug. daily 10am-6pm, $15 adults, $12 seniors, students, and military, youth under 17 free), a shrine to the history, arcana, and heroes of the game, complete with a lifesize talking hologram of Roger Federer. Even the setting is infused with tennis history; the museum grounds once housed the Newport Casino, a social club that hosted the first U.S. National Men's Singles Championship in 1881, and the museum's impeccable grass courts may be booked for games ($80/half hr, $120/ hr). At the other end of the block, the **Audrain Automobile Museum** (222 Bellevue Ave., 401/856-4420, www.audrainautomuseum. org, Tues.-Sun. 10am-4pm, $12 adults, $10 seniors, $8 military and students, children under 6 free) is a celebration of the finest cars and motorcycles ever made; the museum exhibits rotate completely every few months to bring in vehicles from several private collections. Recent exhibitions have focused on American muscle cars, a rare collection of prewar vehicles, custom hot rods, and "speed machines," a show that included Michael Schumacher's Ferrari F310B and a Porsche 918 Spyder with a top speed of 214 mph.

Entertainment and Events

Nightlife

Thames Street is the heart of the action, and some of the waterfront's restaurants double as the area's most appealing bars. **The Black Pearl, Diego's, Midtown Oyster Bar,** and **Fluke Wine, Bar & Kitchen** are all appealing places to cozy up to a pint or cocktail, and the walkable district is so compact that it's easy to wander until you find a happening place. One safe bet is **O'Brien's Pub** (501 Thames St., 401/648-4597, daily 11am-1am), an easygoing spot with a big bar and outdoor seating that's bustling all year. Another is **Clarke Cooke House** (26 Bannisters Wharf, 401/849-2900, www.bannistersnewport.com, Mon.-Fri. 5pm-11pm, Sat.-Sun. 11:30am-11pm) where you can watch the sunset from the back patio, then stay through the evening, when things get pretty lively.

When summertime crowds overwhelm Thames Street, however, locals retreat to the watering holes on Broadway, a few of which retain enough seedy charm to be a refreshing change from the waterfront. One favorite spot is **Pour Judgement** (32 Broadway, 401/619-2115, www.pour-judgementnewport.com, Mon.-Fri. 11am-1am, Sat. 11:30am-1am, Sun. 10am-1am), which combines a pleasantly divey feel—neon signs, bric-a-brac—with great craft beers and a surprisingly appealing menu of bar food and healthier options. Regulars love the wings, the burgers, and the sloppily delicious gouda cheese fries. Just down the block is **The Fastnet Pub** (1 Broadway, 401/845-9311, daily 11am-1am), a cavernous Irish bar with a bit of sailor flair (the Fastnet is a legendary offshore sailing race in the UK). Dartboards, table tennis, and a pool table are the ideal backdrop for Guinness pints and Irish whiskey.

More history-minded barflies stop by **The White Horse Tavern** (26 Marlborough St., 401/849-3600, www. whitehorsetavern.us, 11:30am-2:30pm Mon.-Sat., noon-3pm Sun., and daily 5:30pm-10pm) to channel colonial-era conspirators, Newport pirates, and founding fathers—the atmospheric bar is one of a handful of claimants to "oldest tavern in America," and might just take the award. The White Horse has been serving drinks since 1673 and retains clapboard walls and huge ceiling beams typical of original 17th-century architecture. The dinner menu is more dated than historic, but it's worth a visit just to enjoy the remarkable space.

Festivals and Events
From yacht races to film festivals, Newport has one of the busiest event calendars in New England. The season kicks off with the **Newport Oyster Festival** (late May, www.bowenswharf.com/events, tickets $27), a two-day bivalve blowout with oyster farmers from around the state and live music, followed by the **Newport Flower Show** (last weekend in June, www.newportmansions.org/events/newport-flower-show, tickets $20 adults, $6 youth 6-17), when the Preservation Society's mansions open their grounds for juried shows, garden parties, and afternoon teas. See the city's salty side at the **Newport International Boat Show** (mid-Sept., www.newportboatshow.com). All year round, visitors can attend screenings by **Newport Film** (401/649-2784, www.newportfilm.com), often in some of the city's most dramatic settings, from Gilded Age mansions to seaside gardens.

★ Music Festivals
For two weekends each summer, Newport fills to the brim with music lovers, drawn to two of the country's most important—and historic—festivals. **Newport Jazz Festival** (www.newportjazzfest.org) is the original, a three-day extravaganza that always includes some of the genre's biggest names. Dizzy Gillespie and Billie Holiday played the 1954 festival, and Miles Davis, Duke Ellington, and Ella Fitzgerald each released live albums of their Newport performances. Five years later, **Newport Folk Festival** (www.newportfolk.org) kicked off with a memorable show that included the debut performance of 18-year old Joan

Baez (who invited Bob Dylan to join her on stage in 1963). He came back in 1964 and 1965, when he famously played his first live electric set; after being booed by some members of the audience, he didn't return to the festival for 37 years.

Both festivals remain vital, and artists that range from rock and roll to R&B pack the fields at Fort Adams State Park. To make the festivals a part of your road trip, start planning soon—tickets and many of accommodations in the area sell out the previous winter, and prices skyrocket during both weekends. Visit the festival websites for more information, and be aware of the festivals while planning your trip; if you're not in town *for* the festivals, you'd likely rather be somewhere else entirely.

Shopping

As in all New England tourist towns, there are plenty of fudge shops and kitschy souvenir stores around Newport, but there are also some beautiful places to browse nautical knickknacks, clothing, and gifts.

Thames Street and Downtown
Tempting shops are sprinkled all along the waterfront, but a good place to start would be the cavernous **Armory Antiques and Fine Art** (365 Thames St., 401/848-2398, daily 10am-5pm), where dozens of dealers pile up everything from ships in bottles to leather-bound books and fine china. A bit closer to the center, **Cabbage Rose** (493 Thames St., 401/846-7006, daily 11am-7pm) charms with pretty accessories and locally printed T-shirts.

From lithographs of J-class sloops to oil paintings of Newport beaches, **Arnold Art** (210 Thames St., 800/352-2234, www.arnoldart.com, Mon.-Sat. 9:30am-5:30pm, Sun. noon-5pm) brings together marine artists like Keith Reynolds and Helena Sturtevant—some of the area's most recognizable.

Bellevue Shopping District

Tony boutiques around Bellevue Avenue sell charming bits of the Newport lifestyle, like the perfectly sweet **Cottage & Garden** (9 Bridge St., 401/848-8477, www.cottageandgardennewport.com, Mar.-June and Sept.-Jan. Tues.-Sat. 10am-5pm, July-Aug. Tues.-Sat. 10am-5pm, Sun. noon-5pm), where displays of vintage furnishings, antiques, and garden supplies are arranged just so. Pick out lush, natural gifts at **Farmaesthetics** (144 Bellevue Ave., 401/619-4199, www.farmaesthetics.com, Wed.-Sun. 11am-5pm) a light-filled shop loaded with herbal cosmetics and beauty products, then stock up on yacht-party fashions in **Angela Moore** (190 Bellevue Ave., 401/619-1900, www.angelamoore.com, Mon.-Sat. 10am-5:30pm, Sun. noon-5pm).

Sports and Recreation

Beaches

Much of Newport's coastline is rocky and rugged, but those salty points shelter wonderful beaches that are bustling all summer—though some are livelier than others.

Watch surfers catch waves and take a ride on the vintage carousel at **Easton's Beach** (aka First Beach, 175 Memorial Blvd., 401/845-5810, parking $20 weekends, $10 weekdays), a 0.75-mile stretch of sand that fills up with a friendly crowd of families. With ice cream shops and frozen lemonade trucks, this is a sweetly nostalgic place to enjoy the sun, and the on-site **Rosie's Beach Store** rents out umbrellas, chairs, and boogie boards. It's sometimes possible to find free parking on the side streets off Memorial Boulevard.

A few miles past Easton's Beach is **Sachuest Beach** (aka Second Beach, 474 Sachuest Point Rd., 401/847-1993, parking $20 weekends, $10 weekdays), where there are better waves and sometimes a thinner crowd. This beach is also the home of **Rhody Surf** (401/206-9283, www.rhodysurf.com, private lessons $95 one person, $165 two people, plus $65 for each additional person), which offers surfboard rentals and surfing lessons with certified instructors. The western edge of the beach catches the biggest swell, while the eastern end is calmer, so toss out your beach blanket accordingly.

A rocky cove shelters **Gooseberry Beach** (123 Ocean Ave., parking $20), making it a good choice for quiet swims and smaller children, and the beach is often less crowded than other places in town. Open-topped kayaks are available for rent, but the nearby beach club is not open to the public so it's worth bringing your own supplies. Avoid the Bellevue Avenue traffic and expensive parking by hopping on public transportation; Gooseberry Beach is just under a mile from the final stop on the RIPTA #67 bus route.

Boating

Aspiring yachties and ambitious landlubbers can hit the harbor in 12-meter America's Cup sailboats—a class of racing boats designed for the prestigious America's Cup race—with a pair of local charter companies. **America's Cup Charters** (63 Mill St., 401/849-5868, www.americascupcharters.com, $75 2-hr sail adult or $40 child under 11, $195 3-hr racing experience) has the largest fleet of winning boats in the world, while **12 Meter Charters** (12 Bowens Wharf, 401/851-1216, www.12metercharters.com, $79 2-hr harbor sail, $125 3-hr racing experience) has a slightly smaller, but equally impressive quiver of sailing yachts.

Slower moving and breathtakingly beautiful, old-fashioned schooners are among the prettiest sails on Narragansett Bay, and they're notably more comfortable than the sleek and speedy America's Cup boats. The 80-foot, teak-trimmed *Aquidneck* (32 Bowen's Wharf, 401/849-3333, www.sightsailing.com, $30 1.75-hr sightseeing cruise, $39 sunset sail, $5 discount for children 6-12) has gaff-rigged sails and a broad, comfortable deck that's perfect for a glamorous turn around the coast. Two-masted, wooden *Madeleine* (24 Bannister's Wharf, 401/847-0298, www.cruisenewport.com, $30 1.5-hr sightseeing cruise, $40 sunset sail, $5 discount for children under 12) is 72 feet and impossibly elegant, with a pretty mermaid figurehead to lead the way across the water.

Experienced sailors rent their own boat from **Sail Newport** (60 Fort Adams Dr., 401/846-1983, www.sailnewport.org, from $85 3-hr keelboat, from $225 9-hr keelboat) after being checked out by a staff member, then hit the harbor at the helm of a J22 or a Rhodes 19.

Parks

In addition to the seven-mile **Cliff Walk** and the trails at **Fort Adams State Park** there are plenty of ways to escape the crowds on scenic trails near the sea.

Remember: it's important to be aware of ticks while hiking in this area.

With woodland habitat, streams, and fields **Norman Bird Sanctuary** (583 Third Beach Rd., Middletown, 401/846-2577, www.normanbirdsanctuary.org, daily 9am-5pm, $3) attracts a diverse range of birds, from bobolinks to black-crowned night herons. Seven miles of hiking trails thread through 325 acres; the 1.4-mile **Nelson Pond Trail** traces a ridge covered with cedar and oak trees stunted by the wind and salt air, while the 1.2-mile **Valley Trail** passes through one the preserve's most diverse areas. Each of the tree species that grows within Norman Bird Sanctuary may be found along the trail, including four species of oak and eastern red cedar, the area's only native conifer.

Borrow a pair of binoculars and a wildlife identification guide from the visitors center at **Sachuest Point National Wildlife Refuge** (Sachuest Point Rd., Middletown, 401/364-9124, www.fws.

America's Cup sailing with 12 Meter Charters

gov, daily 10am-4pm, free), then watch for snowy owls, harlequin ducks, and the incredibly adorable New England cottontail rabbits. The 1.5-mile **Ocean View Loop** offers lots of water access and can be linked to the 1.2-mile **Flint Point** trail for a longer walk. Don't miss the explanation of the area's fascinating geological history at the visitors center—the rock record in the refuge retains traces of Rhode Island's 356 million year old run-in with present-day Africa.

Spectator Sports

Grab a wiener and some popcorn, then watch the Collegiate League **Newport Gulls** go to bat at **Cardines Field** (W. Marlborough St. and America's Cup Ave., 401/845-6832, www.newportgulls.com, $4 adults, $2 seniors and youth 13-18, $1 under 13), where there's baseball two or three times a week from early June through the August playoffs. The historic field offers an old-fashioned taste of the sport that's largely been lost in the corporatized professional leagues and is a blissful, family-friendly way to spend a summer evening.

On Saturday afternoons from June through September, Newport dons its pearls and polo shirts for the matches at **Newport Polo** (250 Linden Ln., Portsmouth, 401/846-0200, www.nptpolo.com, lawn seating $12 adults, youth under 16 free). It's the perfect place to bring an elegant picnic and enjoy the sunshine as national and international teams hook, bump, and pass their way through a series of chukkas, or periods. At halftime, spectators are invited onto the field to stomp the grass back into place after being torn up by flying hooves. Matches begin at 5pm and gates open at 1pm (noon in Sept.), so plan to arrive early for prime picnic spots.

Food

Bustling Thames Street is lined with fudge shops, fine dining, and everything in between, including some of Newport's best seafood restaurants. It's the heart of the tourist scene and can get jammed with visitors, but joining the summer crowds by the water is just part of the Newport experience. In recent years, however, a cluster of hip, locals-oriented places have opened on Broadway, and when Thames Street starts looking like an out-of-control yacht party, it's worth heading over there to enjoy a meal away from the din.

Thames Street

A spare, minimalist dining room is the perfect backdrop for showstopping food at ★ **Tallulah on Thames** (464 Thames St., 401/849-2433, www.tallulahonthames.com, May-Oct. Wed.-Sat. 5:30pm-close, tasting menus $68-94), where the 5- or 6-course small-plate menus feature local and seasonal ingredients. The offerings change frequently, but a recent meal included duck confit tart with mushroom duxelle and duck jus, grilled octopus with piquillo pepper jam, and chocolate cremeux alongside chipotle ice cream and cinnamon meringue. The food is elegant, but you can leave on your boat shoes—the dress code is a summery, New England casual.

Seafood stars at the modern, romantic **Fluke Wine, Bar & Kitchen** (41 Bowen's Wharf, 401/849-7778, www.flukewinebar.com, May-mid-Oct. daily 5pm-late; mid-Oct.-Apr. Wed.-Sat. 5pm-late, mains $28-36), which takes up three sunny floors on Bowen's Wharf with views of the water. Crispy oysters with mango pepper relish and chili mayo are a perennial favorite, as is the ultra-local Point Judith fluke. Grab a linen-topped table in the downstairs dining room for a leisurely meal, or head to the 3rd floor, where the casual bar is the perfect place to enjoy rounds of oysters and drinks from Fluke's menu of excellent cocktails.

Cozy up to the bar at ★ **The Black Pearl** (Bannisters Wharf, 401/846-5264, www.blackpearlnewport.com, daily 11:30am-midnight, $8-30) for a bowl of award-winning chowder—rumor has it that The Black Pearl won Newport's chowder cook-off so frequently they got barred from entry. The casual tavern is the place to be here, where you can rub elbows with sailors and sightseers in a room that feels like a piece of maritime history.

You can watch all of Newport come and go at **Midtown Oyster Bar** (345 Thames St., 401/619-4100, www.midtownoyster.com, daily dinner 11:30am-4pm and 5pm-10pm, bar 11am-1am, lunch $10-17, dinner $10-36), a popular hangout with a raw bar, dining room, and comfortable pub. The outdoor decks are dreamy on hot summer evenings, and you can wander around until you find the perfect place to sit. Mains like caramelized sea scallops with cauliflower mash are appealing and super-fresh, but the appetizers tend to be Midtown's most creative options; tuna tartare tacos are a

favorite with regulars, and the charred octopus is a highlight. The bar's especially good on Tuesdays, when you can get a free trio of oysters with a featured drink.

Even if it weren't for the fresh, creative Mexican food, **Diego's** (11 Bowen's Wharf, 401/619-2640, www.diegosnewport.com, Mon.-Fri. 11:30am-1am, Sat.-Sun. 9am-1am, $13-18) youthful, rock-and-roll atmosphere would set it apart in elegant Newport. Mexican wrestlers' masks, mason jar cocktails, and punk music are tonic after a morning in the Gilded Age, and the house drinks are among the best in town. Spiced sangrias are displayed at the bar, along with an apothecary's assortment of funky drink ingredients, from rosebuds to tamarind. Crispy pork belly tacos come with a local fruit pico de gallo and chipotle *crema,* and the over-the-top crack fries have a cult following—order them "dirty Donald" style for a dollop of spicy duck gravy.

Broadway

Newport's best burgers are served with piles of fresh toppings and minimal fuss at ★ **Mission** (29 Marlborough St., 401/619-5560, www.missionnpt.com, Sun. and Tues.-Thurs. 11am-9pm, Fri.-Sat. 11am-10pm, $8-10), a casual spot just off Broadway. Organic, grass-fed beef is freshly ground for burgers and hot dogs, and the restaurant uses Newport-grown potatoes for its crisp, golden, hand-cut fries. Counter service can be poky, and tables in the small dining rooms fill up quickly, but with an excellent selection of canned beers, impeccable food, and very un-Newport prices, Mission is a rare find.

Settle in with a good book and better coffee at the Broadway outpost of **Empire Tea & Coffee** (22 Broadway, 401/619-1388, ext. 1, www.empireteaandcoffee.com, daily 6am-9pm, $3-6), a rambling café with plenty of spots to work and read. Wireless internet, well-made espresso,

Rhode Island's Iconic Foods

Little Rhody boasts some of New England's most distinctive menu items, from snail salad to hot wieners.

* **Clam Cakes:** Go to **Flo's Clam Shack** (4 Wave Ave., Middletown, 401/847-8141, www.flosclamshacks.com, daily 11am-9pm, $5-22) for classic clam cakes. These deep-fried lumps of batter, spices, and clam meat resemble seafood fritters, perfect when dunked in a bowl of clear, broth-based chowder.

* **Coffee Milk and Cabinets:** Rhode Island's state drink is the unassuming **coffee milk,** a sweet blend of cold milk and coffee syrup that's available everywhere (the two major labels are almost identical, but each claims passionate partisans). Order a milk shake here, and you'll get sweetened milk; the frosty, blended ice cream drink is called a **cabinet,** and the very last word in cabinets is the **Awful Awful** from **Newport Creamery** (Newport Mall, 181 Bellevue Ave., 401/846-6332, www.newportcreamery.com, Sun.-Thurs. 7am-9pm, Fri.-Sat. 7am-10pm, $4-10). It's "awful big, awful good."

* **Hot Wieners:** Order one of these distinctive sausages "all the way," and it will come in a steamed bun topped with beef sauce, chopped onions, and a bump of celery salt. Try the classic version (with a side of coffee milk) at the Providence location of **Olneyville New York System Restaurant** (18 Plainfield St., Providence, 401/621-9500, www.olneyvillenewyorksystem.com, Sun.-Thurs. 11am-2am, Fri.-Sat. 11am-3am, $3-8) ... just don't call it a hot dog.

* **Jonnycakes:** The Algonquin tribe taught early settlers to make cakes from cornmeal—and legend has it that that's the origin of these crisp, fried corn cakes that are a Rhode Island breakfast staple. There's a (hotly contested) handful of ways to prepare the simple cakes, but state law decrees that they may not contain sugar, flour, or an *h* (don't even try ordering "johnnycakes"). Try some topped with butter and syrup at Newport's unassuming **Bishop's 4th St. Diner** (184 Admiral Kalbfus Rd., 401/847-2069, Mon.-Fri. 6am-2pm, Sat.-Sun. 6:30am-2pm, $4-9).

* **Snail Salad:** It's getting harder to find this Italian-influenced Rhode Island classic, but you can still order a plate at **Champlin's Seafood** (256 Great Island Rd., Narragansett, 401/783-3152, www.champlins.com, Apr.-Oct. daily 9am-6pm, $9-21), about 25 minutes away from Newport, made fresh using snails from the nearby bay. With several days' notice, **Newport Wine Cellar & Gourmet** (13 Memorial Blvd., 401/619-3882, www.newportwinecellar.com, Mon.-Sat. 10am-7pm, Sun. noon-5pm) can often prepare an order.

* **Pizza Strips:** For reasons lost to history, Rhode Islanders prefer their pizza devoid of cheese and cut into dense rectangular slivers. The chewy crust is topped with marinara sauce, and they're available at Italian bakeries around the state. One Providence favorite is **Buono's Italian Bakery** (559 Hartford Ave., Providence, 401/421-4554, www.buonositalianbakery.com, $3-6).

* **Quahogs and Stuffies:** Hard-shelled clams are called quahogs (pronounced koh-hogs) in the Ocean State, and there are dozens of ways to prepare the briny bivalves. Head back to **Flo's Clam Shack** (4 Wave Ave., Middletown, 401/847-8141, www.flosclamshacks.com, daily 11am-9pm, $5-22) to try them as **stuffies**—the chopped clam meat is mixed with bread and spices, then baked in the shell. Some versions are spiced up with *chourica* sausage, a reminder of Rhode Island's Portuguese heritage.

and excellent teas make this an appealing place to while away a rainy day.

It's worth getting up early to beat the weekend breakfast crowd at the homey **Corner Café** (110 Broadway, 401/846-0606, www.cornercafenewport.com, Mon.-Wed. 7am-2:30pm, Thurs. 7am-9:30pm, Fri.-Sat. 7am-10pm, Sun. 7am-4pm, $5-15). Hearty omelets come with herb-flecked home fries, and regulars love the Portuguese French toast, but there are pages of options that cover the entire breakfast canon. Morning's the real draw here, but a lunch menu of salads and sandwiches and the evening pizza lineup are respectable options for an unpretentious meal.

Bellevue and Beyond

Tucked into the same tony block as the International Tennis Hall of Fame and the Audrain Automobile Museum, **Annie's** (176 Bellevue Ave., 401/849-6731, www.anniesewport.com, daily 7:30am-4:30pm, $5-18) is refreshingly old-fashioned and unpretentious. Homey booths and a diminutive diner counter are pleasant places to sit down to a bowl of lobster bisque or corn and clam chowder, and hearty breakfast plates are served all day. House-made corned beef hash and home fries are a local favorite.

Another respite from Bellevue glitz is ★ **Meg's Aussie Milk Bar** (111 Bellevue Ave., 401/619-4811, www.megsmilkbar.com, Mon.-Sat. 8am-3pm, $5-12), a cozy breakfast and lunch place run by a Newport local and her Australian husband. Breakfast classics are very reasonably priced, and a lunchtime lineup of soups, salads, and sandwiches are the perfect fuel for browsing the mansions and/or hitting the beach. Australian knickknacks and menu items are an enjoyable touch; hand-sized meat pies are comforting treats, and the uninitiated should try ordering a "Tim Tam Slam" with their hot drink—it's an Aussie tradition worth globalizing.

An Awful Awful from the **Newport Creamery** (Newport Mall, 181 Bellevue Ave., 401/846-6332, www.newportcreamery.com, Sun.-Thurs. 7am-9pm, Fri.-Sat. 7am-10pm, $4-10) is a summertime tradition in Rhode Island; the name of the thick ice cream shake stands for "awful big, awful good." A somewhat generic selection of sandwiches and burgers rounds out the menu, and the low prices make the Newport Creamery a decent option for families, but this place is all about the ice cream.

There's another outpost of **Empire Tea & Coffee** (112 William St., 401/619-1388, ext. 4, www.empireteaandcoffee.com, Sun.-Thurs., 6am.-6pm, Fri.-Sat. 6am-8pm, $3-6) just off Bellevue Avenue, which is a convenient place to stop for light lunches, like salads and paninis, along with a coffee, tea, and wireless Internet while exploring the sights.

Head past the sandy crescent of Easton's Beach for another Rhode Island food pilgrimage; ★ **Flo's Clam Shack** (4 Wave Ave., Middletown, 401/847-8141, www.flosclamshacks.com, daily 11am-9pm, $5-22) has been ruling the old-school seafood scene since 1936. Buoys, lobster traps, fishing nets, and Rhode Island kitsch hang from every surface, and the menu features the all the seafood shack classics: golden fried clams come piled atop french fries and coleslaw, generous lobster rolls and oyster rolls overflow from a toasted, buttered hot dog bun, and chowder arrives creamy, clear, or red. Flo's does brisk business in Rhode Island-style clam cakes, a fried, hush puppy–like dumpling speckled with bits of clam meat that can be ordered singly or by the dozen. When coming to Flo's during the summer months, be prepared to wait in line; there's a small parking lot out back, otherwise try across the street near the park.

Head north from Bellevue Avenue and you can try another Rhode Island classic, johnnycakes, at Newport's unassuming

Bishop's 4th St. Diner (184 Admiral Kalbfus Rd., 401/847-2069, Mon.-Fri. 6am-2pm, Sat.-Sun. 6:30am-2pm, $4-9).

From sandy beaches to polo matches, there are plenty of prime picnic spots in town. Pick up basic supplies at the centrally located **Stop & Shop** (250 Bellevue Ave., 401/848-7200, daily 7am-10pm), or pack your hamper with more elegant fare at **Picnic Gourmet** (26 Bellevue Ave., 401/619-1181, www.picnicnewport.com, daily 7am-7pm), which spreads out a tempting array of house pastries, baguette sandwiches, soups, and specialty cheeses.

Another excellent stop is **Newport Wine Cellar & Gourmet** (13 Memorial Blvd., 401/619-3882, www.newportwinecellar.com, Mon.-Sat. 10am-7pm, Sun. noon-5pm), offering ready-to-eat salads, fresh bread, and cheese that pairs well with an excellent wine selection.

Find local provisions at the **Aquidneck Growers Market** (Sat. market year-round 9am-1pm, 909 E. Main Rd. Middletown; Wed. market late-May-Oct. 2pm-6pm, Memorial Blvd between Chapel and Edgar, Newport; 401/848-0099, www.aquidneckgrowersmarket.org), a good place to meet farmers, bakers, fishers, and chefs.

Accommodations and Camping

There's an inn on every corner in Newport's compact downtown, but finding a bed that won't break the bank can be a challenge in peak season. Rooms fill up months in advance for popular festival weekends, and many places maintain a two-night minimum on the weekends. That said, there are some incredible places to stay in town, ranging from homey dorms to aristocratic suites, and off-season prices are considerably lower than those listed.

Camping

Twenty minutes north of downtown, the **Melville Ponds Campground** (181 Bradford Ave., Portsmouth, 401/682-2424, www.melvillepondscampground.com, Apr.-mid-Nov., tent sites $32, RVs $55-70) is a friendly place to put down stakes, with hot showers, picnic tables, fire rings, and a pretty stream through the property. Consult the map on the campground website before booking, as some sites are a fairly long walk from the bathhouses, and beware of holiday weekends and Newport's festival dates, as sites go up in price and have a 2- or 3-day minimum.

With an excellent location near Second Beach and the Sachuest Point NWR, **Second Beach Family Campground** (474 Sachuest Point Rd., Middletown, 401/846-6273, www.middletownri.com, May-Sept. RVs $60-70) has full hookups, but offers few other amenities. Tents are not allowed.

Under $100

With a central location and a homey atmosphere, **William Gyles Guesthouse: Newport International Hostel** (16 Howard St., 401/662-9709, www.newporthostel.com, May-Nov., dorm beds $29-49, doubles $49-149) is an unbeatable budget option for solo travelers and a convivial place to meet other visitors. The hostel's four bed, single-gender dorms are slightly cramped but filled with light, and a cozy living room, kitchen, and outdoor porch are available for guest use. The hostel's friendly tone is set by the owner, an adventurous traveler who's generous with tips for exploring the area, sometimes offers spontaneous city tours, and has a fleet of bicycles available for rent. A simple breakfast of cereal, toast, tea, and coffee is provided, and the hostel has wireless Internet, but no parking.

$100-150

The compact rooms at ★ **Crow's Nest at the Seaman's Church Institute** (18 Market Sq., 401/847-4260, www.crowsnestnewport.com, $135-150) are neat as a pin, decorated with sweet quilts and images of the sea. This unique accommodation was designed as a haven for seamen and fishermen on shore leave, and the Seaman's Church Institute's profits still go to providing services for "the men and women of the sea," as well as other people in need. All rooms share clean communal bathrooms, and visitors have access to the extraordinary ocean-themed Seaman's Chapel and a library stocked with all the books you need to plan a round-the-world sailing trip. The Crow's Nest is a wonderful find in Newport; fishers, military, and mariners should inquire about discounts.

$150-250

Just a short walk from the harbor front, the **Burbank Rose** (111 Memorial Blvd. W., 401/849-9457, www.theburbankrose.com, $129-220, parking $18/day) feels like a glimpse into Newport's past—simple rooms are furnished with old-fashioned charm, and the owner prepares freshly baked pastries for the generous continental breakfast. Three suites are available with a small kitchen and sitting room, and every room has a coffeemaker, flat-screen television and private bath. The steep, narrow stairs are as authentic as the hospitality, and 3rd-floor suites may be a challenge for some guests.

Over $250

With an unbeatable location on the Thames Street waterfront, LEED-certified ★ **Forty 1° North** (351 Thames St., 401/846-8018, www.41north.com, $350-1,100) eschews Newport's beachy pastels for a palette of muted grays and iridescent highlights—the result is a kind of mermaid modernism. Artfully placed design books, stunning harbor views, and elegant indoor-outdoor spaces are lightened up with a billiard room and excellent in-room bars; forget whiskey nips in plastic bottles, Forty offers pints of decent spirits along with cocktail shakers and martini glasses. And for travelers arriving in Newport on their own yachts, Forty 1° North has a private, full-service marina—for the rest of us, it's easy to while away an afternoon on the dock, enjoying a cocktail and watching the dock lines fly.

The ultraromantic ★ **Castle Hill Inn** (590 Ocean Dr., 401/849-3800, www.castlehillinn.com, $650-900) commands sweeping views of the water and feels like a world apart. Follow rocky footpaths to the Castle Hill Lighthouse, bring a drink down to Grace Kelly Beach, or cruise to downtown on the inn's motor launch. The Relais & Chateaux property offers elegant service, and the rooms are furnished with beautifully uncluttered Newport style, along with luxe linens and all the amenities; rates include a sumptuous breakfast and afternoon tea. If a night at the Castle Hill Inn isn't in your travel budget, it's worth stopping by the inn's iconic lawn on a warm afternoon to sip a drink and watch the sails drift past.

Candy-colored decor offers a cheeky, modern take on Newport's over-the-top style at ★ **Gilded** (23 Brinley St., 401/619-7758, www.gildedhotel.com, $300-500). The irreverent design is refreshing and fun, rooms are stocked with iPads, plush linen, smart televisions, and kimono robes, and you can brush up your bank shot or wicket skills at the on-site billiard room and croquet green. Breakfast is a selection of small plates that's perfect for light appetites, but might send hungry travelers looking for more.

Guests at the historic **Admiral Fitzroy Inn** (398 Thames St., 866/848-8780, www.admiralfitzroy.com, $279-329, free parking) can escape the ruckus on Thames Street with a rooftop deck and thoughtfully decorated rooms that are light-filled and comfortable. Hot croissants and baked goods are served in an airy breakfast room, along with fresh fruit, yogurt, and granola. An elevator provides wheelchair access to all rooms (though not the rooftop terrace). Don't miss the Admiral Fitzroy barometer in the lobby—like the inn itself, the barometer was named for the British naval officer and scientist that captained the HMS *Beagle* during Darwin's famous expedition, and who revolutionized weather forecasting.

Information and Services

Stock up on brochures, maps, and any other kind of information on the area at the centrally located **Newport County Convention & Visitors Bureau** (23 America's Cup Ave., 401/845-9110, www.discovernewport.org, daily 9am-5pm). There's also parking on-site.

The area's major hospital is **Newport Hospital** (11 Friendship St., 401/846-6400, www.lifespan.org/newport). Local pharmacies include **Rite Aid** (268 Bellevue Ave., 401/846-1631, www.riteaid.com) and **CVS** (181 Bellevue Ave., 401/846-7800, www.cvs.com, pharmacy hours Mon.-Fri. 8am-9pm, Sat.-Sun. 8am-8pm). A handful of banks are found on Thames Street, and several ATMs are located on Thames Street and on Bellevue Avenue, as well as at the bus station and in convenience stores. Free **Internet** access is available in several local cafés and at the majority of hotels (offered to guests only) in town. Faxing and shipping services are offered at **The UPS Store** (270 Bellevue Ave., 401/848-7600, www.theupsstore.com).

Getting Around

Newport's Thames Street area and Bellevue Avenue can get clogged with traffic during peak season, and **parking** can also be a challenge during summer months; the largest public lot is at **Gateway Center** (23 America's Cup Ave., $2/half hr, $1.50 each additional half hour, $24.50 all day maximum), and metered parking is available in the center for $2/hour.

For visitors who prefer to leave their cars parked, it's easy to visit the main attractions on Bellevue Avenue on the #67 **RIPTA buses** ($2, www.ripta.com/67), which run frequently every day of the week. Another good way to get around is by **bicycle**; rent one at **Mansion Rentals** (113 Memorial Blvd. W, 401/619-5778, www.mansionrentalsri.com, daily 9am-7pm, $7 per hr or $25 full day). Taxi service is available from **Atlantic Taxi Service** (401/239-6600, www.atlantictaxinewport.com), or you can get squired around in a two-wheeled pedicab by **Newport Pedicab** (401/432-5498, www.newportpedicab.com).

Cape Cod and the Islands

Cape Cod unfurls into the ocean from the southeastern edge of New England, a ragged hook of sand, bogs, and crashing waves just over an hour from downtown Boston.

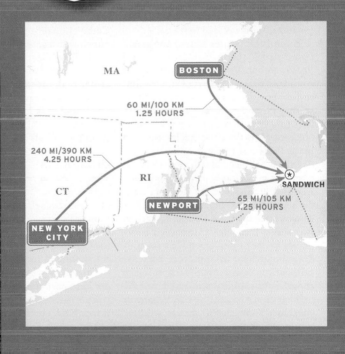

MA

BOSTON

60 MI/100 KM
1.25 HOURS

240 MI/390 KM
4.25 HOURS

RI

CT

SANDWICH

NEWPORT

65 MI/105 KM
1.25 HOURS

NEW YORK
CITY

Endless beaches and sandy cliffs line the Cape Cod National Seashore, while the interior is a maze of rustling cranberry bogs and rolling dunes.

Wild and beautiful, the Cape is the traditional home of the Nauset tribe; it was also the first land sighted when the Mayflower Pilgrims touched down in 1620. In the 18th century, it attracted a rugged population of Portuguese fishers and whalers. In the centuries since, generations of travelers, artists, and renegades have flocked to the Cape for its isolation. Many decided to stay.

Humpback whales patrol the coast from April through October, and Provincetown's historic lighthouses command dramatic views of sunrise and sunset above the sea. The sandy coastline shifts with every storm, but the scenery feels timeless, from Chatham's tony saltbox cottages to the artist shacks scattered in the Provincetown dunes.

Cape Cod's blend of old, new, and wild offers the opportunity to weave between worlds. You can spend the morning wandering world-class galleries in an artists' colony, trace the Cape Cod Rail Trail on two wheels, then catch an evening performance at one of Provincetown's raucous drag shows. Spot wildlife from a kayak, sailboat, or cruise boat, sample clam chowder at a seaside shack, and dance the night away at a beachfront bar. Whatever your thread—whether it's nature, wildlife, history, or culture—you can follow it from Sagamore Bridge to Land's End, where the sand finally gives way to the sea.

Planning Your Time

It's best to find a single region as a home base for your time in the Cape, as moving around the peninsula can be time-consuming when summer traffic hits. For quick chowder-and-cottage overnight stopovers, the Inner Cape is easy to reach and convenient to the mainland—this is also a good base for visiting Nantucket and Martha's Vineyard, a pair of scenic islands that have personalities all their own. The diverse Mid Cape region bundles all the Cape's charms from kitschy tourist joints to picture-perfect villages into a single, compact corridor, where family-friendly Yarmouth and romantic Chatham are excellent getaways.

When you turn the 90-degree corner at Chatham to the Lower Cape, though, things begin to get wilder (in every sense). Come here to explore the lonely dunes and sprawling beaches of the Cape Cod National Seashore, or sip planter's punch with a crowd of shirtless tea dancers in Provincetown, known locally as "the end of the world." P-town's bustling center is all the more thrilling for being so isolated; it's easy to get away from the hustle and walk to rustic artists' shacks, discover thriving wildlife, and catch stunning sunsets from Pilgrim Point.

Orientation

The writer Henry David Thoreau called Cape Cod the "bared and bended arm of Massachusetts: the shoulder is at Buzzard's Bay . . . and the sandy fist at Provincetown." It's a good description of the Cape's eccentric shape. Severed from the mainland by the Cape Cod Canal, the historic towns of Cape Cod's "shoulder" are part of the Inner Cape, and if you keep driving east, you'll be traveling through the Lower Cape.

Make a 90-degree turn at Chatham, then you'll arrive at the oak forests of Mid Cape. Thoreau's "sandy fist" is what Codders call the Outer Cape, the slender passage that extends from Truro to Provincetown.

For driving purposes, the Cape is simple; it's accessed by the Sagamore Bridge if approaching from the north, and the Bourne Bridge when driving from the

Highlights

★ **Cape Cod's Clam Shacks:** Don't leave the Cape without sampling fried fare and hearty soups at a clam shack; forget the Kennedys, these rustic seafood joints are Cape Cod's real democratic power-houses, attracting celebrities, politicians, and sunburned families (page 296).

★ **Cape Cod Rail Trail:** The going's always easy on this 22-mile, mostly flat bicycle path, even when traffic is hopelessly snarled on the Cape's one highway (page 299).

★ **Cape Cod National Seashore:** Stroll miles of sandy beaches with nothing but waves between you Portugal (page 308).

★ **Provincetown's Drag Shows:** People come to P-town to let it all hang out—and so do the wisecracking, arch performers in the community's legendary drag performances (page 315).

★ **Whale-Watching Tours:** Whales, dolphins, and sharks flock to the nutrient-rich waters at the tip of Cape Cod. In recent years, long-endangered right whales have begun returning to the coast (page 318).

★ **Aquinnah Cliffs:** Learn about Martha's Vineyard's Wampanoag heritage in this stunning setting. Cliffs washed in brilliant hues, a historic lighthouse, and perfect beaches are a highlight of the rural up-island landscape (page 337).

★ **Nantucket Whaling Museum:** Scrimshaw, harpoons, and a giant skeleton bring *Moby-Dick* to life (page 342).

Cape Cod and the Islands

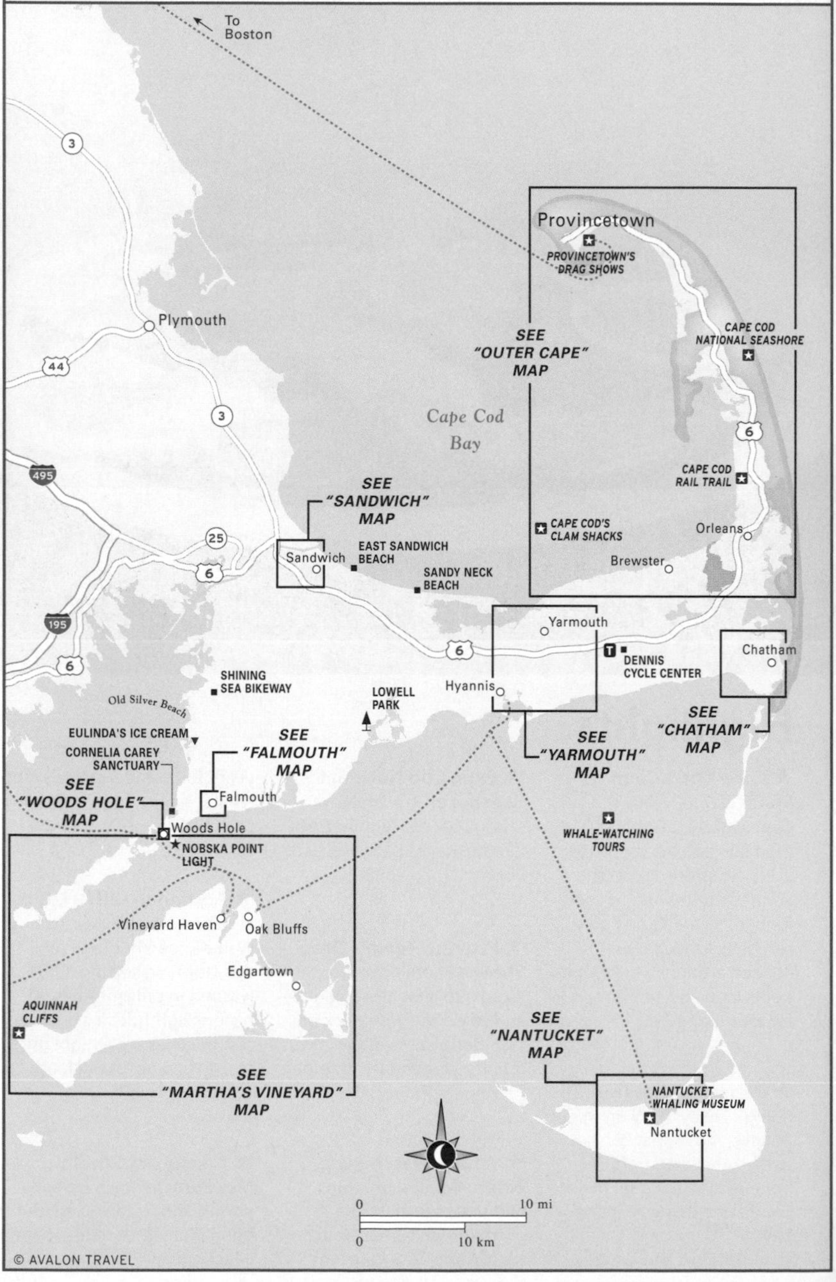

To Boston

3

Plymouth

44

3

495

25

6

195

6

SEE "SANDWICH" MAP

Sandwich

EAST SANDWICH BEACH

SANDY NECK BEACH

Cape Cod Bay

SEE "OUTER CAPE" MAP

Provincetown

PROVINCETOWN'S DRAG SHOWS

CAPE COD NATIONAL SEASHORE

6

CAPE COD RAIL TRAIL

CAPE COD'S CLAM SHACKS

Brewster

Orleans

Yarmouth

6

DENNIS CYCLE CENTER

Chatham

SEE "CHATHAM" MAP

Hyannis

SEE "YARMOUTH" MAP

SHINING SEA BIKEWAY

Old Silver Beach

EULINDA'S ICE CREAM

CORNELIA CAREY SANCTUARY

SEE "WOODS HOLE" MAP

LOWELL PARK

SEE "FALMOUTH" MAP

Falmouth

Woods Hole

NOBSKA POINT LIGHT

WHALE-WATCHING TOURS

Vineyard Haven

Oak Bluffs

Edgartown

AQUINNAH CLIFFS

SEE "MARTHA'S VINEYARD" MAP

SEE "NANTUCKET" MAP

NANTUCKET WHALING MUSEUM

Nantucket

0   10 mi

0   10 km

© AVALON TRAVEL

Best Accommodations

★ **Woods Hole Inn, Woods Hole:** Keep it green at this luxurious inn near a world-class oceanographic institute (page 297).

★ **Chatham Inn at 359 Main, Chatham:** Find old-school luxury at an inn that's walking distance from the sea (page 307).

★ **North of Highland Camping Area, North Truro:** Pitch your tent beneath the pines and walk to some of the Cape's finest beaches (page 312).

★ **Inn at the Oaks, Eastham:** Sleep in this comfortable, historic Victorian where Henry Beston wrote the *The Outermost House* (page 312).

★ **Land's End Inn, Provincetown:** Watch the sun rise over P-town's lighthouses from this exquisite inn furnished with art nouveau antiques and contemporary art (page 321).

★ **Charles & Charles, Vineyard Haven:** Find all the comforts and none of the fuss of a traditional bed-and-breakfast, along with bicycles to explore the island (page 328).

★ **HI Martha's Vineyard Hostel, Edgartown:** A simple, convivial gathering place in the center of the island is the perfect home base for exploring beaches and meeting travelers (page 336).

★ **Star of the Sea HI Nantucket:** Enjoy beach access and priceless views from a friendly hostel housed in an 1873 lifesaving station (page 346).

★ **21 Broad, Nantucket:** Beach blanket chic meets high style on a cobblestone street in the heart of Nantucket town (page 347).

west. Route 6 runs from the Sagamore Bridge to Land's End and is paralleled by two smaller highways on the Mid Cape, Route 6A and Route 28.

Getting to Cape Cod and the Islands

Cape Cod has notorious summer traffic, and on busy weekends, Route 6 can be backed up for miles. When planning a drive to Cape Cod, it's best to **avoid Friday and Sunday afternoons** at all cost, as those are the times that Boston weekenders flood to the beach.

Driving from Boston
60 miles, 1.25 hours
To reach Cape Cod from Boston, leave the city on **I-93 South,** following the interstate for 10 miles, then use Exit 7 to merge onto **Route 3 South.** Upon reaching the

Sagamore Bridge, Route 3 continues into **Route 6.** Cross the Sagamore Bridge, then use Exit 1C to merge onto **Route 6A,** turning right at the base of the ramp. Route 6A passes through downtown **Sandwich** (60 mi, 1.25 hrs).

For **Falmouth** and **Woods Hole,** cross the Sagamore Bridge, then use Exit 1C to merge onto Route 6A, turning left at the base of the ramp. At the **Bourne Rotary,** take the exit for **Route 28 South.** For all other Cape Cod destinations, including **Provincetown** (115 mi, 2.25 hrs), continue straight from the Sagamore Bridge on **Route 6.**

Driving from Newport
65 miles, 1.25 hours
Head north on **Route 114** out of the city, then use the right two lanes to exit onto **Route 24 North.** Two miles after crossing the **Massachusetts border,** merge onto **I-195 East** for 25 miles. Take Exit 22A to

Best Restaurants

★ **Clam Shack of Falmouth:** Enjoy piles of fried fish and clams while watching the fishing fleet come and go at this gem (page 295).

★ **The 41 70, Woods Hole:** The draw at this hot spot is its updated take on coastal cuisine, with modern fare that makes good use of locally grown—and often indigenous—ingredients (page 296).

★ **Chatham Pier Fish Market, Chatham:** With super-fresh seafood straight from the dock, this unpretentious waterside market is the perfect place to grab a bite while watching for whales and sharks (page 306).

★ **PB Boulangerie Bistro, Wellfleet:** The Cape Cod Rail Trail ends by this sweet French bakery, which is the perfect place to refuel with a *chocolatine* or *tarte au citron* (page 311).

★ **Canteen, Provincetown:** Rub shoulders with locals and tourists enjoying seafood classics with creative sides (page 320).

★ **Portuguese Bakery, Provincetown:** Enjoy the tasty heritage of Cape Cod's Portuguese community in the form of egg tarts and pillowy bread (page 320).

★ **20byNine, Oak Bluffs:** Creative small plates make this one of the Vineyard's most exciting places to rub elbows with island foodies in a teeny-tiny dining room (page 331).

★ **The Port Hunter, Edgartown:** Local seafood and produce give island roots to this hip tavern and restaurant, which adds a contemporary edge to Edgartown's elegant food scene (page 336).

★ **Larsen's Fish Market, Chilmark:** Take a seat by a lobster-trap table for a rustic meal of seafood by the docks (page 339).

★ **Company of the Cauldron, Nantucket:** While away an evening over an elegant, prix fixe menu at this ultraromantic Nantucket gem (page 346).

merge onto **Route 25 East** toward Cape Cod. Take Exit 3 onto **Route 6 East.** Cross the **Sagamore Bridge,** then use Exit 1C to merge onto **Route 6A,** turning right at the base of the ramp. Route 6A passes through downtown **Sandwich** (65 mi, 1.25 hrs).

For **Falmouth** and **Woods Hole,** stay on Route 25 to cross the **Bourne Bridge** and, at the **Bourne Rotary,** exit onto **Route 28 South.** For all other Cape Cod destinations, including **Provincetown** (120 mi, 2.5 hrs), continue straight from the Sagamore Bridge on **Route 6.**

Driving from New York City
240 miles, 4.25 hours
Leave New York City heading north on **FDR Drive.** Use the left lane to access Exit 17 to the **Robert F. Kennedy Bridge** ($8 toll, cash only), then stay left to merge onto **I-278 East.** After 4.5 miles, I-278 East merges with **I-95 North** ($1.75 toll, cash only). Stay on I-95 for approximately **165 miles** and then, in **Providence, Rhode Island,** take Exit 19 to merge onto **I-195 East.** Take Exit 22A to merge onto **Route 25 East** toward Cape Cod. Take Exit 3 onto **Route 6 East.** Cross the **Sagamore Bridge,** then use Exit 1C to merge onto **Route 6A,** turning right at the base of the ramp. Route 6A passes through downtown **Sandwich** (240 mi, 4.25 hrs).

For **Falmouth** and **Woods Hole,** stay on Route 25 to cross the **Bourne Bridge** and, at the **Bourne Rotary,** exit onto **Route 28 South.** For all other Cape Cod

Two Days in Cape Cod

With two days to explore the Cape, it's worth driving all the way out past the elbow to the **Lower Cape,** which offers unmatched access to nature, and **Provincetown,** which provides nightlife and culture and makes a good home base.

Day 1

Make your first stop the visitors center at **Cape Cod National Seashore,** to get the background on the area's equally wild geology and history, then spend the rest of the morning walking, swimming, or lounging at one of the park's many fine beaches.

After lunch at **Canteen,** dive into the downtown Provincetown scene, visiting **art galleries** and **boutiques,** and taking in unmatched views of "the end of the world" from the **Pilgrim Monument.** Snag a harbor-side window at the **Lobster Pot** for a classic seafood dinner—or perhaps join the shirtless crowd at the **tea dance**—then kick off the evening with a drag show by one of the town's resident queens.

Day 2

Stop by the **Portuguese Bakery** for snacks to bring on an early morning **whale-watching tour,** and keep your eyes open for the pilot, humpback, and minke whales that thrive in the **Stellwagen Bank National Marine Sanctuary.** Spend the afternoon in the

sand of your choice: Head to **Race Point Beach** to lounge in the sunshine, or take your walking shoes to the **dunes,** where footpaths lead to the rustic **dune shacks** that have attracted generations of artists.

If you're headed to Martha's Vineyard or Nantucket, little **Woods Hole** is a good jumping-off place, and it's worth saving time to visit the town's **lighthouse** and the **Clam Shack of Falmouth** before hopping a boat to the islands.

Cape Cod For Families

Yarmouth or **Brewster** makes a perfect home base for families, both with easy access to the beaches of the **Cape Cod National Seashore** and plenty of kid-friendly ways to keep busy when you're not playing in the sand. Get oriented in the national seashore visitors center, then hit **Coast Guard Beach** for a day of playing in the waves. When you've had enough sun and sand, go to town to play a round of **minigolf** or explore gleefully macabre art at the **Edward Gorey House.**

On day two, rent a fleet of bicycles to take on the **Cape Cod Rail Trail,** saving time to stop along the way for ice cream cones, French pastries, and jaunts to small beaches. By the time the sun sets, you'll be sufficiently tired out to enjoy both of the double features at the old-fashioned **Wellfleet Drive-In Theatre.**

destinations, including **Provincetown** (300 mi, 5.25 hrs), continue straight from the Sagamore Bridge on **Route 6.**

Getting There by Ferry, Air, Train, or Bus
Ferry

A pair of passenger ferries makes the trip from Boston to Provincetown several times daily in high season. **Bay State Cruise Company** (World Trade Center, 200 Seaport Blvd., Boston, 617/748-1428,

www.baystatecruises.com, mid-May-mid-Oct. $59 one-way/$88 round-trip adults, $55/$78 seniors, $39/$65 children 3-12, $6/12 bike). Somewhat newer, slicker, and more comfortable, **Boston Harbor Cruises** (1 Long Wharf, Boston, 617/227-4321, www.bostonharborcruises.com, mid-May-mid-Oct. $58 one-way/$88 round-trip adults, $53/$76 seniors, $39/$65 children 3-11, $23/33 children under 3, $6/12 bike) makes the same trip in a catamaran.

Air

Cape Air (508/771-6944, www.flycapeair. com) runs daily flights from Boston to Provincetown, as well as daily flights from Boston, Providence, and the Islands (Nantucket and Martha's Vineyard) to **Barnstable Municipal Airport** (480 Barnstable Rd., Hyannis, 508/775-2020, www.town.barnstable.ma.us).

Train

From Memorial Day to Labor Day (end of May-early Sept.), the **CapeFLYER** (508/775-8504, www.capeflyer.com) has service from Boston's South Station Friday-Sunday to **Buzzards Bay** (1.5 hrs, $20/35 for one-way/round-trip) and **Hyannis** (2.5 hrs, $22/40 for one-way/ round-trip), where buses connect to destinations around the Cape.

Bus

Peter Pan Bus (800/343-9999, www.peterpanbus.com) lines connect Boston with Falmouth and Woods Hole (1.75 hrs, $31/57 one-way/round-trip), with several daily departures from Logan Airport and South Station.

Buses by **Plymouth & Brockton** (508/746-0378, www.p-b.com) leave daily from Logan Airport and South Station, with stops at most Cape Cod towns including **Hyannis** (2.25 hrs, $26/47 one-way/round-trip) and **Provincetown** (3.5 hrs, $37/67 one-way/round-trip).

Inner Cape

If the Cape is a place apart, then the Cape Cod Canal is what protects the lifelong residents and weekend trippers from the rest of the world. As soon as you cross the Bourne or Sagamore Bridge, interstate highways sliver into smaller roads that wind past historic towns and fishing villages. From historic **Sandwich** to the bustling villages of **Falmouth and Woods Hole,** the Inner Cape is an easy place to get a quick taste of Cape Cod without driving all the way to Provincetown. These towns also make good stops for travelers heading for the Martha's Vineyard or Nantucket ferries. Route 6 is the main route between towns along the northern edge of the Inner Cape, but with extra time to explore, Route 6A is especially scenic, lined with cranberry bogs and antiques stores.

Sandwich

Refugees from Boston's chaotic traffic are relieved to find this quiet town just a few miles past the Sagamore Bridge. Founded 17 years after the Pilgrims touched down, Cape Cod's oldest town remains quaintly old-fashioned, with saltbox houses, tree-lined streets, and a gray-shingled grist-mill at the edge of a swan pond. Sandwich is the place to exhale, slow down, and adapt to the pace of life on the Cape. Spend an afternoon exploring small historic sites, browsing antiques, or pedaling along the seven-mile canal that divides Cape Cod from the rest of the world.

Sights
Cape Cod Canal Visitors Center

Sailing around Cape Cod's shifting sands was painfully slow and shockingly dangerous. The early 17th-century colonists were the first to dream of a canal that would provide a shortcut. Despite repeated surveying, the real digging didn't start until 1909, when New York financier August Belmont Jr. broke ground on a project that would drag on to 1916. The mammoth undertaking was slowed by the enormous, ice age boulders that had to be blown apart by hand-placed, underwater dynamite charges. When Belmont's toll scheme never became profitable, the canal was turned over to the U.S. Army Corps of Engineers. Learn the whole story at the fascinating **Cape Cod Canal Visitors Center** (60 Ed Moffit Dr., 508/833-9678, www.capecodcanal. us, early May-late Oct. daily 10am-5pm, free), where kid-friendly interactive displays bring the canal's construction, shipping, and ecology to life. Take the helm

Sandwich

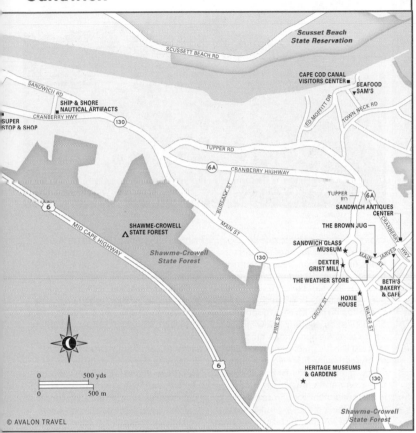

of a 40-foot patrol boat, learn to signal using marine flags, and pick up maps of the **bike trail** (www.capecodbikeguide.com/canal.asp) that links the Bourne and Sagamore Bridges and offers unparalleled views of boat traffic.

Heritage Museums & Gardens

Explore pharmaceutical mogul J. K. Lilly's obsessive collections of classic cars, art, and Americana at **Heritage Museums & Gardens** (67 Grove St., 508/888-3300, www.heritagemuseumsandgardens.org, mid-Apr.-mid-Oct. daily 10am-5pm, $18 adults, $8 children 3-11, free children

under 2) on his superbly maintained former estate. One hundred acres of display gardens wrap around living mazes and labyrinths that bloom with wisteria, honeysuckle, and hyacinth. Inside the museum, browse three sprawling galleries that house a vintage carousel, automobiles, art, and traveling exhibitions, along with a noteworthy collection of Nantucket baskets, scrimshaw, weathervanes and other New England folk art. The grounds are especially breathtaking in late May during the **rhododendron festival,** which draws flower lovers from around the world.

At Home on the Cape

Cape Cod-style homes

Cape Cod lent its name to one of America's most ubiquitous architectural styles, but the region's real signature is the wood-framed, asymmetrical home known as the "**saltbox**," a reference to the wooden boxes once used to store salt under sloping lids. It's easy to spot the distinctive houses around New England; when facing the home head-on, they look just like the simple, English style of houses that the first colonists built, with two rooms on the 1st floor, two on the second, and a squat brick chimney in the center of the roof. From the side, however, the rooflines extend almost to the ground. When a blustery gale is blowing off the ocean, the houses look like they've hunched their backs against the chilly wind.

Legend has it that the style of house became popular when settlers sought to avoid Queen Anne's tax on homes greater than one story (the thinking goes that the roofline would exempt the house from the extra levy), but growing colonial families were likely a bigger factor. Adding an extended roofline is a relatively simple way of expanding the living space on the 1st floor of a boxy home, and the additional area generally included a central kitchen, a bedroom, and a dairy, which was sometimes sunk into the ground for natural cooling. Cape Cod's most historic

saltbox is the **Hoxie House** (18 Water St., 508/888-4361, late May-mid-Oct. Mon.-Sat. 11am-4:30pm, Sun. 1pm-4:30pm, $4 adults, $3 children 9-17) in Sandwich.

Cape Cod houses are just as historic—though they weren't called Cape Cod houses until the early 19th century. They were also adapted from an English building style, with similarities to cottages in Cornwall and Devon. They're generally a story and a half high, with four rooms on the lower floor, a central chimney and staircase, and a pair of 2nd-floor bedrooms with sloping roofs and windows on the gable ends. Cape Cod houses are endlessly adaptable and can take on a patchwork appearance as years go by. Henry David Thoreau said that it looked like each inhabitant "had punched a hole where his necessities required it…without regard to outside effect. There were windows for the grown folks, and windows for the children—three or four apiece." To see a historic example of a Cape Cod house (albeit one with a gambrel roof), visit the **Atwood House Museum** (347 Stage Harbor Rd., Chatham, 508/945-2493, www.chatham-historicalsociety.org, June and Sept.-Oct. Tues.-Sat. 1pm-4pm, July-Aug. Tues.-Fri. 10am-4pm and Sat. 1pm-4pm, $6 adults, $3 students 8-18, free for children 7 and under).

Other Sights

Get a taste of life in 17th-century Sandwich at a historic saltbox house—the oldest house on Cape Cod. Named for a 19th-century whaling captain, the **Hoxie House** (18 Water St., 508/888-4361, late May-mid-Oct. Mon.-Sat. 11am-4:30pm, Sun. 1pm-4:30pm, $4 adults, $3 children 9-17) is carefully maintained with period antiques, and the enthusiastic docents are full of information about how early Cape Codders worked, played, ate and—occasionally—bathed.

Just down the road from the Hoxie House is the 1654 **Dexter Grist Mill** (2 Water St., 508/888-4361, late May-mid-Oct. Mon.-Sat. 11am-4:30pm, Sun. 1pm-4:30pm, $4 adults, $3 children); with a working water wheel and shingles faded to silver gray, it's a pretty spot for taking photos of the swans that bob around in the adjacent pond. Take a picnic to enjoy by the water's edge, and bring some bread to feed the swans, but don't think about abandoning your personal geese and ducks there—a very specific sign warns of a steep fine if you're apprehended.

The Boston Sandwich & Glass Company supplied 19th-century Americans with mold-blown glassware that imitated the cut glass from England and Ireland at much lower prices. See historic pieces and glassblowing demonstrations at the **Sandwich Glass Museum** (129 Main St., 508/888-0251, www.sandwichglassmuseum.org, Feb.-Mar. Wed.-Sun. 9:30am-4pm, Apr.-Dec. 9:30am-5pm, $9 adults, $2 children 6-14, under 6 free), which also has an excellent on-site shop full of traditional and contemporary glass pieces.

Shopping

Boutiques and souvenir shops cluster around Main Street and Jarves Street in downtown Sandwich. It's easy to while away an afternoon browsing art, antiques, and cottage-y home furnishings.

If antique barometers and state-of-the-art weather systems are more your style, however, don't miss **The Weather Store** (146 Main St., 800/646-1203, www.theweatherstore.com, Mon.-Fri. 10am-5pm, Sat. 10am-1pm), where you'll find everything you need to know which way the wind blows. It's a fascinating place stocked with beautiful tide charts, compasses, hygrometers, brass telescopes, and other esoterica, as well as practical tools for modern-day sailors.

The bits and bobs of Cape Cod life sift into the **Sandwich Antiques Center** (131 Route 6A, 508/833-3600, www.sandwichantiquescenter.com, daily 10am-5pm) along with some unique find and a good selection of Sandwich glass.

Visitors in search of maritime antiques, signal flags, and ship wheels will find their hearts' desire at **Ship & Shore Nautical Artifacts** (165 Cranberry Hwy., Sagamore, 508/888-9545, www.nauticalartifacts.com, Mon.-Sat. 10am-6pm Sun. noon-5pm), a museum-like shop that's two miles from the center of Sandwich.

Sports and Recreation

If you can find a place to park or leave your car in town, **East Sandwich Beach** (parking at western end of N. Shore Blvd., parking $15) offers grass-covered dunes and soft sand with serene views to the north. To get a closer look at the area's fragile dunes and salt marshes, walk the 1,350-foot **boardwalk to Town Neck Beach** (parking at the end of Boardwalk Rd., $10). The walk is especially scenic at sunset, when the dune grass glows a dusky pink, and is a favorite among bird-watchers.

There's more parking (and people) farther east at **Sandy Neck Beach** (425 Sandy Neck Rd., Barnstable, 508/362-8300, Memorial Day-Labor Day $20 weekend parking, $15 weekday parking, off-season parking free), six miles of pebbly sand rimmed by rolling dunes that extend all the way to Barnstable, where the beach's main access points are located. A network of walking trails threads between the dunes, from a 0.5-mile loop to a

13-mile round-trip hike that goes within sight distance of the Sandy Neck lighthouse. Campfires are allowed on Sandy Neck Beach after 7pm.

Food

Stock up for an elegant picnic at **The Brown Jug** (155 Main St., 508/888-4669, www.thebrownjug.com, Tues.-Sat. 10am-6pm, Sun. noon-7pm, $7-20), which has an excellent selection of wines, cheeses, and other goodies. The real treat, though, is the wood-fired pizza, which is among the best on the Cape. Toppings are mostly traditional, and they emerge from the oven blistered and bubbling, with a thin crust that is cooked just right. The menu also includes sandwiches, salads, and house-baked pastries, and while seating inside the shop is limited, the outdoor patio is a sunny place to enjoy a slice in fine weather.

The cavernous dining room and counter service at **Seafood Sam's** (6 Coast Guard Rd., 508/888-4629, www.seafoodsams.com, Sun.-Thurs. 11:30am-8:30pm, Fri.-Sat. 11am-9pm, $5-21) might not win awards for ambience, but that can be just the ticket when your party is caked with sand and looking for lunch. Fried whole belly clams, lobster bisque, and clam chowder are favorites among regulars, and mid-day specials (11am-4pm) include well-priced plates of seafood with coleslaw and sides.

The busy ovens at **Beth's Bakery and Café** (16 Sunrise Ln., 508/888-7716, www.bethsbakery.net, Mon.-Thurs. 8am-3pm, Fri.-Sat. 8am-4pm, Sun. 9am-3pm, $4-10) turn out a tempting array of scones, cinnamon rolls, and cookies. Homey decor and comfortable seats make this a pleasant place to linger over tea and a treat, and a simple lunch menu of salads, soups, and sandwiches is freshly prepared and appealing.

Pick up basics at **Super Stop & Shop** (65 Rte. 6A, 508/833-1302, Mon.-Sat. 6am-midnight, Sun. 6am-10pm).

boardwalk to Town Neck Beach

Camping

The pine-shaded campsites at **Shawme-Crowell State Forest** (42 Main St., 508/888-0351, $20 tents, $55-60 yurts) are just outside of Sandwich three miles past the Sagamore Bridge. It's the perfect base for visiting the Inner Cape, and with 285 sites, it tends to have more vacancies than the popular campgrounds near Provincetown. For groups, the yurts are a particularly good deal, through the simple wall tents don't come with linens—bring your own sleeping bag.

Information

Information about Sandwich and surrounding towns is available at the **Sandwich Visitor Center** (Rte. 130, 774/338-5605, www.capecodcanalchamber.org, mid-May-early Oct. daily 10am-5pm), though the volunteer-run spot does occasionally close for lack of staff.

Falmouth and Woods Hole

Many travelers pass through Falmouth and Woods Hole on their way to the Martha's Vineyard ferry, but a scenic harbor, summery beaches, and a world-renowned oceanographic center make this a fine Cape Cod destination of its own. Falmouth loves to boast that it was the childhood home of Katherine Lee Bates, a professor and poet who wrote "America the Beautiful," but visitors may be more impressed with the town's beloved clam shack, a Cape Cod classic at the water's edge that's a pilgrimage spot for great piles of fried seafood.

Sights

Woods Hole Oceanographic Institution

The scientists from the Woods Hole Oceanographic Institution, or WHOI (pronounced "hooey"), spend their time exploring sunken ships, tracking the global climate, and keeping an eye on the critters that live beneath the ocean surface, from whelks to whales. Learn about their work at the small **Ocean Science Exhibit Center** (15 School St., Woods Hole, 508/548-1400, www.whoi.edu/main/ocean-science-exhibit-center, late Apr.-May Mon.-Fri. 10am-4:40pm; June-Oct. Mon.-Sat. 10am-4:30pm; Nov.-Dec. Tues.-Fri. 10am-4:30pm, $3 suggested donation), which has a replica of the Alvin submersible that first explored the wreck of *Titanic,* as well as exhibits and videos on some of the ocean's weirdest, wonderful life-forms.

Get in insider's look at WHOI's latest work by joining one of the institute's free, volunteer-led **walking tours** of the dock area and research facilities that aren't regularly open to the public (1.25 hrs, 93 Water St., 508/289-2252, July-Aug. Mon.-Fri. 10:30am and 1:30pm, reservations required).

Woods Hole Science Aquarium

Do your own research on the adorable—and adorably ugly—things of the deep at the small, kid-friendly **Woods Hole**

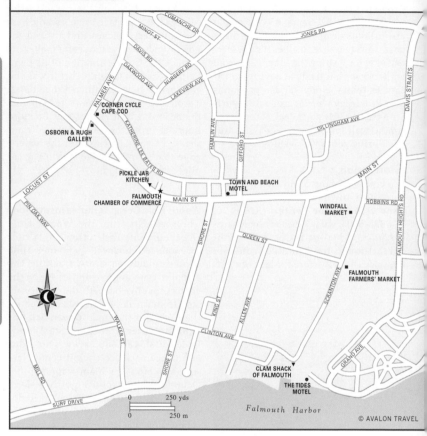

Falmouth

Science Aquarium (166 Water St., Woods Hole, 508/495-2001, www.aquarium. nefsc.noaa.gov, Tues.-Sat. 11am-4pm, donations accepted) that's just down the street from WHOI. The aquarium is home to around 140 species of native New England fish and invertebrates, and kid-friendly touch tanks are a fun, hands-on break from all the learning. Time your visit to see the fascinating seal feeding at 11am and 4pm most days; the seals are rescues that can't survive in the wild, including a blind seal named Bumper that survived a shark attack and is living the good life on hand-fed diet of fresh fish.

Nobska Point Light

Sailors shooting the narrow channel between Woods Hole and Nonamesset Island don't have much leeway, and the 1828 **Nobska Point Light** (233 Nobska Rd., Woods Hole, www.friendsofnobska. org) helped guide a staggering amount of maritime traffic before the Cape Cod Canal shortened their trip. Through much of the 19th century, lighthouse keepers recorded each passing vessel; in 1829, 10,000 boats were spotted from the Nobska light. Even in the days of sophisticated satellite navigation, the light and foghorn are reassuring presences

Woods Hole

WATER ST

THE 41 70

OCEAN SCIENCE
EXHIBIT CENTER ★

★ WOODS HOLE
OCEANOGRAPHIC
INSTITUTION

SCHOOL ST

WOODS HOLE
INN

QUICK'S HOLE
TAQUERIA

LUSCOMBE AVE

WATER ST

PIE IN THE SKY ▼
BAKERY & CAFE

LUSCOMBE AVE

0   50 yds
0   50 m

VINEYARD HAVEN
AND OAK BLUFFS
FERRY TERMINALS

COWDRY RD

CRANE ST

© AVALON TRAVEL

to passing mariners, and Nobska is a sublime place to watch the sun set over Buzzards Bay, with views that stretch clear to Martha's Vineyard.

Entertainment and Events

June's 3-day **Arts Alive** event brings artists from around the Cape, and in early October, Falmouth's **JazzFest** features headliners in venues across town (www. artsfalmouth.org).

Shopping

There's a smattering of art galleries, boutiques, and trinket shops along Main Street in Falmouth, but this isn't a shopping destination in particular. The husband-and-wife **Osborn & Rugh Gallery** (114 Palmer Ave., Falmouth, 508/548-2100, www.osborneandrughgallery. com) is worth a stop, though, to browse oil paintings and watercolors of the Cape Cod landscape.

Sports and Recreation

Beaches

Soft sand and warm water Buzzards Bay make **Old Silver Beach** (Quaker Rd., Falmouth, May-Sept. parking $20) a favorite among locals and visitors alike, and it's among the best places to thrown

out your beach blanket on the entire Inner Cape. There are restrooms, showers, and a snack bar on-site, but parking can be an issue during high season.

Biking

Get out of the car and off the road on the 10.7-mile **Shining Sea Bikeway** (www. woodshole.com/bikepath.html) that runs from North Falmouth to Woods Hole, winding past beaches, cranberry bogs, and salt marshes. Parking is available at the northern terminus, on the north side of Route 151 in North Falmouth, just west of Route 28A. For a shorter trip, start in Falmouth Village, 3.6 miles north of Woods Hole; park on Depot Avenue, west of the main road. As the bike path arrives in Woods Hole, it's easy to take a short side trip past **Nobska Point Light;** turn on to Fay Road, which curves past the lighthouse and rejoins the bike path (the road portion of this ride is narrow and winding, however, and might not be a good option for riders with children).

Maps of the bike path are available on the **Falmouth Chamber of Commerce** (20 Academy Ln., Falmouth, 508/548-8500, www.falmouthchamber.com) website. Find a pair of wheels at **Corner Cycle Cape Cod** (115 Palmer Ave., Falmouth, 508/540-4195, www.cornercycle.com, Mon.-Sat. 10am-6pm, Sun. noon-5pm, $12 per hr, $17 half-day, $25 full-day rentals, child trailer available), which also keeps maps of the path in stock.

Hiking

Walk "the path to the knob" at **Cornelia Carey Sanctuary** (Quissett Harbor Rd., Woods Hole), a 12-acre reserve with striking views of Buzzards Bay. A 1.2-mile loop trail winds through thick forest on the way to the water's edge, then crosses a narrow causeway to "the knob," a scenic spot for watching birds, boats, and the setting sun.

Food

The harbor-side ★ **Clam Shack of Falmouth** (227 Clinton Ave., Falmouth,

★ Cape Cod's Clam Shacks

The peninsula's got enough starched linen for a year of fine dining, but find Cape Codders far from home, and the meal they're dreaming of is probably served in a shack. The free-standing, seasonal spots are a truly democratic experience, as everyone from fishers to day-tripping families stop by for great mounds of fried clams, onion rings, coleslaw, and lobster rolls. Just about every clam shack in New England posts a weathered sign claiming to be "famous" for something; here are some Cape Cod favorites that really are:

Clam Shack of Falmouth, Falmouth: Belly up to a pile of seafood while watching the fishing fleet come and go from a rooftop deck. Shrimp rolls and lobster rolls are another favorite here. (227 Clinton Ave., 508/540-7758, late May-early Sept. daily 11:30am-7:30pm, cash only, $6-21)

Captain Frosty's Fish & Chips, Dennis: Just a couple of miles outside downtown Yarmouth, this popular seafood joint and dairy is the place to be for local families. If you can find a place to park, don't miss the chance for crab rolls and golden onion rings, which go beautifully with a thick, frosty frappe—that's a milk shake for you non-Yankees. (219 Rte. 6A, 508/385-8548, www.captainfrosty.com, Apr.-Sept. Wed.-Mon. 8am-11pm, $5-22)

Cap't Cass Rock Harbor Seafood, Orleans: There isn't much to see in little Orleans, but it's a quick detour on the way to or from other Cape Cod destinations. The weathered buoys that deck the outside of this tiny shack are like lures for hungry locals, and this homey spot can still feel like a slice of old New England, with handwritten signs and gingham curtains. The fried scallops have a loyal following, as do the lobster and crab rolls that boast "all meat—no filler." (117 Rock Harbor Rd., May-Oct. daily 11am-2pm, cash only $8-18)

Arnold's Lobster & Clam Bar, Eastham: With kid's meals served on Frisbees, minigolf, and a faux "shack" built inside a spotless cafeteria, Arnold's is pure Cape Cod vacationland camp, but the fried seafood, chowder, and lobster rolls keep even the locals coming back. Aficionados love the hot lobster rolls and onion rings, and there's outdoor seating and an excellent raw bar on-site. (3580 Rte. 6, 508/255-2575, www.arnoldsrestaurant.com, late May-Oct. daily 11:30am-9pm, $5-20)

508/540-7758, late May-early Sept. daily 11:30am-7:30pm, $6-21 cash only) has the fryolator covered. Fried clams and scallops are lightly battered and succulent. Shrimp rolls and lobster rolls are also favorites.

A perennial favorite for whiling away the time before the ferry is the sweet-as-can-be ★ **Pie in the Sky Bakery & Cafe** (10 Water St., Woods Hole, 508/540-5475, www.pieintheskywoodshole.com, daily 5am-10pm, $3-9). The freshly baked pastries are the stars here, from fruit pies to bread pudding and brioche, but a lunch menu of salads, soups, and sandwiches (at distinctly un-Cape prices) is satisfying and simple. Grab a cup of organic, house-roasted coffee inside the colorful café, or settle into a seat on the sunny deck.

At ★ **The 41 70** (71 Water St., Woods Hole, 508/457-3100, www.the4170.com, daily 11am-7pm, winter hours may vary, $21-38), chef Brandon Baltzley blends an adventurous, avant-garde cooking style with an appreciation for Cape Cod's classic foods and cultural heritage, like milk-poached cod with spruce, apples, and brown bread, or the bread basket of Portuguese sweet bread and chorizo butter. The cozy dining room is built to look like the hull of a ship, with floor-to-ceiling windows and an outdoor deck.

Super-fresh ingredients and bright flavors make the **Pickle Jar Kitchen** (170 Main St., Falmouth, 508/540-6760, www.picklejarkitchen.com, Thurs.-Mon. 7am-3pm, $4-14) an inviting spot for breakfast and lunch in downtown Falmouth. Regulars love the vegetarian-friendly options and house-made hash, as well as substantial salads, hearty sandwiches, and absurdly delicious deep-fried pickle appetizers. The brightly painted casual dining room fills up quickly on weekend mornings, so come early to snag a table. If you haven't guessed, many of the menu items come with delicious house pickles, which are also available by the pound.

Joining the crowd at **Eulinda's Ice Cream** (634 West Falmouth Hwy., West Falmouth, 508/457-1060, late Apr.-Oct daily noon-10pm, $2-6) is a summertime tradition in Falmouth. The tiny shack serves a long list of ice cream flavors, sundaes are piled with hot fudge and whipped cream, and frappes are thick and creamy—keep in mind that a New England milk shake is a thin, flavored milk, and frappes are blended drinks made with ice cream.

Get your seafood in taco form and "wicked fresh" at **Quick's Hole Taqueria** (6 Luscombe Ave., Woods Hole, 508/495-0792, www.quicksholewickedfresh.com, Apr.-Sept. 11am-1am, $9-25), an offbeat spot with counter-service Mexican food, local beer, and a sunny deck. The lobster tacos win raves, but there are plenty of options for landlubbers and vegans, like pulled pork burritos or tacos piled with fire-roasted veggies.

Pick up organic produce and gourmets food at the small **Windfall Market** (77 Scranton Ave., Falmouth, 508/548-0099, www.windfallmarket.com, Mon.-Sat. 8am-8pm, Sun. 8am-7pm) and more standard fare at Falmouth's **Super Stop & Shop** (20 Teakettle Hwy., Falmouth, 508/540-7481, Mon.-Sat. 6am-midnight, Sun. 7am-10pm). Find local pastries, hand-made souvenirs, and produce at the **Falmouth Farmers' Market** (180 Scranton Ave., Falmouth, www.falmouthfarmersmarket.org, late May-early Oct. Thurs. noon-6pm).

Accommodations

$100-150

Good budget options are scanty in this part of the Cape, which makes **Town and Beach Motel** (382 Main St., Falmouth, 508/548-1380, www.townandbeachmotel.com, $95-175) an excellent find. The rooms in the low-rise building are somewhere between outdated and vintage, but the motel is walking distance from the village, and nautical bedspreads and wood-paneled walls feel like an unpretentious taste of a different time.

$150-250

Another pleasantly retro place to land is **The Tides Motel** (267 Clinton Ave., Falmouth, 508/548-3126, www.tidesmotelcapecod.com, $185 d, $250 6-person suite). The Tides has basic, sunny rooms that are spotlessly clean, but what keeps this spot a perennial favorite is the motel's private beach; 1st-floor rooms can open a door to the sand, with a pair of beach chairs for watching boats go in and out of Falmouth's narrow harbor.

Over $250

Charmingly decorated rooms, complimentary bikes, and thoughtful amenities make the ★ **Woods Hole Inn** (28 Water St., Woods Hole, 508/508-495-0258, www.woodsholeinn.com, $295-449) feel like a place to escape to, as do the sumptuous breakfasts. In keeping with the town's science and conservation bent, the inn makes an effort to keep it green with local products, biodegradable cleaners, and employees that bike to work.

Information

Info for Falmouth and Woods Hole is available from the **Falmouth Chamber of Commerce** (20 Academy Ln., Falmouth, 508/548-8500, www.falmouthchamber.com, Mon.-Fri. 8:30am-4:30pm, also Memorial Day-Labor Day Sat. 10am-2pm).

Getting Around

Route 28 connects Woods Hole and Falmouth with Sandwich (23 mi, 0.5 hr). The **Cape Cod Regional Transit Authority** (800/352-7155, www.capecodtransit.org, hourly $2 adults, $1 children) runs the **SeaLine** bus from Woods Hole along the coast to Hyannis and Barnstable, while the **Sandwich** line brings riders from the Sagamore Bridge to Hyannis, where there are connecting buses to all over the cape.

Mid Cape and Lower Cape

This stretch of the Cape is where vacationland hits a fever pitch, with a healthy (and sometimes hilarious) mix of olde New England meets Moby Dick-themed minigolf. It's one of the easiest places to settle in with a family, is easy driving distance from Cape Cod National Seashore, and boasts the refined, old-fashioned town of Chatham, the access point for Monomoy National Wildlife Refuge. The Nantucket ferry departs from the Mid Cape's biggest town, Hyannis; it's not as quaint as other Cape towns, but has a few excellent budget accommodations.

Yarmouth

A cluster of Yarmouths—West Yarmouth, South Yarmouth, and Yarmouth Port—straddle the Mid Cape. On the northern edge of the Cape, Yarmouth Port is all white-steepled churches and old-fashioned homes, but the south is packed with family-friendly vacation kitsch that visitors tend to love or hate, so choose your Yarmouth accordingly.

Sights

Fans of cheerfully macabre art won't want to miss the **Edward Gorey House** (8 Strawberry Ln., Yarmouth Port, 508/362-3909, www.edwardgorey-house.org, mid-Apr.-early July Thurs.-Sat. 11am-4pm and Sun noon-4pm; early July-early Oct. Wed.-Sat. 11am-4pm and Sun. noon-4pm; mid-Oct-Dec. Fri.-Sat. 11am-4pm, Sun. noon-4pm, $8 adults, $5 students and seniors, $2 children 6-12, free children under 6), now an intimate museum that celebrates his work and devotion to animal welfare. The author, illustrator, and costume designer might be best known for the intro to "Masterpiece Mystery." His drawings and rhymes in the *Gashlycrumb Tinies*—"A is for Amy who fell down the stairs; B is for Basil, assaulted by bears"—are as delightful today as they were in 1963. In addition to guided tours, the museum also has a scavenger hunt that's great for kids.

Take aim at Captain Ahab, lighthouses, and an eye-catching pink whale at **Putter's Paradise miniature golf** (119 Rte. 28, West Yarmouth, 508/771-7394, www.puttersparadise.net, Apr.-Oct. daily 9am-10pm, hours may vary in spring and fall, $8.50 adults, $7.50 children under 5-12, $6.50 children under 5). It's a summertime ritual for many visitors, and the friendly staff, Cape-themed courses, and ice cream stand make it a favorite for families. Check the website for coupons.

The Cape Cod Astronomical Society opens doors to **Werner Schmidt Observatory** (210 Station Ave., Dennis-Yarmouth High School, South Yarmouth, 508/398-4765, www.ccas.ws, late-June-Aug. Thurs. 7:30pm lecture, 8:30pm star party, free) on Thursday nights in the summer, and joining a "star party" offers the chance to take in the skies above the Cape through 16" and 18" telescopes.

Shopping

Stock up on beach reading at the **Parnassus Book Service** (220 Rte. 6A, Yarmouth Port, 508/362-6420, www.parnassusbooks.com, May-Sept. Mon.-Sat. 9am-5pm, Sun. noon-5pm; hours vary in winter), which carries thousands of used volumes along with new books

Yarmouth

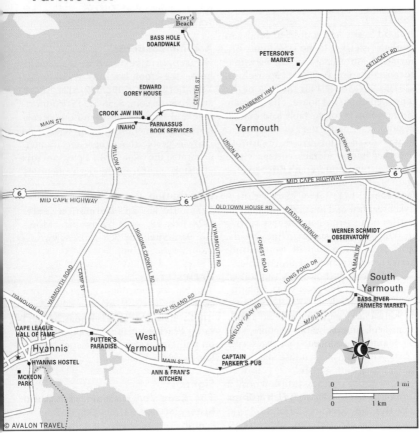

on the Cape and a complete catalog of Edward Gorey. An outdoor extension is open around the clock on the honor system.

Sports and Recreation
Beaches
The **Bass Hole Boardwalk** crosses 900 feet of tidal marshes beside **Gray's Beach** (Center Street, Yarmouth Port, parking $15), the perfect vantage point for watching scurrying crabs, shorebirds, and tidal sloughs, though the bugs can be daunting on calm days. The beach itself is small, sandy, and sheltered from waves, and the roped-in swimming area is a popular choice for families with small children.

★ Cape Cod Rail Trail
The paved, mostly flat **Cape Cod Rail Trail** follows 22 miles of former railroad track between South Dennis and Wellfleet, passing ponds, forests, and short spurs to reach the coast. There is parking at the trailhead in South Dennis (Rte. 134, 0.5-mile south of Rte. 6 on the left, free), and if you're renting your wheels, there's parking available at **Dennis Cycle Center** (249 Great Western Rd., South Dennis, 508/398-0011, www.denniscyclecenter.

com, $14 2 hrs, $22 all day), which is located on the bike path.

Food

Seafood lovers weary of fried food can get their fish fix at **Inaho** (157 Route 6A, Yarmouth Port, 508/362-5522, www.inahocapecod.com, Tues.-Sat. 5pm-close, $20-35), a sushi restaurant in a perky converted Cape Cod house. The intimate dining room is comfortable and casual. Regulars rave about the raw scallops in an avocado shell and ultra-fresh sashimi.

Tucked into an adorable cottage with a striped awning, **Ann & Fran's Kitchen** (471 Main St., West Yarmouth, 508/775-7771, 7am-2pm, $8-12) serves classic diner-style breakfast and lunch. Pancakes and waffles of all stripes and hearty savory breakfasts bring in summertime crowds, but this is a local favorite year-round. Arrive early or plan to wait for a table.

Thick, creamy chowder is the star of the show at **Captain Parker's Pub** (668 Rte. 28, West Yarmouth, 508/771-4266, www.captainparkers.com, July-Aug. daily 11am-10pm, Sept.-June daily 11am-9:30pm, $12-27), a family-friendly pub that also serves hearty American steak house classics in the laid-back dining room.

A few miles northeast of downtown Yarmouth, **Captain Frosty's Fish & Chips** (219 Rte. 6A, Dennis, 508/385-8548, www.captainfrosty.com, Apr.-Sept. Wed.-Mon. 8am-11pm, $5-22) is a classic family seafood stop, with thick ice cream frappes that go perfectly with big piles of onion rings and soft crab rolls. The clam chowder is another favorite, packed with a generous helping of clams, and creamy as can be. Stand in line to order at the counter, then wait for your food at outdoor picnic tables.

Stock up on locally grown berries, fresh bread, and all things artisanal at **Bass River Farmers Market** (311 Old Main St., Yarmouth, www.bassriverfarmersmarket.org, mid-June-mid-Sept., Thurs. and Sun. 9am-1:30pm).

You can find picnic supplies—and just about anything else you need—at locally owned **Peterson's Market** (918 Rte. 6A, Yarmouth Port, 508/362-2147, www.smithfieldmarkets.com, daily 7am-9pm).

Accommodations

Housed in a restored sea captain's home, the **Crook Jaw Inn** (186 Main St., Yarmouth Port, 5098/362-6111, www.crookjawinn.com, $155-175) is comfortable and friendly with fabulous breakfasts. The owner, Brian, is gracious and knowledgeable about the Cape, and has decorated the rooms with a pleasant mix of historic charm and modern amenities.

Information

Yarmouth has an **information center** (424 Rte. 28, West Yarmouth, Mon.-Sat. 9am-5pm, 508/778-1008, www.yarmouthcapecod.com).

Brewster

This bayside town doesn't have much of a center, but its wealth of natural beauty—from wooded parks to salt marshes and sandy beaches—make it a good jumping-off point for exploring the Cape's wilder, less-developed side.

Sights

The **Cape Cod Museum of Natural History** (869 Rte. 6A, 508/896-3867, www.ccmnh.org, June-Sept. 30 daily 9:30am-4pm, Oct.-Dec. Wed.-Sun. 11am-3pm; Feb.-Mar. Thurs.-Sun. 1am-3pm; Apr.-May Wed.-Sun. 11am-3pm, $11 adults, $8 seniors, $6 children 3-12, free children under 3, $1 discount outside peak season) brings the Cape's geology and natural history to life with wave tanks, interactive exhibits, and art. During summer months, visitors can meet the vivid butterflies in the Pollinator House, and a trail behind the museum leads to salt marshes and a beach that attracts flocks of migratory birds.

Shopping

Brewster's not much of a shopping hot

Brewster and Orleans

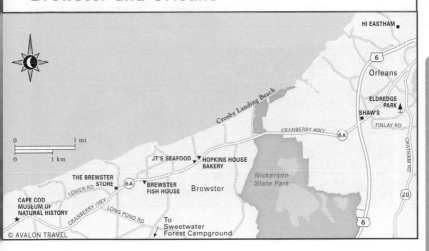

spot, but **The Brewster Store** (1935 Rte. 6A, 508/896-3744, www.brewsterstore. com, May-Aug. daily 9:30am-6pm, Sept.-Apr. daily 10am-5pm) is an old-timey favorite, with penny candy, beach toys, housewares, and antiques. Homesteaders and preppers take note: The Brewster Store is one of New England's premier destinations for oil lamp parts, lamp oil, and hurricane globes.

Sports and Recreation
Beaches
For kid-friendly tidepools and swimming, **Crosby Landing Beach** (Crosby Lane, 508/896-4511, day parking $20) is ideal. If the tide's not too high, walk out to the shallow sandbar to enjoy the warm bay water.

Hiking and Biking
With dense pine forests and freshwater kettle ponds, **Nickerson State Park** (3488 Main St., 508/896-3491, day parking $10) can feel like it's miles away from the coast. **Hiking trails** wrap around the edges of the ponds and **biking trails** wind through the woods, then extend to the Cape Cod Rail Trail. Nickerson does

have a bit of very scenic beach, though; plan your visit to the low tide to walk the intertidal **Namskaket Sea Path,** which crosses 1.5 miles of coastal dunes and tide flats. The state park also has a 400-site campground (tent sites from $27, yurts from $50).

Food
The sunny picnic tables at **JT's Seafood** (2689 Rte. 6A, 508/896-3355, www.jt-seafood.com, $5-25) fill up with families tucked into great piles of beer-battered fish-and-chips, steamers, and lobster rolls that come with little cups of drawn butter. JT's also has a popular ice cream window with hard- and soft-serve ice cream and banana splits.

Fresh baked muffins and scones are the highlight of **Hopkins House Bakery** (2727 Rte. 6A, 508/896-3450, www.hopkinshousebakery.com, $2-8), in a rambling Cape Cod that's also home to a country store filled with antiques and folk art. Regulars swear by the hermit cookies, a chewy, spicy New England classic stuffed with dried fruits and nuts.

Built in a former seafood market, the **Brewster Fish House** (2208 Rte. 6A,

Cape Cod Baseball

summer game in the Cape Cod Baseball League

As the beaches fill and clam shacks open their doors, some of the most talented college baseball players descend on the Cape for a season in the **Cape Cod Baseball League** (www.capecodbaseball.org), one of 11 summer leagues across the country. Teams like the Brewster Whitecaps, Chatham Anglers, and Hyannis Harbor Hawks have sent over 1,000 players to the Major League, and Cape Cod regulars have seen some big names in their small-town venues, including Hall of Famers Harold "Pie" Traynor, Carlton Fisk, Frank Thomas, and Craig Biggio. The league is volunteer run, charges no admission, and many of the young players are hosted in local homes. Attending a game is a fun way to take part in a Cape Cod tradition, and there are games most days of the week from the second week of June through early August. Check the website for an updated schedule, but here are some favorite places to catch a game:

Lowell Park, Cotuit: Home field of the Cotuit Kettleers, Lowell Park is the most picturesque baseball diamond on Cape Cod: an old-fashioned field and bleachers surrounded by dense forest

that looks like the backdrop for a Norman Rockwell painting (www.kettleers.org).

McKeon Park, Hyannis: You can smell the ocean (along with the peanuts and Crackerjacks) when you watch the Hyannis Harbor Hawks go to bat in the heart of the Mid Cape. Head to the "Osprey's Nest" on the third base line for the best views of the action (www.harborhawks.org).

Eldredge Park, Orleans: Bring a blanket or lawn chair to this laid-back park, which has terraced hills along both baselines, but come early—the Orleans Firebirds have a devoted fan base that arrives hours before the first at-bat to stake their claim on prized pieces of grass (www.orleansfirebirds.com).

To get the whole story behind the Cape Cod Baseball League, visit the **Cape League Hall of Fame** (397 Main St., Hyannis, 508/790-3077, www.capecodbaseball.org, mid-Apr.-May and Nov. Mon.-Sat. 10am-4pm, Sun. noon-4pm, June-Oct. Mon.-Sat. 9am-5pm, Sun. noon-5pm, $10 adults, $7 seniors, $5 children 8-17, under 8 free), part of the John F. Kennedy Museum.

508/896-7867, www.brewsterfishhouse.com, daily 11:30am-3pm and 5pm-9pm, $17-38) serves thoughtful presentations of fish and steak house fare that transcend clam shack fare. Friendly service, local ingredients, and a cottage filled with nautical decor and fish portraits make this a Mid Cape favorite.

Part fishing shack, part grandma's kitchen, **Cap't Cass Rock Harbor Seafood** (117 Rock Harbor Rd., Orleans, May-Oct. daily 11am 2pm, cash only $8-18) serves piles of seafood with little ado: paper plates slapped onto vinyl tablecloths, an old-fashioned counter, and maritime bric-a-brac on every wall. Generous portions and an "Old Cape" vibe make this little spot worth the six-mile detour from Brewster—and Cap't Cass' is BYOB, so pick up a bottle of beer or wine on the way.

Stop by **Shaw's** (9 West Rd., Orleans, 508/240-1021, daily 6am-10pm) for picnic supplies and other groceries.

Camping

Wooded sites, fire pits, and playgrounds make **Sweetwater Forest Campground** (676 Harwich Rd., 508/896-3773, www.sweetwaterforest.com, Apr.-Oct. $36 tent sites, $55 30-amp hookups, $60 50-amp hookups) one of the most pleasant, family-friendly places to camp on Cape Cod. Tent campers should try to book the B-area sites, which are just a short walk away from the campground's pleasant pond, which you can explore in the campground's fleet of rental canoes ($5/hr).

Equally appealing (and closer to the beach), the campground at **Nickerson State Park** (3488 Main St., 508/896-3491, tent sites from $27, yurts from $50) has 400 sites, yurts, and ponds stocked with trout. Bring a sleeping bag to sleep in the yurts, and beware the poison ivy that creeps around many of the campsites.

Information

Brewster has an **information center** (2198 Rte. 6A, 508/896-3500, www.brewster-capecod.com, June-early Sept. Mon.-Sun.

9am-3pm), where knowledgeable staffers can answer most questions off the tops of their heads.

Chatham

Perfectly placed on the outer edge of Cape Cod's "elbow," Chatham is an elegant spot with sweet boutiques, a compact downtown, and many year-round residents, which is perhaps why it's quieter than other towns on the Mid Cape. There are plenty of family-friendly beaches for sand castles and sunbathing here, as well as the most convenient access to the shifting sands of the Monomoy National Wildlife Refuge. Its barrier islands are habitat for an extraordinary population of birds, including protected piping plover and the roseate tern.

Sights

It's easy to see why sailing off the Chatham coast would be treacherous work on the clearest day. "Nowhere on the Cape's shorelines has the sea kept busier than among these storm-bitten sands," wrote Provincetown author Josef Berger in 1937, "Monomoy lies beckoning like the bony finger of death which it has been to countless ships." When twin beams at **Chatham Lighthouse** (37 Main St., tours May-Oct. Wed. 1pm-3:30pm, free) were illuminated in 1808, they must have seemed like a godsend to mariners in a storm; the lighthouse still serves sailors to this day. With a red-roofed Coast Guard station and a snapping flag, it's picture-postcard smart. You may spot seals, whales, and flocks of migratory birds just off the nearby beach.

Learn about life in historic Cape Cod at the small but well-curated **Atwood House Museum** (347 Stage Harbor Rd., 508/945-2493, www.chathamhistorical-society.org, June and Sept.-Oct. Tues.-Sat. 1pm-4pm, July-Aug. Tues.-Fri. 10am-4pm and Sat. 1pm-4pm, $6 adults, $3 students 8-18, free for children 7 and under), located in an old Cape Cod house with a gambrel roof. Knowledgeable docents

Chatham

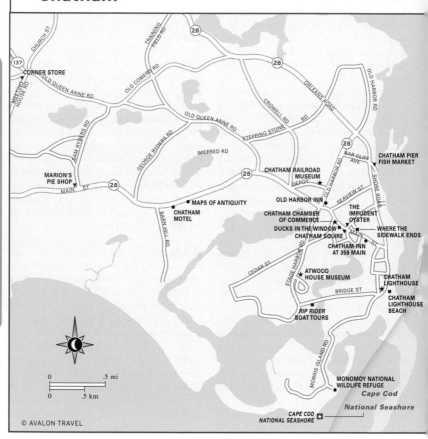

© AVALON TRAVEL

decked in period attire help animate the museum's stories of sea captains, shipwrecks, and day-to-day life.

Brightly painted, "railroad Gothic" detailing makes Chatham's 1887 railway depot an eye-catching home for the **Chatham Railroad Museum** (153 Depot Rd., 508/945-5100, www.chathamrailroadmuseum.com, mid-June-mid-Sept. Tues.-Sat. 10am-4pm, free). It doesn't take long to browse the small collection model trains, railroad history exhibits, and the fully restored wooden caboose, but it's an interesting glimpse of the golden age of rail.

Shopping

Most of the action in Chatham (shopping and otherwise) is clustered on Main Street. You'll find sweet boutiques, upscale design shops, and souvenir joints on the walkable stretch between Old Harbor Road and Willow Bend. Pick up disco ducks, mad scientist ducks, and "celebriducks" at **Ducks in the Window** (507 Main St., 508/945-0334, www.ducksinthewindow.com, daily 11am-5pm, extended hours during peak times), the undisputed claimant to the Cape's largest rubber duck collection. Find beach reads and local authors at **Where the**

Sidewalk Ends (432 Main St., 508/945-0499, www.booksonthecape.com, July-Sept. 9am-9:30pm, Oct.-June 10am 5pm), a welcoming bookstore with a small café. A bit beyond the action is the gallery-like **Maps of Antiquity** (1409 Main St., 508/945-1660, www.mapsofantiquity.com, Mon.-Sat. 10am-5pm, Sun. noon-5pm), which has a wonderful collection of historic New England maps as well as maps featuring constellations, cupids, and sea monsters.

Sports and Recreation
Beaches
The most scenic place to hit the sand is at the **Chatham Lighthouse Beach** (Shore Rd., 30-min parking free, full-day $15), which has views of the historic lighthouse and Monomoy National Wildlife Refuge. It's a good place for spotting passing seals (and occasionally the sharks that love them). Because of the often rough water and strong currents, only good swimmers should think about going past the breakers. Find warmer, calmer water at **Harding's Beach** (Harding's Beach Rd., West Chatham, parking $15), which also has lifeguards, a bathhouse, and bigger parking lots.

Boating
At the time of writing in 2016, the Monomoy National Wildlife Refuge has plans to begin operating **boat tours** of the islands, but currently the only way to visit is with a private captain. Among the best tours are those run by Captain Keith Lincoln aboard the *Rip Rider* (80 Bridge St., 508/237-0420, www.monomoyislandferry.com, 1.5-hr cruises $35 adults, $30 children under 10), a 32-foot motorized tour boat that visits colonies of grey and harbor seals.

Hiking
The sand that stretches south from Chatham forms a pair of barrier islands that are essential habitat for migrating birds; over 10 species make their nests in the **Monomoy National Wildlife Refuge.** Many of the refuge's 7,604 acres are designated wilderness with limited access, but exploring the rest by boat is a remarkable experience. Start at the **Monomoy National Wildlife Refuge Visitor Center** (30 Wikis Way, Morris Island, Chatham, 508/945-0594, www.fws.gov/refuge/Monomoy, Oct.-May Mon.-Fri. 8am-5pm, June-Sept. Mon.-Sun. 8am-5pm), which has exhibits, maps, and information about accessing the islands. It's worth keeping in mind that as the visitors center is volunteer-run, the off-season hours are aspirational—if there are no volunteers, the doors stay closed so call ahead. The 40-acre Morris Island is the only part of the refuge that's accessible by car. A 78-mile **hiking trail** leaves from the visitors center along the shore and coastal forests.

Paddling
To see the islands under your own power, join a guided paddling tour by **Cape Kayaks** (508/247-7402, www.capekayaking.com, 3-hr tours $60); wind and open water mean that tours of the refuge are best suited to those with some paddling experience, but the company offers easier trips into coastal salt marshes and tidal rivers that are good for beginners.

Food
Thick wedges of fruit or savory pie are a summertime tradition for many Chatham visitors. **Marion's Pie Shop** (2022 Main St., 508/432-9439, www.marionspieshopofchatham.com, Oct.-Apr. Tues.-Sat. 8am-5pm, May-Sept. Mon.-Sat. 8am-6pm, Sun. 8am-4pm, $3-18) started as a home bakery in 1947. The hearty potpies are a comforting option, but don't miss the wild blueberry pie in season.

Pick up supplies for a top-notch picnic at **Corner Store** (1403 Old Queen Anne Rd., 508/432-1077, www.freshfastfun.com, daily 6:30am-6:30pm, $6-10), whose burrito bar, sandwiches, and homey whoopie pies are super-fresh and simple. Breakfast burritos stuffed with scrambled eggs, home fries, and tomato salsa are a highlight.

Watch the fishing boats come and go as you eat at ★ **Chatham Pier Fish Market** (45 Barcliff Ave., 508/945-3474, www.chathampierfishmarket.com, May-Sept. daily 10am-7pm, $7-27), a simple takeout shack that's right by the docks. Big portions of fish-and-chips, fried clams, and creamy chowder make this spot a perennial favorite; eat at the picnic tables in the parking lot, or head to the second-story observation deck for views of the harbor.

The seafood menu at **The Impudent Oyster** (15 Chatham Bars Ave., 508/945-3545, daily 11:30am-9pm, $14-35) leans more toward international classics like pesca fra diablo and shrimp scampi, mixed in with substantial salads and sandwiches. In a small, shingled building just off Main Street, dark wood paneling and a cozy dining room make for a warm, welcoming feel—reservations are essential on busy weekends.

In a building that rambles along Main Street, the **Chatham Squire** (487 Main St., 508/945-0945, www.thesquire.com, Mon.-Sat. 11:30am-1am, Sun. noon-1am, $9-25) is the kind of bar where people bring their kids. Choose a spot in the homey dining room for salads, pastas, and hearty mains alongside fried bar food classics, or head to the pub side to drink local drafts in a room lined with antique license plates and Cape Cod bric-a-brac. A seat at the bar is a friendly place to meet locals and other visitors.

Accommodations
Under $100
Busy and a bit pedestrian, Hyannis is 20 miles west of Chatham, but with the only hostel in the Mid Cape area, it's a decent home base for solo budget travelers who want access to Chatham and Monomoy. In a well-maintained home in downtown Hyannis, the **Hyannis Hostel** (111 Ocean St., Hyannis, 508/775-7990, late May-Oct. $35-40 dorms, $79-99 private rooms) is

seals at the Monomoy National Wildlife Refuge

the best option for single travelers in the Mid Cape and has decent private rooms as well. Comfortable common spaces make this a good spot to meet other travelers, and the kitchen and free parking are good perks; the hostel can get loud, so bring earplugs.

$150-250
Just outside of town, the **Chatham Motel** (1487 Main St., 800/770-5545, $130-185) is perfectly tidy, bright and updated, and an excellent deal for the area. Refrigerators, coffeemakers, and a swimming pool make this a relaxed place to stay.

Over $250
Old-fashioned and romantic, the **Old Harbor Inn** (22 Old Harbor Rd., 800/942-4434, www.chathamoldharborinn.com, $299-449) is a sweet bed-and-breakfast filled with thoughtful extras. Elegant common spaces are furnished in English Country style, and the inn is walking distance to Chatham's lighthouse and beach.

With beautiful design and luxurious touches, ★ **Chatham Inn at 359 Main** (359 Main St., 508/945-9232, www.359main. com, $319-499) feels perfectly beachy and refined. Guests get all the usual amenities plus a full breakfast, afternoon cookies, and common spaces that include an outdoor terrace and a cozy room for games and drinks.

Information
The Chatham Chamber of Commerce operates a **seasonal visitors booth** (533 Main St., 508/945-5199, www.chathaminfo.com, mid-May-mid-Oct. Mon.-Sun. 10am-5pm) with information on parking in the area, hotels with current vacancies, and beaches and boat landings. Information is also available year-round at the **main chamber office** (2377 Main St., 508/945-5199, www. chathaminfo.com, mid-May-mid-Oct. Mon.-Sat. 10am-5pm, mid-Oct.-mid-May Thurs.-Sat. 10am-2pm).

Getting Around
Route 6 and Route 28 run parallel for the length of the Mid Cape, linking up a series of small towns that runs together. To reach Chatham from Yarmouth, follow Route 6 east to Old Queen Anne Road, which merges with Route 28 just before entering downtown (16 mi, 0.5 hr).

Outer Cape

When Cape Cod makes a sharp, left-hand turn at Orleans, the peninsula narrows to a sandy slip of land that's just under a mile across in places. But the slender Outer Cape is lined with the stunning beaches and the National Seashore, which make it the finest place to experience the sea at its most beautiful. Locals call the distant tip of Cape Cod "the end of the world." Staying at the end of the Cape offers the chance to move between windblown beaches and the wild, waterfront parties of Provincetown.

Eastham, Wellfleet, and Truro

It would be easy to miss Eastham, whose most compelling places are tucked behind a strip of generic storefronts on Route 6A, but the small town is the main gateway to Cape Cod National Seashore. Tiny Wellfleet, though, is a wonderful destination, its small village center filled with galleries and restaurants. Wellfleet's oysters are among the best in the East, and its excellent bird sanctuary makes for a fascinating visit year-round. Continue north along the Cape, and you'll pass through map dot Truro, which has one of the finest places to camp along the Outer Cape. All three laid-back communities are excellent bases for exploring the Cape Cod National Seashore, but are close enough to Provincetown for a night on the town.

Sights

★ Cape Cod National Seashore

The **Cape Cod National Seashore** is an utterly beautiful swath of coastline. Start your exploration of the park's 43,000 acres at the **Salt Pond Visitor Center** (Rte. 6 at Nauset Rd., Eastham, 508/255-3421, www.nps.gov/caco, daily 9am-4:30pm, extended hours in summer), which stocks maps and information on where to find the best bike trails, lighthouses, and picnic areas. The rangers are deft hands at directing visitors to the finest places to swim, hike, and explore.

For a scenic walk it's hard to beat a stroll down **Coast Guard Beach** to **Nauset Light,** a 1.5-mile stretch that's among the finest in the Northeast. The stairs to Nauset Light often get washed away in winter storms and may not be accessible in early season. Coast Guard Beach is also a particularly good place to watch wildlife from shore: Keep your eyes peeled for seals and whales, which flock to the food-rich waters of the **Stellwagen Bank National Marine Sanctuary.**

The oldest windmill on Cape Cod is **Eastham Windmill** (Rte. 6 and Samoset Rd., Eastham, 508/240-5900), built in the mid-17th century in Plymouth, moved to Provincetown in the latter part of that century, and finally moved to Eastham in 1793. Tours are offered in summertime.

Entertainment and Events

Catch a double feature beneath the stars at the **Wellfleet Drive-In Theatre** (51 Rte. 6, Wellfleet, 508/349-7176, www.wellfleet-cinemas.com, May-Sept. daily, $10 adults, $7.50 seniors and children 4-11, under 4 free, cash only), which is also the site of a sprawling flea market on Saturdays and Sundays (call 508/349-0541 for updated flea market information).

If life in Wellfleet seems suspiciously quiet for a beach town, it's just because the party's at **The Beachcomber** (1120 Cahoon Hollow Rd., Wellfleet, 508/318-4877, www.thebeachcomber.com, daily 11:30am-1am), an insanely popular beach bar and restaurant that's mostly known just as "da coma." Live music, powerful drinks, and an excellent location keep this place packed all summer; a laid-back daytime crowd of families is replaced by a raging crew of 20-somethings as the moon pops out of the ocean.

Learn the basics of opening oysters, or test your skills against the pros in the annual shucking contest at **Wellfleet Oyster Fest** (mid-Oct., www.wellfleetoysterfest.org), when the whole town turns out to celebrate its fabulous shellfish.

Shopping

Wellfleet's walkable town center is packed with over 20 **art galleries**, mostly concentrated on Commercial Street and Bank Street. The Wellfleet Art Galleries Association maintains an art map that most of the galleries keep in stock; favorites include **Left Bank Gallery** (25 Commercial St., Wellfleet, 508/349-9451, www.leftbankgallery.com, Thurs.-Sat. and Mon. 10am-5pm, Sun. 11am-4pm), which has a large selection of works that celebrate coastal landscapes, including home furnishings, and **Blue Heron Gallery** (20 Bank St., Wellfleet,

Outer Cape

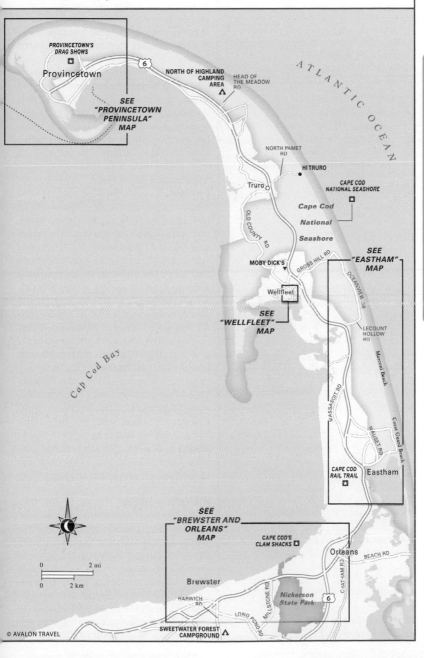

PROVINCETOWN'S
DRAG SHOWS

Provincetown

6

NORTH OF HIGHLAND
CAMPING
AREA

HEAD OF
THE MEADOW
RD

SEE
"PROVINCETOWN
PENINSULA"
MAP

ATLANTIC OCEAN

NORTH PAMET
RD

HI TRURO

Truro

CAPE COD
NATIONAL SEASHORE

Cape Cod

OLD COUNTY RD

National

Seashore

GROSS HILL RD

MOBY DICK'S

Wellfleet

SEE
"EASTHAM"
MAP

OCEANVIEW DR

LECOUNT
HOLLOW
RD

SEE
"WELLFLEET"
MAP

Marconi Beach

Cap Cod Bay

MASSASOIT RD

NAUSET RD

Coast Guard Beach

CAPE COD
RAIL TRAIL

Eastham

SEE
"BREWSTER AND
ORLEANS"
MAP

CAPE COD'S
CLAM SHACKS

Orleans

BEACH RD

CHATHAM RD

6

0   2 mi

0   2 km

Brewster

HARWICH
RD

MILLSTONE RD

LONG POND RD

Nickerson
State Park

© AVALON TRAVEL

SWEETWATER FOREST
CAMPGROUND

Eastham

508/349-6724, www.blueheronfineart. com, July-Aug. daily 10am-6pm, Sept.-Jun. daily 10am-5pm), whose contemporary work is displayed in an airy, relaxed space surrounded by pretty gardens.

There are art shops and boutiques in between Wellfleet's pretty galleries, and one fabulous bookstore-cum-seafood joint: **The Bookstore and Restaurant** (50 Kendrick Ave., Wellfleet, 508/349-3154, www.wellfleetoyster.com, daily 11:30am-8pm) carries rare and antique books (perhaps infused with a light, briny scent from the neighboring oyster beds).

Sports and Recreation
Beaches
The finest beaches on the Cape are those in Cape Cod National Seashore, which has miles of sand for walking, swimming, and soaking up the sun. And fishers and seals aren't the only thing you'll spot from the Cape's beaches—the Atlantic coast is a destination for surfers. Hard-core riders hit the beaches when hurricanes stir up enormous swells, but relatively gentle waves and sandy bottoms mean that Cape Cod's surf breaks are very beginner-friendly. Wellfleet's **Marconi Beach** and **Whitecrest Beach** are a good place to start; pick up a rental board at **Sickday** (361 Main St., Wellfleet, 508/214-4158, www.sickday.cc, Mon.-Sat. 9am-9pm, $30 board, $18 wetsuit). For beginning surfers, **Sacred Surf School** (4900 Rte. 6, Eastham, 508/415-1555, www.sacredsurf-school.com, $75-145) offers very well reviewed private and group lessons.

Hiking and Biking
Spot migratory birds in the salt marshes, barrier beaches, and pine forests of **Wellfleet Bay Wildlife Sanctuary** (291 Rte. 6, Wellfleet, 508/349-2615, www.massaudubon.org, mid-Oct.-late May Tues.-Sun. 8:30am-5pm, late May-mid-Oct. daily 8:30am-5:30pm, $5 adults, $3 seniors and children). Five miles of walking trails wind through the property, and it's common to see fiddler crabs, herons,

and kingfishers along the way. Inside the sanctuary's small nature center are aquariums and art focused on Cape Cod's coastal ecosystems.

The 22-mile **Cape Cod Rail Trail** ends in Wellfleet at LeCount Hollow Road (parking $5). If you're renting wheels in town, you can leave your vehicle at **The Little Capistrano Bike Shop** (1446 Rte. 6, Wellfleet, 508/349-2363, www.littlecapistranobikeshop.com, May-Oct. daily 9am-5pm, bikes from $13 2 hrs and $23 24 hrs); this is also a good stop for maps and advice.

Food

Eastham

Arnold's Lobster & Clam Bar (3580 Rte. 6, 508/255-2575, www.arnoldsrestaurant.com, late May-Oct. daily 11:30am-9pm, $5-20) is a Cape Cod clam shack that's spit-shined and streamlined, and it's about as kid-friendly as it gets. Children's meals come on Frisbees, and the "shack" is in a shiny indoor cafeteria. In addition to well-made standards like fried seafood, lobster rolls, and chowder, Arnold's has a raw bar with ultra-fresh seafood and oysters.

Even oyster farmers need a break from chowder sometimes, and the unexpected, vibrant **Karoo Restaurant** (3 Main St., 508/255-8288, www.karoorestaurants.com, Wed.-Sun. 4:30pm-8:30pm, $12-19) delivers with hearty South African foods like curried lamb stew and peri-peri chicken. Bright, South African flourishes and friendly service make this a lively place to dine, and Karoo has a good selection of vegetarian options as well.

A staggering array of hand-cut cake doughnuts are the starring attraction at **Hole in One** (4295 Rte. 6, 508/255-9446, www.theholecapecod.com, daily 5am-2pm, $2-9); the sweet treats are worth the wait even when the line stretches out of the door. Arrive early to enjoy yours with coffee at a long counter lined with classic diner stools.

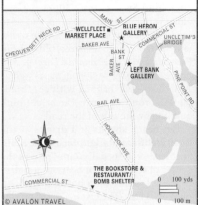

Wellfleet

Wellfleet's got its very own spiffed-up clam shack, and **Moby Dick's** (3225 Rte. 6, 508/349-9795, www.mobydicksrestaurant.com, late May-Oct. daily 11:30am-9:30pm, $7-21) is a favorite for relaxed, family-friendly seafood. Locals are divided about whose chowder and clams win out, but the BYO drinks policy at this spot might just tip the balance.

Surely the first (and only) of its kind, **The Bookstore and Restaurant** (50 Kendrick Ave., 508/349-3154, www.wellfleetoyster.com, daily 11:30am-8pm, $15-29) is just what the name suggests—plus an oyster farm. Order a dozen on the half shell here, and you know they came from just across the street at the family's oyster beds; shellfish and fish stews are the stars of the menu, which also has burgers, salads, and pastas for landlubbers. There's nothing fancy about this place, but seating on the deck is the perfect place to watch a Wellfleet sunset, and the downstairs bar—the **Bomb Shelter**—is a pleasantly divey bar with pool, foosball, and a local crowd most nights of the week.

Cyclists riding the length of the Cape Cod Rail Trail train their sights on the Paris-perfect tarts and éclairs at ★ **PB Boulangerie Bistro** (15 Lecount Hollow Rd., 508/349-1600, www.

pbboulangeriebistro.com, bakery daily 7am-7pm, $3-8, bistro Fri.-Sat. 5pm-10pm and Sun. 10am-2:30pm, $9-35), along with beautiful croissants and oozy croque monsieur sandwiches. The weekend bistro menu features old-school French classics like *canard à l'orange* and house-made *pâté de campagne,* as well as American-style brunch with continental flair. You won't miss the bright pink building by the side of the road.

Get beach snacks and drinks at the little **Wellfleet Marketplace** (295 Main St., 508/349-3156, daily 7am-7pm) in the center of town, which also has a deli—if you're looking for a bottle to go with bivalves, grab "The Oyster," a California sauvignon blanc that funds a Wellfleet wild oyster restoration project: 1 bottle equals 100 seed oysters.

Accommodations and Camping

You can't beat the location of ★ **North of Highland Camping Area** (52 Head of the Meadow Rd., North Truro, 508/487-1191, www.capecodcamping.com, late May-mid-Oct. $44 campsite, $14 additional vehicle, rates are for two adults, extra people $14 adults and $4 children), which is a short walk from Head of the Meadow Beach, one of the prettiest along the Cape Cod National Seashore. Scattered in a sandy pine forest are 237 sites with picnic tables, and the campground has laundry facilities, showers, and a recreation hall with games and a fireplace. There are no fires in the camping area, but there's often a stack of free wood available that you can haul to the beach (free beach fire permits are available by calling the Truro fire dept. at 508/487-7548).

The Lower Cape has a pair of hostels affiliated with Hostelling International USA: **HI Eastham** (75 Goody Hallet Dr., Eastham, 508/255-2785, mid-June-mid-Sept., $37 dorms, $155 4- to 5-person private cabins) feels like a return to summer camp, with mess hall picnic tables, bunk beds, and a quiet, wooded location. The facilities are dated, but tidy, and include

board games and volleyball courts. **HI Truro** (111 N. Pamet Rd., Truro, 508/349-3889, late June-early Sept., dorms $47) has beautiful sea views—the building was originally constructed as a Coast Guard Station—and you can reach the beach by a sandy trail through the dunes. Both hostels provide breakfast and have communal kitchens.

In a cheerfully painted Victorian home, ★ **Inn at the Oaks** (3085 Rte. 6, Eastham, 508/255-1886, www.innattheoaks.com, $195-395) retains a historic feel that's fresh, bright, and accommodating. The inn is full of nautical flourishes and tempting spots to curl up with a book, the generous continental breakfast includes fresh fruit and baked goods, and warm homemade cookies appear like clockwork in the afternoon. Henry Beston stayed at the inn while visiting the Cape and writing his classic book *The Outermost House,* which helped inspire the creation of Cape Cod National Seashore.

Information

The **Eastham Tourist Information Booth** (1700 Rte. 6 at Governor Prence Rd., Eastham, 508/255-3444, www.easthamchamber.com, May-Oct. daily 9am-7pm) doles out information on local businesses, maps, and local tides.

Provincetown

Provincetown's eclectic population of artists, writers, and creative types like to call it "the end of the world." This curling, shifting plot of sand does feel like a place apart. It's easy to imagine how barren it looked when the Mayflower Pilgrims stopped in November of 1620 to pen the famous Provincetown compact on the shore. As the Native American Nauset tribe knew, however, there was a bounty beneath the waves: Provincetown eventually grew into a thriving fishing and whaling village with a strong Portuguese heritage.

Provincetown Peninsula

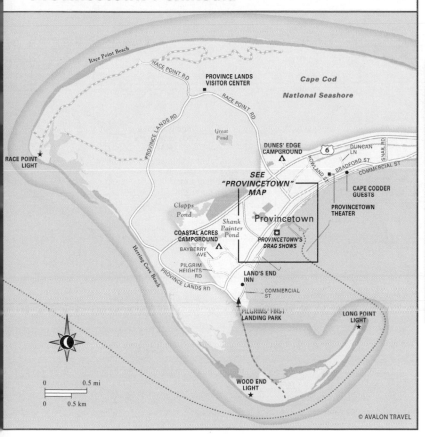

By the late 19th century, the village had become a destination for painters, playwrights, and novelists drawn to the spot's scenic isolation. Rustic shacks began to appear amid the rolling sand and wild roses, creating what became the oldest artist colony in the United States. Over the years, luminaries from Eugene O'Neill to Jack Kerouac, Norman Mailer and Jackson Pollock came to the end of the Cape to work amid the dunes.

Even as the town has acquired a measure of wealth and commercialism, the undeveloped dunes and shacks remain a refuge. Perhaps because of its creative spirit and spontaneity, P-town has been one of America's most popular LGBT vacation spots for decades. On any summer Saturday evening, Commercial Street is a bustling mix of vacationing families, drag show touts, wedding processions, and revelers kicking off parties that will still be going strong at sunrise.

Sights
Lighthouses

Provincetown's three lighthouses are among the prettiest on the Cape. The most easily accessible is the 45-foot cast-iron **Race Point Light** (Race Point Beach,

Provincetown

Clapps Pond & Evans Field

ALDEN ST

Pilgrim Bark Park

JEROME SMITH RD

WINSLOW ST

CAPTAIN BERTIE'S WY

PROVINCE RD

THE BIKE SHACK

STOP & SHOP

COURT ST

WINTHROP'S

BROWN ST

SHANK PAINTER RD

FRITZ'S WY

WINTHROP ST

MONTELLO ST

CONANT ST

PLEASANT ST

WHORFS CT

CREEK RD

FRANKLIN ST

NICKERSON ST

MECHANIC ST

BRADFORD ST

CENTRAL ST

ATLANTIC AVE

LOMMERCIAL ST

CEMETERY RD

CONWELL ST

PEARL ST

STANDISH ST

HARRY KEMP HWY

BREWSTER ST

PRISCILLA ALDEN

MILLER RD

DYER ST

BRADFORD ST

LOVETTS CT

BANGS ST

KILEY CT

HORSE LN

COMMERCIAL ST

Motta Field

Provincetown

SEE "DOWNTOWN PROVINCETOWN" MAP

PROVINCETOWN'S DRAG SHOWS

MacMillan Wharf

BOATSLIP BEACH CLUB

ROSE & CROWN GUEST HOUSE

FLYER'S BOAT RENTALS

LOVELAND

ALBERT MEROLA GALLERY

GALLERY VOYEUR

PROVINCETOWN ART ASSOCIATION AND MUSEUM

JULIE HELLER EAST

| 0 | | 250 yds |
| 0 | | 250 m |

© AVALON TRAVEL

Rte. 6, 508/487-9930, www.racepoint-lighthouse.org), built in 1876 to replace an existing stone structure. It can be reached by a 30-minute walk over marsh grass and sand to the far edge of the cape from the parking lot at **Province Lands Visitor Center** (171 Race Point Rd., 508/487-1256, May-Oct. daily 9am-5pm). It's open for tours on the first and third Saturdays from June to October between 10am and 2pm. You can also stay in the adjoining keeper's house during the summer, when it becomes a bed-and-breakfast.

The other two beacons stand sentinel on the bay side of Provincetown's curving claw. You can hike 1.25 miles across the breakwater at the west end of town to reach **Wood End Light.** From there, continue another 1.5 miles to **Long Point Light.** Most of the walk is along soft sand, so it can take *much* longer than you expect. Another way to reach Long Point Light is on a boat shuttle from **Flyer's Boatyard** (MacMillan Pier, slip #8, 508/487-0898, www.flyersrentals.com, daily hourly departures 10am-5pm during summer months, $10 one-way, $15 round-trip).

Pilgrim Monument & Provincetown Museum

Before the Pilgrims touched down at Plymouth Rock, they spent five weeks in Provincetown, where they wrote the Mayflower Compact and met the Nauset Indians for the first time. The **Pilgrim Monument** (High Pole Hill Rd., 508/487-1310, www.pilgrim-monument.org, Apr.-May and mid-Sept.-Nov. daily 9am-5pm, June-mid-Sept. daily, $12 adults, $10 seniors and students, $2 children 4-12, free children under 4, free parking with admission) that memorializes their landfall is an Italianate tower dominating the skyline and offering unmatched views. After you make it up (and down) the tower's 60 ramps and 116 steps, visit the small **Provincetown Museum,** whose classically kitschy dioramas depict the story of the Pilgrims in living color. The museum also has an interesting collection of Wampanoag artifacts, Cape Cod furniture, household items, and ephemera.

Provincetown Art

Decades of artists that fell for the life and lines of Cape Cod mean a downtown that's packed with galleries, right between the T-shirt shops and drag bars. The majority are on Commercial Street between Montello Street to the west, and Howland Street, at the eastern edge of the strip. From east to west, some not-to-be-missed galleries include **Julie Heller East** (465 Commercial St., 508/487-2166, www.juliehellergallery.com, Thurs.-Mon. 11am-5pm), where the art historian owner curates a collection of historic and modern Provincetown artists that's a fascinating look at the Cape's evolving art, and **Gallery Voyeur** (444 Commercial St., 508/487-3678, www.voy-art.com, late May-June daily 11am-4pm, July-late Sept. daily 11am-4pm and 6pm-10pm) to see Johniene Papandreas's large-format portraits. The **Albert Merola Gallery** (424 Commercial St., 508/487-4424, www.albertmerolagallery.com) also has a good collection of contemporary and historic work from the Cape. Opening hours are typically 11am-4pm daily in season (June-Sept.) though can be variable, especially in off-season, so call ahead for information or to make an appointment. If you were only to make one stop for art in Provincetown, however, the **Provincetown Art Association and Museum** (460 Commercial St., 508/487-1750, www.paam.org, Oct.-May Thurs.-Sun. noon-5pm, June-Sept. Tues.-Thurs. 11am-8pm, Fri. 11am-8pm, Sat.-Mon. 11am-5pm, $10, free after 5pm Fri.) is a treasure trove of Cape Cod and Provincetown art.

Other Sights

Step on the same ground that the Pilgrims did at **Pilgrim's First Landing Park** at the west end of Commercial Street. A plaque there memorializes the Pilgrims' touchdown on November 21, 1620.

It would be easy to read away a rainy day on the coast at the **Provincetown Public Library** (356 Commercial St., 508/487-7094, www.provincetownlibrary.org, Mon.-Thurs. 10am-8pm, Fri. 10am-5pm, Sat.-Sun. 1pm-5pm, Mon. 10am-8pm), which has a great collection of book on the area. Stop in anyway to look at the half-size replica of the *Rose Dorothea* fishing schooner, which sails the stacks on the library's 2nd floor.

To learn more about **Stellwagen Bank National Marine Sanctuary** visit the free **exhibit center** (205-209 Commercial St., 781/545-8026, www.stellwagen.noaa.gov, July-Aug. daily 11am-6pm, June and Sept. Fri.-Sat. 11am-6pm, free), which explains the unique habitat with touch screen computer exhibits and other displays.

Entertainment and Events
★ Drag Shows

The drag scene is a classic P-town experience. You don't need to look for a drag show in Provincetown, as one is likely to find you—watch for flamboyantly dressed performers careening down Commercial Street on foot, bicycle, and

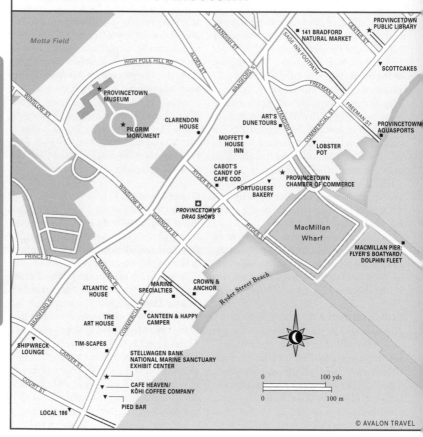

Downtown Provincetown

PROVINCETOWN PUBLIC LIBRARY

Motta Field

141 BRADFORD NATURAL MARKET

SCOTTCAKES

HIGH POLE HILL RD

PROVINCETOWN MUSEUM

CLARENDON HOUSE

ART'S DUNE TOURS

PILGRIM MONUMENT

MOFFETT HOUSE INN

PROVINCETOWN AQUASPORTS

LOBSTER POT

CABOT'S CANDY OF CAPE COD

PROVINCETOWN CHAMBER OF COMMERCE

PORTUGUESE BAKERY

PROVINCETOWN'S DRAG SHOWS

MacMillan Wharf

PRINCE ST

MACMILLAN PIER: FLYER'S BOATYARD/ DOLPHIN FLEET

CROWN & ANCHOR

MARINE SPECIALTIES

Ryder Street Beach

ATLANTIC HOUSE

THE ART HOUSE

CANTEEN & HAPPY CAMPER

SHIPWRECK LOUNGE

TIM-SCAPES

STELLWAGEN BANK NATIONAL MARINE SANCTUARY EXHIBIT CENTER

CAFE HEAVEN/ KŌHI COFFEE COMPANY

0   100 yds

0   100 m

PIED BAR

LOCAL 186

© AVALON TRAVEL

moped. The performances are an irreverent blend of Provincetown's deep LGBT roots and sheer, touristy commercialism. Shows range from classy song and dance numbers to raunchy humor with big hair, big smiles, and outsize personalities.

The surreal **Dina Martina** is a fixture of the scene, with regular appearances at the **Crown & Anchor** (247 Commercial St., 508/487-1430, www.onlyatthecrown. com, $28). Dina's offbeat monologues and comically bad singing make her a P-town favorite. With vampy, pinup charm, **Jinkx Monsoon** brings a fun theatricality to her routine, and she makes

frequent appearances at **The Art House** (214 Commercial St., 508/487-9222, www. ptownarthouse.com, $32), another popular venue for drag shows. Drag queen residencies come and go; if there's a performer you'd like to see, it's worth looking up where their show is now. To find out what's happening, pick up a copy of the free *Provincetown Magazine,* which is available in many downtown shops and at the visitor's bureau. The magazine is updated each Wednesday.

Nightlife

The nightclub scene is as LGBT-friendly

as any in New England. Some venues are scene-specific, while others have open door policies. Festivities kick off early at the late-afternoon **Tea Dance** at the **Boatslip Beach Club** (161 Commercial St., 508/487-1669, www.boatslipresort. com, summertime daily 4pm-7pm, spring and fall weekends 4pm-7pm), where revelers sip dangerously powerful planter's punch, which sloughs both inhibitions and clothing.

Predominantly for men, the **Atlantic House** (4-6 Masonic Pl., 508/487-3821, www.ahouse.com) is a classic gay nightclub with underwear-clad bartenders, smoke machines, and an upstairs **Macho Bar** (10pm-1am) that features lots of leather, Levi's, and sexy videos on continuous loop. The Atlantic House is also comprised of the **Little Bar** (noon-1am) and **Big Room bar** (10pm-1am). The lesbian crowd tends to be a bit more subdued in P-town, but the ladies kick up their heels at the **Pied Bar** (193 Commercial St., 508/487-1527, www. piedbar.net, May-June and Oct.-Nov. Sat.-Sun. noon-midnight, July-Aug. daily noon-midnight), which is open to all comers. Most of the patrons stay fully clothed at the **Shipwreck Lounge** (10 Carver St., 508/487-1472, www.ptown-lounge.com, daily 5pm-1am), which feels like a cozy beach house living room with excellent cocktails.

Theater
Local thespians date the beginning of American drama to 1916, when the first Eugene O'Neill play was performed on P-Town's Lewis Wharf. The theater community was reborn in 2001 with the construction of the beautiful 200-seat **Provincetown Theater** (238 Bradford St., 508/487-7487, www.provincetowntheater. org, $20-75), which stages everything from campy musicals to heart-wrenching original dramas.

Festivals and Events
Filmmaker John Waters is a regular at the **Provincetown International Film Festival** (508/487-3456, www.p-townfilmfest.org, mid-June), which showcases truly independent films. The town's thriving fishing community celebrates its heritage during the weekend-long **Provincetown Portuguese Festival** (508/487-0086, www.provincetownportuguesefestival. com, late June, free) that culminates with the annual "Blessing of the Fleet." The **Fourth of July Celebration** (508/487-7000, www.p-townchamber.com, July 4, free) has the best beachside fireworks on the Cape. Last but not least, **Carnival Week** (508/487-2313, www.p-town.org, late Aug.) is a seven-day Mardi Gras that features a parade, elaborate dance parties, and performances by internationally renowned drag queens.

But during the summer months in Provincetown, it seems like every week is a "week," with a different slice of the scene seizing a piece of the calendar, from bears (stop by in early July to fête large, hairy men with a leather-vest take on masculinity) to whales (come the last week in July to celebrate the marine mammal).

Shopping
Art galleries, penny candy stores, and sex shops line Commercial Street, which is the best place in Cape Cod to browse for souvenirs and unique gifts. A few boutiques stock wonderfully curated collections of clothes and accessories. Browse for "bohemian marine" treasures at **Loveland** (120 Commercial St., 508/413-9500, www.lovelandprovincetown.com, May-June Thurs.-Sun. noon-6pm, July-Aug. daily 11am-11pm, Sept. daily noon-6pm). At **Tim-Scapes** (208 Commercial St., 917/626-4052, www.tim-scapes.com, late May-early Sept. daily 11am-8pm, Sept.-May Sat.-Sun. 11am-5pm), artist Tim Convery uses duct tape to create bold graphic designs. Find diving bells, antique life-saving rings, and other intriguing flotsam at **Marine Specialties** (235 Commercial St., 508/487-1730,

Sun.-Fri. noon-5pm, Sat. 11am-6pm), and stock up on penny candy or saltwater taffy at **Cabot's Candy of Cape Cod** (276 Commercial St., 508/487-3550, www.cabotscandy.com, daily 11am-7pm).

Sports and Recreation
★ Whale-Watching Tours

Just north of Land's End is a shallow, sandy rise in the ocean floor called Stellwagen Bank, where nutrient-rich upwelling and a U.S. National Marine Sanctuary attract a diverse population of dolphins, sea turtles, and whales. From April-October, whales migrate to this coast to feed on schooling fish, and a dozen tour operators offer trips into the sanctuary to spot humpback, finback, minke, sei, and pilot whales. In the winter of 2016, a cluster of endangered right whales appeared off the Cape Cod coast, a sign that the struggling population has found a safe, nourishing place to feed; a whale-watching tour is a rare chance to spot one of the known 500-some surviving right whales.

The **Dolphin Fleet** (MacMillan Pier, 800/826-9300, www.whalewatch.com, mid-Apr.-Oct., $47 adults, $31 children 5-12, free children under 5) departs many times a day during the season from downtown Providence, with open decks, enclosed cabins, and free tickets if no whales are sighted. Onboard naturalists help identify any fins and flukes you spot, and, though they're not always operated, some of their boats are equipped with hydrophones for listening for whale vocalizations. Tours last 3-4 hours.

Beaches

Stunning **Race Point Beach** is an eight-mile stretch of crashing waves and soft sand edged with dune grass. To access the beach, park at the **Province Lands Visitor Center** (171 Race Point Rd., 508/487-1256, May-Oct. daily 9am-5pm), which has observation decks, interpretive displays, and a knowledgeable staff. For sunsets

over the surf, it's hard to beat a spot at **Herring Cove Beach** a peaceful swath that's just a few miles from the center of Provincetown. Turn right at the parking lot to set up at the family-oriented part of the beach, or turn left to reach the more swinging real estate, where visitors tend to self-sort by gender and orientation.

Like other beaches in the Cape Cod National Seashore, parking fees and entrance fees are collected in season ($20 cars, $10 motorcycles, $3 pedestrians). Parking lots get crowded, so it's worthwhile to access the beaches by public transport or bicycle. Shuttles leave Macmillan Wharf for Race Point every 15-30 minutes 7am-8pm and for Herring Cove every 20 minutes 9am-a half hour before sunset. To get to Race Point by bike, head down Conwell Street to Race Point Road, where a bike path parallels the roadway. For Herring Cove, cyclists have two options: they can ride right on Route 6, or take the longer but nicer ride along the bike path through the Province Lands. Pick up the trail at the Beech Forest Parking Area off of Race Point Road.

Boating and Fishing

Rent anything from a kayak to a 19-foot sloop at **Flyer's Boat Rentals** (131A Commercial St., 508/487-0898, www.flyersrentals.com, starting at $30), which also offers two-hour sailing lessons ($130 one person, $30 each additional person). Find a stand-up paddleboard at **Provincetown Aquasports** (333R Commercial St., 508/413-9563, www.ptownaquasports.com, $20/hr, $50 full-day). The 73-foot gaff-rigged schooner *Bay Lady II* (20 Berry Ln., 508/487-9308, www.sailcapecod.com, $28-33 adults, $15 children) sails several times daily for the Corn Hill bluffs and Long Point Light. Sportfishing boats lining Macmillan Wharf include the *Ginny G* (508/246-3656, www.ginnygcapecodcharters.com), which goes in search of bluefish, bass, cod, and tuna.

Hiking and Biking

Just across from Provincetown's vibrant downtown are the **Province Lands,** a rugged, shifting stretch of dunes that can feel wild and otherworldly, a transporting reminder of why generations of artists came to the Cape to escape the world. The sand is held together with webs of wild, five-petaled roses and grass, sagging fences, and a few spiny scrub pines, and is especially stunning in the fall, when the plants take on a subtle rusty hue. The artists' shacks are the only rustic structures in the dunes, without electricity or running water.

A good place to orient yourself to the dune's natural history, plants, and trails is the **Province Lands Visitor Center** (171 Race Point Rd., 508/487-1256, May-Oct. daily 9am-5pm), which offers ranger guided hikes and outings.

To see the dune's historic and scenic highlights, though, you can't beat local knowledge, and **Art's Dune Tours** (4 Standish St., 508/487-1950, www.artsdunetours.com, Apr.-Nov., $29 adults, $18 children 6-11, free children under 6) has operated tours of the sand in 4x4 vehicles since 1946. Art's offers every possible variation on the dune tour—add a sunset, clambake, lighthouse, lake or kayak trip—and has several departures daily.

One of the best **walking trails** into the dunes starts at **Snail Road** off Route 6. Limited parking is available. A sandy road leads to a path that winds past dunes, shacks, and hollows to the shore. It's just a mile or so to the beach, but wandering up and over soft dunes takes much longer than hiking on firm ground. The trail braids and splits at times, so take note of your route throughout the walk and bring shoes and plenty of water—the sand gets surprisingly hot.

Or do as P-town locals do: Park your car and explore on two wheels. An excellent network of bike path and

Top to bottom: Provincetown's Commercial Street; Provincetown dunes; Canteen.

bike-friendly roads make it easy. The 5.45-mile **Province Lands Bike Trail** is a dreamy route through dunes with spurs to Race Point Beach and Herring Cove Beach. Pick up a map of the trail at **Province Lands Visitors Center** (Race Point Rd., 508/487-1256, May-Oct. daily 9am-5pm) or at a bike shop in town. To rent a bike, stop by **The Bike Shack** (63 Shank Painter Rd., 918/660-7183, www. provincetownbikeshack.com, bike starting at $10/hr or $17/day), whose fleet includes beach cruisers, road and mountain bikes, and baby trailers.

Food

Provincetown is lined with excellent places to eat, mostly clustered around Commercial Street. Business hours can vary with season and demand; restaurants sometimes close early on slow nights or keep serving as long as the tables are full. It's always worth calling ahead.

It's hard not to love ★ **Canteen** (225 Commercial St., 508/487-3800, www. thecanteenptown.com, daily 10am-8pm, off-season hours and days vary, $7-19), a tourist joint that's also a local favorite. The nautical theme of this casual lunch spot is bright and hip. The lack of elbow room at large communal tables makes it easy to make friends over plates of excellent fish-and-chips, crispy brussels sprouts, house-made Portuguese sausage, and a good selection of local beers on draft. Its little sibling next door, **Happy Camper** (227 Commercial St., 508/487-3800, www.happycamper.cool, daily 10am-8pm, off-season hours and days vary, $2-8) takes a summery-cool approach to doughnuts and ice cream.

The distinctive neon sign at the **Lobster Pot** (321 Commercial St., 508/487-0842, www.ptownlobsterpot. com, late April/early May-Nov. daily 11:30am-9:00pm, $16-27) has been signaling chowder-hungry crowds for years. Among the dozens of places that claim "best chowder" on the Cape, the Lobster Pot is a strong contender. The Portuguese soup is another favorite dish that's steeped in Cape Cod history, and the long menu meanders onto lobster, steaks, tacos, and sushi. The cavernous restaurant has table seating on two levels, and a bar upstairs—the 2nd floor has better views. The raw bar is a good alternative when the wait for a table gets long.

Decked with bright, big art and handwritten menu boards, **Cafe Heaven** (199 Commercial St., 508/487-9639, Apr.-Nov., daily 8am-2pm and 6pm-10pm, $7-16) is a cheerful spot for breakfasting on piles of French toast, home fries, pancakes, and fruit. The compact café stays busy throughout the day, serving sandwiches on homemade bread, hearty soups, and salads.

Enjoy a chewy, sugary taste of Cape Cod's heritage at ★ **Portuguese Bakery** (299 Commercial St., 508/487-1803, Apr.-Nov. daily 8am-5pm, $2-8), which piles their shelves with fried-dough *malasadas,* lightly caramelized egg tarts, and cream-filled *bolas de berlim.*

Burgers made with pasture-raised beef and topped with everything from fried avocado to lobster are the stars of the menu at **Local 186** (186 Commercial St., 508/478-7555, www.local186.com, May-Oct. 11am-1am, $13-22), a stylish restaurant with butcher charts painted on the walls and a sunny porch for prime people-watching. A solid draft list and creative cocktails round out the menu of clams, oysters, and salads.

When pink-frosted cupcakes are all that will do, head to **ScottCakes** (353 Commercial St., 508/487-7465, www. scottcakes.com, daily 11am-midnight, $3), where pink-frosted cupcakes are all that's on the menu. The simple yellow cakes are a P-town icon and the pink hole-in-the-wall bakeshop is just as sweet. Where else can you find a "legalize gay cupcakes" T-shirt?

Find the best coffee in Provincetown at the stylish, diminutive **Kōhi Coffee Company** (199 Commercial St.,

774/538-6467, www.kohicoffee.com, daily 7:30am-5pm, $3-7), which brews organic, single-origin beans into espresso and pour-over drinks. On hot days, the lightly sweet, chicory and coffee blend in the New Orleans Iced is sublime. The tiny shop has a prime spot between the beach and Commercial Street.

Shop for natural, organic food and healthy ready-to-eat options at **141 Bradford Natural Market** (141 Bradford St., 508/487-9784, www.the141market.com, Mon.-Wed. 8am-7pm, Thurs.-Sat. 8am-8pm, Sun. 9am-6pm), or pick up supplies at **Stop & Shop** (56 Shank Painter Rd., 508/487-4903, Mon.-Sat. 6am-9pm, Sun. 7am-9pm).

Accommodations and Camping
Camping

Just a 10-minute walk from Provincetown, **Dunes' Edge Campground** (386 Rte. 6, 508/487-9815, www.thetrustees.org, late May-early Oct., basic sites $35-49, hookups $50-61) has 85 tent sites in a wooded area with coin operated hot showers and laundry. The sites are small and relatively densely packed, so the campground can get pretty noisy on busy weekends. Sites often fill up weeks in advance, but a handful are released each morning, so it's worth calling on the same day. Slightly seedy but very friendly, **Coastal Acres Campground** (76R Bayberry Ave., 508/487-1700, www.coastalacresprovincetown.com, Apr.-Nov., basic sites $36, hookups $60) is a mile from downtown, with grassy sites and serviceable facilities.

Under $100

The simple rooms at **Cape Codder Guests** (570 Commercial St., 508/487-0131, www.capecodderguests.com, May-Nov., rooms $65-90, apartment $185) don't have phones, televisions, or private baths, but they're perfectly clean and comfortably furnished in an old-fashioned home with a blooming garden. The guesthouse also has a private beach with a sundeck and a nearby parking lot.

$100-150

A painted figurehead greets guests arriving at the **Rose & Crown Guest House** (158 Commercial St., 508/487-3332, www.roseandcrownptown.com, rooms $75-125, apartments $150-180, parking $10), a unique place to stay in the center of town. Rooms are small but imaginatively designed; one is decked out with purple fabrics and Victorian antiques, another features exposed beams and a stately brass bed. Three less-expensive rooms upstairs share a bath.

Cozy and relaxed, **Moffett House Inn** (296A Commercial St., 508/487-6615, www.moffetthouse.com, free continental breakfast July-Aug., $80-140) feels like a family vacation house that just happens to be walking distance from the action on Commercial Street. Limited parking is available on-site for $5-18 per night, or guests can get discounted access to a nearby parking lot ($20). For guests that take advantage of the two bicycles provided with each room, the Moffett House Inn is one of the best deals in town.

$150-250

There are just six rooms in the **Clarendon House** (118 Bradford St., 508/680-4444, www.theclarendonhouse.com, June-Jan., $175-235, free parking), which was updated in 2016 with furniture that's old-fashioned but thoroughly unstuffy. The friendly owners are a highlight, as are full breakfasts and around-the-clock snacks, coffee, and tea.

The adjoining keeper's house at **Race Point Light** (Race Point Beach, Rte. 6, 508/487-9930, www.racepointlighthouse.org, $165-205) is a summer bed-and-breakfast, whose three simple rooms boast the most dramatic location on the Cape.

Over $250

The elegant, secluded ★ **Land's End Inn** (22 Commercial St., 508/487-0706, www.landsendinn.com, $405-680, free parking) commands sweeping views of the ocean, so guests can watch the sun rise—and set—from a glassed-in tower. The owner's exceptional collection of art nouveau antiques fills every conceivable nook of the common areas, while guest rooms feature skylights, interior balconies, and domed ceilings. A breakfast buffet, afternoon wine bar, and 24-hour tea and coffee make this a soothing place to watch the tide come in.

Information

The **Provincetown Chamber of Commerce** (307 Commercial St. at Lopes Sq., 508/487-3424, www.p-town-chamber.com, May-Oct. daily 9am-5pm, Nov.-Dec. and Mar.-Apr. Mon.-Tues. and Thurs.-Sat. 10am-3pm, Jan.-Feb. Mon. and Fri. 10am-3pm) runs a visitors center just off the ferry landing.

Getting Around

The Cape Cod Transit Authority runs the **Breeze shuttle** (800/352-7155, www.the-breeze.info), which provides transport to the airport, beaches, and town center. Or travel in style with the vintage **Mercedes Cab** (508/487-3333).

Martha's Vineyard

Celebrity vacation spot, family retreat, rural getaway . . . after more than two hundred years of summer people, Martha's Vineyard's diversity still comes as a surprise. It's easy to find your own slice of this wonderfully scenic island, whose quaint villages and tourist traps are interspersed with coastal dunes, pale beaches, and farmland. The Wampanoag tribe has a stronger presence here then elsewhere in the Cape and islands, and families of Vineyard sailors, farmers, and fishers still maintain deep roots.

It's a fun place to explore on a day trip to Oak Bluffs or Edgartown, but really experiencing the Vineyard means taking the time to discover back roads and up-island fishing villages. While the island has a reputation as an expensive retreat, prices aren't far off from those on Cape Cod. A wonderful hostel and campground offer a taste of Vineyard life on a budget.

Residents divide the island into **down-island** (east) and **up-island** (west). The former is home to the island's three main population centers: touristy Vineyard Haven, posh Edgartown, and charming Oak Bluffs. Up-island is more rural, with the cow pastures of West Tisbury and Chilmark sharing space with the scenic fishing village of Menemsha and the cliffs of Aquinnah.

Getting to Martha's Vineyard

Ferries to the Vineyard leave from Cape Cod, Nantucket, and departure points farther afield in New York, Massachusetts, and New Jersey.

From Woods Hole to Vineyard Haven or Oak Bluffs, take the year-round **Steamship Authority** (508/477-8600, www.steamshipauthority.com, 0.75 hr, round-trip tickets $17 adults, $9 children, $8 bicycles, $87 cars). From Falmouth to Oak Bluffs, take the passenger-only **Island Queen** (508/457-0598, www.is-landqueen.com, late May-mid-Oct, 0.5 hr, round-trip tickets $20 adults, $10 children, $8 bicycles). **Hy-Line Cruises** (800/492-8082, www.hylinecruises.com, May-Oct., 1 hr, from Hyannis $59 adults, $19 children, $7 bicycles or from Nantucket $65 adults, $24 children, $7 bicycles) connects Hyannis and Nantucket with Vineyard Haven.

From New Bedford, New York City, Boston, and New Jersey take the **Seastreak** (800/262-8743, www.seast-reak.com, May-Oct. round-trip tickets from $70 adults, $40 children, $14 bicycles). During the summer, many flights a day are offered by **Cape Air** (508/771-6944, www.flycapeair.com) from Boston, New Bedford, Hyannis, and Nantucket.

Getting Around

The **Martha's Vineyard Regional Transit**

One Day in Martha's Vineyard

Morning
Pack your bathing suit and walking shoes, and catch the first boat of the day to Oak Bluffs, a bustling community whose star attractions are walking distance from the ferry landing. After picking up pastries-to-go at the **Martha's Vineyard Gourmet Café and Bakery,** take a stroll through the winding streets of **The Campground,** a onetime Methodist revival camp lined with sweet Carpenter Gothic cottages in vibrant colors; then check out the statelier Victorians that surround the town green.

Afternoon
Enjoy the rural up-island scenery by heading north on the island bus to **Aquinnah**

Cliffs and **Gay Head Light,** where you can meet members of the Vineyard's Wampanoag at the nearby shops.

Save room for pie after a seafood lunch at **Aquinnah Shop Restaurant,** then walk down to the nearby beach to watch for celebrities and soak up the sun before catching a bus back to Oak Bluffs, where a tempting array of souvenir shops, fudge stores, and boutiques stay bustling all summer.

Evening
Make your way back to Oak Bluffs as the sun begins to set, but before you leave for the mainland, try to snag the brass ring at the **Flying Horses Carousel,** the oldest in the United States.

Authority (508/693-9440, www.vineyardtransit.com) runs buses between all of the towns. A bicycle or moped is an excellent way to explore the extensive bike paths and pretty winding roads. Try **Martha's Bike Rentals** (4 Lagoon Pond Rd., Vineyard Haven, 800/559-0312, www.marthasbikerentals.com, Apr.-Nov., 1-day rental from $27) or **Ride-On Mopeds and Bikes** (9 Oak Bluffs Ave., Oak Bluffs, 508/693-2076, www.mvmoped.com).

Unless you are going to be spending a lot of time up-island, having a car is more trouble than it's worth, but **AAA Island Auto Rentals** (196 Main St., Edgartown; Five Corners, Vineyard Haven; 800/627-6333 www.aaaislandautorentals.com) offers free pickup in Edgartown, Oak Bluffs, and Vineyard Haven.

Vineyard Haven
Ferries arriving in this compact harbor town thread past world-class sailing yachts, tall ships, and fishing boats guarded by an attractive pair of lighthouses. With tourist shops, historic homes, and a pair of public beaches right in town, Vineyard Haven is the first stop

for most visitors to the island. Even at its most crowded it's remarkably charming.

Sights
The finest examples of mid-19th-century captain's houses are clustered in the **William Street Historic District** that runs south from Woodlawn Avenue to just past Camp Street. The best way to see the homes is following self-guided walking tour available at the **Chamber of Commerce** (24 Beach St., 508/693-0085, www.mvy.com, Mon.-Fri. 9am-5pm).

It's an easy, two-mile jaunt from downtown Vineyard Haven to **West Chop Light** (W. Chop Rd.). While the historic lighthouse isn't open to the public, the low picket fence allows for great views from the road.

Shopping
The walkable center of Vineyard Haven is crowded with beachy boutiques and souvenir shops, but the mother of all tourist traps is the **Black Dog Bakery and General Store** (3 Water St., 508/338-4440, www.theblackdog.com, daily 8am-6pm), which sells everything imaginable emblazoned with the company's distinctive

Martha's Vineyard

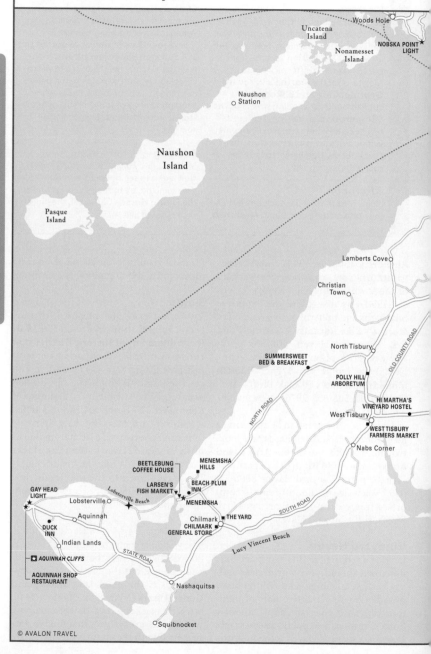

Woods Hole

Uncatena
Island

Nonamesset
Island

NOBSKA POINT
LIGHT

Naushon
Station

Naushon
Island

Pasque
Island

Lamberts Cove

Christian
Town

OLD COUNTY ROAD

North Tisbury

SUMMERSWEET
BED & BREAKFAST

POLLY HILL
ARBORETUM

HI MARTHA'S
VINEYARD HOSTEL

West Tisbury

WEST TISBURY
FARMERS MARKET

Nabs Corner

NORTH ROAD

MENEMSHA
HILLS

BEETLEBUNG
COFFEE HOUSE

BEACH PLUM
INN

LARSEN'S
FISH MARKET

GAY HEAD
LIGHT

Lobsterville Beach

MENEMSHA

Lobsterville

THE YARD

AQUINNAH

Chilmark

SOUTH ROAD

CHILMARK
GENERAL STORE

DUCK
INN

Lucy Vincent Beach

Indian Lands

AQUINNAH CLIFFS

STATE ROAD

AQUINNAH SHOP
RESTAURANT

Nashaquitsa

Squibnocket

© AVALON TRAVEL

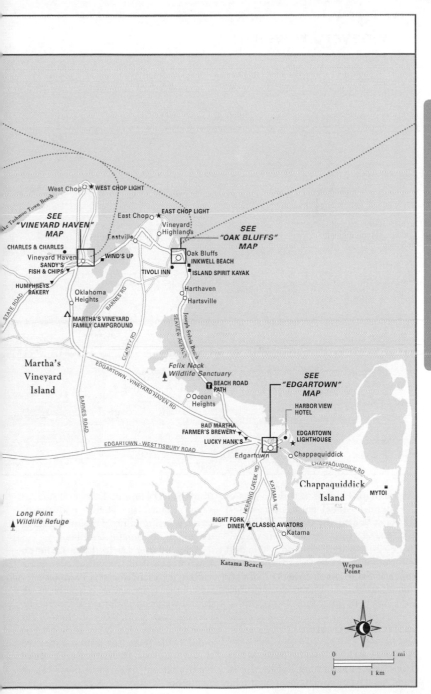

West Chop ○ ★ WEST CHOP LIGHT

Lake Tashmoo Town Beach

SEE
"VINEYARD HAVEN"
MAP

East Chop ○ ★ EAST CHOP LIGHT

Vineyard
Highlands ○

SEE
"OAK BLUFFS"
MAP

Eastville

CHARLES & CHARLES ●

Vineyard Haven ■ WIND'S UP
SANDY'S □
FISH & CHIPS ▼

Oak Bluffs ○
INKWELL BEACH 🏖

TIVOLI INN ▲

ISLAND SPIRIT KAYAK

HUMPHREYS ▼
BAKERY

STATE ROAD

Oklahoma
Heights ○

BARNES RD

Harthaven ○

Hartsville ○

△
MARTHA'S VINEYARD
FAMILY CAMPGROUND

COUNTY RD

SEAVIEW AVENUE

Joseph Sylvia Beach

Martha's
Vineyard
Island

EDGARTOWN - VINEYARD HAVEN RD

Felix Neck ▲
Wildlife Sanctuary

SEE
"EDGARTOWN"
MAP

BARNES ROAD

🚻 BEACH ROAD
PATH

Ocean ○
Heights

HARBOR VIEW
HOTEL

EDGARTOWN - WEST TISBURY ROAD

BAD MARTHA
FARMER'S BREWERY ▼
LUCKY HANK'S ▼

EDGARTOWN
LIGHTHOUSE
★

Edgartown ■ ○ Chappaquiddick

CHAPPAQUIDDICK RD

HERRING CREEK RD

KATAMA RD

Chappaquiddick
Island

MYTOI ■

Long Point ▲
Wildlife Refuge

RIGHT FORK ▼
DINER ▼ CLASSIC AVIATORS

○ Katama

Katama Beach

Wepua
Point

0 ———— 1 mi
0 ———— 1 km

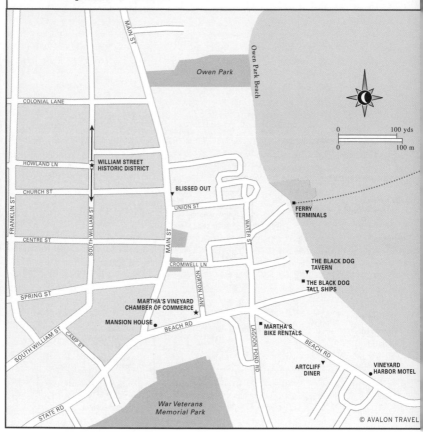

Vineyard Haven

Owen Park

Owen Park Beach

0   100 yds
0   100 m

COLONIAL LANE

MAIN ST

MAIN ST

HOWLAND LN

CHURCH ST

CENTRE ST

SPRING ST

FRANKLIN ST

SOUTH WILLIAM ST

WILLIAM STREET
HISTORIC DISTRICT

BLISSED OUT

UNION ST

MAIN ST

CROMWELL LN

NORTON LANE

WATER ST

FERRY
TERMINALS

THE BLACK DOG
TAVERN

THE BLACK DOG
TALL SHIPS

MARTHA'S VINEYARD
CHAMBER OF COMMERCE

MANSION HOUSE

BEACH RD

MARTHA'S
BIKE RENTALS

LAGOON POND RD

BEACH RD

SOUTH WILLIAM ST

CAMP ST

STATE RD

War Veterans
Memorial Park

ARTCLIFF
DINER

VINEYARD
HARBOR MOTEL

© AVALON TRAVEL

canine logo. Find beautiful images of the island by local photographer Jeff Serusa at **Seaworthy Gallery** (34 Beach Rd., 508/693-0153, www.seaworthygallerymv.info, daily 10am-5pm). The best selection of books by local authors is at **Bunch of Grapes Bookstore** (35 Main St., 508/693-2291, www.bunchofgrapes.com, Mon.-Sat. 9am-6pm, Sun. 11am-5pm).

Sports and Recreation
Beaches
Just a thin strip of sand off Main Street, **Owen Park Beach** might not be the island's most scenic, but its location not far from the ferry terminal is a good stop for a first or last swim. There are lifeguards on duty during summer months, making it a popular option for families.

A bit farther afield, **Lake Tashmoo Town Beach** is at the outlet between a shallow lake and the sea, so swimmers can choose between the warm, brackish inland water or cooler ocean shoreline. Parking is very limited at Tashmoo, but it's a relatively flat, three-mile bike or moped ride from downtown Vineyard Haven; follow Herring Creek Road northwest out of town to dead end at Tashmoo.

Biking

Plenty of bike paths and fellow cyclists mean that riding on Martha's Vineyard is easier (and safer) than anywhere in New England. Bring your own, or rent from **Martha's Bike Rentals** (4 Lagoon Pond Rd., 800/559-0312, www.marthasbikerentals.com, Apr.-Nov., 1-day rental from $27), where you can also pick up biking maps of the island. Popular rides from Vineyard Haven include the four-mile loop ride to **West Chop Light** on quiet roads, or the seven-mile bike path to **Edgartown.** Biking maps are also available at the town's visitors center.

Boating

All eyes are on the soaring canvas and proud bowsprits of the schooners *Alabama* and *Shenandoah* as they cruise the Vineyard Haven harbor. Both are part of **The Black Dog Tall Ships** (Black Dog Wharf, 20 Beach St., 508/693-1699, www.theblackdogtallships.com, late May-early Oct., 3-hour sail $75 adults or $50 children 4-12). Its fleet makes several daily outings during the summer season. Aspiring sailors can take a turn raising sails or manning the helm.

Paddling

Explore the coast at your own pace with a rental from **Wind's Up** (199 Beach Rd., 508/693-4252, www.windsupmv.com, June-Sept. daily 10am-5pm, rentals from $16/hr or $50/day). Find anything with a paddle from kayaks to canoes and SUPs, or rent a Sunfish or 15-foot sloop. The shop also offers lessons from $50 per person.

Food

Classic diner fare and friendly service have kept the **Artcliff Diner** (39 Beach Rd., 508/693-1224, daily 5am-3pm, $7-16) a Vineyard favorite for years. It's usually packed all day with fishers and vacationing families. Hearty omelets and the almond-crusted French toast are favorites among regulars, who grab counter seats right by the coffeepot.

The organic smoothies and vegan wraps at **Blissed Out** (65 Main St., 508/693-0083, Mon.-Sat. 9am-4pm, $9-14) come with hefty, Vineyard prices, but they're a welcome change from the fried fare that many of the island's casual restaurants serve. The cozy, little shop has a friendly, hippie vibe.

Homey cookies, fresh doughnuts, and hearty sandwiches are the draw at **Humphrey's Bakery** (455 State Rd., 508/693-6518, www.humphreysmv.com, Mon.-Sat. 5am-4pm, Sun. 9am-2pm, $3-12), a cozy shop with brightly painted chairs and a devoted following. The most beloved sandwich is the Turkey Gobbler, a Thanksgiving inspired behemoth filled with roasted turkey, stuffing, and housemade cranberry sauce.

Tuck into fried clams, fish cakes, and chowder at **Sandy's Fish and Chips,** inside **John's Fish Market** (5 Martin Rd., 508/693-1220, daily 11am-7pm, call for off-season hours, $7-24), one of the best places on the island for clam shack fare. There's nowhere to sit inside the basic market, but in fine weather you can eat at the parking lot tables or order seafood to go.

If you've been rolling your eyes at the sea of Black Dog T-shirts, caps and bumper stickers, **The Black Dog Tavern** (21 Beach St. Extension, 508/693-9223, www.theblackdog.com, daily 7am-4pm, 5pm-9pm, $14-31) may come as a pleasant surprise. It's real and rustic, decked with grainy images of old-fashioned schooners and excellent views of the harbor. Island specialties like quahog or codfish chowder are good, as are the hearty breakfasts. The tavern is mobbed from the beginning of summer until the leaves change.

Accommodations and Camping

Oak-shaded sites, playgrounds, and a spot right on the bicycle path make **Martha's Vineyard Family Campground** (569 Edgartown Rd., 508/693-3772, www.campmv.com, mid-May-mid-Oct., tent sites with 2 adults $58, additional adult

$15, additional child $5, cabins $145-165) an excellent choice for families. Cabins are clean and comfortable with an outside gas grill and picnic tables (no cooking equipment), and the larger, 2-room cabins sleep 6 people in double beds and bunks.

The rooms at **Vineyard Harbor Motel** (60 Beach Rd., 508/693-3334, www.vineyardharbormotel.com, $225-355) are somewhat dated and worn, but the waterfront location, private beach, and sunny decks make it an excellent find. Some rooms have full kitchens with cooking supplies. Suites are an excellent choice for families.

Tchotchke-leery travelers will appreciate the ★ **Charles & Charles** (85 Summer St., 508/338-2351, www.charlesandcharlesmv.com, $250-300) guarantee of "no decorative plates on the walls!" The intimate, six-room inn delivers a charming blend of modern design and New England style. On sunny days, it's hard to beat their poolside breakfast. Perks like free bicycles, luxurious linens and soaps, and comfy beds make it a wonderful spot to land. The inn is a 10-minute walk from the ferry.

The historic **Mansion House** (9 Main St., 508/693-2200, $309-400) has an unbeatable location a few minutes' walk from the ferry dock. Bright, comfortable rooms and an on-site health club make it a great getaway. Don't miss the rooftop lounge, which is stocked with cold lemonade in the afternoons and has panoramic views.

Information

The **Martha's Vineyard Chamber of Commerce** (24 Beach St., 508/693-0085, www.mvy.com, Mon.-Fri. 9am-5pm) is stocked with maps and brochures. Its website has a helpful listing of last-minute rooms on the island.

Oak Bluffs

Walking through Oak Bluffs' gingerbread cottages and brightly painted homes feels like a glimpse of a different New England, when charismatic preachers packed enthusiastic crowds into summertime revivals. The town's most distinctive neighborhood is Wesleyan Grove, a cluster of Carpenter Gothic homes surrounding an open-air Tabernacle, the site of popular 19th-century Methodist camp meetings. The elaborate, whimsical style of those cottages spreads throughout the town: the grassy common is lined with hundreds of miniature homes that face an old-fashioned gazebo where bands play weekly concerts.

The historic heart of Martha's Vineyard's African American community, Oak Bluffs was a longtime favorite of intellectuals and luminaries like novelist Dorothy West and Edward Brooke, America's first popularly elected African American senator. It's still a popular vacation spot for black Americans.

With great access to beaches, atmospheric neighborhoods, and wonderful parks, Oak Bluffs is far-and-away the best family destination on Martha's Vineyard.

Sights

Don't miss strolling through the adorable cottages in **Wesleyan Grove,** which center around the open-air **Trinity Park Tabernacle** (80 Trinity Park, 508/693-0525, www.mvcma.org), an area known as **The Campground.** It's easy enough to explore on your own, but for a bit of perspective on the neighborhood's history, time your visit to join one of the Martha's Vineyard Campground Meeting Association's **walking tours** (www.mvcma.org, July-Aug. Tues. and Thurs. 10am, 1.5-hr tours $12 walkups or $10 online registration), which start at the Tabernacle.

A perennial favorite is the **Flying Horses Carousel** (15 Oak Bluffs Ave., 508/693-9481, daily 11am-4:30pm, call for off-season hours, $2.50), a National Landmark and the oldest operating platform carousel in the United States. During summer months, throngs of children wait to ride one of 20 carved wooden horses and take turns grabbing for the brass ring, accompanied by

Oak Bluffs

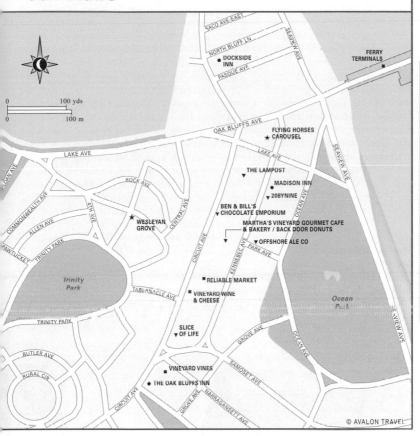

a 1923 Wurlitzer Band Organ that plays the original paper rolls.

With commanding views of the sea, the **East Chop Light** (229 E. Chop Dr., www.mvmuseum.org) is a fine place for a picnic. The 1.5-mile walk or ride from downtown passes through an exclusive neighborhood lined with beautiful homes. The Martha's Vineyard Museum offers tours of the lighthouse on Sunday evenings in the summer.

Entertainment and Events

Summer on the Vineyard officially kicks off with the **Oak Bluffs Harbor Festival** (www.oakbluffsmv.com, mid-June), when the waterfront fills with live music, craft vendors, and food booths, and the annual chalk-art contest sees fierce competition. One of the most anticipated nights of the summer is the **Grand Illumination** (Campground, 508/693-0525, mid-Aug.), when the gingerbread cottages of the Oak Bluffs revival camp are lit up with thousands of paper lanterns. Depending on your frame of mind, the effect can be romantic or intensely spiritual.

Several bars in Oak Bluffs feature live music at night, including **Offshore Brewing Company** (Kennebec Ave.,

508/693-2626, www.offshoreale.com, Sun.-Tues. 5pm-8:30pm, Thurs.-Sat. 5pm-9pm) and **The Lampost** (6 Circuit Ave., 508/693-4032, www.lampostmv. com, Mon.-Sun. 4pm-1am), which also offers a sweaty dance floor catering to the under-30 set.

Shopping

Most of Oak Bluffs' shops line **Circuit Avenue,** which runs through the heart of downtown and is easy to explore on foot. The most iconic shop in town might be **Vineyard Vines** (56 Narragansett Ave., 508/687-9841, www.vineyardvines.com, Mon. and Thurs.-Sat. 10am-6pm, Sun. 11am-5pm), a nautical-themed boutique that's spread Vineyard-prep and spouting whale logos across the United States.

Sports and Recreation
Beaches

The **Joseph Sylvia Beach** (Beach Rd. between Oak Bluffs and Edgartown) is four miles of perfect sand that's excellent for swimming and sunbathing. Even on busy days, you can find a spot to stake your umbrella. The slender spit is joined by the American Legion Memorial Bridge, but ask directions and you'll get blank looks. Locals just call it the Jaws Bridge—scenes from the original 1975 movie were filmed here. It's a popular (but illegal) spot for jumping in the water.

Walking distance from downtown on the ocean side of Seaview Avenue, between Nantucket Avenue and Ocean Park, **Inkwell Beach** has calm water and a lifeguard, making it a popular spot for families with young children. Historically this was a gathering place for the town's African American community; the name was originally a sneering racial reference, but it's since been adopted by Martha's Vineyard's black residents as a point of pride.

Biking

The six-mile **Beach Road Path** that connects Oak Bluffs and Edgartown is a

gingerbread cottages in Oak Bluffs

wonderful way to see the island, with places to hop off the path and onto the sand all along the way. Rent a bike from **Anderson's Bike Rentals** (23 Circuit Ave. Extension, 508/693-9346, www.andersonsbikerentals.com, May-Oct., 1-day rental from $20).

Boating and Fishing
The tide ponds and lagoons around the island are perfect for maneuvering in and out of by kayak. **Island Spirit Kayak** (Beach Rd., 508/693-9727, www.islandspirit-kayak.com) leads paddling tours that emphasize island geology and wildlife, and also rents boats that can be delivered to the shoreline of your choice ($65 half-day and $120 full-day kayak tours, kayak rentals from $20/hr to $55 24 hrs). Island Spirit is located on the outlet from Sengekontacket Pond to the ocean, so paddlers can turn inland to paddle in warm, still water, or explore along the beach.

For anglers, the *Skipper* (Oak Bluffs Harbor, 508/693-1238, www.mvskipper.

com, half-day trips $65 adults, $55 children 12 and under) bills itself as a "party fishing boat," which takes family-friendly trips in search of fluke, flounder, and striped bass.

Food
Crushed peanut shells litter the floor at ★ **Offshore Ale Co.** (30 Kennebec Ave., 508/693-2626, www.offshoreale.com, Sun.-Tues. 11:30am-4pm and 5pm-8:30pm, Thurs.-Sat. 11:30am-4pm and 5pm-9pm, $11-32), a warehouse turned brewpub in Oak Bluffs with nautical decor and a friendly atmosphere. Brick-oven pizzas and hamburgers join traditional Vineyard fare like fisherman's stew and thick, creamy chowder. Offshore Ale Co. keeps nine beers on tap and has live music most weeks.

If the fried green tomato BLT sandwich were the only thing on the menu, it would still be worth a trip to **Slice of Life** (50 Circuit Ave., 508/693-3838, www.sliceoflifemv.com, Tues.-Sat. 11am-8pm, Sun. 8am-2pm, $10-22), a sunny café furnished with intimate tables and folding chairs. Thin crust pizzas, goodie-loaded salads, and addictive truffle fries round out the menu. Sunday brunch is very popular—arrive early to get a seat on the enclosed porch.

Upscale food on the Vineyard can be a little lackluster, which makes ★ **20byNine** (16 Kennebec Ave., 508/338-2065, www.20bynine.com, Wed.-Mon. 5:30pm-midnight, summer brunch Sun. 10am-2pm, $24-30) a gem. Small plates of charcuterie, cheeses, and seafood are packed with flavor. The entire menu is designed to share, which might be the secret to this tiny gastropub's intimate, convivial feel. Chef Scott Cummings sources many ingredients locally and the house cocktail menu is a highlight (no "sharkaritas" here).

Show up at **Martha's Vineyard Gourmet Café and Bakery** (5 Post Office Sq., 508/693-3688, www.mvbakery.com, Apr.-Oct. Mon.-Sat. 7am-5pm, Sun.

7am-2pm, $3-9) during normal business hours to pick up sweet and savory baked goods that make prime picnic fare. This place really starts hopping at night, though, when doughnut lovers line up around back. Noshing on a fresh apple fritter in the alleyway **Back Door Donuts** (Thurs.-Sat. 7pm-1am) might be a well-known tradition, but it still feels like you're in on a sweet, gooey secret.

Martha's Vineyard has more fudge and ice cream shops than you could shake a waffle cone at, but **Ben & Bill's Chocolate Emporium** (20 Circuit Ave., 508/696-0008, www.benandbills.com, Apr.-Oct., Mon.-Fri. 11am-8pm, Sat.-Sun. 11am-9pm, extended hours midsummer, $2-10) is one of the best. Drop into the dark-walled interior for a handful of candy from old-fashioned bins of saltwater taffy and brittle, or get a cone of the absurdly rich butter pecan crunch ice cream.

Pick up supplies and snacks at the town's small grocery store, **Reliable Market** (36 Circuit Ave., 508/693-1102, www.thereliablemarket.com, Mon.-Sat. 8:30am-6pm, Sun. 9am-1pm). Gourmet treats, spirits, and wine are available just up the street at **Vineyard Wine & Cheese** (38 Circuit Ave., 508/693-0943, Apr.-Dec. daily 9am-6pm).

Accommodations

Oak Bluffs' inns are welcoming and comfortable. Prices plummet in the off-season. Some of the privately owned historic cottages in **The Campground** (www.mvcma.org, starting at $2,000/week) are available to rent for visits of a week or more.

$150-250

Country charm and a friendly innkeeper make the **Tivoli Inn** (125 Circuit Ave., 508/693-7928, www.tivoliinn.com, $125-315) a good, relatively lower-budget option. It's a leisurely walk from downtown. Continental breakfast is a full spread of breads, pastries, and cereal served on the gracious porch in fine weather. Less expensive rooms have a tidy shared bathroom.

Brightly painted rooms and pleasant common spaces are the draw at the **Madison Inn** (18 Kennebec Ave., 508/644-8226, www.madisoninnmv.com, $199-269), which also has unexpected amenities for the price. Start the day with coffee and teas, snack on cookies, ice cream, and fruit at will, and use beach towels, toys, chairs, and umbrellas. Rooms also come with white noise machines, which is good, as the walls are a bit thin.

Over $250

With a prime spot on the waterfront, the **Dockside Inn** (9 Circuit Ave. Extension, 508/693-2966, www.vineyardinns.com, $259-409) is simple and immaculate. Bits of modern flair keep the historic building feeling fresh. A comfortable seat on the deep, wraparound porch is a dreamy place to watch sails float by. The enclosed garden has a hot tub. Higher priced rooms accommodate four or five people, an excellent deal for the location.

A pink wedding cake of a house at the top of the main drag, **The Oak Bluffs Inn** (64 Circuit Ave., 800/955-6235, www.oakbluffsinn.com, Apr.-Oct., $225-695) is appointed with a tasteful mix of modern country furniture and old English antiques. The informal, lived-in air and afternoon cookies and lemonade on the porch make it a sweetly hospitable place to stay.

Edgartown

Romantic and old-fashioned, Edgartown is Martha's Vineyard's most elegant destination, with historic homes, narrow lanes, and fine dining. It's also a fine day trip via the Falmouth passenger ferry. The compact center is easy to explore on foot.

Sights

Get a glimpse of Vineyard life before the fudge shops and celebrities at the

Martha's Vineyard Museum (59 School St., 508/627-4441, www.mvmuseum. org, late May-mid-Oct. Mon.-Sat. 10am-5pm, Sun. noon-5pm, mid-Oct.-late May Mon.-Sat. 10am-4pm, $10 adults, $9 seniors, $5 children 6-12, under 6 free). Kid-focused history exhibits make it a pleasant break from the beach. Artifacts from Martha's Vineyard's Wampanoag people, whalers, and early colonists offer a broad perspective on the island's past. The gorgeous Fresnel lens in the center of the compound used to shine from the Gay Head Light.

On an island that offers every possible angle of ocean views, the finest place to watch the sunrise may be **Edgartown Lighthouse** (121 North Water St.). Located on a slow strip of sand surrounded by calm bay water, it looks like it was placed by a landscape architect (as opposed to the U.S. Coast Guard). The lighthouse is a 10-minute walk from the ferry landing in downtown Edgartown; follow North Water Street northeast, and when the Harbor View Hotel is on your left, take the short, sandy path to the right that leads toward shore.

Perhaps the best way to soak in Edgartown's historic charm is on foot, and it's easy to see the town's highlights in an hour of walking. A good place to start is the **Edgartown Visitors Center** (29 Church St.), where you can pick up maps of the town; highlights include the nearby **Old Whaling Church** (89 Main St.), an impressive Greek Revival building whose clock tower is visible far out at sea, the **Dr. Daniel Fisher House** and the **Vincent House** (both 99 Main St.), the oldest unaltered house on Martha's Vineyard. From late May through mid-October, the **Martha's Vineyard Preservation Trust** opens these three properties for 45-minute guided tours (508/627-4440, www. mvpreservation.org, Mon. Fri., $10).

Entertainment and Events

Edgartown is pretty sedate by Vineyard standards, but you can catch live shows (and try your hand at the lawn games) at **Bad Martha Farmer's Brewery** (270 Upper Main St., 508/939-4415, www.bad-marthabeer.com, May-Oct. Thurs.-Sun. noon-7pm, $4-10). A mason jar full of the flagship Martha's Vineyard Ale pairs beautifully with a seat in the sunny garden.

Middle-of-the-road island fare like clam chowder and burgers will do in a pinch, but beer and atmosphere are the real draws at **The Newes from America Pub** (23 Kelley St., 508/627-7900, daily 11:30am-11pm, $7-19), a year-round mainstay with dark wood, brick walls, live music, and sports.

Try some of the island's best bites at the **Martha's Vineyard Food and Wine Festival** (mid-Oct., www.mvfoodandwine.com), which brings local chefs, producers, and artisans together for an indulgent weekend that benefits island agriculture and schools.

Shopping

Main Street is full of elegant shops that make for an appealing afternoon of browsing. Start at **Peases Point Way** and head toward the water, then turn left on **Water Street.** For two entirely different takes on Vineyard style, stop by **Island Outfitters** (27 North Water St., 508/627-7281, www.islandoutfitters.com, Mon.-Sat. 10am-6pm, Sun. 11am-5pm), where you can get a whole cottage full off preppie outfits from Vineyard Vines and Lilly Pulitzer. Just up the street is **The Boneyard Surf Shop** (47 Main St., 508/627-7907, www.theboneyardsurfshop.com, daily 10am-6pm), which has a more punk rock take on island fashion, including surf-themed clothes and swimwear.

Sports and Recreation
Beaches

To access the slender **Joseph Sylvia State Beach** from Edgartown, just hop on the scenic bike path that fronts Beach Road. Don't let the fact that scenes from *Jaws* were filmed here dissuade you; this beach

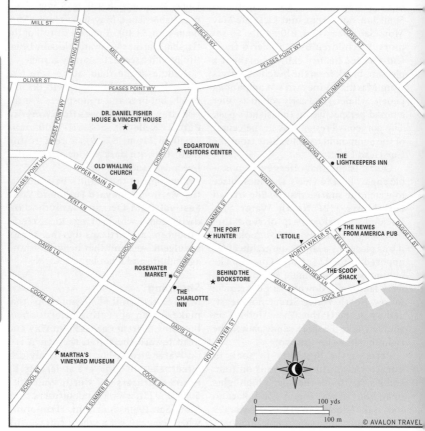

Edgartown

MILL ST
PIERCES WY
MORSE ST
PLANTING FIELD WY
MILL ST
PEASES POINT WY
PEASES POINT WY
OLIVER ST
NORTH SUMMER ST
PEASES POINT WY
DR. DANIEL FISHER
HOUSE & VINCENT HOUSE ★
EDGARTOWN
★ VISITORS CENTER
SIMPSONS LN
PEASES POINT WY
OLD WHALING
CHURCH
THE
● LIGHTKEEPERS INN
UPPER MAIN ST
CHURCH ST
WINTER ST
PENT LN
N SUMMER ST
THE PORT
★ HUNTER
L'ETOILE
THE NEWES
▼ FROM AMERICA PUB
DAVIS LN
SCHOOL ST
S SUMMER ST
ROSEWATER
MARKET
BEHIND THE
★ BOOKSTORE
NORTH WATER ST
KELLEY ST
DAGGETT ST
● THE
CHARLOTTE
INN
MAHEW LN
MAIN ST
THE SCOOP
SHACK ▼
COOKE ST
DAVIS LN
DOCK ST
SOUTH WATER ST
★ MARTHA'S
VINEYARD MUSEUM
SCHOOL ST
S SUMMER ST
COOKE ST

0   100 yds
0   100 m
© AVALON TRAVEL

is a good choice for less confident swimmers, as it's fairly sheltered from ocean swells.

A more dramatic landscape is **Katama Beach,** a narrow barrier beach three miles south of Edgartown, with surf crashing on one side and a warm saltwater lagoon on the other. Follow South Water Street southeast from downtown, then turn left on Katama Road to find the beach parking area.

Boating
Set sail from Edgartown's harbor on the *Magic Carpet* (508/627-5889, www. sailmagiccarpet.com, June-Oct. 2-hour sails $65), a beautiful 56-foot yawl—a two-masted sailboat that's rigged fore and aft. The friendly and experienced owners Todd and Lee plot a course with views of the most elegant homes along the coast.

Flying
Strap on leather goggles for a bird's-eye view of the island on a ride in a 60-year-old cherry-red biplane. **Classic Aviators** (Katama Airfield, 508/627-7677, www.biplanemv.com, starting at $199/2-person tours) runs sightseeing trips that range

from 15 minutes to one hour, buzzing over the island's beaches and towns in the company of an experienced guide.

Hiking and Biking

Pick up a cycling map at Edgartown's visitors center and hop on one of the paths that connect to island beaches and forest. There are countless places to hit the beach along the **six-mile trail** that connects Edgartown and Oak Bluffs and a relatively flat, **three-mile bike path** leads to Katama Beach on the south shore.

To really get away from it all, take your bike to the less-developed **Chappaquiddick Island,** which is connected to Edgartown by a small **passenger ferry** (53 Dock St., vehicle waiting line forms on Daggett St., 508/627-9427, www.chappyferry.com, round-trip tickets $4 passenger, $6 with bike) that runs all day, year-round. A single, four-mile paved road leads from Chappaquiddick's ferry dock across the island. Other roads are sandy (and potentially challenging on a bicycle). As you might expect from an island off an island off Cape Cod, Chappaquiddick is wild and scenic; it's a perfect place to escape the crowds. Hop off your bike to visit **Mytoi** (Dike Rd., 508/627-7689, www.thetrustees.org, year-round daily sunrise to sunset, free), a 14-acre Japanese garden with beautifully landscaped ponds, forests, and walking trails.

Back in Edgartown, you can spot wood ducks, ospreys, and even nesting barn owls at the **Felix Neck Wildlife Sanctuary** (100 Felix Neck Dr., off Edgartown-Vineyard Haven Rd., 508/627-4850, www.massaudubon.org, Mon.-Sat. 9am-4pm, trails dawn to dusk, $4 adults, $3 seniors and children), a rambling preserve of salt marsh and beach meadow. The sanctuary has four miles of walking trails (including one mile accessible to those in wheelchairs) that take in a diverse range of Vineyard ecosystems.

Paddling

Rent a kayak at **Joseph Sylvia State Beach** from **Island Spirit Kayak** (Beach Rd., Oak Bluffs, 508/693-9727, www.islandspirit-kayak.com, $65 half-day, $120 full-day kayak tours, kayak rentals from $20/hr to $55 24 hrs), which also delivers around the island.

Food

It's easy to miss the tiny café that's tucked behind Edgartown Books, but ★ **Behind the Bookstore** (46 Main St., 774/549-9278, www.btbmv.com, mid-Apr.-Dec. daily 7am-5pm, later hours and dinner during peak season, $5-15) is among the most appealing places to eat in town. Seats are available on an enclosed, sunny patio, the espresso is from Intelligentsia Coffee, and the menu's full of fresh, flavorful gems like farro and black rice grain bowls and gem lettuce and fennel salad. The dinner menu is only served in the middle of the summer, and includes more elaborate (and expensive) seafood plates and mains.

If you can get yourself out to the Katama Airfield, the **Right Fork Diner** (12 Mattakesett Way, 508/627-5522, daily 7am-2pm, $5-14) is a strong contender for the best diner on the Vineyard. Watch small planes touch down as you dig into hearty omelets and scrambles, soups, salads, and sandwiches.

Comfort food made with plenty of local ingredients is the draw at ★ **Lucky Hank's** (218 Upper Main St., 508/939-4082, www.luckyhanksmv.com, Fri.-Tues. 8am-9pm, Sat.-Sun. 8am-2:30pm, $7-27), a small restaurant in a cozy converted home. Dinner plates like duck cassoulet and cod amandine are hearty and full-flavored. Brunch is very popular (pancakes get rave reviews).

Romantic and softly lit, **L'Etoile** (22 North Water St., 508/627-5187, www.letoile.net, May-Nov. Thurs.-Sun. 5:30-close, $30-55) is Edgartown's last word on date night. The French-inspired menu changes frequently, but fois gras, Katama

Bay oysters, and beautifully fileted trout are perennial favorites. The dinner menu is also available in the more relaxed bar, which is a fine place for cocktails and snacks.

A little bit hipper than the Edgartown average, ★ **The Port Hunter** (55 Main St., 508/627-7747, www.theporthunter.com, late May-Oct., Mon.-Sat. 5:30pm-1am, $17-40) feels like a lively telegram from the next generation of Vineyard chefs. An emphasis on local fish and products is welcome, and the smoked bluefish, oysters, and fish served whole are highlights. As dinnertime winds down, this becomes a happening spot downtown, with live music, shuffleboard, and powerful drinks.

Old-fashioned candy and offbeat ice cream flavors keep **The Scoop Shack** (22 Dock St., 508/627-7829, daily 11am-11pm, $4-8) bustling all summer. The house made s'mores ice cream is summer vacation in a cone.

Find prepared foods, gourmet treats, and baked goods at **Rosewater Market** (20 South Summer St., 508/627-1270, www.rosewatermv.com, Mon.-Sat. 7am-5pm), which stocks many products made on-island. It also has a simple, thoughtful take-away menu. More basic provisions are available at the town's **Stop & Shop** (225 Upper Main St., 508/627-9522, Mon.-Sat. 7am-10pm, Sun. 7am-9pm).

Accommodations

Plan ahead if you'd like to stay at ★ **HI Martha's Vineyard Hostel** (525 Edgartown-West Tisbury Rd., 508/693-2665, May-Oct., dorms $37-39, private rooms $99-150), the island's only hostel—it's a fabulous deal. Enjoy a generous breakfast, volleyball courts, kitchen, and relaxed common spaces. While it's located in the rural center of the island, it's easy to reach by bike and bus; the #6 bus from Edgartown stops just in front.

The quaint, airy suites at **The Lightkeepers Inn** (25 Simpsons Rd., 508/627-4600, www.thelightkeepersinn.

sailing off Martha's Vineyard

com, 4-person suites $215-350) are just a short walk from the ferry dock. Kitchenettes, coffeemakers, and sitting areas make these comfortable places for a family. The inn's bright blue shutters and shingled exteriors exemplify classic Vineyard style.

Sunrise is best viewed with a cup of coffee from the porch of the **Harborview Hotel** (131 N. Water St., 508/627-7000, www.harbor-view.com, $499-800). The sprawling historic building looks out over the town's scenic lighthouse. Rooms in the main building have wonderful sea views, while the Captain's Cottage suites are a good choice for families, with kitchens, living rooms, and dining areas stocked with luxe amenities.

The Charlotte Inn (27 S. Summer St., 508/627-4151, www.relaischateaux. com, $395-795) is a romantic old-world retreat. The elegant house is furnished with English antiques, the perfectly tended gardens overflow with blooming flowers and hidden sitting areas, and an à la carte menu is available in a glass-walled dining room.

Up-Island

With all of its celebrity sightings and souvenir shops, it's a real surprise is that much of Martha's Vineyard's remains fundamentally rural. Up-island roads wind past cattle barns, sleepy corner stores, and fishing villages. While it's nice to have a car to really do justice to the area, frequent buses pass by all the major sites. Although up-island roads are quite narrow and often have no shoulder, experienced cyclists can certainly make the trip. The Vineyard buses have racks that accommodate three or four bikes, so it's possible to bike out to Gay Head and return on the bus, but you may find that others had the same idea, and end up waiting some time for a bus with an open rack.

Addresses on Martha's Vineyard can be confusing, and some destinations listed in Vineyard Haven turn out to be right in the center of the island, but Aquinnah and Chilmark stake out the slightly bulbous, left-hand corner of the island, and are the gateway to the teeny Menemsha fishing community.

Sights
★ Aquinnah Cliffs
Striped with wild layers of ochre clay, green sand, and glittering quartz, the **Aquinnah Cliffs** are a stunning and dramatic sight that has drawn mainland tourists for centuries. The cliffs also feature in Wampanoag stories about the island's formation; the legendary, supernatural giant Moshup resided in a den beside the cliffs, where he lived off a hearty diet of roasted whales—one per meal. When he saw a whale approach the shore, he'd kill it by heaving it against the cliffs, then cook it over the enormous fire that he tended all day and all night. Streaming red whale blood, black coals, and pale bones stained the cliffs, lodging in each layer, still visible to this day.

The walkway to the cliff overlook is lined by shops and information booths maintained by the Wampanoag and is a great place to learn more about their history and culture.

Gay Head Light

In rusty brick that echoes the nearby cliffs, the **Gay Head Light** (9 Aquinnah Cir., Aquinnah, www.mvmuseum.org, late May-late June Sat.-Sun. 11am-4pm, late June-mid-Oct. daily 11am-4pm, $5, under 12 free) is among the most picturesque in New England. A lighthouse was built on this spot in 1799, just on the edge of the cliff—a little too close, as it turned out. The lighthouse was moved back from the erosion-prone cliff in 1844, and a second time in 2015.

Menemsha Harbor

Fishing villages don't get any prettier than old-fashioned **Menemsha Harbor,** where weathered, gray-shingled shacks stand watch over an active fleet of trawlers and lobster boats. Watch the Vineyard's fishers bring in the day's catch while nibbling on clam shack fare. If you're exploring by bike, Menemsha is connected by a convenient, but somewhat unpredictable bike ferry, so you don't have to climb back up the big hill that leads in to town. Does the town look familiar? It's the site of the fictional Amity Island in the movie *Jaws.*

Entertainment and Events

The dancing at **The Yard** (1 The Yard, off Middle Rd. near Beetlebung Corner, Chilmark, 508/645-9662, www.dancetheyard.org) ranges from top-notch contemporary and tap performances to joyful, themed public dance hall events (registration required).

Every Sunday during the warmer months, local artists and crafters display their wares at the **Vineyard Artisans Fair** (Grange Hall, West Tisbury, www.vineyardartisans.com, June-Sept. Sun. 10am-2pm, July-Aug. Thurs. 10am-2pm). There is always a good selection of watercolors and photography of island scenes.

The week following the Grand Illumination is the annual Martha's Vineyard Agricultural Society **Livestock Show and Fair** (West Tisbury, 508/693-4343, www.marthasvineyardagriculturalsociety.org), which for almost 150 years has celebrated the farming history of the island. Displays include sheep and cow pens, wood-chopping competitions, country bands, fireworks, and, of course, a Ferris wheel.

Shopping

At first glance, the shops that line the path to the Aquinnah Cliffs lookout seem like run-of-the-mill kitsch, but they're worth exploring further. Located on traditional Wampanoag land, many of the shops are operated by tribe members selling handmade gifts among the T-shirts. Wampum jewelry made from shells, hand-thrown pottery, and silver make exquisite souvenirs.

Sports and Recreation
Beaches

One of the finest up-island beaches is **Lucy Vincent Beach,** which is only open to Chilmark residents and renters in the summer (and is reason enough to make friends with a local). For the rest of us, Aquinnah's **Lobsterville Beach** is a favorite for beachcombing, with plenty of shells and sea glass washing up on the shore. Bring your bike, however, as there is no parking along the road.

The beach at the base of the Aquinnah Cliffs is no longer accessible, but the **Aquinnah Public Beach** is a beautiful, family-friendly spot to spend the afternoon; the beach is a 10-minute walk from the parking lot (summer parking fee $15).

Boating

Cruise around the sweet Menemsha Harbor with a kayak, stand-up paddleboard, powerboat, or sailboat from **Book-A-Boat** (Menemsha waterfront,

508/645-2400, www.bookaboatmv.com, rentals from $40 half day and $60 full day). Fish with Captain Buddy Vanderhoop of **Tomahawk Charters** (508/645-3201, www.tomahawkcharters.com, half-day charters from $700), a local fishing celebrity and Wampanoag tribal member.

Hiking and Biking

The Vineyard's off-road bike paths don't reach up-island, but experienced cyclists can make the trip from Edgartown (18 miles) or Vineyard Haven (16.5 miles). A bike ferry crosses the short channel at Menemsha starting in late May, but hours are a bit sporadic.

Three miles of hiking trails thread through the **Menemsha Hills** (North Rd., Chilmark) passing wetland, woodland, and coastal plain on the way up **Prospect Hill**—at a towering 308 feet above sea level, it's just shy of the tallest point on the Vineyard, Peaked Hill, which has an extra three feet of height. In August, the high-bush blueberries along the path make for blissful grazing.

Island naturalist Polly Hill gathered nearly 1,000 different species of plants at the **Polly Hill Arboretum** (809 State Rd., West Tisbury, 508/693-9426, www.pollyhillarboretum.org, sunrise-sunset daily, $5, children under 12 free), which has miles of walking paths through wildflower meadows and woodland of dogwood and magnolia.

The 600-acre **Long Point Wildlife Refuge** (Long Point Rd., West Tisbury, fees June-Sept. $10 car, $5 cyclist or pedestrian, children under 15 free) wraps around the long, narrow Long Cove Pond, and ends in a wildly scenic barrier beach. Two miles of hiking trails pass through coastal dunes and dry forest, and paddleboards and kayaks are available to rent on-site (from $30/hr).

Food

A meal at the **Aquinnah Shop Restaurant** (27 Aquinnah Cir., 508/645-3867, www.theaquinnahshop.com, May-Oct. Mon.-Fri. 9am-3pm, Sat.-Sun. 8am-4pm, reduced hours in shoulder season, $12-30) feels like eating at the end of the world, with stunning views of ocean and cliffs. Seafood basics like fish-and-chips or lobster rolls are solid bets, but save room for pie—the owner bakes it daily with fresh peaches, blueberries, and seasonal fruits.

Dig into Katama Bay oysters, lobster bisque, and steamers at ★ **Larsen's Fish Market** (29 Basin Rd., Menemsha 508/645-2680, www.larsensfishmarket.com, May-Oct. daily 9am-6pm, $5-18), where you can watch the fishing fleet unload from a seat at the outdoor tables—lobster traps topped with unfinished plywood.

The hip little **Beetlebung Coffee House** (24 Menemsha, 508/645-9956, late June-Sept. daily 8am-7pm, $4-14) has good alternatives to Menemsha's seafood shack fare. Hearty sandwiches, smoothies, and bagels are fresh and appealing, and the coffee is the best in town.

The **Beach Plum Inn** (50 Beach Plum Ln., Menemsha, 508/645-9454, www.beachpluminn.com, May-Oct. Mon.-Sat. 5:30pm-10pm, call for off-season hours, $30-42) has one of the island's finest restaurants, with a rustic, romantic garden aesthetic and beautifully cooked food. The menu changes with the season, but always includes seafood, meat, and vegetarian options.

Meet the Vineyard's farmers at the **West Tisbury Farmers Market** (Grange Hall, West Tisbury, 508/693-4359, www.thewesttisburyfarmersmarket.com, June-Oct. Sat. 9am-noon, mid-June-late Aug. Wed. 9am-noon), where you can also find prepared foods and handicrafts.

Part old-fashioned general store, part overpriced tourist trap, the **Chilmark General Store** (7 State Rd., Chilmark, 508/645-3739, www.chilmarkgeneralstore.com, mid-May-June and Sept.-early Oct. Sun.-Fri.7am-3pm, Sat. 7am-5pm, June-Sept. daily 7am-7pm) has picnic supplies, souvenirs and a decent menu of pizza and sandwiches.

Accommodations

$150-250

Visiting **Summersweet Bed & Breakfast** (9 Shaler's Way, Chilmark, 508/645-8017, www.summersweet.org, $215-225), with just two guest rooms, feels like staying with friends. The owners, Gail and Don, are nice as can be, and the rural location, hearty breakfasts, and decor are a taste of the old Vineyard. A comfortable deck, hammock, and yard are appealing places to relax, and guests have access to beautiful Lucy Vincent Beach.

Over $250

The secluded **Duck Inn** (10 Duck Pond Way, Aquinnah, 508/645-9018, www. gayheadrealty.com, $155-315) is located in an 18th-century home with bohemian furnishings and a knockout ocean view. One room has a bathtub in the middle; another is swept at night with the beam from Gay Head Light. The personable owner is a 30-year island resident who gives therapeutic massages and makes killer organic breakfasts.

On the other side of the island, the **Beach Plum Inn** (50 Beach Plum Ln., Menemsha, 508/645-9454, www.beach-pluminn.com, $320-535) is a secluded retreat, with six acres of hilltop property overlooking Vineyard Sound and the Elizabeth Islands. Rates include a full breakfast and a coveted pass to the residents-only Lucy Vincent Beach, one of the most beautiful on the island.

Information and Services

Find all the maps and information you need to get around the island—plus advice on accommodations and dining—at **Martha's Vineyard Chamber of Commerce** (24 Beach Rd., Vineyard Haven, 508/693-0085, www.mvy.com, Mon.-Fri. 9am-5pm).

The island's full-service hospital is **Martha's Vineyard Hospital** (One Hospital Rd., Oak Bluffs, 508/693-0410, www.mvhospital.com), with emergency services offered 24 hours a day. Fill prescription needs at **Leslie's Pharmacy** (65 Main St., Vineyard Haven, 508/693-1010, Mon.-Sat. 8:30am-5:30pm, Sun. 9am-2pm). The commercial centers of Edgartown and Vineyard Haven are home to several **banks.** Each also has an **ATM**—which are also scattered around the streets of those towns, as well as in Oak Bluffs.

Major cell phone networks function within the main towns, but can be undependable in the island's less-crowded areas. Free **Internet access** and terminals are offered at the **Vineyard Haven Public Library** (200 Main St., Vineyard Haven, 508/696-4211, www.vhlibrary.org, Mon., Wed., and Sat. 10am-5:30pm; Tues. and Thurs. 10am-8pm; Fri. 1pm-5:30pm; Sun. noon-4pm) and **Edgartown Free Public Library** (58 North Water St., Edgartown, 508/627-4221, www.edgartownlibrary. org, Mon., Thurs., Fri., and Sat. 10am-5pm; Tues. and Wed. 10am-8pm).

Nantucket

With cobblestone streets and misty beaches, pretty Nantucket is a dreamy world unto itself, a tiny curve of sand that points out toward the sea. It's among the most exclusive (and expensive) destinations in New England, but before the blue bloods and boutiques arrived, the island had a salty history of Native Americans, colonial refugees, and whalers. Then, as now, Nantucket seemed like the last place on earth: early colonists arrived fleeing restrictive mainland towns and found Wampanoag residents who'd fled the European encroachments on Cape Cod—the island's name means "the faraway place" in their language.

That faraway place took an outsize role on the world stage when Nantucketers began pursuing whales, first off the coast, then into deeper and deeper waters. For a century and a half, Nantucket men left the island to hunt whales for years at a time, producing a vast flood of oil that

Nantucket

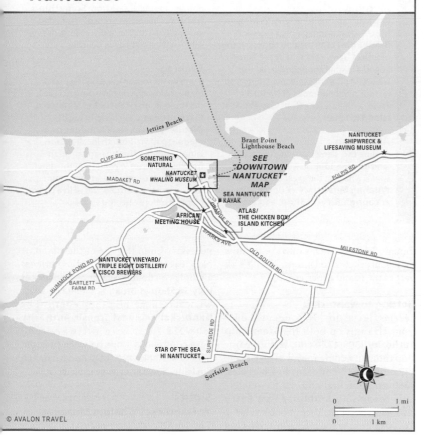

Jetties Beach

Brant Point
Lighthouse Beach

NANTUCKET
SHIPWRECK &
LIFESAVING MUSEUM

**SEE
"DOWNTOWN
NANTUCKET"
MAP**

CLIFF RD

SOMETHING
NATURAL

NANTUCKET
WHALING MUSEUM

MADAKET RD

SEA NANTUCKET
KAYAK

POLPIS RD

AFRICAN
MEETING HOUSE

ATLAS/
THE CHICKEN BOX/
ISLAND KITCHEN

GRANGE ST

SPARKS AVE

MILESTONE RD

OLD SOUTH RD

HUMMOCK POND RD

NANTUCKET VINEYARD/
TRIPLE EIGHT DISTILLERY/
CISCO BREWERS

BARTLETT
FARM RD

SURFSIDE RD

STAR OF THE SEA
HI NANTUCKET

Surfside Beach

0   1 mi

0   1 km

© AVALON TRAVEL

helped ease the screaming machinery of the industrial revolution and light 18th-century homes. It was a harsh, addictive trade to depend on, flush with money and unimaginably dangerous; it's the world of Herman Melville's *Moby-Dick,* and of the doomed whale ship *Essex,* and it ended as suddenly as it began when the world's whale population plummeted in the mid-19th century.

These days, Nantucket is the finest place to see the historic architecture of maritime New England; picture-perfect saltbox houses are crowned with widow's walks and five-petaled roses, and residents still "go laning," strolling the narrow streets that wind through the center. It's impossibly charming on foggy summer mornings when the harbor is smooth as glass, or when the whole island takes cover as nor'easter storms rage across the coast. It's taken deep pockets and a vigilant zoning laws to maintain the island's character, though, and at times, Nantucket has a sanitized, exclusive homogeneity; enormous, identically colored houses line the coast in some places, and bone-deep preppiness may leave some visitors wishing for a bit of grit and color. In Melville's words,

One Day in Nantucket

Morning
Catch an early morning ferry from Hyannis, then find a spot on deck to watch **Brant Point Lighthouse** appear at the mouth of Nantucket's sheltered harbor. Spend a leisurely hour going "laning," wandering the cobblestone streets and historic neighborhoods of Nantucket Town, with time for a hearty breakfast at **Island Kitchen.**

Afternoon
Explore the island's whaling history (and go nose-to-nose with a mammoth sperm whale) at the excellent **Nantucket Whaling Museum.** Pick up some wheels at **Young's Bicycle Shop,** and get homemade picnic fare from **Something Natural,** then take to one of Nantucket's many bike paths to explore rolling, dunes, salt marshes, and scenic beaches.

Evening
If you've booked an evening ferry back to the mainland, you have time to visit the three-in-one **Nantucket Vineyard, Cisco Brewers, and Triple Eight Distillery,** which has live music on an outdoor patio to go with locally made wine, spirits, and beer. Snag one of the free shuttle buses leaving from the downtown visitors center during the summer, then watch the sun go down with a crowd of locals before catching your boat.

though, "these extravaganzas only show that Nantucket is no Illinois," and it's all part of the island experience.

Getting to Nantucket
Ferries leave for Nantucket Town from Hyannis on both the **Steamship Authority** (508/477-8600, www.steamshipauthority.com, round trip-tickets $37 adults, $19 children, $14 bicycles, $280 car, 2.25 hrs) and the passenger-only **Steamship Authority Fast Ferry** ($69 adults, $34 children, $14 bicycles, 1 hr). Also leaving from Hyannis: **Hy-Line Cruises High Speed Ferry** (508/778-2600, www.hylinecruises.com, round-trip tickets $77 adults, $51 children 5-12, $14 bicycles, 1 hr). You can also get to Nantucket from Oak Bluffs on Martha's Vineyard (late June-early Sept.).

During the summer, many flights a day are offered by **Cape Air** (508/771-6944, www.flycapeair.com) from Boston, Hyannis, and Martha's Vineyard.

Getting Around
The cost of traveling to Nantucket with your own car is prohibitive, and while several agencies rent vehicles from Nantucket Airport, a car isn't really necessary given the size of the island. A bicycle is a fun choice, as is a scooter: rent a single- or double-seater at **Nantucket Bicycle Shop** (4 Broad St., 508/228-1999, www.nantucketbikeshop.com). The **Nantucket Regional Transit Authority** (508/228-7025, www.nrtawave.com) does continuous loops between Straight Wharf in Nantucket Town and Madaket, Surfside, Siasconset, and the airport.

Sights
★ Nantucket Whaling Museum
The world's whaling industries have a lasting legacy of destruction that obliterated some species of whale, and left others teetering at the brink of extinction. Now that the oil in our cars, machines, and furnaces comes from the below the ground it's easy to forget that it used to roll off whaling ships in great wooden vats, the fruit of dangerous hunting trips that could last for years. Standing between a fragile, open whaleboat and the 46-foot skeleton of a sperm whale puts it all in perspective at the wonderful **Nantucket Whaling Museum** (15 Broad St., 508/228-1894, www.nha.org, late May-late Oct. daily 10am-5pm; call or check online for off-season hours, $20

Downtown Nantucket

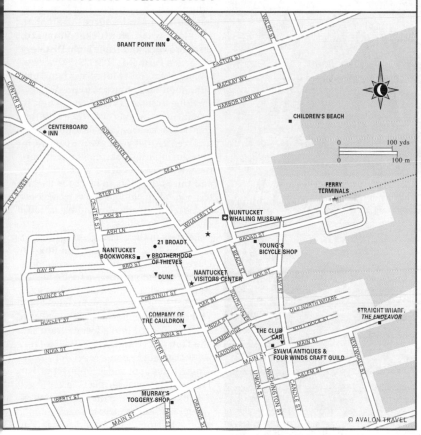

adults, $15 seniors, $5 children 6 and over, free children under 6). Explore a fully restored candle making factory and see the souvenirs that Nantucket whalers brought home from around the world, and the scrimshaw and carvings they made to pass long hours belowdecks.

Other Sights

The shoals around Nantucket have wrecked hundreds of ships throughout the years, and many more lives would have been lost without the islanders that plunged into the breakers to look for survivors. Hear their stories at the **Nantucket**

Shipwreck & Lifesaving Museum (158 Polpis Rd., 508/228-2505, www.nantucketshipwreck.org, late May-mid-Oct. daily 10am-5pm, $10 adults, $7 seniors and students, $5 youth 6-17), which is 3.5 miles from town by the Polpis bicycle path. The small **African Meeting House** (29 York St., 508/228-9833, www.afroammuseum.org/afmnantucket.htm, June-Sept. Mon.-Fri. 10am-4pm, Sat. 10am-2pm, Sun. noon-4pm, $5 adults, $3 seniors and youth 13-17, under 13 free) dates to 1827, when it was used as a meeting place and schoolhouse for escaped slaves, Cape Verdeans and Native Americans.

Entertainment and Events

With long, dark winters and party-fueled summers, it's no surprise that Nantucket has an on-island source of alcohol. Locally owned **Nantucket Vineyard, Cisco Brewers, and Triple Eight Distillery** (5 Bartlett Farm Rd., 508/325-5929, www. ciscobrewers.com, Mon.-Sat. 11am-7pm, Sun. noon-6pm, tours $20) produce everything from aged rum to pinot noir in a facility just outside of town, with a free shuttle service from the downtown visitors' center that runs every 20-30 minutes during high season. Guided tours include tastes of spirits, wine and beer, and this is the place to be in the late afternoon, when outdoor shows by regional and local bands attract a laid-back crowd of locals and visitors.

Later on in the evening, things can get pretty raucous at **The Chicken Box** (16 Dave St., 508/228-9717, www.thechickenbox.com, noon-1am)—a fried-chicken stand turned roadhouse—with reggae and rock bands several nights a week; it's a hike from downtown, so plan to return in a cab. Tucked into a former train car, **The Club Car** (1 Main St., 508/228-1101, www.theclubcar.com, May-Oct. daily, dining 11am-3pm and 5:30pm-10pm, bar 11am-1am) is an atmospheric place to get a drink downtown, with a nightly sing-along piano show, elegant snacks, and a good selection of wine. Music starts at 8:30pm.

Nantucket lights up the first weekend in December for **Christmas Stroll Weekend** (www.christmasstroll.com), when the town goes all out with period carolers, nautical Santas, and lighthouses dressed for the holidays. Once the weather warms up, there's the **Daffodil Festival** (508/228-1700, www.nantucketchamber.org) in April, which takes over with parades of blossom-festooned antique cars and a tailgating picnic.

Top to bottom: lighthouse in Nantucket; canoe; whale boat and whale bones at the Nantucket Whaling Museum.

Shopping

If you're searching for shops on Nantucket, you won't have to look for long; the entire downtown is lined with boutiques and stores, with the biggest concentration along Main Street. There are a few classic Nantucket souvenirs, though, that are distinct in the Cape Cod area. There's a fine selection of **Nantucket lightship baskets** at **Four Winds Craft Guild** inside **Sylvia Antiques** (15 Main St., 508/228-9623, www.fourwindscraftguild.com, Mon. and Wed.-Sat. 10am-5pm, Sun. 11am-3pm), and you can pick up all sorts of clothes in distinctive "Nantucket red"— actually a faded pink — at **Murray's Toggery Shop** (62 Main St., 508/228-0437, www.nantucketreds.com, Mon.-Sat. 10am-5pm), a longtime preppy pilgrimage spot. Legend has it that every inn on the island used to stock guest rooms with a copy of *Moby-Dick*, which is full of Nantucket references and over seven hundred pages long. Unsurprisingly, most visitors didn't finish the book before leaving, so more and more disappeared with every departing ferry; buy your own copy at **Nantucket Bookworks** (25 Broad St., 508/228-4000, www.nantucketbookworks.com, Mon.-Thurs. 10am-8pm, Fri.-Sat. 10am-9pm, Sun. 10am-6pm), which also has an excellent collection of works by local authors.

Sports and Recreation
Beaches

Nantucket's beaches are soft and sandy, and they're the center of life on the island, when fine weather turns all eyes to the sea. The first one you'll spot as you approach the coast on the ferry is **Brant Point Lighthouse Beach** (on Brant Point, at the tip of Easton St.) at the mouth of Nantucket's sheltered harbor. It's a quiet and very small beach, about a 15-minute walk from town. As it has no facilities or lifeguard, it's frequented mostly by those looking for a brief stroll or a view of the lighthouse or town. A quick five-minute walk from town, just around the bend in the harbor toward Brant Point, is **Children's Beach.** With very few waves, a small park, a lifeguard on-duty, and restrooms, it's a perfect spot to take the tykes. On the outskirts of town, equipped with lifeguards and restrooms, is **Jetties** (508/228-5358, www.nantucketchamber.org). There's also a playground; a concession stand selling burgers, ice cream, and such; and boat rentals. Take a shuttle or ride a bike to the island's south side to reach **Surfside** (www.nantucketchamber.org), a big, wide stretch of sand that catches a heavy swell and has an excellent snack bar.

Biking

With off-road paths, mellow traffic, and gentle terrain, a bicycle is one of the best ways to explore the island. You can pick up wheels just off the ferry at **Young's Bicycle Shop** (6 Broad St., 508/228-1151, www.youngsbicycleshop.com, daily 9am-5pm, $20/hr to $35 24-hr rental). They stock helpful maps of popular bike rides, and their website has links to a number of the best, with step-by-step instructions and maps. The 4.2-mile self-guided tour of downtown takes in the lighthouse and Nantucket's most historic neighborhoods; other good choices are the flat, 3.5-mile ride to **Surfside Beach,** or the scenic, 19-mile ride that heads out to **Sconset** via Milestone and comes back on the Polpis bike path.

Boating

One of the most peaceful ways to see the island is from the water; **Sea Nantucket Kayak** (76 Washington St., 508/228-7499, www.seanantucketkayak.com, daily 9am-5pm, boats from $25/hr to $55 for all day) rents kayaks and stand-up paddleboards from a waterfront location that's walking distance from downtown, with tips on where to paddle.

To explore the harbor under sail, book a place on *The Endeavor* (Straight Wharf, Slip 1015, 508/228-5585, www.endeavorsailing.com, 1.5-hr daytime sails $45, sunset sails $60), a 31-foot Friendship sloop that makes four trips a day with Captain Jim Genthner.

Food

Slipping into the basement door at **Brotherhood of Thieves** (23 Broad St., 508/228-2551, www.brother-hoodofthieves.com, daily 11:30am-late, $13-26) feels like discovering a shined-up sailor pub, with brick walls, thick wooden beams, and long, dark wooden tables. Burgers, sturdy mains, and bar food are well-prepared (if unremarkable), and a seat at the bar is an excellent place for striking up conversations. When the basement is crowded, more seating is available upstairs, but the dining rooms seems a bit too brightly lit after the atmospheric gloom on the lower level.

Pick up a sandwich on the way to the beach, or just eat at the sunny picnic tables outside **Something Natural** (50 Cliff Rd., 508/228-0504, www.somethingna-tural.com, Apr.-Oct. daily 8am-3pm, $5-13.50). House-made bread and super-fresh ingredients make the menu of simple sandwiches an appealing option, especially when combined with a thin, crispy chocolate chip cookie. Skip the wait by calling in your order.

Simple breakfasts and affordable lunch and dinner plates make ★ **Island Kitchen** (1 Chins Way, 508/228-2639, www.nan-tucketislandkitchen.com, Sun.-Mon. 7am-2pm, Tues.-Sat. 7am-2pm and 5:30pm-close, $6-18) a year-round favorite, and the meal-sized salads are a refreshing break if you've been living off chowder and clam shack fare. Diner-like counter seating looks into the small, open kitchen, and the tables at this casual joint fill up quickly, so arrive early on weekends or come prepared to wait.

The roaring fire and comfortable chairs at **Atlas** (130 Pleasant St., 508/825-5495, www.atlasnantucket.com, daily 6pm-1pm, $16-32) may leave you wishing for a cold, foggy evening to enjoy the hearty, creative menu of barbecue and seafood. Slabs of ribs and tender pulled pork are highlights of the menu, and this is an excellent place to stop by for a drink and snacks; classic cocktails are prepared with thoughtful ingredients, and the beer list is gathered from craft breweries around the country.

A pale, minimalist dining room is a serene backdrop for the showstopping food at **Dune** (20 Broad St., 508/228-5550, www.dunenantucket.com, lunch mid-May-Oct. daily 11:30am-2:30pm, dinner year-round Tues.-Sat. 5:30pm-9:30pm, $45-65); the menu changes seasonally, but always features elegant seafood presentations with brightly flavored sides that lean French. The rich corn chowder is a perennial favorite, and the soft shell crab is a crispy, crunchy bite of heaven.

Another destination-worth restaurant is ★ **Company of the Cauldron** (5 India St., 508/228-4016, www.companyofthe-cauldron.com, Mon.-Sat. 7pm-close, $75-100), an intimate, romantic spot with fixed-priced dinners that are among the best on the island. Fresh flowers and candles encourage a leisurely feel, and the restaurant has just one seating each evening, so reservations are essential.

Accommodations

With the exception of an excellent hostel, it is very challenging to find a place to sleep for under $350 dollars during Nantucket's peak season, put prices drop dramatically in the shoulder season, when crowds start to thin. Simple rooms are available on Airbnb for less than the commercial options, but still start at $150 in the summer.

One of New England's most memorable hostels, the ★ **Star of the Sea HI Nantucket** (31 Western Ave., 508/228-0433, www.hiusa.org, late May-late Sept., $42) was built as a lifesaving station in 1873 and included on the National Register of Historic Places. It's just across the street from Surfside Beach, so it can be easily reached by bike or an island shuttle, and has a fire pit, grill, communal kitchen, and a good-size breakfast.

Walking distance from the lighthouse, **Brant Point Inn** (6 N. Beach St., 508/228-5442, www.brantpointinn.com, $225-295) is one of the better values in town, and the hospitable owner makes this a particularly welcoming place to stay. Home-made muffins for breakfast and a gracious front porch with comfy rocking chairs are nice touches, as are the beach chairs and umbrellas that are available to guests.

Friendly and old-fashioned, the **Centerboard Inn** (8 Chester St., 508/283-7156, www.centerboardinn.com, $399-550) is a romantic option in the former home of a whaling captain. The owners have meticulously restored the building's Victorian details and added luxurious, comfortable common spaces that feel like a retreat. Board games, beach chairs, an appealing breakfast, and an afternoon wine and cheese hour are fun touches, and the inn's three-bed studio is a good option for families, especially during shoulder season.

The airy decor at ★ **21 Broad** (21 Broad St., 508/228-4749, www.21broadhotel. com, $450-689) is a vibrant blend of modern lines and Nantucket style, both urban and beachy. Elegant extras are less stuffy than at other high-end hotels on the island: a mix your own cocktail bar, small plate breakfasts, in-room iPads,

and an on-site steam room are more fun than formal. During the summer, a deck with an outdoor fireplace is a haven in the heart of downtown Nantucket.

Information and Services

Get the lowdown on where to stay, where to eat, and how to get there from the centrally located **Nantucket Visitors Center** (25 Federal St., 508/228-0925, www.nantucket-ma.gov, Apr.-Nov. daily 9am-5pm, Dec.-May Mon.-Sat. 9am-5pm), which maintains a list of the rooms that are available each day.

The island's only emergency medical facility is **Nantucket Cottage Hospital** (57 Prospect St., 508/825-8100, www.nantuckethospital.org), which offers 24-hour care. Fill prescription needs at **Island Pharmacy** (122 Pleasant St., 508/228-6400, www.islandrx.com, Mon.-Fri. 8am-7pm, Sat.-Sun. 8am-6pm).

Nantucket Town's Main Street is home to two banks, **Nantucket Bank** (104 Pleasant St. and 2 Orange St., 508/228-0580, www.nantucketbank. com, Mon.-Thurs. 8:30am-3:30pm, Fri. 8:30am-5pm, Sat. 8:30am-12:30pm) and **Pacific National Bank** (61 Main St., 508/228-1917). Both have **ATMs**—as does the nearby **A & P** (Straight Wharf, 508/228-1700) grocery store. Be aware each charges a fee of $2-3 if you are not on its network. Cell phone service can be unreliable on Nantucket.

New York City

Take in Broadway lights and lofty skyscrapers in this iconic city, whose neighborhoods, museums, and street scenes are American touchstones.

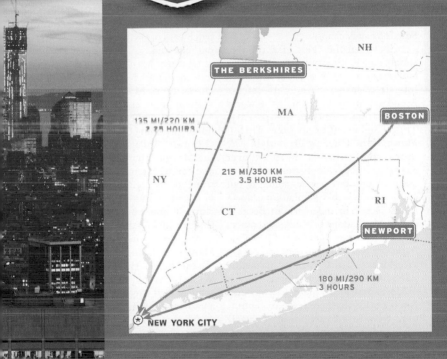

THE BERKSHIRES

NH

MA

BOSTON

135 MI/220 KM
2.25 HOURS

215 MI/350 KM
3.5 HOURS

NY

RI

CT

NEWPORT

180 MI/290 KM
3 HOURS

★ NEW YORK CITY

The Big Apple needs no introduction, and while New York City is *not* part of New England, it's a grand place to launch or conclude an epic trip through the Northeast.

For most first-time visitors, a trip to New York means discovering the classic sights: crossing the New York Harbor to Ellis Island and the Statue of Liberty, peering over the edge of the Empire State Building, ordering a pastrami sandwich, and immersing yourself in Times Square's gaudy chaos.

In between the "best-ofs," though, simply take in the city's unique rhythms and prepare for the unexpected. Duck into street-corner pizza joints, catch a Broadway show, and watch the world drift by from a bench in Central Park. The five boroughs of New York—Manhattan, Queens, Brooklyn, the Bronx, and Staten Island—sprawl over 303 square miles of immigrant neighborhoods, glamorous avenues, and grit, but you can walk across Manhattan Island's widest section in under an hour. Because of this, Manhattan's bristling skyscrapers are easy to explore on foot and by public transport, and there's no better way to get a feel for New York life than by hitting the sidewalks and subway platforms.

Meet some locals along the way and you'll notice that, contrary to reputation, New Yorkers tend to be gregarious, kind, and funny. One piece of the NYC typecast hits home, however—many New Yorkers think their bright lights and bustling streets are the center of the known universe. To find out why, take a long walk down Broadway, head to Wall Street for the closing bell, or hit the town at 4am, when the "City that Never Sleeps" is still going full-steam.

Planning Your Time

If New York City is your New England gateway, plan to visit car-free, exploring the city before picking up your rental (or after returning it). Make a beeline for Manhattan, where you'll need at least a couple of days if you'd like to see the primary sights, with additional time to get farther afield.

Orientation

New York City is divided into five boroughs: the Bronx, Queens, Brooklyn, Staten Island, and Manhattan. Most of the key tourist attractions are located in Manhattan, which is divided into a patchwork of smaller neighborhoods laid out on a grid.

Uptown Manhattan generally refers to the area north of 59th Street. Downtown Manhattan, or Lower Manhattan, refers to the island south of 14th Street and encompasses neighborhoods including SoHo, the East Village, Greenwich Village, the Lower East Side, the Meatpacking District, the Bowery, and Nolita. Midtown Manhattan loosely stretches between these zones, and some of its more famous neighborhoods include Times Square, Hell's Kitchen, Chelsea, and Gramercy Park.

Avenues run north-south on Manhattan Island, from 1st Avenue on the east side to 11th Avenue on the west. While the avenues are in numeric order, some named streets are interspersed: It's a four-block hike from 3rd Avenue to 5th Avenue, crossing Lexington, Park, and Madison Avenues.

Streets run (mostly) east-west; starting at Houston Street, numbered streets rise as you head uptown. When reading an address, note that 5th Avenue is the dividing line between east and west. Below Houston Street, streets begin to snarl and go off the grid—from there, a map is essential.

Highlights

★ **Central Park:** The United States' most famous park is even bigger and more beautiful than you thought (page 356).

★ **The Metropolitan Museum of Art:** Explore everything from antiquities to the cutting edge in the largest art museum in the United States (page 356).

★ **The High Line:** Follow a trail of public art and modern landscape architecture over a reincarnated piece of railway (page 360).

★ **The Museum of Modern Art (MoMA):** Find the world's largest collection of modern art and world-class traveling exhibitions (page 361).

★ **National September 11 Memorial & Museum:** Pay tribute to some of New York's most tragic stories at this moving monument (page 362).

★ **One World Observatory:** Soar through New York history to the tip top floors of the Western Hemisphere's tallest sky-scraper (page 364).

★ **Ellis Island and the Statue of Liberty:** Get an immigrants' view of New York Harbor at this iconic gateway to the United States, then see the famous French gift carrying a torch for freedom (page 364).

★ **Broadway Shows:** Watch the ol' song and dance on the Great White Way, the nerve center of New York's musical theater (page 365).

New York City

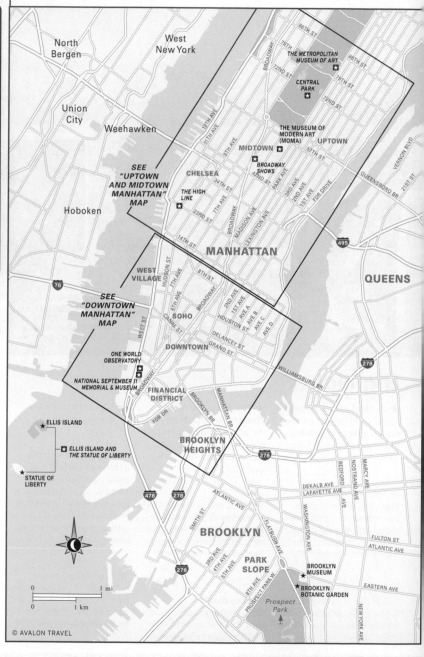

North Bergen

West New York

Union City

Weehawken

Hoboken

SEE "UPTOWN AND MIDTOWN MANHATTAN" MAP

SEE "DOWNTOWN MANHATTAN" MAP

THE METROPOLITAN MUSEUM OF ART

CENTRAL PARK

THE MUSEUM OF MODERN ART (MOMA)

MIDTOWN

UPTOWN

CHELSEA

BROADWAY SHOWS

THE HIGH LINE

MANHATTAN

QUEENS

WEST VILLAGE

SOHO

DOWNTOWN

ONE WORLD OBSERVATORY

NATIONAL SEPTEMBER 11 MEMORIAL & MUSEUM

FINANCIAL DISTRICT

BROOKLYN HEIGHTS

ELLIS ISLAND

ELLIS ISLAND AND THE STATUE OF LIBERTY

STATUE OF LIBERTY

BROOKLYN

PARK SLOPE

BROOKLYN MUSEUM

BROOKLYN BOTANIC GARDEN

Prospect Park

12TH AVE
11TH AVE
8TH AVE
7TH AVE
34TH ST
23RD ST
14TH ST
HUDSON ST
8TH ST
BROADWAY
MADISON AVE
LEXINGTON AVE
2ND AVE
1ST AVE
AVE A
AVE B
AVE C
AVE D
HOUSTON ST
DELANCEY ST
GRAND ST
CANAL ST
WEST ST
FOR DR
BROOKLYN BR
MANHATTAN BR
WILLIAMSBURG BR

BROADWAY
72ND ST
78TH ST
86TH ST
57TH ST
42ND ST
3RD AVE
PARK AVE
FDR DRIVE
VERNON BLVD
QUEENSBORO BR
21ST ST

78
495
278
478
278
278

SMITH ST
ATLANTIC AVE
3RD AVE
4TH AVE
5TH AVE
8TH AVE
FLATBUSH AVE
WASHINGTON AVE
DEKALB AVE
LAFAYETTE AVE
BEDFORD AVE
NOSTRAND AVE
MARCY AVE
FULTON ST
ATLANTIC AVE
EASTERN AVE
NEW YORK AVE
PROSPECT PARK W

0   1 mi
0   1 km

© AVALON TRAVEL

Best Accommodations

★ **New York Budget Inn:** Find dorm beds, doughnuts, and a lively group of fellow travelers blocks away from the Empire State Building (page 372).

★ **American Dream Bed and Breakfast:** Hostel prices meet bed-and-breakfast hospitality in this friendly Midtown option (page 372).

★ **The Pod Hotel:** Tiny rooms have techy touches and modern style for an up-to-the-minute feel (page 372).

★ **citizenM:** Chic decor and a rooftop bar make this the hippest place to sleep In Midtown—and oversize beds ensure sweet dreams In the heart of Times Square chaos (page 372).

★ **The Jane:** Design that evokes the golden age of travel fills these tiny rooms with adventurous charm (page 373).

★ **The Bowery House:** These budget digs come with some authentic NYC grit—and a rooftop patio with million-dollar views (page 373).

Getting to New York City

Driving from Boston
215 miles, 3.5 hours

Leave Boston on **I-93 South,** then use Exit 20A-20B to merge onto **I-90 West,** which you'll follow for **52 miles** ($7.25 toll, cash only). Take Exit 9 for **I-84 South,** following signs to New York City, continuing on I-84 for **41 miles.** Take Exit 57 to **Route 15 South,** then Exit 86 onto **I-91 South.** After 17 miles, use Exit 17 to merge back onto **Route 15 South** for **30 miles.**

Take Exit 52, merging onto **Route 108 South/Route 8 South** for 5 miles before exiting onto **I-95 South.** Continue for **45 miles,** then stay left to continue onto **I-278 West,** following signs for Manhattan. Use Exit 46 for Manhattan/FDR Drive, continuing onto **Robert F. Kennedy Bridge** ($8 toll, cash only). Take Exit 10 for destinations in Midtown.

Driving from Newport
180 miles, 3 hours

Leave downtown Newport on **Route 238,** then turn west on Route 138 across the **Newport Bridge** ($4 toll, cash

only). Exit onto **Route 1 North** toward Providence after 8.5 miles, then stay left to continue onto **Route 4 North.** Take Exit 5 to turn left onto **Route 102 North,** staying on it for about 8 miles, then turn left onto **Route 3 South** for 4.4 miles, and merge onto **I-95 South.**

Continue for **137 miles,** then stay left to continue onto **I 278 West,** following signs for Manhattan. Use Exit 46 for Manhattan/FDR Drive, continuing onto **Robert F. Kennedy Bridge** ($8 toll, cash only). Take Exit 10 for destinations in Midtown.

Driving from the Berkshires
135 miles, 2.25 hours

From **Great Barrington, Massachusetts,** leave town on **Route 7 South,** then turn right onto **Route 23 West** for 17 miles. Turn right to merge onto the **Taconic State Parkway**—among New York state's most **scenic** drives, passing through Hudson Valley farms and forest.

Follow the Taconic Parkway for about **85 miles,** then exit onto the **Saw Mill Parkway South** for 16 miles. Keep right at the fork to continue onto **Henry Hudson Parkway/Route 9A South,** which crosses the **Henry Hudson Bridge** ($5.50 toll, assessed and billed automatically). Turn left on surface streets for destinations in Midtown.

Best Restaurants

★ **Daniel:** The last word in New York City's fancy French dining, Chef Daniel Boulud's eponymous restaurant is full of pomp and fine preparations (page 369).

★ **The Halal Guys:** Take food truck fare back to its bare-bones, cabbie-feeding roots at a stall that serves great piles of chicken and rice at (almost) any hour of day or night (page 369).

★ **Gramercy Tavern:** Dine farm-to-table in the heart of Midtown in the convivial bar or elegant dining room (page 370).

★ **Veselka:** Find homey, Ukrainian dishes like borscht and pierogi at any hour of the day or night (page 370).

★ **Momofuku Noodle Bar:** Visit the restaurant where Chef David Chang's creative Korean empire began—the

pork buns and noodle bowls are still the best in town (page 371).

★ **Katz's Delicatessen:** Locals and first-time visitors both line up for sandwiches piled with pastrami at the quintessential New York deli—just don't lose your ticket (page 371).

★ **Russ & Daughters:** Visit the "appetizing" shop or café for Jewish deli classics, chewy bagels, lox, and caviar (page 371).

★ **Balthazar:** SoHo's take on a French bistro is the place to see and be seen over plates of steak frites and oyster towers (page 371).

★ **John's of Bleecker Street:** Brave the lines to get the perfect New York pie from this simple, landmark pizza joint (page 371).

Getting There by Air, Train, or Bus
Air

Three airports serve New York City: **John F. Kennedy International Airport** (JFK, 718/244-4444), **LaGuardia Airport** (LGA, 718/533-3400), and **Newark Liberty International Airport** (EWR, 973/961-6000) in New Jersey. Coming or going, taxis between JFK and Manhattan have a flat rate of $52, plus a $0.50 New York state surcharge, not including bridge/tunnel tolls and tips. From LaGuardia, taxis charge regular metered fare, with the cost running approximately $25-37, not including tolls and tips to Manhattan, with meters starting at $2.50. From Newark, a taxi charges $17.50 on top of the regular metered fare, plus tolls and tip.

For inexpensive transportation to and from JFK, the Port Authority operates the **AirTrain** (www.panynj.gov/airtrain), a light-rail that connects all airport

terminals to the subway system. You can access the AirTrain from the Sutphin Boulevard stop on the E line or via the Howard Beach stop on the A line (take a train marked "Far Rockaway"). You can also take the Long Island Rail Road from Penn Station to the AirTrain at Jamaica Station. The cost of a one-way trip on the AirTrain is $5. You can pay the fare using a pay-per-ride MetroCard or purchase tickets in the station.

The **Port Authority of New York and New Jersey** (www.panynj.gov) operates booths that provide information on rates and connections to private limousine and van companies. Its **Air-Ride service** (800/247-7433) provides recorded information about bus, shuttle, and private car services from area airports. Shuttle options include **Olympia/Coach Usa Airport Express** (908/354-3330 or 877/863-9275, www.coachusa.com) and **Supershuttle** (212/209-7000 or 800/258-3826, www.supershuttle.com).

Driving the Connecticut Coast

Great piles of suburban wealth do little to dispel Connecticut's reputation as an NYC bedroom community, but the coast is dotted with pretty towns and sandy beaches that could easily occupy a day or two of slowed-down exploration. Follow Route 1 all the way down (or up) the coast between Rhode Island and New York, hopping off onto I-95 where you want to save time.

Explore Sailing History

With a deeply sheltered harbor that straddles the Mystic River, lovely **Mystic** is all seaside charm, with colonial buildings and fields of bristling masts. Its show-stopping attraction is **Mystic Seaport** (75 Greenmanville Ave., Mystic, 888/973-2767, www.mysticseaport.org, daily 9am-5pm, $26 adults, $24 seniors, $17 youth 6-17, children under 6 free), the largest maritime museum in the United States, which recreates a 19th-century coastal village complete with costumed docents, ship smiths, riggers, and coopers in old buildings that were shipped from around New England.

Hit the Beach

The stretch of road from the **Connecticut River** (which divides the towns of Old Saybrook and Old Lyme) to **Guilford** is among the most appealing on the coast, a landscape shot through with inlets and marshland, dotted with ice cream shops and country boutiques. A crown jewel is breezy, beautiful **Hammonasset Beach** (1288 Boston Post Rd., Madison, 203/245-8743, www.ct.gov, $15 weekdays, $22 weekends). If the shore's too pretty to leave behind, there's a **campground** on-site ($30 primitive sites, $45 hookups, $80 primitive cabins).

Eat Classic Coastal Food

Another classic Connecticut coastal experience is stopping for seafood at **The Place** (901 Boston Post Rd., Guilford, 203/453-9276, www.theplaceguilford.com, late Apr.-Oct. Mon.-Thurs. 5pm-9pm, Fri. 5pm-10pm, Sat. 1pm-10pm, Sun. noon-9pm, $10-26), a rough-and-tumble outdoor joint in **Guilford** with tree stumps for chairs, smoky roasted clams, and big communal tables.

Go to College

Despite the blue-blooded university at the heart of **New Haven,** the sprawling seaport's reputation has always been more grit than glam. That's changed in recent years, and the city center is an energetic mix of new businesses and art galleries abutting older neighborhoods. The highlight is still **Yale University** (Sachem St., New Haven, 203/432-2300), whose campus displays Gothic and Victorian architecture. **Guided tours** (Mon.-Fri. 10:30am and 2pm, Sat.-Sun. 1:30pm) last a little over an hour, or download a map and take a **self-guided MP3 tour** (http://visitorcenter.yale.edu). The campus also has several fine (and free) museums: Visit the **Yale University Art Gallery** (1111 Chapel St., 203/432-0600, www.artgallery.yale.edu, Sept.-June Tues.-Wed. and Fri. 10am-5pm, Thurs. 10am-8pm, Sat.-Sun. 11am-5pm; July-Aug. Tues.-Fri. 10am-5pm and Sat.-Sun. 11am-5pm) to see a vast collection that includes works by Chuck Close and Dorothea Lange, along with pieces from around the world. The **Yale Center for British Art** (1080 Chapel St., 877/247-8278, www.britishart.yale.edu, Tues.-Sat. 10am-5pm, Sun. noon-5pm) is home to the largest collection of British artwork outside the UK.

If you get hungry while in town, note that New Haven's other claim to fame is a distinctive take on thin-crust pizza known as "apizza." It's got a charred, slightly sour crust and an oblong shape, and the plain version comes topped with oregano, tomato sauce, and pecorino romano. If you want chewy strings of mozzarella cheese, order yours with "mootz." A great place to get your first pie is **Sally's Apizza** (237 Wooster St., New Haven, 203/624-5271, www.sallysapizza.com, Wed.-Thurs. 4pm-9pm, Fri. 4pm-10pm, Sat. 3pm-10pm, Sun. 3pm-9pm, $7-10, cash only).

Train

Penn Station (33rd St. between 7th Ave. and 8th Ave.) serves passengers arriving on **Amtrak** (800/872-7245 or 212/630-6401, www.amtrak.com) as well as **New Jersey Transit** (973/275-5555 or 718/330-1234, www.njtransit.com), **Long Island Rail Road** (718/217-5477, http://mta.info/lirr), and the subway's A, C, E, 1, 2, and 3 trains. Visitors arrive at New York's other main station, **Grand Central Terminal** (89 E. 42nd St.), via **Metro-North Railroad** (212/532-4900, www.mta.info/mnr) and the 4, 5, 6, 7, and S subway lines (NYC Transit, 718/330-1234).

Bus

The Midtown **Port Authority Bus Terminal** (625 8th Ave., 212/435-7000) is the main long-distance bus hub for the city, linking New York City with destinations all over New England. Carriers include **Greyhound** (www.greyhound.com), **Peter Pan** (800/343-9999, www.peterpanbus.com), and discount bus service **Megabus** (www.megabus.com). A good way to find fares to other destinations in New England is on the search site **Wanderu** (www.wanderu.com), which aggregates bus and train schedules with real-time fares.

Sights

Uptown
★ Central Park

Designed by Frederick Law Olmsted and Calvert Vaux in the mid-19th century, **Central Park** (between 5th Ave. and Central Park W., 59th St. and 110th St., 212/310-6600, www.centralparknyc.org, daily 6am-1am) was the first landscaped recreational area in the United States. In 1856, the city purchased most of the park's present 843 acres, displacing a number of poor communities and shantytowns in the process. Many of Central Park's most prominent attractions have been beloved landmarks since it opened

in 1876, such as the wild-looking **Ramble,** tranquil **Central Park Mall,** and lovely **Bethesda Terrace and Fountain.** Today, it remains an impressively large and beautiful park, a beloved respite from the relentlessly urban landscape that surrounds it.

Though open year-round, the park truly comes alive in the warmer months. Each summer brings a host of outdoor performances, including free concerts by the Metropolitan Opera and New York Philharmonic, the Shakespeare in the Park festival, and the often-raucous SummerStage. Recreational activities abound, including softball on the **Great Lawn,** boating on the lake, tai chi on the North Meadow, and bicycling, jogging, and horseback riding. Squirrels and chipmunks run wild throughout, while the park's famous red-tailed hawks soar overhead. More than 130 species from polar bears to tropical toucans live in naturally designed habitats at the **Central Park Zoo** (off 5th Ave. near 64th St., www.centralparkzoo.com, $18 adults, $15 seniors, $13 children, free under 2, discounts with online purchase).

A wonderful way to explore the park is by bicycle: A **Citi Bike** (www.citibikenyc.com) station is located at the intersection of Central Park South and 6th Avenue, but for a longer ride it's worth renting a bike at **Central Park Bike Tours** (203 West 58th St., 212/541-9759, www.centralparkbiketours.com, rentals from $10).

Some favorite stops to visit by bike are the John Lennon memorial at **Strawberry Fields,** whimsical **Belvedere Castle,** and **The Pond,** where park views have a perfect backdrop of skyscrapers.

Visiting families shouldn't miss the **Central Park Carousel** (1802 65th St. Tranverse, daily 10am-6pm, $3), where 57 hand-carved horses and pair of chariots have gone round and round since 1908.

★ The Metropolitan Museum of Art

Undisputed crown jewel of Museum Mile, a stretch of 5th Avenue that includes

Two Days in New York City

Day 1

Cue the Sinatra, pull on some walking shoes, and see the hits in 48 hours: Grab a bagel (any bagel) and head to the **One World Observatory** to get your bearings from the tallest building in the hemisphere. Head back down to planet earth to visit the nearby **National September 11 Memorial & Museum,** commemorating the nearly 3,000 people killed in the 2001 terrorist attack. Continue to **Battery Park** for a ferry to the **Statue of Liberty and Ellis Island,** making it back in time for **sunset** on New York Harbor and dinner—farm-to-table at **Gramercy Tavern, Momofuku** pork buns, or just a hot dog at **Katz's Delicatessen**?

Day 2

Slow down for a morning of modernists and old masters at **The Metropolitan Museum of Art,** then find a bit of fresh air and greenery in nearby **Central Park.** Stroll the peaceful **Strawberry Fields,** climb to the top of **Belvedere Castle** and take a spin around the **Central Park Carousel.** You might want to take a nap by **The Pond,** so you can clap all the way through the final bow at a **Broadway show.**

some of the city's most important collections, the **Metropolitan Museum of Art** (1000 5th Ave., 212/535-7710, www.metmuseum.org, Sun. and Tues.-Thurs. 9:30am-5:30pm, Fri.-Sat. 9:30am-9pm, admission by donation) houses one of the world's largest and most diverse collections, with works ranging from the prehistoric era to the 21st century, from design to drawing.

The museum first opened in 1870 with a Roman sarcophagus, and now the Met boasts more than two million objects in its permanent holdings. Among its major collections are important classical antiquities, Asian prints, American decorative arts, and European paintings, including notable works by Vermeer, Monet, and Van Gogh. The Egyptian Art wing, one of the Met's top attractions, incorporates ancient jewelry and funerary statues, as well as the impressive Temple of Dendur, an entire sandstone shrine dating back to the 1st century BC, which has been fully reassembled in the Met's window-filled north wing.

The museum has three vast floors divided into numerous rooms and wings, and it's impossible to view the entire collection in a single trip. Exploring the museum's website beforehand and picking up a map in the Great Hall will help you prioritize. There are also free tours and knowledgeable museum staffers to point you in the right direction. For bird's-eye views of Central Park, have a glass of wine in the rooftop sculpture garden and café, open from May through fall, weather permitting. You'll notice that the $25 entrance fee is "suggested." The museum, which does not pay rent to the city of New York, has come under fire because many visitors feel obligated to pay full price, but the ticket price is truly optional. If you'd like to pay a reduced rate or not at all, plan to wait in line at a cash-only cashier's window, as credit card kiosks and online sales all charge the full amount.

Midtown
Empire State Building

Completed in 1931 during the height of the skyscraper craze, the 102-story **Empire State Building** (350 5th Ave., 212/736-3100, www.esbnyc.com, daily 8am-2am, last elevator 1:15am) is one of New York's most recognizable landmarks. A 1,454-foot limestone monument to progress, it remains a fixture in the popular imagination, in part because of its long cinematic history. It served as a romantic rendezvous point in *An Affair to Remember,* was destroyed by aliens in

SIGHTS

Independence Day, and saw the giant ape's last stand in *King Kong.*

Taking the ear-popping elevator ride to the 86th-floor main observation deck means waiting in three interminable lines (metal detector, ticketing, and elevator) and shelling out $32 ($26 children 6-12, under 6 free), but visitors are rewarded with panoramic views of the city, stretching for up to 80 miles in all directions, as well as an exhibit featuring history and memorabilia from the construction of the skyscraper. If you're willing to pay an extra $20, you can ascend even higher, to the 102nd-floor observatory. To experience the Empire State Building without a crushing crowd, buy tickets online before arriving and plan to come before 11am.

Throughout the city, the building's most visible feature is its tower floodlights, which illuminate the exterior of the 72nd floor to the base of the TV antenna at the top. Equipped with LED lights that sparkle in over 16 million tones, the illumination changes day to day to mark holidays, sports victories, and other special occasions.

Chrysler Building

What the Empire State Building has in stature, the **Chrysler Building** (405 Lexington Ave., 212/682-3070, Mon.-Fri. 8am-6pm) achieves in style. At the time of its construction between 1928 and 1930, another building at 40 Wall Street was vying for the title of tallest in the city. To keep his competitors guessing, the building's architect, William Van Alen, hid his final plans for the top of the structure, which included a seven-story spire. At the last minute, workers raised the spire right through what spectators had assumed was the roof and riveted it into place. It was the first human-made structure to reach over 1,000 feet. However, its run at the top lasted only for about 40 days until the Empire State Building was completed, usurping its title as the highest building in the world.

From the outside, the 1,046-foot granite-and-glass structure, with its protruding gargoyles (designed to resemble the hood ornaments of Plymouth cars), is topped by a distinctive crown ornamentation of stainless steel cladding. The luxurious lobby (once a car showroom) is the only interior space open to the public, giving visitors a chance to peek past the security gates at the marble walls, polished nickel chrome decorations that embellish the stairway railings, *très* deco light fixtures, and mural by Edward Trumbull depicting early 20th-century technological triumphs.

Grand Central Terminal

Roughly 750,000 people pass through **Grand Central Terminal** (89 E. 42nd St., 212/340-2583, www.grandcentralterminal.com, daily 5:30am-2am) every day, headed for the city's busiest subway station (five lines pass through underground) and the Metro North commuter trains. Completed in 1913 under the auspices of transportation magnate Cornelius Vanderbilt, the station is all pomp and classical grandeur. The Beaux-Arts facade on 42nd Street looks more like the entrance to a Roman coliseum than a rail station, with its pair of Corinthian columns supporting sculptures of Hercules, Minerva, and Mercury (the Roman god of speed and commerce). With its towering ceilings and famous four-sided clock at the center, the station's Main Concourse is one of the most spectacular public spaces in the world. It's almost always alive with activity, especially during rush hour. Above it all, the cerulean blue ceiling depicts zodiac constellations with fiber-optic lights that really twinkle.

Not long ago Grand Central was considered an eyesore, as years of wear and neglect had slowly drained it of its splendor and significance. A decade of renovations brought the station back to its former glory, and since the restoration was completed in 1998, Grand Central has become a destination unto

Uptown and Midtown Manhattan

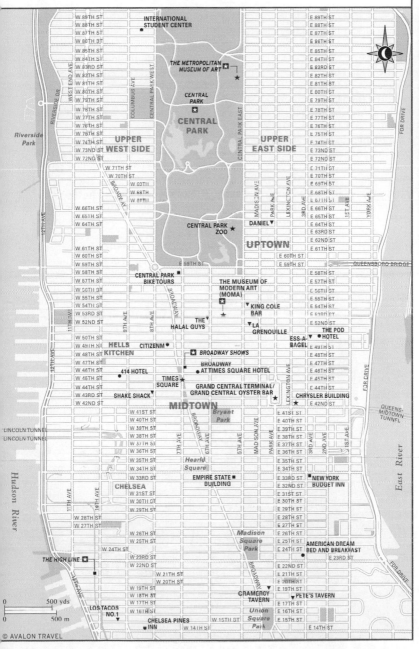

INTERNATIONAL STUDENT CENTER

THE METROPOLITAN MUSEUM OF ART ★

CENTRAL PARK

CENTRAL PARK

UPPER WEST SIDE

RIVERSIDE DR

WEST END AVE

CENTRAL PARK WEST

COLUMBUS AVE

12TH AVE

BROADWAY

Riverside Park

Hudson River

UPPER EAST SIDE

CENTRAL PARK EAST

MADISON AVE

PARK AVE

LEXINGTON AVE

3RD AVE

1ST AVE

YORK AVE

FDR DRIVE

CENTRAL PARK ZOO ★

DANIEL ▼

UPTOWN

QUEENSBORO BRIDGE

CENTRAL PARK BIKE TOURS ■

THE MUSEUM OF MODERN ART (MOMA) ◻

KING COLE BAR ▼

11TH AVE

8TH AVE

9TH AVE

THE HALAL GUYS ▼

LA GRENOUILLE ▼

ESS-A-BAGEL ▼

THE POD HOTEL ●

HELLS KITCHEN

CITIZENM ●

BROADWAY SHOWS ◻

414 HOTEL ●

BROADWAY AT TIMES SQUARE HOTEL ●

TIMES SQUARE ★

SHAKE SHACK ▼

GRAND CENTRAL TERMINAL/ GRAND CENTRAL OYSTER BAR ★

CHRYSLER BUILDING

MIDTOWN

Bryant Park

BROADWAY

7TH AVE

6TH AVE

5TH AVE

MADISON AVE

PARK AVE

3RD AVE

2ND AVE

1ST AVE

LEXINGTON AVE

FDR DRIVE

LINCOLN TUNNEL
LINCOLN TUNNEL

QUEENS-MIDTOWN TUNNEL

Herald Square

EMPIRE STATE BUILDING ■

NEW YORK BUDGET INN ■

CHELSEA

11TH AVE

10TH AVE

East River

Madison Square Park

AMERICAN DREAM BED AND BREAKFAST ●

THE HIGH LINE ◻

BROADWAY

GRAMERCY TAVERN ▼

PETE'S TAVERN ▼

0   500 yds
0   500 m

LOS TACOS NO. 1 ▼

CHELSEA PINES INN ●

Union Square Park

© AVALON TRAVEL

itself, with an impressive food hall and a range of shops along the lower concourse. Many locals stop in even without a train to catch, as the beloved Grand Central Oyster Bar is a longtime favorite restaurant.

★ The High Line

A triumph in innovative urban planning, **The High Line** (Gansevoort St. and Washington St. to W. 34th St., between 10th Ave. and 11th Ave., 212/500-6035, www.thehighline.org, Dec.-Mar. daily 7am-7pm, Apr.-May and Oct.-Nov. daily 7am-10pm, June-Sept. daily 7am-11pm) is a picturesque 1.45-mile stretch of public walkways, sundecks, and gardens, built atop an elevated rail bed that runs along Manhattan's west side. Cutting through the Chelsea gallery district and offering views of Midtown skyscrapers on one side and the Hudson River on the other, the park is open year-round (and fully accessible by wheelchair). A vestige of the neighborhood's industrial past, the

elevated railway was built in the 1930s, replacing the street-level freight trains that carried goods from the Meatpacking District to the warehouses and docks farther north. After falling into disuse in the 1980s, the structure was threatened with demolition (most of the original 13 miles of track were destroyed in the 1960s). In response, a local community-based organization, Friends of the High Line, launched a campaign for the its preservation.

Together with the City of New York, Friends of the High Line began long-term planning for a new public park atop the structure. The first segment of The High Line was opened to the public in 2009, with the final stretch, encompassing the former rail yards, completed in 2014.

Since then, The High Line has become a focal point of the neighborhood, with a crop of trendy hotels, great restaurants, and shops opening along its route, in addition to ongoing public art

walking The High Line

projects throughout the park, sponsored by Friends of the High Line. **Free public tours** of The High Line offer a fascinating look at the park's design and artwork, and stargazing evenings take place during summer months; check the website for the schedule.

Times Square

With its crowds, chaos, and iconic bright lights, **Times Square** (between Broadway and 7th Ave., W. 42nd St. and W. 47th St., 212/768-1560, www.timessquarenyc. org) is a massive commercial intersection, shimmering with all of New York's energy and electricity. Lured by the shopping, the theaters, the mega-restaurants, and the occasional street performances, people from all walks of life crowd the sidewalks along Broadway, some of which have expanded pedestrian areas. Larger-than-life billboards have always been a hallmark of Times Square, and nowadays dozens of dazzling, multimedia "spectaculars" vie for attention. Even the police

station and the subway stops sport glittering logos.

Named after the *New York Times* offices on 43rd Street and Broadway, Times Square was originally synonymous with theater, vaudeville, and cabaret. During the Great Depression, Broadway attendance dwindled, and seedier businesses moved in. By the 1960s, Times Square had developed a tawdry and unsafe reputation. However, after a cleanup effort in the 1990s, the area became far more tourist-friendly (if a bit generic), with new landmarks like the Hard Rock Café and Disney Store. More than 330,000 pedestrians are estimated to pass through Times Square every day, some hoping to snag tickets for a same-day show at the TKTS booth, others gathering outside MTV Studios at 1515 Broadway.

One of the most visible new "attractions" in Times Square is the throng of characters—from grinning Lady Liberties to topless women and matted Sesame Street puppets—who charge visitors wanting photos with them. The flamboyant figures aren't without controversy (and they're now confined to "activity zones"), but some have become minor celebrities in their own rights: A strolling, strumming "Naked Cowboy" is a longtime favorite who made headlines by running for president of the United States in 2012 (he's more conservative than one might presume).

★ The Museum of Modern Art (MoMA)

Holding the largest collection of modern art in the world, **The Museum of Modern Art** (11 W. 53rd St., 212/708-9400, www. moma.org, Wed.-Thurs. and Sat.-Mon. 10:30am-5:30pm, Fri. 10:30am-8pm; late June-late Sept. also Tues. 10:30am-5:30pm, $25 adults, $19 seniors, $14 students, free youth 16 and under) has an elegant, minimalist exterior that belies the many vibrant works on display inside. Founded during the Great Depression in 1929, the museum moved to its location

on 53rd Street in 1939. Since then, the building has gone through many alterations; in 2004, the space was totally redesigned by Japanese architect Yoshio Taniguchi. Currently, the museum is planning a massive expansion to two adjoining buildings, including the former American Folk Art Museum.

MoMA's permanent collection and its temporary exhibitions are on display in galleries surrounding a six-story atrium, facing the museum's signature sculpture garden (which is now free and open to the public). To view the permanent collection, head to the 4th and 5th floors' Painting and Sculpture galleries, where you'll find such iconic works as Picasso's *Les Demoiselles d'Avignon* and Van Gogh's *Starry Night,* among other modern masterpieces. The museum continues to acquire works by art superstars, such as Cindy Sherman and Richard Serra, as well as up-and-coming artists. Its temporary exhibitions are almost always worth the trip in themselves. Admission is free every Friday night 4pm to 8pm.

Downtown
★ National September 11 Memorial & Museum

Ten years after the tragedy on September 11, 2001, the former World Trade Center site was reopened as the **National September 11 Memorial** (between Church St. and West Side Hwy., Liberty St. and Vesey St., 212/266-5200, www.911memorial.org, daily 7:30am-9pm), an eight-acre, tree-filled public plaza designed as the centerpiece to a new business and transportation complex. Two elegant pools were built in the footprints of the former Twin Towers, with the names of almost 3,000 victims from the terrorist attacks in New York City, Pennsylvania, and the Pentagon in 2001, as well as the 1993 World Trade Center bombing, etched in bronze panels

Top to bottom: the September 11 Memorial; Statue of Liberty; inside One World Observatory.

Downtown Manhattan

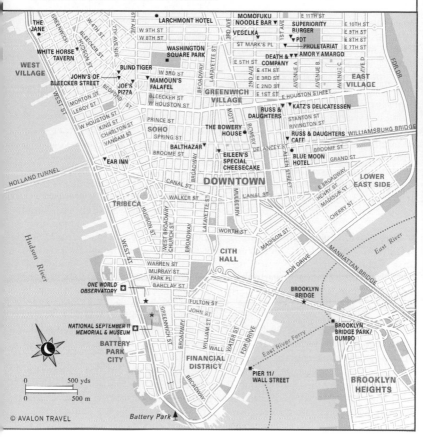

© AVALON TRAVEL

surrounding them. Among the hundreds of white oaks filling the plaza is a lone pear tree that survived the collapse of the towers; after its rehabilitation, the "survivor tree" was returned to the site.

In early 2014, the **National September 11 Memorial & Museum** (Sept.-Apr. daily 9am-7pm, last entry 5pm; closed Sept. 11, $24 adults, $18 seniors, veterans, American students, $15 youth 7-17, under 7 free) opened on the grounds. Filling a spacious, multistory, belowground exhibition space, the museum chronicles the events on the day of the terrorist attacks, history of the Twin Towers, and larger geopolitical context of the time. Exhibits include artifacts recovered from the demolished towers, such as a badly mangled fire truck, and a somber memorial room covered floor-to-ceiling with photos of the victims. Anyone who remembers the events of September 11, 2001, will be moved by the exhibits, but the museum is also a tourist attraction, occasionally inspiring a less-than-somber atmosphere, to the chagrin of some New Yorkers. The high admission price, along with the inclusion of a gift shop inside the museum, also stirred up some controversy among locals when the space first opened. Reserve tickets online to bypass the long line at the entrance.

One World Trade Center

Built on the site of the original World Trade Center, the shining tower of **One World Trade Center** (285 Fulton St., www.onewtc.com, daily 9am-10pm) is the tallest skyscraper in the Western Hemisphere, rising above the Manhattan skyline to a symbolic 1,776 feet. Architect David Childs designed a footprint identical to the original Twin Towers, but the resemblance to the squared-off original buildings ends there: Freedom Tower, as it's often called, is sheathed in glass that reflects the sky and the surrounding buildings.

★ One World Observatory

Between floors 100-102 is **One World Observatory** (844/696-1776, www.oneworldobservatory.com, May-early Sept. daily 9am-10pm, early Sept.-June daily 9am-8pm, $34 adults, $32 seniors, $28 children 6-12, under 6 free), which has stunning views of the city and multimedia presentations on the local history and landscape. Along with the floor-to-ceiling windows, the elevator ride to the top is a highlight; video screens depict the changing NYC landscape as you rise through the floors, passing images of the original, swampy site as it grew into a village, town, and city. The finest time to visit is sunrise and sunset, when all of Manhattan seems to glow. Consider the weather when planning your trip, as the top of the building can be shrouded in mist on cloudy days. Buy tickets online to avoid waiting in line.

★ Ellis Island and the Statue of Liberty

A gift to the United States from France after the Union victory in the Civil War, the **Statue of Liberty** (board ferry at Battery Park/State St. at Battery Pl., visitor information 212/363-3200 or ferry 877/523-9849, www.nps.gov/stli, daily 9:30am-5pm, closed Dec. 25) has become a symbol the country's finest aspirations. Designed by sculptor Frédéric Auguste Bartholdi, with internal structural engineering designed by Gustave Eiffel (of Eiffel Tower fame), the statue arrived in 1885 without a pedestal to support its 225-ton weight. Prompted by the urgings of newspaper magnate Joseph Pulitzer, thousands of Americans made donations to pay for the base's construction, and in 1886, the statue was assembled and dedicated on Bedloe's Island, now known as Liberty Island.

Across the harbor, **Ellis Island** (www.ellisisland.org, daily 9:30am-5pm, closed Dec. 25) was once the nation's main immigration checkpoint. More than 12 million people passed through the site from 1892 until it closed in 1954, though immigration slowed considerably after the 1920s. After years of disuse, the main building of the former immigration complex was completely restored, reopening in 1976 as an interesting museum, displaying photos and artifacts from the island's past.

Statue Cruises (201-604-2800, www.statuecruises.com, reserve and pedestal tickets $18 adults, $14 seniors, $9 children; crown tickets $21 adults, $17 seniors, $14 children) is the only company authorized to provide transportation to Liberty and Ellis Islands. Ferries depart every 15 minutes from Battery Park in New York (and hourly from Liberty State Park in New Jersey), and include full access to both Liberty Island and Ellis Island. While tickets are sold onsite in Battery Park, it's worth booking ahead; tickets to the statue's pedestal are the same price as basic "reserve" access tickets to Liberty Island, but a limited number are given out, and crown tickets are booked months in advance for busy periods.

Entertainment and Events

★ Broadway Shows

The 40 historic theaters classified as Broadway houses are mostly located in the 10 blocks surrounding Times Square, around the eponymous north-south thoroughfare. Broadway shows all play in these houses (productions classified as off-Broadway run in smaller theaters), and most are performed six evenings a week, along with two matinees. Prices run the gamut from a fancy New York hamburger to the cost of a transatlantic flight.

Spending an hour or so in line at **TKTS** (in Times Square, at South Street Seaport, or in downtown Brooklyn) can get you a good deal on discounted same-day tickets for Broadway and off Broadway shows that haven't sold out. Signs near the booth list the possibilities for that day, and the useful **TKTS app** (www.tdf. org) gives real-time updates about what shows are available. Some theaters release same-day tickets and sell day-of standing room tickets. If you're between the ages of 18 and 35, you qualify for discounted tickets through the **Roundabout Theatre Company's HipTix program** (www. roundabouttheatre.com) and **Lincoln Center Theater's LinkTix program** (www. lct.org/linctix).

Shows are constantly changing, but the most successful productions are long-running and spectacular: Favorites include **Wicked** (www.wickedthemusical. com), a musical retelling of the *Wizard of Oz* story, and **Kinky Boots** (www.kinky-bootsthemusical.com), but the historical hip-hop show **Hamilton** (www.hamilton-broadway.com) is easily the hottest ticket on the street (and the hardest to get; the breakaway success and Tony Awards monster has broken records with its $850 premium tickets).

Beyond the shows themselves, Broadway has a fascinating history stretching back to the early 20th century (with lots of backstage drama and rumored hauntings). Unfortunately, most of the theaters are closed to the public unless you're attending a show, so the best way to explore Broadway lore is on tours—they don't grant inside access to theaters, but are a fun way to learn about show business in New York. One of the best is offered by **Broadway Up Close** (917/841-0187, www.broadwayupclose. com, $35 adults, $30 children 12 and under), with a 1.75-hour walking tour led by professional actors who give enthusiastic renditions of Broadway history and gossip.

Nightlife
Classic NYC Bars

The poet Dylan Thomas drank his last (18) whiskeys at the **White Horse Tavern** (567 Hudson St., 212/989-3956, Sun.-Thurs. 11am-1:30am, Fri.-Sat. 11am-3:30am, cash only), an atmospheric Greenwich Village bar that's been frequented by a who's who of literary legends, from James Baldwin and Norman Mailer to an entire cadre of Beat poets. The food is dubious, but the beer and whiskey are cheap. Find something entirely different at **King Cole Bar** (2 E. 55th St., 212/753-4500, www.stregisnewyork. com, Mon.-Sat. 11:30am-1am, Sun. noon-midnight) in the St. Regis Hotel, where you can sip a very expensive cocktail with a well-heeled Midtown crowd. The real highlight, though, is getting to take in the stunning Maxfield Parrish mural that provides the finest bar backdrop in the city.

All dark wood and pressed-tin ceilings, **Pete's Tavern** (129 E. 18th St., 212/473-7676, www.petestavern.com, daily 11am-2:30am) is one of the oldest bars in New York City. The writer O. Henry was a regular here, and it remains a cozy place to duck off the sidewalk for a beer. Another bar that jostles for position as oldest in the city is the raucous **Ear**

Inn (326 Spring St., 212/226-9060, www. earinn.com, daily 11:30am-4am), which has served time as a sailor and longshore workers' bar, Prohibition-era speakeasy, and all-around time capsule. Come here for a colorful cross section of the city and live music some nights.

Craft Beer and Cocktail Bars

Three of Manhattans best cocktail bars are strolling-distance apart in the East Village: Bartenders in suspenders and snappy bow ties serve lengthy apprenticeships before ever pouring a drink at **Death & Company** (433 E. 6th St., 212/388-0882, www.deathandcompany. com, Sun.-Thurs. 6pm-2am, Fri.-Sat. 6pm-3am), whose creative cocktail recipes are unusual and intensive—think eyedroppers, beakers, and unpronounceable ingredients. Tiny **Amor y Amargo** (443 E. 6th St., 212/614-6818, www.amoryamargony.com, Sun.-Thurs. 5pm-1am, Fri.-Sat. 5pm-2am) is just steps away and specializes in esoteric bitters and equally bitter *amari* apertifs with Italian flair. In-the-know patrons enter **PDT**—it stands for "please don't tell"—through the vintage phone booth in the back of **Crif Dogs** (113 St. Mark's Place, 212/614-0386, www. pdtnyc.com, Sun.-Thurs. 6pm-2am, Fri.-Sat. 6pm.-3am). Decor is updated speakeasy chic, cocktails are extraordinary, and reservations are a good idea.

Plenty of Manhattanites got their craft beer baptism at **Blind Tiger** (281 Bleecker St., 212/462-4682, www.blindtigeralehouse.com, daily 11:30am-4am), an unpretentious-looking draft joint with a very respectable brew list and knowledgeable bartenders. Skinny as a pilsner glass, **Proletariat** (102 St. Mark's Place, 212/777-6707, www.proletariatny.com, Mon.-Thurs. 5pm-2am, Fri.-Sun. 2pm-2am) is another craft beer gem that pulls offbeat brews from all over.

Festivals and Events

It's hard to find a weekend in New York without some kind of festival happening, from the massive and colorful **Puerto Rican Day Parade** (www.nprdpinc.org, second Sun. every June) to arts celebrations of all kinds, including the prestigious **New York Film Festival** (www. filmlinc.org/nyff, late Sept.-early Oct.). A few standouts include the iconic **Macy's Parade** on Thanksgiving Day (212/494-2922, www.macys.com/parade) and **Rockefeller Center Christmas Tree Lighting Ceremony** (212/632-3975, www. rockefeller.com/events). People from around the United States watch the **Times Square New Year's Eve** (www.newyearseve.nyc) celebration, and the wonderfully energetic **NYC Pride** (212/807-7433, www.nycpride.org, June) event is one of the best in the country.

Unless you're planning a trip around one of these destination events, however, it's worth simply checking through the city's event listings. A good place to start is the *New York Times* **Arts and Entertainment Guide** (www.nytimes. com/events). You can also pick up a free copy of the *Village Voice* (www.villagevoice.com/calendar), or check out **NYC. com**. Magazine *Time Out New York* (www. timeout.com/newyork) also offers extensive weekly listings.

Shopping

The classic place to shop New York's elegant department stores is **5th Avenue,** between 49th and 60th Streets, where behemoths like **Bergdorf Goodman** (754 5th Ave., 212/7533-7300, www.bergdorfgoodman.com, Mon.-Sat. 10am-8pm, Sun. 11am-7pm) and **Tiffany & Co.** (727 5th Ave., 212/755-8000, www.tiffany. com, Mon.-Sat. 10am-7pm, Sun. noon-6pm) line the iconic street.

To experience the city's more creative side, head to **SoHo** (the shopping district is bordered by Canal and Houston Streets, and Sullivan and Lafayette Streets), where name brand and indie boutiques abound and a gallery-like

One Day in Brooklyn

Once a working-class enclave, Brooklyn today is a hipster darling and creative hot spot—a destination in its own right.

Morning
Frequent subway trains link Manhattan and Brooklyn, but it's far more fun to arrive on the **East River Ferry** (800/533-3779, www.eastriverferry.com, one-way $4 weekdays, $6 weekends, $1 bicycle surcharge). For a sightseeing trip down the East River (a more direct boat departs from Pier 11/Wall St.), catch the ferry at East 34th Street/Midtown. If you've gotten an early start, hop off in **Williamsburg** (N. 6th St./N. Williamsburg ferry stop) to explore this legendary hipster haven en route to other parts of Brooklyn. Walk up **North 6th Street,** which is packed with restaurants and shops, and then, three blocks from the water, turn onto one of the neighborhood's trendiest strips, **Bedford Avenue.**

The other classic way to reach Brooklyn is by **walking across the Brooklyn Bridge,** a 1.3-mile trip with amazing views. The longest suspension bridge in the world when it opened in 1883, the Brooklyn Bridge remains one of the city's most important landmarks. From Manhattan, access it from the Brooklyn Bridge/City Hall metro station. Budget an hour for the walk, as the pedestrian lane can be crowded.

Continue by foot or ferry (Brooklyn Bridge Park/DUMBO stop) to **DUMBO** (that's "down under the Manhattan bridge overpass"), the perfect place to take in Brooklyn's creative culture. The blocks between the Manhattan and Brooklyn Bridges afford plentiful places to stop, but don't miss **Mighty Tanaka** (111 Front St., #224, www.mightytanaka.com, Wed.-Sun. noon-6pm), which specializes in street art, or supercool gallery **Smack Mellon** (92 Plymouth St., www.smackmellon.org, Wed.-Sun. noon-6pm).

Afternoon
Duck back under the bridge to reach **Brooklyn Bridge Park,** which has winding paths along the **East River Waterfront,** an ideal spot for a picnic

and people-watching: Find supplies at **Foragers Market** (56 Adams St., 718/801-8400, www.foragersmarket. com, Mon.-Fri. 8am-10pm, Sat. 9am-10pm, Sun. 9am-9pm), or call ahead for a thin pie from **Juliana's Pizza** (19 Old Fulton St., 718/596-6700, www.julianaspizza. com, lunch daily 11:30am-3:15pm, dinner Sun.-Thurs. 4pm-10pm and Fri.-Sat. 4pm-10:30pm, $17-32). Afterward, grab a locally made scoop at the **Brooklyn Ice Cream Factory** (1 Water St., 718/246-3963, www. brooklynicecreamfactory.com, daily noon-10pm, $4-7), which you can lick on the way to **Brooklyn Heights,** an upscale neighborhood with some of the borough's classic brownstone houses (some of the best are along **Willow** and **Cranberry St.**).

Hop a subway train (lines 2 or 3) at the nearby Clark Street station and get off at the Grand Army Plaza stop, continuing on foot into **Prospect Park,** a 585-acre enclave. Amble aimlessly or explore the park's attractions, like the wonderful **Brooklyn Botanic Garden** (990 Washington Ave., 718/623-7200, www. bbg.org, Tues.-Fri. 8am-6pm, Sat.-Sun. 10am-6pm, $12 adults, $6 seniors and students 12 and over, under 12 free) or **Brooklyn Museum** (200 Eastern Pkwy., 718/638-5000, www.brooklynmuseum. org, Fri.-Sun. and Wed. 11am-6pm, Thurs. 11am-10pm, $16 adults, $10 seniors and students, youth 19 and under free), which has old-world masterpieces and contemporary art.

Evening
Park Slope, the tree-lined neighborhood on Prospect Park's northwest side, is a great spot to grab a coffee at local roaster **Gorilla Coffee** (472 Bergen St., 347/987-3766, www.gorillacoffee.com, Mon.-Sat. 7am-9pm, Sun. 8am-9pm, $2-7), high-end deli sandwich at **BKLYN Larder** (228 Flatbush Ave., 718/783-1250, www. bklynlarder.com, Mon.-Fri. 8am-9pm, Sat. 8am-8pm, Sun. 8am-7pm, $9-13), or drink at tire-shop-turned-bar **Mission Dolores** (249 4th Ave., 347/547-5606, www.missiondolores.com, Mon.-Tues. 4pm-2am, Wed.-Thurs. 2pm-2am, Fri. 2pm-4am, Sat. 12:30pm-4am, Sun. 12:30pm-2am, $6-12).

minimalism recalls the area's past as an arts district. Two favorite stops for local fashionistas are **Opening Ceremony** (35 Howard St., 212/219-2688, www.openingceremony.com, Mon.-Wed. and Fri.-Sat. 11am-8pm, Thurs. 10am-9pm, Sun. noon-7pm), and **A.P.C.** (131 Mercer St., 212/966-9685, www.apc.fr, Mon.-Thurs. 11am-7:30pm, Fri.-Sat. 11am-8pm, Sun. noon-6pm), which share a minimalist aesthetic and a passionate following.

On the **Lower East Side** (Orchard St. and Ludlow St., between E. Houston St. and Rivington St.), small storefronts sell the latest in urban gear and cutting-edge fashion, like ultramodern sneakers and graphic tees. Graffiti artist Claw Money sells her own line of street-inspired fashion at **Claw and Co.** (101 Delancy St., 212/995-2440, www.clawandco.com, daily noon-7:30pm), and a collective of local designers displays their work in **The Dressing Room** (75a Orchard St., 212/966-7330, www.thedressingroomnyc.com, Tues.-Wed. 1pm-midnight, Thurs.-Sat. 1pm-2am, Sun. 1:30pm-8pm), which is also a bar.

Meanwhile, pretty boutiques displaying sweet frocks are the norm along the tree-lined streets of **Nolita** (Mulberry St. to Elizabeth St., between Broome St. and Houston St.). Find chic designs with a bit of grit at Anya Ponorovskaya (251 Elizabeth St., 212/966-9650, www.apnorovskaya.com, Wed.-Mon. 11am-8pm, Tues. 11am-7pm), and a fragrance to match from the custom scents at Le Labo (233 Elizabeth St., 212/219-2230, www.lelabofragrances.com, daily 11am-7pm).

Sports and Recreation

Parks
Central Park is New York's most extraordinary green space, but there are parks scattered throughout the city. Occupying the southernmost tip of Manhattan,

Top to bottom: The Pond in Central Park; Manhattan skyline; Yankee Stadium.

25-acre **Battery Park** (State St. at Battery Pl., 212/344-3491, www.thebattery.org) is the jumping-off point for visitors headed to Liberty and Ellis Islands. The park itself features sculptures, harbor-facing benches, and the Castle Clinton National Monument, a small sandstone fort that was the first U.S. immigration center, which is adjacent to the site of the earliest Dutch fort in New Amsterdam. Weary Wall Street workers jog off stress on the **Battery Park City Esplanade** (212-267-9700, www.bpcparks.org) along the Hudson River.

Washington Square Park (between W. 4th St. and Waverly Pl., University St. and Macdougal St., 212/639-9675, www.nycgovparks.org) is a Greenwich Village institution, attracting dog-walking celebrities, boa constrictor-wearing locals, NYU students, and fire-juggling street performers. Its famous triumphal arch stands at the foot of 5th Avenue.

Spectator Sports
From the **Yankees** to the **Mets** and the **New York Knickerbockers,** New York City's sports include some of the most recognizable, best-loved, and widely hated teams in the United States (sometimes all at once). The baseball teams play a hectic schedule of up to five games a week, so it's often possible to get tickets a day or two before the game. Head to **Yankee Stadium** (1 E. 161st St., Bronx) in the Bronx to see the **Yankees** (718/293-4300, www.newyork.yankees.mlb.com, tickets from $20), one of the city's two Major League baseball teams. The **New York Mets** (718/507-8499, www.newyork.mets.mlb.com, tickets from $20) play at **Citi Field** (123-01 Roosevelt Ave., Queens), near LaGuardia Airport. When choosing seats, it's worth avoiding the very cheapest tickets in the stadium's 400 level, where the ball is barely visible, and spend the money to sit in the 100 or 200 level, where tickets start at $50.

The **New York Knickerbockers** (877/695-3865, www.nba.com/knicks,

tickets from $81), or Knicks, are one of just two founding NBA teams still based in their original city—the word *knicker-bocker* refers to early Dutch settlers who wore their pants rolled up above their knees. This team plays home games at **Madison Square Garden** (4 Pennsylvania Plaza), sometimes called the "Mecca of Basketball," and attending a game there is a classic New York experience. If you'd like to catch a sports game in the city, and aren't too picky about who you see, check the resale site **Stub Hub** (www.stubhub.com) for last-minute deals.

Food

New York City overflows with amazing food options, from roadside "street meat" carts slinging gyros and hot dogs to high-end institutions and foodie hot spots. Narrowing down the choices is almost impossible, as the restaurant scene seems to change daily. Some places, however, serve meals worthy of planning a trip around, whether you're splashing out for the dinner of a lifetime, finding wiseguy joints that feel like NYC movie sets, or just visiting New York's culinary touchstones.

Uptown
Artfully choreographed service, refined contemporary French cuisine, and a delightfully elegant atmosphere keep ★ **Daniel** (60 E. 65th St., 212/288-0033, www.danielnyc.com, Mon.-Sat. 5:30pm-10:30pm, tasting menu $230) among the finest restaurants in the United States. This is an opulent, reserve-a-month-ahead destination for a memorable evening.

Midtown
Before food trucks became as ubiquitous as artisanal doughnuts, ★ **The Halal Guys** (W. 53rd St. at 6th Ave., 347/527-1505, www.thehalalguys.com, Sun.-Thurs. 10am-4am, Fri.-Sat.

10am-5:30am, $5-9) were slinging gyros and chicken over rice to a devoted following of Muslim cabdrivers. The little food cart has grown into a chain, but locals and tourists still love the original location for filling, cheap food in Midtown at (almost) any hour. Don't forget to ask for extra white sauce.

As classic as Grand Central itself, the landmark **Grand Central Oyster Bar** (Grand Central Terminal, Lower Level, 212/490-6650, www.oysterbarny.com, Mon.-Fri. 11:30am-9:30pm, Sat. noon-9:30pm, $20-35) serves the freshest of fish in a sprawling, subterranean space with vaulted ceilings. Bustling commuter noise is the backdrop as you cozy up to oysters on the half shell and a glass of champagne, but the most renowned dish is the oyster pan roast, a creamy stew with six Blue Point oysters ladled over triangles of toasted white bread. Not everyone loves it, but it's classic old New York.

A pioneer of farm-to-table, seasonal fare, ★ **Gramercy Tavern** (42 E. 20th St., 212/477-0777, www.gramercytavern.com, Sun.-Thurs. noon-11pm, Fri.-Sat. noon-midnight, tavern menu and dining room lunch $23-30, fixed menu $125) serves gorgeous seasonal food in a casual tavern and more formal dining room. For an affordable version of this exquisite New York destination, come at lunch to order off the à la carte menu, but the kitchen really shines on the nuanced multicourse dinners.

Back when a fancy meal out was synonymous with food from the Continent, **La Grenouille** (3 E. 52nd St., 212/752-1495, www.la-grenouille.com, Tues.-Sat. noon-2:30pm and 5pm-10:30pm, lunch $30-50, prix fixe dinner $148) was the place to see and be seen over quenelles or a soufflé. Old-world flower arrangement and manners remain at this elegant restaurant, and the food is exquisitely unreconstructed. Don't fail to order the garlicky, delicate, namesake frog legs.

Some of New York's finest turn out at **Ess-a-Bagel** (831 3rd Ave., 212/980-1010, www.ess-a-bagel.com, under $15), where police officers rub elbows with lawyers at tiny faux-marble tables. The smoked fish and spreads leave most competitors' versions in the dust.

Now a chain of counter-service burger restaurants, **Shake Shack** (691 8th Ave., 646/435-0135, www.shakeshack.com, daily 11am-midnight, $5-10) first enchanted New Yorkers from a cart set up in Midtown's Madison Square Park with its very good, affordable burgers and creamy frozen custard. You can find the Shake Shack all over the city now, but the location near Times Square is particularly welcome in that sea of overpriced, touristy table mills.

Downtown

In 1971, falafel was pretty darn exotic for the many Greenwich Village residents, who took their first bite at **Mamoun's Falafel** (119 Macdougal St., 212/674-8685, www.mamouns.com, daily 11am-5am, $3.50-12), a friendly Middle Eastern restaurant that still draws crowds of locals. The food is fresh, flavorful, and cheap, and while most come for the standards—falafel sandwiches, shish kebobs, shawarma—the menu also includes *mambrumeh,* a filo pastry that oozes honey and chopped pistachios. There are just a few places to sit in the eatery, but Washington Square Park is just a short walk away.

For the true, hole-in-the-wall New York pizza experience, **Joe's Pizza** (7 Carmine St., 212/255-3946, www.joespizzanyc.com, daily 10am-4:40am, $5-10) is a wonderful option, with its thin, crisp-chewy crusts, an atmospherically grimy dining room, and melted cheese that stretches the length of your arm. Regulars love the pepperoni slice for a quick lunch (and it's worth bringing it to Washington Park for a very New York picnic).

It's easy to see why ★ **Veselka** (144 2nd Ave., 212/228-9682, www.veselka.com, $5-12) is a favorite for hearty Ukrainian fare and people-watching, open 24 hours a day. Eggs Benedict come on top of hefty potato pancakes and short rib pierogi are pillowy and rich, served alongside applesauce, sour cream, and cabbage.

Since David Chang hit the New York culinary scene in 2004, he's been dominating headlines with his edgy cuisine, blending Korean flavors with . . . anything he wants. The East Village's ★ **Momofuku Noodle Bar** (171 1st Ave., www.noodlebar-ny.momofuku.com, lunch Mon.-Fri. noon-4:30pm and Sat.-Sun. noon-4pm, dinner Sun.-Thurs. 5:30pm-11pm and Fri.-Sat. 5:30pm-1am, $14-18) is the original, with spare decor and a menu of steamed buns, noodles, fried chicken, and fermented things that continue to win raves.

From the gruff service to the melt-in-your-mouth pastrami sandwiches (on rye, of course!), ★ **Katz's Delicatessen** (205 E. Houston St., 212/254-2246, Mon.-Wed. 8am-10:30pm, Thurs. 8am-midnight, Fri.-Sat. 24 hrs, Sun. noon-10:30pm, $16-23) is a legend. In the years since it opened in 1888, sandwiches have gotten a bit pricey, but they're enormous (although it's possible to order a half sandwich), truly delicious, and thoroughly old-school. Take a number, then guard it with your life until you leave the restaurant—pay on the way out.

Another Lower East Side behemoth, ★ **Russ & Daughters** (179 E. Houston St., 212/475-4880, www.russanddaughters.com, Mon.-Fri. 8am-8pm, Sat. 8am-7pm, Sun. 8am-5:30pm, $3-12) is a shop, not a restaurant, but this is the place to go for a bagel-and-lox picnic to rule them all. Grab a ticket when you step in the door of the "appetizing store," which has smoked and cured fish, caviar, bagels from the Bagel Hole in Brooklyn, and enough babka and rugelach for a month of Sundays. The same family also runs the appealing **Russ & Daughters Cafe** (127 Orchard St., 212/475-4880, www.russanddaughters.com, Mon.-Fri. 10am-10pm, Sat.-Sun. 8am-10pm) nearby, if you'd like your food on a plate.

A SoHo icon, ★ **Balthazar** (80 Spring St., 212/965-1414, www.balthazarny.com, breakfast Mon.-Fri. 7:30am-11:30am and Sat.-Sun. 9am-4pm, lunch Mon.-Fri. noon-4:30pm, dinner Sun.-Thurs. 5:30pm-midnight and Fri.-Sat. 5:30pm-1am, $20-50) serves wonderful bistro fare to a mix of celebrities, local power brokers, and ladies who lunch. The experience easily justifies the prices.

The coal-fired brick ovens at ★ **John's of Bleecker Street** (278 Bleecker St., 212/243-1680, www.johnsbrickovenpizza.com, Sun.-Thurs. 11:30am-11:30pm, Fri.-Sat. 11:30am-midnight, pizzas $20-30) have been turning out thin, crispy pies topped with traditional ingredients for almost a century. It's a classic pizza joint with wooden booths and pitchers of beer, and a strong contender for best old-school pizza in the city.

Vegetarian comfort food is infused with verve and a little of chef-owner (and drummer) Brooks Headley's punk rock spirit at **Superiority Burger** (430 E. 9th St., 212/256-1192, www.superiorityburger.com, Wed.-Mon. 11:30am-10pm, $5-9), which has a tiny menu and just a few places to sit. Since opening in 2015 it's won accolades from eaters of all stripes, and it's a bargain for some of the most creative meat-free food around.

In a city not known for great Mexican food, **Los Tacos No. 1** (75 9th Ave., 212/256-0343, www.lostacos1.com, daily 11am-9pm, $8-10) is an island of authentic, street-style tacos. *Adobada* tacos and carne asada are favorites here, as are the giant vats of creamy, sweet *horchata*. No seating.

Anyone on a mission to find New York City's best cheesecake would do well to start at **Eileen's Special Cheesecake** (17 Cleveland Pl., 212/966-5585, www.eileenscheesecake.com, Mon.-Fri. 9am-9pm, Sat.-Sun. 10am-7pm, $3-6), where the slices are ultrarich and fluffy. Miniature versions make it dangerously easy to try all flavors, from a plain version topped with strawberries to the luscious salted caramel.

Accommodations

Uptown

If you're between the ages of 15 and 35, the **International Student Center** (38 W. 88th St., 212/787-7706, www.nystudent-center.org, 8- or 10-bed dorms $50) is a convivial budget option that recalls the early years of hosteling: homey, ad hoc decor, a good-size kitchen and common space, and no wireless Internet or air-conditioning. It's wonderfully convenient to Central Park and public transport.

Midtown
Hostels

With a perfect location two blocks from the 33rd Street subway station, ★ **New York Budget Inn** (200 E. 34th St., 212/689-6500, www.newyorkbudgetinn.com, four-bed dorms $65-75, private rooms $80-120 with shared bath, $160 with private bath) is the best of Manhattan's flock of hostels. Four-bed dorms are utilitarian but very clean, with enough shared bathrooms that they never seem crowded. Private rooms have single beds, double beds, or three bunk beds, some with en suite, private baths. There's no real common space for meeting other travelers, which means you have to make friends in true, New York style—over the breakfast of coffee and doughnuts served in the lobby.

$100-200

Stylish, artful touches elevate the budget-friendly ★ **American Dream Bed and Breakfast** (168 E. 24th St., 646/884-3881, $110 s, $168 d, $192 t), which has minimalist private rooms and shared bathrooms. A breakfast of homemade waffles is served with fruit, cereal, toast, and hot drinks, and snacks are available throughout the day. The rooms, which have a double-single bunk bed, all come with air-conditioning, television, and a heater, but try to book one with a window, as the windowless versions are a bit claustrophobic.

$200-300

In the spirit of New York, ★ **The Pod Hotel** (230 E. 51st St. or 145 E. 39th St., 212/355-0300, www.thepodhotel.com, $250-280) uses thoughtful design to compensate for cramped quarters. Super-small, economical guest rooms are clean and brightly decorated, and the cheerful lobby has a backpacker-cool vibe. Rooms all have televisions, safes, iPod docks, and individually controlled heating and cooling units. The location on 39th Street has a super-hip in-house restaurant, Salvation Taco, run by Michelin-starred celebrity chef April Bloomfield.

Just one block away from lights, cameras, and action at Times Square, the **Broadway at Times Square Hotel** (129 W. 46th St., 800/567-7720, $250-290) has modern (if forgettable) style and an unbeatable location, particularly if you're planning to spend a late night out at the theater. All rooms have coffeemakers, televisions, air-conditioning, and safes, and some have a refrigerator and microwave. Continental breakfast is included.

Over $300

It's hard to believe that bed-and-breakfast **414 Hotel** (414 W. 46th St., 212/399-0006, www.414hotel.com, $325-360), located on a quiet tree-lined street, is a few blocks from Times Square. The rooms, many overlooking a small patio, are clean and stylish.

Ultracool and filled with contemporary art, ★ **citizenM** (218 W. 50th, 212/461-3638, www.citizenm.com, $220-380) has free movies, 24-hour snacks, rain showers, and utterly enormous beds. The location right on Times Square is in the heart of the action downtown, but a gym, yoga terrace, and rooftop bar with panoramic views would make it easy to never leave the premises.

Downtown
$100-200
Simple rooms and shared bathrooms keep prices low at the **Larchmont Hotel** (27 W. 11th St., 212/989-1333, www.larchmonthotel.com, $145-165), which is tucked away on a quiet side street in Greenwich Village. A continental breakfast is served in the cramped basement dining room, and while everything inside has seen better days, the price is hard to beat, and the building itself is an early 20th-century Beaux-Arts charmer.

Itty-bitty rooms accommodate little more than a bed and a wall-mounted flat-screen TV at ★ **The Jane** (113 Jane St., 212/924-6700, www.thejanenyc.com, $135-325) but the enchanting old-fashioned design, fantastic location in the Meatpacking District, free bike rental, and low nightly rates offset the reduced space. Rooms are inspired by boat and train cabins, encouraging the sense that the miniscule spaces are something of an adventure. The Captains Cabins have private baths, all others share clean hallway bathrooms.

In trendy little Nolita, ★ **The Bowery House** (220 Bowery, 212/837-2373, www.theboweryhouse.com, $89-99 s, $119-164 d) is one of Manhattan's more unusual options. Miniscule, private "cabins" have lattice ceilings that let in the central air-conditioning and quite a bit of noise from other residents (earplugs are provided). This was once temporary housing for WWII veterans, then became something of a flophouse for the neighborhood. These days, though, hip common spaces are decked out with custom artwork, and there's a rooftop garden with views of the Brooklyn Bridge and Chrysler Building. If the word "flophouse" evokes New York's gritty, poetic history, this is just the place for you—if not, look elsewhere.

$200-300
Tenement dwellers never had it so good: A former tenement, the **Blue Moon Hotel** (100 Orchard St., 212/533-9080, www.bluemoon-nyc.com, dorms $70-85, private rooms $254-460) has been transformed into a boutique hotel that retains bits and bobs of Victorian charm, such as pressed tin, newspaper clippings, and a lobby ideal for catching up on the *New York Times*. The rooms themselves are pretty standard fare, and the continental breakfast is skimpy, but you're just around the corner from Russ & Daughters.

Over $300
Vintage movie posters give the rooms at the **Chelsea Pines Inn** (317 W. 14th St., 888/546-2700, www.chelseapinesinn.com, $270-360) a whimsical feel, and the friendly owners make it a charming place to say (if you can get past the brownstone's three flights of stairs). The guest lounge, indoor greenhouse, and enclosed patio garden are green havens in this bustling neighborhood, and they're always stocked with espresso, tea, snacks, and coffee. An ample cold breakfast is served.

Near JFK Airport
As is usual, the hotels near JFK are entirely forgettable, but all offer airport shuttles and some are a bit more appealing than the competition.

$100-200
Lay your head at the **Days Inn Jamaica-JFK Airport** (144-26 153rd Ct., Jamaica, 718/527-9025, www.daysinn.com, $170-210) for basic, clean rooms in a somewhat scruffy neighborhood close to the airport. Free parking is available until checkout time, and a 24-hour shuttle leaves for the airport every hour on the half hour, and returns from the airport every 20-30 minutes. An ample (if not particularly appealing) free breakfast is served in the lobby.

$200-300
Efficient and well-run, the **Courtyard New York JFK Airport** (145-11 N. Conduit Ave., Jamaica, 718/848-2121, www.

marriott.com, $244-280) is a noticeable step up from the cheaper options. Bits of colorful flair leaven the corporate-feeling rooms and common spaces, and there's a fitness room and small bistro that sells continental and hot breakfasts. Limited parking is available at $22 per night, and a 24-hour shuttle makes the short trip to the airport every 30 minutes.

Updates in 2015 make the **Hampton Inn JFK** (144-10 135th Ave., Jamaica, 718/322-7933, www.hamptoninn3.hilton.com, $220-280) a comfortable place to stay, with free hot breakfasts, an onsite gym, and 24-hour shuttle. Shuttle service from the airport to the hotel is on-demand (though some travelers have complained that service is not always prompt), and shuttles to the airport leave every 30 minutes 4am-2pm, and every hour from 2pm-4am. Valet parking is $21.

Information and Services

Information

NYC & Company (810 7th Ave., 212/484-1200, www.nycgo.com, daily 9am-5pm) is the official tourism organization in the city. Maps, brochures, and other informational materials are available at the visitors centers.

Attraction Passes

A dizzying array of sightseeing passes are available for exploring New York, and choosing one that's well suited to your plans can offer substantial savings. The **New York City Pass** (www.citypass.com, $116 adults, $92 youth 6-17) includes admission to six sites over nine days (though the list of admissions is padded by including the technically by-donation Met and American Museum of Natural History), so it is only worthwhile if you're planning to visit all the sites on the list. For shorter trips to the city, a better option is

the **New York City Explorer Pass** (www.smartdestinations.com, from $77 adults, $60 children), which allows you to select the sites you're interested in; this pass is an especially good value if you plan to do a hop-on, hop-off bus tour.

Services
Emergencies

For immediate emergency medical and police service, dial **911.**

These hospitals operate 24-hour emergency rooms: **Lenox Hill Hospital** (100 E. 77th St., 212/434-2000 or 212/434-3030, www.lenoxhillhospital.org), **Mount Sinai Hospital** (Madison Ave. at 100th St., 212/241-6500, www.mountsinai.org), and **St. Luke's-Roosevelt Hospital** (1000 10th Ave. at 59th St., 212/523-4000, www.stlukeshospitalnyc.org).

Getting Around

Public Transit

The **subway** is the cheapest and often fastest way to get around. Riders pay their fare via **MetroCards,** which are sold in machines in every subway station. It costs $2.75 for a single-ride card, though you'll save both time and money by buying more than one ride at a time. The pay-per-ride MetroCard, which can be loaded up with $5-100, gives you a 5 percent bonus on your purchase and includes automatic free transfer between subways and buses. A weekly subway pass costs $31, and a 30-day pass costs $116.50; passes allow unlimited rides for one person. Large route maps are mounted at all stations and are available for free at any subway station booth. Subway line and schedule information is also available at the **Metropolitan Transportation Authority** website (www.mta.info) and information line (718-330-1234), as well as via the MTA's smartphone app, the Weekender.

MetroCards are also accepted on city buses, as is exact change in coins (no pennies or half dollars). The fare for a single ride is $2.75 for local buses and $6.50 on express buses. Transfers to and from connecting buses or subways are free with use of a MetroCard. On buses and subways, up to three children under 44 inches tall ride for free when accompanied by an adult, and seniors and people with disabilities receive a discounted $1.35 fare on regular buses, and $3.25 on express buses, though only at off-peak hours. Most buses have maps posted and wheelchair lifts.

Taxi

Metered **yellow cabs** have an initial $2.50 fare, which increases at $0.50 increments for every one-fifth of a mile traveled or 60 seconds idle. There is a $0.50 surcharge daily 8pm-6am and a $1 surcharge weekdays 4pm-8pm, plus a $0.50 New York state surcharge.

During **rush hour**, it's often faster to take the subway, as hailing a cab can be nearly impossible. At other times, especially at night, taking a cab is the most convenient way to get around. Open cabs tend to cruise for fares on avenues and crosstown arteries, and near hotels, nightclubs, and other crowded areas.

Cabs can be particularly scarce on busy nights like New Year's Eve or during storms. In these instances, it makes good sense to call a car service; rates tend to be comparable to a cab ride. App-based car services like Uber and Lyft are increasingly popular. Here are a few car service options:

- **AJ Luxury Car & Limo** (212-228-1111, www.allencarlimo.com)

- **Carmel Car Service** (212-666-6666 or 866-666-6666, www.carmellimo.com)

- **Dial 7 Car & Limousine Service** (212-777-7777, www.dial7.com)

- **Uber** (www.uber.com)

- **Lyft** (www.lyft.com)

Bike

New and expanded bike paths have made Manhattan a much easier and safer place to traverse by bicycle. In 2013, New York's first bike-share program, **Citi Bike** (855-245-3311, www.citibikenyc.com), began operation, with over 300 stations located across Manhattan and Brooklyn. For riders over the age of 16, Citi Bike offers two short-term rental options, a **24-hour pass** ($12) and **3-day pass** ($24), which can be purchased with a credit card at any Citi Bike station. All Citi Bikes must be returned to a designated station within 30 minutes or risk additional fees. If you want to take a longer ride, you'll need to swap your bike for another one at a designated station, at no cost. You can download the Citi Bike app to your smartphone to locate nearby stations.

Car

Driving around New York City is not for the faint of heart, and parking overnight in Manhattan can rival the cost of a cheap hotel. If you do need to park in New York, it's worth consulting an **NYC parking site** (www.nycbestparking.com), which shows fares in real time, or the free parking app **SpotHero,** which allows you to book discounted sites.

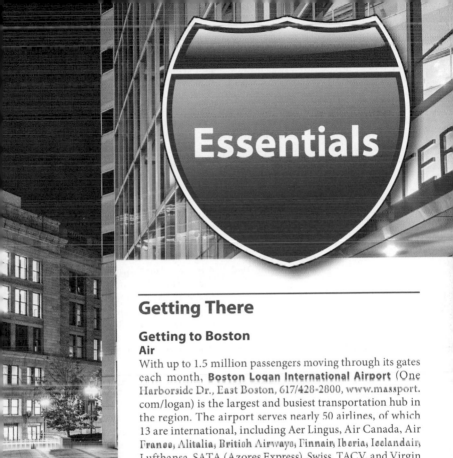

Essentials

Getting There

Getting to Boston
Air

With up to 1.5 million passengers moving through its gates each month, **Boston Logan International Airport** (One Harborside Dr., East Boston, 617/428-2800, www.massport. com/logan) is the largest and busiest transportation hub in the region. The airport serves nearly 50 airlines, of which 13 are international, including Aer Lingus, Air Canada, Air France, Alitalia, British Airways, Finnair, Iberia, Icelandair, Lufthansa, SATA (Azores Express), Swiss, TACV, and Virgin Atlantic Airways. International flights arrive in Terminal E. From the airport, a variety of options take passengers to downtown Boston, which is only a mile away. The most efficient way to get into the city is via taxi, though expect to pay a minimum of $25 for downtown locations, or shared van service to downtown and Back Bay for $20-25 per person.

Far cheaper (and almost as quick) is the **Silver Line bus** (www.mbta.com); inbound rides on SL1 from Logan Airport to Boston's South Station are free and leave from stops directly in front of each terminal. Buses leave several times an hour, 5am-1am, and reach South Station in 15-25 minutes. If you're continuing to downtown stops or Cambridge, request a free transfer for the MBTA Red Line subway route.

Train

Amtrak (800/872-7245, www.amtrak.com) runs frequent trains along the Northeast corridor to Boston, including the **Acela Express,** the United States' first high-speed service, from New York (3.5 hrs) and Washington DC (6 hrs). Unless you are in a rush, though, it can often make more sense to save $100 and take the **Northeast Regional** service, which also runs to Boston from New York (4.5 hrs) and Washington DC (7 hrs), stopping along the way in New Haven, New London, Providence, and several smaller cities on the Connecticut and Rhode Island coasts.

From the west, Amtrak's **Lake Shore Limited** route offers service to Boston from Buffalo, New York (12 hrs) and Cleveland, Ohio (15 hrs), stopping along the way in Springfield and Worcester in Massachusetts. Connecting to that route, Amtrak's **Adirondack** route offers service between New York City and Montreal, Quebec (12 hrs).

Bus

New England is accessible from many domestic and Canadian locations via **Greyhound Bus Lines** (800/231-2222, www.greyhound.com). Nearby major cities offering service to Boston include New York (4.5 hrs), Philadelphia (7.5 hrs), Montreal (7.5 hrs), Washington DC (10.5 hrs), Buffalo (10.5 hrs), Toronto (14 hrs), and Cleveland (16 hrs). The discounter carrier **Megabus** (www.megabus.com) services many major cities, as well, and booking in advance (particularly on less popular days) can mean very cheap fares. While not the quickest way to travel, the bus can be an attractive alternative for those on a budget or traveling to more rural or remoter regions not served by rail or air.

A good way to search public transport on different carries is the site **Wanderu** (www.wanderu.com), which combines information about trains and buses.

Getting to New York City
Air

Three airports serve New York City: **John F. Kennedy International Airport** (JFK, 718/244-4444), **LaGuardia Airport** (LGA, 718/533-3400), and **Newark Liberty International Airport** (EWR,

973/961-6000) in New Jersey. Coming or going, taxis between JFK and Manhattan have a flat rate of $52, plus a $0.50 New York State surcharge, not including bridge/tunnel tolls and tips. From LaGuardia, taxis charge regular metered fare, with the cost running approximately $25-37, not including tolls and tips to Manhattan, with meters starting at $2.50. From Newark, a taxi charges $17.50 on top of the regular metered fare, plus tolls and tip.

For inexpensive transportation to and from JFK, the Port Authority operates the **AirTrain** (www.panynj.gov/airtrain), a light-rail that connects all airport terminals to the subway system. You can access the AirTrain from the Sutphin Boulevard stop on the E line, or via the Howard Beach stop on the A line (take a train marked "Far Rockaway"). You can also take the Long Island Rail Road from Penn Station to the AirTrain at Jamaica Station. The cost of a one-way trip on the AirTrain is $5. You can pay the fare using a pay-per-ride MetroCard or purchase tickets in the station.

The **Port Authority of New York and New Jersey** (www.panynj.gov) operates booths that provide information on rates and connections to private limousine and van companies. Its **Air-Ride service** (800/247-7433) provides recorded information about bus, shuttle, and private car services from area airports. Shuttle options include **Olympia/Coach Usa Airport Express** (908/354-3330 or 877/863-9275, www.coachusa.com) and **Supershuttle** (212/209-7000 or 800/258-3826, www.supershuttle.com).

Train

Penn Station (33rd St. between 7th Ave. and 8th Ave.) serves passengers arriving on **Amtrak** (800/872-7245 or 212/630-6401, www.amtrak.com) as well as **New Jersey Transit** (973/275-5555 or 718/330-1234, www.njtransit.com), **Long Island Rail Road** (718/217-5477, http://mta.info/lirr), and the subway's A, C, E, 1, 2, and 3 trains. Visitors arrive at New York's other main station, **Grand Central Terminal** (89 E. 42nd St.), via **Metro-North Railroad** (212/532-4900, www.mta.info/mnr) and the 4, 5, 6, 7, and S subway lines (NYC Transit, 718/330-1234).

Bus

The Midtown **Port Authority Bus Terminal** (625 8th Ave., 212/435-7000) is the main bus hub for the city, and services leave for destinations all over New England, including **Greyhound** (800/231-2222, www.greyhound.com), **Peter Pan**, (800/343-9999, www.peterpanbus.com), and discount carrier **Megabus** (www.megabus.com).

A good way to find fares to destinations in New England is on the search site **Wanderu** (www.wanderu.com), which aggregates bus and train schedules with real-time fares.

Road Rules

Car Rental

The major car rental companies have branches at even small airports around New England. To reserve a car in advance, it's often better to use a car rental search aggregator (as with airline tickets), such as **Cheap Tickets** (www.cheaptickets.com) or **Orbitz** (www.orbitz.com). Rentals can be found as cheaply as $15 a day, though more standard rates start at $25 a day. While searching for cars, be aware that one-way rentals often have a surcharge, especially when beginning or ending your trip in a smaller city. Most car rental companies offer several kinds of insurance: The collision damage waiver covers damage to the rental car, and liability covers damage to others, though personal car insurance may already cover this. To rent a car, drivers must be at least 21 years of age with a valid driver's license. Drivers between 21 and 24 years of age may be limited to certain models, and some companies charge a "young driver" fee in addition to the rental price.

Inquire directly with major car rental companies for details: **Alamo** (800/462-5266, www.alamo.com), **Avis** (800/331-1212, www.avis.com), **Budget** (800/527-0700, www.budget.com), **Dollar** (800/800-4000, www.dollar.com), **Enterprise** (800/261-7331, www.enterprise.com), **Hertz** (800/654-3131, www.hertz.com), **National** (800/227-7368, www.nationalcar.com), or **Thrifty** (800/367-2277, www.thrifty.com).

RV Rental

Weeklong RV rentals start at $900, and mileage is generally a supplemental charge. Check with **Cruise America** (800/671-8042, www.cruiseamerica.com) and **USA RV Rentals** (877/778-9569, www.usarvrentals.com) for availability. If beginning and ending your trip in New York City, camper rentals are available from **Escape Campervans** (877/270-8267, www.escapecampervans.com) from $123/day, including 100 miles each day. An RV-accessible campsite can cost upwards of $50. Note that RVs aren't as well suited to New England driving as they are to the wide open roads of the American West.

Many RV rental companies require that drivers be 25 years of age or above, though some allow drivers between 21 and 24 years old for an additional fee. A standard driver's license is sufficient for operating an RV.

Driving Rules

Seat belts are required in all New England states outside of "Live Free or Die" New Hampshire, where they're only required for those under 18 years of age. All states have child safety seat requirements—child safety seats are available as an add-on with any car rental. Talking on a **handheld cell phone** is banned for drivers in New York, Vermont, and New Hampshire, and **texting while driving** is illegal in all New England states.

All states in New England now have

move-over laws that mandate slowing down and changing lanes (when safe) while passing stopped police cars and emergency vehicles. Some Massachusetts, New Hampshire, New York, Rhode Island, and Maine highways have **tolls** ($1-10), so it's worth traveling with cash.

Road Conditions

If traveling in summer and fall, the most challenging road issue is the extensive roadwork that takes place during the snow-free months. Find detailed information about roadwork and **traffic conditions** at www.newengland511. org. State by state information is available for **Massachusetts** (www.massdot. state.ma.us), **New Hampshire** (www. nh.gov/dot), **Maine** (www.maine.gov/ mdot), **Rhode Island** (www.dot.ri.gov), **Connecticut** (www.ct.gov/dot), and **New York** (www.nyc.gov/html/dot).

The two-lane highways that connect much of rural New England can get clogged with traffic, but the only places where it's truly important to plan around the busy times are Boston and New York City. If renting a car, wait until you leave the city to pick it up, and try to avoid the weekday hours of 6am-10am and 3pm-7pm.

When traveling in rural areas, hitting a **deer** or **moose** on the road is a significant concern, especially when driving at dawn or dusk. Slow down, keep an eye on the edge of the road, and pay close attention to the "wildlife crossing" signs denoting animal corridors.

Parking

Outside the tourist hot spots and cities, parking is easy and inexpensive throughout New England. In Boston and New York City, it's worth planning ahead and either avoiding parking by leaving your car outside the city (both cities have long-term parking at commuter train stations) or booking a parking spot in advance. The free app **SpotHero** (www.spothero. com) is a good choice for finding and booking discounted spaces in parking garages throughout both cities.

Many cities have now converted to credit-card meters—some require a ticket be left in the car, and some don't. Many (but not all) meters are free on Sundays. If you're driving an RV, note that large, chain hotels often have parking spots which can accommodate the vehicles, but smaller inns and bed-and-breakfasts may not.

Tolls

Some of the interstates and bridges in New England and New York require tolls, and the state-run systems are a bit of a patchwork, with some requiring cash, a few accepting credit cards, and others using license-plate recognition software. Many toll stations have an express **EZ-Pass** lane (www.e-zpassiag.com), which uses electronic sensors to deduct the toll from a prepaid account; visitors with an EZ-Pass from elsewhere in the United States can use their EZ-Pass in New England with their own vehicle or with a rental vehicle of the same vehicle class.

A few toll locations are transitioning to cashless tolls which operate using either the EZ-Pass or by taking a photo of your license plate and then forwarding on the bill. Unfortunately for rental car drivers, some rental agencies tack on a processing charge to this, adding as much as $5 a day to the tolls. Inquire directly with your rental agency.

International Drivers Licenses

International visitors need to secure an **International Driving Permit** from their home countries before coming to the United States. They should also bring the government-issued driving permit from their home countries. They are expected to be familiar with the driving regulations of the states they will visit. More information is available online: http://ghsa. org/html/stateinfo/bystate/index.html.

Maps and Tourist Information

Each of the destinations covered in this book has tourist information offices stocked with free maps that are great for navigating by car or bicycle. To obtain these maps (and other guides) in advance, contact the tourist offices for each state: **Massachusetts** (www.massvacation.com), **New Hampshire** (www.visitnh.gov), **Maine** (www.visitmaine.com), **Vermont** (www.vermontvacation.com), **Rhode Island** (www.visitrhodeisland.com), **Connecticut** (www.ctvisit.com), and **New York** (www.iloveny.com).

Roadside Assistance

In an emergency, dial **911** from any phone for police and emergency services. The **American Automobile Association** (www.northernnewengland.aaa.com, 800/222-4357) offers roadside assistance including jump-start, towing, and flat tire services. Depending on your situation, it may be more cost-effective to join AAA on the spot than pay out of pocket for a tow truck. If traveling in a rental car, roadside assistance may be offered by your agency.

Visas and Officialdom

Passports and Visas

Visitors from other countries must have a **valid passport** and **visa.** Visitors with current passports from one of the following countries qualify for **visa waivers:** Andorra, Australia, Austria, Belgium, Brunei, Chile, Czech Republic, Denmark, Estonia, Finland, France, Germany, Greece, Hungary, Iceland, Ireland, Italy, Japan, Latvia, Liechtenstein, Lithuania, Luxembourg, Malta, Monaco, the Netherlands, New Zealand, Norway, Portugal, San Marino, Singapore, Slovakia, Slovenia, South Korea, Spain, Sweden, Switzerland, Taiwan, and the United Kingdom. They must apply online with the Electronic System for Travel Authorization at www.cbp.gov and hold a **return plane ticket** to their home countries less than 90 days from their time of entry. Holders of **Canadian passports** don't need visas or waivers. In most countries, the local U.S. embassy can provide a **tourist visa.** Plan for at least two weeks for visa processing, longer during the busy summer season (June-Aug.). More information is available online at http://travel.state.gov.

Embassies and Consulates

New York City and Boston are home to consulates from around the world. Travelers in legal trouble or those who have lost their passports should contact the consulate of their home country immediately. The **U.S. State Department** (www.state.gov) has contact info for all foreign embassies and consulates. The **British Consulate** (www.gov.uk) has offices in the **Boston** area (1 Broadway, Cambridge, 617/245-4500) and **New York City** (845 3rd Ave., 212/745-0200). The **Australian Consulate** has an office in **New York City** (150 East 42nd St., 34th floor, 212/351-6600), and the **Canadian Consulate-General** is in **Boston** (3 Copley Place #400, 617/247-5100) and **New York City** (1251 Avenue of the Americas, 212/596-1628).

Customs

Foreigners and U.S. citizens age 21 or older may import (free of duty) the following: 1L of alcohol, 200 cigarettes (one carton), 50 cigars (non-Cuban), and $100 worth of gifts. International travelers must declare amounts that exceed $10,000 in cash (U.S. or foreign), traveler's checks, or money orders. Meat products, fruits, and vegetables are prohibited due to health and safety regulations.

Travel Tips

Conduct and Customs

The legal **drinking age** in the United States is 21. If you look younger than 35, expect to have your ID checked not only in bars and clubs, but also before you purchase alcohol in restaurants, wineries, and markets. Young-looking international travelers should bring their passports, as some locations may not accept other identification such as international driver's licenses.

Smoking is banned in many places, including bars, clubs, and restaurants. Many hotels, motels, and inns are also nonsmoking. Smokers should request a smoking room when making reservations.

Money

The currency is the **U.S. dollar ($)**. Most businesses accept the **major credit cards** Visa, MasterCard, Discover, and American Express. ATM and debit cards work at many stores and restaurants, and ATMs are available throughout the region. You can **change currency** at any international airport or bank. Currency exchange may be easier in large cities and more difficult in rural and wilderness areas.

Banking hours tend to be 8am-5pm Monday-Friday, 9am-noon Saturday. Never count on a bank being open on Sunday. There are **24-hour ATMs** not only at banks but at many markets, bars, and hotels. A **convenience fee** of $2-4 per transaction may apply.

Internet Access and Cell Service

Wireless Internet is available in most cafés, as well as many other businesses. Local libraries are a good place to find computers with Internet access free of charge, as most make these services available to visitors. Most hotels and bed-and-breakfasts offer free wireless Internet, though some smaller, rural inns may not.

While all New England cities have full cell coverage, many rural areas do not, so it's worth having access to a paper map when traveling through the countryside.

Hotel and Motel Chains

Hotel and motel chains like **Best Western** (800/780-7234, www.bestwestern.com), **Motel 6** (800/557-3435, www.motel6. com), **Days Inn** (800/225-3297, www. daysinn.com), and **Super 8** (800/454-3213, www.super8.com) are easy to find in urban areas. Many offer discount rates (depending on season) and reasonable amenities. Expect higher rates during the summer (June-Sept.). For the most part, it's easiest and cheapest to book these through an online travel site such as www.priceline.com, www.kayak.com, and www.hotels.com.

Traveling with Children

Travel all over New England is quite family-friendly. Most hotels offer cribs in the room upon request, and public transportation and attractions offer discounted fares for children. The majority of restaurants are happy to offer high chairs, and many have kids' menus. Some higher-end bed-and-breakfasts, though, do not welcome younger children, and upscale restaurants may look askance at small diners.

Children will enjoy aquariums, amusement parks, and, perhaps most of all, beaches. Many beaches and parks are equipped with bathrooms. You'll also find several good family-friendly restaurant and hotel options. Generally hotels allow up to four in a room, so be sure to inquire about a suite if necessary.

The main concerns when traveling the highway with children is that the long drive can make them antsy, and the twists and turns can cause nausea, even for parents. Make plenty of stops to allow your young ones to burn off some energy and for everyone to use the bathroom, stretch their legs, and breathe in the fresh air. Bring plenty of car-fun activities to keep your kids busy, like books and travel games.

Senior Travelers

If you are over 60 years of age, ask about potential discounts. Nearly all attractions, amusement parks, theaters, and museums offer discount benefits to seniors. Be sure to have some form of valid identification such as a driver's license or passport.

Access for Travelers with Disabilities

Public transportation in the vast majority of New England is wheelchair-accessible, as are most major hotels, museums, and public buildings. Even many beaches and campgrounds in Massachusetts are accessible, though the remoter the destination, the greater the possibility that it will not be. As common sense would dictate, call ahead and plan accordingly.

The greatest challenge for travelers in wheelchairs in New England may be accessing historic neighborhoods and inns which have not been retrofitted with wider doorways and elevators. Some inns have converted one or more rooms with roll-in showers, while others are completely inaccessible.

Those with permanent disabilities, including the visually impaired, should inquire about a free **Access Pass** (888/275-8747, ext. 3) from the National Park Service. It is offered as part of the America the Beautiful—National Park and Federal Recreational Lands Pass Series. You can obtain an Access Pass in person at any federal recreation site or by submitting a completed application (www.nps.gov/findapark/passes.htm, $10 processing fee may apply) by mail. The pass does not provide benefits for special recreation permits or concessionaire fees.

Gay and Lesbian Travelers

Few regions in the country are friendlier to LGBT visitors than New England. Same-sex marriage is legal in every state, and cities like Boston, Portland, and Providence have significant and thriving gay and lesbian communities. Meanwhile, resort towns such as Provincetown, Massachusetts, and Ogunquit, Maine, are major destinations for LGBT visitors from around the world.

Environmental Concerns

Each state has environmental concerns that involve water pollution, disruption of fish and wildlife habitat, and emissions. You can do your part as a visitor and protect the natural environment by doing the following: Stay on trails and do not stomp on plantlife; utilize pet waste receptacles in pet-friendly campgrounds; protect water sources by camping at least 150 feet from lakes and streams; leave rocks and plants as you find them; light fires only where permitted and use only established fire pits; pack it in, pack it out—check your campsite for garbage and properly dispose of it or take it with you.

Health and Safety

People travel to New England from all over the globe simply to receive care from the area's doctors and hospitals, which are widely regarded as among the best. That said, certain precautions will help you stay as safe as possible. If immediate help is needed, always **dial 911,** otherwise go to the nearest 24-hour hospital emergency room.

Compared with the rest of the nation, New England is relatively low in crime, and many of its rural areas are virtually crime-free. Cities are, not surprisingly, a different story. But even in Boston and New York, if you follow the basic rules of common sense (take precautions in watching your belongings, avoid walking alone late at night, and be aware of

Ticks and Lyme Disease

Forget snakes, bears, and moose—ask a New Englander what wildlife they're scared of, and they'll say **ticks.** The eight-legged creatures are tiny—from the size of a poppyseed to just under 3 millimeters—and easy to miss. Some are carriers of **Lyme disease,** a dangerous bacterial infection. Not all ticks can carry Lyme disease, but the deer tick sometimes does, and it's the most common species in the Northeast. Taking the following precautions will help protect against Lyme:

* Wear long pants tucked into your socks when walking through high grass and bushy areas.

* Use insect repellent that contains DEET, which is effective against ticks.

* Shower within a few hours of coming

inside, and check carefully for ticks. If you find a tick, use tweezers to grasp it near to your skin, and firmly remove without twisting. Don't worry if the mouth parts remain in the skin; once the tick is separated from the body, it can no longer transmit the bacteria that cause Lyme.

Carefully checking for ticks once a day is a good practice. Don't panic if you find a tick, as it takes around 36 hours for the bacteria to spread. The first symptoms of Lyme disease are often flu-like, and occur 3-30 days after infection. They're often accompanied by a rash or bull's-eye redness around the bite. If you experience these symptoms, it's smart to visit a doctor. Prompt treatment of Lyme disease is generally effective, but the disease can be fatal if untreated.

your surroundings), odds are safety won't be a problem.

In the New England countryside, one of the biggest threats to visitors' safety can be their own lack of outdoors savvy and preparedness. Whether summiting White Mountain peaks or on a day hike, it's important to stay aware of weather conditions and bring maps, extra clothes, and sufficient food and water.

Carry your **medical card** and a list of any **medications** you are taking. Keep a **first-aid kit** in your car or luggage, and take it with you when hiking. A good kit should include sterile gauze pads, butterfly bandages, adhesive tape, antibiotic ointment, alcohol wipes, pain relievers for both adults and children, and a multipurpose pocketknife.

Whether you're in a large city, resort area, small town, or even a wilderness area, take precautions against **theft.** Don't leave any valuables in the car. If you must, keep them out of sight in the trunk or a compartment with a lock if available.

Keep wallets, purses, cameras, mobile phones, and other small electronics on your person if possible.

Internet Resources

The websites maintained by state tourism agencies can be surprisingly useful, with tips on finding scenic byways, events, and on-call staff.

New England
Discover New England
www.discovernewengland.org
This site highlights seasonal events and current happenings in every corner of New England, and suggests driving tours and weather information, plus gives a brief primer on each state.

NewEngland.com
www.newengland.com
Run by the folks behind *Yankee* magazine, this site is packed with local

landmarks, recommended itineraries, foliage reports, event listings, and vacation planners.

New England Towns
www.newenglandtowns.org
Read selective, quirky histories of small New England towns, plus little-known facts and statistics.

Fall Foliage Reports
Get in-depth and up-to-date foliage reports on each state, starting in early September and throughout autumn, from the following websites: **Vermont** (www.vermont.com/foliage.cfm), **New Hampshire** (www.visitnh.gov/vacation-ideas/Foliage-Tracker), **Maine** (www.maine.gov/dacf/mfs/projects/fall_foliage), and **Massachusetts** (www.massvacation.com).

Destination Websites
Expect to find basic background information about the destination, plus essentials such as hours, locations, entrance fees, driving directions, and special deals or packages currently offered.

Massachusetts
Greater Boston Convention & Visitors Bureau
www.bostonusa.com
The site provides a full a list of events throughout the year and visitor information on lodging, restaurants, sights, shopping, and transportation.

The Freedom Trail Foundation
www.thefreedomtrail.org
Find tourist info, historical background notes, and the latest news on tours and events for the 16 historical sites that make up Boston's Freedom Trail.

The Berkshires
www.berkshires.org
This site offers lots of advice on dining and lodging in the area, plus other diversions such as spas, concerts, family

outings, outdoor excursions, plus a list of current getaway deals.

Cape Cod Chamber of Commerce
www.capecodchamber.org
Find full business listings, information on where to stay and eat, backgrounds on the 15 towns that make up Cape Cod, help on getting around the area, plus information on golfing, baseball, football, and other sporting in the area on this website.

Nantucket Island
www.nantucket.net
Plan your island vacation with this site's easy listings of local restaurants, hotels and inns, beaches, and museums. There's also plenty of information on where and how to go boating, fishing, golfing, and biking, plus a section on where to take kids around the island.

Martha's Vineyard Island
www.mvy.com
From diving and sailing to horseback riding and beach-going, this site details all there is to do on and around Martha's Vineyard. It also lists accommodations and restaurants, posts a calendar of events and festivals, and provides information on car rentals and ferries, as well as vacation rentals. The last-minute lodging feature of this website is particularly useful.

Maine
Maine Tourism
www.visitmaine.com
This site offers information on everything to see and do in Maine, including fall foliage, outdoor recreation, family-friendly outings, restaurants, shopping, events, and accommodations.

Portland, ME
www.visitportland.com
With coverage that stretches across southern Maine, this site is an excellent resource for trip planning.

Acadia National Park, ME
www.nps.gov/acad

Maps, campground information and booking services, and online passes are available on this site.

New Hampshire
New Hampshire Tourism
www.visitnh.gov

Find all kinds of visitors' information on the state, including local foliage reports, travel itineraries, online photo galleries, deals on seasonal travel packages, and lodging and restaurant listings.

Mt. Washington Valley, NH
www.mtwashingtonvalley.org

Just about anything happening in the valley shows up on this site: local events throughout the year, dogsledding and cross-country skiing—plus how to find the best local crafters and artists, as well as shopping, restaurant, and hotel listings.

Vermont
Vermont Tourism
www.vermontvacation.com

Here you'll find information on nightlife and dining, shopping, accommodations, ski resorts, local churches, and businesses, plus help on getting around the area by public transportation and finding local festivals.

Rhode Island
Providence Chamber of Commerce
www.goprovidence.com

This site offers information not just on visiting Providence, but on moving there as well.

Newport, RI
www.discovernewport.org

Find full listings of local businesses on the site, along with useful visitor information on events, historic sites, and shows by area and neighborhood.

The Preservation Society of Newport County
www.newportmansions.org

The Preservation Society operates the majority of mansions open to the public in Newport. Find out more about the history and character of each one on this in-depth site—plus essentials such as events, hours, and online ticketing.

Connecticut
Connecticut Tourism
www.ctvisit.com

Built primarily for visitors to the state, this site lists weekend getaway itineraries and events happening throughout the year. It also offers help on getting to and around the different counties, and special deals on hotels.

Mystic, CT
www.mystic.org

The town's official site lists everything currently happening within it, from the aquarium's exhibits to the Seaport's presentations. Also find restaurant, hotel, and shopping listings.

Suggested Reading

Reference
Feintuch, Bert, ed. *The Encyclopedia of New England.* New Haven, CT: Yale University Press, 2005. A good book to read *before* you go, this 1,600-page, eight-pound tome will tell you everything you want to know about New England and then some, including entries on Walden Pond, fried clams, Ben & Jerry's, and the Red Sox. Instead of a disjointed alphabetical arrangement, the book cogently organizes contents by subject matter.

History
Cronon, William. *Changes in the Land: Indians, Colonists, and the Ecology of New England.* New York: Hill and

Wang, 1983. The classic study of early New England history debunks myths and shatters preconceptions about Pilgrims and Native Americans and how each interacted with the landscape.

Fairbrother, Trevor. *Painting Summer in New England.* New Haven, CT: Yale University Press, 2006. From a recent exhibition of the same name at the Peabody Essex Museum, this beautiful art book includes dozens of paintings by American Impressionists, along with stories about the artists.

Howard, Brett. *Boston: A Social History.* New York: Hawthorn, 1976. Detailing the impact of the city's leaders and most prominent families over the centuries, Howard shows the impact Boston Brahmins have had on local politics and cultural landscape.

McCullough, David. *1776.* New York: Simon & Schuster, 2005. Rather than writing a start-to-finish account of the Revolution, McCullough drills down to the pivotal year in which the fortunes of George Washington turned, from the tense standoff of the siege of Boston to the ultimate victories at Trenton and Princeton.

Paine, Lincoln P. *Down East: A Maritime History of Maine.* Gardiner, ME: Tilbury House Publishers, 2000. A look back at more than four centuries of pirates, privateers, lobstermen, and windjammers from a maritime historian and native Downeaster.

Rappeleye, Charles. *Sons of Providence: The Brown Brothers, the Slave Trade, and the American Revolution.* New York: Simon & Schuster, 2006. A fascinating journey into the heart of colonial America, told through the history of the most enlightened city in the New World which nevertheless founded its fortune on the slave trade.

Vowell, Sarah. *The Wordy Shipmates.* New York: Riverhead, 2007. The popular essayist and National Public Radio contributor not only writes one of the most irreverent and entertaining histories of the early days of Puritan and Pilgrim New England, but makes those ancient times surprisingly relevant to our own United States.

Woodard, Colin. *The Lobster Coast: Rebels, Rusticators, and the Struggle for a Forgotten Frontier.* New York: Viking, 2004. From early Scotch-Irish woodchoppers to 20th-century oil painters, this clearly written account populates the map of Maine with colorful historical characters.

Natural History and Ecology

Albers, Jan. *Hands on the Land: A Natural History of the Vermont Landscape.* Boston: MIT Press, 2002. In a gorgeous oversized book, Albers details the various factors—geological, ecological, and economic—that have transformed the Green Mountain State.

Kessler, Brad. *Goat Song: A Seasonal Life, A Short History of Herding, and the Art of Making Cheese.* New York: Scribner, 2009. In this lovely and earnest little book, longtime writer Kessler sets out to live the dream that tugs at many of us: leaving the city to go back to live a simpler life out on the farm. What he finds in two years of raising goats is nothing short of connection to our most mythic religious archetypes.

Kurlansky, Mark. *Cod: A Biography of the Fish that Changed the World.* New York: Penguin, 1998. The settlement and economic rise of New England is inseparable from the plentiful groundfish that once populated its waters in astounding numbers.

National Audubon Society. *National Audubon Society Regional Guide to New England.* New York: Knopf, 1998. The amateur naturalist would do well to pick up this guide, which details many local species of trees, wildflowers, reptiles, and mammals with 1,500 full-color illustrations.

Wessels, Tom. *Reading the Forested Landscape: A Natural History of*

New England. Woodstock, VT: Countryman Press, 2005. A good read before heading off into the hills, this book helps put features of the landscape into their proper context.

Literature

Douglass, Frederick. *Narrative of the Life of Frederick Douglass, An American Slave: Written By Himself.* 1845, Signet Classics, 2005. The quintessential slave narrative includes details of Douglass's life as an abolitionist in Boston.

Frost, Robert. *The Poetry of Robert Frost: The Collected Poems, Complete and Unabridged.* Henry Holt and Co., 1979. The New England landscape infuses Frost's poetry, much of which was written in Vermont and New Hampshire.

Hawthorne, Nathaniel. *The House of Seven Gables.* 1851, Signet Classics, 2001. The tragic story of several interlocking families is set in a house that still exists in Salem.

James, Henry. *The Bostonians.* 1886, Modern Library Classics, 2003. Beacon Hill comes alive in this evocation of 19th-century Boston.

Jewett, Sarah Orne. *The Country of the Pointed Firs.* 1896, Dover, 2011. Maine's customs, dialect, and traditions come to life in this often-overlooked masterpiece.

Melville, Herman. *Moby-Dick.* 1851, Penguin Classics, 2002. From the opening scene in New Bedford, Massachusetts, this classic tale brings New England's grand, tragic whaling history to the page; written from Melville's country home in the Berkshires.

Stegner, Wallace. *Crossing To Safety.* 1987, Random House, 2002. A quintessential Western author tells a finely woven story of love and loss with the backdrop of northern Vermont.

Thoreau, Henry David. *Walden.* 1854, Modern Library Classics, 2000. The classic account of Thoreau's two years living a hermit's life on Walden Pond is a philosophical treatise, a timeless glimpse into 19th-century rural New England, and inspiration for the modern-day environmental movement. Look for an edition that includes *The Maine Woods* and *Cape Cod,* travelogues that blend the author's sharp eye and wry sense of humor.

Wharton, Edith. *The Age of Innocence.* 1920, CreateSpace, 2015. A stormy romance brings the Gilded Age New York and Newport society to life.

Contemporary Fiction and Memoir

Bergman, Megan Mayhew. *Birds of a Lesser Paradise.* Simon & Schuster, 2012. Writing from a farm in Vermont, Bergman draws New England's cows, chickens, and exotic birds into her intimate short stories.

Beston, Henry. *The Outermost House: A Year of Life on the Great Beach of Cape Cod.* New York: Owl Books, 1928. Beston's attempt to "go Thoreau" by living for a year in a small house in the dunes remains the most joyous evocation of Cape Cod's unique ecology.

Elder, John. *Reading the Mountains of Home.* 1998, Harvard University Press, 1999. With the company of Robert Frost's poetry, a Vermont writer watches a year unfold in the Green Mountains.

Greenlaw, Linda. *The Lobster Chronicles: Life on a Very Small Island.* New York: Hyperion, 2003. The sword boat captain featured in Sebastian Junger's nonfiction book *The Perfect Storm* returns with a fascinating memoir of her return to her family's home on Isle Au Haut in Maine to try her hand at the lobstering business.

Irving, John. Many of the most popular books of this cult American novelist are set in New England. For example, *The Cider House Rules* is centered around an orphanage in Maine, *The*

World According to Garp takes place in part at a New England boarding school, and *A Prayer for Owen Meany* concerns several generations of a troubled New England family.

MacDonald, Michael Patrick. *All Souls: A Family Story from Southie.* New York: Ballantine, 2000. In writing his moving memoir of Irish American life, MacDonald does for South Boston what Frank McCourt did for Dublin.

Guidebooks

Appalachian Mountain Club Books (www.outdoors.org/publications) publishes dozens of guides considered gospel by outdoors enthusiasts in the region. They are jam-packed with no-nonsense directions for hiking and canoeing every inch of the New England wilderness. Among them are the *White Mountain Guide* and *Maine Mountain Guide,* as well as several guides for canoeing and kayaking.

Corbett, William. *Literary New England: A History and Guide.* New York: Faber and Faber, 1993. An excellent guide to sights associated with poets and writers who called New England home, it includes detailed directions to hard-to-find graves, historic sites, and houses.

Crouch, Andy. *The Good Beer Guide to New England.* Hanover, NH: University Press of New England, 2006. Don't know your Whale's Tail from your Smuttynose? This detailed guide to breweries in the region is the ultimate New England pub crawl.

Dojny, Brooke. *The New England Clam Shack Cookbook.* North Adams, MA: Storey Publishing, 2003. In addition to providing recipes for stuffed quahogs and other favorites, this book offers a guide to some of the best clam shacks, lobster pounds, and chowder houses in all six states.

Hartnett, Robert. *Maine Lighthouses Map & Guide.* Howes Cave, NY: Hartnett House Map Publishing, 2000. A fold-out map that provides detailed directions to every lighthouse along the rocky fingers of the Maine coast. Hartnett also publishes a map to lighthouses in Massachusetts and New Hampshire (yes, there are two).

Kershner, Bruce, and Robert Leverett. *The Sierra Club Guide to the Ancient Forests of the Northeast.* San Francisco: Sierra Club Books, 2004. Despite centuries of human habitation and exploitation, a surprising number of old-growth stands still exist in New England. This guide takes you inside their mossy interiors, and explains what makes old-growth forests so unique.

Tourville, Jacqueline. *Moon New England Hiking.* Berkeley, CA: Avalon Travel, 2010. By the same publisher as Moon Handbooks, this guide features plenty of hiking trails to get your boots muddy.

INDEX

393

400

INDEX

LIST OF MAPS

PHOTO CREDITS

ALSO AVAILABLE

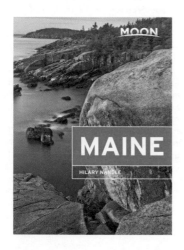

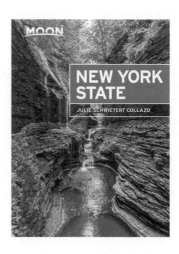

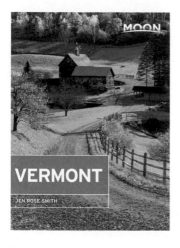

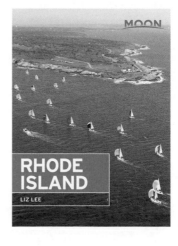

MAP SYMBOLS

≡≡≡	Expressway	○	City/Town	✈	Airport	⚓	Golf Course
≡≡≡	Primary Road	◉	State Capital	✗	Airfield	P	Parking Area
	Secondary Road	⊛	National Capital	▲	Mountain	≜	Archaeological Site
- - - - -	Unpaved Road	★	Point of Interest	✛	Unique Natural Feature	♠	Church
———	Feature Trail	•	Accommodation				Gas Station
- - - - -	Other Trail	▼	Restaurant/Bar	⌇	Waterfall		Glacier
··········	Ferry	■	Other Location	▲	Park		Mangrove
	Pedestrian Walkway	▲	Campground	▣	Trailhead		Reef
ⅢⅢⅢⅢ	Stairs			⚡	Skiing Area		Swamp

CONVERSION TABLES

°C = (°F - 32) / 1.8
°F = (°C x 1.8) + 32
1 inch = 2.54 centimeters (cm)
1 foot = 0.304 meters (m)
1 yard = 0.914 meters
1 mile = 1.6093 kilometers (km)
1 km = 0.6214 miles
1 fathom = 1.8288 m
1 chain = 20.1168 m
1 furlong = 201.168 m
1 acre = 0.4047 hectares
1 sq km = 100 hectares
1 sq mile = 2.59 square km
1 ounce = 28.35 grams
1 pound = 0.4536 kilograms
1 short ton = 0.90718 metric ton
1 short ton = 2,000 pounds
1 long ton = 1.016 metric tons
1 long ton = 2,240 pounds
1 metric ton = 1,000 kilograms
1 quart = 0.94635 liters
1 US gallon = 3.7854 liters
1 Imperial gallon = 4.5459 liters
1 nautical mile = 1.852 km

°FAHRENHEIT	°CELSIUS	
230	110	
220		
210	100	WATER BOILS
200		
190	90	
180	80	
170		
160	70	
150		
140	60	
130		
120	50	
110		
100	40	
90		
80	30	
70		
60	20	
50		
40	10	
30		
20	0	WATER FREEZES
10		
0	-10	
-10		
-20	-20	
-30	-30	
-40	-40	

(clock face with hours 1–12 on outer and 13–24 on inner ring)

INCH: 0 1 2 3 4

CM: 0 1 2 3 4 5 6 7 8 9 10

MOON NEW ENGLAND ROAD TRIP
Avalon Travel
An imprint of Perseus Books
A Hachette Book Group company
1700 Fourth Street
Berkeley, CA 94710, USA
www.moon.com

Editors: Nikki Ioakimedes, Kevin McLain, Kristi Mitsuda
Series Manager: Sabrina Young
Copy Editor: Ashley Benning
Graphics Coordinator: Rue Flaherty
Production Coordinator: Rue Flaherty
Cover Design: Erin Seaward-Hiatt
Interior Design: Darren Alessi
Moon Logo: Tim McGrath
Map Editor: Albert Angulo
Cartographers: Albert Angulo, Brian Shotwell, Moon Street Cartography (Durango, CO)
Indexer: Rachel Kuhn

ISBN-13: 978-1-63121-246-8
ISSN: 2475-4749

Printing History
1st Edition — June 2017
5 4 3 2 1